Basic Skills in English

9

Contents of the Teacher's Edition

Components of *Basic Skills in English*

Student Texts

Red Level
Grade 7

Green Level
Grade 8

Orange Level
Grade 9

Blue Level
Grade 10

Yellow Level
Grade 11

Purple Level
Grade 12

Teacher's Editions

Practice Books/Duplicating Masters

Diagnostic and Mastery Tests

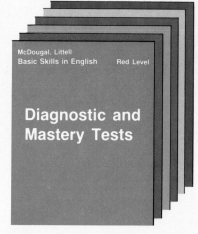

The only English series for students reading *below* grade level . . . with content that is *on* grade level!

Ever since its introduction, *Basic Skills in English* has been the only series of its kind—a composition/grammar series for students reading below grade level. It's a program designed to teach all essential skills while helping students learn with confidence and achieve success.

The 1985 edition maintains the tone, format, and clear instruction that teachers praised in the earlier edition. It then builds on this success with more practice exercises, greatly expanded instruction in the process of writing, and new material on study and research skills, speaking and listening, critical thinking, and more. *Basic Skills in English* provides:

Clear, readable presentation for below-level readers

The series offers a controlled reading level, a one-step-at-a-time approach, and success-directed lessons. As a result, students read with ease and master skills gradually, gaining confidence as they progress (see pages T4–T5).

Comprehensive coverage of on-level skills

Students reading below grade level need the same skills and preparation that average students do. That's why *Basic Skills in English* provides thorough instruction in all the language basics: composition, grammar, and related language skills (see pages T6–T7).

So complete, you can be sure your students will learn all essential English skills.

All students need the same skills, regardless of their reading abilities. That's why *Basic Skills in English* teaches all of the essential concepts and skills that students are expected to master at their grade level. It's a comprehensive program that provides instruction in *all* the language basics: composition; grammar, usage, and mechanics; and related language skills.

Composition

In-depth writing instruction teaches students the skills and techniques they'll need to write effectively:

Process of Writing
Students learn the three stages of the process of writing . . . pre-writing, writing, and revising . . . then use the process consistently throughout the program.

Types of writing
The series teaches students the various elements and techniques that characterize narrative, descriptive, and explanatory writing.

Forms of writing
Students learn and practice the different forms of writing that they will use in school and in everyday life. Lessons on sentences, paragraphs, compositions, reports, and research papers give students the essential skills they need.

Part 5 **Replay**

Revising Your Narrative Paragraph

Here's the Idea After you have written the first draft of your
Then return to it
You may want to
language. As you
stions:

cific details?
in chronological

ases to make the

l attention to the
e of verbs. Try to
ike *is*, *seems*, or
e *races*, *sings*, or
is a stronger sen-

ecific verbs. For
itute for the gen-
ffled, *strolled*, or
ust decide which
ing.
ization, and word
ect any errors in
lling.

n from a narrative.

rock. Despite his
as though he were

nily of thirteen
en when I got a
a hotel up in
he highway and
spent my time
llers, cleaning
ns. Then I got

Part 4 **Time Will Tell**

Writing the First Draft

-writing notes
tails organized
point of view.
ou start to tell
rder of events

chronological
will also allow
events. Study

e time

nning
dle

sitional words
t to use, such
ne, or *by next*

Part 1 **Tell a Tale**

Pre-Writing: The Narrative Paragraph

Here's the Idea The next four writing sections will teach you how to write different kinds of paragraphs. As you study each type of paragraph, notice that the process of writing is always the same. However, each type of paragraph is developed and organized differently. In this section, you will learn how to develop and organize a **narrative paragraph.**

A narrative tells a story. When you write about an experience at the state fair or your first trip in an airplane, you are writing a narrative. A narrative does not have to be a true story. For example, Rudyard Kipling wrote about a mongoose called Rikki Tikki Tavi, who saves his human and animal friends by slaying two evil cobras. Kipling's story is an imaginary narrative.

When you choose a topic for your narrative paragraph, select a story you can tell well in this length. To help you limit your story, ask questions about it. Ask *who? what? when? where? why?* and *how?* The answers you get will give you the details you need to zero-in on your topic.

After you have selected and limited your topic, think about it. How will you develop your story? Any story, even one brief enough to be told in a single paragraph, is made up of many small incidents or events. Suppose you decided to write about your first ride on a roller coaster. This story would be made up of many events. First, you buy your ticket. Then you wait in line. Finally, it's your turn. You board the roller coaster. These are the kinds of specific details that will help you to tell your story.

A good story also contains sensory details. There are screams as the roller coaster descends. There are the colored lights that decorate the amusement park. There is the smell of popcorn and hot dogs. Details will bring your narrative to life.

106

Grammar, usage, and mechanics

Basic Skills in English offers exceptionally clear, to-the-point instruction in grammar, usage, and mechanics. A flexible handbook format allows for developmental teaching, skills review, and student reference. And each section includes a wealth of varied exercises that are both fun and instructive. The series pays special attention to problems of usage and speech that often present difficulties for less able students.

Related language skills

Separate chapters teach the related skills students need for effective communication and for successful learning in every subject area:

Critical thinking
Topics include distinguishing fact and opinion, avoiding errors in reasoning, and drawing conclusions.

Vocabulary
The series develops skills such as discovering word meaning from context and recognizing word parts.

Levels of language
Students learn about standard and nonstandard English, slang, jargon, regional language, and more.

Life skills
Letters, forms, applications, résumés, and interviews are a few of the topics taught throughout the program.

Study and research
Students learn skills such as following directions, completing research, and preparing for tests.

Speaking and listening
Skills include presenting formal and informal speeches, evaluating speeches, and participating in group discussions.

Part 1 Pairs of Verbs That Are Often Confused

See how the following pairs of verbs are used. Study the difference in their meanings. Avoid making mistakes when you use them.

Can and May

Use *can* when you are talking about being able to do something. *Can* has no principal parts. Another form of *can* is *could*.
Use *may* when you are asking or giving permission. *May* is used only as a helping verb. It has no principal parts. Another form of *may* is *might*.

Can you see me?	*Might* we leave early?
Tara *could* not see the screen.	You *may go* to the party.

Exercise Use *can* and *may* correctly.

Number your paper from 1 to 10. Write the correct verb from the two given in parentheses.

1. (May, Can) you write backwards?
2. (May, Can) I help you with anything for the Halloween party?
3. Yes, you (can, may) go to Robert's party.
4. (Can, May) that little stove heat this whole room?
5. (May, Can) Melinda and I go out in the canoe?
6. (May, Can) you read the bottom line without your glasses?
7. A catbird (can, may) imitate other birds.
8. (May, Can) I please be excused?
9. (Can, May) Eduardo go to the par
10. My little brother (may, can) count

392

Part 1 **Fact-Finding Mission**

Facts and Opinions

Here's the Idea Your mind is like a computer. In it you have stored thousands and thousands of ideas. These ideas may be facts or opinions.

Facts are ideas that can be proved true. They tell about people, things, and events. The following are facts:

1. Many television shows are written by more than one person.
2. President Lincoln signed the Emancipation Proclamation.
3. Vampire bats have sharp, V-shaped teeth.

Facts can be proved in three different ways:

1. Some facts can be proved through observation. You can prove them by using your senses of sight, smell, hearing, taste, and touch. For example, you can use your sense of sight to prove the first fact listed above. All you have to do is watch the credits that follow most television shows.
2. Some facts can be proved by asking an expert. This is someone who has special knowledge, training, or experience. You can prove the second fact by asking a history teacher.
3. Some facts can be proved by checking a reliable written source. A **reliable source** is one you can count on to give you accurate information. You can prove the third fact listed above by reading about vampire bats in an encyclopedia.

Opinions are very different from facts because they cannot be proved true. The following statements are opinions:

1. Everyone should learn to ice skate.
2. Pandas are beautiful and funny.

These statements tell how some people feel about things. Other people might feel differently. That is why these statements can't be proved.

218

T5

As students progress, they build on the success they've already achieved.

Success-directed lessons, a controlled reading level, and a one-step-at-a-time approach combine to make concepts more accessible to students. As a result, they read with ease and master skills gradually, gaining confidence as they progress.

Success-directed lessons

The short, highly-structured lessons are fail-proof . . . every student can achieve success.

Here's the Idea
The main idea of the lesson is presented in a clear, concise manner. Explanations are especially easy to understand.

Check It Out
High-interest examples and models illustrate the main idea of the lesson. Questions help students focus on key points.

Try Your Skill
These highly-structured, success-directed exercises allow students to apply the skill they have learned.

Keep This in Mind
For further reinforcement, a boxed summary highlights the main idea of the lesson.

Now Write
The second exercise is a writing application that gives students independent practice in using the skill.

Part 1 **Sensational!**

Pre-Writing: Using Sensory Details

Here's the Idea A descriptive composition paints a picture with words. It might describe a scene, such as a park in the city. It might describe a thing, such as a cab. It might also describe a person, such as a clown.

Begin planning your word picture by choosing and narrowing a subject. Next, begin gathering sensory details by observing your subject in person or by working from memory. Then list as many sensory details as you can. Ask yourself how your subject looks, sounds, smells, tastes, and feels.

When you finish making your notes, read them over carefully. Cross out any details that will not help you to describe your subject. Then organize your notes in spatial order. Group your details around two or three main ideas. Each of these idea groups will become a paragraph in your composition.

Next, put your main ideas and the details grouped around them into a logical order. You will probably want to use spatial order to show how all the parts of your subject are related.

Check It Out Look at these pre-writing notes.

Topic: Grandma Sarah's apartment

Grandma Sarah and the sea
   lives in New Bedford, near harbor—busy
   fishing boats—treasures from Grandfather's sailing days
bedroom
   four-poster bed, maple, (center),—Chinese clock (red dragons)—oval mirror—sea chests, leather, wood, brass—smells of fresh-washed linen, lavender
favorite corner
   window facing sea—colorful seashells—when the window is open, smell of salt and sea—muffled clang of harbor buoy—comfortable rocking chair

174

Popeye, the talking parrot
   has a perch near the rocking chair—pale green parrot—loud squawks—"You old sea dog!"

- What senses have been used to gather the details in these pre-writing notes?
- What main ideas have the details been clustered around? How have these idea clusters been organized?

Try Your Skill Below are some pre-writing notes for a descriptive composition about a pizza parlor. Along with the notes are three main ideas. Decide which notes belong with which main idea. Cluster the notes around that main idea.

Main Ideas:	Regina's Pizzeria (outside)	Regina's Pizzeria (inside)	Regina's is the best pizza
Details:	small, old building	10 wooden tables	
	red and white checked placemats	crispy crust	
	neon sign	refrigerator for soda	
	mushrooms, pepperoni	oldies jukebox	
		long lines	
		creamy cheese	

Keep This in Mind

- Gather sensory details to develop your description.
- Group your details around several main ideas.
- Use spatial order to organize your composition.

Now Write Make a list of some people, places, and things that you would like to describe. Choose the one that interests you the most. Use your senses to gather details about your subject. Group your details around several main ideas. Then, organize your main ideas and details in the order you want your reader to notice them.

175

Controlled reading level

While the content of each text is on grade level, the readability has been carefully controlled so that it does not interfere with the concepts.

The language and tone of the instruction is encouraging and conveys confidence in the student's ability. To further motivate students, the text uses lively, high-interest models and exercises.

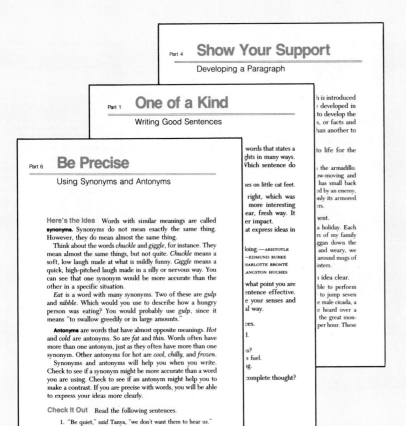

Part 4 **Show Your Support**

Developing a Paragraph

Part 1 **One of a Kind**

Writing Good Sentences

Part 6 **Be Precise**

Using Synonyms and Antonyms

Here's the Idea Words with similar meanings are called **synonyms.** Synonyms do not mean exactly the same thing. However, they do mean almost the same thing.

Think about the words *chuckle* and *giggle*, for instance. They mean almost the same things, but not quite. *Chuckle* means a soft, low laugh made at what is mildly funny. *Giggle* means a quick, high-pitched laugh made in a silly or nervous way. You can see that one synonym would be more accurate than the other in a specific situation.

Eat is a word with many synonyms. Two of these are *gulp* and *nibble*. Which would you use to describe how a hungry person was eating? You would probably use *gulp*, since it means "to swallow greedily or in large amounts."

Antonyms are words that have almost opposite meanings. *Hot* and *cold* are antonyms. So are *fat* and *thin*. Words often have more than one antonym, just as they often have more than one synonym. Other antonyms for hot are *cool*, *chilly*, and *frozen*.

Synonyms and antonyms will help you when you write. Check to see if a synonym might be more accurate than a word you are using. Check to see if an antonym might help you to make a contrast. If you are precise with words, you will be able to express your ideas more clearly.

Check It Out Read the following sentences.

1. "Be quiet," *said* Tanya, "we don't want them to hear us."
   barked   called   shrieked   whispered
2. Is your job *dull*, or is it _____?" asked Ron.
   busy   exciting   important   valuable

12

One-step-at-a-time approach

Each lesson follows a consistent, manageable format that focuses on one . . . and only one . . . topic at a time.

Single-concept lessons
So that students master skills gradually, lessons focus on a single skill and develop it. Later lessons review and build on the concept, helping students retain what they've learned.

Developmental sequence
Instruction moves logically from the word, to the sentence, to the paragraph, and on to longer types of writing.

Using the Teacher's Edition

The Teacher's Edition for each level provides step-by-step teaching strategies for presenting, developing, reinforcing, and reviewing each lesson.

Full-size student pages
Student pages are reproduced full size for ease in reading.

Objectives
Knowing what the objectives are can make your teaching more directed and purposeful.

Section 6 Objectives
1. To study the steps in the writing process
2. To learn different ways of choosing a subject
3. To understand and apply the process of narrowing a topic
4. To learn how to write direct, interesting topic sentences
5. To learn how to gather information through personal observation, brainstorming, and research
6. To learn how to develop paragraphs by using details, examples, or facts and figures
7. To recognize the four different methods of paragraph organization
8. To understand how to write a first draft
9. To gain skill in writing a paragraph ending that sums up the main idea of the paragraph in an interesting way
10. To understand the purpose of revising and to gain important revising skills

Preparing the Students
Refer once again to the poster developed throughout Section 5. Highlight the main points and explain that in Section 6, students will learn to apply what they have learned about paragraphs.

Additional Resources
Mastery Test — page 19 in the test booklet
Practice Book — pages 26–34
Duplicating Masters — pages 26–34

WRITING SECTION 6

Writing a Paragraph

Part 1 **Stepping Stones**
Writing as a Process

Part 2 **A Matter of Choice**
Pre-Writing: Choosing a Subject

Part 3 **Straight and Narrow**
Pre-Writing: Narrowing a Topic

Part 4 **Direct Contact**
Pre-Writing: Writing a Topic Sentence

Part 5 **Round Up**
Pre-Writing: Developing a Paragraph

Part 6 **Let's Get Organized**
Pre-Writing: Organizing a Paragraph

Part 7 **Blazing the Trail**
Writing the First Draft

Part 8 **Stop Sign**
The First Draft: Ending a Paragraph

Part 9 **Famous Last Words**
Revising Your Paragraph

61

Teaching Special Populations
LD LD students may have great difficulty with Writing Sections 6–18. Some students may be unable to even write more than a sentence or two. Work through these sections slowly and methodically with your LD students.

To arouse interest in and overcome resistance to writing, bring to class pictures (photographs, posters, reproductions of fine art), interesting magazine articles (especially those accompanied by illustrations), exciting stories, and unusual objects. Use these to illustrate different types of writing and as focal points for the students' writing.

Some LD students may find it easier to talk out their sentences and paragraphs than to write them. A tape recorder will enable these students to replay their sentences and perhaps even to improve them.

However you choose to use these writing sections with your LD students, you must modify your expectations. Let your knowledge of your students' abilities be your guide.

ESL ESL students will benefit from frequent brainstorming opportunities. Be sure that they understand suggested ideas and their relation to the subject.

ESL students may need help in locating and using reference materials. You may want to work through Writing Section 20, **Using the Library,** before teaching the writing sections.

Encourage these students to talk about their writing. Pair them with native speakers so that they can check their progress at each stage of the process of writing.

If these students have trouble writing in English, assign a native English speaker to write down what they can express orally.

Preparing the students
The Teacher's Edition suggests ideas for motivating and preparing students prior to every new section.

Additional resources
A detailed list directs you to extra practice, review, and tests.

Teaching special populations
At the beginning of each writing section and at the end of each handbook, the Teacher's Edition explains difficulties faced by the special student. Strategies are presented for helping students for whom English is a second language, students with learning disabilities, and students who speak nonstandard dialects.

Lesson objectives
Objectives are clearly stated in terms of student performance.

Presenting the lesson
Teaching suggestions stress points to emphasize, possible areas of difficulty, and ways to use the exercises effectively.

Answers
For your convenience, exercise answers are printed on or beside the student page.

Optional practice
Additional ideas are provided for drill, review, or reinforcement.

Part 9

Objective
To understand the purpose of revising and to gain important revising skills

Presenting the Lesson

1. Read aloud and discuss **Here's the Idea.** Have students turn to the contents page for the Handbook section as reference for any questions about mechanics.
2. Discuss **Check It Out.** Read the first draft aloud and then the revised version. Point out how the added details and corrected grammar enhance the paragraph.
3. Assign **Try Your Skill.** Discuss the revisions after the students are finished.
4. Read aloud **Keep This in Mind** and then assign **Now Write.**

Individualizing the Lesson

Less-Advanced Students
Do the first two sentences in **Try Your Skill** on the board so that the students can see how proofreading symbols are used. Then assign the remainder of the sentences to be corrected individually.

Advanced Students
Have students revise the following paragraph:

Archery can be fun. you need to be strong to do it. Just slinging the bow is difficult, Pulling back on the bow takes strength and consintration. Robin hood made it look so easy. That bullseye seems to get even smaller as you try too hit it with the arrow. You must be careful that the string or arrow does not scrape you're arm as you release.

Part 9 **Famous Last Words**

Revising Your Paragraph

Here's the Idea The third and final step of the writing process is revising. When you revise, you take a fresh look at what you have written. You make changes so that your writing is the best it can be.

At this point, you will have to work very carefully and thoughtfully. First, check your ideas. Be sure your paragraph has a good topic sentence. See that all of your details help to develop the main idea of your paragraph. Are there any unrelated details? Could you add any details that would improve your paragraph?

Next, check the order of your details. Have you chosen a method of organization that suits the kind of paragraph you are writing?

Now look at the ending sentence of your paragraph. Is the ending interesting? Does it work well with the rest of the paragraph? Does it sum up the main idea of your paragraph?

Finally, check the language you have used. Is it direct, lively, and interesting? Try reading aloud what you have written. Sometimes your ears will catch what your eyes miss.

After revising your ideas, your organization, and your language, proofread your work. Be sure you have used correct grammar, capitalization, punctuation, and spelling. Use a dictionary and the Handbook sections of this book to help you proofread your paragraph.

Check It Out Read the following paragraph. Notice how the author has revised it.

- What are some specific things the writer has done to make this paragraph better?

78

At the corner of Elm Street and Fourth Avenue was a house. My friend George and me used to play in it when we were little. The house had boarded up windows and old brick walls, There were a lot of trees around it. On bad days, the wind would rush through the house. George and me would dare each other to go in. We'd give all kinds of excuses not to go in.

Try Your Skill Read the following sentences. Proofread each one for errors in grammar, spelling, punctuation, and capitalization.

1. Black bear's hibarnat every Winter.
2. juan leeped from the truck to the grownd.
3. When you are tired its hard to get up and jog.
4. Put on these Ear muffs on your head.
5. I seen mr. Roberts run toward the gym.

Keep This in Mind

- Revising is the final step in the process of writing.
- Revise your first draft to improve your ideas, organization, and word choice.
- Proofread to find and correct errors in grammar, capitalization, punctuation, and spelling.

Now Write Use what you have learned in this lesson about revising to revise the first draft of your paragraph. When you are satisfied with your paragraph, write it in its final form. Make your work as neat as possible. Proofread the paragraph, reading it aloud one last time. Save your paragraph.

79

Optional Practice
Tell students to exchange with a partner the paragraphs they have been writing, and to check each other's paragraphs for the following:

- Completeness of sentences
- Mechanics such as capitalization and punctuation of sentences and indentation of the paragraph
- Spelling
- A direct, interesting topic sentence
- Sentences that develop the idea in the topic sentence
- An ending that sums up the main idea

Have each student write any suggestions for improvement on a separate sheet of paper.

Extending the Lesson
Introduce the idea of putting out a collection of students' writing. Explain that periodically you will ask for samples of their writing to save for the collection. Encourage students to turn in copies of their completed paragraphs.

On-page teaching suggestions
The text provides ideas for motivating the student, presenting the lesson, and providing enrichment.

Individualizing
Each section provides approaches for adjusting the basic lesson to different levels of ability or skill development.

Extending the lesson
An enrichment lesson or exercise suggests way students can apply the concepts outside of the English classroom.

Guidelines for evaluating composition
Special pages offer guidelines for teaching and evaluating student writing, including an evaluation form.

Other McDougal, Littell Programs

Building English Skills

Building English Skills is the only complete, developmental grammar and composition program for grades 1–12. Skills are developed sequentially from one grade to the next, with each level reinforcing and extending the skills learned earlier.

The McDougal, Littell Literature Series

The *McDougal, Littell Literature* Series for grades 7–12 provides an in-depth presentation of literary types at every level to give students a strong grasp of the possibilities of each genre.

Reading Literature Series

Reading Literature is a new literature program for grades 7–12 that combines high-quality literature selections with developmental instruction in reading skills. The program builds skills in comprehension, reading literature, vocabulary, and writing. In addition, related skills such as study and research, speaking and listening, and critical thinking are reinforced throughout.

Teaching Special Populations

Many classrooms in our society include students with special language needs. Some of these students may have learning disabilities (LD). Others may be learning English as their second language (ESL). Still others may speak a nonstandard dialect of English (NSD). These students are likely to encounter special difficulties in mastering some of the concepts and acquiring some of the skills presented in *Basic Skills in English*.

The purpose of this section is to make the classroom teacher aware of these students and the learning difficulties they may face. A teacher who understands the special needs of these students can make certain that they are not penalized for learning deficiencies beyond their control. At the same time, the teacher will be better equipped to help these students fulfill their potential.

The text for *Basic Skills in English* has been reviewed by consultants whose areas of expertise include the problems faced by LD, ESL and NSD students in the English classroom. Our consultants' general suggestions for adapting *Basic Skills in English* to the special needs of these students are provided on the following pages. Additionally, specific suggestions for teaching special populations are presented at the beginning of each writing section and at the back of this book.

Special Consultants

Rebecca Benjamin, Educational Consultant, Albuquerque, New Mexico

Grace Massey Holt, Instructor of English as a Second Language, California State University, Sacramento, California

Dr. Eleanor Wall Thonis, District Psychologist, Wheatland School District, Wheatland, California

Karen Bustelo Wehle, S.L.D. Teacher, Leon County School District, Tallahassee, Florida

Virginia Woods, Secondary Resource Teacher, Dripping Springs Independent School District, Dripping Springs, Texas

Following are some general strategies for modifying lessons and assignments to help LD, ESL, and NSD students overcome some of their difficulties.

Learning Disabled Students

LD students typically have average or above average potential. However, specific areas of deficiency, which vary from student to student, can make the processing of information and the acquisition of skills difficult. There are many learning problems that can be included under the general heading "learning disabilities."

Specific areas of dysfunction include auditory memory, auditory discrimination, visual memory, visual discrimination, fine motor coordination, gross motor coordination, written expression, and oral expression.

It is important for the teacher to realize that these learning difficulties are beyond the students' control. Learning disabilities may be the result of brain damage, central nervous system dysfunction, mild cerebral palsy, or other physical impairment. Therefore, what may appear to be inattentiveness or an uncooperative attitude on the part of a student may actually be a sign of his or her inability to learn through conventional methods. Nevertheless, learning disabled students can compensate for their handicaps and overcome their problems. This is most likely to occur when teachers understand their students' strengths and limitations and are willing to adjust assignments and the presentation of material to maximize the chances for success.

Whenever possible, the teacher should work with counselors and special education teachers to determine the specific nature of a student's disability. This will allow the teacher to devise strategies for circumventing the disability. Some general strategies that apply to many kinds of learning disabilities are presented here. How-ever, the teacher is encouraged to improvise new methods and to modify material as necessary for individual students.

General Areas of Difficulty

Whatever the nature of a student's disability, there are certain predictable problems that will impede his or her efforts to learn:

1. short attention span
2. poor memory
3. difficulty in generalizing
4. hyperactivity
5. distractability
6. low motivation
7. poor motor coordination

These problems of concentration and memory are usually compounded by low levels of acquired skills:

1. low reading level
2. inability to organize work and ideas
3. laborious and illegible handwriting

General Strategies

There are several strategies the teacher can use to counter learning disabilities.

1. Seat the students in the front of the classroom where there are no obstructions to sight or hearing.
2. Present essential information both orally and in writing. Reinforce written material in the text with oral explanation or with tape recordings made by the teacher, the student, or the student's parents. Write oral instructions and assignments on the board, and provide a written study guide that highlights the key points of oral presentations.
3. Supply visual aids whenever possible, to reinforce

material from the text. Simple charts, diagrams, photographs, and other illustrations may help to clarify the relationships among ideas.

4. Repeat important ideas frequently and begin each lesson with a summary of the material covered the previous day. This will help students to compensate for poor short- and long-term memory. Repeat assignments more than once, and give them both orally and in writing.

5. Demonstrate the correct way to complete an assignment. Work one or more problems on the board, showing the students how to go about answering them. Break down the assignment into steps, and be sure that the order of the steps is clear.

6. Give two grades for written work, one for content and another for mechanics. This two-grade system rewards students for good ideas despite mechanical shortcomings. Do not penalize students with visual disabilities for misspellings.

7. Allow students to answer test questions orally, either directly to the teacher or into a tape recorder. This can help to eliminate the anxiety caused by the prospect of writing under the pressure of time.

8. Help the students find shortcuts so that they can avoid writing long or difficult words repeatedly. When complete words or sentences are unnecessary, devise abbreviatons. For example, use *D.*, *Int.*, *Imp.*, and *E* instead of *Declarative, Interrogative, Imperative,* and *Exclamatory* for completing exercises on the types of sentences. Allow LD students to print rather than write if printing is easier and more legible. You might also suggest that students with writing difficulties learn to type.

Modification of Material

The teacher may find that some modification of the course material in *Basic Skills in English* will be necessary so that learning disabled students can keep pace with the rest of the class.

1. Break long-term assignments into shorter, individual tasks that can be assigned on a step-by-step, short-term basis.

2. Shorten and simplify all regularly assigned work; these students must put extra time and effort into completing their work. When possible, allow the students to select one, or a few, of several questions, topics, or exercises.

3. Simplify the assignments for written paragraphs and compositions, and allow students to work with partners or to put first drafts on tape.

4. If the reading level of a Section is too advanced, explain important vocabulary words and concepts before asking the students to read it.

5. Either supplement or replace difficult terms from the text with simpler ones. For example, when teaching the types of sentences, supplement or replace the terms *Declarative, Interrogative, Imperative,* and *Exclamatory* with words like *Statement, Question, Command,* and *Strong Feeling.*

6. Review "Study and Research Skills" with LD students several times during the year. This chapter will help them to overcome their difficulties in organizing work and ideas.

English as a Second Language

Students whose first language is not English face a number of challenges. These vary in difficulty depending on their native language and culture and their familiarity with American language and culture. In general, speakers of Indo-European languages, such as German and Spanish, will probably have fewer problems learning English grammar and adapting to American culture than will, for example, speakers of Oriental languages. However, most ESL students share one distinct disadvantage: they lack their classmates' years of experience with the English language, experience which is necessary to the thorough understanding of most standard textbooks. For these students, the problems of using textbooks fall into two categories: difficulty with the complexity of language and unfamiliarity with cultural references.

The Sections of *Basic Skills in English* are written at a level that may be difficult for many ESL students. Moreover, the exercises and assignments require students to analyze and manipulate a language that many ESL students will not yet have acquired fully. Once a teacher is aware of these problems, he or she can implement certain techniques for reducing the difficulties ESL students face.

General Strategies for Countering Language Barriers

To help students overcome these difficulties posed by an unfamiliar language, the following strategies may be employed:

1. Introduce new topics at a slower pace, and provide guided practice with increased feedback and monitoring.
2. Read aloud the essential parts of each Section, allowing time for explanation, examples, and the answering of questions.
3. In explaining any abstract concept such as "unity," it is better to go to the specific example first, pointing out the elements that show unity before giving the definition. Beginning from the concrete and particular enables ESL students to follow to the general or abstract.
4. Shorten assignments for these students and allow extra time for the acquisition of concepts.
5. Simplify all activities and exercises linguistically

whenever possible. Exercises from intermediate ESL books would be helpful.
6. Build into the activities as many visuals, manipulatives, and concrete experiences as possible. The teacher may have to illustrate and demonstrate meanings as if with small children. However, these aids should not be presented in a condescending manner—the age and intelligence of the students must be respected.
7. Suggest that students work as a group whenever possible. Allowing each student to go through activities with the group before having to do it individually gives him or her enough concrete practice and confidence to try it alone.
8. Correct written exercises and compositions carefully so that students will not continue to practice mistakes.
9. Precede *every* writing activity for ESL students with a similar oral activity; these students must have opportunities to speak and express themselves *before* writing. This procedure provides students with an opportunity to separate the tasks of clarifying ideas and translating them into correct written form.
10. Encourage ESL students to keep journals in English, recording thoughts and impressions without concern for grammar, spelling, and pronunciation. It will help them to develop fluency and build confidence and enjoyment in their writing, and it will free them from anxieties about absolute correctness.
11. To reduce the demands on the teacher's time, recruit advanced students to help the ESL students understand written materials and to monitor their practice.

General Strategies for Countering Culture Differences

The other major problem area for ESL students will be

the many cultural references that appear in the text. Some ESL students will have trouble determining gender from proper names alone. They may also have difficulty understanding references to national holidays, sports, individual teams, famous people, geography, foods, and popular culture. Slang, jargon, and idiomatic expressions are tied directly to a specific culture and are often impossible to translate. The following approaches could alleviate these problems:

1. Encourage class discussion to clarify cultural references and provide general information to the whole class. This and other oral work will greatly facilitate the ESL student's acquisition of English.
2. Encourage discussion of differences and similarities between ESL student's language and English. In covering verb tenses, for example, ask the ESL student to explain how his or her language expresses ideas of time. Such comparisons would benefit the American students by exposing them to aspects of language that are not part of their own linguistic experience.
3. Encourage ESL students to write about their native customs, holidays, geography, celebrities, and foods.
4. Encourage ESL students to read material, at an appropriate level, about specifically American people, places, and events. You might even provide these students with newspapers and popular magazines to read and discuss. This will help them acquire the common stock of information familiar to most Americans.

Speakers of Nonstandard Dialects

Everyone speaks some sort of dialect. The speech of Americans in one section of the country differs in at least some aspects of pronunciation, vocabulary, and grammar from the speech of people in other sections.

In addition, certain social, ethnic, and racial groups share a distinct way of speaking. Sometimes, however, the dialect common to a particular group departs so much for the most widely used and accepted dialects that it is termed "nonstandard." It is with students who speak such a dialect that this section is concerned.

Teachers must be aware that nonstandard dialects are legitimate language variations. These dialects follow regular phonological and semantic rules and serve the needs of the speech communities that use them. Speakers of "nonstandard" dialects are not necessarily careless speakers of English, nor should the variant features of these dialects be considered "errors." On the other hand, speakers of these dialects should be led to recognize that they cannot participate fully in mainstream American culture and society without understanding and effectively employing its language, standard English.

General Strategies

The teacher of NSD students should bear in mind that one need not, and indeed should not, eradicate one dialect in order to teach another. Instead, the teacher should implement the following strategies:

1. Encourage students to learn the patterns and usages of standard English for use in contexts where it is considered more appropriate: for academic writing and speech; in job applications and interviews; at work, if co-workers or superiors use standard English.
2. Encourage students to use the dialect that sounds natural both to speaker and listener in informal, casual, and family settings.
3. Tape-record samples of speech from various settings: playing fields, family gatherings, classrooms, committee meetings. Guide students in analyzing the vocabulary, sentence patterns, and grammar

used in these different contexts. This practice will make them see that various forms exist within a single language, each form being appropriate in a certain setting. It has proven to be a non-threatening way to increase all students' awareness of linguistic variation and to demonstrate that shifting from one form of speech to another does not involve a loss of identity.

4. When covering the Writing Sections have the NSD students keep journals, in whatever dialect is natural and comfortable, of thoughts, feelings, impressions, and experiences. Read the journals periodically and comment in writing about potential uses for the material in later compositions. Do not "correct" variations from standard usage or point out misspellings. Such nonjudgmental reading, discussion, and subsequent use of the journal entries will reinforce the lesson that writing in standard English is not abandoning one's identity but communicating it to a wider audience.

5. Establish small-group "workshops" consisting of four or five students, and have them collaborate in making suggestions for revision of written work. This strategy educates all of the students about the various dialects spoken in class.

6. Take note of the areas of grammatical variations that appear in the NSD students' written work, and be prepared to help the students with any problems that arise from these differences. Speakers of so-called Black English, for example, may have trouble with verb usage, for some of the principles of standard grammar and usage do not match their speech patterns. For similar reasons speakers of Hawaiian dialect may encounter difficulties with articles and pronouns. Other groups may have trouble with word order in sentences. Provide extra coaching, more details explanations, and additional practice, until the students have mastered the unfamiliar parts of standard dialect.

Specific suggestions for teaching composition to special populations appear at the beginning of each Composition Section of this book.

Specific suggestions for teaching grammar, usage, and mechanics to special populations appear at the end of this book.

Basic Skills in English

Purple Level
Yellow Level
Blue Level
Orange Level
Green Level
Red Level

Basic Skills in English

Orange Level

Joy Littell, EDITORIAL DIRECTOR

McDougal, Littell & Company
Evanston, Illinois
New York   Dallas   Sacramento

AUTHORS

Joy Littell, Editorial Director, McDougal, Littell & Company

The Editorial Staff of McDougal, Littell & Company

Kraft and Kraft, Developers of Educational Materials, Newburyport, Massachusetts

CONSULTANTS

Carole B. Bencich, Coordinator of Secondary Language Arts, Brevard County School Board, Rockledge, Florida

Dr. Sheila F. S. Ford, Coordinator for Secondary Language Arts, Spring Branch Independent School District, Houston, Texas

Marietta H. Hickman, English Department Chairman, Wake Forest-Rolesville High School, Wake Forest, North Carolina

Mary Evans Roberts, Supervisor of English and Language Arts, Savannah-Chatham Public Schools, Savannah, Georgia

ISBN: 0-86609-488-1   TE ISBN: 0-86609-490-3

Acknowledgments

Simon & Schuster: for entries from *Webster's New World Dictionary,* Students Edition; copyright © 1981 by Simon & Schuster, Inc. Macmillan Publishing Company: the Handbook section contains, in revised form, some materials that appeared originally in *The Macmillan English Series, Grade 7,* by Thomas Clark Pollock et. al., © 1963 by Macmillan Company. Used by arrangement. (Acknowledgments are continued on page 730.)

85 86

Composition

Handbook

Section 1 Objectives

1. To know that English is constantly growing and changing
2. To know three of the ways that English grows: by borrowing, by making words from people's names, and by clipping
3. To know that new words enter the language from special fields
4. To learn word meanings by using the direct context clues of restatement and definition
5. To learn word meanings by using the context clue of examples
6. To learn word meanings by using the context clues of comparison and contrast
7. To learn word meanings by drawing inferences from context
8. To recognize and use synonyms and antonyms to make written work more precise
9. To recognize base words in unfamiliar words
10. To learn common prefixes and to recognize them in unfamiliar words
11. To learn common suffixes and to recognize them in unfamiliar words

Preparing the Students

Ask students to define the word *vocabulary*. Explain that this section will present concrete ways to build vocabulary by studying the history, the use, and the structure of words.

Additional Resources

Mastery Test — pages 11–12 in the test booklet
Practice Book — pages 1–10
Duplicating Masters — pages 1–10

Building Your Vocabulary

Teaching Special Populations

LD As most learning disabled students have difficulty with both reading and writing, teachers should allow them as much time as possible. Shorten exercises or devise new ones that are tailored to your students' needs.

Give LD students constant guidance, and make periodic checks to see whether they are following instructions correctly. To compensate for students' reading problems, it is often useful to go over sections of the text orally. Additional exercises can be found in the Practice Book and under **Optional Practice** and **Extending the Lesson** in the teacher's notes.

Some LD students may have difficulty inferring meanings from context. Monitor these students' progress and encourage them by asking questions that help pin down meanings. Use a list of common prefixes, suffixes, and the words that contain them as the basis for simple exercises. Students could also be asked to memorize prefix and suffix meanings from flashcards.

To make sure students understand the difference between synonyms and antonyms, conduct synonym and antonym "bees" or exercises in which students match words and their synonyms.

ESL Many students for whom English is a second language lack the skills necessary to infer the meaning of new words. Pretest to determine the range of your ESL students' vocabulary, and take time to develop definitions in a variety of contexts. Make sure students un-

It's Alive!

Learning About Language

derstand the *primary* meaning of each word. Try using visual cues, role playing, and native English speakers to help during practice sessions. Allow ESL students extra time for exercises. Also try dictating shorter sentences to students before asking them for their own examples.

NSD Some students who speak a nonstandard dialect, aware that their pronunciation problems reinforce spelling errors, may resist using new words. Encourage these students and go over spelling rules. When teaching synonyms, ask NSD students to keep a list of the standard words that are equivalent in meaning to the nonstandard forms they have been using.

Part 1

Objectives

1. To know that the English language is constantly growing and changing

2. To know three of the ways that English grows: by borrowing, by making words from people's names, and by clipping

Presenting the Lesson

1. Read aloud and discuss **Here's the Idea.** Highlight the three ways that English grows. Then ask students for additional examples of borrowing, making words from people's names, and clipping.

Here's the Idea   English is a living language. It keeps growing and changing. In the process of change, some words are dropped from common use. Others are added. Words are added to the English language in several ways.

One major way in which English grows is by **borrowing.** Many words used in the United States are not native English words. They come from other languages. Borrowed words include American Indian words, like *pecan;* French words, like *bureau;* Spanish words, like *tornado;* and Italian words, like *pizza.*

Another way English gains new words is by making **words from people's names.** For instance, a person named Louis Braille was blinded in an accident in 1812 when he was three years old. When he was fifteen years old, Braille invented a language system based on raised dots that the blind could read. *Braille* later became the word naming this system.

English also grows when a new word is made from part of another word. This process is called **clipping.** Clipping creates the word *auto* from *automobile.* It creates *fan* from *fanatic.*

Can you see how English is enriched by the addition of new words? As you add words to your own vocabulary, you will be able to express ideas in interesting and more precise ways.

Check It Out   Read the following examples.

1. The word *cole slaw* is borrowed from Dutch, *plaza* from Spanish, and *yogurt* from Turkish.

2. The word *bowie* knife is made from the name of Colonel James Bowie, *Morse* code from Samuel Morse, and *pasteurize* from Louis Pasteur.

3. The word *flu* is clipped from *influenza, gym* from *gymnasium,* and *jet* from *jet airplane.*

- Do you see how the English language is enriched by new words?
- What does your dictionary tell you about these examples?

Try Your Skill   Can you guess where each of the following words came from? Use a dictionary to help you find the answers.

Spanish
ranch

Hindi
shampoo

American Indian
skunk

Dutch
wagon

dorm clipped form of *dormitory*

lab clipped form of *laboratory*

math clipped form of *mathematics*

sub clipped form of *submarine* or *substitute*

Use a dictionary to answer the following questions.

1. For whom was the Franklin stove named? Benjamin Franklin
2. For whom was the poinsettia named? Joel R. Poinsett
3. For whom is the month of August named? Augustus Caesar

Keep This in Mind

- English is a living language. It changes continually.
- New words are added by borrowing, by making words from people's names, and by clipping.

Now Write   Use a dictionary to help you find out how each of these words came into English. Write your answers in complete sentences. Label your paper **It's Alive!** and put it into your folder.

cotton	Bunsen burner	bus
laugh	marathon	memo
train	saxophone	taxi

3

Objective

To know that new words enter the language from special fields

Presenting the Lesson

1. Read aloud and discuss **Here's the Idea.** Discuss words that have come into the language from fields other than science and technology, such as *knockout*, *game plan*, (sports) and *motif* (music). Ask students to give other examples.

2. Discuss **Check It Out.** Ask students why they think previously-existing words might be used in new situations. Point out the relationship between the old meaning of the word and the new meaning.

3. Assign **Try Your Skill.** Remind the class that members of different professions may use the same word but attach different meanings to it.

4. Read **Keep This in Mind.** Then assign **Now Write.**

Individualizing the Lesson

Less-Advanced Students

Have students do **Try Your Skill** as an in-class assignment. Ask them to make up sentences showing they understand the different meanings of each word they discuss.

Advanced Students

Ask students to think of technical words that are now used commonly: *software, feedback, blastoff,* and so on. Have students make a classroom display of these words and add to the display whenever they come across more of these words in their reading.

4

Speaking of the Future

New Language for Special Fields

Here's the Idea   You live in a time of rapid change. Every day brings new discoveries, inventions, fashions, and fads. As the world changes, your language changes with it. New words are created to describe new ideas. Old words are given new meanings. In short, your language grows and develops like a living thing.

Most of the new words that enter your language are from the fields of science and technology. The word *quasar,* for example, was created in 1965. It describes a new kind of object in space discovered by astronomers. The word *memory* was given a new meaning by computer scientists in the 1950's. They used the word to describe the part of a computer that stores information. To understand the world of the future, you will have to understand many new words. Whenever you read or hear one of these new words, try to find out its meaning. Then try to use the word in your own speech and writing. This will help to prepare you for life in this modern age.

Check It Out   Read the following list of recently-created words.

Computer Science	Space Science	Entertainment
debugging	light-year	video-cassette
hardware	black hole	pay television
terminal	space shuttle	video-disc
microcomputer	nebula	music video

- Which of these terms are made from previously-existing words? What were their original meanings?
- Which of these words are brand new?

4

Try Your Skill   Using a dictionary, answer the following questions.

1. What does the word *fault* mean to a geologist? To a tennis pro? fracture in rock strata / error in service

2. What is a *printout?* What existing words were used to make this new term? printed output of computer

3. What is a *bug* to a computer scientist? defect in computer

4. What are the various meanings of the word *magnitude?* What does this word mean to an astronomer? important, loud, brightness of star

5. What does *video* mean in such words as *video-cassette*, *video game*, and *videotape?* image or picture portion to be played back on TV

Keep This in Mind

· Your language changes as the world changes.
· New words are created, and existing words take on new meanings to describe the world today.

Now Write   Look through some magazines dealing with science and computers. Make a list of ten new terms from these fields. Using a dictionary, write the meaning of each new term. Then, use each term in a sentence that shows your understanding of its meaning. Label your paper **Speaking of the Future.** Save it in your folder.

Optional Practice

Ask students what fields the following words come from. Have students look up the meanings of the words in a recently published dictionary.

holograph	beta-blocker
transistor	microchip
quark	input
photography	medicine
electronics	electronics
physics	computer science

Extending the Lesson

Have students look through their science and social studies texts for new words or "old" words with new meanings. Have them make up a class dictionary of these words. Each entry in the dictionary should contain the meaning of the word, what field or fields it is used in, and a sentence showing how the word is used.

Objective

To learn word meanings by using the direct context clues of restatement and definition

Presenting the Lesson

1. Read aloud and discuss **Here's the Idea.** Review the terms *context, definition,* and *restatement.*

2. Discuss the meanings of the italicized words in **Check It Out.** Ask the class what context clues are used. Ask which clues are definition and which are restatement. Have the class point out the key words or commas used to indicate the meanings in restatements.

3. Assign **Try Your Skill.** Ask students to point out the context clues.

4. Read **Keep This in Mind.** Assign **Now Write.**

Individualizing the Lesson

Less-Advanced Students

Do the first two sentences in **Try Your Skill** orally, asking students to point out the context clues. Then, have the students finish the exercise on their own.

Advanced Students

Ask students to think of five words they know that the rest of the class is not likely to know. The words may be specific to a hobby, skill, or other area of interest. They could also come from different areas of study, such as science or social studies. Have the students write sentences for each of their own words, being sure to include definition and restatement context clues. Then have

Direct Answers

Context: Definition and Restatement

Here's the Idea When you see an unfamiliar word, do you look it up in a dictionary? Do you ask someone for the definition? There is another method that you can use. You can try to learn the meaning of an unfamiliar word by thinking about the context. **Context** means the words and sentences around a word. The most direct context clues to the meaning of a word are definition and restatement.

When **definition** is used, the meaning of a new word is stated in a direct way.

> Jamie placed the bowl inside the *kiln*. A *kiln* is an oven for baking pottery.

When **restatement** is used, the meaning of a new word is usually signaled by key words, like *or, is called, that is, which is,* or *in other words.* A comma or a pair of commas may also be used to signal the meaning of the new word.

> The sailboat *careened*, or leaned sideways, in the storm.
> Shakespeare was a master at exposing the *foibles*, or minor weaknesses, of the characters in his plays.

Do you see how helpful these context clues are? As you read, look for similar clues. You will be able to add many new words to your vocabulary.

Check It Out Read these examples.

1. Have you used an *almanac?* An almanac is a book published each year that lists facts about many subjects.
2. A Channel 5 *editorial*, a statement of opinion made by the station manager, criticized the new mayor.

3. We learned about the Ming *dynasty*, which is the series of Chinese rulers from the Ming family.

4. World leaders met recently to discuss *disarmament*. Disarmament is the reduction of military forces and equipment.

5. In the future many homes may be heated by *solar* energy; that is, energy that comes from the sun.

- What clues indicate definition or restatement?
- What is the meaning of each italicized word?

Try Your Skill   Use context clues to find the meanings of the italicized words. Then write definitions for these words.

1. The doctor charged only a *nominal*, or very small, fee.

2. The *marimba*, a kind of xylophone, makes lovely, ringing sounds.

3. As a hockey player Dave was *aggressive*; that is, he was bold and forceful.

4. The government sent troops after the *insurgents*. An insurgent is a rebel.

5. A *southpaw*, or left-handed pitcher, has the advantage when facing a left-handed batter.

Keep This in Mind

- You can often learn the meanings of unfamiliar words by thinking about their context.
- The most direct context clues are definition and restatement.

Now Write   Imagine that you are writing for young readers. You want to use the following words: *cheetah, drum, landlubber, marathon, oxygen,* and *volunteer.* Check the meanings of the words in a dictionary. Then use each word in a sentence, using a definition or restatement to give the meaning of the word. Label your paper **Direct Answers.** Put it into your folder.

them write their sentences on the board, asking the rest of the class to figure out the meanings.

Optional Practice

Ask the students to determine the meanings of the italicized words in the following sentences.

1. Ricardo was the *beneficiary* of his Uncle's will; in other words, he received his uncle's money.

2. Marc figured out the *cryptogram*, a message written in secret code.

3. Helena looked *regal* in her new gown. That is, she looked like royalty.

4. The governor's speech was filled with *clichés*. Clichés are words and phrases that everyone uses until they become dull.

5. After studying for the test, everyone became *fatigued*, or very tired.

Extending the Lesson

1. Ask students to imagine that a prehistoric man is visiting their town. List ten things on the chalkboard that the prehistoric man might not recognize. Have students write sentences using the context clues of definition or restatement for five of the items.

2. Ask students to bring their science books to class. Select a page and have students identify as many new words as possible by using the context clues of definition and restatement.

Part 4

Objective

To learn word meanings by using the context clue of examples

Presenting the Lesson

1. Read the title of the lesson and review with the class the meaning of *context*.

2. Read aloud and discuss **Here's the Idea.** Emphasize that an example does not give a precise definition but rather the general idea of a word. Write the common key words on the chalkboard for student reference.

3. Assign and discuss **Check It Out.** Have students define the italicized words. Ask them to identify the key words that introduced the context clues.

4. Assign and discuss **Try Your Skill.**

5. Read **Keep This in Mind** aloud.

6. Assign **Now Write.**

Individualizing the Lesson

Less-Advanced Students

Do the first two sentences in **Try Your Skill** orally. Ask different students to point out the context clues and key words. Then have the students finish the exercise on their own.

Advanced Students

Have students look through their literature book for three words they do not know. After they look up the words in the dictionary, have them write sentences using the words. The sentences should use an example as a context clue.

8

Ample Examples

Context Clues: Examples

Here's the Idea Writers may supply the meanings of unfamiliar words by giving **examples** in the context. A familiar example may give you the clue you need to define a word you do not know. For instance, do you know what a *pugilist* is? Read the following sentence.

America's great *pugilists*, like Rocky Marciano and Muhammad Ali, shared the qualities of determination and discipline.

Do you recognize the names of famous boxers? If so, you know that the word *pugilist* must mean "professional boxer." From this sentence you can see that examples do not always tell you exactly what an unfamiliar word means. However, they do give you a general idea of the word.

Several key words and phrases alert you to the use of examples. Here are some of the more common ones:

like	for example
other	for instance
this, these	such as
especially	

When you see an unfamiliar word, check the context for any of these key words and phrases.

Check It Out Read the following sentences.

1. Alexis collects foreign *currencies*, such as pounds, pesos, francs, yen, and lira.
2. *Carbonated* beverages, such as ginger ale and root beer, give Kate the hiccups.

8

3. Hawaii, Samoa, Tahiti, and other *Polynesian* islands are located in the Pacific.

4. Many chemical elements, such as *neon* or hydrogen, exist in the form of gas.

- What words or phrases indicate that examples are used?
- What is the meaning of each italicized word?

Try Your Skill   As you read the following sentences, write what you think each italicized word means.

1. The planets bear the names of *Neptune, Mars,* and other Roman gods.

2. *Mesquite,* like many thorny trees, grows in desert areas of the southwestern U.S.

3. On a clear night, *constellations,* such as the Big Dipper and Little Dipper, can be seen in the sky.

4. Some parts of an automobile engine, the *carburetor* for example, may need adjustment from time to time.

5. Some *tubers,* especially potatoes and yams, are grown on this farm.

Keep This in Mind

- Examples in context help you to learn the meaning of an unfamiliar word. Such key words as *like, other,* and *for example* signal the use of examples.

Now Write   Choose three of these words: *cotton, dolphins, peaches, softball.* Write a sentence for each, using an example to explain the word. Be sure to include key words that signal examples. Use a dictionary to help you. Label your paper **Ample Examples.** Put your work into your folder.

Optional Practice

Ask students to determine the meanings of the italicized words in the following sentences.

1. On the counter were catsup, relish, and other *condiments*.

2. We put basil, rosemary, thyme, and other *herbs* into the turkey dressing for flavoring.

3. Millie will not eat *crustaceans* such as shrimp, lobster, and crab.

4. *Conifers,* especially pine and fir trees, lined the driveway.

5. The police officer received a reward for her acts of *heroism*. She rescued a baby from a burning building, and then saved the baby's brother and sister.

Extending the Lesson

Play a game with context clues. Have each student find one or two unfamiliar words in the dictionary. Instruct students to write their words in sentences, using examples as context clues. When this preparation has been completed, divide the class into two teams. Explain that the object of the game is to have the other team correctly guess the meaning of the unfamiliar word. For each word guessed correctly, the presenting team gets a point. The number of guesses allowed for each word is optional. The team with the most points wins the game. Have the entire class try to write sentences using examples to define the words that weren't correctly guessed.

Part 5

Drawing Parallels

Context Clues: Comparison and Contrast

Objective

To learn word meanings by using the context clues of comparison and contrast

Presenting the Lesson

1. Briefly review the context clues learned in the preceding chapters: *restatement*, *definition*, and *examples*.

2. Read aloud and discuss **Here's the Idea.** Highlight the terms *comparison* and *contrast*. Point out that a comparison uses a similar word to explain a new word and that a contrast uses an opposite word to explain a new word. Write the key words and phrases that signal the context clues of comparison and contrast on the chalkboard for student reference.

3. Discuss **Check It Out.** For each sentence ask the students three questions. Is a comparison or a contrast used? What key words signaled the comparison or contrast? What is the meaning of the italicized word?

4. Assign and discuss **Try Your Skill.** Remind students to look for the key words that signal comparisons or contrasts.

5. Assign **Now Write.**

Individualizing the Lesson

Less-Advanced Students

1. Have students do **Try Your Skill** with a partner, or working in groups.

2. Have students write the dictionary definition for each italicized word in **Try Your Skill** and compare it to the definitions they had worked

Here's the Idea   Two other kinds of context clues can help you figure out the meanings of unfamiliar words. They are comparison and contrast. These context clues will tell you what an unfamiliar word is like or unlike.

When **comparison** is used, an unfamiliar word is compared with a similar word that is known to you. Look at this sentence:

The cat's *amber* eyes were like the color of honey.

You may not know exactly what *amber* means, but through comparison you know it is like the color of honey.

When **contrast** is used, an unfamiliar word is compared with an opposite word that is known to you. Read this sentence:

Unlike Jill, who is very talkative, Monica is *laconic*.

The word *laconic* may be unfamiliar to you. However, from the context, key words and phrases help give you the meaning. These are the most common context clues:

Comparison: as, like, in the same way, just as, similar to
Contrast: although, but, unlike, on the contrary, on the other hand, however

Check It Out   As you read the following sentences, use the context clues to find the meanings of the italicized words.

1. Although driver education is not required in some states, it is *mandatory* in this state.

2. No scent is as *tantalizing* as the sweet aroma of homemade apple pie.

3. The sound of the rain was as *persistent* as the ticking of the clock on the mantle.

4. In contrast to how depressed they had been after four straight losses, the players were *jubilant* after their victory.

- What key words signal that comparison is used?
- What key words signal that contrast is used?

Try Your Skill Write what you think the italicized words mean according to the context clues.

1. The *discordant* music sounded like pots and pans clanging together.

2. Unlike a pullover sweater, which must be pulled on over the head, a *cardigan* can be unbuttoned and put on like a shirt.

3. Although Kim gave us enthusiastic praise for our work on the play, Jean's remarks were *perfunctory*.

4. The *desolate* house looked as though it were haunted.

5. Although Roy is careful about spending money, his brother Andy is *extravagant*.

Keep This in Mind

- Comparison is a context clue that shows how things are similar. Such key words as *like* and *as* signal comparison.
- Contrast is a context clue that shows how things are different. Such key words as *but, unlike,* and *on the contrary* signal contrast.

Now Write Choose four of these words: *sour, transparent, enormous, miniscule, lively, ridiculous.* Write a sentence for each, using a comparison or contrast to explain the word. Use a dictionary if necessary. Use key words to signal each context clue. Label your paper **Drawing Parallels.** Keep your work in your folder.

out for the same words through context clues. Discuss the differences.

Advanced Students

Have the students use each italicized word in **Try Your Skill** in an original sentence.

Optional Practice

Have the students follow the directions for **Try Your Skill,** using the following sentences.

1. The *avocado,* unlike other fruits, is not sweet.
2. I was *anxious,* but everyone else seemed calm and relaxed.
3. The cheerleaders were *exuberant,* but the fans remained sadly silent.
4. Although Ralph dressed *somberly,* he was a cheerful, happy person.
5. The dough was as *elastic* as a rubber band.

Extending the Lesson

Copy the following sentences for the students. Have them define the italicized words, using their knowledge of fairy tales and the use of context clues.

1. Unlike hardworking Cinderella, the stepsisters were *slothful.*
2. In contrast to Cinderella's rags, they wore only the finest *raiment.*
3. Like Peter Pan, I want to be a *perpetual* child.
4. If you *prevaricate* as Pinocchio did, your nose will grow, too.
5. Like the giant who lived at the top of Jack's beanstalk, he was *mammoth* in size.

Part 6

Objective

To learn word meanings by drawing inferences from context

Presenting the Lesson

1. Read aloud and discuss **Here's the Idea.**

2. Discuss **Check It Out.** Ask students to list all of the characteristics of a *gourmet* that are given in the paragraph.

a. To a gourmet, good food is one of life's pleasures.

b. A peanut butter and jelly sandwich is not for a gourmet.

c. A bologna sandwich is not for a gourmet.

d. Only carefully prepared food is fit for a gourmet.

e. Gourmets eat only what they enjoy.

Ask students to infer the definition of *gourmet* from these facts.

3. Assign and discuss **Try Your Skill.** For each paragraph, ask students the meaning of the italicized word. Refine the definition by reviewing the facts that the students used to reach their conclusions about the word meanings.

4. Read **Keep This in Mind** aloud.

5. Assign **Now Write.** Remind students not to define the word *daydream* directly.

Individualizing the Lesson

Less-Advanced Students

1. These students are likely to have difficulty understanding the concept of inference. Have them practice using the kinds of inferences that they make in daily life.

Between the Lines

Inferring Word Meanings

Here's the Idea Sometimes the context in which an unfamiliar word appears does not give direct clues to the meaning of the word. The context may only hint at the meaning of an unfamiliar word. You must read between the lines to find clues. Then you draw a conclusion about what the word means. This process of reading between the lines to reach a conclusion is called **inference.**

The main idea of a whole paragraph can center on the meaning of an unfamiliar word. For example, as you read the following paragraph, try to **infer** the meaning of *kibitzer.*

> When you are playing cards, there are few things more irritating than a *kibitzer.* Kibitzers love to stand behind you and smile or groan as you pick up your cards. By doing this, they manage to give the other players a clear idea of your hand. Kibitzers also love to give you advice. In fact, they will criticize you if you don't follow their suggestions.

From this paragraph you can infer that a kibitzer is a person who bothers people, in this case cardplayers, by offering unwanted advice.

Check It Out Read the following paragraph.

> My friend Mark is a *gourmet.* Mark says that good food is one of life's greatest pleasures. He does not care for most of the food I usually eat. Yesterday, for example, Mark turned down a peanut butter and jelly sandwich I offered him. He also refused a bologna sandwich. I think Mark would rather go hungry than eat something that is not carefully prepared and that he does not completely enjoy eating.

- What can you infer about the meaning of *gourmet?*

Try Your Skill As you read the following paragraphs, try to infer the meanings of the italicized words. Then, write definitions for them.

1. My brother is an *avid* reader. He is like my mother; they would both rather read than eat or sleep. I suspect that if nothing else were available, my brother would probably read the phone book.

2. Sally is far more *gregarious* than her two older sisters. They are quiet girls who seldom go out. Sally considers it a waste of time to stay home when she could be out with her friends.

3. My sister is much more *frugal* than I am. She carries a little notebook in her purse and keeps track of every penny she spends. She never buys anything without checking to see if she can buy it cheaper at another store. Each month her bank account grows. I don't think she ever buys anything without giving it long and careful thought.

Keep This in Mind

- Inference is the process of reading between the lines to draw a conclusion about the meaning of a word. Sometimes inferences can be drawn from the main idea of a paragraph.

Now Write Imagine that you are writing for young readers about daydreams. You want to hint at the meaning of the word *daydream* without defining it directly. Write three or four sentences about daydreaming. Label your paper **Between the Lines** and put your work into your folder.

Part 7

Objective

To recognize and use synonyms and antonyms to make written work more precise

Presenting the Lesson

1. Read aloud and discuss **Here's the Idea.** Review the definitions of *synonym* and *antonym*. Write them on the chalkboard for student reference. Emphasize that synonyms do not mean exactly the same thing and that writers try to use the word that best fits the meaning of a sentence.

2. Discuss **Check It Out.** After the class decides which synonym is best in number 1, ask them to think of sentences in which the other three synonyms could be used properly. After discussing which antonym is correct for number 2, ask the class to suggest antonyms for the three remaining words.

3. Assign and discuss **Try Your Skill.**

4. Read **Keep This in Mind.**

5. Assign **Now Write.**

Individualizing the Lesson

Less-Advanced Students

1. Go over the synonym choices in **Try Your Skill** with the students. Make sure they understand the connotations of each word before they choose the appropriate synonym.

2. Have students complete the exercise with a partner, or in groups.

Words of a Feather

Using Synonyms and Antonyms

Here's the Idea   Many English words have similar meanings. They are called **synonyms.** Examples are *pick, choose,* and *select.* Sometimes there is only a slight difference between the meanings of synonyms. However, because of that slight difference, one word will fit into the context of a sentence better than its synonyms. For example, you might *pick* a card, *choose* a partner, and *select* the best answer.

Each synonym has its own meaning. Here are three synonyms: *slip, err,* and *blunder.* They all mean "to do something incorrectly." But are they exactly the same? Read these examples.

> I *slipped* in calling him by my brother's name.
> The report *erred* in calling Columbus a Spaniard.
> Henry *blundered* by failing to stop at the stop sign.

From these examples, you can see that *slipped* suggests that a person made a minor, unintentional mistake. *Erred* suggests that a person overlooked or misunderstood something. *Blundered* suggests that a person made a careless mistake, perhaps a serious mistake.

Using the correct word is important. The wrong word will give the wrong idea. The more synonyms you know, the more exact your writing will be.

Antonyms are words with opposite meanings. They include such pairs of words as *fast—slow, in—out, loud—soft,* and *strong—weak.* Antonyms serve several useful functions. They, too, add precision to your writing. They can also serve to point out contrasts. For example, "The basketball player was so tall that he made his six-foot-tall coach look short."

Check It Out   Read the following sentences.

1. The fruit salad was so *good,* I had a second helping.
   helpful   proper   pleasant   delicious
2. Barbara is a cheerful person. Jim, on the other hand, is usually *sad.*
   heartbroken   gloomy   grave   displeased

- Which is the best synonym for *good?* Why?
- Which antonym for *cheerful* is more appropriate than *sad?* Why?

Try Your Skill   Each of the following sentences contains an italicized word that does not quite fit the context of the sentence. Below each sentence are four synonyms. On your paper, write the sentence, using the most appropriate synonym.

1. Tim answered the question in a *small* voice.
   ordinary   humble   <u>soft</u>   tiny
2. The lifeguard *moved* into the water when she heard a cry.
   <u>leaped</u>   skipped   walked   wandered
3. The pilot tested his instruments to be sure they were *right.*
   <u>accurate</u>   suitable   fitting   true

Keep This in Mind

- Synonyms are words with nearly the same meaning.
- Antonyms are words with opposite meanings. Antonyms, as well as synonyms, help you write precisely.

Now Write   Choose two of the italicized words in **Try Your Skill.** Check their meanings in the dictionary. Use each word correctly in a sentence of your own. Then use an antonym of *small* or *right* in a sentence. Label your paper **Words of a Feather** and put your work into your folder.

15

After students have done **Try Your Skill,** have them write sentences using the synonyms that are left. Tell them to make their sentences illustrate the shades of difference in meaning among the synonyms.

Optional Practice

Have students use antonyms to compare each of the following.

Example: two buildings
One building is *modern,* and the other one is *old-fashioned.*

two pets	two moods
two seasons	two teachers
two cars	two TV programs

Extending the Lesson

1. Show students how to find synonyms and antonyms in the dictionary. Ask students to find synonyms for the following words: *civil, speech.* Ask students to find antonyms for these words: *silent, likely.*

2. Introduce the class to Roget's *Thesaurus.* If a classroom set is available, have the students find synonyms for common words like *walk, talk, cold, hot, pretty, nice, slow, fast,* etc. Remind students that synonyms do not mean exactly the same thing and that they must be precise in choosing the correct word for a sentence.

Part 8

Objective

To recognize base words in unfamiliar words

Presenting the Lesson

1. Read aloud and discuss **Here's the Idea.** Emphasize that finding base words, sometimes called root words, can help to define an unfamiliar word.

2. Discuss **Check It Out.** Once students find the six base words, point out that the spelling of the base word is sometimes changed when parts are added to the words. Use the three examples in the lesson: *unbelievable, disbelieving,* and *uncaring.* (See pages 695–697 of the Handbook for spelling rules.)

3. Assign **Try Your Skill.** Have students explain any spelling changes that they make.

4. Read **Keep This in Mind.**

5. Assign **Now Write.** Have students compare their lists in class.

Presenting the Lesson

Less-Advanced Students

Have students use dictionaries to help them determine the base words in **Try Your Skill.** Ask volunteers to write the words on the board and analyze the word parts for the class.

Advanced Students

Have students give definitions for the words listed in **Try Your Skill.** They should write the meaning of the base word and the new meaning formed by the addition of prefixes and suffixes.

16

Base Hit

Learning Word Parts: Base Words

Here's the Idea   A **base word** is a word on which other words are based. Word parts may be added at the beginning of a base word or at the end. Sometimes word parts are added at both places. For instance, *misuse, useful,* and *reusable* are all formed by adding word parts to the base word *use.*

Often the base word is clear, as it is in the word *misprint.* Here the base word is clearly *print.* In some words, though, you may have to look more carefully. Can you find the base word in *indirectness?* To find it, you have to remove a word part from each end of the base word. Then you see that *direct* is the base word.

Being aware of base words helps you to enlarge your vocabulary. You can look at an unfamiliar word and recognize within it a word you already know. This gives you some idea of what the unfamiliar word means.

Check It Out   Look at each group of words below.

believe	reader	helpful
unbelievable	readable	helpless
disbelieving	misread	helper
uncaring	misunderstand	unreasonable
careful	understandable	reasonable
careless	misunderstanding	reasonably

- What is the base word in each group of words?

Try Your Skill   Read each word below and determine what the base word is. Number your paper from 1 to 20 and write the correct base word.

1. washable
2. extraordinary
3. misfortune
4. heater
5. misspell
6. thoughtless
7. harmful
8. review
9. improvement
10. actor
11. foreground
12. enjoyment
13. remake
14. interaction
15. joyful
16. nonbreakable
17. mispronounce
18. sickness
19. fearless
20. renew

Keep This in Mind

- A base word is a word on which other words are based. Word parts may be added at the beginning of a base word, at the end, or at both places. Recognizing base words will help you to determine the meaning of longer, unfamiliar words.

Now Write   Using any newspaper or magazine available to you, find ten words that contain base words. Copy each word as it appears in context. Then write the base word. You may want to use a dictionary to help you. Label your paper **Base Hit** and keep it in your folder.

Optional Practice

Have students identify the base words in *distasteful, unfortunately, happiness,* and *preschool.* Then ask them to think of other base words that can be expanded with additional word parts.

Extending the Lesson

Have a contest to see who can make the most words from the following base words. This can be done individually, in pairs, or in small groups. Set a time limit for the contest, and allow the use of the dictionary if each student or team has one.

| like | real | elect | inform |
| happy | wash | chill | sense |

Part 9

In First Place

Objective

To learn common prefixes and to recognize them in unfamiliar words

Presenting the Lesson

1. Read aloud and discuss **Here's the Idea.** Highlight the definition of *prefix*. Help students to remember the meaning by explaining that the prefix *pre-* means *before*. Examine these additional examples to see if students can determine which words are base words with prefixes and which have no prefixes.

untie   under   missile   misspell

Point out that adding a prefix never changes the spelling of the base word. Review the six prefixes introduced in the section and ask students to memorize their meanings.

2. Discuss **Check It Out.** Ask students for other examples of words that begin with each prefix.

3. Assign and discuss **Try Your Skill.**

4. Read **Keep This in Mind.**

5. Assign **Now Write.**

Individualizing the Lesson

Less-Advanced Students

1. Do the first five items in **Try Your Skill** orally. Ask student volunteers to write the words on the board, analyze the word parts for the class, and give word meanings.

2. Have the class finish the exercise with partners, or in groups.

Learning Word Parts: Prefixes

Here's the Idea   A **prefix** is a word part added to the beginning of a base word. The word part *re-* is a prefix in *rebuild* and *recall.* A prefix has its own meaning that changes the meaning of the base word. Some prefixes may have more than one meaning. The prefix *re-* means "again" or "back." *Rebuild* means "to build again," while *recall* means "to call back."

Watch out for words that seem to begin with a prefix but really do not. The word *reason,* for example, does not contain the prefix *re-.* To determine whether a word has a prefix, look at what remains if you omit the prefix. *Reorder* becomes *order,* a base word, and "to order again" makes sense. *Reason,* however, becomes *ason,* which is not a word. Not all words contain prefixes.

Here is a list of common prefixes, their meanings, and examples of each. When you know these six prefixes, you can figure out the meanings of hundreds of English words.

Prefix	Meaning	Example
extra-	"outside, beyond"	extraordinary
fore-	"before, front"	forehead
inter-	"between, among"	international
mis-	"wrong, bad"	misplace
non-	"not"	nonstop
re-	"again" or "back"	rerun, repay

Check It Out   Read the following words and their definitions. Notice how the meanings of the prefix and base word combine to create a new word with a new meaning.

extracurricular—"outside the regular courses offered by a school"
forewarn—"to warn before"
interplanetary—"between planets"
misdeed—"a wrong act, a crime"
nonfiction—"not imaginary, real"
redo—"to do again"
replace—"to put back"

- What is the prefix in each example? What is the base word?

Try Your Skill Many of the words below have prefixes. Some do not. For each word that has a prefix, write the meaning of the prefix plus the base word. For example, for the word *retype* you would write: again + type.

1. misfit — bad + fit
2. interstate — between + state
3. ready
4. reschedule — again + schedule
5. foresee — before + see
6. foreign
7. replay — again + play
8. none
9. extralegal — beyond + legal
10. miserable
11. nonactive — not + active
12. misfortune — bad + fortune
13. extrasensory — outside + sensory
14. forerunner — before + runner
15. return — back + turn

Advanced Students

Have students write the words from **Try Your Skill** in original sentences. Tell them to use as many words from the list as they can in each sentence.

Optional Practice

1. Have students use a dictionary to find two words beginning with each prefix listed on page 18.

2. Have students match the following prefixes with the base words to form new words. Have them check a dictionary to make sure they have made real words.

mis-	cover
non-	prove
re-	spell
inter-	heat
	national
	order
	direct
	connect

Extending the Lesson

Introduce these additional prefixes. Have the students find the definition of each in a dictionary and write one example of a word using that prefix.

trans-	super-
bi-	un-
sub-	dis-

Keep This in Mind

- A prefix is a word part that is added to the beginning of a base word. Each prefix has a meaning of its own that changes the meaning of a base word.

Now Write Use a dictionary to find six words, each containing one of the six prefixes you have learned. List new words and define them. As a final step, study the words and make them part of your vocabulary. Label your paper **In First Place.** Put your work into your folder.

Part 10

End of the Line

Objective

To learn common suffixes and to recognize them in unfamiliar words

Presenting the Lesson

1. Review the terms *base word* and *prefix*.

2. Read aloud and discuss **Here's the Idea.** Highlight the meaning of the word *suffix.* Emphasize that the spelling of the base word may change when a suffix is added. Review the spelling rules for final silent *e,* words ending in *y,* adding *-ness,* and doubling the final consonant. Read the list of suffixes and ask the students to memorize them. Ask students for additional examples of the use of the suffixes.

3. Discuss **Check It Out.** (If students are still having trouble spelling suffixes, refer them to the Handbook, pages 695–697.)

4. Assign and review **Try Your Skill.** If necessary, review the spelling rules for dropping a silent *e* and for changing *y* to *i.*

5. Read **Keep This in Mind.**

6. Assign **Now Write.**

Individualizing the Lesson

Less-Advanced Students

1. Do the first half of **Try Your Skill** orally in class.

2. If the class needs more practice in spelling suffixes correctly, assign the exercises on page 696 in the Handbook.

Learning Words Parts: Suffixes

Here's the Idea A word part that is added at the end of a word is called a **suffix.** In *wonderful,* the suffix is *-ful.* Suffixes change the meanings of words just as prefixes do.

Sometimes the spelling of a base word changes when a suffix is added. For example, a letter may be dropped from the base word. *Love* becomes *lovable.* Sometimes the final consonant may be doubled. *Win* becomes *winner.* At other times, the final letter of the base word may be changed. *Happy* becomes *happiness.*

The following list shows seven common suffixes with their meanings. Examples are also given.

Suffix	Meaning	Example
-able or **-ible**	"can be, having this quality"	movable, sensible
-er or **-or**	"a person or thing that does something"	leader, generator
-less	"without"	helpless
-ful	"full of"	joyful
-ous	"full of"	mysterious
-ment	"the state or quality of being"	movement
-ness	"the state or quality of being"	sadness

Check It Out Read the following words and their definitions. Notice how the meanings of the suffix and base word combine to create a new word with a new meaning.

washable—"can be washed"
survivor—"a person who survives"
valueless—"without value or worth"
harmful—"full of harm"
envious—"full of envy"
contentment—"the state of being content, satisfied"
greediness—"the quality of being greedy"

- What is the suffix in each word? In which words is the spelling of the base word changed?

Try Your Skill   Number your paper from 1 to 16. Find the suffix in each word below. Then write the base word and the meaning of the suffix for each word. For example, for the word *sensible* you would write: sense + having this quality.

drive + person who can
1. driver
deaf + state of being
2. deafness
use + full of
3. useful
fame + quality of
4. famous
improve + quality of
5. improvement
tax + can be
6. taxable
operate + person who can
7. operator
thought + without
8. thoughtless

glamor + full of
9. glamorous
wait + person who does
10. waiter
gentle + state of
11. gentleness
return + can be
12. returnable
direct + person who does
13. director
doubt + full of
14. doubtful
study + full of
15. studious
thank + full of
16. thankful

Keep This in Mind

- A suffix is a word part added to the end of a base word. A suffix has a meaning of its own that changes the meaning of a base word. Sometimes the spelling of a base word is changed when a suffix is added.

Now Write   Use a dictionary to find seven words, each containing one of the seven suffixes you have learned. List the words and define them. Label your paper **End of the Line** and keep it in your folder.

Have students divide into groups. Each group should choose one suffix and then try to find as many words as they can that use that suffix. They should use dictionaries to check their work. Display the results in the classroom.

Optional Practice

Introduce these additional suffixes to the class. Have students find the definitions of each in the dictionary and write one example of a word that contains that suffix.

-tion   -age
-ly   -ship
-hood   -ist

Extending the Lesson

Distribute newspaper articles to the class. First, have students list all of the words that they can find using the seven suffixes that they have learned. Next, have them define the words. Last, if a change was made in the spelling of the base word, have the students put a star next to the word.

Section 2 Objectives

1. To review the basic characteristics of dictionaries

2. To use guide words to locate words in a dictionary

3. To know and to use the information in a dictionary entry: syllabification, pronunciation, part of speech, special forms or endings, history, definition, and synonyms and antonyms

4. To practice using context to determine the correct dictionary definition of a word

Preparing the Students

Choose a word, look it up in three different dictionaries, and reproduce each entry. Distribute copies to the students and discuss the similarities and differences among the entries. Then take the students to the school library and show them the dictionaries available to them. Ask them to compare their classroom dictionary with an unabridged dictionary. Compare those with the *Oxford English Dictionary* if one is available. Explain that there are specialized dictionaries and show students several examples.

Additional Resources

Mastery Test — pages 13–14 in the test booklet

Practice Book — pages 11–14

Duplicating Masters — pages 11-14

Using a Dictionary

Teaching Special Populations

LD It may be necessary to simplify sets of instructions for these students. Also, give LD students additional exercises to review alphabetizing skills. Check from time to time that students are managing to find words in the dictionary.

ESL ESL students may have pronunciation difficulties that inhibit their attempts to find words in a dictionary. Carefully pronounce each word aloud and emphasize phonemes that may not appear in the students' native languages. Construct a simplified chart to demonstrate the relationship between diacritical marks, syllables, and how sounds are produced. Use contextual examples to demonstrate a word's multiple meanings.

Pretest to determine ESL students' familiarity with parts of speech. (See Handbook Sections 3–12.) Since some languages do not permit multiple functions for particular words, you should offer plenty of concrete examples. Try pairing students with native English speakers and provide extra guidance when dealing with dictionary entries for irregular verbs.

NSD Ask students to look up the meaning and pronunciation of any unfamiliar words they come across. Check to make sure students who frequently mispronounce words can find these words in the dictionary. Encourage NSD students to keep a private list of nonstandard words they often use, together with the standard equivalents.

Part 1

Objectives

To review the basic characteristics of dictionaries

Presenting the Lesson

1. Read aloud and discuss **Here's the Idea.** Refer to the classroom dictionaries. Study the list of terms, symbols, and abbreviations. Also check to see what other information is included in addition to the dictionary itself (tables, lists, etc.).

2. Discuss **Check It Out.**

3. Assign **Try Your Skill.** Check the alphabetical order in class.

4. Read **Keep This in Mind.**

5. Assign **Now Write.** Have students record the name of the dictionary they use. Be aware that answers may vary slightly depending on what dictionary was used.

Individualizing the Lesson

Less-Advanced Students

1. Before assigning **Try Your Skill,** have students alphabetize the first names of everyone in the class. Have each student print his or her name on a card. Then use the cards to show the students how to approach the task of alphabetizing systematically. Put all the cards with names starting with the same letter in groups. Then arrange the names within a group by the second letter, and so on.

2. Do **Try Your Skill** on the board as in-class exercise.

In So Many Words

How To Use a Dictionary

Here's the Idea A dictionary is a useful tool. This handy reference book contains lists of words and information about the words. When you read, you will see unfamiliar words. A dictionary will help you understand the meanings of these words. When you write, you may be unsure about the spelling or usage of some words. A dictionary helps then, too.

There are many kinds of dictionaries. Some are written for people of certain age groups. Some dictionaries cover only one major subject. Even general dictionaries differ. Some are unabridged, or complete. Many are abridged, or shortened. Each dictionary has its own terms, symbols, abbreviations, and organization. It is important, then, to become familiar with the dictionary you use.

All dictionaries have one thing in common, however. Words are always arranged in alphabetical order, which allows you to find a word quickly. Words beginning with *a* come before words beginning with *b*. If two words begin with the same letter, they are alphabetized by the second letter. If the first two letters are the same, look at the third letter, and so on. The following sequence of words is in alphabetical order: *transfer, transistor, translate, transmission, transparent,* and *transplant.*

Check It Out Look at the bottom portion of a dictionary page shown on the next page.

- How is each column of words listed? What words are new to you?
- What special symbols are used in this dictionary?

he·red·i·ty (hə red′ə tē) *n.*, *pl.* **-ties** [< Fr. < L. *hereditas*, heirship < *heres*, heir: for IE. base see GO] **1.** the transmission of characteristics from parents to offspring by means of genes in the chromosomes **2.** all the characteristics that one inherits genetically

Her·e·ford (hur′fərd, her′ə-) *n.* [orig. bred in *Herefordshire*, England] any of a breed of beef cattle having a white face and a red body with white markings

here·in (hir in′) *adv.* **1.** in here; in or into this place **2.** in this writing [her name is listed *herein*] **3.** in this matter, detail, etc. [you don't speak clearly and *herein* you are at fault]

here·in·a·bove (hir′in ə buv′) *adv.* in the preceding part (of this document, speech, etc.): also **here′in·be·fore′** (-bi fôr′)

here·in·af·ter (-af′tər) *adv.* in the following part (of this document, speech, etc.): also **here′in·be·low′** (-bi lō′)

HEREFORD COW

her·mit (hur′mit) *n.* [< OFr. < LL. < LGr. < Gr. *erēmitēs* < *erēmos*, solitary] a person who lives by himself away from others, often for religious reasons; recluse **her·mit′ic, her·mit′i·cal** *adj.* **—her′mit·like′** *adj.*

her·mit·age (-ij) *n.* **1.** the place where a hermit lives **2.** a place where a person can live away from other people; retreat

hermit crab any of various soft-bellied crabs that live in the empty shells of certain mollusks, as snails

☆**hermit thrush** a N. American thrush with a brown body, spotted breast, and reddish-brown tail

Her·mon (hur′man), **Mount** mountain on the border between Syria & Lebanon

Her·mo·sil·lo (er′mô sē′yô) city in NW Mexico: pop. 197,000

her·ni·a (hur′nē ə) *n.*, *pl.* **-ni·as, -ni·ae** (-ē) [L.: for IE. base see CORD] the sticking out of all or part of an organ, esp. a part of the intestine, through a tear in the wall of the surrounding structure; rupture **—her′ni·al** *adj.*

HERMIT CRAB
(to 18 in. long)

---

fat, āpe, cär; ten, ēven; is, bite; gō, hôrn, tōōl, look; oil, out; up, fur; get; joy; yet; chin; she; thin, *then*; zh, leisure; ŋ, ring; ə for *a* in *ago*, *e* in *agent*, *i* in *sanity*, *o* in *comply*, *u* in *focus*; ' as in *able* (ā′b'l); Fr. bal; ë, Fr. coeur; ö, Fr. feu; Fr. mon; ö, Fr. coq; ü, Fr. duc; r, Fr. cri; H, G. ich; kh, G. doch; ‡foreign; ☆ Americanism; < derived from. See inside front cover.

Try Your Skill   Arrange the following list of words in alphabetical order: *tie, mill, soft, art, article, brook, tiger, tight, sofa, softly, milk, bronze, soggy, artificial, tie-dye, tile.* answers below

---

Keep This in Mind

- A dictionary is a reference book that lists words alphabetically and gives an explanation for each word.
- Become familiar with the abbreviations, symbols, and organization of the dictionary you use.

Think of ten words that begin with the same letter and arrange the words in alphabetical order. Write a definition for each word. Use a dictionary to help you. Label your paper **In So Many Words** and keep it in your folder.

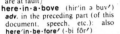

art	sofa	tiger
article	soft	tight
artificial	softly	tile
brook	soggy	
bronze	tie	
milk	tie-dye	
mill		

25

Advanced Students

Assign each student a specialized dictionary to investigate and report on to the class. Have them report on dictionaries of etymology, slang dictionaries, bilingual dictionaries, rhyming dictionaries, etc. Ask them to bring in specialized dictionaries from home if they have any.

Optional Practice

Discuss the use of glossaries in textbooks. Have students compare the information found in a glossary entry to that found in a dictionary entry. Remind students to use their glossaries when they need quick and handy reference.

Extending the Lesson

To develop accuracy and speed in looking up words in the dictionary, have races. Give students a short list of words. They are to write down the page number of their classroom dictionary on which the word appears. The first student to have finished correctly is the winner. As students become more adept, make the lists longer.

Objective

To use guide words to locate words in a dictionary

Presenting the Lesson

1. Read aloud and discuss **Here's the Idea.** Refer to the classroom dictionaries to locate guide words.

2. Discuss **Check It Out.** Using the classroom dictionaries, ask volunteers to state the guide words for the pages on which these words would be found: *lotus, walk, apple, sliver,* and *belt.*

3. Assign **Try Your Skill.** Check the answers in class.

4. Read **Keep This in Mind** aloud and then assign **Now Write.**

Individualizing the Lesson

Less-Advanced Students

1. Use a classroom dictionary to show students where guide words are located and to demonstrate their use. If the classroom dictionary varies from the dictionary illustrated in the text, make sure that students understand the differences.

2. Have students do **Try Your Skill** as a group exercise.

Advanced Students

Have students write the actual guide words in their classroom dictionaries for the words in **Try Your Skill.**

Lead the Way

How To Use Guide Words

Here's the Idea   Most dictionaries have two **guide words** on each page. The guide words appear in large, bold print at the top of the page. Guide words tell you at a glance the range of words on each page. The guide word on the left is the same as the first entry word on the page. The guide word on the right is the same as the last entry word on the page. Every other word on the page is somewhere between the two words in alphabetical order. Look at this top portion of a dictionary page.

| **Maxine** | 593 | **meager** |

Max·ine (mak sēn′) [fem. of *Max:* see MAXIMILIAN] a feminine name
Max·well (maks′wel, -wəl), **James Clerk** (klärk) 1831–79; Scot. physicist
May¹ (mā) *n.* [OFr. < L. < *Maia,* goddess of increase] **1.** the fifth month of the year, having 31 days **2.** the springtime of life; youth
May² (mā) [contr. of MARY, MARGARET] a feminine name
may (mā) *v.aux. pt.* **might** [OE. *mæg* < IE. base *magh-,* to be able] a helping verb followed by an infinitive (without *to*) and meaning: **1.** to be possible or likely to *[it may rain]* **2.** to be allowed or have permission to *[you may go]* **3.** to be able to as a result *[they died that we may be free]* **4.** it is to be wished or hoped that *[may he rest in peace]* —see SYN. at CAN¹
Ma·ya (mä′yə) *n.* **1.** *pl.* **Ma′yas, Ma′ya** a member of a tribe of Indians in SE Mexico and Central America, who had a highly developed civilization **2.** their language —*adj.* of the Mayas — **Ma′yan** *adj., n.*
Ma·ya·güez (mä′yä gwes′) seaport in W Puerto Rico: pop. 69,000
☆ **May apple 1.** a woodland plant with shield-shaped leaves and a single large, white flower, found in the eastern U.S. **2.** its yellow, oval fruit
may·be (mā′bē) *adv.* [ME. (for *it may be*)] perhaps
May·day (mā′dā′) *n.* [< Fr. (*venez*) *m'aider,* (come) help me] the international radiotelephone signal for help, used by ships and aircraft in distress
May Day May 1: as a traditional spring festival, often celebrated by dancing, crowning a May queen, etc.; as an international labor holiday, observed in many countries by parades, demonstrations, etc.

maze (māz) *n.* [< OE. *amasian,* to amaze & pp. *amasod,* puzzled] **1.** a confusing, intricate network of winding pathways; labyrinth, specif. one used in psychological experiments and tests **2.** a state of confusion or bewilderment — **ma′zy** *adj.* **-zi·er, -zi·est** —**ma′zi·ly** *adv.* —**ma′zi·ness** *n.*
ma·zur·ka, ma·zour·ka (mə-zur′kə, -zoor′-) *n.* [Pol. *mazurka,* woman from Mazovia, region of C Poland] **1.** a lively Polish dance like the polka **2.** music for this, generally in 3/4 or 3/8 time

MAZE

Maz·zi·ni (mät tsē′nē, mäd dzē′nē), **Giu·sep·pe** (jōō zep′pe) 1805–72; It. patriot & revolutionist
M.B.A. Master of Business Administration
M·ba·ba·ne ('m bä bä′nä) capital of Swaziland: pop. 14,000
MBS Mutual Broadcasting System
Mc-, Mᶜ- *same as* MAC-
M.C. **1.** Master of Ceremonies **2.** Member of Congress
☆ **Mc·Car·thy·ism** (mə kär′thē iz′m) *n.* [after J. *McCarthy,* U.S. senator (1946–57)] the use of careless, often false, accusations and methods of investigating that violate civil liberties
Mc·Clel·lan (mə klel′ən), **George Brin·ton** (brin′t'n) 1826–85; Union general in the Civil War
Mc·Cor·mick (mə kôr′mik), **Cyrus Hall** (hôl) 1809–84, U.S. inventor of the reaping machine
Mc·Coy (mə koi′), **the (real)** [Slang] the real person or thing, not a substitute

Dictionary guide words help you find the word you need. First look for guide words that have the same first letter as the word you need. Then look for guide words having the same second letter. Keep looking for guide words that are more and more like the word you want.

Check It Out Look at the top portion of a dictionary page shown on the facing page.

- What are the guide words for this page? Would you find the word *meager* on this page? Which way would you turn to find the word *maximum? meal? mature? meaning?*

Try Your Skill Write the following sets of guide words on your paper: *raga/raise, raised/Ramses, seal/seating, seatmate/second nature*. Write each of the following words under the appropriate set of guide words. Then arrange each list in alphabetical order.

1 rain	1 raid	3 search	2 ramp
2 rally	1 ragged	3 seat	4 second cousin
4 Seattle	2 ram	2 raisin	2 ramble
3 seam	4 second base	4 second	1 raise
3 seaport	2 railroad	3 season	4 seaweed

Keep This in Mind

- Guide words show the alphabetical range of words on each page of the dictionary. The left guide word is the same as the first word on the page. The right guide word is the same as the last word on the page.

Now Write If you were writing a composition about musical instruments, you might have to look up the following words: *kettledrum, lute, mandolin, oboe, sitar, sousaphone, viola,* and *zither*. Find each word in a dictionary. On your paper, list each word and write the guide words that appear on the page where the word is found. Choose four of the words and write four sentences. Use one of the words in each sentence. Label your paper **Lead the Way** and put it into your folder.

Using their own dictionaries, have students copy the guide words they find for the following words.

teller, add, acid, career, drip, newt, lathe, dollar, tepid, rain

Extending the Lesson

Ask students to make a list of ten words that relate to a hobby or interest of theirs. Instruct them to look up the words in the classroom dictionary. Next to each word, they are to write the guide words that appear on the page. Then ask them to define their words.

Objective

To know and to use the information in a dictionary entry: syllabification, pronunciation, part of speech, special forms or endings, history, definition, and synonyms and antonyms

Presenting the Lesson

1. Read aloud and discuss **Here's the Idea.** Make a list of all the information included in a dictionary entry on the chalkboard. Then choose sample words and study the entries in the classroom dictionaries. Ask students if they can find anything on the dictionary page that has not been explained.

2. Discuss **Check It Out.** Again ask students if there is anything on the sample dictionary page they don't understand.

3. Assign **Try Your Skill.**

4. Read **Keep This in Mind** and then assign **Now Write.** Have students record the title of the dictionary they use. Ask volunteers to share their findings with the class.

Individualizing the Lesson

Less-Advanced Students

1. These students may have trouble understanding this part. Go over the notations in the dictionary, writing them on the board for easy reference.

2. Choose another word and substitute it for the word *condition* in **Check It Out.** Use the students' classroom dictionaries and answer the questions in group discussion.

3. Do **Try Your Skill** orally.

28

Upon My Word!

How To Read a Dictionary Entry

Here's the Idea   A dictionary entry explains the meaning of a word. In addition, an entry contains much other information that is useful. All of the information will not be contained in every entry. Also, the information will not be arranged in the same order in every dictionary. Most dictionaries, however, will give you the following information.

The **entry word** itself is shown in bold type and divided. For example, the word *vacation* is entered as **va·ca·tion.** When writing, you may have to divide a word at the end of a line. Use the dictionary to find the correct division.

The **pronunciation** of a word is usually given within parentheses. Special symbols help you to sound out the word. The word is divided into syllables, and an accent mark tells you which syllable to stress. For example, *auditorium* appears as (ô′ də tôr′ ē əm).

The **part of speech** is given by an abbreviation in bold print. For example, *noun* is abbreviated *n.* Usually you will find a list of abbreviations in the front of your dictionary.

Sometimes a word can be used as more than one part of speech. If so, the other parts of speech will also be given.

If a word has **special forms** or **endings,** they will be included next in the entry. For example, the entry for the irregular verb *do* includes the forms **did, done,** and **doing.** Plural endings of some nouns are also given. For the noun *potato,* for instance, the plural ending **-toes** is given.

The **origin,** or **history,** of a word is next, usually in brackets. Symbols are used. The symbol < means "came from." The abbreviations *OE., Fr.,* and *L.* stand for "Old English," "French," and "Latin." Look up unfamiliar abbreviations.

28

Definitions are given in a numbered list. Usually the most common definition is first. If a word has a special meaning in a particular field, the dictionary mentions the field. For example, one definition of *love* is *"Tennis—a score of zero."*

A word may have a meaning that is generally used informally. This is a colloquial meaning. The dictionary indicates this by using an abbreviation. For example, one definition of *buzz* is "[Colloq.] a telephone call." The dictionary also indicates slang, which is very informal, popular language. For example, one definition of *bread* is "[Slang] money."

Synonyms and **antonyms** may also be listed. Some entries may include a *synonymy*—a group of synonyms and their shades of meaning. Sometimes, the notation *"see **SYN.** at"* may direct you to a synonymy under a different entry.

Do you see how helpful a dictionary can be? Be familiar with the way an entry is given in the dictionaries you use.

Check It Out   Read this dictionary entry.

> **con·di·tion** (kən dish′ən) *n.* [< OFr. < L. *condicio*, agreement < *com-*, together + *dicere*, to speak] **1.** anything required before the performance or completion of something else; provision; stipulation *[conditions* set for a cease-fire*]* **2.** prerequisite *[*some consider wealth a *condition* of happiness*]* **3.** anything that has an effect on the nature of something else; circumstance *[conditions* were favorable for business*]* **4.** manner or state of being *[*a house in a dilapidated *condition]* **5.** *a)* state of health *[*the patient's *condition] b)* [Colloq.] an illness; ailment *[*a lung *condition]* **6.** a proper or healthy state *[*athletes out of *condition]* **7.** social position; rank; station ☆**8.** the requirement that a student make up deficiencies in a subject in order to pass it **9.** *Law* a clause in a contract, will, etc. that revokes or modifies all or part of it if a certain thing happens —*vt.* **1.** to impose a condition or conditions on **2.** to be a condition of; determine, modify, or influence *[*factors which *condition* our lives*]* **3.** to bring into a proper or desired condition *[*training camps help to *condition* a team*]* **4.** *Psychol. a)* to develop a conditioned reflex or behavior pattern in *b)* to cause to become accustomed *(to) [*to *condition* women to annual fashion changes*]* —*see **SYN.** at STATE —**on condition that** provided that —**con·di′tion·er** *n.*

· How many syllables are there in *condition?* Where is the pronunciation given? What part of speech is *condi-*

Advanced Students

Have students answer the questions in **Try Your Skill** for the word *shell.*

Optional Practice

Make a copy of a page from a dictionary. Have students find the following parts on the page.

1. Tell them to circle an *entry word*.
2. Have them circle the *part of speech*, and then write it out fully in the margin next to the entry word.
3. Tell them to find the *origin* of an entry word and to write it out fully in the margin next to the entry word.
4. Tell them to underline any *colloquial* or *slang* expressions given.
5. Tell them to put a star next to any *synonyms* or *antonyms* given.

Extending the Lesson

Ask each student to skim through his or her dictionary and make up interesting questions about ten different words. Here are some sample questions.

What was the Greek word from which *stomach* originated?
What are the two ways to make *cactus* plural?

Collect the questions, duplicate the best ones, and have a dictionary treasure hunt in class.

tion? Is it used as any other part of speech? From what languages did the word come? What is the most common definition? Are there any definitions used in special fields? Are any synonyms mentioned?

Try Your Skill   Read the following dictionary entry.

scene (sēn) *n.* [< MFr. < L. < Gr. *skene*, tent, stage: for IE. base see SHINE]   **1.** the place in which any event occurs *[the scene of the crime]*   **2.** the setting of the action of a play, story, etc. *[the scene of Hamlet is Denmark]*   **3.** a division of a play, usually part of an act   **4.** a part of a play, story, etc. that is a single, continuous unit of action *[a deathbed scene]*   **5.** *same as* SCENERY (sense 1)   **6.** a view, landscape, etc. *[a peaceful autumn scene]*   **7.** a show of strong feeling before others *[she made a scene in court]*   **8.** a real or imaginary event, esp. as described *[she witnessed a distressing scene on her way home]*   **9.** [Colloq.] a particular area of interest or activity *[the poetry scene]* —see *SYN.* at VIEW —**behind the scenes 1.** backstage   **2.** in private or in secrecy —☆**make the scene** [Slang]   **1.** to be present   **2.** to participate actively or successfully

1. How is the word *scene* pronounced?
2. What part of speech is it?
3. What is the most common meaning?
4. What is a synonym for *scene?*
5. What slang phrase includes the word *scene?*

Keep This in Mind

· A dictionary entry contains the meanings of a word and other helpful information. Entries may differ in different dictionaries.

Now Write   Use a dictionary to find words with these characteristics. Each word should have one characteristic.

1. has two pronunciations
2. has three parts of speech
3. has come from Spanish
4. has an informal meaning
5. has an antonym
6. has a synonym

A Number of Choices

How To Find the Meaning of a Word

Here's the Idea When you see an unfamiliar word, you look it up in a dictionary. What do you do if the word has several meanings? How can you tell which is the right one? Most of the time the context will help you find the right meaning.

For example, the simple word *run* has a surprising number of meanings. *Webster's New World Dictionary, Students Edition,* gives forty-nine meanings for *run* as a verb. The same entry lists twenty meanings for *run* as a noun, two for *run* as an adjective, and twenty phrases that include *run*. In each sentence below, the context helps you to determine the meaning of *run*.

1. I had to *run* to catch the bus this morning.
(In this context, *run* means "move swiftly.")
2. The Mississippi River *runs* into the Gulf of Mexico.
(In this context, *runs* means "flows.")
3. Red hair and freckles *run* in our family.
(In this context, *run* means "continue to occur.")
4. Jim Rice's double brought in the winning *run*.
(In this context, *run* means "scoring point.")

You can see that a single entry can contain many different meanings for a word.

Sometimes, however, the same word seems to appear in more than one entry. You will find the word *bat*, for example, entered three times: *bat*[1], a noun, means "a club used to hit a ball"; *bat*[2], also a noun, means "a mouselike mammal that flies at night"; and *bat*[3], a verb, means "to blink, as to *bat an eye.*" In each of the three entries, the word *bat* has a different meaning and a different origin. Such a word is called a *homograph*. A homograph has the same spelling, but it may have different

31

Part 4

Objective

To practice using context to determine the correct dictionary definition of a word

Presenting the Lesson

1. Read aloud and discuss **Here's the Idea.** Review the meaning of *context.* Emphasize the importance of reading through all the entries to find the applicable definition.

2. Discuss **Check It Out.** If students are not familiar with the abbreviations, refer them to the front of their classroom dictionaries.

3. Assign and discuss **Try Your Skill.**

4. Read **Keep This in Mind** and then assign **Now Write.**

Individualizing the Lesson

Less-Advanced Students

Be sure students understand that a word can have several *similar* meanings, or several *different* meanings. For example, a word like *bed* has several meanings but all are extentions of one idea (furniture to lie on, flower bed, river bed, etc.). A word like *bureau* has two completely different meanings (chest of drawers, division of government).

Advanced Students

Ask students to think of words that have more than one meaning. Have them write down only the definitions of the word and let the rest of the class guess the word (example: a cord; a system of pipes or wires connecting the telephone system; a

31

long thin mark; a border; descendants of a common ancestor—*line*).

Optional Practice

Have students write sentences for words with different meanings. They should write a different sentence for each different meaning. For example, *sharp* has four different meanings, while *case* has three, and *ring* has five.

Extending the Lesson

As a class, look up each of these words in the classroom dictionary. Divide the entries among the students. Instruct them to write a sentence for each dictionary entry that they were assigned. Collect all of the sentences and compile them by word. Duplicate them and give each student a copy of the sentences. Then ask students to put the number of the correct dictionary entry next to the appropriate sentence.

fit	post	bridge
low	egg	cope

pronunciations. You can see that each entry is not a shade of meaning of the same word, but it is really a different word. If you see a word with more than one entry, read all the entries to find the meaning you want.

Check It Out   Read the dictionary entries below.

> **school**[1] (sko͞ol) **n.** [OE. *scol* < L. *schola* < Gr. *schole*, leisure (esp. as used for study), school < IE. base *segh-*, to hold] **1.** a place or institution for teaching and learning [a public *school*, dancing *school*] **2.** *a)* the building or buildings, classrooms, etc. of a school   *b)* all of its students and teachers [most of the *school* attends the games]   *c)* a regular session of teaching at a school [*school* begins next week] **3.** *a)* attendance at a school [to miss *school* for a week]   *b)* the process of being educated at a school [he finished *school* at seventeen] **4.** any situation or experience through which one gains knowledge, training, etc. [the *school* of hard knocks] **5.** a particular division of an institution of learning, esp. of a university [the *school* of law] **6.** a group following the same teachings, beliefs, methods, etc. [the Impressionist *school*] **7.** a way of life [a gentleman of the old *school*] —**vt.** **1.** to teach; instruct; educate [he was *schooled* in the old methods] **2.** to discipline or control [to *school* oneself to be patient] —**adj.** of a school or schools —see **SYN.** at TEACH
>
> **school**[2] (skool) **n.** [Du., a crowd]   a large number of fish or water animals of the same kind swimming or feeding together —**vi.** to move together in such a school —see **SYN.** at GROUP

- Which definition of *school*[1] fits the context of the following sentence? I missed *school* last Monday.
- From what language did *school*[1] come? *school*[2]? What parts of speech is *school*[1] used as? *school*[2]? Under what word would you find a synonym for *school*[1]? *school*[2]?

Try Your Skill   Read the following dictionary entries. Then read the five sentences. Decide which meaning of *shock* fits the context of each sentence. Write your answer.

> **shock**[1] (shäk) **n.** [< Fr. < MFr. *choquer*, prob. < MDu. *schokken*, to collide] **1.** a sudden, powerful blow, shake, disturbance, etc. [the *shock* of an earthquake] **2.** *a)* a sudden and strong upsetting of the mind or feelings *b)* something causing this [her accident was a *shock* to us] **3.** the violent effect on the body of an electric current passed through it

4. [Colloq.] *short for* SHOCK ABSORBER: *used in pl.* **5.** *Med.* a disorder caused by severe injury or damage to the body, loss of blood, etc., and marked by a sharp drop in blood pressure, a rapid pulse, etc. **—vt. 1.** to disturb emotionally; astonish, horrify, etc. [*her words shocked us*] **2.** to cause a physical shock to **3.** to produce electric shock in **—vi.** to be shocked, distressed, etc. [*one who does not shock easily*] **—shock′er n.**

SYN.—shock suggests a violent disturbance of the mind or emotions caused by an unexpected, overwhelming event that comes as a blow [*shocked* by her sudden death]; **startle** implies a slight shock of surprise or alarm, often one that causes a person to jump or flinch [*startled* by the clap of thunder]; **paralyze** suggests such extreme shock as to make one unable to move for a time [*paralyzed* with fear]; to **stun** is to shock with such force as to make one numb, dazed, or speechless [*stunned* by the disaster]

shock² (shak) **n.** [prob. via MDu. or MLowG. *schok*] a number of sheaves of grain, as corn or wheat, stacked together on end to cure and dry **—vt., vi.** to gather in shocks

shock³ (shak) **n.** [< ? SHOCK²] a thick, bushy or tangled mass, as of hair

1. I was *shocked* by the violence in the TV movie.
   <small>sudden upset of feelings</small>
2. The *shocks* of wheat cast long shadows across the field.
   <small>grain stacked together</small>
3. A *shock* of hair kept falling in Betsy's eyes as she wrote.
   <small>thick mass of hair</small>
4. The mechanic replaced the worn *shocks* in the Chevy.
   <small>shock absorber</small>
5. Grandpa Willie is in Forbes Hospital suffering from *shock*.
   <small>physical disorder</small>

Keep This in Mind

- When you look up an unfamiliar word in the dictionary, decide which meaning fits the context.
- Sometimes a word has more than one entry, with a different origin and meaning for each. Again, use the context to help you find the meaning.

Now Write   Look up two of the following words in the dictionary: *bark, lean, part,* and *sound.* If the word appears in more than one entry, read through all the entries. Write three definitions for each of the two words. Then write a sentence using each of the meanings you have written. Label your paper **A Number of Choices** and put it into your folder.

Section **3** Objectives

1. To recognize and learn the appropriate uses of standard and nonstandard English

2. To recognize slang as a type of nonstandard English

3. To recognize that many activities have their own specialized vocabularies called *jargon*

Preparing the Students

Ask students if they think that all language is appropriate in all situations. Ask them if slang is always appropriate. Ask them if some language can be used only in a technical situation. Tell students that this section will help them to recognize different kinds of language and to know when to use each kind.

Additional Resources

Mastery Test — page 15 in the test booklet

Practice Book — pages 15–17

Duplicating Masters — pages 15-17

Teaching Special Populations

LD Give LD students simplified instructions for **Check It Out, Try Your Skill** and **Now Write.** You may also wish to shorten some exercises and pair students with others who read well.

ESL Distinguishing between standard and nonstandard usage depends upon a native cultural awareness that many ESL students do not yet have. Demonstrate to students when and where each form of

The Right Language at the Right Time

usage is appropriate. Also remember that foreign language speakers often mistake slang (particularly that used on television) for standard English.

Some nonstandard usage by ESL students results from foreign grammatical rules being applied to English. Double negatives and verbs at the ends of sentences, for instance, are correct forms in many languages. When students have difficulty with subject-verb agreement, refer them to Handbook Section 15. Also use native English speakers to act out situations that demonstrate appropriate and inappropriate usage.

NSD This section is invaluable for NSD students. Remember that even nonstandard dialects employ distinctions between standard and nonstandard usage. Tell students that their dialect is neither wrong nor bad, but stress that there *is* a standard dialect that most people speak. Learning this dialect will help them communicate with the greatest number of people.

Point out to students that slang is an extremely limited form of communication. To demonstrate how quickly slang becomes dated, write some lines of dialogue using contemporary slang and slang, say, from about ten years ago. (For inspiration you might turn to the reruns of some older television shows.) Then have two volunteers act out the piece. Encourage NSD students to provide their own examples of situations in which slang is and isn't appropriate.

A Proper Time

Objectives

To recognize and learn the appropriate uses of standard and nonstandard English

Presenting the Lesson

1. Read aloud and discuss **Here's the Idea.** Write the terms *Standard English* and *Nonstandard English* on the board. Ask students for sentence examples using nonstandard English. Write the examples on the board. Then ask students to change the sentences so that they use standard English. Emphasize that only standard English is acceptable in all situations.

2. Have students read and discuss **Check It Out.** Refer to Handbook Sections 4 and 5, pages 403–428, if students have difficulty seeing what is nonstandard about the sentences in the second column.

3. Assign and discuss **Try Your Skill.** If students need help, refer them to the appropriate Handbook sections.

4. Read **Keep This in Mind.** Assign **Now Write.** Ask several volunteers to read their revised descriptions aloud.

Individualizing the Lesson

Less-Advanced Students

Do **Check It Out** and **Try Your Skill** orally. Help students find the appropriate usage rule for each item.

Using Standard and Nonstandard English

Here's the Idea   You wouldn't wear a bathing suit to a concert. Neither would you get all dressed up to go to the beach. Similarly, different types of language are suitable for different situations. There are two types, or levels, of language from which you can choose. They are called **standard English** and **nonstandard English.** These two types of language are described in the following chart:

Two Levels of Language

	Standard English	Nonstandard English
Definition	Standard English is language that follows the rules of good grammar and usage.	Nonstandard English is language that does not follow the rules of good grammar and usage.
Use	Standard English is acceptable in all situations.	Nonstandard English is unacceptable in all situations except very casual conversation with friends.
Examples	1. He doesn't care. 2. Those chairs are broken. 3. I'm not going.	1. He don't care. 2. Them chairs is broke. 3. I ain't going.

Notice that nonstandard English is unacceptable in most situations. Get into the habit of using standard English.

Check It Out   Read the following pairs of sentences.

Standard	Nonstandard
1. We are done with our work.	1. We done with our work.
2. She didn't say anything.	2. She didn't say nothing.
3. We saw those photo-graphs.	3. We seen them photo-graphs.
4. He and I are brothers.	4. Him and me are brothers.
5. Are you the winner?	5. Is you the winner?

· What is nonstandard about the second sentence in each pair?

Try Your Skill   From each pair, choose the sentence that is written in standard English.

1. I don't know if she like you, but I think she do.
   I don't know if she likes you, but I think she does.
2. John and me went to the bake sale.
   John and I went to the bake sale.
3. I want to know where he went.
   I want to know where he gone.
4. We couldn't figure out why he did it.
   We couldn't figure out why he done it.

Keep This in Mind

· Standard English is appropriate in any situation.
· Use standard English when you speak or write.

Now Write   Write a short description of a movie, concert, or sports event. Exchange your paper with a classmate. Circle any examples of nonstandard English in your classmate's paper. Then, take back your own paper and revise it. Replace any nonstandard English with standard English. Save your work.

Part 2

Objectives

To recognize slang as a type of nonstandard English

Presenting the Lesson

1. Ask students for a definition of the word *slang,* and then read **Here's the Idea.** Discuss why slang can become dated so quickly, and ask students for examples of slang that they no longer use because it is not in style.

2. Discuss **Check It Out.** Bring a dictionary of slang to class and read to the class some examples of slang that was once popular. Ask them what they think will happen in five years time to the slang that they speak now.

3. Assign **Try Your Skill.** Read the students' papers aloud. Point out how many synonyms there are for each slang word in standard English.

4. Read **Keep This in Mind** aloud, and then assign **Now Write.** Have volunteers read their terms aloud.

Individualizing the Lesson

Less-Advanced Students

Some of these students may not recognize the words they use as slang. It might help to have them visualize the words that they speak. Ask them to describe in standard English what they see when they say *bummer, uptight,* or *cool.* Point out how much more specific in description the standard words are than the slang words.

Here Today

Using and Misusing Slang

Here's the Idea   **Slang** is a type of nonstandard English made up of fad words and phrases. Most slang is temporary. It lives a brief, colorful life. Then, it disappears and is replaced by newer slang. For example, the following slang terms were popular during the 1950's:

cool cat   hep   wowsville

Today these terms sound dated. They have been replaced by the slang of the 1980's.

You are probably familiar with many slang words and phrases in use today. Some of these terms may even be part of your everyday speech. If you do use slang terms regularly, be aware that slang is not acceptable in most formal situations. Slang should never be used in compositions, reports, business letters, or talks. Slang may be used in casual conversation with friends. It may also be used to make dialogue in a short story sound realistic.

If you do not know whether a particular word is slang, look it up in a dictionary. If the word is not in the dictionary, or if it is labeled *slang,* avoid using it in formal speech and writing.

Check It Out   The following slang terms all have the same meaning. However, each term was popular at a different time during the past seventy years. Read this list of terms.

the cat's pajamas	out of sight
the bee's knees	groovy
swell	neat
peachy	far out

- Can you guess the meaning shared by these terms?
- Are any of these terms popular today? What does this tell you about the nature of slang?

Try Your Skill   Identify the slang terms in the following sentences. Then, rewrite each sentence. Replace each slang term with a standard word or phrase.

1. The accident was a real bummer.
2. Don't be so uptight. Try to relax.
3. Your performance will be fine if you just play it cool.
4. These new fashions have a lot of pizazz.
5. Some guy left a package for you.

> ### Keep This in Mind
> - Slang is a type of nonstandard English made of fad words and phrases.
> - Use slang only in casual conversation or when writing dialogue for a short story.
> - Do not use slang in compositions, reports, business letters, or talks.

Now Write   Working with a partner, make a list of slang terms that are now popular. Write the definition of each term. Then, ask some older people to tell you what slang terms they used when they were young. Make a list of these terms and define them. Label your paper **Here Today.** Save it in your folder.

Advanced Students

Have students divide into groups. Have them write and then act in skits in which formal language is used on the playing field or in the locker room, and slang is used in a government meeting, or law court. Encourage humor (which should clearly illustrate the importance of using the right language at the right time).

Optional Practice

Have students "police" each other's speech patterns for one or two class sessions, giving tickets for slang expressions used in class. Students who receive the tickets must write the standard word as their "fine."

Extending the Lesson

Have students write a dictionary of slang that they and their class-mates use. For every slang expression they write and define, they should list at least three synonyms in standard English. They could photocopy their work for distribution to other classes.

Part 3

Objectives

To recognize that many activities have their own specialized vocabularies called *jargon*

Presenting the Lesson

1. Read **Here's the Idea.** Ask students for other examples of jargon they are familiar with. You might refer them back to Part 2 of Section 1, and ask if any of those words are jargon. (Most are not because they are clearly understood by most people.)

2. Read **Check It Out.** Point out that sometimes members of different professions use the same words but attach different meanings to them. For example, what might *zone defense,* or *forward* mean to someone in the army?

3. Assign **Try Your Skill.** Remind the class that their sentences should be related to the theater.

4. Read **Keep This in Mind** and then assign **Now Write.**

Individualizing the Lesson

Less-Advanced Students

Do **Try Your Skill** as an in-class exercise.

Advanced Students

Have the students choose five examples of jargon from any field and follow the instructions from **Try Your Skill** for them.

A Way of Speaking

Using and Misusing Jargon

Here's the Idea   Many activities have their own special vocabularies. These special vocabularies are called **jargon.** People who work in specialized fields use jargon to communicate with one another quickly. For example, when one auto mechanic talks to another, he or she will use words like *rings, manifold, lifters, catalytic converter,* and *headers.* The mechanics understand one another because they are speaking the jargon of their own field. A person who doesn't know anything about cars will be mystified by such language.

Whenever you speak or write about a specialized activity, be careful about the use of jargon. If you know that your audience is familiar with the activity, you can use as much jargon as you want. However, if your audience is not familiar with the activity, you should avoid jargon completely. If you must use a jargon word, define it right away. Otherwise, your reader or listener will not understand what you are saying.

Check It Out   Read the following words from the jargon of basketball:

> center court
> foul
> double-dribble
> rim shot
> zone defense
> forward

- How many of these words do you know?
- Which of these words would be understood only by someone who knows a great deal about basketball?

- Which of these words have other meanings outside of basketball?

Try Your Skill The following words are from the jargon of the theater. Look up each word in the dictionary. Find out how this word is used by theater people. Then, write two sentences. In the first sentence, make a statement using the word. In the second sentence, define the word. Sentences will vary.

Example: *teasers*

       a. The lights were hidden behind *teasers*.

       b. *Teasers* are rows of very short curtains that hang above the stage.

1. blocking   to work out the movements of the actors
2. scrim   hanging curtain used as backdrop
3. book   the words of a play
4. properties   articles used in the setting
5. proscenium   the apron of a stage

Keep This in Mind

- Many activities have their own special vocabulary called *jargon*.
- Use jargon only when you are sure your audience is familiar with it.

Now Write Choose a special activity that you enjoy a great deal. This may be a sport, a hobby, or a class in school. Make a list of the jargon words that are used by people who perform this activity. Then, write a paragraph describing the activity. When you use a jargon word in the paragraph, make sure you define it. Label your paper **A Way of Speaking.** Save it in your folder.

Have students give two examples of jargon from each field listed below. They might have to check a dictionary or encyclopedia for the answers.

1. medicine
2. banking
3. teaching
4. cosmetics
5. carpentry

Extending the Lesson

Below is a list of words used as jargon by the professions listed next to them. Have students define the word as it is used in each profession. They should use a dictionary to check their work.

1. *culture*—biologist and sociologist
2. *fault*—geologist and tennis pro
3. *bumper*—farmer and auto mechanic
4. *book*—librarian and talent agent

Section 4 Objectives

1. To know what makes a good sentence
2. To write clear, succinct sentences
3. To avoid writing sentences that are repetitive or that state unsupported opinions
4. To avoid padding a sentence with useless expressions
5. To avoid overloading a sentence with too many ideas

Preparing the Students

Write the following groups of words on the chalkboard.

1. Maria, Frank and Katy
2. Is dancing a polka
3. Leo squashed a bug

Read the groups aloud and ask students in what way they are different. Explain that only number 3 is a sentence. Ask the class what should be added to number 3 (a period). Discuss what the students know about sentences. Three things should be brought up.

1. A sentence expresses a complete thought.
2. A sentence has a subject and a predicate. (See pages 343–371 of the Handbook for review.)
3. A sentence begins with a capital letter and ends with a period, a question mark, or an exclamation point.

Additional Resources

Mastery Test — page 16 in the test booklet

Practice Book — pages 18–21

Duplicating Masters — pages 18–21

Writing Effective Sentences

Teaching Special Populations

LD Even experienced writers sometimes find it difficult to distinguish between complete and incomplete thoughts. LD students will require daily drill and simplified examples to help them determine what constitutes a complete thought.

Some LD students may become confused when asked to perform simultaneously the various tasks required of them in the instructions. You may wish to shorten exercises and simplify instructions. **Now Write,** Part 1, for example, can be simplified as follows:

Write five sentences:
1. one that describes something,
2. one that tells about an action,
3. one that tells what something is,
4. one that tells how to do something,
5. one that tells why something should be done.

Read over your sentences when you have finished. Make sure they are clear, complete, and correct. Add changes or corrections.

ESL Concepts such as *empty, padded,* or *overloaded* must be clearly defined before ESL students are asked to apply them to sentences. First complete several exercises as a group, and show students what particular features make these sentences weak or unclear.

NSD NSD students will find this section useful because nonstandard dialect relies heavily on sentences that sound empty to the average speaker. By having constant exposure to well-formed sentences, NSD students should find it easier to produce good syntax and standard English.

Part **1**

Part 1

Make Your Point

Objectives

1. To know what makes a good sentence

2. To write clear, succinct sentences

Presenting the Lesson

1. Read aloud and discuss **Here's the Idea.** Highlight the definition of *sentence*. Then discuss what makes a sentence good. Ask students to paraphrase the thoughts presented in the four example sentences.

2. Discuss **Check It Out.** Ask students what makes each sentence interesting. Point out that word choice is important. Use *wailed* in sentence 2 as an example. Also point out that using a question can be direct, as in sentence 4.

3. Assign and discuss **Try Your Skill.** Remind students that a sentence expresses a single, complete thought. Encourage students to revise their work until each sentence is clear and direct.

4. Read **Keep This in Mind** and then assign **Now Write.** Stress the importance of revising the sentences until they are clear and to the point.

Individualizing the Lesson

Less-Advanced Students

Do **Try Your Skill** as an in-class exercise. Write ideas for the sentences on the board, and then revise each sentence with the students' help. Use **Here's the Idea** to stimulate discussion about when and why revision may be necessary.

Writing Sentences

Here's the Idea   You have seen how important it is to choose words carefully in order to express an idea. The next step is to learn to make your words work together in sentences. A **sentence** is a group of words that expresses a complete thought.

A good sentence makes a point. It expresses an idea in a direct, clear, fresh way. A single sentence can be imaginative and powerful.

Some sentences express an idea particularly well. Consider the examples below:

> Dogs do not dislike poor families.—CHINESE PROVERB

> A thought comes when it wishes, not when I wish.
> —FRIEDRICH NIETZSCHE

> Courage is the price that life exacts for granting peace.
> —AMELIA EARHART

> Some books are to be tasted, others to be swallowed, and some few to be chewed and digested.—FRANCIS BACON

Sentences such as these have been remembered because each makes a point in a lively and original way. When you write a sentence, you will also want to express your idea in a clear and interesting way.

Check It Out   Read the following sentences.

1. Lee walked slowly to the end of the diving board and stared down at the water.
2. Police sirens wailed through the night.
3. In the winter, thermostats should be set at sixty-eight degrees to conserve fuel.

4. Do you know how to write a check?

5. An oboe is a musical instrument that makes a high, sad sound.

- Does each sentence express a single complete thought? Is each sentence clear and direct?

Try Your Skill   Write one sentence in response to each direction below. Make your sentences clear and interesting. Use real or imaginary details.

1. Tell one thing you enjoy doing.
2. Describe a pet you'd like to own.
3. Explain how you travel to school.
4. Explain why everyone should vote in an election.
5. Explain what a sister is.
6. Describe your favorite article of clothing.
7. Tell one event that made you feel like a success.
8. Explain why you like a certain friend.

Keep This in Mind

- A sentence is a group of words that expresses a complete thought. A good sentence is clear and interesting.

Now Write   Write one sentence that tells an event that happened. Write one sentence that describes something. Write one that explains how something is made. Write one that explains why something should be done. Write one that explains what something is. Your sentences may tell only part of a larger idea. However, the point of each sentence should be clear to a reader. Choose your words carefully. Include real or imaginary details. When you are finished, read and revise your work until you are satisfied with it. Label your paper **Make Your Point.** Put your work into your folder.

Have students write two sentences for each direction in **Try Your Skill.** Stress the need for revision to make a sentence lively and original.

Optional Practice

Have students go through their literature book and look for sentences they find imaginative and powerful. Copy and distribute these sentences and discuss with the class what makes the sentences good. You might want to point out humor, interesting comparisons, and specific vocabulary choices if the students don't recognize these things on their own.

Extending the Lesson

1. Collect the **Now Write** papers from this lesson. Compile a sample of the sentences, both good and bad, and reproduce them. Distribute copies to the students and discuss the sentences. Remind students to keep the criteria for a good sentence in mind: a sentence should express a complete thought, and it should be clear and interesting. Ask for suggestions for revisions to improve the weak sentences. Discuss the elements that make the good sentences good.

2. Display a series of photographs around the room. They should be intriguing subjects— faces of people, landscapes, city shots, animals, etc. Have students write a sentence to accompany each photograph. A good source for interesting pictures is old copies of *National Geographic.*

Part 2

Objective

To avoid writing sentences that are repetitive or that state unsupported opinions

Presenting the Lesson

1. Read aloud and discuss **Here's the Idea.** Emphasize that both kinds of empty sentences should be avoided. Repetitive sentences should be simplified, and unsupported statements should be backed up with facts.

2. Discuss **Check It Out.** After revising the sentences, ask students when sentences 3 and 5 would be acceptable. Explain that although each sentence cannot stand alone, each would be usable as a part of a paragraph or composition on the topic.

3. Assign **Try Your Skill.** Remind students to revise their sentences until they are clear and concise.

4. Read **Keep This in Mind** aloud and then assign **Now Write.**

Individualizing the Lesson

Less-Advanced Students

Do **Try Your Skill** as an oral exercise. Write **Keep This in Mind** on the board as a reinforcement as the students correct these empty sentences.

Advanced Students

Have students write five sentences based on strong opinions they hold. Tell them to revise any empty sentences they may have written. Then have the class exchange papers and check for any

Running on Empty

Avoiding Empty Sentences

Here's the Idea   Some sentences do not express an idea clearly or completely. They are called **empty sentences.** One type of empty sentence repeats an idea.

Chuck has a huge appetite, and he always wants to eat.

Appetite means "the desire to eat," so the second part of the sentence is unnecessary. Avoid repetition. Make the sentence simpler or add more information.

Chuck has a huge appetite.
Chuck has a huge appetite, especially for sweets.

Another type of empty sentence makes a statement or offers an opinion without supplying facts, reasons, or examples to back it up. Readers are left hanging. Read the example below:

The movie rating system should be eliminated.

Such a strong statement is empty of meaning for a reader unless it is explained. Supporting evidence may be given in the same sentence or in another sentence.

The movie rating system should be eliminated so that movies, like other forms of entertainment, are open to everyone.
The movie rating system should be eliminated. Like other forms of entertainment, movies should be open to everyone.

In some instances, a strong opinion may be developed in a longer piece of writing, such as a paragraph or a composition.

Check It Out   Read the following empty sentences.

1. Bicycling is the best form of exercise.
2. I paid a great deal for this watch, which was very expensive.

3. Everyone should have a hobby.

4. A motorcycle offers an exciting ride, and I'd like to ride a motorcycle.

5. Everyone should be required to pass a basic skills test in order to earn a high school diploma.

- Which sentences repeat an idea? Which sentences offer an unsupported opinion?
- How would you improve these empty sentences?

Try Your Skill   Rewrite each of these empty sentences.

1. My tooth aches and I am in pain.

2. It is a good book because I like it.

3. Every citizen should be required to serve his or her country for one year.

4. The loggers chopped down all the trees, and none were left standing.

5. All licensed drivers should have to take a driving test every five years.

Keep This in Mind

- Sentences that repeat ideas or offer unsupported opinions are empty sentences.
- Improve a sentence that repeats an idea by making it simpler or by adding information. Improve a sentence with an unsupported opinion by including reasons or facts that support the opinion.

Now Write   Label your paper *Empty Sentences*. Find, or write, two examples of each kind of empty sentence. Improve the sentences by avoiding repetition or by including reasons or facts. Keep your work in your folder.

sentences that still offer unsupported opinions.

Optional Practice

Have students revise the following empty sentences. Answers will vary.

1. When I'm in college I will enjoy being a college student.
2. Summer jobs are hard to get.
3. Everyone should exercise regularly.
4. In planning his career, he was making plans to work.
5. Most people are interested in sports because sports are very interesting.
6. Small cars are the best cars to drive.
7. The school year should be longer.
8. We ate all the popcorn, and there was none left.
9. That was a good movie and I really liked it.
10. Dogs make the best pets.

Extending the Lesson

Give students practice in writing their own sentences. Ask them to write a good sentence for each of the following topics. Pair the students so that they can check each other's work for empty sentences.

dessert
the football team
the marching band
health food
grizzly bears
circus elephants
curfew for teenagers
favorite animals

Part 3

Objective

To avoid padding a sentence with useless expressions

Presenting the Lesson

1. Read aloud and discuss **Here's the Idea.** Review the list of expressions to be avoided. Carefully examine the model padded sentences and the improved versions. Explain that although people often pad sentences when they speak, it is not acceptable to write padded sentences.

2. Discuss **Check It Out.**

3. Assign and discuss **Try Your Skill.** Have volunteers share their improved sentences with the class.

4. Read **Keep This in Mind** and then assign **Now Write.**

Individualizing the Lesson

Less-Advanced Students

Do the first three sentences in **Try Your Skill** with the class. If they have trouble finding the unnecessary words and phrases, ask them to find the verb and subject of the sentence. Then have them go over every other word in the sentence and ask themselves the question, "Is this word necessary to the meaning of the sentence?" Have them finish the exercise working in a group, or with a partner.

Advanced Students

Explain to students that one of the reasons people use padding is that they try to put themselves into every sentence they write. Point out how

48

Slim Down

Avoiding Padded Sentences

Here's the Idea   Some sentences do not make a point directly. They contain useless words and phrases that bury the main idea. Such sentences are called **padded sentences.**

There are several common phrases that add nothing to the meaning of a sentence and should be avoided. Here are some of these expressions that pad a sentence.

because of the fact that	what I mean is
due to the fact that	what I believe is
on account of the fact that	what I'm saying is
the thing is	I mean
my feeling is	you see
I am going to write about	well

You can usually improve a padded sentence by omitting the useless expressions. Sometimes, however, you have to rewrite the sentence completely.

Padded: I couldn't go out on Thursday because of the fact that I had a report to write.

Improved: I couldn't go out on Thursday because I had a report to write.

Padded: On account of the fact that he is a good cook, Jack wanted to get a job in a restaurant after school.

Improved: Jack, a good cook, wanted to work in a restaurant after school.

Check It Out   Read the following padded sentences.

1. What I'm trying to say is that my drawings are of places in my neighborhood.

2. Betty was late for school because, you know, she forgot to set her alarm clock.

48

3. I'm going to write about what happened the week I cooked dinner for my family.

4. Because of the fact that it rained, the class picnic was postponed.

· How would you improve each of these padded sentences?

Try Your Skill   Improve the padded sentences below. Either eliminate any unnecessary words and phrases, or rewrite the entire sentence.

1. My feeling is that this chair is very comfortable.

2. I'm upset due to the fact that I have three tests this week.

3. The thing is that my older sister never wants to hear my opinions.

4. Owing to the fact that this book is overdue, I should return it to the library immediately.

5. The point is that the prices of food, clothing, and housing are rising steadily.

Keep This in Mind

· Sentences containing unnecessary words are padded sentences. Improve a padded sentence by omitting the useless expressions or by revising the sentence.

Now Write   Label your paper *Padded Sentences*. Find, or write, four examples of padded sentences. Improve the sentences. Eliminate unnecessary phrases or rewrite the sentence. Keep your paper in your folder.

many of the expressions listed on page 48 are in the first person or contain a personal pronoun.

Then ask students if there is any other kind of pattern in the list of padding on page 48 (using the word *fact*).

Optional Practice

Have students improve the following padded sentences. Answers will vary.

1. What I believe is that you succeed through your own efforts.

2. Due to the fact that it was foggy, the two cars collided.

3. The thing is that nobody could understand why Dave was so afraid of the dark.

4. My feeling is that this is going to be a great movie!

Extending the Lesson

Ask students to rewrite these sentences eliminating the padding. Answers will vary.

1. Because of the fact that I was running a temperature, the school nurse sent me home.

2. What I'm saying is girls should be eligible for athletic scholarships, too.

3. What I mean is that Larry's poster should win the contest because of the fact that it is the cleverest.

4. This paper is going to tell about the two kinds of skiing.

5. Owing to the fact that I am tired, I am going home.

Slow Down

Avoiding Overloaded Sentences

Objective

To avoid overloading a sentence with too many ideas

Presenting the Lesson

1. Read aloud and discuss **Here's the Idea.** Point out that the best way to avoid writing overloaded sentences is to remember that a sentence should contain only one main idea.

2. Read and discuss **Check It Out.** Emphasize that the way to improve overloading is to break the sentence into smaller parts.

3. Assign **Try Your Skill.** Ask volunteers to share their improved sentences with the class.

4. Read **Keep This in Mind.** Then assign **Now Write.** Have students work in pairs to check each other's work.

Individualizing the Lesson

Less-Advanced Students

1. To emphasize why overloaded sentences need revision, have a student read aloud the sentences in number 1 in **Try Your Skill.** Make sure the person reading only pauses for periods.

2. Have the students do **Try Your Skill** with a partner.

Advanced Students

Have students write a paragraph in which a nervous or excited character relates an incident in one long sentence. Then have students exchange papers and revise their partner's work.

Here's the Idea   Padded sentences contain too many words. **Overloaded sentences** contain too many ideas. Read the overloaded sentences below.

> It was a snowstorm, and the black and white cat sat on the porch and watched as a flock of birds came to the feeder, and the cat waited, ready to pounce.

From this example, you can see that in an overloaded sentence, too many ideas run together. Confusion results. You cannot tell which of the many ideas is the main one. The best way to avoid overloaded sentences is to separate each main idea into its own sentence.

Look at the example sentence again. Notice that *and* is used much too often. *And* is a useful word, but it can be overused. When *and* is used to connect two equal parts of one idea, it is being used correctly. When *and* is used to connect different ideas or ideas that are not equally important, it confuses readers. It leads them to believe that there is a connection when there is none.

A sentence usually contains only one main idea. You can improve an overloaded sentence by breaking it into several shorter sentences.

> During the snowstorm, the black and white cat sat on the porch. As a flock of birds came to the feeder, the cat watched and waited. It was ready to pounce.

Check It Out   Read the following overloaded sentence.

Overloaded: I explained to Marlene and Richard how I do my homework and I said that I do my science first, and then I concentrate on math and French, and once I start I don't stop until it's finished.

Improved: I explained to Marlene and Richard how I do my homework. I said that I do my science first, and then I concentrate on math and French. Once I start, I don't stop until it's finished.

• How has this overloaded sentence been improved?

Try Your Skill Improve the following overloaded sentences.

1. One play turned Sunday's football game around. Two of the Dallas Cowboys tackled the Green Bay Packers' quarterback, and his pass went right into the hands of one of the Cowboys, and the crowd roared, and the Cowboy who intercepted the pass ran it seventy-three yards for a touchdown.

2. My brother is in a rock group. He has an electric guitar, with two amplifiers, and he plays it every day, and the sounds he gets from it are amazing, and his group is going to play at a school dance on Friday.

3. It was the day before the wedding, and the bride and groom sat together in the kitchen, and the refrigerator hummed, and the television screamed in the next room, and they didn't say a word to each other.

Keep This in Mind

• Sentences that contain too many ideas are overloaded sentences. Improve an overloaded sentence by breaking it into several shorter sentences.

Now Write Label your paper *Overloaded Sentences*. Find or write three examples of overloaded sentences. Improve the sentences by breaking them into several shorter sentences. Keep your paper in your folder.

Optional Practice

Have students improve the following sentences. Answers will vary.

1. Tawna got a white bike for her birthday and it is a ten-speed, and it has a real leather saddle.

2. My family picked apples at an orchard, and we learned how to tell which apples were ripe, and how to climb ladders to reach the top branches, and when we got home we made apple pie and then we made applesauce.

3. I went into the building and I waited for the elevator, and when it didn't come I had to walk up five flights of stairs.

4. We have a fountain in the center of town and everyone in town uses it for a meeting place and there are benches and flowers on all sides of the fountain.

Extending the Lesson

Excerpt a paragraph or two from a magazine article that would appeal to your class. Combine the sentences with commas and conjunctions until you have a series of overloaded sentences. Make copies of the sentences and distribute them to the students. Have them make the necessary revisions.

Section 5 Objectives

1. To combine sentences that express ideas of equal importance

2. To combine sentence parts and eliminate repeated words

3. To add single words from one sentence to another

4. To use combining skills in revision

Preparing the Students

Explain to the class that a good writer is able to find more than one way to express an idea, and is also able to choose the best of several ways. Explain that this section will help students achieve this kind of flexibility in their writing. It will also help them write smoother, clearer sentences.

Additional Resources

Mastery Test — page 17 in the test booklet

Practice Book — pages 22–25

Duplicating Masters — pages 22–25

52

Sentence Combining

Teaching Special Populations

LD For LD students it may be necessary to shorten some of the sentences in these combining exercises. Also, to make instructions doubly clear, list on the chalkboard those steps necessary for completing each exercise. Remind students constantly of the specific meaning of coordinating conjunctions used to join sentences.

ESL Like many foreign language speakers, ESL students often prefer to use shorter syntactic constructions. They may be alarmed at the prospect of joining sentences. Make sure students fully understand the meaning of sentences to be combined. Guide them in distinguishing the similarity in content or the logical relationship between sentences, as well as the function of each coordinating conjunction. Provide extra examples of sentences that should be combined, and some examples of those that should not.

NSD Demonstrate to students how sentence combining adds variety to otherwise bland or unclear writing. Remember that nonstandard dialect often uses nonstandard conventions to signal the logical relationship between sentence parts. Tell NSD students that proper use of coordinating conjunctions and punctuation will enable them to convey these relationships more precisely.

Objective

To combine sentences that express ideas of equal importance

Presenting the Lesson

1. Read and discuss **Here's the Idea.** Emphasize the critical effect that the choice of *and, but,* and *or* has on the meaning of the sentence. Stress that the comma is also an important part of this combining technique.

2. Discuss **Check It Out.** Make sure students know the meaning of the words *similar, contrasting,* and *equal importance.*

3. Assign **Try Your Skill.** Ask students what would happen if they used a different word to combine these sentences.

4. Read **Keep This in Mind** aloud.

5. Assign **Now Write.**

Individualizing the Lesson

Less-Advanced Students

Before students begin **Try Your Skill,** discuss how the sentences in each pair are related.

Advanced Students

Have students replace the second sentence in each pair in **Try Your Skill** with another sentence that can be combined with the first.

Join the Crowd

Combining Sentences

Here's the Idea   One way to make your writing interesting is to vary the length of your sentences. Too many short, simple sentences can make your writing sound choppy and dull. You can often combine two short sentences into one longer sentence.

Sometimes two sentences state similar ideas. Both ideas are equally important. Such sentences can usually be joined by a comma and the word *and.*

Karen played the piano. Felipe sang.

Karen played the piano**, and** Felipe sang.

At other times, two sentences state contrasting ideas of equal importance. Sentences like these can usually be joined with a comma and the word *but.*

Bill fed the cat. She wasn't hungry.

Bill fed the cat**, but** she wasn't hungry.

Occasionally, two sentences offer a choice between ideas of equal importance. Such sentences can usually be joined with a comma and the word *or.*

Will Sheila play on the varsity team this year? Will she play on the junior varsity again?

Will Sheila play on the varsity team this year**, or** will she play on the junior varsity again?

Check It Out   Study the following sentences.

1. Melinda attended the meeting, but Alice did not.
2. You can use a calculator, or you can add the figures yourself.
3. The thunder rumbled, and lightning filled the sky.

- Which sentence combines similar ideas of equal importance?
- Which sentence combines contrasting ideas of equal importance?
- Which sentence combines ideas of equal importance and offers a choice between them?

Try Your Skill   Combine each pair of sentences. Follow the directions in parentheses.

1. Should we go on ahead? Should we wait for the rest of the campers? (Join with **, or.**)
2. The lights dimmed. A hush fell over the audience. (Join with **, and.**)
3. Strange sounds came from the woods. I wasn't afraid. (Join with **, but.**)
4. Mark wants to become an actor. Rosa wants to skate in the Olympics. (Join with **, and.**)

Keep This in Mind

- Use a comma and *and* to combine sentences that state similar ideas of equal importance.
- Use a comma and *but* to combine sentences that state contrasting ideas of equal importance.
- Use a comma and *or* to combine sentences that offer a choice between ideas of equal importance.

Now Write   Combine each pair of sentences using **, and** or **, but** or **, or.**

1. Ted arrived on flight 112. His father met him at the airport.
2. Lightning struck a generator. The city went dark.
3. An eclipse will occur next month. It won't be total.
4. Did you correct the problem? Is the engine still stalling?

Label your paper **Join the Crowd.** Save it in your folder.

55

Part 2

Objective

To combine sentence parts and eliminate repeated words

Presenting the Lesson

1. Tell students that the connecting words *and, but,* and *or* can also be used to combine parts of sentences. Review the relationships of those words. Then read and discuss **Here's the Idea.** Stress that *only* sentence parts that express related ideas of equal importance can be joined.

2. Read and discuss **Check It Out.** Point out that the comma is not used when combining sentence parts.

3. Do **Try Your Skill** orally.

4. Read **Keep This in Mind.**

5. Assign **Now Write.**

Individualizing the Lesson

Less-Advanced Students

1. Review the difference in punctuation between the following two sentences. Explain that commas are used between complete sentences, not sentence parts.

Harold likes to swim, and he likes to jog.
Harold likes to swim and jog.

2. If students have trouble knowing what words to leave out in **Now Write,** have them underline repeated words before they begin to join the sentences.

Advanced Students

Have students replace the second sentence in each pair in **Try Your Skill** with another sentence that

Taking Part

Combining Sentence Parts

Here's the Idea   Sometimes two sentences contain many of the same words. This is usually a sign of dull writing. You can improve these weak sentences by combining them. To do this, take part of one sentence and join it to the other sentence.

Sentence parts that state similar ideas of equal importance can usually be joined with *and.*

Mark repairs automobiles. *Mark repairs* motorcycles.

Mark repairs automobiles **and** motorcycles.

Notice that the repeated words in italics were dropped in the combined sentence.

Sentence parts that state contrasting ideas can usually be joined with *but.*

Joan loves science fiction movies. Joan hates horror films.

Joan loves science fiction movies **but** hates horror films.

Sentence parts that offer a choice between ideas of equal importance can usually be joined with *or.*

Will you vote for Enrico? *Will you vote for* Melinda?
Will you vote for Enrico **or** Melinda?

Check It Out   Study the following examples.

1. Her voice was strong. *Her voice was* unsteady.
   Her voice was strong but unsteady.
2. Will we meet tomorrow? *Will we meet* Friday?
   Will we meet tomorrow or Friday?
3. Buses are not permitted on the bridge. Trucks *are not permitted on the bridge.*
   Buses and trucks are not permitted on the bridge.

- Which example combines similar sentence parts of equal importance?
- Which example combines contrasting sentence parts of equal importance?
- Which example combines sentence parts that offer a contrast between ideas of equal importance?

Try Your Skill   Join each pair of sentences according to the directions in parentheses. Leave out the italicized words.

1. Betty enjoys science fiction. *Betty enjoys* mysteries. (Join with **and.**)
2. We can hold a book sale. *We can hold* a car wash. (Join with **or.**)
3. The rolls were crispy outside. *The rolls were* chewy inside. (Join with **but.**)
4. Hiking boots must be sturdy. *Hiking boots must be* comfortable. (Join with **and.**)

Keep This in Mind

- Use *and* to join sentence parts that state similar ideas of equal importance.
- Use *but* to join sentence parts that state contrasting ideas of equal importance.
- Use *or* to join sentence parts that offer a choice between ideas of equal importance.

Now Write   Join each pair of sentences. Use *and, but,* or *or.*

1. Did you buy a paperback copy? Did you buy the hardback edition?
2. The bears found the honey. The bears ate it eagerly.
3. Ted located the fuse box. Ted couldn't find a fuse.
4. We could go to a movie. We could stay at home.

Label your paper **Taking Part.** Save it in your folder.

has parts that can be combined with the first.

Optional Practice

Have students decide whether any of the sentences in **Try Your Skill** can be combined with any other word than the one suggested. Ask how this would affect the meaning of the sentence.

Extending the Lesson

Have students look through previous writing assignments for sentences that can be revised by combining.

Part 3

Objective

To add single words from one sentence to another

Presenting the Lesson

1. Read and discuss **Here's the Idea.** Point out to the class that in each example a word is added from the second sentence to describe another word in the first sentence. Be sure students understand that sometimes the form of a word must be changed before it can be added to a sentence.

2. Read and discuss **Check It Out.** Emphasize that the main idea of each sentence should not be changed when the sentences are combined.

3. Assign **Try Your Skill.** List the ending changes on the board for reinforcement.

4. Read **Keep This in Mind** aloud and then assign **Now Write.**

Individualizing the Lesson

Less-Advanced Students

Have the students do **Try Your Skill** with a partner.

Advanced Students

Write the following sentence on the board.

We sang.

Ask students to suggest sentences that are related to the main idea of the sentence above. Write these sentences on the board. Then ask students to combine these sentences with the first sentence by adding key words.

In Addition

Combining by Adding Single Words

Here's the Idea   Sometimes the second sentence in a pair contains only one important word. All the other words in the sentence are unnecessary. In such cases, the one important word can be added to the first sentence.

> The jugglers were followed by a trapeze act. *The trapeze act was* daring.

> The jugglers were followed by a **daring** trapeze act.

Notice that the words in italics were dropped. The word *daring* was then added to the first sentence.

Sometimes the form of the important word must be changed before it is added to another sentence. You may have to change the ending of the word by adding *-ing, -ed,* or *-ly.*

> A police officer stopped the car. *The car was traveling at great* speed.

> A police officer stopped the **speeding** car.

> The paper is on the teacher's desk. *The paper is* complete.

> The **completed** paper is on the teacher's desk.

> Susan sang. *It was* beautiful.

> Susan sang **beautifully.**

Check It Out   Study the following examples.

1. Marsha discarded some of her records. *They were* old.
   Marsha discarded some of her old records.

2. The sidewalk was covered with pigeons. *The pigeons* cooed.
   The sidewalk was covered with cooing pigeons.

3. The doctor rushed to the quarterback. *He was in a* daze.
   The doctor rushed to the dazed quarterback.

4. The candidate spoke to the press. *The candidate was* brief.
   The candidate spoke briefly to the press.

- What words were added to make the combined sentences?
- What words had to change form?

Try Your Skill Combine each pair of sentences. Leave out the words in italics. Remember that the word you add to the first sentence may have to change form.

1. Crustaceans have shells. *Their shells are* hard.
2. The campers built a fire. *The fire* blazed.
3. The scientist examined the moon rocks. *The scientist was* careful.
4. Ramon could not work in the room. *There was too much* clutter *in the room.*

Keep This in Mind

- Some sentences can be combined by adding a single word from one sentence to the other.
- When adding a word to a sentence, you may have to change the ending of the word to *-ing*, *-ed*, or *-ly*.

Now Write Combine each group of sentences by adding a word to the first sentence. Leave out the words in italics.

1. Nitrogen is a gas. *It is* colorless.
2. The captain told us a tale. *The tale* frightened *us.*
3. We bought some popcorn. *The popcorn had* butter *on it.*
4. The astronauts opened the hatch. *They were* cautious.

Label your paper **In Addition.** Save it in your folder.

Optional Practice

Have students create their own sentences to be combined by their classmates.

Extending the Lesson

Have students look through their previous writing assignments, this time looking for sentences to be combined by adding words from one sentence to another.

Part 4

Objective

To use combining skills in revision

Presenting the Lesson

1. Read **Here's the Idea.** Write the three ways to combine related ideas in sentences on the board. Emphasize that combining sentences is a skill that adds interest and clarity to students' writing.

2. Read and discuss **Check It Out.** Ask for ideas for combining sentences in the paragraph. Then assign **Try Your Skill.** Compare the directions and their results to the students' suggestions.

3. Read **Keep This in Mind.**

4. Assign **Now Write.** Tell the class to read all the sentences at least twice before they combine them.

Individualizing the Lesson

Less-Advanced Students

Do **Try Your Skill** as an in-class exercise. If students have trouble with rewriting the paragraph, then do the first half of **Now Write** with them. Then let them do the second half with a partner.

Advanced Students

Have students combine the sentences in each of the following groups into a single sentence. Answers will vary.

1. I was sitting in a room. The room was brightly lit. I was watching a TV show. The TV show was funny.

2. I was reading a book. I was sitting on the couch. It was an interesting book.

3. Next summer I may get a job. I could go to summer school.

A Winning Combination

Using Combining Skills in Writing

Here's the Idea Sometimes two sentences state closely-related ideas. A reader may better understand how the ideas are related if the sentences are combined. You have learned several ways to combine related ideas in sentences.

1. You can combine two sentences by using a comma and the words *and, but,* or *or.*

2. You can join parts of sentences by using just the words *and, but,* or *or.*

3. You can combine sentences by adding an important word from one sentence to the other. To do this, you sometimes must change the form of the added word by adding *-ing, -ed,* or *-ly.*

Use the combining skills you have learned whenever you revise your writing. Combining sentences will help you to show how your ideas are related. It will also add variety to your sentences.

Check It Out Read the following paragraph.

1. The pilot glanced at his instrument panel. The pilot's glance was quick. 2. His fuel was low. One of his engines had been struck by lightning. 3. The pilot could ditch the plane in the lake. He could try to make an emergency landing on the highway. 4. He decided to send a distress signal. He decided to make an emergency landing.

- Would this be a better paragraph if some of the sentences were combined? Explain your answer.

Try Your Skill   Rewrite the paragraph given in **Check It Out.**
Follow these directions:

1. Combine the first pair of sentences. Add *-ly* to the important word in the second sentence. Take out the repeated words.

2. Combine the second pair of sentences by using a comma and *and*.

3. Combine the third pair of sentences by using a comma and *or*.

4. Combine the fourth pair of sentences by using just the word *and* to join together sentence parts.

Keep This in Mind

- Use sentence combining when you revise your writing.
- Combine sentences to show relationships between ideas.
- Combine sentences to add variety to your writing.

Now Write   Read the following paragraph. Then revise it, using the sentence combining techniques you have learned. Follow the directions in parentheses.

Gorillas look mean. They are actually very gentle. (Join the two sentences with a comma and the word *but.*) Most gorillas are friendly. Most gorillas are shy. (Combine sentence parts with the word *but.*) They need companionship. They prefer to live in groups. (Join the sentence parts with the word *and.*) Gorillas sometimes act fierce. Gorillas act fierce if something frightens them. (Change the form of the word *frightens* by adding *-ed.* Then, add this word to the first sentence.) They stand on their hind legs. They beat their chests. (Join the sentence parts with the word *and.*) They do this out of fear. Human beings need not worry about being attacked. (Join the two sentences with *and.*).

Label your paper **A Winning Combination.** Save it in your folder.

61

Optional Practice

Have students combine the following pairs of sentences. Answers below.

1. Scientists know that the world has had periods of great cold that have come regularly. Scientists know that periods of great cold have then disappeared. (Combine sentence parts with the word *and*.)

2. They don't know why. They are trying to discover what causes climate changes. (Join the two sentences with a comma and the word *but*.)

3. They find clues in rocks, glaciers, and the ocean floor. These clues are important. (Add the word *important* to the first sentence.)

4. They put clues together. They learn more about climate patterns. (Combine sentence parts with the word *and*.)

Extending the Lesson

Use several samples of unrevised writing from your files to provide examples of sentences that can be combined. Duplicate the examples or use an overhead projector. Have students discuss which combining techniques can be used for each and why.

1. Scientists know that the world has had periods of great cold that have come regularly and then disappeared.

2. They don't know why, but they are trying to discover what causes climate changes.

3. They find important clues in rocks, glaciers, and the ocean floor.

4. They put clues together and learn more about climate patterns.

Section 6 Objectives

1. To understand that a paragraph is a group of sentences that develop one main idea

2. To recognize unity in a paragraph

3. To recognize and write effective topic sentences

4. To understand that the main idea of a paragraph may be developed by sensory details, by specific examples, by facts and statistics, or by incidents or anecdotes

5. To recognize the three kinds of paragraphs: narrative, descriptive, and explanatory

Preparing the Students

Point out the units of writing covered in this book: the word, the sentence, the paragraph, and the composition. Describe the paragraph as a unit of writing that is an important building block for many other types of writing.

Tell students that in this section they will learn about some of the qualities of well-written paragraphs. They will also study three different kinds of paragraphs.

Additional Resources

Mastery Test — pages 18–19 in the test booklet

Practice Book — pages 26–30

Duplicating Masters — pages 26–30

Teaching Special Populations

LD Before asking LD students to write, review all the **Try Your Skill** sections together as a group. Use the following graphic method to show students how sentences in a

A Look at Paragraphs

paragraph are connected: list the sentences vertically (in sequence) on the chalkboard, join them with arrows, then ask students to explain how each sentence adds to the main idea.

Whenever necessary, go over and simplify instructions. The instructions for **Now Write** Part 1 can be simplified as follows:

Look at paragraph 2 above. Find the two sentences that do not belong and underline them. Rewrite the paragraph, leaving out the sentences you underlined.

Before they are able to differentiate between types of paragraphs, LD students may need additional, easily distinguishable examples of each kind.

ESL Make sure that ESL students understand the vocabulary and meaning of all the sample paragraphs. Those students who still find it difficult to distinguish between types of paragraphs may be helped by your reading the examples aloud. The various inflections and tonal changes will help students distinguish narrative, descriptive, and explanatory elements.

When teaching ideas of *unity, coherence, topic sentence,* and so on, have students work in pairs and discuss the respective elements in each paragraph.

NSD Make sure that NSD students have extensive practice in this section. Remember that in nonstandard dialect run-on sentences often substitute for normal methods of achieving paragraph unity. Show students where the unity and coherence of their paragraphs can be improved. Encourage them to use more details and examples.

Objective

To understand that a paragraph is a group of sentences that develop one main idea

Presenting the Lesson

1. Read aloud and discuss **Here's the Idea.** Emphasize the definition of *paragraph.* Encourage students to restate the definition in their own words.

2. Assign **Check It Out.** Then discuss with students why these groups of sentences are paragraphs. Have students state the main idea of each paragraph. Discuss with them how each sentence of each paragraph develops the main idea.

3. Assign and discuss **Try Your Skill.** Number 1 is the paragraph. Have students state the main idea of the paragraph. Point out that the second group of sentences is not a paragraph because it does not stick to one topic. Ask students to name the various topics covered in number 2.

4. Read **Keep This in Mind** and then assign **Now Write.** Remind students to revise their work so that all of the sentences develop one main idea. Review with students the fundamentals of good sentences.

Tell students to watch out for empty, padded, and overloaded sentences. Also remind students to indent the first line of a paragraph.

Individualizing the Lesson

Less-Advanced Students

Have students read aloud the

Group Work

Defining a Paragraph

Here's the Idea   A **paragraph** is a group of sentences that develop one main idea. All the sentences in a paragraph should work together to make that one idea clear.

As you read the following groups of sentences, notice how sentences in each group work together.

1   Neither the mist nor the strange moans of nighttime desert dwellers troubled Artoo Detoo. He made his careful way up the rocky gully. He was hunting for the easiest pathway to the top. His squarish, broad footpads made clicking sounds. The sounds seemed loud in the evening light as the sand underfoot gave way to gravel.

—GEORGE LUCAS

2   Holmes was certainly not a difficult man to live with. He was quiet in his ways, and his habits were regular. It was rare for him to be up after ten at night, and he had invariably breakfasted and gone out before I rose in the morning. Sometimes he spent his day at the chemical laboratory, sometimes in the dissecting rooms, and occasionally in long walks, which appeared to take him into the lowest portions of the city.

—SIR ARTHUR CONAN DOYLE

3   Melons were gathered as they were consumed. In the autumn, pumpkins and beans were gathered and placed in bags or baskets; ears of corn were tied together by the husks, and then the harvest was carried on the backs of ponies up to our homes. Here the corn was shelled, and all the harvest stored away in caves or other secluded places to be used in winter.

—GERONIMO

Check It Out   Take another look at the three groups of sentences. The first group tells part of a story. The second group describes a person. The third group describes one aspect of Apache Indian life. Are these groups of sentences paragraphs?

- Does each group of sentences deal with one main idea? Does every sentence in a group say something about the main idea?

Try Your Skill   Read the groups of sentences below. One of them is a paragraph. One is not. For the group that is a paragraph, write the main idea. For the group that is not a paragraph, explain why it is not.

1   Insects that live together in large colonies are called social insects. Ants and bees are both social insects. Each of these insects has one particular job to do that helps to keep the whole society alive. These insects live in large groups because there are so many different jobs required. All the members must do their own jobs well and must cooperate with the others.

2   Television is a relaxing form of entertainment. Dancing and sports require you to move around a lot. You can watch television while lying down. Most people need to lie down after they've played a strenuous game. Basketball can be especially tiring, unless of course you're watching it on TV.

Keep This in Mind

- A paragraph is a group of sentences that develop one main idea. Every sentence in the group should deal with that idea.

Now Write   Look again at the group of sentences in **Try Your Skill** that do not make a good paragraph. Write the first sentence of that paragraph. Then write several more sentences that help to explain the first sentence. Label your paper **Group Work** and put it into your folder.

Objective

To recognize unity in a paragraph

Presenting the Lesson

1. Review the definition of *paragraph* and then read aloud **Here's the Idea.** Discuss the meaning of *unity* and ask the students to define other words from the same root (*unit, unify, united*, etc.).

2. Have a student read **Check It Out** aloud. Determine the main point of the sample paragraph (that "necessity is the mother of invention") and discuss how unity is achieved in the paragraph.

3. Assign and discuss **Try Your Skill.** Remind students to read the paragraph once to determine the main idea and then again to determine if all the sentences tell about that main idea.

4. Read aloud **Keep This in Mind.**

5. Assign **Now Write.**

Individualizing the Lesson

Less-Advanced Students

1. For **Try Your Skill,** do sample paragraph 1 as a class. Determine the main point and then question the relevance of each sentence. Assign 2 and 3 to be done independently.

2. Before students begin their **Now Write** assignment, demonstrate on the chalkboard how they might proceed. Ask for a topic from the class, and then have the students suggest sentences that could be used to develop that idea.

All for One

Recognizing Unity in a Paragraph

Here's the Idea   A paragraph should develop one idea. All the sentences in a paragraph should tell something about that main idea. When they do, a paragraph has **unity.**

Look at the following paragraph. Notice how all the sentences tell something about a family trip that was rained out.

> Huddled together, the Robb family viewed their soggy surroundings. Tiny rivers of rain trickled through the holes in their canvas tent. The once-fluffy sleeping bags had absorbed a great deal of water. They were like enormous sponges. Soaked bits of twigs and pine needles clung to everyone's wet clothes. In miserable agreement, the entire Robb family vowed never to go camping again.

Check It Out   Now read the following paragraph.

> It is often said that necessity is the mother of invention. That was certainly true just before Christmas in 1818. A mouse had chewed a hole in the bellows of a church organ in Oberndorf, Austria. The organ would not play. Quickly, Franz Gruber wrote a song that could be played on a guitar instead. On Christmas Eve he played the guitar, and the choir sang the new carol. Because of a hungry mouse, "Silent Night" is now sung all over the world every Christmas Eve.

  • Do all of the sentences relate to one main idea? Does the paragraph have unity?

Try Your Skill   Each paragraph below has at least one sentence that is not related to the main idea. Such sentences prevent the paragraph from having unity. For each paragraph, write the sentence or sentences that do not belong.

1   Solving word problems in math is not so hard. First, you have to figure out what question you are trying to answer. Then you must decide what figuring you need to do. Next, see which numbers and facts are necessary for the solution and which are thrown in to trick you. ~~Some people have trouble with math, while others just breeze through it.~~ Following these steps will help you to solve word problems more easily.

2   The legend of Johnny Appleseed is based on the life of a real person. His name was John Chapman. He was born in 1775. He died in 1845. Because of Johnny Appleseed, apples are now an important crop. They are grown from coast to coast. ~~The state of Washington produces more apples than any other state.~~

3   Physical education classes in school teach more than just team sports. They teach individual sports as well, such as running, swimming, and tennis. A person can continue these individual sports for life. Team sports, however, may be hard to keep up with outside of school. ~~People should organize teams where they work.~~

Keep This in Mind

- All the sentences in a paragraph should develop one main idea. Then a paragraph has unity.

Now Write   Label your paper **All for One.** Write the name of a person whom you admire, a place you have visited, or a sport that you enjoy. Number your paper from 1 to 5. Then write five sentences that say something about your topic. Keep your work in your folder.

One for All

Objective

To recognize and write effective topic sentences

Presenting the Lesson

1. Review the definition of *unity* and then read **Here's the Idea.** Discuss how topic sentences add unity to paragraphs.

2. Read **Check It Out** aloud and have students respond to the questions.

3. Assign **Try Your Skill** to be done during class. When the students have finished, ask volunteers to explain their choices. Make sure they understand that all the sentences in a paragraph support the topic sentences.

4. Review **Keep This in Mind** with the class.

5. For **Now Write** ask students to divide their paper into thirds. Have them write the main idea for each paragraph on one-third of the paper. Then, under each main idea, have them compose a topic sentence.

Individualizing the Lesson

Less-Advanced Students

1. Begin **Try Your Skill** by doing the first item orally. Then have students do 2 and 3 on their own.

2. For **Now Write,** have the class brainstorm possible topics. Write their ideas on the chalkboard. Then select one and do a demonstration of the exercise following the suggestions in Step 5 of **Presenting the Lesson.**

Using a Topic Sentence

Here's the Idea   You know that a good paragraph develops just one main idea. How do you express one idea briefly and clearly? The best way is to write a topic sentence. The **topic sentence** of a paragraph states the main idea. The rest of the sentences should support the idea expressed in the topic sentence.

A topic sentence often begins a paragraph. This helps the writer and the reader. First, the topic sentence helps the writer to keep in mind what it is that he or she wants to say. Second, the topic sentence tells the reader what the paragraph is going to be about.

Check It Out   Read the paragraph below.

Many animals need the companionship of other animals. In fact, some animals suffer without it. A race horse, for instance, often has an animal companion that shares its stall. This companion might be a dog, a cat, or even a goat. As long as its companion is around, the race horse will perform well. If the companion leaves or dies, though, the horse may lose all its spirit.

· Which sentence is the topic sentence? What is the main idea of this paragraph?

Try Your Skill   Read the groups of sentences below. Each group has one sentence in it that states the main idea of the whole group. This sentence is the topic sentence. On a piece of paper, write the topic sentence of each group.

1.   (a) It continued for several decades.
     (b) Those from Europe arrived on the East Coast, while the Japanese landed in California.

(c) In 1890, a new wave of immigration into this country began.
(d) People poured in from Europe, Russia, and Japan.
(e) The immigrants helped each other adjust to their new home.

2. (a) Others, like bats, use a kind of radar to keep them safe and help them locate prey.
   (b) They are especially adapted to night life.
   (c) Some animals, like cats, have other features like long whiskers that keep them from bumping into things.
   (d) Nocturnal animals sleep by day and hunt by night.
   (e) They usually have very keen vision and extra sharp hearing.

3. (a) This happened right after the new music teacher came.
   (b) Now it plays rock music, jazz, and country and western as well.
   (c) All these changes have made it one of the most popular after-school activities.
   (d) The school band has really changed.
   (e) The band used to play only marching music and school songs.

Keep This in Mind

- A topic sentence often begins a paragraph. The topic sentence states the main idea of the paragraph.

Now Write Think of three topics that you might want to write a paragraph about. You might want to write about something that happened to you. You might want to write about some place you enjoy. Decide what the main idea of each paragraph would be. Then write a topic sentence for each paragraph that states that main idea. Write the title of this lesson, **One for All,** at the top of your paper. Then put your work into your folder.

Advanced Students

Have students look through their textbooks for a brief paragraph that has a clearly defined topic sentence. Ask them to copy the sentences of that paragraph in scrambled order, exchange papers, and follow the directions for **Try Your Skill.**

Optional Practice

1. Select five to ten well-written paragraphs from student work or from other sources. Duplicate them and have students underline the topic sentence in each.

2. Select five to ten well-written paragraphs. Reproduce them, omitting the topic sentence. Leave blank lines where the topic sentences should be. Have students write a good topic sentence for each paragraph.

Extending the Lesson

Duplicate several one-paragraph newspaper articles for the class. Have students read them aloud and determine which sentence serves as a topic sentence. Then ask the students to write a headline which states the main idea of the article.

Objective

To understand that the main idea of a paragraph may be developed by sensory details, by specific examples, by facts and statistics, or by incidents or anecdotes

Presenting the Lesson

1. Review the function of a topic sentence.

2. Write the following terms on the chalkboard: *sensory details, specific examples, facts and statistics, incidents or anecdotes.* Discuss the terms and write a brief definition next to each. Have students use dictionaries if necessary.

3. Read **Here's the Idea,** and analyze the development of each type of paragraph. For the first paragraph, have students identify the main idea and list the sensory details that develop that idea. For the second paragraph, find the topic sentence and list the specific examples that follow it. Proceed in this manner with the last two paragraphs as well.

4. Read and discuss **Check It Out.** Remind students to refer to the notes on the chalkboard as they answer the questions.

5. Assign and discuss **Try Your Skill.** Students will discover that some topics can be developed in more than one way. Ask students to be very specific in explaining how they would develop each paragraph.

6. Read **Keep This in Mind** aloud. Review the methods of development one more time.

70

An Idea Takes Shape

Developing a Paragraph

Here's the Idea   A topic sentence presents the main idea of a paragraph. This idea is developed with sensory details, examples, facts and statistics, or incidents or anecdotes.

Sensory details are details that appeal to the senses of sight, sound, hearing, touch, or taste.

> Miss Adela Strangeworth came daintily along Main Street on her way to the grocery. The sun was shining, the air was fresh and clear after the night's heavy rain, and everything in Miss Strangeworth's little town looked washed and bright. Miss Strangeworth took deep breaths and thought that there was nothing in the world like a fragrant summer day.
>
> —SHIRLEY JACKSON

One or more **examples** can be used to develop a paragraph that begins with a general statement.

> Many nationalities have a starchy food that they use as a base for most meals. People in many Oriental countries use rice. South Americans and Mexicans eat many foods with a corn-meal base. A basic starch, in some form, is used all over the world.

Facts and statistics can prove a point or make an idea clear.

> A person's life expectancy depends on the country where the person lives. Australian men have a life expectancy of 67.6 years. Men in Peru can expect to live only 52.6 years. People in Chad have the lowest life expectancies. For men, it is only 29 years. For women, it is 35 years. Women in Norway have the highest life expectancy. They can expect to live 78.7 years.

Incidents or anecdotes (very short stories) can be used to illustrate a point.

> Chris was always there when I needed him. I remember how awful I felt after the Centerville game last year. We had played

terribly. We looked like a bunch of kindergarten kids out on the field. After the game, Chris met me outside the locker room. All the way home, he didn't say a word. He knew I didn't want to talk. When we got to my house, he smiled and said, "Hey, it's only a game." I needed to hear that then. Chris understood.

Check It Out   Read the following paragraph.

When the fog rolls in, the harbor is veiled in mystery. All the warehouses look haunted. Fishermen appear ghostly as they wend their way along hidden piers to invisible boats. The powerful beam from the lighthouse pierces the thick white curtain, warning ships of danger. Most eerie of all is a mournful voice that seems to come from nowhere—the foghorn.

- Is the topic sentence developed by sensory details? examples? facts and statistics? incidents or anecdotes?

Try Your Skill   Read the topics listed below and decide how you might develop each of them. Write *Sensory Details, Specific Examples, Facts and Statistics,* or *Incidents or Anedotes.*

1. the most popular video games
2. a perfect summer day
3. the costs of running this school
4. incredible feats of strength

Keep This in Mind

- The main idea of a paragraph may be developed by sensory details, by specific examples, by facts and statistics, or by incidents or anecdotes.

Now Write   Choose one of the four topics in **Try Your Skill.** Write a topic sentence. List sensory details, examples, facts and statistics, or an incident or anecdote that you could use to develop it. Label your paper **An Idea Takes Shape.** Keep your work.

7. Assign **Now Write** and allow class time for the students to begin. Offer individual help to students who are having trouble with the assignment.

Individualizing the Lesson

Less-Advanced Students

1. For **Check It Out,** have students identify the topic sentence (sentence 1), and ask a volunteer to write it on the chalkboard. Then list the sensory details used in the paragraph.

2. For **Now Write,** choose one topic to demonstrate the exercise on the chalkboard. Then have students choose one of the remaining three topics to work from.

Advanced Students

Have students do the **Now Write** exercise for two topics instead of one. Allow them to select their own topics for **Now Write** if they prefer to do so. Be sure to review their choices, screening out unmanageable topics.

Optional Practice

Have the class choose a general topic. Discuss with students how they might develop it according to each of the methods presented in this chapter.

Extending the Lesson

Divide the class into four groups, and assign each group one type of paragraph development. Have each group find examples of one type of development in a paragraph from any of their text books. Ask them to write out their examples and make a bulletin board display.

Objective

To recognize the three kinds of paragraphs: narrative, descriptive, and explanatory

Presenting the Lesson

1. Write the terms *narrative, descriptive,* and *explanatory* on the chalkboard. Read **Here's the Idea** and write a short definition next to each term.

2. Discuss **Check It Out.** When discussing the narrative paragraph, ask students to note the sequence of events in the story. When discussing the descriptive paragraph, ask students to find all of the words that appeal to the senses. When discussing the explanatory paragraph, point out the importance of following a logical order.

3. Assign and discuss **Try Your Skill.** Ask students to explain their choice of narrative, descriptive, or explanatory paragraphs.

4. Read aloud **Keep This in Mind** and refer to the definitions on the chalkboard.

5. Assign **Now Write.**

Individualizing the Lesson

Less-Advanced Students

If necessary, supply additional narrative, descriptive, and explanatory paragraphs for students to identify.

Advanced Students

Ask volunteers to explain the process followed so far in their **Now Write** work (from general topic, to

Read the Labels

Recognizing Three Kinds of Paragraphs

Here's the Idea A paragraph may tell a story, describe something, or explain something. Each kind of paragraph has a different name and presents an idea in a different way.

Narrative paragraphs tell a story or tell about something that happened. The events may be real or imaginary.

Descriptive paragraphs use words to create pictures. Descriptions appeal to all the senses.

Explanatory paragraphs may tell *how* to do something, or *how* something happens or works. They can also tell *why* something is or should be done, or *what* something is.

Check It Out Notice how the subject of dogs is presented in three different ways in three different kinds of paragraphs.

1   The dog waited until everyone was out of the apartment, and then jumped up to sleep on Ben's bed. Later in the afternoon, however, footsteps sounded in the hall and a key turned in the lock. The dog reacted quickly. It leaped from the bed immediately. When Ben came into his room, the dog was lying quietly curled up on the rug. However, Ben could see from the rumpled blankets where the dog had been.

2   The dog looked like a miniature wolf. It had stiff, grey fur that formed a thick mat on its back and soft tufts on its legs. The dog's ears were pointed. Its eyes were shiny and black. The animal made no sound as it entered the room.

3   When you train a dog to come to you, don't give it a chance to make a wrong move. Instead, put it on a long leash or rope. Then stand a few feet from the dog and say "Come" in a friendly voice. Tug gently on the rope as you do this. When the dog gets up close to you, reward it so that it knows it has done the right thing.

- Which paragraph is narrative? Which is descriptive? Which is explanatory?

Try Your Skill   As you read these topic sentences, decide what kind of paragraph they would probably be part of. Write *Narrative, Descriptive,* or *Explanatory.*

1. The streets were covered by a soft carpet of snow that muffled all sounds. Descriptive

2. One morning right after breakfast, the phone rang. Narrative

3. My first subway trip was a disaster. Narrative

4. The best way to lift something heavy without straining your back is to start with the proper posture. Explanatory

5. An abacus is a frame containing movable beads that is used for teaching arithmetic. Explanatory

6. I believe that the Walker School should not be closed.
Explanatory

Keep This in Mind

- Narrative paragraphs tell a story or relate events.
- Descriptive paragraphs create word pictures by appealing to the senses.
- Explanatory paragraphs tell *how* to do something, *how* something happens or works, *why* something is or should be done, or *what* something is.

Now Write   Read over your topic sentence and list of related sentences from **Now Write** in **An Idea Takes Shape.** Which of the three types of paragraphs would you use for your topic? Write the name for that type of paragraph on your paper. Explain why it is the best type to use with your topic. Label your paper **Read the Labels** and keep it in your folder.

Section 7 Objectives

1. To understand that writing is a process that has three main stages: pre-writing, writing the first draft, and revising

2. To develop techniques for choosing a topic

3. To learn how to narrow a topic

4. To consider purpose and audience when planning a paragraph

5. To learn how to write effective topic sentences

6. To learn how to gather information for a paragraph

7. To learn how to choose an appropriate method for organizing details

8. To learn how to write a first draft

9. To learn how to write an effective ending sentence

10. To understand how to revise and proofread

Preparing the Students

To introduce the idea of process, have students imagine that they are reporters assigned to write articles for a publication on careers. Ask them what they would have to do in order to write their articles. List their responses on the board.

Point out to students that good writing is done in stages, and that a considerable amount of work is done before the actual writing of a piece. Explain that this section will help them learn about the steps in the process of writing.

Additional Resources

Mastery Test — pages 20–21 in the test booklet

Practice Book — pages 31–40

Duplicating Masters — pages 31–40

Writing a Paragraph

75

Teaching Special Populations

LD It is crucial that teachers allot more time for guiding students individually through the stages of writing in Sections 7–20. Try to make evaluations of each student's progress based on your knowledge of his or her capability.

Offer students interesting secondary material: magazine articles, pictures, short stories, and short films can all be used to good effect. Have students respond verbally to this material then use their responses as an occasion for writing.

Some LD students may find it easier to record their "first drafts" using a tape recorder. They may then replay the sentences and improve on them. However you approach these exercises, try to be patient and offer positive reinforcement. Encourage even the most elementary responses.

ESL To boost students' confidence and increase their understanding of what is required, it may be best to conduct pre-writing exercises (brainstorming, for example) as a group activity.

When teaching the writing sections, have native English speakers act as guides. Also use these sections to help students expand their vocabulary and their knowledge of reference materials. In fact it may be useful to work through Section 22, **Using the Library,** before starting the writing sections.

NSD To help NSD students overcome their feeling of insecurity, you should stress the importance of first drafts. Emphasize that most writers use nonstandard expressions in their first drafts, and that revisions can be made at a later stage.

Objective

To understand that writing is a process that has three main stages: pre-writing, writing the first draft, and revising

Presenting the Lesson

1. Refer to the discussion in **Preparing the Students,** and review the meaning of *process.* Write the three stages of the process of writing on the chalkboard, and then read and discuss **Here's the Idea.**

In discussing pre-writing, remind students that they did some pre-writing activities as they studied the previous section. Tell them that the main goal for the second stage, writing the first draft, is to get their thoughts down on paper. Explain that in stage three, revising, they will make changes and corrections.

2. Discuss **Check It Out,** tracing the process followed by this writer. Ask students to suggest revisions of the first draft.

3. Read and discuss **Try Your Skill.** Go through the revised paragraph sentence by sentence. Ask students to explain why the writer made each revision.

4. Read **Keep This in Mind** aloud.

5. Assign **Now Write.** Explain the concept of journal writing to the class. Tell them that it does not contain finished writing, but ideas, feelings, and experiences.

Individualizing the Lesson

Less-Advanced Students

To help these students become more comfortable with writing, use

Paragraph in Progress

Writing as a Process

Here's the Idea   You have learned what a paragraph is and how a paragraph can be developed. Now you are ready to learn how to write a paragraph of your own.

If you are going to complete any task successfully, you must think it out carefully. Writing is no exception. The best way to be sure that your writing is clear, well-developed, and lively is to follow a step-by-step process called the **process of writing.**

The process of writing has three main stages. The first stage is called **pre-writing.** It includes all of the planning that you do before you write. During this stage, you will choose and narrow a topic. Then you will gather details to develop your topic. Finally, you will arrange your ideas in a logical order.

The second stage is called **writing the first draft.** At this stage in the process, you turn your pre-writing notes into a paragraph. You let your thoughts flow freely. You write your ideas in good order. You needn't worry about grammar and mechanics at this point. You will have time later to correct your mistakes.

The third stage in the process of writing is called **revising.** During this stage you will improve your ideas and your writing style. You will also proofread your first draft to find and correct any errors in grammar and mechanics.

Use the process of writing whenever you write. It will help to make you a better writer.

Check It Out   Read the following notes and paragraph.

General Topic:	a summer adventure
Narrowed Topic:	a weekend in Wisconsin
Pre-Writing Notes:	swimming, water skiing, fishing for trout, no TV—didn't miss it, cabin on lake, sandy beach, blackberry pie

First Draft: Our weekend at the lake was great. We swam all the time and water skied. One day we went fishing I caught a trout. There wasnt any TV. We didn't even notice. The cabin was right on Lake Michigan. The beach was sandy. At night we ate on the porch. There was blackberries by the cabin. Mom made a pie. Next year I hope we go back.

- What two steps in the process of writing did this writer complete? What step hasn't been done yet?

Try Your Skill   Here is the revised paragraph about a weekend in Wisconsin. Correct the two errors that remain.

> wasn't, were
>
> Our weekend ~in a cabin~ at the lake was great. We swam all the time and water-skied. ~every day.~ One day we went fishing ~and We ate it for supper.~ I caught a trout. There wasnt any TV. ~but~ We didn't even notice. The cabin was right on ~a sandy beach at~ Lake Michigan. The beach was sandy. At night we ate on the ~screened-in~ porch. There was blackberries by the cabin. Mom made a pie. ~wild~ ~growing~ Next year I hope we go back. ~On Sunday,~

Keep This in Mind

- Pre-writing is the planning you do before you begin writing.
- Writing the first draft is writing a rough version of your paragraph.
- Revising is improving what you have written.

Now Write   A journal can help you become a better writer. Get a notebook and try to write in it every day. For today, write about something interesting that you saw or read about recently.

the first five or ten minutes of class each day for journal writing. Suggest interesting topics and encourage the students to experiment with many kinds of writing (personal experience, argument, poetry, description, editorials, etc.).

Advanced Students

Institute daily journal writing and put the students in charge of suggesting the topics. Tell them to be creative with ideas and form.

Periodically check students' journals, without reading the work, to encourage students to write something every day. Stress that a journal is their source book for writing ideas.

Optional Practice

Have students list all the pre-writing work they might have to do to write an essay on a well-known community event such as the Fourth of July celebration, a sidewalk sale, etc. (decide on a specific topic, research the history of the event, interview people involved with it, and organize the information).

Extending the Lesson

1. Discuss other activities that follow stages similar to those in the writing process (cooking, drawing, composing music, etc.). Discuss what ways the approach to these arts is similar to and different from writing.

2. Have students interview classmates and teachers on how they approach a writing task. Discuss the results in class.

Part 2

Objective

To develop techniques for choosing a topic

Presenting the Lesson

1. Ask students to recall favorite writing they have done. Discuss their responses and determine why those stories, essays, etc. stand out in the students' minds.

2. Read and discuss **Here's the Idea.** In class, practice each of the techniques covered in the text.

For *journal writing,* present the students with a question, idea, or article to which they can respond in their journals.

For *brainstorming,* demonstrate the method on the chalkboard and then have the students try it in their journals.

For *reading,* distribute reading material to students and ask them to look through it. Ask them to come up with at least three topics based on their reading. They should write their ideas in their journals.

3. Read and discuss **Check It Out.**

4. Read and assign **Try Your Skill.** When students are finished, ask volunteers to write their brainstorming notes on the chalkboard.

5. Review **Keep This in Mind.**

6. Assign **Now Write.** Tell students to use at least two different methods for deriving their ideas.

Individualizing the Lesson

Less-Advanced Students

Before assigning **Now Write,** have each student name a topic that he

Something To Say

Pre-Writing: Choosing Subjects

Here's the Idea   Students often wonder what makes a subject worth writing about. In general, the best topics are those that a writer is most interested in. To write well about a topic, you must feel that you really have something important to say.

Where do you find these kinds of topics? You might be surprised to learn that the best topics are already right in your head. You have many ideas, feelings, and memories of past experiences that would be interesting for others to read about. To discover these topics, try using one of these methods:

Look in your journal. Your journal contains your thoughts and feelings about people, places, and events. If they interest you, you can make them interesting for your reader.

Brainstorm. Brainstorming is a word game that can lead to interesting writing ideas. You can brainstorm by yourself or with friends. Start with a word or a general idea such as *the park.* List everything that comes into your mind when you think of the park. You could come up with writing ideas such as "weekend ice hockey games," or "the botanical gardens." Each of those ideas could lead to writing possibilities.

Read. Browse through some books, magazines, and newspapers that interest you. Read some articles, stories, or poems. Look at some photographs. These are all good sources of ideas.

Check It Out   Imagine that one student started a class brainstorming session with the word *animals.* Look at the "idea tree" that the class brainstormed from that one word.

- What ideas could you add to this idea tree?
- What possible writing ideas can you find in the idea tree?

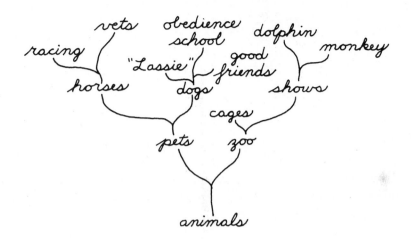

Try Your Skill Here are five broad topics that one student came up with. She looked in her journal and leafed through a book of photographs. Choose one of these subjects and do some brainstorming. When you are finished, look over your notes. In your journal, write down at least three possible writing ideas.

heroes   fashions   holidays   winning   my sister/brother

> **Keep This in Mind**
>
> • Choose a topic that interests you and that you know something about.
> • You can find writing ideas in your journal, by brainstorming, and by reading.

Now Write Make a list of topics that interest you and that you know something about. Use the methods you learned about in this lesson. Come up with at least five or six writing ideas. Save your list in your folder.

or she would like to write about. Then have students work on the exercise in class.

Advanced Students

In addition to a list of topics they already know something about, have students also make a list of topics they would like to write about but would need to research first.

Optional Practice

Have students use each of the three techniques to arrive at writing ideas on the general topic "Important People in My Life," or on another topic agreed upon by the class.

Extending the Lesson

Bring in a newspaper article on a controversial topic (the banning of video games, for example). Have students react to the article in their journals.

Part 3

Objective

To learn how to narrow a topic

Presenting the Lesson

1. Read and discuss **Here's the Idea.** Point out how the writer can move from a very broad idea to a specific topic suitable for one paragraph.

2. Read and discuss **Check It Out,** emphasizing the effectiveness of specific details.

3. Remind students of the definition of a paragraph (sentences relating to *one* idea). Assign and discuss **Try Your Skill.**

4. Review **Keep This in Mind.**

5. Assign **Now Write.**

Individualizing the Lesson

Less-Advanced Students

1. For **Try Your Skill,** do the first two topics orally with the class. Write the questions (*who, what, when, where, why, how*) on the chalkboard, and list suggestions from the class next to each question.

2. For **Now Write** check each student's topic for suitability. Have students list the six questions on their paper and then proceed with the exercise.

Advanced Students

Ask for volunteers to write their **Now Write** assignment on the chalkboard, giving a step-by-step explanation of how they arrived at their ideas.

Zero In

Pre-Writing: Narrowing a Topic

Here's the Idea   If you write a paragraph about a topic that is too general, you will probably find it hard to say anything interesting. Some subjects are too broad to write about in a paragraph. If you started with a general topic like "recreation," you might end up with a dull paragraph like this:

> Recreation is as important as work. I enjoy cooking out of doors with my family. I like to swim, skate, and play soccer. There is never enough time to do all the things I enjoy.

If you narrowed the topic, however, you could focus on just one recreational activity. One good way to narrow a topic is to ask questions about it. Such questions might begin with *who, what, when, where, why,* and *how.*

For instance, if your general subject is recreation, you might ask *What?* about it, to get a list of activities you enjoy.

swimming   skating   soccer   outdoor cooking

Now you would choose one of these activities to explore further. Suppose you choose *outdoor cooking.* Begin asking other questions about it, like these:

When?   summers, weekends, holidays (July 4, Labor Day)
Who?   me, my family, friends
Where?   backyard, park, beach

As you make your notes, you will probably remember specific times when you cooked outdoors. You might remember the Fourth of July cookout you planned for your family—the time when a thunderstorm struck just as you got everything ready. Now you have discovered a topic that can be covered well in one paragraph: an Independence Day cookout disaster.

Check It Out Read this paragraph.

My Independence Day cookout for my family turned into a disaster. When it was time to start the fire, I discovered we were out of charcoal. Wondering why I hadn't checked this detail sooner, I ran to the store and bought more. After several starts, I finally had a strong fire going. Then I hauled dishes, silverware, napkins, and extra chairs out onto the lawn. I brought out creamy cole slaw, hot German potato salad, mustard, ketchup, and platters of sliced tomatoes and sweet onions. Just as I was putting the first hot dogs and hamburgers on the grill, I felt several drops of rain splatter on my arm. The drops of rain soon became a downpour. Screaming for help, I began grabbing the waterlogged food. The next time I plan a cookout, I'll check the weather forecast first.

- What makes this paragraph more interesting than the one in **Here's the Idea?** What does this tell you about the importance of narrowing a topic?

Try Your Skill Choose one of these general topics. Ask *Who? What? When? Where? Why?* or *How?* Use your answers to develop a topic that could be covered in one paragraph.

travel   television   music   friends   art   hobbies

> **Keep This in Mind**
>
> - Narrow a general topic by asking *who, what, when, where, why, and how* questions. Be sure that your narrowed topic can be covered well in one paragraph.

Now Write Look at your list of topics from the last lesson. Choose one topic. Ask *who, what, when, where, why,* and *how* questions about it. Use your answers to narrow the topic so that it can be covered well in one paragraph. Save your work.

81

Part 4

Objective

To consider purpose and audience when planning a paragraph

Presenting the Lesson

1. Write *purpose* and *audience* on the chalkboard. Discuss possible definitions of each word and then read **Here's the Idea.** To illustrate each term, ask students to recall the purpose of the paragraph about the cookout in Part 3, page 81 (to tell about a disastrous event). Ask them to determine the intended audience (classmates).

2. Read aloud and discuss **Check It Out.**

3. Assign and discuss **Try Your Skill.** Explain to the class that in longer pieces of writing, they will write out a statement of their topic and purpose (*thesis statement*).

4. Read **Keep This in Mind** aloud.

5. Assign **Now Write.**

Individualizing the Lesson

Less-Advanced Students

Do **Try Your Skill** orally in class. Lead the class through decisions for several different purpose/audience pairs.

Advanced Students

1. Have each student bring in three newspaper or magazine articles clearly intended for three different audiences.

2. Have students find several articles that have different purposes. Tell them to be prepared to explain those purposes to the class.

What's the Point?

Pre-Writing: Purpose and Audience

Here's the Idea   Now that you have a topic to write about, you should stop to consider two important questions: "What is the purpose of my paragraph?" and "For whom am I writing?"

Anything you write has a **purpose.** The purpose of your paragraph is what you hope to accomplish with your writing. Your purpose might be to tell a story or to describe someone or something. Your purpose might also be to define a word, explain a process, or express an opinion. If you know your purpose *before* you begin writing, you will write a better paragraph. Knowing your purpose will help you to see your topic more clearly. It will also help you to choose the right kinds of details to develop your topic.

The readers you have in mind are called your **audience.** As you continue planning your paragraph, ask yourself what your audience is like. What age are your readers? Knowing this will help you choose the right vocabulary for your paragraph. What are your audience's interests and opinions? Answering this question will tell you whether you have chosen a topic that your audience is likely to enjoy. Consider whether your audience knows a little, a lot, or nothing at all about your chosen topic. Then you will know how detailed your information should be. Learn as much as you can about your readers. Then you can write a paragraph just for them.

Check It Out   Look over these possible purposes and audiences for a paragraph about dancing.

<pre>
              Topic: dancing
  Possible Purposes: to tell about my first high-school dance
                       to describe the grace of a ballet dancer
                       to define a dancing term
                       to explain how to do a new dance
                       to explain why I like or dislike
                         dancing
 Possible Audiences: a teacher who likes to dance
                       a classmate
                       a friend I am writing a letter to
                       someone who disapproves of dancing
</pre>

- How would these different purposes and audiences change the way you developed this paragraph?

Try Your Skill   Choose one of the purposes listed in **Check It Out** and one of the possible audiences. Then explain how you would develop a paragraph for that purpose and audience. What vocabulary would you use? How detailed would your information have to be?

Keep This in Mind

- Your purpose is your reason for writing.
- Your audience is the person or persons for whom you are writing.
- Knowing your purpose and your audience will help you to write a better paragraph.

Now Write   Look at the topic you chose in **Zero In**. Decide what your purpose is. Name your audience and write a brief description of them. Save your paper in your folder.

Optional Practice

Have students determine whether the audience for the following paragraph would be adults, children, or scientists. Ask them to explain their decision.

How would you like to cuddle a sweet little baby shark? You wouldn't? Well, you're smart! Shark pups may be little, but they sure aren't sweet and cuddly. They're rough and tough ter- rors right from the start....

Sandra M.T. Cole

If necessary, point out that the tone, vocabulary ("sweet and cud- dly," "rough and tough," etc.), and punctuation indicate that the au- dience is children.

Extending the Lesson

Divide students into pairs. Have them write down a topic, purpose, and audience, and then exchange papers. Each student must devise a plan for a paragraph according to the specifications received. For ex- ample, one assignment might read:

topic—vacation
audience—principal
purpose—to convince that spring va- cation is too short

Part 5

Objective

To learn how to write effective topic sentences

Presenting the Lesson

1. Review the definition of *topic sentence.* Write the term on the chalkboard.

2. Read and discuss **Here's the Idea,** emphasizing the qualities of a good topic sentence. Write *direct, interesting,* and *informative* next to the term on the board.

3. Read and discuss **Check It Out.** Point out that items 1 and 3 are too dull and vague.

4. Assign and discuss **Try Your Skill.** Remind students to write sentences without unnecessary words and to be specific about *how* and *why* in the sentences.

5. Read aloud **Keep This in Mind.**

6. Assign **Now Write.** Ask students to underline the specific information in their topic sentences.

Individualizing the Lesson

Less-Advanced Students

1. Have volunteers revise the sentences in **Try Your Skill** on the chalkboard. Discuss their revisions.

2. As students work on **Now Write,** check their topic sentences and offer advice while they are composing. It will probably be best to emphasize the idea of specific information since the terms *direct* and *interesting* describe more abstract qualities.

Make It Direct

Pre-Writing: Topic Sentences

Here's the Idea   Narrowing a topic gives you a clear idea of your subject. Writing a clear topic sentence helps you to make your subject clear for your audience.

A good topic sentence states the main idea of your paragraph. In other words, it tells the reader what your paragraph is about.

A well-written topic sentence is direct and interesting. It should introduce the topic, not *you.* Don't write a topic sentence like this one:

> In this paragraph I will explain why women live longer than men.

This sentence takes too long to get to the point. It contains unnecessary words. Look at this revised topic sentence.

> Women live longer than men for three important reasons.

This sentence is direct. It gets right to the point. Furthermore, it is interesting. It makes the reader want to read on to discover *why* women live longer than men.

A well-written topic sentence is informative. It gives specific information about a paragraph. Don't write a general statement like this one.

> Swimming regularly is good for you.

This sentence is not specific enough. It doesn't say *how* or *why* swimming is good for you. Read the revised topic sentence.

> Swimming regularly improves physical fitness in two important ways.

This sentence tells the reader exactly what your paragraph is about.

Check It Out
Read the topic sentences below.

1. My paragraph is about the day of my history exam.
2. Learning to roller skate requires practice, patience, and padding.
3. The city of Los Angeles is nice.
4. Bees live in a highly organized society where every bee has a specific job to do.

- Which sentences are well-written topic sentences? Which ones are not? Give reasons for your answers.

Try Your Skill
Below are five poorly written topic sentences. Rewrite each of the sentences. Make each rewritten sentence direct, interesting, and informative.

1. There is an animal that is the biggest land animal in the world, and it is an African elephant.
2. When I look around me at everyone else in school, it seems as if every person I see is wearing some kind of ring.
3. It is easy to learn how to juggle.
4. I have a cousin named Bobby who is a nice person and has a hobby that I'm sure will be interesting to you.
5. I like to watch game shows.

Keep This in Mind

- A topic sentence states the main idea of a paragraph.
- A topic sentence should be direct, interesting, and informative.

Now Write
Look at the topic you narrowed in Part 3, **Zero In.** Write two or three different topic sentences that state the main idea of your topic. Write sentences that are direct, interesting, and informative. Save your topic sentences in your folder.

Part 6

Objective

To learn how to gather information for a paragraph

Presenting the Lesson

1. Read and discuss **Here's the Idea.** Write each development method on the chalkboard. Ask students to think of topics for which they could gather information by these methods. List the students' ideas for each method.

2. Read and discuss **Check It Out.** Have the students explain why some details don't develop the narrowed topic.

3. Assign and discuss **Try Your Skill.** Have each student explain what kind of details he or she used.

4. Read **Keep This in Mind** aloud.

5. Assign **Now Write.**

Individualizing the Lesson

Less-Advanced Students

1. Do **Try Your Skill** as a class. Then present another topic and repeat the exercise. Ask for volunteers to work at the chalkboard as the others work at their seats.

2. Begin **Now Write** in class and check to see that students are producing usable pre-writing notes. Allow some class time for a research trip to the library.

Advanced Students

For extra practice in gathering information, have students interview each other. Before they start, have the class decide on a focus for the interviews (a special skill or hobby,

Now What?

Pre-Writing: Developing a Paragraph

Here's the Idea   You have chosen and narrowed a topic for a paragraph. You have identified your purpose and your audience. You have written an interesting and informative topic sentence. Now you are ready to develop your topic. In Section 6, you learned that you can develop a paragraph in four ways. You can use sensory details, specific examples, facts and statistics, or incidents or anecdotes. The type of development you use depends on your topic and your purpose.

One way to gather information is through **observation.** If you are planning a description, you can observe your subject first-hand, and write down all of the sensory details you notice.

You can also gather information by **brainstorming.** Think about your subject. Write down all of the details and examples that come to mind.

Another way to find information for your paragraph is by doing **research.** If you need facts and statistics, the library is the place to go. Read about your subject in books, magazines, newspapers, and encyclopedias. Take notes as you read.

Finally, you can gather information by searching your own **experiences.** The incidents and anecdotes that you need to illustrate a point can come from day-to-day experiences.

Check It Out   Here is a list of pre-writing notes that one student made for a paragraph. The broad topic was *Nursing*. The narrowed topic was *A Candy-Striper's Day*.

Saturday afternoons
Dad drives Ken to band practice
Dad drives me to the hospital
Uniform must be clean

Some unpleasant jobs
Ms. Kim—my supervisor
Hospital is brand new
Make patients comfortable
Difficult patients
Serve meals, change beds, talk to patients
Favorite patient—Mr. Francesco
Want to be a doctor
Best job—feeding babies in nursery

- Do all the student's notes develop the narrowed topic? Which details do not?
- What methods do you think the student used to gather the information? Explain your answer.

Try Your Skill   Here is a narrowed topic for a paragraph. Make a list of details, examples, or facts and figures that you might use to develop the topic. Compare your pre-writing notes with those of your classmates.

the kitchen: the activity center of our home

Keep This in Mind

- The type of information you look for depends on your topic and your purpose.
- You can gather information for your paragraph through observation, by brainstorming, through research, and from your experiences.

Now Write   Review the topic you narrowed in **Zero In**. Decide what type of information you need to develop your paragraph. Use one or more of the methods described in this lesson to gather your information. Save your pre-writing notes in your folder.

career plans, etc.) and plan good questions based on that focus. Tell students to save their notes.

Optional Practice

1. Ask students which of the four methods they would be most likely to use in gathering material for the following topics.

1. The first day of kindergarten (personal experience, brainstorming)
2. A description of their bedroom (observation)
3. How a spider spins a web (research)

2. Give students the general topic *homework*. Ask them how they might develop the topic with details from *observation*. What might the narrowed topic be? How would it change if it were to be developed with details from *experience* or *research*?

Extending the Lesson

Have each student find three different paragraphs in published sources—one based on the writer's observations, one based on research, and one developed with an incident or anecdote. Using these paragraphs as examples, make a bulletin board display that shows three ways to gather information.

Objective

To learn how to choose an appropriate method for organizing details

Presenting the Lesson

1. Review the kinds of details that students have been working with in these parts: sensory details, specific examples, facts and statistics, incidents or anecdotes.

2. Read and discuss **Here's the Idea.** Write the methods of organization and a brief definition of each on the chalkboard. Students will probably grasp chronological and spatial order quite easily, but they will need more help with order of importance and general to specific order. Be prepared with several sample paragraphs illustrating each kind of order.

3. Read and discuss **Check It Out.**

4. Assign and discuss **Try Your Skill.**

5. Before students begin **Now Write,** have each one tell how he or she might organize the pre-writing notes and why. Then, assign the exercise.

Individualizing the Lesson

Less-Advanced Students

1. Go through the sample paragraph in **Try Your Skill** sentence by sentence. Have the class work together to reorganize the sentences chronologically.

2. Have students who are having trouble understanding organization work with a partner on **Now Write.**

Make Arrangements

Pre-Writing: Organizing a Paragraph

Here's the Idea   After you have gathered details to develop your main idea, you are ready for the next pre-writing step. Now you have to organize your notes by arranging them in an order that makes sense.

What is a logical order? The type of paragraph you are planning will give you a clue. Different types of paragraphs are organized in different ways.

If you are writing a paragraph that tells a story, you will arrange your pre-writing notes in **chronological order.** This is the order in which events happened or should happen. Chronological order is also the best way to organize an explanation that tells how to do something or how something happens or works.

A paragraph that describes someone or something calls for a different kind of organization. You would present your details in the order that you want your reader to notice them. This is called **spatial order.**

The pre-writing notes for a paragraph that explains *why* something is or should be are best arranged in the **order of their importance.** You begin with the least important reason and build toward the most important.

If you are writing a paragraph that defines a word or an idea, you would organize your details from the **general to the specific.**

Check It Out   Here is a poorly organized paragraph.

When you start jogging, take it easy. Switch between running and walking. Even Olympic runners had to begin somewhere. Be sure to limber up first. Don't get discouraged. Your muscles may be tight. Soon you will be able to run a mile or more. Your strength and energy will gradually increase.

- What is the writer trying to do in this paragraph?
- Why is the organization confusing?
- What kind of organization would be best for this paragraph?

Explain your answers.

Try Your Skill   This paragraph is not well organized. Re-arrange the sentences in a logical order. Tell what order you used.

Monday was a disaster. I walked into my math class twenty minutes late . On my long walk to school, I lost my pen. I missed my bus. On the bus going home, I realized I had forgotten to buy a ticket to the conference basketball game. Now I would have to pay full price at the door. After lunch, I found out that I had read the wrong story for English. Tuesday has got to be better! I had forgotten to set my alarm before I went to sleep. My lunch was left on the kitchen table, next to my math homework.

Keep This in Mind

- Pre-writing notes can be arranged in chronological order, spatial order, the order of importance, or general to specific order.
- Choose the kind of organization that best suits the type of paragraph you are writing.

Now Write   Look at the pre-writing notes that you wrote in **Now What?** Arrange your notes in an order that makes sense for the type of paragraph you are writing. Save your notes in your folder.

Part 8

Part 8

Discovery

Writing the First Draft

Objective

To learn how to write a first draft

Presenting the Lesson

1. Read and discuss **Here's the Idea,** emphasizing the temporary nature of a first draft. Tell students to expect to make changes during and after writing this draft. Discuss why it is best not to worry about mechanics while writing a first draft.

2. Go over the sample first draft in **Check It Out** with the class. Refer back to the notes in Part 6, pages 86–87.

3. For **Try Your Skill,** discuss with the class the importance of heroes and heroines in their lives. Then have students follow this procedure: formulate some thoughts on heroes and heroines using some or all of the examples listed, and adding new ones if necessary; determine purpose and audience; write a topic sentence that expresses a clear opinion about the role of heroes and heroines; organize the details, making needed additions and changes; then, write a first draft.

4. Review **Keep This in Mind.**

5. Assign **Now Write.** Encourage students to examine their notes carefully, keeping the process of writing a first draft in mind.

Individualizing the Lesson

Less-Advanced Students

1. Do **Check It Out** as a group. Ask students to imagine why the writer made the changes he or she did.

Here's the Idea All of the planning you have been doing in pre-writing is about to pay off. Now you are ready to write the first draft of your paragraph.

A first draft is sometimes called a discovery draft. Discovering new ideas, better ways to use language, and different types of organization are all part of writing a first draft.

At this important stage in the process of writing, try to write freely. Concentrate on discovering what it is that you want to say. Don't worry about making errors in punctuation or spelling. There will be time later to find and correct these mistakes. To give yourself room to make corrections later, write your first draft on every other line of your paper.

As you write, refer to your pre-writing notes. You may discover some details that do not help you to develop your topic or to accomplish your purpose. These details should be left out of your paragraph. At the same time, new ideas and details may also occur to you. You may also realize that the organization of your ideas could be improved. You might want to change the order of your sentences to make your ideas clearer.

Keep in mind that your first draft is not the final copy of your paragraph. Making changes is an important part of writing a first draft. Use this draft to experiment and discover.

Check It Out Read the following first draft. It was written from the pre-writing notes in Part 6. Look back at those notes to see how the writer used them to write this paragraph.

Being a Candy Striper is a good experience. Every Saturday, my dad drives my brother to band practice. Then he drops me off at the county hospital. I check in with my supervisor, Ms. Kim. She assigns us our jobs for the day. I like feeding the babies in the nursery. I want to be a doctor someday. Some patients are difficult. One of my favorite patients is Mr. Francesco. Our main job is to make patients comfortable. We change sheets deliver meals and do other things. Some jobs aren't the greatest. Ms. Kim reminds us that everything we do is important.

- Are there any details in the pre-writing notes on pages 86–87 that were left out of the first draft? Why?
- Did the writer add any new ideas that weren't in the pre-writing notes?

Try Your Skill   Write a brief first draft from these pre-writing notes. You may change the order of details. You may leave out some ideas if you wish. You will want to add other details that occur to you. Before you begin writing, decide on your purpose and your audience.

Topic: Heroes and heroines are an important part of our lives.
Notes: Cartoon characters—Spider Man, Wonder Woman
Sports heroes—baseball, football, Olympics
People who risk their lives—police, firefighters
Historical figures—political figures, war heroes, doctors and scientists

Keep This in Mind

- The first draft is the first written version of your paragraph.
- Use the first draft to experiment with your ideas and to discover new ones.
- Write freely without worrying about making errors in grammar or mechanics.

Now Write   Reread the pre-writing notes that you organized in Part 7. Write the first draft of your paragraph. Use the guidelines in this lesson as you write. Save your first draft.

91

91

2. Do **Try Your Skill** as a group. Have a volunteer write the students' ideas on the chalkboard. First, ask for suggestions on narrowing the topic and making more complete notes. Then set a purpose, write a topic sentence, organize the details, and write a first draft.

Advanced Students

1. Require students to add at least three more details to their pre-writing notes before beginning **Now Write.**

2. Have students continue working on their interviews from the **Advanced Students** section in Part 7. Have them design good topic sentences if they have not done so already. Then they should prepare their first drafts.

Optional Practice

Have the students exchange first drafts with partners, or read them aloud in small groups. Ask the audience to comment on the strengths of each paragraph, keeping in mind specific detail and organization.

Extending the Lesson

Have students reflect in their journals on their experience so far in writing paragraphs. Ask them to talk about the problems and the successes they have had.

Objective

To learn how to write an effective ending sentence

Presenting the Lesson

1. Read and discuss **Here's the Idea.** Emphasize the idea that a good ending sentence should sum up the point of the paragraph in an interesting way.

2. Read and discuss **Check It Out.**

3. Assign and discuss **Try Your Skill.** Duplicate the students' ending sentences or use an overhead projector. Compare the sentences.

4. Have a student read **Keep This in Mind** aloud.

5. Assign **Now Write.** When the students are finished, ask volunteers to read their drafts aloud, leaving out the ending sentences. Have class members suggest suitable last sentences for each paragraph; compare them with the one the writer composed. Tell the writers to feel free to alter their sentences if they prefer ideas from other members of the class.

Individualizing the Lesson

Less-Advanced Students

1. For **Try Your Skill,** do the first item orally and then assign the remaining two. You may wish to supply additional practice paragraphs if necessary.

2. Look at and discuss the closing sentence in the sample paragraph that appears in Part 3, **Check It Out,** page 81.

Finish It Off

The First Draft: Ending a Paragraph

Here's the Idea   The last step in writing the first draft of a paragraph is coming up with an ending sentence. What does a good ending sentence do? It sums up in an interesting way what has been said in the paragraph.

An ending sentence should not add any new information to a paragraph. Suppose you wrote a paragraph about how to polish gemstones to make jewelry. Your last sentence should not be about how to clean silver jewelry. Instead, your concluding sentence should sum up what you said about polishing stones.

An ending sentence should also be interesting. If it is, your reader will be more likely to remember what your paragraph was about.

If you are having difficulty writing a concluding sentence, look at your topic sentence. What is the main idea? Your ending sentence should sum up that main idea in different words.

Check It Out   Read the following paragraph.

Sometimes when I'm in shop class I look like a creature from outer space. My safety goggles and respirator make it hard to tell that I'm human. The goggles cover the whole top half of my face. The respirator covers most of the lower half. Sometimes I am covered with sawdust. I certainly do not look as if I belong on this earth.

 · Does the ending sentence sum up the main idea of the paragraph? Is the ending sentence interesting?

Try Your Skill   Read these three paragraphs. Rewrite the poorly written ending sentences. Try to make your ending sentences interesting. Be sure that they sum up the main ideas.

1   The new band uniforms are designed to be neat and trim. They are fashioned from a soft navy blue material that refuses to wrinkle. The jackets have white collars, white cuffs, and a white pocket. The pants have a broad white stripe down each leg. *I have been in the band for two years.*

2   The bleachers were bursting with eager baseball fans. Many waved Cubs pennants or wore Cubs T-Shirts. One young man organized a cheering section. People discussed the players and the standings. *Everyone agreed that it was a warm day.*

3   The only time I had ever ridden a horse, I felt like a character in a comedy. First, the saddle slid off when I tried to mount the horse. Then my boot stuck in the stirrup. Worst of all, the horse ignored me completely. As my friends rode out of sight, the horse lowered its head and nibbled the grass. *My horse was obviously hungry.*

Keep This in Mind

- A good ending sentence should sum up the main idea of the paragraph in an interesting way.

Now Write   Write a strong ending sentence for your paragraph. First, read your paragraph to yourself. Then write an ending that sums up the main idea. Make the ending interesting. Save your work in your folder.

Advanced Students

After finishing **Now Write,** students should write the closing sentence for their interview assignment. Have them exchange papers and make suggestions for improvement.

Optional Practice

Ask students to imagine a final sentence for this paragraph from Jane Howard's essay "All Happy Clans Are Alike."

Call it a clan, call it a network, call it a tribe, call it a family. Whatever you call it, whoever you are, you need one. You need one because you are human. You didn't come from nowhere. Before you, around you, and presumably after you, there are others. Some of these others must matter a lot—to you, and if you are very lucky, to one another. Their welfare must be nearly as important to you as your own. . . .

If necessary, point out that the second sentence is the topic sentence. Compare students' ending sentences with Howard's: "Even if you live alone, even if your solitude is [by choice], you still cannot do without a clan or a tribe."

Extending the Lesson

Present students with paragraphs that lack ending sentences. Ask them to write a good closing sentence for each one.

Objective

To understand how to revise and proofread a draft

Presenting the Lesson

1. Ask students to suggest what a writer might look for when revising a paragraph. Then read and discuss **Here's the Idea.** Outline this procedure for the students to follow.

1. Read the topic sentence to determine whether the main idea is clear.

2. Read each sentence, asking whether it helps develop the main idea. Should some details be added or deleted?

3. Check the organization for logical, effective presentation of ideas.

4. Determine whether the ending sentence is effective.

5. Read the paragraph for style, making improvements in word choice and sentence structure.

6. Proofread for errors in grammar, punctuation, and spelling. Refer to the Handbook if necessary.

2. Go over **Check It Out** in class, comparing the sample paragraph with the first draft on pages 90–91.

3. Discuss the paragraph in **Try Your Skill.** Have students rewrite the topic sentence so that it mentions fashions and recreation. Then sort through the details, reorganizing them and adding more specific information where necessary.

4. Review **Keep This In Mind.**

5. Assign **Now Write.**

94

Part 10 # Polishing Up

Revising Your Paragraph

Here's the Idea Revising is the final step in the process of writing. The purpose of revision is to make your writing the best it can be. Revision is your chance to see what is good about your paragraph and what should be improved.

First you will revise the ideas in your paragraph. Be sure that your topic sentence is direct, interesting, and informative. Keep in mind your purpose for writing. Does your paragraph do what you set out to do? Remember your audience. Is your paragraph right for the people who will be reading it?

Fine-tune the ideas that you used to develop your paragraph. Ask yourself whether all of the details develop the main idea. Cross out any ideas that do not develop your topic sentence.

Carefully go over the organization of your paragraph. Does the order of your details make sense? Would using a different method of organization make your ideas clearer?

When you are satisfied with your ideas and your organization, look at the language you have used. Is it lively and interesting? Have you used strong, specific verbs? Are your adjectives vivid? Is your word choice suitable for your audience? Add or change words until you are satisfied.

Finally, proofread your paragraph for errors in grammar, capitalization, punctuation, and spelling. When you have revised your paragraph completely, make a final copy of it. Proofread and correct this final copy.

Check It Out Read this revised paragraph.

- Name some specific ways the writer has changed and improved this paragraph.

My volunteer work as   great

~~Being a Candy Striper is a good~~ experience. Every Saturday,
has been
my dad ~~drives my brother to hockey practice. Then~~ he drops me
                                    First,
off at the county hospital. I check in with my supervisor, Ms.
                                 My favorite job is
Kim. She assigns us our jobs for the day. ~~I like~~ feeding the babies
in the nursery. ~~I want to be a doctor someday.~~ Some patients are
        Other patients are a joy.   *He is always telling*
                                                    stories
difficult. One of my favorite older patients is Mr. Francesco. *and joking*
                                                              around.
~~Our main job is to make the patients comfortable.~~ We change
                              work   *like*
sheets, deliver meals, and do other ~~things~~. Some jobs aren't the *cleaning*
                                                                    up after
greatest. Ms. Kim reminds us that everything we do is important. *sick*
        always   *Being a candy*   *patients,*
                        striper has taught me many
                        lessons about people and life.

Try Your Skill   Read this first draft. Use the guidelines in
this lesson to revise it.

   Fads are hear today and gone tomorrow. Mini-skirts have
been in and out of fashion. Personally, I like jeens. Hairstyles are
"in" one year and "out" the next. Their are also fads in recreation. Like skateboards hula hoops and certain games. I remember when everyone wore deely-boppers. You can go broke
keeping up with all the latest fads. Save your money.

Keep This in Mind

· Revise the ideas, organization, and word choice of
   your paragraph. Proofread your paragraph.

Now Write   Use the guidelines in this lesson to revise the
first draft of your paragraph. When you are satisfied with your
paragraph, make a final copy. Save your paragraph.

95

Individualizing the Lesson

Less-Advanced Students

   Before students revise their
drafts, have each student specify
two or three changes they intend to
make. Then have them proceed with
Now Write.

Advanced Students

   Have students revise and then
put together a booklet of their interviews. They should select a good
title and provide illustrations or photographs to go with the text.

Optional Practice

   Duplicate for students three or
four samples of paragraphs that
need revising. Have them determine
the areas of weakness and then rewrite the paragraphs.

Extending the Lesson

   1. Invite someone who writes pro-
fessionally to talk to the class about
the writing process he or she follows. Ask the person to bring actual
notes and drafts, if possible.
   2. Put together a publication of
the students' paragraphs. Have a
student committee work on the organization and layout. Duplicate
and distribute the booklet throughout the school.

95

Section 8 Objectives

1. To understand the three main stages of the writing process: pre-writing, writing the first draft, and revising

2. To understand and correctly use proofreading symbols

Presenting the Section

If possible, obtain pictures of the construction of a building—before, during, and after. Or else, you can have students imagine what such photographs would look like. Discuss the kinds of planning and work necessary to get from one stage to the next (from empty construction site, to building in progress, to finished product). Ask students why a builder might have to change his plans once the construction has started.

Tell students that they use a similar process even when involved in much simpler tasks. For example, talk about packing a suitcase in terms of planning, carrying out the plans, considering the results, and making the needed adjustments.

Explain to students that this section will present them with a look at each stage of the writing process. They will see that this process also involves planning, carrying out the plans, and making changes.

When you discuss pre-writing, be sure the students are familiar with all the activities that are part of this stage of the process of writing: selecting and limiting a topic, gathering ideas and details, and evaluating and organizing information. Refer the students to the illustration of pre-writing notes on page 99.

The Process of Writing

Also be sure the students know the different methods for gathering ideas and details (brainstorming, observation, and library research) and the different methods of organizing information (chronological order, spatial order, order of importance, and general to specific order). Review all of these methods with your students.

The idea of a first draft may be foreign to some of your students. Stress that a first draft is an opportunity to experiment with language and ideas. Be sure that students understand that it is all right to change their ideas and organization during this stage of the process.

Stress the importance of revising to your students. Be sure they understand that revising is more than just fixing misspellings or adding missing punctuation. Revising is a chance to improve the entire paragraph or composition, including ideas and organization. Look over the revised paragraph on page 102 with your students. Ask them to tell you how it is different from the first draft on page 100.

You may want to introduce your students to the following techniques for revising their work.

Peer evaluation—In pairs or small groups, students critique each other's writing.

Conference—Oral evaluations by the teacher concentrate on both strengths and problems.

Editorial group—Students assigned the roles of author, editor, and proofreader work together on an assignment.

Group questioning—After one student in a group reads a piece of

97

writing aloud, the other students ask questions focusing on what they still want to know about the subject.

Clinics—In workshops, students with similar writing problems receive instruction from the teacher.

Tutoring—A student who is weak in some area is paired with a student who is stronger in the same area.

Review the proofreading symbols on page 101 with your students. Tell them to use these symbols when they revise their work.

Additional Resources

Practice Book — pages 41–42

Duplicating Masters — pages 41–42

Teaching Special Populations

LD See **Teaching Special Populations,** page 75.

ESL Guide students through the reading of this section, and use class discussion to clarify difficult concepts. Students may also benefit from being paired with a native English speaker during the pre-writing stages. Carefully monitor each student's spelling, capitalization, grammar, and punctuation, providing additional practice whenever needed. Be prepared to accept some written passages that are bland but grammatically correct.

NSD See **Teaching Special Populations,** page 75.

The Process of Writing

As you work your way through the composition chapters in this book, you will do many kinds of writing. You will write stories and describe people and places. You will state your opinions, explain processes, and define words and ideas. Although the type of writing you do will change, the way you approach your writing will not. You will always use the process of writing to plan, write, and revise your paragraphs and compositions.

The three main stages in the process of writing are **Pre-Writing, Writing the First Draft,** and **Revising.** If you complete these three stages carefully, your writing will be clear and well organized. It will also have unity. When you have mastered the process, writing will be much easier for you.

In this chapter you can review the process of writing. First, read about each stage of the process. Then look at the example that shows what one student wrote during each stage.

Pre-Writing Success is usually the result of careful planning. That is why an actor rehearses before opening night. That is why an artist draws many sketches before beginning a painting. That is also why the pre-writing, or planning, stage of the process of writing is so important. What you do *before* you write will determine how successful you will be *when* you write.

Before you write, you must choose a good subject. You can discover interesting things to write about in a variety of ways. You can brainstorm, look through your journal, and do some reading in books, newspapers, and magazines. When you have chosen a subject, narrow it so that you can cover it well in a given length.

Make a list of interesting details about your subject. You will use these details to develop your subject. These might include sensory details, specific examples, facts and statistics, or incidents or anecdotes. You can gather these kinds of details through observation, brainstorming, and research.

When you have enough details, you must organize them. Organizing is a very important pre-writing step. If your details are not well organized, your writing will not be clear. First, look carefully at your list. Cross out any details that do not develop your topic. Then arrange the remaining details in a logical order. You might use chronological order, spatial order, the order of importance, or general to specific order. Be sure to choose an order that suits the type of writing you are doing.

Pre-Writing

You list possible topics and select one.

You list details, choose those that develop your topic, and organize them.

topics

Julie's new job — Grandpa's workshop
storm at the beach — the band room

details — scratchy

floor covered with sawdust — oak candlesticks
Gramps is 65 years old — smell of wood
boards against the wall — sweet?
workbench — blueprints —
  planes, T-square — rolled up
We live on Taylor Avenue — lathe and jig saw
  hum — buzz

Writing the First Draft At this point in the process of writing, you are ready to write your first draft. This is perhaps the most exciting stage of the process. Now you will turn your ideas into sentences and paragraphs. Simply put your pencil to paper and write. Let your ideas flow freely. Don't fuss with the

99

Use of Writing Folders

Throughout this series, students are asked to keep their independent **Now Write** assignments in folders. Depending on your school's policy, you may issue these folders to students or ask them to purchase their own. Both you and your students need to keep track of writing assignments in separate writing folders for reasons that are as practical as they are educationally sound:

1. Students should be encouraged to write in the classroom and to keep assignments there.

2. Both you and your students need a permanent record of assignments completed. Assignments can be compared in order to see measurable progress, and in order to determine grades.

3. As students see a growing body of material that reflects their own ideas and interests, writing folders become special, personal collections. In this way, writing becomes a more positive experience.

writing. Don't be concerned about grammar or mechanics. Don't get slowed down by trying to make your writing perfect at this stage. This is a time to experiment, to discover what you want to say about your subject and how you want to say it. You will have time later to revise what you have written. Skip lines as you write. Then you will have plenty of space to add details, make corrections, and improve what you have written.

Writing the First Draft

> Gramp's favorite spot is his workshop. Its neat. It smells great. His work bench has a hammer, a T-square, planes, jars of nails, and other stuff. Wood is against the walls. On the floor is sawdust and wood shavings. He's got a lathe and a jig-saw. Theres other things like blueprints. And candlesticks. He made them on the lathe. Like I said, Gramp's workshop is neat.

Revising When you have finished your first draft, you are ready for the third stage of the process of writing—revising. At this stage of the process you must work carefully and thoughtfully with what you have written. Did you include everything you wanted to? Do you like what you've written? Is it interesting? Your goal is to improve your writing. Here are some questions you should ask yourself as you revise your first draft.

1. Have I written a good topic sentence for each paragraph? Is it direct and informative? Is it interesting enough to capture the reader's attention?

2. Have I included enough details to develop my topic completely? Have I left out any details that do not relate to my main idea?

3. Have I arranged my details in a logical order? Does the order suit the type of writing I am doing?

4. Have I used lively, vivid language?

5. Have I written a strong ending? Does it bring my writing to a satisfactory conclusion?

Proofreading   The last step in revising is called proofreading. Read your first draft carefully. Find and correct any errors you made in grammar, capitalization, punctuation, and spelling. Check a dictionary and the Handbook sections of this book as you proofread.

As you revise your first draft, use the following proofreading marks to show your corrections and changes.

Proofreading Symbols

Symbol	Meaning	Example
∧	add	would gone *have*
≡	capitalize	United states
/	make lower case	our club President
∿	reverse	t h i e r
ℓ	take out	finished the the race
¶	make new paragraph	....be over. New ideas
⊙	period	....and stop Before we
∧	add comma	Red, blue and green are

Notice how the paragraph has been revised.

Revising

Gramp's favorite spot is his ['s]
behind our house. The workshop is filled with the sweet smell
workshop. ~~Its neat. It smells great~~ of pine
and
~~His~~ (Gramps's) work bench, has a hammer, a 's cedar. is cluttered with
several
T-square, planes, jars of nails,
tools. Boards are stacked
and other ~~stuff~~. ~~Wood is~~ against
covered with
the walls. ~~On the floor is~~ sawdust
also has
and wood shavings. ~~He's got~~ a lathe
that hum and buzz as he works.
and a jig-saw. Theres other things
Rolled-up are piled on a shelf above the bench.
like blueprints. And candlesticks. of solid oak
stand waiting for sanding and staining. Now that he's
~~He made them on the lathe. Like I~~
retired, Gramps spends hours in his workshop
~~said, Gramps workshop is neat.~~
every day. It has become his second home.

Making the Final Copy   When you are satisfied that your writing is clear and correct, write it in its final form. The final copy of your paragraph, composition, or report is important. This is the only copy of your work that your readers will see. Rewrite your work carefully. Include all of the changes that you made when you revised. Make your work as neat as possible.

When you have finished your final copy, proofread your work one last time. Neatly correct any errors you find. If you find that you've made more than three mistakes, you may want to redo your final copy. Remember, you want to make a good impression on your readers.

102

Gramps's favorite spot is his workshop behind our house. The workshop is filled with the sweet smell of pine and cedar. Gramps's workbench is cluttered with hammers, a T-square, several planes, jars of nails, and other tools. He also has a lathe and a jig-saw that hum and buzz as he works. Boards are stacked against the walls. The floor is covered with sawdust and wood shavings. Rolled-up blueprints are piled on a shelf above the bench. Candlesticks of solid oak stand waiting for sanding and staining. Now that he's retired, Gramps spends hours in his workshop every day. It has become his second home.

Now you are ready to begin your writing adventures. Whenever and whatever you write, complete all the stages of the process of writing. Each time you write, you will be learning something about writing and about yourself.

Section **9** Objectives

1. To learn how to develop a narrative paragraph with incidents and sensory details

2. To use chronological order to organize the incidents in a narrative paragraph

3. To recognize and use the first-person and the third-person points of view

4. To use transitions to show chronological order

5. To learn to revise a narrative paragraph

Preparing the Students

Ask for a volunteer to tell about the funniest or most surprising thing that has happened to him or her recently. Explain to the class that such a story is also called a narrative. Remind students that they have already been introduced to the three different kinds of paragraphs in Section 6, pages 72–73. Ask if anyone can recall the other two types (descriptive and explanatory). Tell students that in this section they will learn special techniques for writing a good narrative paragraph.

Additional Resources

Mastery Test — page 22 in the test booklet

Practice Book — pages 43–47

Duplicating Masters — pages 43–47

The Narrative Paragraph

Teaching Special Populations

LD See **Teaching Special Populations,** page 75.

ESL ESL students may have trouble with verb and pronoun forms in narrative paragraphs. Emphasize those sections of the text that deal with chronological order and explain the vocabulary related to time. Give students numerous examples of the change of form in third-person singular present tense verbs. Try assigning exercises in which students must change first-person constructions to third person, and vice versa. Combine these examples with practice in using the third-person point of view.

NSD See **Teaching Special Populations,** page 75. Use this section to give NSD students extra practice in pronoun agreement. In their first drafts, have students circle each pronoun they use and draw an arrow to its antecedent.

Objective

To learn how to develop a narrative paragraph with incidents and sensory details

Presenting the Lesson

1. Review the purpose of a narrative (to tell a story), and then read and discuss the first two paragraphs of **Here's the Idea.**

2. Tell students that the next two paragraphs of **Here's the Idea** describe how to begin writing a narrative paragraph. Be sure they understand what is meant by *incident.*

3. Before reading the final paragraph of **Here's the Idea,** read the following paragraph to students and ask them what is wrong with it.

I got on the bus to go downtown and noticed that there were very few seats. There was one vacancy next to a boy about my age, so I sat down next to him. The bus ride was pretty long, but by the time I got off, I realized that the boy next to me had been my good friend in kindergarten.

Discuss the fact that while the paragraph does tell a story, it is not very interesting. It does not set the scene at all and it does not tell us how the narrator felt about seeing his old friend. Read the final paragraph of **Here's the Idea** and then ask students to suggest some sensory details that would improve the paragraph about the bus ride.

4. Read and discuss **Check It Out.**

5. Assign and discuss **Try Your Skill.** Ask for a few volunteers to write their notes on the chalkboard

106

The Big Event

Pre-Writing: Developing a Narrative

Here's the Idea   You have learned what a paragraph is and how to write one. You have also learned how the process of writing can help you to write better paragraphs. Now you are going to learn how to write specific types of paragraphs.

There are several different types of paragraphs you can write. The kind of paragraph you write will depend on your purpose for writing. If your purpose is to tell a story, you will write a **narrative paragraph.** A narrative can be a true story, such as an account of your first dance class. Or a narrative can be an imaginary story, set in a different time or in another world.

As in any other kind of writing, the first pre-writing step is to choose and narrow a topic. Try to remember or to imagine an interesting or exciting event. Be sure the topic you choose is narrow enough to be covered well in one paragraph.

When you have chosen an event to write about, begin listing the details that will help you to tell your story. An event is made up of many smaller events, or incidents. For example, suppose the story you want to tell concerns your first ride on a New York City subway. This event includes such incidents as paying your fare and checking the subway map to figure out how to get to your destination. The event also includes such incidents as going down to the subway platform, boarding the train, and so on. Most of the pre-writing notes you make for your narrative paragraph will be the incidents that tell your story.

To make your narrative paragraph really interesting, however, you also need to include good sensory details. For example, how did the ticket agent *look*? How do subway trains *sound*? Add sensory details to each incident that you list. They will make your narrative come alive for your reader.

106

Check It Out   Read this narrative paragraph.

A faint, scratchy noise awakened me. In seconds I saw that someone was lifting the screen on my window. Just as I was about to cry out, I heard a loud thud. Then I heard hisses, snarls, and a scream. I jumped out of bed and switched on the light. Max, my cat, was sitting beside the open window, licking his paws. I peered into the darkness, then hugged Max, my protector.

· What incidents tell the story of Max and the burglar?
· What sensory details did the writer include?

Try Your Skill   Below are four situations. Choose one situation and make some pre-writing notes for it. First, list the incidents that would tell the story. Then add good sensory details to the incidents.

1. I had done my homework, but the teacher didn't know that, and I couldn't find my paper.
2. As Gwen shut the door, she suddenly realized that she had locked the key inside.
3. It took Tom a few minutes to realize that he was invisible.
4. Once in a while a strange thing happens to me.

Keep This in Mind

· A narrative paragraph tells a real or an imaginary story.
· A narrative is developed with incidents and sensory details.

Now Write   Choose an interesting story you would like to tell. Narrow your topic so that your story can be told in one paragraph. Then gather details to develop your narrative. List the incidents that will tell your story. Include good sensory details. Save your pre-writing notes in your folder.

107

and explain how they found their sensory details (memory, observation, imagination, etc.).

6. Review **Keep This In Mind.**

7. Assign **Now Write.** Instruct students to include good sensory details to bring the scene to life. If they are having trouble choosing a story, have them look through their journals for ideas.

Individualizing the Lesson

Less-Advanced Students

For **Try Your Skill,** do the first sentence orally in class. Write the students' ideas on the chalkboard. Then assign the exercise.

Advanced Students

Have these students make two sets of pre-writing notes for **Now Write.** The two narratives could be thematically related (childhood experiences, great successes, etc.).

Optional Practice

Choose a narrative paragraph from the student's literature text and duplicate it or read it to the students. Have them list the incidents and the sensory details in the paragraph.

Extending the Lesson

Have students bring in comic strips that tell a story. Have them write a narrative paragraph based on the incidents in one comic.

Part 2

Objective

To use chronological order to organize the incidents in a narrative paragraph.

Presenting the Lesson

1. Read and discuss **Here's the Idea.** Be sure students understand the term *chronological order.* Have them list the incidents in the sample paragraph.

2. Read and discuss **Check It Out.** Ask students to find words in the paragraph that tell "time" order (*awakened, too, early,* etc.).

3. Assign **Try Your Skill.** Ask students to look for "time" words that will help them recognize chronological order.

4. Read **Keep This In Mind** aloud.

5. Assign **Now Write.** Encourage the students to add more information to their notes as they organize.

Individualizing The Lesson

Less-Advanced Students

1. For **Check It Out,** have students list the separate incidents in the narrative.

2. Do paragraph 1 in **Try Your Skill** as a group. Assign paragraph 2.

3. Ask for some volunteers to write the **Now Write** exercise on the chalkboard. Have the class ask questions about the narratives. Show the writers how to add the necessary details to their notes.

Advanced Students

1. Explain that chronological order does not always start at the beginning of an event and move

Time Will Tell

Pre-Writing: Using Chronological Order

Here's the Idea   To be a good storyteller, you need to plan your story before you write it. You began planning your story when you chose a topic and made pre-writing notes for it. Now you must organize your pre-writing notes. You must decide on a logical order in which to present your details.

The best order for a narrative paragraph is **chronological order.** Chronological order is the order of time. Your story should start with the first incident that happened and move along in time to the last incident.

Look at this narrative paragraph. Notice that the incidents are told in the order in which they happened.

> Outside, blinking against the sun, I left my bike in the rack and wandered down the street. Something was happening in front of the dime store. I could see a crowd of kids gathered at the doors while a policeman attempted to keep order. I slipped inside behind his back. The place was a madhouse. It was jammed with hundreds of shrieking children. They all pressed toward one of the aisles. Some kind of demonstration was going on.
>
> —FRANK CONROY

Check It Out   Now read this narrative.

> His father's voice awakened him. Stretching his back against the mattress, he looked over at his parents' end of the sleeping porch. He saw that his mother was up too, though he could tell that it was still early. He lay on his back quietly. He watched a spider that dangled on a golden, shining thread from the rolled canvas of the blinds. The spider came down in tiny jerks, its legs wriggling, and went up again in the beam of sun. Then, from the other room, he heard his father's voice, loud and cheerful.
>
> —WALLACE STEGNER

- Are the events in this narrative in chronological order? Explain your answer.

Try Your Skill   Below are two lists of pre-writing notes for narratives. Read them. Then write the incidents in each list in chronological order.

1. 2(a) In the town square, we saw a statue of an insect—the boll weevil.
   6(b) The farmers decided that the boll weevil had actually helped them, and they erected the statue.
   1(c) Last fall, my family visited Enterprise, Alabama.
   4(d) Then boll weevils came and destroyed the cotton crop.
   3(e) We learned that many years ago, most of the people in Enterprise had grown cotton for a living.
   5(f) When that happened, the farmers tried raising peanuts and made more money than before.
2. 1(a) A gorilla walked into a restaurant and ordered a sandwich.
   4(b) When the waitress took the gorilla's money, she said that she did not often see gorillas in the restaurant.
   5(c) The gorilla told her that at those prices she would not see many more, either.
   2(d) The waitress was shocked to see a gorilla but brought the sandwich.
   3(e) Because the waitress thought that a gorilla would be easily fooled, she charged it twenty dollars.

Keep This in Mind

- Use chronological order to organize the incidents in a narrative paragraph.

Now Write   Take out the pre-writing notes you made in the last lesson, **The Big Event.** Arrange the notes in chronological order. Save your organized pre-writing notes in your folder.

progressively toward the end. Ask students to find examples of movies or books that start in the middle or the end of the action and move backwards in time to previous events (flashback).

2. For **Now Write,** students may either develop both sets of pre-writing notes from Part 1, or select just one set to work on. Require them to add at least five pieces of information to their notes.

Optional Practice

Show students a picture of an action scene or of interaction between two or three people. Have students determine what is happening *now*, what might have happened *before*, and what will happen *next*. Explain that they are dealing with *chronological order.*

Extending the Lesson

1. Select several narrative paragraphs from student work or other sources. Scramble the sentences, copy the altered paragraphs, and distribute them to the class. Have students organize the sentences into chronological order.

2. Have students bring in brief newspaper articles and trace the chronology of the incidents covered in the story.

Objective

To recognize and use the first-person and the third-person points of view

Presenting the Lesson

1. Read and discuss **Here's the Idea.** Then review the terms *point of view, first-person,* and *third-person.*

2. Read and discuss **Check It Out.** Point out how the first-person narrative allows the reader to feel more a part of the narrator's experiences, while the third-person narrative has a more objective feeling.

3. Assign **Try Your Skill.**

4. Read and discuss **Keep This in Mind.**

5. Assign **Now Write.** Before doing the exercise, have each student tell one advantage and one disadvantage of using the first-person and third-person points of view for his or her paragraph.

Individualizing the Lesson

Less-Advanced Students

1. Do **Try Your Skill** orally. Write the students' suggestions on the chalkboard. After completing the two paragraphs, discuss the different effects of the two points of view.

2. Have students look through their literature anthology and identify stories written from the first-person point of view, and from the third-person point of view.

Advanced Students

Have students choose a great moment in history, a moment they would like to have witnessed. Have

Insiders and Outsiders

Pre-Writing: Choosing a Point of View

Here's the Idea Who knows more about an avalanche? A person watching it from a distance or a person in its path? Actually, both know something about the avalanche, but they know different things. They have different **points of view.**

There are also different points of view in writing. "Point of view" means the eyes and mind through which something is written. In your narrative paragraph, you might use the first-person point of view or the third-person point of view.

When you use the **first-person point of view,** you use the pronoun *I. I* is the narrator, the one who tells the story. *I* tells only what he or she can see. This first-person narrator cannot tell what anyone else is thinking or feeling. You will probably use the first-person point of view when you write about something that happened to you. You can also write from the first-person point of view in a story that you make up.

Another point of view you can use is the **third-person point of view.** When you write from this point of view, you use the pronouns *he* and *she.* The narrator can see and hear everything that goes on, but the narrator is not a character in the story. You will probably use the third-person point of view to write about something that happened to other people.

Choosing a point of view is an important decision when you write a narrative. Once you have chosen an appropriate point of view, stick to it. Otherwise, your reader will be confused.

Check It Out Read the following two paragraphs.

1   At the base camp, the group of climbers was watching for the return of Andrew. He had not returned from what should have been an easy climb to check supplies on the ridge. Finally, Andrew's red parka was sighted. Far above him, however, a wall

of snow suddenly broke away from a rocky ledge. The massive cloud of snow roared down the mountain.

2   Near the top of the snowbound ridge the air was sharp and cold. I was exhausted. I was afraid I would not make it back to the camp. Just as I began my crawl to the tents, I heard an awesome rumbling. I felt my heart racing, but I was too weak to move.

- From which point of view is each paragraph written?
- Which words helped you identify each point of view?

Try Your Skill   Use these pre-writing notes to write two paragraphs. Write one paragraph from the first-person point of view. Write the other from the third-person point of view.

Waded across the river on a sandbar
Water got deeper and deeper
Up to knees, chest, chin
Halfway across, tripped on a hidden rock
Fell, was swept underwater
Was carried downstream

Keep This in Mind

- Point of view is the eyes and mind through which a story is told.
- The pronoun *I* signals the first-person point of view. *I* is the narrator.
- The pronouns *he* and *she* signal the third-person point of view. The narrator is not a part of the story.
- Choose a point of view and stick to it.

Now Write   Review your pre-writing notes and choose a point of view for your narrative paragraph. Write *third person* or *first person* at the end of your notes. Save your notes.

the students gather details about the event and then narrate it either in the first-person or in the third-person.

Optional Practice

Have students identify the point of view in the following passages.

> It was very cold the year I tore a ligament in my right leg and fell in love with soft-eyed brown-haired angel-on-earth Emma Haines and got a job as a messenger boy after school...
> –William Saroyan

> Charlie Bates was on his way home from work when the eight lanes of traffic around him slowed to a crawl and finally came to a standstill. He was on a high, curving overpass that looked down on the city's twelve-lane freeway system. As far as Charlie could see, cars were jammed end to end, lane to lane, and nothing moved.
> –James D. Houston

If necessary point out the use of *I* and *my* in paragraph 1, and *he, his, him* in paragraph 2.

Extending the Lesson

Display pictures of people doing interesting things. Ask students to select one picture and to write a paragraph about the picture using the first-person point of view. Collect the paragraphs and read them aloud. See if the class can match the paragraphs with the pictures.

Part 4

Objective

To use transitions to show chronological order

Presenting the Lesson

1. Read and discuss **Here's the Idea.** Talk about the term *transition* and the meaning of the prefix *trans.* Go over the list of transitional words and phrases and have the students think of a sentence for each one. Explain that a transition not only links two thoughts but also expresses chronological order.

2. Read and discuss **Check It Out.**

3. Assign **Try Your Skill.** Then ask students to explain their choices of transitional words and phrases.

4. Read **Keep This in Mind.**

5. Assign **Now Write.**

Individualizing the Lesson

Less-Advanced Students

1. Do **Check It Out** orally. Discuss the function of each transition.

2. Have students work on **Try Your Skill** in small groups.

3. To build momentum for the first drafts, ask each student to read his or her opening sentence aloud. Ask the class to speculate on what might happen in each narrative.

Advanced Students

Ask each student to find a well-written narrative paragraph that contains at least three transitions. Have volunteers write their paragraphs on the chalkboard, leaving a blank space for the transitions.

Good Timing

Writing the First Draft

Here's the Idea   In the last three lessons you have been planning your narrative paragraph. Now you are ready to write the first draft. As you write, you want to make sure that the order of the incidents that tell your story is clear.

You can make the order of incidents clear by using transitions. These are words and phrases that carry a reader from one thought to the next. Here is a list of transitional words and phrases that are often used in narratives.

first	while	at the beginning	before
then	soon	in the middle	after
next	later	afterwards	by the time
finally	when	at the end	at the same time

This list shows some of the most common transitional words and phrases. However, there are many others. For example, you might use such phrases as *at that instant, before noon, two weeks later,* or *next year.* Whenever you write a narrative, use a variety of transitional words and phrases to show chronological order.

Check It Out   Read the following narrative paragraph.

He sat motionless a minute longer. Then, his hand crept nervously onto the table and pushed a button. The room darkened. At that moment, a long section of wall became transparent, revealing a dozen silvery models of spaceships. He quickly touched another button. The models faded. At the same time the opposite wall showed the construction of a neutron-drive spaceship. A few seconds later, when he pushed a third button, another picture showed a section of Earth's surface. It also revealed in the far distance, the tiny reddish globe of Mars. Finally, a tiny rocket rose from the section of Earth and spread its silvery sails.

—FRITZ LEIBER

- Find the transitional words and phrases in this paragraph. Do they help to make the order of the incidents clear?

Try Your Skill Read the following paragraph. Then rewrite the paragraph, adding transitions to show the order of the incidents.

The taxi driver stomped on the gas pedal. The taxi sped up Grand Avenue. We reached a busy intersection. A bus pulled out in front of us. The driver slammed on the brakes. The taxi driver rolled down his window and hollered at the bus driver.

Keep This in Mind

- Transitional words and phrases make the order of events in a narrative clear.
- In a narrative, include transitions to show chronological order.

Now Write Write the first draft of your narrative paragraph. Use transitional words and phrases to show your reader the order of events. Save your first draft in your folder.

Challenge the class to guess what words or phrases belong in the blanks.

Optional Practice

Have students identify the transitions in the following passage.

(Kipkoech and Charles Cherviyat) left home at age five, scrabbled at farm work for four years and then entered Kenya's system of free primary schools. They ran barefoot races with their schoolmates, and began winning. Later, in Munich, Kipkoech set the world junior record for 1,500 meters, and Charles did the same for 5,000. After a rocky spring, Charles qualified for the Kenyan Olympic Squad at the last moment.

–Time

Extending the Lesson

1. Read a short story aloud in class. Ask students to write a one-paragraph summary of the plot. Remind them to use transitions.

2. Oral story-telling can help students become sensitive to the elements of narrative. If possible have someone who often tells stories (librarian, speech teacher, etc.) read a narrative to the class or use a record or tape. Afterwards, discuss with the class how the specific details, the chronological order, the point of view, and the transitions all worked together to make the story-telling interesting.

Part 5

Instant Replay

Revising Your Narrative Paragraph

Objective

To learn to revise a narrative paragraph

Presenting the Lesson

1. Read **Here's the Idea** aloud. Go over the five questions to ask when revising. Then discuss the qualities of strong verbs. Remind students that careful proofreading will help them produce a good final draft.

2. Assign and discuss **Check It Out.**

3. Assign **Try Your Skill.** Have students read their revised paragraphs aloud. Ask students if they can think of even more synonyms for the words in italics. List their suggestions on the board.

4. Discuss each point in **Keep This in Mind.**

5. Assign **Now Write.**

Individualizing the Lesson

Less-Advanced Students

1. Do **Try Your Skill** orally. Write the revised paragraph on the chalkboard.

2. Have students begin **Now Write** in class. Remind them to refer to the questions listed in **Here's the Idea.** You should write those questions on the chalkboard for reinforcement.

Advanced Students

To make **Try Your Skill** more challenging, have students create certain effects in their revisions. Tell some students to convey a tense, serious mood, and others to treat the topic humorously. Have some

Here's the Idea   You have completed the first draft of your narrative paragraph. Read it over carefully. How well does it tell your story? How might your first draft be improved? Now is the time to carefully revise what you have written. As you revise your first draft, keep these questions in mind.

1. Will the topic sentence capture the reader's interest?
2. Have I included good sensory details?
3. Are the incidents arranged in chronological order?
4. Did I stick to one point of view throughout my story?
5. Have I used transitional words and phrases to show time order?

As you revise your paragraph, you may see other ways to improve the narrative. A good way to make your writing interesting and lively is to use strong, specific verbs.

A verb is a word that tells what happens or what is. The strongest verbs show action, like *gallop*, *snarl*, and *climb*. Weak verbs just show state of being, like *is*, *become*, and *seems*. As you improve your narrative, change weak state-of-being verbs to strong action verbs whenever possible. For example, suppose you wrote "Jerry was in the pool." You could make this sentence more interesting by revising it to "Jerry swam across the pool," or "Jerry dove into the pool."

The verbs you use should be as specific as possible. Specific verbs give your reader a clear picture of the action you are describing. You might replace a general verb like *moved* with a more specific one like *raced*, *crawled*, *danced*, or *leaped*.

Remember to proofread your paragraph. Find and correct any errors in grammar, capitalization, punctuation, and spelling.

Check It Out   Read the following paragraph.

I tramped today through miles of open, snow-clad country. I slipped in the ruts of the road or ploughed through the drifts in the fields with such a sense of adventure as I cannot describe.

—DAVID GRAYSON

- Pick out strong specific verbs in the paragraph. How do they make the paragraph come to life?

Try Your Skill   Revise the following narrative paragraph. Improve it by adding transitions and by replacing the verbs in italics with stronger, more specific verbs.

Katrina *was* on the diving board. She *looked* straight ahead. She *put* her arms out in front of her. She *put* her arms down and bounced on the board. She *put* her arms up. She *was* in the air, arching forward. She *went* toward the water. She entered the water. The crowd *was* loud.

Keep This in Mind

- Review your narrative paragraph to make it clear, lively, and interesting.
- Arrange the details in chronological order.
- Use transitions to show time order.
- Replace weak, general verbs with strong, specific ones.
- Keep the same point of view throughout the story.

Now Write   Revise your narrative paragraph, following the guidelines in this lesson. Then make a final copy. Proofread your paragraph one last time. Save your narrative in your folder.

students give the impression that Katrina's dive is a success, and others that the dive is a failure. Another possibility is to show that the diver does not really care how well she does.

Optional Practice

Have students find the strong verbs in the following passage.

Tornadoes most often <u>sweep</u> across the central plains of the United States. They usually <u>strike</u> in the spring. At that time, warm air from the south <u>crashes</u> into cooler air from the north. Thunderstorms form, and sometimes the storms cause tornadoes.

–*National Geographic World*

Extending the Lesson

1. Have students form small groups and decide on a topic sentence. One student starts writing and stops after one minute. The paragraph is passed around until each person in the group has had two chances to write. Have group members read the resulting narratives aloud to the class.

2. Put together a publication of the students' own narrative paragraphs. Have students illustrate the paragraphs.

Section 10 Objectives

1. To develop a descriptive paragraph with specific sensory details
2. To learn to organize details in spatial order
3. To recognize that words create a specific mood
4. To learn to use transitions to show spatial order
5. To learn to revise a descriptive paragraph

Preparing the Students

Ask students to discuss the difference between the words *describe* and *narrate*. Point out that the purpose of a narration is to tell about an action, or what happened, while a description paints a picture of a scene, often with little or no action. Remind the class that whether they write a narrative or description depends on their purpose for writing. Explain to students that in this section they will learn how to write a descriptive paragraph.

Additional Resources

Mastery Test — page 23 in the test booklet
Practice Book — pages 48–52
Duplicating Masters — pages 48–52

The Descriptive Paragraph

Teaching Special Populations

LD See **Teaching Special Populations,** page 75.

ESL Students will have to expand their vocabulary in order to write effective descriptive paragraphs. Concentrate your exercises on vocabulary associated with the senses. Provide students with concrete examples of different textures, tastes, smells, and sounds, and have them describe the experiences in complete sentences. Bear in mind that sensory words can be culturally biased: for example, some languages employ a wider variety of sensory words than English, while others may use single terms to describe combinations such as texture and taste.

Help ESL students become familiar with the concepts and vocabulary associated with spatial order. Try pairing students with partners and have them issue instructions to one another using words that indicate spatial relationships (*beneath, to the left, inside, behind,* and so on). Show students a large poster or photograph and have them use these words to describe where the objects in the picture are in relation to each other.

NSD See **Teaching Special Populations,** page 75.

Part 1

Objective

To develop a descriptive paragraph with specific sensory details

Presenting the Lesson

1. Choose a place familiar to all of the students (school cafeteria, auditorium, playing field, etc.), and ask them for words and phrases to describe that place. Write their suggestions on the chalkboard. Most of the ideas will probably be sensory details.

Then ask students to name the five senses. Explain that vivid descriptions depend on good sensory details. Check the list of details on the board to see if all of the senses are represented.

2. Read and discuss **Here's the Idea.** Point out that both methods of gathering details can generate long lists of usable information.

3. Read and discuss **Check It Out.** Before answering the questions, write the five senses on the chalkboard.

4. Assign **Try Your Skill.** Tell students to be sure to use all five senses. Have them share their lists with the class.

5. Review **Keep This in Mind.**

6. Assign **Now Write.**

Individualizing the Lesson

Less-Advanced Students

1. Do **Check It Out** as a class.

2. For **Try Your Skill,** first have students list the five senses. Then, using that list, describe the first place with the class orally. Then have the students do the exercise

118

In a Sense

Pre-Writing: Gathering Sensory Details

Here's the Idea   Have you ever experienced something that impressed you so much you wanted to share your experience with others? Maybe it was your first view of the Grand Canyon. It may have been a wonderful Mexican dinner you had at a friend's house. Perhaps it was a sleek imported sports car you saw at the auto show. One way you can share these kinds of experiences is by writing **descriptive paragraphs.**

The purpose of a descriptive paragraph is to describe a person, place, or thing as clearly and as vividly as possible. To accomplish this goal, you will want to develop your description with sensory details. Sensory details tell about things that can be seen, heard, touched, smelled, or tasted.

Sensory details can be gathered in two ways. The best way is through personal observation. Suppose you wanted to describe the lion house at the zoo. You would go to the lion house with a notebook and observe. You would write down everything you saw, heard, touched, smelled, or tasted.

Another way to gather sensory details is by searching your memory. Suppose you were at the Grand Canyon last summer and now you want to describe what you saw. You would think back to your experience and write down as many sensory details as you can remember. What did the colors look like? Was the air scented by the nearby pine forests? Could you hear any animals at night? If you have photos of the canyon, look them over carefully. They may jog your memory.

Check It Out   Read this descriptive paragraph.

The brittle air stung Sonja's cheeks as her sleigh glided along the snow-packed road. As the horse clip-clopped homeward, his brass harness bells jingled. White steam puffed from his nostrils.

118

The sleigh whooshed past black, leafless trees silhouetted against the sunset. Through the blur of branches, Sonja watched the last light turn the sky rosy-pink. Woodsmoke drifted toward her, and the familiar scent told her they were almost home.

- Did the writer use sensory details? Which senses do the details appeal to? Give examples.

Try Your Skill   Choose one of the following places to describe. Make a list of sensory details related to the place you choose.

> a neighborhood restaurant
> the school library
> inside a pet store
> a subway on a hot day
> your kitchen

Keep This in Mind

- In a description, use sensory details to describe your subject.
- Gather sensory details through observation or from memory.

Now Write   Think of a person, place, or thing that you would like to describe. Be sure you can describe your subject in one paragraph. Make a list of sensory details that tell about your subject. You can gather these details from personal observation or from your memory. Save your pre-writing notes in your folder.

individually, writing at least one detail for each sense on their list. The same approach can be used for **Now Write.**

Advanced Students

Add a sixth sense to the students' list of senses: the *kinesthetic* sense, or *motion*. Go back through the sample paragraph in **Check It Out** and ask the class to identify motion words (*glided, puffed, whooshed, drifted,* for example). Then have students consider motion as well as the other five senses when they do **Try Your Skill** and **Now Write.**

Optional Practice

Have students identify and classify the sensory details in the following passage.

> Just opposite the diners seated at the table, the immense fireplace, filled with bright flames, cast a lively heat on the backs of the row on the right. Three spits were turning on which there were chickens, pigeons, and legs of mutton; and an appetizing odor of roast beef and gravy dripping over the nicely browned skin rose from the hearth, increased the jovialness, and made everybody's mouth water.
> –Guy de Maupassant

Extending the Lesson

Have students find one sentence in their literature books that represents each one of the senses. Then have them illustrate these sentences. Make a bulletin board display of the students' sentences and art work.

Part 2

Objective

To learn to organize details in spatial order

Presenting the Lesson

1. Read and discuss **Here's the Idea.** Be certain that students understand the meaning of *spatial order*. Give additional examples, if necessary. Explain that in describing a clown, a writer might start with the clown's big feet and work up to his floppy hat or vice versa. Point out that there is no one right order for describing an object; however, it is important for the writer to use some spatial order so that his description is clear to the reader.

2. Discuss **Check It Out.** Ask students if this paragraph could be organized any other way.

3. Assign **Try Your Skill.**

4. Read **Keep This in Mind** aloud.

5. Before beginning **Now Write,** have each student explain how he or she plans to organize the details for this exercise.

Individualizing the Lesson

Less-Advanced Students

Give these students extra practice in gathering and organizing details. Have them make pre-writing notes for descriptions of actual objects or of scenes represented in pictures. Then have them arrange those notes in spatial order.

Advanced Students

To emphasize the idea that there may be several ways to describe a given subject, have students plan

120

Words in Space

Pre-Writing: Using Spatial Order

Here's the Idea   In a well-written description, the writer and the reader share an experience. If the writer is describing a forest, the reader should notice the details of the forest just as the writer noticed them. That is why it is so important that the details that develop a description be well organized.

One way to organize a description is to use **spatial order.** In other words, you arrange your details in the order that you want your reader to notice them. Begin with whatever detail you want your reader to notice first. This might be the most obvious detail or the detail that made the biggest impression on you. Then arrange the other details in an order that shows how they are related to the first detail. You might describe your subject from top to bottom, right to left, near to far, and so on.

Suppose that you want to describe a harbor scene. You might want to begin by focusing the reader's attention on a large oil tanker in the middle of the harbor. Then you might have your description move around this central subject. Mention the two tugboats near the ship. Then describe the darkening sky above it. Finally, describe the sun setting in the distance. You will have arranged your description in spatial order.

Check It Out   Read the following description of a mountain.

Our mountain has towered above the village since time began. Its base is densely wooded with birches and fir trees. Where trees had been cut down long ago, wild blackberries grow. A well-beaten path winds upwards through woods and berry patches, all the way to the tree line. Shrubs sparsely cover the middle of our

120

mountain, and above that nothing grows. The top third of it is gray granite, deeply etched with crevasses, and a challenge for us young climbers.

- How does this description use spatial order?

Try Your Skill Turn to your folder. Find the list of details that you gathered for **Try Your Skill** in Part 1 of this section. Arrange those details in spatial order, the order in which you want your reader to notice them.

Keep This in Mind

- Use spatial order to organize the pre-writing notes for your description.
- Arrange your details in the order that you want your reader to notice them.

Now Write Use spatial order to organize the pre-writing notes for your descriptive paragraph. Arrange your sensory details in the order that you want your reader to notice them. Save your organized notes in your folder.

two different approaches toward describing the same thing. Students may select an object or scene from memory, or use photographs or actual objects for their inspiration.

Have them make two sets of pre-writing notes and then arrange their notes in spatial order. Ask each student to explain his or her two strategies. Discuss the different effects each method would create.

Optional Practice

Have students analyze the spatial order in this passage from John Steinbeck's *The Red Pony*. Ask them to identify the sensory details, as well.

...He looked down on the little hills and ridges below and then out at the huge green Salinas Valley. He could see the white town of Salinas far out in the flat and the flash of its windows under the waving sun. Directly below him, in an oak tree, a crow congress had convened. The tree was black with crows all cawing at once. Then Jody's eyes followed the wagon road down from the ridge where he stood, and lost it behind a hill, and picked it up again on the other side.

Extending the Lesson

Bring five or six photographs or art prints to class and display them. Ask students to choose one to describe. Remind them to find an object to use as the focus of the description. Then ask them to write a paragraph describing that photograph or print. Read the descriptions of each picture to the class. Discuss the spatial order used in each.

Objective

To recognize that words create a specific mood

Presenting the Lesson

1. Read aloud and discuss **Here's the Idea.** Ask students to explain the meaning of *mood* in their own words. Discuss the fact that adjectives can have a positive or a negative effect on readers. Ask the class to list positive and negative adjectives describing the classroom.

2. Discuss **Check It Out.**

3. Assign **Try Your Skill.** Have students tell you their lists of mood words. Put the words on the board and challenge the class to find even more words.

4. Read **Keep This in Mind** and then assign **Now Write.**

Individualizing the Lesson

Less-Advanced Students

For more practice in creating mood, do the following exercise with the class. Write a brief, "neutral" sentence on the chalkboard ("The boy practiced his piano lesson" or "The girl sat on the couch," for example). Then ask volunteers to come to the board and rewrite the sentence so that it conveys a specific mood (happy, sad, confused, silly, serious, angry, satisfied, etc.). Students may change the sentence in any way.

Discuss the revisions, emphasizing the words responsible for creating the mood. Then repeat the exercise with new sentences and different volunteers.

In the Mood

Pre-Writing: Creating Mood

Here's the Idea   People have many different moods. They express their moods by the way they talk, look, and act. Writing has mood, too. **Mood** is the feeling suggested by a piece of writing. A story might suggest a feeling of excitement or mystery. A description might suggest great beauty or great sadness. Writers express mood through the language they use.

Suppose two writers are describing a house. The first writer wants to suggest a feeling of sadness and despair. She might use words like these:

Nouns	Adjectives	Verbs	Adverbs
shack	dingy	litters	haphazardly
box	musty	tilts	dimly
shanty	drab	crumbles	loosely

A second writer wants to suggest a feeling of cheer and brightness. He might use words like these:

Nouns	Adjectives	Verbs	Adverbs
household	trim	nestles	snugly
homestead	sunny	protects	comfortably
cottage	cozy	surrounds	warmly

As you plan your description, think about the mood you want to create. Then make lists of nouns, adjectives, verbs, and adverbs you might use to help you suggest that feeling.

Check It Out   Read the following descriptive paragraph.

The kitchen, worn by our boots and lives, was scruffy, cluttered, and warm. The furniture seemed never the same but was shuffled around each day. A fireplace crackled with coal and beech twigs. The mantel was littered with fine old china, and oddly shaped potatoes. On the floor were strips of muddy matting. The windows were filled with plants. The walls were hung with several clocks and calendars. There were also six tables of different sizes, some stuffed armchairs, four boxes, books and papers on every chair, a sofa for cats, and a piano for dust and photographs.

—LAURIE LEE

- What feeling is suggested by this paragraph?
- What words help to create that mood?

Try Your Skill   Suppose you wanted to describe a park. Winter is over and spring is in bloom. There are children in the playground. A group of girls is playing softball on the diamond. People are walking along the pathways.

The feeling you want to suggest in your description is one of beauty and rebirth. Make a list of nouns, adjectives, verbs, and adverbs that will help you to create this mood. Compare your list with those of your classmates.

Keep This in Mind

- *Mood* is the feeling suggested by a piece of writing.
- Writers express mood through the language they use.

Now Write   Think about the descriptive paragraph you have been planning. What kind of feeling would you like the paragraph to suggest to your reader? Make a list of nouns, adjectives, verbs, and adverbs to help you create that mood. List as many words as you can think of. When you write your first draft, choose the best words from your list to help you create the mood you want in your paragraph. Save your list in your folder.

Part 4

Objective

To learn to use transitions to show spatial order

Presenting the Lesson

1. Read and discuss **Here's the Idea,** emphasizing the list of transitions. You might return to the Steinbeck passage in **Optional Practice,** Part 2 and have the students analyze the use of transitions in that description.

2. Read aloud and discuss **Check It Out.**

3. Assign **Try Your Skill.** Make sure students know the meanings of the words *triangle, rectangle, square,* and *circle.*

4. Review **Keep This in Mind.**

5. Assign **Now Write.** Remind students to keep the mood of their paragraphs in mind as they write their first draft.

Individualizing the Lesson

Less-Advanced Students

The exercise in **Try Your Skill** may be too difficult for these students. Either do it together as a group, or substitute another assignment. For example, you might ask each student to bring in a photograph with several objects or people in it, and write a description of that photo. Then display the photos with no names on them. Read the descriptions aloud and ask the class to match each piece of writing with the appropriate photograph.

In Place

Writing the First Draft

Here's the Idea Throughout this chapter, you have been planning your descriptive paragraph. After you gathered your sensory details, you arranged them in the order that you wanted the reader to notice them. Now you can write your first draft. How can you make the order of your details clear?

There are certain transitional words and phrases that can help you to make spatial order clear. These words and phrases help the reader to get a clear picture of the subject.

Here are some familiar transitional words and phrases.

above	beside	in the center	over
against	between	low	side by side
alongside	by	near	south
ahead of	down	next to	to the left
at the end of	east	north	to the right
at the top	facing	on	toward
around	high	on the bottom	throughout
behind	in	on the corner	under
below	in back of	on the edge	up
beneath	in front of	outside	west

Check It Out Read the following paragraph.

The dashboard of my sister's sports car looks like the instrument panel of a jumbo jet. Directly in the middle of the dashboard is a large green radio dial. Below the dial are the knobs for volume and fine tuning. To the left of the radio are the levers and switches for the headlights, wipers, and air vents. In front of the driver are the speedometer and the gauges for gas, engine temperature, and oil. Below the dashboard is a stereo tape deck.

· Which words and phrases show spatial order?

Try Your Skill Look at the illustration below. Decide how you would describe it to another person. Write a description of the illustration. Include each shape, and use specific transitional words and phrases. Make the spatial order clear.

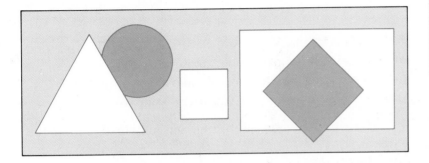

Keep This in Mind

• In a description, include transitions that show spatial order.

Now Write Write the first draft of your descriptive paragraph. Follow your organized pre-writing notes as you write. Use transitional words and phrases to make the spatial order clear. Remember, you want the reader to share your experience, so make your description as clear as possible. As you write, use words from the list you developed in the last lesson to create a specific mood. Save your first draft in your folder.

Objective

To learn to revise a descriptive paragraph

Presenting the Lesson

1. Read and discuss **Here's the Idea.** Review the questions to ask when revising.

2. Read **Try Your Skill** aloud. Discuss possible revisions and then assign the exercise.

3. Read and discuss **Check It Out.** Ask students to identify the adjectives that help paint a vivid word picture.

4. Read **Keep This in Mind.**

5. Assign **Now Write.** Require students to make at least three substantial revisions in their paragraphs.

Individualizing the Lesson

Less-Advanced Students

1. You might supply additional sample paragraphs for revision after students have completed **Try Your Skill.**

2. Begin **Now Write** in class by leading students through the questions in **Here's the Idea.** First, have them check their topic sentences, then sensory details, and so on.

Advanced Students

1. Have students exchange papers and offer advice to each other for the **Now Write** revisions.

2. For an extra writing project, have students write one-paragraph descriptions of various school scenes. Tell them to be sure to choose scenes with contrasting

126

Share the Experience

Revising Your Descriptive Paragraph

Here's the Idea   When you have completed the first draft of your descriptive paragraph, revise it to make it clearer and more interesting. Try to make it come alive for the reader. Ask yourself these questions as you revise your work.

1. Have I written an interesting and informative topic sentence?

2. Have I developed my description with good sensory details?

3. Have I used spatial order to arrange the details?

4. Have I included transitional words and phrases to make the spatial order clear?

5. Have I used words to suggest a particular feeling or mood?

When you have revised the ideas, the language, and the organization of your description, proofread it. Find and correct any errors in grammar, capitalization, punctuation, and spelling.

Check It Out   Read the following description of a Sunday breakfast.

I love Sunday breakfasts in our family. Every one of them is the same. The family gathers around the kitchen table in the center of the room. The six of us sit there for hours, eating and talking. The old maple table is jammed with plates of chewy bagels, cream cheese, fried eggs, and smoked fish. From one corner of the table drifts the strong, rich aroma of coffee. Over the center of the table hangs a lamp with a stained glass shade. It is in the center that we spread out the Sunday newspapers that we all read at the end of our meal.

- Does the topic sentence introduce the subject of the paragraph?
- What sensory details has the writer included?
- Has the writer used transitional words and phrases? What are they?
- Does this paragraph suggest mood? Explain your answer.

Try Your Skill   Here is the first draft of a descriptive paragraph. As you read it, notice that it does not paint a very vivid word picture. It has strong verbs, but it also needs strong adjectives to bring the scene to life. Revise the paragraph, adding strong adjectives. Replace any weak, overused adjectives with more vivid ones.

It was a bad flood. A wall of water burst through the dam upstream. It tore down the valley and wiped out crops for miles. The water ripped out trees by their roots. It swept away cars and even houses with its force. The damage was unbelievable. A trail of destruction was left by the flood.

Keep This in Mind

- Include strong sensory details in your description.
- Organize your details in the order that you want your reader to notice them.
- Include transitions that show spatial order.
- Use language that helps you to create a particular mood.

Now Write   Use the guidelines in this lesson to revise the first draft of your descriptive paragraph. Include language to create a mood and to make your description more vivid. When your description is as clear and as interesting as you can make it, proofread it. Then make a final copy. Save your descriptive paragraph in your folder.

moods. Publish the final drafts in a booklet for distribution to the school community.

Optional Practice

Have students rewrite the following passage, making it convey a happy mood.

...I walked around feeling weak, as if at any moment I would collapse in a heap. If I rested my head on my desk, in an instant I fell asleep; the walk to and from school wore me out, so that I moved at the speed of an old jalopy.
–Jamaica Kincaid

Extending the Lesson

1. Have each student make an illustration to go with his or her descriptive paragraph. Display the students' work in a bulletin board display.
2. Make a display that demonstrates the process the students have followed, from pre-writing through proofreading. Use actual student notes, drafts, etc. for the display.

Section 11 Objectives

1. To learn to list all of the steps involved in a process

2. To arrange the steps in the order that they happen or should be done

3. To write a first draft using a good topic sentence and effective transitions

4. To learn to revise a first draft, checking for logical order and clear transitions

Preparing the Students

Read aloud to the class a descriptive paragraph, a narrative paragraph, and an explanatory paragraph. Ask the students to discuss the ways in which the three paragraphs differ, and why. Focus on the writer's purpose and how it determines the type of paragraph he or she will write.

To illustrate the effect of purpose (and to review the three categories of paragraphs), try the following exercise. Write the general subject "Sports" on the chalkboard. Then have the students think of three specific topics for different types of paragraphs: for descriptive paragraphs (the school gym during a basketball game, for example), for narrative paragraphs (personal experiences as participants or observers at athletic events), and for explanatory paragraphs telling *how* (instructions for how to play or win a certain game).

Tell the class that this section will deal with one kind of explanatory paragraph, the paragraph that explains *how*.

The Explanatory Paragraph

Telling *How*

Part 1 **Get into It**
Pre-Writing: Explaining a Process

Part 2 **One, Two, Three**
Pre-Writing: Using Step-by-Step Order

Part 3 **Follow the Plan**
Writing the First Draft

Part 4 **Clearing Things Up**
Revising Your Explanatory *How* Paragraph

Additional Resources

Mastery Test — page 24 in the test booklet
Practice Book — pages 53–56
Duplicating Masters — pages 53–56

Teaching Special Populations

LD See **Teaching Special Populations,** page 75. Remind LD students of how step-by-step order is used in explanatory paragraphs. Make sure students understand the vocabulary associated with sequence and progression.

ESL Make certain that ESL students are familiar with those transitional words and phrases commonly used in explanatory paragraphs. Also, you may wish to modify some of the topics and exercises (Part 1, **Check It Out,** for example) that rely on unfamiliar cultural experiences. Whenever you can, include topics that are appropriate to ESL students' background (how to use a wok to stir-fry vegetables, how to cultivate bonsai, how to wrap parcels securely for international mailing, and so on).

Be especially careful when explaining the vocabulary associated with time. Devote extra time to those students whose native languages may not include such words.

NSD See **Teaching Special Populations,** page 75. Pair students with fluent English speakers and have them work together on translating rough notes in nonstandard dialect into explanatory paragraphs that use standard English.

Objective

To learn to list all of the steps involved in a process

Presenting the Lesson

1. Ask students to mention some kinds of *how* paragraphs they have read or written (instructions for cooking, for operating appliances, for training animals, etc.). Then read and discuss **Here's the Idea.** Emphasize the importance of dividing a process into distinct steps.

2. Read and discuss **Check It Out.**

3. Assign **Try Your Skill.** Have students read their lists aloud. Encourage them to add to their lists as they hear others' ideas.

4. Read **Keep This in Mind** aloud.

5. Assign **Now Write.**

Individualizing the Lesson

Less-Advanced Students

1. Do **Check It Out** orally in class.

2. For **Try Your Skill** have the whole class brainstorm topics and write them on the chalkboard. Students may use ideas from that list as they compile their own lists.

3. For **Now Write,** ask some volunteers to do the exercise on the chalkboard. Have the class discuss whether enough steps are included, and whether the wording is clear.

Advanced Students

After completing **Now Write,** have the students exchange papers and offer advice to each other on the thoroughness and clarity of the lists.

Get into It

Pre-Writing: Explaining a Process

Here's the Idea   An explanatory paragraph explains. It explains *why* something should be so or *what* something is. An explanatory paragraph can also explain *how* to do something or *how* something happens or works.

An explanatory *how* paragraph may explain how to do a science experiment or a type of math problem. An explanatory paragraph may also explain how a pacemaker works or how stars are formed. You can write an explanatory *how* paragraph to explain any process or skill that you know well. Be sure, though, that you choose a topic that can be developed well in one paragraph.

When you have chosen your topic, you need to list the details that will develop your paragraph. Because you are explaining a process, you must write down all the steps in that process. Suppose your topic was "How Paper Is Made." Your pre-writing notes would include each step in the process, from cutting down the trees to finishing the product.

As you write your pre-writing notes, make sure that you include all of the steps in the process. Write each step clearly and simply, so that your explanation is easy to understand.

Check It Out   Read this explanatory *how* paragraph.

There is a technique to the difficult art of hitting a baseball. First, enter the batter's box. Place your feet to maintain your balance. Next, grip the bat firmly and hold it off your shoulder. After that, concentrate on watching the pitch. Swing the bat evenly to meet the ball. Be sure to follow through with your swing. Finally, as the ball sails deep into the outfield, head to first base.

· What process is explained? Is each step explained clearly and simply?

Try Your Skill   Take the first pre-writing step in writing an explanatory *how* paragraph. Brainstorm for some processes that you know well enough to explain, step-by-step. Your topics might be about how to do something, how something happens, or how something works. Make a list of at least five topics that you could write about. Be sure each topic is narrow enough to be covered well in one paragraph. Save your list of topics in your folder.

Keep This in Mind

· An explanatory *how* paragraph explains how to do something or how something happens or works.
· Make sure that all of the steps in the process are included.
· Explain each step clearly and simply.

Now Write   Look back at the topics you developed in **Try Your Skill.** Choose one topic that you could explain well in a paragraph. Write the topic at the top of a piece of paper. Then, list the steps that are involved in the process. Don't leave out any steps. Write each step clearly and simply. Save your pre-writing notes in your folder.

Part 2

Objective

To arrange the steps in the order that they happen or should be done

Presenting the Lesson

1. Read and discuss **Here's the Idea.** Emphasize the importance of including all steps in the process and placing them in clear chronological order.

2. Read and discuss **Check It Out.** Ask the class what would happen if any of the steps were out of order. (Example: what would happen if you put the bacon over the tomatoes and then were told to cook the bacon?) Stress again the importance of including all steps and putting them in chronological order.

3. Assign and discuss **Try Your Skill.**

4. Review **Keep This in Mind.**

5. Assign **Now Write.**

Individualizing the Lesson

Less-Advanced Students

For **Try Your Skill,** have students work in pairs or small groups. Have each group then report on its answers to the class.

Supply additional exercises like **Try Your Skill** if necessary. Then ask for volunteers to explain their step-by-step organization to the class.

Advanced Students

List on the board the names of children's games that all your students are familiar with (hopscotch, red rover, ring-around-the-rosie, London bridge, etc.). Then have them choose one game and list the

132

One, Two, Three

Pre-Writing: Using Step-by-Step Order

Here's the Idea   Imagine a cook trying to make a seafood gumbo from a recipe that is all mixed up. Think about a mechanic fixing the brakes on a car using instructions that have several missing steps. In both cases, the results might be disastrous. A written explanation of how to do something or how something happens or works must be complete. It must also be carefully organized. Then the reader will be able to follow the explanation easily.

The best way to organize your explanatory *how* paragraph is to use **step-by-step order.** This is the order in which a process happens or should be done. You begin with the first step in the process and then proceed, step by step, to the last step. Step-by-step order is similar to chronological order. In both cases, details are organized according to a natural time order.

As you organize your pre-writing notes, check again to make sure that no steps are missing.

Check It Out   Read this paragraph.

A bacon-lettuce-and-tomato sandwich is delicious and easy to make. First, slowly cook several pieces of bacon until crisp. Second, spread a thin layer of mayonnaise on two pieces of toast. Next, place lettuce on one piece of toast. After that, put tomato slices on the lettuce and bacon strips over the tomatoes. Finally, close and slice your sandwich. Enjoy your lunch!

- Does this explanatory *how* paragraph explain a process step by step?
- What transitions are used to show step-by-step order?

Try Your Skill   Here are two sets of instructions that are confused. Organize the steps in each process into step-by-step order.

How To Take a Photograph

1. Focus on your subject, holding the camera steady. 3
2. Choose your subject. 1
3. Gently squeeze the shutter release button. 4
4. Stand so that the source of light is behind you. 2

How To Make Pancakes

1. When the edges bubble up, flip each pancake over. 5
2. Beat the batter until it's smooth. 2
3. Lightly grease a frying pan and preheat it. 3
4. Serve with butter, maple syrup, or powdered sugar. 7
5. First, combine two cups of pancake mix, one egg, and one and one-third cups of milk. 1
6. Cook pancakes until golden brown. 6
7. Pour small amounts of batter into the pan. 4

Keep This in Mind

· In an explanatory *how* paragraph, explain the process step by step.
· Arrange the steps in the order that they happen or should be done.

Now Write   Organize your pre-writing notes into step-by-step order. Arrange the steps in the order that they happen or should be done. Make sure you haven't left out any important steps. Save your organized pre-writing notes in your folder.

steps for playing it in chronological order. You might have one student read the instructions while others try to follow them.

Optional Practice

Ask students to think of processes that can be demonstrated in the classroom (how to make or do something). Have each student select a topic and list the steps involved. Then, as the writer reads his or her list aloud, have another student follow the directions. Also, students should take note of any difficulties encountered by the person following the directions. Have them give specific reasons why these complications arise. Students should bring to class any materials necessary for their own demonstration.

Extending the Lesson

1. Make a master list of all the subjects taken by the students, including art, physical education, etc. Distribute the lists and see who can be the first to name two processes associated with each subject. Students may work individually or in groups.

2. Hide an object in the classroom as the students watch. Tell them to list the steps a person would have to take to find the object, starting from the doorway. Write their suggestions on the chalkboard and have a volunteer follow the instructions to test them. Then, send someone out of the class and hide the object in a different place. Repeat the writing of instructions and ask for a volunteer to read his or her list to the student trying to find the object.

Part 3

Follow the Plan

Objective

To write a first draft using a good topic sentence and effective transitions

Presenting the Lesson

1. Read and discuss **Here's the Idea.** Review the list of transitions and talk about the functions of such words and phrases. Point out that transitional words help the reader to understand the steps in the process.

2. Read and discuss **Check It Out.** Ask students if they could substitute any other transitional words or phrases for those used in this paragraph. Explain that there are many possible choices.

3. Assign and discuss **Try Your Skill.** Have students decide what the main idea of the paragraph is before they write their topic sentence. Ask for volunteers to read their paragraphs aloud.

4. Read **Keep This in Mind** aloud.

5. Assign **Now Write.**

Individualizing the Lesson

Less-Advanced Students

1. Do **Try Your Skill** together in class. Demonstrate with a student volunteer's notes how to rewrite the assigned paragraph. After deciding on the main idea of the paragraph, begin with constructing a good topic sentence. Then show the students how to use transitions to introduce the steps in the process.

2. When the students have completed their revisions have them underline the transitions they used.

Writing the First Draft

Here's the Idea   A builder follows a plan when he or she builds a house. The architect's blueprints are used as a guide. A writer needs a plan to follow, too. As you begin to write your explanatory *how* paragraph, follow your organized pre-writing notes.

To begin your first draft, write a good topic sentence. The topic sentence should tell the reader what process you will be explaining. It should also be interesting enough to capture your reader's attention.

Next, develop your topic sentence by explaining the steps in the process. Write each step clearly and simply. To help the reader follow the step-by-step order of your process, use transitions as you write. Study this list of transitional words and phrases. They are often used in explanatory *how* paragraphs.

first	when	the next step
second	afterwards	at the same time
third	later	while
as	after that	following that
next	at last	the last step
then	finally	

You needn't limit yourself to just these examples. Almost any word or phrase that refers to time order may be helpful to you when you are writing your explanatory *how* paragraph.

Check It Out   Read this paragraph.

You can make an old pair of leather shoes look new by dyeing them a different color. First, pick the new color you want. Second, be sure the leather is clean. Protect the surface you are working on with paper or plastic. Then, using a clean applicator, cover the whole surface of the shoes with leather dye. Make your strokes smooth and even. When the first coat is dry, see if a second coat is needed. After the second coat has completely dried, apply shoe polish and buff the shoes. The last step is to admire your new pair of shoes!

- What process does this explanatory *how* paragraph explain?
- What transitional words and phrases are used to show step-by-step order?

Try Your Skill   The following explanatory paragraph does not have a topic sentence. It also lacks transitions. Rewrite the paragraph, adding a topic sentence and good transitions.

In the bottom of the bag put the heavy items like canned soup, frozen foods, and bottles of ketchup. Wrap frozen foods separately in plastic. Use soft items, such as paper towels, to separate and protect breakable jars and bottles. Put non-crushable, lighter-weight foods like cereal boxes in the bag. Put fresh produce, such as broccoli and apples, in the bag. Place fragile foods, such as strawberries and potato chips, carefully on top.

Keep This in Mind

- In an explanatory *how* paragraph, begin with a good topic sentence. Then explain the process step by step.
- Use transitional words and phrases to show step-by-step order.

Now Write   Write the first draft of your explanatory *how* paragraph. Follow your organized pre-writing notes. Be sure your paragraph has a good topic sentence. Use transitions that show step-by-step order. Save your first draft in your folder.

135

Obtain a "commission" for your students to produce an explanatory piece of writing for actual use in the school. Check with various teachers—science or shop, especially—to see what they might need. Consider instructions for how to use a piece of equipment, how to begin a science project, etc.

Optional Practice

Sometimes it is easier for students to divide a process into steps if they imagine that their audience is young children. The following paragraph is such an example. Read it aloud and have the students list the separate steps. Some students may notice that the writer has not used any transitions. Discuss why she might have made that decision. Then have the students rewrite the paragraph, inserting appropriate transitions. Ask them to explain their choices.

Put a sprouted sprout in a little pot of soil inside a box. Keep the lid on the box, but cut a small hole in it so there's a source of light for the plant. Put the plant in one corner away from the hole and close up the box. Go back in two or three days and you'll find that the plant has grown up and out of the hole. It's called phototropism—the tendency of the shoot to grow toward light.

—Georgia Tasker

Extending the Lesson

Explain that *how* paragraphs can be found everywhere—in cookbooks, in instructions for games, etc. Ask students to bring in as many examples of *how* paragraphs as they can and to make a bulletin board display of them.

Objective

To learn to revise a first draft, checking for logical order and clear transitions

Presenting the Lesson

1. Read and discuss **Here's the Idea.** Write the questions for revising on the chalkboard.

2. Read aloud the sample paragraph in **Check It Out.** Discuss the questions in class.

3. Assign and discuss **Try Your Skill.** Remind the class that no revision is complete without a final reading.

4. Review **Keep This in Mind.**

5. Assign **Now Write.**

Individualizing the Lesson

Less-Advanced Students

1. For **Try Your Skill,** have students work in class, in pairs or small groups. Designate one person in each group as the secretary. When students have completed the exercise, have the secretaries read the revised paragraphs to the class.

2. For **Now Write,** lead students through each question and have them check and revise their paragraphs with you. Emphasize topic sentences, step-by-step order, transitions, and proofreading.

Advanced Students

Have students revise their *how* writings begun in Part 3 of the Teacher's Notes. Ask them to include illustrations and other graphic aids along with their written instructions.

Clearing Things Up

Revising Your Explanatory *How* Paragraph

Here's the Idea   To make an explanatory paragraph clear enough for your reader to follow easily, it is important that you revise it carefully. Read your first draft as if someone else had written it. Ask yourself these questions:

1. Does the topic sentence introduce the process?
2. Is every important step of the process included?
3. Are the steps arranged in the order that they happen or should be done?
4. Is each step explained clearly and simply?
5. Do the transitions help to lead the reader smoothly from one step of the process to the next?

When you are satisfied with your ideas and organization, proofread your paragraph. Correct any errors in grammar, capitalization, punctuation, and spelling. Then you are ready to write your final copy.

Check It Out   Read the following paragraph.

If you are patient, you can become an expert at photographing animals in their natural setting. First, decide what animal you want to photograph. Then dress in camouflage colors and go quietly to the area where the animal lives. The first time you go there, just sit quietly for half an hour so the animal can observe you. If you are still and make no sudden moves, it will see that you are not to be feared. On the second day, return to the area and move in a little closer. Have your camera around your neck, but don't use it. Just sit quietly again. Continue this procedure for several days, each day moving just a little closer. It may take a week or two to get really close to your subject. The final reward for your patience will be good close-up photographs.

- Does the topic sentence introduce the process?
- Are the steps arranged in the order they should be done?
- What transitions did the writer use?

Try Your Skill   Read the following rough draft of an explanatory paragraph. Revise it, making sure to add a good topic sentence and clear transitions. Be sure to proofread the paragraph.

> You take a lump of wet clay. Roll the clay on the table until it is in long ropes. Before you roll the clay, knead it until all the bubbles are out of it. Second, coil the ropes round and round. Now press them together. Now smooth the coils. Now shape your vase or pot. Third, glaze it. Before you glaze it, let it dry for several days. You are ready to put it into a special oven called a kiln. You will have a piece of pottery that you made yourself.

Keep This in Mind

- Revise your explanatory paragraph so that each step is explained clearly and simply.
- Include all the steps in the process. Arrange them in step-by-step order.
- Use transitional words and phrases to show the order of each step.

Now Write   Use the guidelines in this lesson to revise the first draft of your explanatory *how* paragraph. Don't forget to proofread your explanation. Correct any errors in grammar and mechanics. Then make a final copy of your paragraph. Save it in your folder.

Section **12** Objectives

1. To learn to state an opinion and to support it

2. To make a list of accurate facts and logical reasons to support that opinion

3. To arrange supporting facts and reasons in the order of their importance

4. To use transitions to state reasons or facts and the order of their importance

5. To sum up the argument in the concluding sentence

6. To learn to revise the first draft of the explanatory *why* paragraph

Preparing the Students

Show the class some editorials and a letters-to-the-editor column from a newspaper and explain that all these letters and columns tell *why* something is so or why something should be. Then point out that this section will help students to learn how to state an opinion clearly and to support it logically and persuasively.

Additional Resources

Mastery Test — page 25 in the test booklet

Practice Book — pages 57–60

Duplicating Masters — pages 57–60

138

The Explanatory Paragraph

Telling *Why*

Teaching Special Populations

LD See **Teaching Special Populations,** page 75.

ESL Many ESL students have difficulty using modals. Since some languages express mood exclusively by using inflected verbs you should alert students to the need for separate words in English.

You may also find that ESL students are unwilling to state firm opinions in their own writing, or that they consider it impolite to disagree with the teacher. This usually occurs because these students are subject to stricter standards of decorum than their American peers. Try to coax opinions from ESL students, and avoid making them participate in aggressive forms of debate. Help them develop confidence in their own opinions by first assigning uncontroversial topics such as sports and food.

NSD See **Teaching Special Populations,** page 75.

Objectives

1. To learn to state an opinion and to support it

2. To make a list of accurate facts and logical reasons to support that opinion

Presenting the Lesson

1. Write the words *opinion* and *fact* on the board and ask students to define the words. (An opinion is a feeling about something, while a fact can be proven true.) Then read **Here's the Idea.** Point out the different ways to form an opinion (thinking about familiar things, reading newspapers and magazines, etc.). Ask students why they think a topic sentence is the right place to state an opinion. Then explain that to make an opinion worthwhile, students must use facts and reasons to support it.

2. Discuss **Check It Out.** Point out that the better the list of reasons given, the better the opinion is.

3. Assign and discuss **Try Your Skill.** Ask volunteers to share their supporting reasons or facts.

4. Read **Keep This in Mind** and then assign **Now Write.** Remind students who are having trouble thinking of an opinion of the first pre-writing step mentioned in **Here's the Idea.**

Individualizing the Lesson

Less-Advanced Students

1. Do **Try Your Skill** as an in-class lesson. List the facts or reasons the students suggest on the board.

A Matter of Opinion

Pre-Writing: Developing an Opinion

Here's the Idea Not everyone thinks alike. People have different opinions about the world they live in, and they like to express those opinions. People write letters to newspapers and magazines. Newspapers and television stations print and broadcast editorials. People participate in debates. All of these activities have one purpose: the expression of opinions.

You have opinions, too. A good way for you to express your opinion is to write an explanatory *why* paragraph. This kind of paragraph presents an opinion, and then gives reasons to support the opinion. For example, an explanatory *why* paragraph might explain why the public library needs a new building.

The first pre-writing step in planning an explanatory paragraph is to choose an opinion that you want to express. Think about the world around you. Then think about your family, your school, your neighborhood, your after-school job. Look through newspapers and magazines. Ask yourself how you feel about the issues of the day. You will find that you have opinions about many topics. Choose one of them to write about.

When you have chosen an opinion, write a sentence that states your opinion clearly and directly. It can serve as the topic sentence of your paragraph, where it will make your opinion clear to the reader. Read these statements of opinion.

> Computer courses should be required of all high school students.

> The national speed limit should remain at fifty-five miles per hour.

Now you must gather information to back up your opinion. Make a list of accurate facts and logical reasons that support your view. To learn more about the importance of supporting your opinions, see pages 254–255.

Check It Out   Read the following statement of opinion and the list of reasons that support it.

> Swimming is the best sport.
> –It can be enjoyed all year round.
> –It exercises every muscle in your body.
> –People of all ages can swim.
> –Physically handicapped people can enjoy the sport.
> –It can save your life.
> –It is one of the best ways to get in shape.

- Do these reasons explain *why?* Are they clear and logical?

Try Your Skill   Here are five statements of opinion. Choose one. List five facts or reasons to support the opinion. Share your reasons with your classmates. Save your list.

> A pet can benefit a person or family.
> The holiday season is too commercial.
> _____ is the best musical performer or group.
> _____ is a great vacation spot.

Keep This in Mind

- An explanatory *why* paragraph presents your opinion about something.
- Support your opinion with logical reasons and accurate facts.

Now Write   Think of an issue that you feel strongly about. Write a clear, direct statement of your opinion. Then list facts or reasons to support your opinion. Be sure your reasons are logical and your facts accurate. Save your work.

2. For **Now Write,** choose the number of reasons or facts that the students should include in their paragraphs.

3. If students are having trouble seeing the difference between opinion and the facts or reasons needed to support the opinion, have them mentally insert "because" after each opinion or before each supporting statement.

Advanced Students

After students have listed their facts and reasons for **Now Write,** ask them to list any reasons and facts they can think of on the opposite side of the issue. Ask them why it is important to think of these opposing reasons when they write their paragraphs.

Optional Practice

Divide students into groups. Have each group think of an opinion that would be important to them all. Then have them make up a list of facts and reasons to support this opinion. Compare the different opinions and the groups' lists of supporting reasons and see if the class as a whole can add any more to the lists.

Extending the Lesson

Examine the editorials from the daily newspaper. Ask students to state the opinion expressed in each and the facts and reasons used to support that opinion.

Objective

To arrange supporting facts and reasons in the order of their importance

Presenting the Lesson

1. Read and discuss **Here's the Idea.** Review the definition of the *why* paragraph. Explain that the writer of an explanatory *why* paragraph is trying to convince the reader of his or her opinion. Point out that the structure of the explanatory *why* paragraph helps the writer to do this: the opinion is stated clearly in the topic sentence, and the supporting facts or reasons follow directly in order from the least important to the most important.

2. Read and discuss **Check It Out.** Point out the transitional words and phrases in the paragraph that help the reader understand which is the most important reason.

3. Assign **Try Your Skill.**

4. Read **Keep This in Mind** aloud.

5. Assign **Now Write.** Explain that sometimes some reasons are almost equal in importance. In that case, students should put the reason that would be most important to the reader as the last reason.

Individualizing the Lesson

Less-Advanced Students

Let students know that there is no absolute order of importance to be followed. Explain that for other people to accept a writer's opinion they must feel it is reasonable. Point out that discussion can be used as a pre-writing and revising technique:

For What Reasons?

Pre-Writing: Organizing an Opinion

Here's the Idea At the end of a trial, the defense lawyer talks to the jury. The lawyer states his or her opinion—that the person on trial is innocent. Then the lawyer reminds the jury about all the reasons that have been presented during the trial to support that opinion. The lawyer saves the most important reasons for the end of the talk. That way, the jury goes to make its decision with the strongest points fresh in their minds.

When you write your explanatory *why* paragraph, the order in which you present your facts and reasons is important, too. The most effective order is to save your strongest reason for last. Arrange your facts and reasons from the least important idea to the most important. This type of organization is called the **order of importance.**

For example, in a paragraph about the need for a new recreation center, you might include the following reasons:

1. Recreation gives people pleasure.
2. Recreation strengthens you physically and mentally.
3. If people can gather together to enjoy recreation, life in the entire neighborhood will be improved.

You can see that these reasons have been listed in order, from the least important idea to the most important. You will leave your readers with the most powerful reason that supports your opinion.

Check It Out Look at these notes for an explanatory *why* paragraph.

Opinion: Sunlight is the fuel of the future.
Reasons: costs less, does not pollute, is plentiful

Now read the completed paragraph:

> Sunlight can fuel our future. First, sunlight is free. Therefore, there will be only a few major expenses, such as the cost of solar converters. More importantly, the use of sunlight will not pollute the environment. In that way, sunlight is superior to oil and coal. Most importantly, the sun is a never-ending source of energy. Supplies of oil and coal, on the other hand, are being used up. The sun is an energy source on which we can always depend.

- Notice the order of the reasons in this paragraph. Did the writer organize them from the least important idea to the most important? Explain your answer.

Try Your Skill   Reread the list of facts or reasons that you wrote for **Try Your Skill** in Part 1, **A Matter of Opinion.** Organize your list from the least important idea to the most important.

Keep This in Mind

- Organize the facts and reasons that support your opinion from the least important idea to the most important.

Now Write   Look at the statement of opinion and list of reasons that you wrote in **A Matter of Opinion.** Organize your list from the least important idea to the most important. Save your organized pre-writing notes in your folder.

the reactions of friends or classmates can be very helpful in determining an acceptable order for organization.

Advanced Students

Have students hold a debate. Have them decide on an opinion that is important to them (changes needed in grading, new course offerings at your school, etc.). Then let them divide up into pro and con teams. Each team must list facts and reasons to support its side. Make sure the lists are organized in order of importance. Then have students hold the debate.

Optional Practice

Have students use the lists they made up in the **Optional Practice** from Part 1 and put the reasons in the order of their importance.

Extending the Lesson

Have students look through newspapers, magazines, and books for topics that would make interesting explanatory *why* paragraphs. Have them each choose one opinion and illustrate the reasons and facts to support it, using the order of importance. Make a display of their work.

Part 3

Objectives

1. To use transitions to state reasons or facts and the order of their importance

2. To sum up the argument in the concluding sentence

Presenting the Lesson

1. Read and discuss **Here's the Idea.** Stress that even though the students are writing their opinions, they should not put themselves into the paragraph. Ask if the class can think of any other transitional words or phrases that state reasons or put reasons in the order of their importance.

2. Read **Check It Out.** Ask students to list each reason or fact in the paragraph.

3. Read and assign **Try Your Skill.** Ask students to list those transitions that they think would help put the reasons in order of importance.

4. Read **Keep This in Mind** and assign **Now Write.** Tell students that it is not unusual to think of new reasons or facts when writing the first draft. Emphasize that the first draft is a time for making such changes.

Individualizing the Lesson

Less-Advanced Students

Do **Try Your Skill** as an in-class exercise. Have students suggest different topic and ending sentences.

Advanced Students

Have students write a paragraph using the pre-writing notes in **Try Your Skill.**

144

Tryout

Writing the First Draft

Here's the Idea   Once you have made and organized your pre-writing notes, you can begin your first draft.

Begin your explanatory *why* paragraph by stating your opinion in the topic sentence. You may want to use the statement of opinion you wrote in your pre-writing notes. State your opinion clearly and directly. Do not say, "I think that . . . ," or, "In my opinion . . . ." The reader already knows it is your opinion.

After the topic sentence is written, turn your reasons and facts into sentences that support and develop it. Remember to present your reasons in the order of their importance.

Good transitions make your paragraph clear and interesting. There are two kinds of transitions. One kind helps you to state your reasons and facts. The second helps you to show their order of importance. Here are some examples.

To State Reasons or Facts:	because, so, since, if, therefore, as a result
To Put in Order of Importance:	the first reason, second, more important, most important, finally

After you have presented and supported your opinion, you should sum up your ideas with a strong ending sentence.

Check It Out   Read the following paragraph.

Movie theaters are awful places to watch movies. In the first place, they have become very expensive. It can cost up to five dollars for one person to see a movie. Second, popular movies attract crowds. Consequently, moviegoers have to stand in long lines waiting to buy tickets. Also, many movie theaters are messy. Therefore, patrons have to put up with sticky floors and popcorn-filled aisles. Most important, though, is the fact that many moviegoers are rude. They talk and laugh throughout the movie. Why would anyone want to wait in line and pay good money to be treated rudely?

- Does the topic sentence state an opinion clearly?
- What transitional words and phrases help to show reasons? Which help to show the order of importance?
- Does the ending sentence sum up the writer's opinion and reasons?

Try Your Skill   Here is a set of pre-writing notes for an explanatory *why* paragraph. Write a good topic sentence. Organize the reasons in order of importance. Then write a good ending sentence.

Opinion: Fad diets are dangerous.

Reasons: permanent damage to health may result, good balance of foods is necessary for growth, weight usually returns after dieting

Keep This in Mind

- State your opinion clearly and directly in the topic sentence.
- Use good transitional words and phrases. These can help you to present your reasons and show the order of their importance.
- Sum up your opinion and reasons in your ending sentence.

Now Write   Write the first draft of your explanatory *why* paragraph. Include a good topic sentence. Use appropriate transitions. Write an ending sentence that sums up your opinion and reasons. Save your first draft in your folder.

145

Each of the following sentences could be the topic sentence of an explanatory *why* paragraph. Have students choose one sentence and develop it into a first draft of a paragraph.

1. Saturday morning TV shows for children should be improved.
2. Summer vacation is too long.
3. Everyone should be required to take gym.
4. Everyone should have a hobby.

Extending the Lesson

Establish a *source* library for the class to use to check for facts and reasons for their paragraphs. Include dictionaries, encyclopedias, books of lists and world records, and some news and science magazines.

Part 4

Objective

To learn to revise the first draft of the explanatory *why* paragraph

Presenting the Lesson

1. Read and discuss **Here's the Idea.** List the questions to ask on the board for reinforcement.

2. Read and discuss **Check It Out.** Make sure students understand they are to look for more things to correct than just those things listed in **Here's the Idea.**

3. Assign **Try Your Skill.**

4. Read **Keep This in Mind** aloud. Have students copy **Keep This in Mind** in their notebooks to use when revising their first drafts.

5. Assign **Now Write.**

Individualizing the Lesson

Less-Advanced Students

Duplicate the students' revisions and go over them in class. Point out that there is no one correct way to revise.

Advanced Students

Divide the class up into editorial groups. Have each group read the revisions from **Now Write** and offer suggestions for further corrections.

Optional Practice

The following topic sentences give opinions. Have students choose one of the sentences and revise it to make it as interesting as possible. Then have them develop the topic into an explanatory *why* paragraph.

146

A Good Look

Revising Your Explanatory *Why* Paragraph

Here's the Idea   Now that you have written your first draft, take a good look at it. Is your opinion as clear as you can make it? Are your reasons convincing? Ask yourself the following questions as you revise your first draft.

1. Does the topic sentence state my opinion clearly and directly?

2. Have I given enough logical reasons and accurate facts to support my opinion?

3. Are the reasons organized in the most effective order, from the least important idea to the most important?

4. Have I used transitions to present my reasons and make their order clear?

5. Have I ended the paragraph with a strong ending sentence that sums up my opinion and my reasons?

After you have revised your ideas and your organization, proofread your paragraph. Correct any errors in grammar, capitalization, punctuation, and spelling.

Check It Out   Read this first draft of an explanatory *why* paragraph.

In my opinion, the president of the U. S. should get just one six-year time in office. Four years isnt enough time to get programs through. Two more years would let the president help the country more. Another thing is how the president wouldnt have to spend the last year of his or her term campaigning. So the president could spend more time running the country. Most important, if the president didn't have to worry about getting reelected, they wouldn't have to do favors for anybody. The president could just do the best job and then walk away. You wouldn't owe nobody nothing. That's my opinion.

- What specific things in this first draft would you improve? Use the guidelines in this lesson and the other revising skills you have learned to help you decide.

Try Your Skill   Use the guidelines in this lesson and your class discussion to revise the paragraph in **Check It Out.** Improve the topic sentence. Make the sentences clearer and more interesting. Add transitions. Write a better ending sentence. Remember to proofread the paragraph.

Keep This in Mind

- In an explanatory *why* paragraph, state your opinion clearly and directly in your topic sentence.
- Support your opinion with logical reasons and accurate facts.
- Use transitional words and phrases to state your reasons and facts and to show the order of their importance.
- Write an ending sentence that sums up your opinion and reasons.

Now Write   Revise your own explanatory *why* paragraph. Follow the guidelines in this lesson. When you think your paragraph is the best it can be, make a final copy. Save your explanatory *why* paragraph in your folder.

1. I think that big cities (are, are not) the best places to live.
2. _____ is the best movie I've ever seen.
3. I hate rainy days.
4. Everybody should have a pet.

Extending the Lesson

Prepare this lesson with the students' social studies teacher. Have the students search the newspaper for articles giving opinions on controversial subjects related to something being studied in their social studies or civics class. The students should choose one subject, research it, and write two paragraphs about the subject. In the first, they should write an explanatory *why* paragraph explaining one opinion and, in the second, they should write the opposite opinion.

Section **13** Objectives

1. To know the elements of a good definition

2. To learn to develop a good definition

3. To learn to organize a definition from the general to the specific

4. To learn to write a topic sentence that gives the word to be defined, puts the word into a general class, and tells about the word's particular characteristics

5. To develop the first draft with specific details

6. To end the paragraphs with a strong ending sentence

7. To learn to revise the explanatory *what* paragraph

Preparing the Students

Ask students for definitions of various words, such as *tree, dog, pencil, television,* and *book.* Challenge them to make the definitions as specific as possible. Explain that clear definitions help people understand new words, ideas, and things, and that this section will help students to write a clear, understandable definition.

Additional Resources

Mastery Test — page 26 in the test booklet

Practice Book — pages 61–64

Duplicating Masters — pages 61–64

The Explanatory Paragraph

Telling *What*

Part 1 **What's the Point?**
Pre-Writing: Learning About Definitions

Part 2 **What Do You Say?**
Pre-Writing: Developing a Definition

Part 3 **The Plain Truth**
Writing the First Draft

Part 4 **Checkpoint**
Revising Your Definition

Teaching Special Populations

LD See **Teaching Special Populations,** page 75.

ESL Spend more time on oral examples before you ask students to write. Display examples of well-constructed definitions on the chalkboard and show students what ingredients make each definition successful.

Monitor your students' progress in the **Now Write** sections and remember that in some instances (Part 2, **Try Your Skill,** for instance) cultural references may require more detailed explanation than that provided by the text.

NSD See **Teaching Special Populations,** page 75. If students are not averse to reading aloud from one another's writing, have them gather in small groups and exchange paragraphs.

149

What's the Point?

Objective

To know the elements of a good definition

Presenting the Lesson

1. Read and discuss **Here's the Idea.** Make sure students understand the words *general class* and *characteristics.* Explain that a definition tells as much about something as possible so it will be easily recognizable or understood.

2. Read and discuss **Check It Out.** Point out that the topic sentence presents the subject to be defined, the general class of the subject, and the particular characteristics of the subject.

3. Assign **Try Your Skill.** Have students give reasons why paragraph 2 is a good definition and paragraph 1 is not.

4. Read **Keep This in Mind.**

5. Assign **Now Write.** It is suggested that you do this exercise orally with the class.

Individualizing the Lesson

Less-Advanced Students

1. These students might have trouble understanding the concepts of classification and characteristics. Use the following sentence to help them set up their definitions.

A _____ is a(n) _____ that _____.

Example:

A *zebra* is an *animal* that *looks like a horse and has black and white stripes on its body.*

Pre-Writing: Learning About Definitions

Here's the Idea   Do you realize how often you are asked to define things? In class, you may be asked to explain *decimal, adverb, glacier,* or *monarchy.* At home, a grandparent may ask you to explain *break dancing.* A younger brother or sister might want to know what *geography* is.

An explanatory *what* paragraph is a definition of something. The subject might be a real thing, such as a *kiln* or a *laser.* The subject might also be a term or an idea, such as *recession* or *courage.*

A good definition does three things.

1. It presents the subject to be defined.
2. It puts the subject in the general class to which it belongs.
3. It shows the particular characteristics of the subject.

Imagine that you want to define *canary.* First, you would write that a canary is a bird. That puts canary in its general class. Now you have to show how a canary is different from other birds. You could write that a canary is a small bird. That's a start. That shows how canaries are different from large birds, such as pigeons, ravens, and parrots. However, there are many other small birds besides canaries. So you might add that a canary is a songbird. Because there are many small songbirds, you could add that canaries are greenish-yellow in color. Because there are other small, greenish-yellow songbirds, you also add that they are often kept as pets. Now you have a good definition.

> A canary is a small songbird, greenish-yellow in color, that is often kept as a pet.

Check It Out   Read the following explanation.

   A shark is a large ocean fish covered with small, toothlike scales. Sharks have been on earth more than 350 million years. There are about 250 kinds of sharks, but only thirty kinds are dangerous to people. Sharks eat other fish, but they will gobble anything they can. That is an easy task because sharks have more than four rows of teeth, and they grow a new set every two weeks. Sharks have few enemies in the sea.

- Is the topic sentence a definition?
- Does the paragraph define the general class and the particular characteristics of the subject?

Try Your Skill   Read these two explanatory *what* paragraphs. Explain which paragraph is a good definition.

1   A peacock has a huge tail. The tail has very long, beautiful feathers. They are different colors, like green and blue. It looks like a big fan. The bird's neck is long, and it walks strangely. You can see one at the zoo.

2   A mobile is a piece of sculpture that moves. It can be made of almost any materials. Most are made from metal, wood, or paper. The sculpture is designed to balance on slender threads or wires. With even a little breeze the mobile turns in the air.

Keep This in Mind

- An explanatory *what* paragraph explains what something is.
- A good definition puts a subject in its general class. Then it shows the particular characteristics of the subject.

Now Write   Brainstorm a list of objects, terms, and ideas that you could define in an explanatory *what* paragraph. Try to list at least ten possible subjects. Save your list in your folder.

2. Do **Try Your Skill** as an in-class exercise. Ask students to rewrite paragraph 1 as a definition.

Advanced Students

   Have students work in pairs. Have each student make up a definition of an imaginary or mythical animal. Have students exchange papers, and then illustrate the animal based on their partner's definition.

Optional Practice

   Have students put the following words into their general class and then list their particular characteristics.

   motorcycle
   cloud
   chicken pox
   gossip

Extending the Lesson

   Have students bring their science texts to class and then skim through the books to find examples of definitions. Ask some questions about the definitions. Is the subject or word to be defined presented? Is the word being defined put into the general class to which it belongs? Does the definition show the particular characteristics of the word?

Objectives

1. To learn to develop a good definition

2. To learn to organize a definition from the general to the specific

Presenting the Lesson

1. Read and discuss **Here's the Idea.** Stress the fact that the definition should be stated in the topic sentence. To illustrate the difference between definitions developed by facts and figures and definitions developed by personal details, read the dictionary definition of *happiness* and then quote Charles Schultz's *Peanuts:* "Happiness is a warm puppy." Explain that abstract nouns like *happiness, success, love, courage,* etc. are often defined by using personal details. Concrete nouns are usually defined with facts and figures.

2. Read **Check It Out.** Point out that a definition is given in the topic sentence. Have students find the type of organization in the paragraph (general to specific).

3. Assign **Try Your Skill.**

4. Read **Keep This in Mind.**

5. Assign **Now Write.** Ask the students to organize their pre-writing notes from the general to the specific.

Individualizing the Lesson

Less-Advanced Students

Have students do only one topic for **Try Your Skill.** If necessary, do this exercise in class.

What Do You Say?

Pre-Writing: Developing a Definition

Here's the Idea You have learned that there are many different subjects you can define in an explanatory *what* paragraph. You can define an object, such as a *banjo*, a *silo*, an *evergreen*, or a *zircon*. You can also define terms or ideas, such as *checkmate, fear, offside,* or *success.*

In an explanatory *what* paragraph, the subject is defined in the topic sentence. The rest of the paragraph develops that definition as completely as possible. To write a good definition, you must make some pre-writing notes about your subject. You may want to do some research. You may also want to use your own experience.

Some definitions are best developed in a detailed, factual way. For instance, if you define *evergreen*, you will probably use facts and statistics to develop your definition. You may want to use an encyclopedia or a dictionary in order to develop a complete and accurate definition.

Other definitions can best be developed in a detailed, but more personal way. For instance, if you define *courage*, you will probably use specific details from your own experience.

After you have completed your pre-writing notes, organize them. Explanatory *what* paragraphs are usually organized from the general to the specific. In other words, begin with a general statement like, "An artichoke is an odd-looking vegetable that resembles a thistle." Then continue with specific details that help the reader to understand just what an artichoke is.

Check It Out Read the following definition of a leader.

A leader is a person who directs or guides a group. A leader takes control of a situation and sets a good example for his or her followers. My scoutmaster is a leader who shows me how to survive in the woods and how to depend on my own skills. The captain of my basketball team is a leader who sets up the game plan and directs our play. My parents are leaders who show me how to live as a useful family member and a good citizen. I am able to follow the valuable example of these leaders in my life.

- Does this paragraph develop the definition given in the topic sentence?
- Is the paragraph developed by personal details or by facts and statistics?

Try Your Skill Choose two topics from the columns below. For each of your choices, develop a short list of pre-writing notes. You may need to use a dictionary or encyclopedia to help you. You may also want to use personal experiences. Save your notes.

friendship	free throw	jazz
loneliness	arcade	socialism
hero	Middle Ages	word processor
family	haiku	balance beam

Keep This in Mind

- The topic sentence of an explanatory *what* paragraph gives a definition of the subject.
- An explanatory *what* paragraph is developed with personal details or facts and statistics.

Now Write Refer to the list of topics you brainstormed in Part 1. Choose one of those topics to be the subject of your explanatory *what* paragraph. Develop some pre-writing notes about your topic. Use research or your own personal experience. Save your pre-writing notes in your folder.

Part 3

The Plain Truth

Writing the First Draft

Objectives

1. To learn to write a topic sentence that gives the word to be defined, puts the word into a general class, and tells about the word's particular characteristics

2. To develop the first draft with specific details

3. To end the paragraph with a strong ending sentence

Presenting the Lesson

1. Review the three things a good definition does (page 150). Then read and discuss **Here's the Idea.** Point out the importance of the topic sentence to an explanatory *what* paragraph. Ask students why an ending sentence should be strong and interesting.

2. Read and discuss **Check It Out.** Have students compare this paragraph with the paragraph in **Check It Out** on page 151. Point out that the paragraph on page 154 defines an idea or quality while the one on page 151 defines a thing. Ask if there is any difference in the type of examples used in these two paragraphs.

3. Assign **Try Your Skill.**

4. Read **Keep This in Mind.** Then, assign **Now Write.**

Individualizing the Lesson

Less-Advanced Students

1. Have students do only one group of notes for **Try Your Skill.**

2. Assign **Now Write.**

Here's the Idea   The topic sentence of a paragraph tells what the paragraph is all about. In an explanatory *what* paragraph, the topic sentence has other work to do as well. First, it gives the word to be defined. Then, it puts that word into its general class. Finally, the topic sentence tells a little about the particular characteristics of the subject. Here is an example of a good topic sentence for a definition.

An orthodontist is a dentist who straightens teeth.

When you have a clear statement of definition as your topic sentence, expand the definition. Remember, your topic sentence is a general statement. Now you must develop that statement by adding specific details. Use the personal details or facts and statistics that you gathered and organized during pre-writing.

Finish your explanatory *what* paragraph with a strong ending sentence. Leave your reader with an interesting thought or detail about your subject. Here is an example of a strong ending sentence.

Thanks to my orthodontist, I've rediscovered how nice it is to smile.

Check It Out   Read this explanatory *what* paragraph.

Pride is a feeling of respect for yourself. A person may feel pride for doing a job well. He or she may be proud of overcoming some difficult problems, or of scoring well in a game or on a test. Someone may feel pride after helping another person or after refusing to get involved in something wrong. Being proud of yourself is another way of showing you believe in yourself.

- Does this paragraph have a good topic sentence that does three things? What are they?
- What details has the writer included to develop the definition?
- Is there a strong ending sentence? Explain your answer.

Try Your Skill   Look at the two lists of pre-writing notes that you developed for **Try Your Skill** in Part 2. Write a topic sentence for each group of notes. Be sure each topic sentence gives the word to be defined, the general class of the word, and some of its particular characteristics.

Keep This in Mind

- In an explanatory *what* paragraph, define the subject clearly and completely in the topic sentence.
- Develop the definition in the body of the paragraph.
- Write a strong ending sentence to conclude the paragraph.

Now Write   Write the first draft of your explanatory *what* paragraph. Be sure the topic sentence defines your subject. Include details from your pre-writing notes to develop your definition. Write a strong ending sentence. Save your first draft in your folder.

Objective

To learn to revise the explanatory *what* paragraph

Presenting the Lesson

1. Read and discuss **Here's the Idea.** Write the questions to be asked on the board for reinforcement.

2. Read **Check It Out.** Make sure students know the proofreading symbols being used. Review page 101, if necessary.

3. Assign **Try Your Skill.** Compare the finished revisions in class. Point out that there are many correct ways to revise any first draft.

4. Read **Keep This in Mind** and then assign **Now Write.** Refer students to the questions written on the board. Stress that no writing is complete until it has one final proofreading *after* all errors are corrected.

Individualizing the Lesson

Less-Advanced Students

Do **Try Your Skill** as an in-class exercise. As you discuss revisions with the students, make sure they know *why* the corrections are made.

Advanced Students

Have students exchange their revised explanatory *what* paragraphs and offer suggestions for further corrections.

Optional Practice

Have students revise the paragraph they wrote for the **Optional Practice** in Part 3.

Checkpoint

Revising Your Definition

Here's the Idea   If you want your definition to be helpful to your reader, it must be as clear and complete as possible. Careful revision will help you to improve your paragraph. As you revise your paragraph, ask yourself these questions:

1. Does my topic sentence present and define my subject?
2. Have I included enough information to develop my definition completely?
3. Is the information organized from the general to the specific?
4. Does my ending sentence leave the reader with an interesting thought or detail about my subject?

After you have revised your definition, proofread your paragraph. Correct any errors in grammar, capitalization, punctuation, and spelling.

Check It Out   Read this revised explanatory *what* paragraph.

> The lantern festival is a celebration. ^part of the New Year^ It goes for 15 days. The ^Festival^ lantern part comes at the end. Children go ^in Malaysia. The celebration lasts^ through the streets ^parade^ ^fifteen^ with lanterns. They are led by a dragon. Inside the dragon are ^lighted^ ^The children^ ^colorful, papier-maché^ men who make it dance and wriggle. The lanterns help the ^The Malaysian people believe that^ people to find the spirits that fly by the light of the first full ^heavenly^ ^them^ moon of the new year.

- How has the writer improved the topic sentence?
- Is the paragraph organized from the general to the specific? Explain.
- How else has the writer improved this paragraph?

Try Your Skill Revise this rough draft of an explanatory *what* paragraph.

Ice hockey is where you have a hockey stick and a puck. Each team has six players. One is the goalie. He or she wears a mask and lots of protective clothing. The players skate back and forth, between the two goals. Sometimes they get in fights. The team who hits the puck inside the goal the most times wins.

Keep This in Mind

- In an explanatory *what* paragraph, define the subject in the topic sentence.
- Organize your details from the general to the specific.
- Include a strong ending sentence.

Now Write Revise your explanatory *what* paragraph. Follow the guidelines in this lesson. Be sure to proofread your paragraph. Then make a final copy. Save your paragraph in your folder.

Section **14** Objectives

1. To define a composition
2. To know the three parts of a composition: the introduction, the body, and the conclusion
3. To select and narrow a topic for a composition
4. To develop a topic by gathering details
5. To organize details around the main ideas
6. To present these main ideas and details in a suitable order
7. To write a first draft that contains an introduction, a body, and a conclusion
8. To learn to revise the ideas, organization, and word choice in a composition
9. To write an interesting title
10. To produce a neat, clean, final copy of the composition
11. To know and use the guidelines for writing a composition

Preparing the Students

Write the following on the board.

word → sentence → paragraph → composition.

Explain that in order to write a sentence, you must have a knowledge of words. In order to write a good paragraph, you must have a knowledge of sentences. To write a composition, you must know how to write a paragraph. Explain that the set of skills needed for each more complex form of writing is dependent on the skills learned for the more basic forms of writing. Point out to the students that they have studied words, then sentences, and finally the paragraph. The next step is to study compositions.

A Look at Compositions

159

Additional Resources

Mastery Test — pages 27–28 in the test booklet

Practice Book — pages 65–71

Duplicating Masters — pages 65–71

Teaching Special Populations

LD See **Teaching Special Populations,** page 75.

ESL Using concrete examples, demonstrate to students the meaning of general terms such as *introduction, body,* and *conclusion.* Provide students with sample compositions and have them identify the constituent elements.

Remind ESL students that the use of first drafts allows them to put down thoughts freely, in their own style, without fear of criticism. Before allowing students to proceed with their final drafts, go over the first drafts indivdiually and make suggestions as to ways in which the organization and grammar can be improved.

Finally, make sure students expand their vocabulary in the writing exercises. In particular, help ESL students find appropriate transitional words and phrases to help ease the flow of their arguments.

NSD See **Teaching Special Populations,** page 75.

159

Compose Yourself

Objectives

1. To define a composition
2. To know the three parts of a composition: the introduction, the body, and the conclusion

Presenting the Lesson

1. Read aloud and discuss **Here's the Idea.** Write the definition of *composition* on the chalkboard. Point out the differences and similarities between paragraphs and compositions. Write the three parts of a composition on the chalkboard and the function of each.

2. Read aloud "Grandpa's Pond." Ask students to state the main idea of the composition and to label the parts. Point out that the title reflects the main idea of the composition.

3. Assign **Try Your Skill.** Ask students to explain their answer.

4. Read **Keep This in Mind.**

5. Assign **Now Write.**

Individualizing the Lesson

Less-Advanced Students

Do **Try Your Skill** orally with students. If they have trouble identifying the part of the composition, bring in a number of introductory paragraphs, body paragraphs, and concluding paragraphs. Reproduce them and distribute copies to the students. Have them label what part of the composition each paragraph is. Discuss the reasons for their choices.

Learning About Compositions

Here's the Idea You have learned that a paragraph is a group of sentences that develops one main idea. Sometimes, you may have a long story to tell or a detailed description to present. When you want to write about an idea that is too long for one paragraph, you can write a composition.

A **composition** is a group of paragraphs that develops one main idea. Like a paragraph, a composition can be narrative, descriptive, or explanatory.

There are three parts to a composition: an introduction, a body, and a conclusion. The **introduction** is the part that tells what the composition will be about. In this way the introduction is similar to the topic sentence of a paragraph.

The **body** of the composition is the part that develops the main idea. In a narrative, the body contains the events that tell the story. In a description, the body contains the sensory details that help the reader to share an experience. In an explanation, the body contains steps in a process, reasons, or details that define.

The **conclusion** brings the composition to a close. The conclusion may sum up the important ideas in the composition.

Check It Out Read the following composition.

Grandpa's Pond

My grandfather lived in a small house in New Orleans. The house itself was ordinary, but the yard held a surprise. Grandpa had planted and cultivated the entire yard. It resembled a miniature wilderness. The highlight of this scene was a goldfish pond.

The pond was nestled in a shady corner of the yard, beneath a rock mountain that my grandfather made. The water was clear and cool. Beneath the surface the fish swam lazily. Some of them were scarlet, and some were silver-white. Only a few were actually gold.

The lovely green yard and the fish pond were special to Grandpa. His natural creations gave him pleasure and something to care for. He would take his chair into the yard and sit for hours, reading and resting.

Grandpa died six years ago, and his house was sold. The people who bought his house have continued to keep the pond alive. Their children play around the edge of the pond just as my cousins and I did. The pond still brings pleasure. I cannot imagine a better mark for Grandfather to have left on the world.

- What is the main idea of this composition?
- Which part of the composition is the introduction?
- Which is the body? Which is the conclusion?

Try Your Skill   Which part of a composition is this?

The ancient Persians gave New Year's gifts of eggs, symbols of productiveness. The Celtic priests of what is now England gave the people mistletoe, which was considered sacred.

Keep This in Mind

- A composition develops one main idea in several paragraphs.
- A composition should have three parts: an introduction, a body, and a conclusion.

Now Write   Answer these questions in complete sentences.

1. What is a composition?
2. When would you write a composition?
3. What are the three parts of a composition?

1. Have students decide what type of composition "Grandpa's Pond" is.

2. Have students point out the topic sentence in each paragraph of "Grandpa's Pond."

Optional Practice

Ask each student to find a magazine article about one topic, such as sports, pollution, or hobbies. Point out that all compositions have certain things in common, including:

1. an introduction, body, and conclusion
2. organization into paragraphs
3. development with specific details
4. a main idea or topic sentence for each paragraph

Have students identify these elements in the articles they bring to class.

Extending the Lesson

Make sure students understand the similarities between compositions and paragraphs. Then suggest they restrict themselves to five paragraph compositions for your class. Ask them how such a composition would be divided into introduction, body, and conclusion (one paragraph each for introduction and conclusion, and three paragraphs for body).

Part 2

Objectives

1. To select and narrow a topic for a composition

2. To develop a topic by gathering details

Presenting the Lesson

1. Read **Here's the Idea.** Discuss with students what makes a subject too broad or too narrow to work with in a composition. Remind students that finding a subject is the initial pre-writing step in the process of writing. Point out that journals and brainstorming are especially good sources for ideas.

2. Read and discuss **Check It Out.** Ask students to find the parts of this composition. Have them decide where the author found his or her ideas for this composition.

3. Assign **Try Your Skill.** Emphasize that this is a sort of brainstorming exercise, and that students should not try to limit their ideas.

4. Read **Keep This in Mind** and then asign **Now Write.**

Individualizing the Lesson

Less-Advanced Students

1. Hold a class brainstorming session to help students generate details for **Try Your Skill.**

2. Help students narrow the topic they choose for **Now Write.**

Advanced Students

Suggest that one way to narrow a subject is to look for a fresh or unusual angle to it. To demonstrate this, have students brainstorm for unusual viewpoints on a single topic

162

First Steps

Pre-Writing: Developing a Composition

Here's the Idea   When you write a composition, you will use many of the same skills you learned for writing paragraphs. You will choose a subject, gather details, organize your information, write a first draft, and revise.

Choosing a subject is the first step. Look in your journal. Do some reading. Page through a book of photographs. Try brainstorming. Choose a subject that is interesting to you and that you know something about. Work with ideas that are too broad to be covered well in a single paragraph. However, don't choose a subject that is too general.

For example, an explanation of how to eat with chopsticks is just right for a single paragraph. A description of a Japanese dinner, however, is much too broad to be covered well in only a few sentences. At the same time, the topics *Japan* or *Japanese Customs* are too general even for a composition.

When you have chosen a good subject, look for ideas to develop it. These ideas might include sensory details, specific examples, facts and statistics, or incidents or anecdotes. You can discover these ideas by brainstorming, through research, or from your own experiences. To learn more about gathering ideas, see pages 78–79.

Check It Out   Read the following composition.

A Japanese Dinner

When I lived in Baltimore, I had a Japanese friend named Takao Matsudo. One day I had a chance to learn about some of the differences in our ways of life. Takao had invited me to have dinner with his family.

Mr. and Mrs. Matsudo greeted me at the door. They invited me into the kitchen to show me how they cooked each dish we would eat. They showed me the preparation of the stir-fried beef and vegetables, of the rice, and of the green tea.

When we sat down to eat, the Matsudos asked if I wanted to use a fork or chopsticks. I saw that the Matsudos all had chopsticks. Foolishly, I asked for chopsticks, too. I was sure that I could master them. Takao showed me how to hold them. I awkwardly practiced wiggling the chopsticks in the air.

The meal began, but I was struggling. I kept trying to pick up a small morsel of beef. I could not get hold of it. Finally, I grasped my chopsticks more firmly. My tight grasp on the chopsticks made them snap past each other. The food shot across the table.

I stammered an apology over and over again. I was totally flustered, but the Matsudos were not. Mr. Matsudo told me that such problems were common when people first tried chopsticks. After that night, I was invited to many other dinners at the Matsudos' house. Happily, I learned to master chopsticks.

- Was the writer able to cover the topic well?

Try Your Skill Suppose you were going to write a composition about a dinner at your house. What kinds of details would you choose? Think about the subject. Then make pre-writing notes. Write as many details as you can think of.

> ### Keep This in Mind
>
> - Choose a topic that can be handled well in several paragraphs.
> - Develop your composition with sensory details, specific examples, facts and statistics, or incidents or anecdotes.

Now Write Choose a topic you can write about in a composition. Use the information in this lesson to guide your choice. Be sure to choose a topic that interests you. Make some pre-writing notes. Save your notes in your folder.

(example: *weather* can become "How to enjoy a heat wave," or "The benefits of a blizzard").

Optional Practice

Have students think of five specific topics based on each of the following general topics.

grandparents	sports
talents	fads
teenagers	songs

Extending the Lesson

Have students develop an idea file for subjects. Have them go through one edition of a daily newspaper and find interesting topics suggested by front page stories, current events, features, comics, advice columns, and sports columns. Have students keep their ideas in their journals.

Group Effort

Pre-Writing: Organizing a Composition

Part 3

Objectives

1. To organize details around main ideas

2. To present these main ideas and details in a suitable order

Presenting the Lesson

1. Approach **Here's the Idea** paragraph by paragraph. Try to relate the material presented in this part to what the students already know about organizing a paragraph. Make sure students know the difference between a main idea and a supporting idea. Compare main ideas to suitcases into which you put supporting ideas. If necessary, review the ways to organize pre-writing notes on pages 88–89.

2. Read and discuss **Check It Out.** It is suggested this exercise be done as a class activity.

3. Assign **Try Your Skill.**

4. Read **Keep This in Mind** and then assign **Now Write.**

Individualizing the Lesson

Less-Advanced Students

1. Do one topic from **Try Your Skill** with students in class. Then have them do another topic on their own.

2. Work individually with students who are having trouble organizing their ideas for **Now Write.**

Advanced Students

1. Have students read through their list of details for **Now Write.** For each detail, have them add at least one word or phrase that makes the detail more specific and easier to visualize or understand.

Here's the Idea When you learned to write a paragraph, you discovered how important it was to organize your ideas. It is important to organize the ideas for a composition, too. However, because a composition is made up of several paragraphs, you have to organize your ideas a little differently.

Look over your pre-writing notes. Try to find two or three main ideas that run through the notes. For example, suppose your composition is a narrative about going to your first high-school dance. As you read through your pre-writing notes, you might discover that your ideas seem to be about three things: getting a date, getting ready for the dance, and the dance itself. These are your main ideas.

Next, group the details in your notes around the main idea that they tell about. For instance, asking Rob to go to the dance would fall under the main idea "getting a date." Details about the way the gym was decorated, the music the band played, and the refreshments served would be grouped around "the dance itself." Each main idea, along with the details grouped around it, will become a paragraph in the body of your composition.

When all of your details are grouped around main ideas, you are ready to choose an order in which to present them. Choose a method of organization that suits the type of composition you are writing. Because the composition about the school dance is a narrative, you will want to present your ideas in chronological order. First, arrange the main ideas in chronological order. Then do the same for the details grouped around each main idea. You will then have a clearly organized set of notes.

To learn more about the different ways to organize your pre-writing notes, see pages 88–89.

Check It Out Here are some pre-writing notes for a descriptive composition about a supermarket.

shiny purple eggplants	10 kinds of cheese
"Fisherman's Wharf"	bok choy cabbage
creamy pasta salad	silvery rainbow trout
heaping tub of clams	"the Garden Spot"
black, green, and stuffed olives	cole slaw
ripe, red tomatoes	red emperor grapes
"Deli Delites"	huge Mexican shrimp
live lobsters in a tank	sliced baked ham

- What three main ideas do you find in these notes?
- What details would you group around each main idea?
- Do you see how each group of notes could be developed into a paragraph?

Try Your Skill Make a list of ten or twelve details that come to your mind about one of these topics:

a shopping mall   our school   winter sports

Try to group the details around two or three main ideas.

Keep This in Mind

- Group your pre-writing notes around two or three main ideas. Each group of ideas will become a paragraph in your composition.
- Organize your main ideas and the details grouped around them.

Now Write Organize the pre-writing notes you have made for your composition. Group your details around two or three main ideas. Then organize the main ideas and the details grouped around them. Save your organized notes in your folder.

165

2. Have students write the type of organization they will use for **Now Write.**

Optional Practice

Have students find the three main ideas in the following pre-writing notes and then group the remaining ideas under the appropriate main idea.

Summer Jobs

jobs done from your home
growing plants
garage sale
helping in a hospital
babysitting
jobs done as a volunteer
mowing lawns
jobs done for neighbors
helping out a religious organization

Extending the Lesson

Have students view a short film that tells a story. Discuss with students the major events in the film, and list them on the chalkboard. Then have them suggest which details should be grouped around which major event.

Objective

To write a first draft that contains an introduction, a body, and a conclusion

Presenting the Lesson

1. Read and discuss **Here's the Idea.** Write on the chalkboard the words *purpose* and *audience*. Make sure students understand the function of these words as they write their first draft. Emphasize that the first draft is a time to experiment, and that students should not worry about mechanical mistakes at this time.

2. Read **Check It Out.** Have students find the introduction, body, and conclusion of the composition.

3. Assign **Try Your Skill.** Explain to students that most writing, even when it needs revision, has good points. Explain that it is important for students to recognize what is good about their work, as well as what needs correction.

4. Read **Keep This in Mind.** Assign **Now Write.** Remind the class to keep their purpose and audience in mind as they write.

Individualizing the Lesson

Less-Advanced Students

1. Emphasize the importance of a good introductory paragraph to interest the reader in the rest of the composition, and the importance of a conclusion to tie ideas together for the reader.

2. Help students translate their main ideas into composition paragraphs. Provide individual and

Experiment!

Writing the First Draft

Here's the Idea You have already planned and organized your composition. Now you are ready to write the first draft.

As you write your first draft, keep your purpose for writing in mind. Are you telling a story, describing a person, or explaining an opinion? If you know what you are trying to accomplish, you stand a better chance of reaching your goal.

Don't forget your audience as you write. Be sure you include the kind of information your audience needs in order to understand and enjoy your composition. Also, remember to choose language that suits your readers.

Make sure that each part of your composition fulfills its purpose. Write an interesting introductory paragraph that tells the reader what you are writing about. In the body paragraphs, develop your composition clearly and completely with good details. Conclude your composition with a strong ending paragraph that brings your composition to a close.

Finally, keep in mind that a first draft is really a discovery draft. Feel free to experiment with your ideas, your organization, and your language. Add new details. Leave out details that do not help you to develop your main idea. Move sentences and paragraphs around if that helps you to express your ideas more clearly. You will have time during the third step of the writing process to correct any mistakes.

Check It Out Read this first draft.

Stanley Park

My family went to Canada last summer. Our favorite day was spent in Stanley Park. In Vancouver, B.C. It has 1,000 acres of forests, trails, beautiful views, restaurants. And even a zoo and a aquarium.

Stanley Park is a peninsula. Surrounded by water. A lot of it is a dense forest. There is a large pond called Lost Lagoon. Trails wind through the forest and a path goes around the lagoon. Dad liked the rose garden the best. Mom and I watched a cricket match. We all enjoyed walking along the seawall that surrounds the park. Its seven miles long we didn't walk the whole thing. You can get beautiful views of the city the ocean and the mountains. Dad took my picture by the totem poles.

We spent the afternoon at the zoo and the Aquarum. We watched the monkeys and polar bears. Peacocks were walking around. A lot of people had British accents. In the Aquarum we saw amazing sea creatures. The best part was the killer whale show.

That night we ate at a beautiful restaurant in the park. We had a view of the Pacific Ocean. All of us ate fresh samon it is a local specialty. After dinner we went to a concert by the Nylons. Their a fantastic group from Toronto.

Stanley Park is the greatest park. At least that I've been to. I hope I can go back sometime. Youd love it to.

- Does each part of the composition fulfill its purpose?
- Did the writer include enough details?

Try Your Skill   Look again at the first draft in **Check It Out.** Write five things about it that make it a good composition. Then write five things you think need to be improved.

> **Keep This in Mind**
> - Your first draft is a discovery draft. Experiment with your ideas, organization, and language.

Now Write   Use your organized pre-writing notes to write the first draft of your composition. Keep your purpose and audience in mind as you write. Be sure your composition has an introduction, a body, and a conclusion. Save your first draft.

small-group help as needed, guiding the students in expanding ideas and supporting the ideas with relevant details.

Advanced Students

Provide short magazine articles with either the introduction or conclusion missing. Ask students what the purpose of each article is. Then have students write the missing paragraphs.

Optional Practice

Have students work in small groups while developing the bodies of their compositions. After students have written first drafts of their body paragraphs, have them exchange papers with someone else in their group. Tell them to point out any places where the writer could add details to help develop the body.

Extending the Lesson

Read to the class a few famous introductions from well-known novels. Some examples are the beginnings of *Little Women,* and *Pride and Prejudice.* Ask students to think about why these particular introductions are famous. How do they capture a reader's attention?

Fine-Tuning

Revising Your Composition

Part 5

Objective

To learn to revise the ideas, organization, and word choice in a composition

Presenting the Lesson

1. Review the guidelines that students have used for revising paragraphs. Then read and discuss **Here's the Idea**. Point out the similarities between revising a composition and a paragraph. Ask students if they can find any differences.

2. Read **Check It Out**. Compare these revisions with the students' answers in **Try Your Skill** in Part 4.

3. Assign **Try Your Skill**. Use an overhead projector or duplicate the students' revisions in order to compare them.

4. Read **Keep This in Mind** and then assign **Now Write**.

Individualizing the Lesson

Less-Advanced Students

Work with these students as they revise their compositions. Methods such as peer evaluation, reading aloud, and group questioning may help students to improve their first drafts.

Advanced Students

Encourage students to read their compositions aloud during revision, either at home or in small groups in class. Explain that hearing one's own writing often brings to light any problems in the composition.

Here's the Idea   When your first draft is complete, put it away for a day or two. Then reread it. As you do, you will most likely see ways to improve what you have written. You will probably move some words around. You will add words, take out some, and look for errors in grammar and mechanics.

As you revise your first draft, ask yourself these questions.

1. Have I included enough details to develop my topic?

2. Are there any unrelated details that should be taken out?

3. Have I organized my details around two or three main ideas?

4. Will my introductory paragraph capture the reader's attention? Does it tell the reader what my composition is about?

5. Does each paragraph in the body tell about one main idea?

6. Have I arranged my paragraphs and the ideas within them logically?

7. Have I used transitional words and phrases to lead the reader from one idea to the next?

8. Have I used strong and specific verbs? Have I used vivid adjectives?

9. Have I written a good conclusion that sums up my ideas?

Check It Out   Here is part of the first draft of a composition that is in the process of revision.

·   In what specific ways have these paragraphs been improved?

My family went to ^Western^ Canada last summer. Our favorite day was spent ^at^ in Stanley Park. In Vancouver, ~~B.C.~~ *British Columbia.* It has 1,000 acres of forests, trails, beautiful views, restaurants, ~~And~~ *Stanley Park* even a zoo and an aquarium. *The park is a great tourist attraction.*

Stanley Park is a peninsula, ~~Surrounded~~ surrounded by water. ~~A lot~~ *much* of it is a dense *evergreen* forest. There is a large pond called Lost Lagoon. Trails wind through the forest and a path goes around the lagoon. *Near the lagoon is a* ~~Dad~~ liked the rose garden the best. *Dad enjoyed the roses while* Mom and I watched a cricket match. *Then* We all enjoyed walking *along* around the seawall that surrounds the park. It's seven miles long *but* we didn't walk the ~~whole thing~~ *entire length of it.* ~~You can get~~ *The park has* beautiful views of the city, the ocean, and the mountains.

Dad took my picture by the totem poles. *Before we ate our picnic lunch,*

Try Your Skill Use the guidelines in this lesson to revise the last three paragraphs of the composition about Stanley Park. Compare your revision with those of your classmates.

> **Keep This in Mind**
> - Revise your composition to improve your ideas, your organization, and your word choice.
> - Proofread your composition to correct any errors in grammar and mechanics.

Now Write Revise the first draft of your composition. Ask yourself the questions in **Here's the Idea** as you revise. Save your revised composition in your folder.

169

Optional Practice

Hold writing clinics in specific problem areas, and assign students to the clinics that they will benefit from the most. Some examples of clinic topics might be: developing a topic sentence, organization of ideas, writing a conclusion, etc.

Extending the Lesson

Have students seek information on how many drafts professional writers write and how they revise their work. Have them report back to the class on what they find out. Refer them to the library for source material, especially the *Paris Review* series of interviews, "Writers at Work."

Name Game

Writing a Title

Objective

To write an interesting title

Presenting the Lesson

1. Read and discuss **Here's the Idea.** Point out that a title may be serious or humorous, but that it should suggest the main idea of the students' writing.

2. Read **Check It Out.** Stress that a good title is one that is interesting and to the point.

3. Assign **Try Your Skill.** It is suggested you do this exercise orally with the students.

4. Read **Keep This in Mind.**

5. Assign **Now Write.**

Individualizing the Lesson

Less-Advanced Students

Have students write two titles for **Now Write,** and then choose one.

Advanced Students

Have students discuss the function of a title in attracting readers' attention and in giving them an idea about the subject of a composition. Have students find at least five good titles in a magazine or a literature book. Have them explain why each title appeals to them.

Optional Practice

Have students choose some interestingly titled news stories and features from a local newspaper and bring them to class for discussion. Point out any stylistic tricks the writers used in the titles, such as alliteration, puns, and so on.

Here's the Idea You have to make many decisions when you write. You decide whether to write a narrative, a description, or an explanation. You choose a topic. You choose the right kind of details to develop your topic. You select specific words that express your ideas exactly. Writing is a series of such decisions.

For some of your writing, you will also need to write a title that expresses your idea. Most short pieces of writing, such as paragraphs, do not usually have a title. However, most longer pieces of writing, such as compositions and reports, need a title.

A title will probably be the last thing you write. However, a title is the first thing your reader will notice. That is why a good title should attract your reader's interest and attention. A good title should also suggest the main idea of your writing. A good title may be simple and clear, like "To Build a Fire." A good title may sometimes be surprising, like "The Night the Ghost Got In."

Check It Out Look at the following titles of stories you may have read.

"The Rocking Donkey"	"The Lady, or the Tiger?"
"Father's Day"	"After Twenty Years"
"The Colt"	"A Man Who Had No Eyes"
"The Possibility of Evil"	"How John Boscoe Outsung the Devil"

• Are these good titles? Why?

Try Your Skill   Choose four of the following composition topics. Write two possible titles for each topic. Write titles that express the idea of the topic in a simple or surprising way.

1. a story about a family that suddenly becomes wealthy
2. a report on famous zoos
3. a description of your favorite city
4. an explanation of how to make chicken soup
5. a report on solar energy
6. a story about two friends who quarrel
7. an explanation of what thunder is
8. an explanation of why _____ is a good movie

Keep This in Mind

- Write a title for compositions and reports.
- A good title should attract a reader's interest.
- A good title should suggest the main idea of your writing.

Now Write   Write four or five titles that would suit your composition. Be sure each title is interesting and suggests your main idea. Think about the titles you have written. Then, choose one. Write it at the top of your revised composition. Save your composition in your folder.

Home Free

Objective

To produce a neat, clean, final copy of the composition

Presenting the Lesson

1. Ask students what they think the final copy of a composition should look like and why. Then read and discuss **Here's the Idea.** Explain that not only does a neat paper look good, but it is easier for a reader to read through and understand.

2. Read and discuss **Check It Out.** Have students point out each part of the paper that is done correctly.

3. Assign **Try Your Skill.** Tell students that part of their grade on their compositions will be based on how well they followed the rules for a final copy.

4. Read **Keep This in Mind** and then assign **Now Write.** Remind students to write on only one side of their paper. Stress the importance of the final reading after corrections have been made.

Individualizing the Lesson

Less-Advanced Students

Have students make a large chart of the guidelines for writing a final copy. Display the chart so the class can use it for easy reference.

The Final Copy

Here's the Idea After the first draft of your composition has been completely revised, it is time to write the final copy. This copy should be neat, clean, and as free of errors as you can make it.

Write your final copy on clean, white, lined paper. Always use a pen, and not a pencil. If you want to, you may type your paper. In the upper right-hand corner of your paper, put your name, the subject, and the date. On the second line of your paper, write the title of your composition. Remember to center the title.

Copy each line of your composition carefully. Leave at least one inch on the right and left sides of your paper. Leave at least one line blank at the bottom of your paper. Write on only one side of a sheet of paper. If you need more than one sheet, number every sheet after the first one. Write the number of each page at the very top in the center.

When you are done, proofread your final copy one last time. Neatly correct any errors that you find. If you have to cross out more than three or four errors on a page, you should write that page again.

Check It Out On the following page is the beginning of the final copy of the composition about Stanley Park.

- Does this final copy follow the form given in this lesson?

> Jorge Diaz
> English
> December 9, 1985
>
> Stanley Park
> My family went to western
> Canada last summer. Our favorite
> day was spent at Stanley Park
> in Vancouver, British Columbia.
> Stanley Park has 1,000 acres of
> forests, trails, beautiful views,
> restaurants, and even a zoo and
> an aquarium. The park is a great
> tourist attraction.

Try Your Skill　Make a chart that lists all of the guidelines for writing a final copy. Tape this chart somewhere in your folder or notebook where you can refer to it easily.

Keep This in Mind

- The final copy of your composition should be neat and free of errors.

Now Write　Write the final copy of your composition. Proofread it carefully. Be sure it is neat and free of errors. Save your final copy in your folder.

Don't Forget

Guidelines for Writing a Composition

Guidelines for Writing a Composition

Objective

To use the guidelines for writing a composition

Presenting the Lesson

This part is to be used as a review as students progress with their study of writing different kinds of compositions. Point out how these guidelines follow the process of writing the students have been using. Encourage students to refer to these guidelines as often as necessary.

In the next few sections of this book, you will be writing many different kinds of compositions. Whatever type of composition you write, however, the process of writing will remain the same. Here is a checklist of the steps to follow when you write a composition. Refer to these guidelines often as you write your compositions.

Guidelines for Writing a Composition

Pre-Writing

- Choose a topic that interests you and that you know something about.
- Narrow the topic so that you can cover it well in the length of your composition.
- Gather details to develop your topic.
- Group similar details around two or three main ideas.
- Organize your details into an order that suits the type of composition you are writing.

Writing the First Draft

- Begin your composition with an interesting introductory paragraph. It should tell your reader what your composition is about.
- After your introduction, present the body of your composition. Use your organized details to develop your topic. Each group of details will become a paragraph in the body of your composition.
- Use transitional words and phrases to lead your readers from one idea to the next.

- Add, take out, and reorganize your ideas if you need to.
- Finish your composition with a concluding paragraph that sums up your ideas.
- Add an interesting title to your composition.

Revising

- Be sure your composition has an introduction, a body, and a conclusion.
- Check to see that you have included enough details to develop your topic.
- Organize the paragraphs and the ideas within them logically.
- Be sure the topic sentence of each paragraph presents the main idea of that paragraph.
- Use transitional words to make your ideas flow smoothly.
- Make sure you have used vivid language.
- Proofread to find and correct errors in grammar, capitalization, punctuation, and spelling.

Final Copy

- Rewrite your composition neatly in ink on white, lined paper.
- Write your name, subject, and the date in the upper right-hand corner of your paper.
- Proofread your final copy one last time. Neatly correct any errors you find.

Section 15 Objectives

1. To know the basic elements of a narrative composition: setting, characters, plot, and conflict
2. To learn to arrange details in chronological order
3. To understand how to use a flashback
4. To recognize and use appropriately the three kinds of point of view: first-person, third-person limited, and third-person omniscient
5. To write the first draft using an introduction, body, and conclusion
6. To use dialogue and dialogue tags to reveal the feelings of characters
7. To use transitions between and within paragraphs to show chronological order
8. To revise the narrative composition

Preparing the Students

Select a folk tale or a short myth and tell it to the class. Make your presentation both amusing and interesting. Explain that storytellers have been around since the beginning of time to transmit knowledge and to entertain. Point out that when students write a narrative composition, they, too, are becoming storytellers. They should think of the audience that they are writing for and try to make their compositions as interesting and entertaining as possible. Emphasize to the students that the process of writing remains the same.

Additional Resources

Practice Book — pages 72–78
Duplicating Masters — pages 72–78

The Narrative Composition

Teaching Special Populations

LD See **Teaching Special Populations,** page 75. Note particularly that LD students may not have the reading skills necessary for understanding some of the sample passages. Go over these passages orally in class.

ESL Using contextual examples, demonstrate to students the meaning of *setting, characters, plot*, and *conflict*. For extra practice, ask ESL students to translate folk tales from their native cultures and identify narrative elements in these stories. Also ask native English speakers to play the parts of first- and third-person narrators and have ESL students identify the respective points of view.

ESL students will need additional practice in punctuating dialogue. Try tape recording a conversation from a TV program, then have students transcribe correctly the dialogue between characters. Review Handbook Section 19, pages 676–680, as a group. Additional exercises can be found in the Practice Book.

NSD See **Teaching Special Populations,** page 75. Remember also that in writing narratives, NSD students are often loathe to talk about characters not from their own mileau. Encourage students to experiment with different characters and different forms of dialogue. Make sure students understand that nonstandard dialect is only acceptable in the context of written dialogue or in exchanges with their friends.

Have You Heard?

Pre-Writing: Planning a Story

Part **1**

Objective

To know the basic elements of a narrative composition: setting, characters, plot, and conflict

Presenting the Lesson

1. Write the word *narrative* on the chalkboard and have students define it. Then read aloud and discuss **Here's the Idea.** Point out that there are three kinds of conflict mentioned, and ask students to name them. Have students make up examples for each kind. Summarize several short stories that the class has read and discuss the conflicts in each. Point out that the conflict is often introduced in the introduction to a narrative and then is developed in the body.

2. Read **Check It Out.** Point out that a conflict should create suspense; the reader should *want* to find out how it is resolved.

3. Assign **Try Your Skill.** Have students set up their pre-writing notes like those in **Check It Out.**

4. Read **Keep This in Mind** and then assign **Now Write.** Refer students to their journals as well as their imaginations to discover ideas for their narratives.

Individualizing the Lesson

Less-Advanced Students

1. Do **Try Your Skill** as a class exercise. Write the students' answers on the board.

Here's the Idea Have you ever greeted a friend with, "Have you heard about . . . ?" After catching your friend's attention, you probably went on to tell about something important that had just happened.

When you tell your story on paper rather than in person, you are writing a **narrative composition.** Many narratives are based on real life experiences. Others may be entirely made-up, written from the writer's imagination.

Whether a story is true or imaginary, it does more than just relate a series of events. It also makes a point. It tells how people think, feel, act, or react in a specific situation.

Every narrative contains certain basic elements. These elements are the setting, the characters, the plot, and the conflict.

The **setting** tells the reader when and where the story takes place. The time can be in the past, the present, or the future. The place can be a deserted beach, a crowded city street, or a classroom in the year 2000.

The **characters** are those directly involved in the action of the story. Characters may be people or animals.

The **plot** includes all the events that happen within a story. At the heart of the plot is the **conflict.** The conflict is the major difficulty that a character faces. It can be a struggle that one character has with another character. It can also be a struggle with a personal problem or with the forces of nature. The conflict creates interest and involves the reader in your story.

Check It Out Look at these pre-writing notes.

Setting: at home, last year
Characters: my little sister Tracy and me

Plot: Tracy enters a radio contest to win circus tickets, she
            asks for my help in painting her entry

Conflict: me with myself (personal problem)—should I help
            her?

• Does this writing plan contain all the elements necessary for a narrative composition?

Try Your Skill   Alone, or with a writing partner, develop
pre-writing notes for a narrative about "the first day of high
school." Make decisions about each basic element of the narrative. What is the setting? Who are your characters? What is the
plot? What will the conflict be?

Keep This in Mind

• A narrative composition tells a story that makes a
  point.
• The elements of a narrative include setting, characters, plot, and conflict.

Now Write   Think of ideas for some stories you would like to
tell. Is there something you remember from your childhood
that you could turn into a story? Is there a hard choice you have
had to make or some obstacle you have overcome? Think of
conflicts that you have had with other people. Is there a story
idea in your struggles? Is there a distant time or a foreign
setting that sparks your imagination?

Write your answers to these questions and other ideas you
have for real and imaginary stories on a piece of paper. Label
the page "Story File." Save your story file in your folder.

2. Work with students to develop
topics for their compositions. Explain to students that they can select an incident from their own
experiences but write about it as if it
had happened to someone else.

Advanced Students

As a class, have students write a
detailed "biography" for an imaginary character. Explain that the
more real a character is in their own
minds, the more effectively they will
be able to create the character for
their readers. Encourage students
to add many details to the biography.

Optional Practice

Select a short narrative to duplicate for the class. Have students
read the narrative and identify the
setting, characters, plot, and conflict.

Extending the Lesson

Discuss with the students the narrative they read for **Optional Practice.**
Ask them to consider these questions:

1. Where in the story does the conflict
   become apparent?
2. How is the conflict introduced?
3. What specific details in the story
   make the characters seem real?
4. Does the author use sensory details to set the scene?
5. Where in the story is the conflict
   resolved? How is it resolved?

Part 2

Objectives

1. To learn to arrange details in chronological order
2. To understand how to use a flashback

Presenting the Lesson

1. Read aloud and discuss **Here's the Idea.** Make sure that students understand that *chronological* refers to time sequence.

Ask students to define *flashback,* and then to imagine some situations when an author might use a flashback. Ask them to relate any flashbacks they might have seen in a movie or TV show.

2. Read **Check It Out** and discuss the answers in terms of pre-writing skills they have already learned (writing notes, organizing notes, etc.).

3. Assign **Try Your Skill.** Ask volunteers to share their flashbacks with the class.

4. Read **Keep This in Mind.**

5. Assign **Now Write.** Remind students that their pre-writing notes are not written in stone. They may very well want to change some details later.

Individualizing the Lesson

Less-Advanced Students

1. Have students do **Try Your Skill** together in class. Ask them to describe Ann as they see her before they decide on their flashback.

2. Have students work with a partner for **Now Write.**

I Can See It Now!

Pre-Writing: Plotting a Story

Here's the Idea   Every story, real or imaginary, is made up of many small incidents or events called the *plot.* After you decide on an idea for your narrative composition, you are ready to write down all of the events that will tell your story.

As you list these events, try to add some specific details that will make your story more interesting. Jot down names, dates, places, and times. You will also want to add sensory details to your list. Be sure all of your details are accurate.

The events in a story should be arranged in the order in which they occurred. This is called **chronological order.** First organize your notes. Then decide which events are important enough to be covered in separate paragraphs. Also decide which events can be combined into one paragraph.

You may want to interrupt the natural, chronological flow of events to tell the reader about an event that took place before the events in your story. Then you will use a **flashback.**

A flashback tells about an earlier event that says something about the present conflict. Suppose you were writing about an important race between you and an opponent. You might want to insert a scene from an earlier contest when your opponent had beaten you. This flashback could help explain to your reader why you want to win so badly.

Check It Out   Here are the plot details for the story about Tracy.

1. WRKT contest for Super Circus tickets
2. Tracy decides to enter and to win
3. Tracy made dozens of paintings—some pretty bad
4. wanted me to paint so she could win
5. wanted to help her but decided I shouldn't

6. remembered my soapbox derby contest when Dad wouldn't help me

7. learned that doing my best by myself was what mattered

8. Tracy's drawing won!

- Are these events arranged in chronological order?
- Do the notes contain a flashback? What is it?
- Do you see how these notes have been divided into paragraphs?

Try Your Skill Here is part of a narrative composition. Create a flashback that would help to explain why Ann is so angry now. Rewrite this situation and insert your flashback.

Ann was so upset that she could hardly see the numbers on the combination lock of her gym locker. She couldn't believe what her best friend Carla had done to her! Ann jerked open her locker and pulled out her jacket and Spanish notebook. It looked like she'd be doing homework Saturday night, after all.

Keep This in Mind

- The events and details in a narrative composition are usually arranged in chronological order.
- You may interrupt the chronological flow of events to insert a flashback. A flashback is a scene from the past that helps to explain something in the present.

Now Write Choose a topic from the story file you started in the last lesson, **Have You Heard?** Write down the story element, setting, characters, plot, and conflict. Make specific notes about each one. Then list the events that make up your story. Arrange these events in chronological order. If a flashback could add meaning to an event in your story, add it to your list. Save your notes in your folder.

181

Have students plan a simple story about the character whose biography they wrote in the last lesson. Have them make some pre-writing notes about setting, plot, and conflict. Have them arrange their notes in chronological order. If they can include a flashback, so much the better.

Optional Practice

Have the students brainstorm together all the elements necessary for a mystery narrative. After they have decided on setting, characters, and conflict have them put their notes for the plot into a chronological order.

Extending the Lesson

Have students study several short stories as models of narrative compositions (Edgar Allen Poe is a good writer for this). Have the students look for unusual characters and settings, for conflicts and flashbacks. Discuss what makes the stories interesting.

What a View!

Pre-Writing: Choosing a Point of View

Objective

To recognize and use appropriately the three kinds of point of view: first-person, third-person limited, and third-person omniscient

Presenting the Lesson

1. Review the definition of *point of view.* Refer the students to page 110.

2. Read aloud and discuss **Here's the Idea.** Review first-person and third-person point of view and introduce the omniscient point of view. Stress that the meaning of *omniscient* is "knowing all things." Write the three kinds of point of view on the chalkboard. Provide these sentences to give students practice in identifying point of view.

1. I was frightened when I saw the cat burglar climbing down the side of the building.

2. The cat burglar climbed down the side of the building.

3. The cat burglar, feeling pleased with himself for escaping the scene of the crime, climbed down the side of the building.

3. Discuss **Check It Out.** Point out that the pronoun *I* is always used in first-person point of view.

4. Assign **Try Your Skill.** Collect the paragraphs and read examples written from each point of view. Point out that to show the thoughts and feelings of one or more people, the most effective points of view would be first-person or third-person omniscient.

5. Read **Keep This in Mind** aloud.

6. Assign **Now Write.**

Here's the Idea   Who will tell your narrative for you? Before you write, you must select a narrator. The narrator is the person who tells the story. In order to choose a narrator, you must decide on a point of view.

When you use the **first-person point of view,** your story is told by a character involved in the action. This character is identified by the pronoun *I.* When *I* tells the story, the reader knows only what this character knows. If you are telling a story in which you are one of the characters, the first-person point of view is a natural choice.

When you use the **third-person point of view,** your story is told by a narrator who is not a character in the story. The pronouns *he* and *she* are used. There are two types of third-person point of view. The first type is third-person limited.

In the **third-person limited** point of view, the narrator acts as a reporter who tells only what he or she sees and hears. The reader knows what the characters are thinking or feeling only if they say so themselves.

The second third-person point of view is not limited. It is called **omniscient** (om·ni′·shunt), which means "knowing all things." From this point of view, the narrator not only sees and hears everything, but also knows what every character thinks and feels.

Check It Out   Read the following paragraphs. They continue the narrative about Tracy.

When we reached home, Tracy headed straight for the desk where the paints and paper were stored. She took her supplies to the kitchen table and began painting. All afternoon she kept at it. I had never seen anyone concentrate so hard.

Just before supper, Tracy stopped working. She stared at the papers in front of her and then pushed them aside. She propped her elbows on the table, dropped her chin onto her hands, and started to cry. Tracy moaned that her pictures were no good. I tried to tell her that she was wrong, but Tracy would not believe me. At last she calmed down, but she ate hardly any supper. Afterwards, she came to my room to talk.

- Who is the narrator of this story? How is the narrator identified?
- From what point of view is this narrative composition written? How do you know?

Try Your Skill   Rewrite the paragraphs in **Check It Out,** from another point of view.

Keep This in Mind

- In the first-person point of view, the reader knows only what the narrator, *I*, knows.
- In the third-person limited point of view, the reader knows only what the narrator can see and hear. The narrator does not report thoughts or feelings.
- In the third-person omniscient point of view, the reader learns about the thoughts, feelings, and actions of the characters from the "all-knowing" narrator.

Now Write   Reread your pre-writing notes. Decide on a point of view from which to write your narrative. Write *first-person, third-person limited,* or *third-person omniscient* at the side of your notes. Save your notes in your folder.

Individualizing the Lesson

Less-Advanced Students

1. Students might be confused by which pronouns indicate a first-person or third-person point of view. Go over the pronouns in first person and those in third person.

2. Duplicate copies of a narrative composition. Have students identify the point of view.

Advanced Students

Have students find short news articles about different sporting events. Have the students rewrite the accounts, using the facts but writing from a different point of view.

Optional Practice

Discuss with the students the ways a character's personality can be revealed in a narrative: as seen through description by a narrator (omniscient) or observor (third-person limited); and through the character's own speech and actions (first-person). Ask students for examples of narratives that would best fit each point of view, (mystery–first person; adventure story–third person; love story–omniscient, etc.).

Extending the Lesson

Instruct students to divide a sheet of paper into three columns and label each with a point of view. Ask students to turn to the short story section of their literature books. Ask them to read the first paragraph of each story and to identify the point of view used. Then have them write the title under the appropriate heading on their papers.

Objective

To write the first draft using an introduction, body, and conclusion

Presenting the Lesson

1. Read and discuss **Here's the Idea.** Write the headings *Introduction, Body,* and *Conclusion,* on the board. Have students help you list what is contained in each of these sections of a narrative composition.

2. Read **Check It Out.** Ask students to identify what point of view is used in this paragraph. Lead them to the discovery that the story is actually one long flashback.

3. Assign **Try Your Skill.** Duplicate the students' paragraphs so they can compare their work.

4. Read **Keep This in Mind.** Then assign **Now Write.**

Individualizing the Lesson

Less-Advanced Students

Work with students to make sure they have enough details and a real conflict before they begin writing their first draft for **Now Write.**

Advanced Students

Have students exchange their introductions from **Now Write.** Ask them to offer suggestions on improving characterizations and settings.

Optional Practice

Using the notes for a mystery narrative that students wrote together for the **Optional Practice** in Part 2,

It Goes Like This

Writing the First Draft

Here's the Idea   Different types of compositions have different purposes. Some describe, some explain, and some tell stories. All compositions, however, have the same three parts: introduction, body, and conclusion.

In a narrative, the **introduction** presents the characters and sets the scene. As you write your introduction, give specific details about the time and place of the setting. Present the situation that will lead to the conflict. Use the introduction to capture the reader's interest.

The plot is developed in the **body** of the composition. The body includes all the events that tell your story. The body also introduces the story's conflict. The conflict should develop naturally from the story's events. Show the conflict developing through the actions of the characters.

The **conclusion** draws the events of the story to a close. It also settles the conflict. The conclusion should not leave the reader in suspense or with questions in mind. The ending of your story should follow naturally from the events that have come before it. For instance, if your imaginary story is very true-to-life, do not introduce super heroes to "save the day" in the end.

As you write the first draft, follow through with your prewriting decisions. Don't change the point of view. Don't have a character suddenly change his or her personality or attitude unless the change comes from the solution of the conflict.

Check It Out   Read this introduction.

My favorite family snapshot shows my six-year-old sister Tracy riding an elephant. Tracy's adventure began one day last summer when she and I were shopping at Bernsten's Market. Near the check-out counter Tracy spotted a poster that showed elephants, lions, and clowns. Radio station WRKT was inviting children to paint pictures that captured the excitement of the circus. The winning artists and their families would receive free tickets when Super Circus came to Dallas. Tracy told me that she was going to be the winner.

- Does the introduction present the main characters?
- Does the introduction include specific details about the setting? What are they?
- Does the introduction set up a situation that will lead to a conflict?

Try Your Skill   The following introduction to a narrative composition is incomplete. Although the narrator introduces the main characters, there is little to catch the reader's attention. Rewrite the paragraph. Use your imagination. Include specific details about the characters and a setting. Introduce a situation that could lead to a conflict.

> Everyone thinks my older brother is great. As for me, I'm just Jack's younger brother.

Keep This in Mind

- The introduction of a narrative presents the characters, the setting, and the situation that will lead to conflict.
- The body of a narrative develops the plot and conflict of the story.
- The conclusion of a narrative brings the plot to a close and solves the conflict.

Now Write   Using your pre-writing notes, write the introduction for your first draft. Include details about characters and setting. Add a situation that will lead to conflict.

185

have them each write an introduction for the narrative. Have volunteers share their work with the class.

Extending the Lesson

Read or duplicate some short paragraphs that are from the introduction, body, and conclusion of a narrative. Ask students to identify what each part is and why.

185

Objective

To use dialogue and dialogue tags to reveal the feelings of characters

Presenting the Lesson

1. Read aloud and discuss **Here's the Idea.** Emphasize the distinction between a *direct quotation* and an *indirect quotation.* Give these examples.

Mom said, "You may go to Helen's birthday party."
Mom said that you could go to Helen's birthday party.

2. Discuss **Check It Out.** Ask students to describe their impressions of Greg and Tracy from their dialogue and dialogue tags. Tell them to cite specific words that give them that impression.

3. Assign **Try Your Skill.** Remind students to start a new paragraph for each new speaker.

4. Read **Keep This in Mind** and then assign **Now Write.** Remind students that dialogue not only moves the narrative along, but makes a story more interesting.

Individualizing the Lesson

Less-Advanced Students

1. Go over the rules for writing dialogue correctly in Handbook Section 19, pages 679–680.

2. Do **Try Your Skill** in class. Have students first identify where each speaker starts and stops talking. Then have them identify the dialogue tags and decide which dialogue they describe. After students

Speak Up

The First Draft: Dialogue

Here's the Idea A **dialogue** is a conversation between two or more characters. Using dialogue is a way to bring characters to life. It is also a way to show what they are like. A polite character might ask, "Excuse me, sir. Could I pass through?" A bully, however, might snap, "Get out of my way, you."

Dialogue can also move your story along. It is a good way to *show* your readers the developing action. Don't have the narrator say "Jenny got into her car and turned the key. The car wouldn't start." Instead, let dialogue reveal the action.

"There's Jenny getting into her car now," Tom said. He heard the engine sputter and die. "Sounds like her car won't start," he said.

Dialogue always includes **dialogue tags.** A dialogue tag is a short phrase such as *Tina said* or *Rob asked.* Dialogue tags identify the character who is speaking. They also tell how the words are spoken.

Dialogue tags are another way for you to show a character's personality or feelings. Don't always use tags like "he said." Sometimes you can be more precise by writing "she mumbled" or "he insisted" or "Chris snarled."

Always put quotation marks around the speaker's exact words. Begin a new paragraph every time a different speaker talks. For more information about writing dialogue correctly, look at Handbook Section 19 on pages 679–680.

Check It Out Read the following dialogue. It continues the narrative about Tracy.

"Will you help me, Greg? I can't do it all by myself," Tracy pleaded.

"Sure you can," I insisted. "The paintings you did this afternoon are really good."

"You're just saying that because you don't want to help me," she cried. "My pictures are terrible. I'm going to tear them up."

I tried to tell Tracy that she shouldn't tear her pictures, that she would feel better about them in the morning.

Tracy screamed, "You don't care if I win or not!"

"I do care," I said softly, "but this is something you have to do by yourself."

- Does this dialogue reveal anything about Tracy and Greg? Does it move the story forward?
- Does the writer use good dialogue tags?

Try Your Skill Rewrite the following dialogue correctly. Substitute better dialogue tags. Dialogue tags will vary.

"Am I tired," said Janet. "I didn't get to bed until midnight." "Why were you up so late," asked Ron. Janet said, "I was studying for the big test today." "What test," said Ron. "Don't you remember the history test scheduled for today." Ron said that he had forgotten to study.

Keep This in Mind

- Dialogue can reveal the feelings and the personalities of the characters in a narrative. It can also move the story forward.
- Dialogue tags identify who is speaking and how the words are spoken.

Now Write Continue writing the first draft of your narrative composition. Include some dialogue as your story develops. The dialogue should reveal the personality or feelings of the characters. It should also help to move your story along. Save your writing in your folder.

have determined the correct way to punctuate the dialogue, have them finally substitute better dialogue tags.

Advanced Students

Have students work in groups to develop a script for a play based on one of the narratives in their literature book. Show them how dialogue is presented in a script and how dialogue tags become stage directions.

Optional Practice

Ask students to write three sentences for each subject below—one spoken by an adult, one by a teenager, and one by a small child. Remind students to include explaining words.

1. Order breakfast
2. Say hello
3. Say goodbye
4. Ask the price of something

Extending the Lesson

Ask students to bring comic strips to class. Have each student write the text of his or her comic strip in dialogue format. Remind students to punctuate the sentences properly and to indent every time a new speaker begins. Also, explain that they will have to add the dialogue tags for each line of dialogue.

Part 6

Objective

To use transitions between and within paragraphs to show chronological order

Presenting the Lesson

1. Read and discuss **Here's the Idea.** Review the purpose of transitions in a narrative to show chronological order.

2. Discuss **Check It Out.** Review the transitions listed on page 112.

3. Assign **Try Your Skill.** Have volunteers share their paragraphs with the class.

4. Read **Keep This in Mind** and then assign **Now Write.**

Individualizing the Lesson

Less-Advanced Students

Point out that there are many transitional words and phrases to choose from. Have students use a minimum of three different transitional words or phrases when they do **Try Your Skill.**

Advanced Students

Duplicate a short narrative composition and distribute copies to the class. Ask students to underline all the transitions used within the paragraphs and to circle the transitions used between paragraphs.

Optional Practice

Have students narrate the events in a typical day at their school. Write these events in chronological order on the board and ask students to supply transitions to connect the

The Time Is Right

The First Draft: Transitions

Here's the Idea   In narrative compositions, transitions are used for the same reason that they are used in narrative paragraphs. They help to make the order of events clear.

Within a paragraph, transitions form a bridge between sentences. In a composition, transitions also form bridges between paragraphs. They connect the events of one paragraph with those of the next. Transitions also place the events of each paragraph in time. For example, suppose that you wanted to write a composition about an eventful day. If you wrote four paragraphs, they might begin with these transitional phrases: *At breakfast, After lunch, Later that day,* and *Early in the evening.*

Transitions are especially important when you add a flashback. They help to prevent confusion. For example, you could signal the beginning of a flashback with transitional phrases such as *each year, only last week,* or *in the past.* To show your reader that the flashback has ended, you could use a transition such as *now* or *at this moment.*

Check It Out   Read the following paragraphs that continue the narrative about Tracy.

For the next few days I thought maybe I was being too tough on Tracy. Who would ever find out if I helped her a little? After all, she was only six years old. Besides that, she had been working so hard. Didn't she deserve a little help? Yet, as the contest deadline drew nearer, I still could not convince myself. Finally, I knew that I had to stay out of it, and I knew why. I decided to tell Tracy a story.

Five years ago, I had entered a race. I had been building a racer for a soapbox derby, and I had asked Dad to help me. I was sure there was no way I could win without his help. When Dad refused to help me, I felt angry at first. Later, however, Dad talked about the faith he had in me. He believed that I should try to do my best. Then I, too, started to believe that I should. Finally, I understood that I had to win or lose all on my own. Doing my best was what really mattered.

- What transitional words and phrases within each paragraph help to carry the reader from one time to another?
- What transition words and phrases between paragraphs help make the time sequence clear?

Try Your Skill   Add a flashback to the following narrative. Use transitional words or phrases that will help your reader to follow the action into and out of the flashback.

> I got up and ate my breakfast as usual, but I could not get the basketball game off my mind. I slowly drank my orange juice and wondered what the guys at school would say.

Keep This in Mind

- Use transitional words and phrases to make the order of events clear. Use them within paragraphs and between paragraphs.
- Use transitional words and phrases to signal the beginning and ending of a flashback.

Now Write   Finish writing the first draft of your narrative. Use transitional words and phrases to help you show the order of events. Be sure that your conclusion brings your story to a close and successfully settles the conflict. Save this draft in your folder.

events. Then have them supply the transitions they would use if this day happened in the past (*flashback*).

Extending the Lesson

Tell students to pretend that they are being questioned about the disappearance of the leftover pizza from the refrigerator. Ask them to write several paragraphs accounting for their time during the day. Have them underline the transitions.

189

Objective

To revise the narrative composition

Presenting the Lesson

1. Read and discuss **Here's the Idea.** Explain that students will have to read through their compositions a few times in order to think about all the guidelines for revision. Remind them that they will probably want to revise their work more than once, also.

2. Discuss **Check It Out.** Make sure students understand that sections of their composition can be moved around, or deleted, if necessary. Point out that most of the revisions in these paragraphs were to make the narrative more specific.

3. Assign **Try Your Skill.**

4. Read **Keep This in Mind** and then assign **Now Write.** Tell students to be especially careful when checking the punctuation of their dialogue.

Individualizing the Lesson

Less-Advanced Students

Divide the class into small groups. Have students read their **Now Write** papers aloud to the other group members. Ask the members of each group to comment on how well each paper followed the guidelines on page 109.

Advanced Students

Have students read a short story with a surprise ending. Discuss the effectiveness of the endings. Point

190

The Grand Finale

Revising Your Narrative Composition

Here's the Idea The revision stage of the process of writing is your chance to improve your writing. Now you can work to make your narrative as good as it can be.

Read over your first draft several times. As you do, ask yourself the following questions.

1. Does my narrative have a point?
2. Have I introduced the characters and set the scene in my introduction?
3. Is there a conflict at the heart of my story? Is it well developed in the body of my composition?
4. Have I used sensory and specific details to give my readers a clear picture of the action?
5. Have I used a clear time order to present the events?
6. Are flashbacks used effectively?
7. Have I kept the same point of view throughout my story?
8. Does dialogue help move the story along and reveal character traits? Have I used the correct form for writing dialogue?
9. Have I used transitional words and phrases where necessary?
10. Does the conclusion offer a solution for the conflict and bring the events to a close?

After you have finished making improvements in the content and the organization of your story, proofread it. Correct any errors you find in grammar, capitalization, punctuation, and spelling.

Check It Out Here is the conclusion of the narrative composition about Tracy. The writer has just finished revising it.

The revised narrative (with handwritten editing marks):

When (inserted, replacing "The")

Super circus came to Dallas. We were there. Tracys own darwing *a* of a parade of elephents had been a winner in the contest. *WRKT* *my sister.* I had never been prouder of Tracy. Tracy herself was alowed to join the parade of circus performers. Tracy *a* set on top *colorful* of the leed *a* elephent and smiled and waved to everyone. I cheered wildly, waving to Tracy all the while. Tracy had done her best, and she would remember her *special* reward for a long time.

- What are some of the improvements that the writer has made in this revision?

Try Your Skill   Write a final copy of the paragraph in **Check It Out.** The writer overlooked two errors when he revised. Be sure to find and correct them before you write the final copy.

allowed, elephant

Keep This in Mind

- Revision is an opportunity to review your first draft and to make changes in it. Your goal is to make your story the best it can be.

Now Write   Revise your narrative composition. Refer to the guidelines in this lesson. When you are satisfied with the results, make a final copy. Save your narrative composition in your folder.

out to students how the ending, although a surprise, still came about logically from the events in the narrative.

Optional Practice

Duplicate examples of an unrevised student narrative from your files. Discuss the needed revisions with the class.

Extending the Lesson

Select several of the students' narratives to be used in a mock radio dramatization. Students might tape their narratives or present them by reading them aloud. Suggest that students put together an entire radio show, including sound effects and commercials between stories.

Section 16 Objectives

1. To use sensory details to develop a description
2. To group details around main ideas and to use spatial order to organize those details and ideas
3. To know the purpose of the introduction, body, and conclusion of a descriptive composition
4. To use transitions between sentences and paragraphs to make spatial order clear
5. To write a conclusion that summarizes the main ideas in a description
6. To know and use the guidelines for revising a descriptive composition

Preparing the Students

Have students close their eyes and picture the scene described as you read them a description. Ask them what helps them to *see* the description. Explain that this section will show them how to share with other people their own impressions of something they have seen.

Additional Resources

Practice Book — pages 79–82
Duplicating Masters — pages 79–82

The Descriptive Composition

Teaching Special Populations

LD See **Teaching Special Populations,** page 75.

ESL See **Teaching Special Populations,** page 75. For extra practice, you might try the following game: place a variety of small objects in a cloth bag (a toothbrush, a watch, an eggbeater, and so on), and have students determine by touch alone what the items are. Ask students to describe the shape and texture of the objects, using complete sentences. Give students additional lists of words that describe sensory impressions. Have them transcribe new words onto vocabulary cards and keep them on file.

NSD See **Teaching Special Populations,** page 75.

Part 1

Objectives

1. To use sensory details to develop a description

2. To group details around main ideas and to use spatial order to organize those details and ideas

Presenting the Lesson

1. Review what students have learned about writing a descriptive paragraph (Section 10). Then read and discuss **Here's the Idea.** On the chalkboard list the three steps for planning a descriptive composition: choosing and narrowing a subject; making a list of sensory details and grouping them around a few main ideas; organizing the pre-writing notes into spatial order.

2. Discuss **Check It Out.** Ask students what senses are being appealed to in the pre-writing notes.

3. Assign **Try Your Skill.** Remind students who are having trouble to use the *who, what, where, when, how,* and *why* questioning technique to help them narrow the topic and think of supporting details.

4. Read **Keep This in Mind** and then assign **Now Write.**

Individualizing the Lesson

Less-Advanced Students

1. Do one topic from **Try Your Skill** with the class. Then let them do another topic with a partner.

2. Hold a brainstorming session to help students choose and narrow topics for **Now Write.** Have each student tell the class what topics he or she has been considering, and

Show and Tell

Pre-Writing: Using Sensory Details

Here's the Idea   Your senses of smell, hearing, taste, and touch tell you about the world around you. If you use your senses when you write a descriptive composition, your reader will experience through words what you have experienced in real life.

Begin planning your composition by choosing and narrowing a subject. First, select an interesting subject that you would enjoy describing in detail. Make certain you can describe your subject completely in the assigned length of your composition. The subject *Yosemite National Park* is too broad even for a composition. But you could describe a campground or a mountain that you explored in the park.

After you choose your topic, make a list of specific sensory details that describe your subject. Find details that appeal to as many senses as possible. Remember, a good description helps your reader to see, hear, smell, taste, or touch your subject. You can gather your details by observing your subject. You can also work from memory. You might find it helpful to look at a picture of your subject as you list your details.

Now organize your sensory details. First, group your details around a few main ideas. For example, if you are describing a person, you might group your details around looks, clothing, and mannerisms. As your idea groups develop, add other details that occur to you. Each of these idea groups will become a paragraph in your composition.

Next, arrange your main ideas and the details grouped around them in a logical order. The best method for organizing the details in a description is spatial order. Arrange your ideas and details in the order that you want your reader to notice them.

Check It Out   Look at these pre-writing notes.

Topic   The Delicatessen at Saveway Supermarket

red and green striped canopy—colorful display of
   tempting foods—aroma makes my mouth water

center and left side of display case
   roast beef and hams—spicy sausage smell
   cheese (far left)—mild and sharp

right side of display case
   vegetable and macaroni salads (bottom row)
   fruit, gelatin salads (middle row)—like a rainbow
   desserts—pies, puddings, cheesecakes (top row)

shelf above display case
   pickle jars (far right)—smell of garlic
   Greek olives, clams and egg rolls (middle)
   meat slicer (far left)—humming sound

- Notice how spatial order was used to organize details.

Try Your Skill   Choose one of the following topics. Narrow the topic to a *specific* person, place, or thing. Then make a list of interesting sensory details. Group your details around a few main ideas, arranged in spatial order.

a large machine   an unusual animal   an exciting place

Keep This in Mind

- Use sensory details to develop your description.
- Group your details around a few main ideas.
- Use spatial order to organize ideas and details.

Now Write   First, choose and narrow a topic for a descriptive composition. Then, make a list of sensory details to develop your description. Group these details around several main ideas. Organize your notes in spatial order. Save your notes.

have the others ask questions to help the student recall the details that are needed.

Advanced Students

Have students make a list of sensory details that they might see, hear, feel, or smell while looking from the window of an airplane as they land at an airport, and a list of sensory details they might see, hear, feel, or smell while at an airport watching a plane land.

Optional Practice

Have students collect and study travel folders and travel advertisements. Then have each student select a favorite place and prepare to write a brochure describing the city or tourist attraction of their choice. Instruct students to do all of the pre-writing activities for a descriptive composition: narrowing their topic, making a list of sensory details, grouping details around a few main ideas, etc.

Extending the Lesson

Set up a still-life exhibit in the classroom that includes objects to be touched, smelled, tasted, heard, and seen. Have each student examine the exhibit and take notes on the sensory details he or she finds. Compare their notes to the actual exhibit.

Objectives

1. To know the purpose of the introduction, body, and conclusion of a descriptive composition

2. To use transitions between sentences and paragraphs to make spatial order clear

Presenting the Lesson

1. Read and discuss **Here's the Idea.** Write *spatial order* on the board and have students give you its definition. Then ask students for more examples of transitional words and phrases that help make spatial order clear.

2. Read and discuss **Check It Out.** Compare these two paragraphs to the pre-writing notes on page 195. Point out that the more detailed the pre-writing notes are, the clearer and more interesting the paragraph will be.

3. Assign **Try Your Skill.** Have volunteers read their paragraphs aloud to the class.

4. Read **Keep This in Mind.**

5. Assign **Now Write.**

Individualizing the Lesson

Less-Advanced Students

1. Have students do **Try Your Skill** with a partner.

2. Take time to check the development of these students' writing at several stages after they have chosen subjects for **Now Write.** Make sure their sensory details are complete and well organized. Always offer encouragement as well as critical evaluation.

196

Paint a Picture

Writing the First Draft

Here's the Idea   After you have gathered and organized your sensory details, you are ready to write your first draft. Remember, writing is an ongoing process. You can change your pre-writing plans whenever you need to.

Begin your descriptive composition with an **introduction.** Keep in mind that the introduction in a descriptive composition is like the topic sentence of a descriptive paragraph. The introduction presents the person, place, or thing you are describing. Often, the introduction will also describe the setting.

The **body** of the composition describes your subject. It includes the sensory details you collected. Each paragraph develops one of the idea groups from your organized pre-writing notes.

The **conclusion** is the last paragraph of your descriptive composition. It draws your ideas together and brings the composition to a close.

To lead your reader smoothly from sentence to sentence and from paragraph to paragraph, use transitional words and phrases. Words and phrases such as *on the bottom, around, through, to the left, to the right,* and *next to* help to make the order of your details clear.

Check It Out   Here are the introduction and first body paragraph from the description of the delicatessen.

When it is my turn to plan and prepare a family supper, I head for the delicatessen at the rear of Saveway Supermarket. A red-and-green-striped canopy marks the deli counter. Below the canopy is a long display case. Behind its shiny glass, spread out temptingly, lay the wonders of the deli world. The combined aromas of the wide variety of foods make my mouth water.

196

Filling center stage are the meats and cheeses. There is a huge slab of nearly-rare roast beef and several large pink, glazed hams. To the left of these are strings of fragrant sausage and speckled salamis. Beside these meats are blocks of cheese, from mild-flavored Gouda to pungent Limburger.

- Does the introduction describe the setting?
- Point out the sensory details. Which senses are included?
- What transitional words and phrases has the writer used to make the order of the details clear?

Try Your Skill Write the second and third paragraphs for the body of the description of the delicatessen. Use the pre-writing notes on page 195. You may add to them. Be sure your paragraph has a good topic sentence and strong sensory details. Use transitional words and phrases to make the order of your details clear. Share your paragraphs with your class.

Keep This in Mind

- The introduction of a descriptive composition presents the person, place or thing described.
- The body describes the subject. Each paragraph in the body has its own topic sentence and is developed with sensory details.
- The conclusion sums up the description.
- Use transitions between sentences and paragraphs to make spatial order clear.

Now Write Review the pre-writing notes for the description you planned in the last lesson. Use the sensory details that you gathered and organized to write a first draft of your descriptive composition. Write the introduction and the body. Include good transitions as you write. Save your first draft.

197

See It Through

The First Draft: Ending a Description

To write a conclusion that summarizes the main ideas in a description

Presenting the Lesson

1. Read and discuss **Here's the Idea.** Stress that a conclusion should not suddenly change the mood developed in the composition's introduction and body.

2. Read and discuss **Check It Out.** If necessary, review the paragraphs in the text and those the students have written about the delicatessen before reading **Check It Out.**

3. Assign **Try Your Skill.**

4. Read **Keep This in Mind** and then assign **Now Write.** Have students go over the topic sentences of the paragraphs they have already written to help them remember the main ideas in their composition.

Individualizing the Lesson

Less-Advanced Students

1. Have students first list the main ideas from the descriptive composition before they begin to write the conclusion in **Try Your Skill.**

2. Have students work with a partner to do **Try Your Skill.**

Advanced Students

Duplicate descriptive compositions from your files. Analyze the conclusions. Have students identify key ideas in the composition that are repeated in the conclusions.

Here's the Idea A well-written composition needs a strong ending paragraph. This paragraph should sum up the important ideas in the composition.

To write a strong ending, first look back at the topic sentence of each paragraph you have written. Identify the main idea in each sentence. Think about these main ideas as you summarize your description. However, remember that a conclusion should not just repeat what you have already said. Try to express your ideas in a slightly different way.

As you plan your ending paragraph, keep in mind that a good description is not just a list of sensory details. It also should leave your reader with a general feeling or impression about the subject. Is the place you are describing busy and confusing? Is the person kind and sympathetic? Is the object sleek and expensive? In your conclusion, share these feelings and impressions with your reader. They will help you to explain why you found your subject interesting and important.

A good conclusion follows naturally from what has come before it. If you have praised an object throughout your description, don't criticize it in your conclusion. If you have created a feeling of suspense, end on a note of mystery.

Check It Out Here is the topic sentence of the conclusion of the paragraph about the delicatessen.

> As I wait for my order, my eyes feast on the banquet under glass.

- Does the topic sentence of the conclusion tell you that this paragraph will summarize the main ideas of the composition?

Try Your Skill   Reread the descriptive composition about the delicatessen, including the two paragraphs that you wrote. Write an ending paragraph for this composition. Be sure your ending sums up the important ideas in the description. Give the reader your feelings and impressions about the deli. Remember that an ending paragraph should follow naturally from what has come before. Save your conclusion in your folder.

Keep This in Mind

· In your conclusion, summarize the main ideas in your description.
· Include your feelings about and impressions of the subject.
· Your conclusion should follow naturally from what has come before.

Now Write   Write a conclusion for the composition that you have been writing. Summarize the main ideas in your description. Share with the reader your feelings and impressions about the subject. Save your work in your folder.

Optional Practice

Have students read the following body paragraphs from a descriptive composition about a summer evening. Ask them to identify the sensory details that make these paragraphs come to life.

We finish dinner and walk out onto the old porch. It smells musty, as if the recent rain were still caught in its cracked door sills and cobwebs. My father sits in the wicker rocking chair which creaks every time he shifts his weight.

The fireflies are out. My little sister tries to catch one. She pants and puffs after them, but they are always faster than she. Soon the moon rises above the shadows of the trees and the crickets begin their evening symphony.

Extending the Lesson

Tell students that it is important to be a good observer in order to write good descriptions. Have them take a notebook and pencil to a public place where they won't be noticed: a cafeteria, subway station, public library, etc. Tell them to observe one person and take notes on his or her appearance, dress, movements, and speech. Have them save their notes in their journals for later use.

Part 4

The Final Picture

Objective

To know and use the guidelines for revising a descriptive composition

Presenting the Lesson

1. Read and discuss **Here's the Idea.** Have students list the questions for revision in their notebooks to use when they revise their first drafts. Ask them if they can think of anything else to look for when they revise (strong verbs and adjectives, clear and specific details, etc.).

2. Read and discuss **Check It Out.** Ask students if they would have changed anything else in the paragraph and why. Explain that there are many ways to revise the same paragraph.

3. Read and assign **Try Your Skill.**

4. Read **Keep This in Mind** aloud.

5. Read and assign **Now Write.**

Individualizing the Lesson

Less-Advanced Students

Do **Try Your Skill** with students as a class exercise. Use any mistakes that they do not see or understand as the basis for review lessons.

Advanced Students

Have students revise the following sentences to create a more vivid word picture. Remind them to also correct any errors in grammar, capitalization, punctuation, and spelling.

Revising Your Descriptive Composition

Here's the Idea   When you revise your descriptive composition, your goal is to create a vivid word picture There should be enough sensory details to bring your subject to life.

As you reread your first draft, ask yourself these questions.

1. Have I included good sensory details?
2. Are the details arranged in clear spatial order?
3. Have I used transitional words and phrases between and within paragraphs to make the order of my details clear?
4. Does the introduction present the subject of my composition? Will it make the reader want to continue?
5. Does each paragraph have a good topic sentence?
6. Does my conclusion summarize the main ideas in my composition? Does it show how I feel about my subject?

When you are pleased with your ideas and organization, proofread your composition. Correct any errors in grammar, capitalization, punctuation, and spelling.

Check It Out   Here is a paragraph from a descriptive composition. Note the changes the writer made.

> The gymnast stood ~~ready. He waited~~ *at attention,* for the signal. His hands *ing a from the judges.* *covered in chalk,* hung loosely at his sides. ~~His uniform was white.~~ *and* His feet pointed straight ahead. ~~He stood at attention.~~ His arms and neck were *thick and* muscular. ~~He must have worked out with weights.~~ He smiled but he looked nervous. *Suddenly,* A buzzer went off. *loud* *shattered the silence.*

- In what ways has the writer revised this paragraph? How have these changes improved the paragraph?

Try Your Skill   Below is more of the first draft of the descriptive composition about a gymnast. Continue to revise the composition, following the guidelines in this lesson.

The gymnast got on the trampoline. He jumped up and down he bounced higher and higher. He almost touched the cieling. He did flips, somersaults. He didn't look nervous anymore.

His routine was over. He jumped off the trampoline, he looked over at the judges. His score was posted. It was 9.6. The gymnast smiled and walked to the bench.

Keep This in Mind

- Revise your description to help your reader share your experience. Include details that allow your reader to see, hear, touch, taste, and smell what you did.
- Use spatial order to organize your details. Add transitional words and phrases to make the order of the details clear.
- Be sure your introduction catches your reader's interest. It should also introduce the subject of your composition.
- Write a conclusion that sums up your ideas and leaves your reader with a definite feeling or impression about your subject.

Now Write   Use the guidelines in this lesson to revise the first draft of your descriptive composition. When you have completed your revisions, make a final copy. Proofread your composition one last time. Correct any errors neatly. Save your completed composition in your folder.

Answers will vary.

1. The small bird hoped (hopped) on the evergreen branch. And knocked down snow and ice to the ground.
2. The Sun (s) touched the window, and reflected the heat into the room.
3. The smell of the backing (baking) Apples (a) and cinnamon made my mouth water.
4. the (I) attik (attic) dust rised (rose) up and made me sneeze and my eyes tear.
5. The Spring (s) rain made the air, seem clean and fresh. Again.

Optional Practice

Set up peer-editing groups. Make sure that students follow the guidelines for revision in this section as their model for editing. Be sure to make yourself available to help resolve any problems that might arise.

Extending the Lesson

Appoint a student committee to put together booklets made up of the students' revised descriptive compositions. They can design covers and illustrations, duplicate and collate the publications, and distribute them to classmates.

Section **17** Objectives

1. To know how to plan an explanation

2. To organize an explanation in a step-by-step order

3. To use transitions that show time order within and between paragraphs in an explanation

4. To learn to revise the ideas, organization, and word choice in an explanatory composition telling *how*

Preparing the Students

Refer the students back to the paragraphs they wrote for Section 11, the explanatory paragraphs telling *how*. Point out that an explanatory paragraph telling *how* differs from an explanatory composition telling *how* only in length. Emphasize that explanatory compositions are written for subjects that are too complex to be covered in a single paragraph. Explain that this section will teach the skills for writing the explanatory composition telling *how*.

Additional Resources

Practice Book — pages 83–86
Duplicating Masters — pages 83–86

The Explanatory Composition

Telling *How*

Teaching Special Populations

LD See **Teaching Special Populations,** page 75.

ESL Work with students to produce a comprehensive list of transitional words and phrases related to temporal order. (Some examples can be found in the lists on pages 112 and 208.) To make certain students understand the contextual meaning of these items, have them use the words in sentences. Also, arrange for a student to perform a simple action (such as watering a house plant and placing it on a windowsill), then have ESL students describe the action using as many accurate transitional words and phrases as possible. Emphasize to students that transitions have two important functions: they indicate temporal order, and they help readers get from one idea to the next or from one paragraph to the next.

NSD See **Teaching Special Populations,** page 75.

Part 1

Objective

To know how to plan an explanation

Presenting the Lesson

Read aloud and discuss **Here's the Idea.** On the chalkboard, write the steps involved in planning an explanation. (1) Choose a topic. (2) Make sure the topic is not too broad nor too limited for a composition. (3) Make pre-writing notes listing all the steps in the process and any materials, tools, or ingredients needed.

2. Read and discuss **Check It Out.** Ask students if the topic is too broad or too limited for a composition, and why.

3. Assign **Try Your Skill.** It is suggested that this exercise be done as a class discussion.

4. Read **Keep This in Mind.**

5. Assign **Now Write.** Discuss possible topics and their suitability for a composition of this length before the students begin **Now Write.**

Individualizing the Lesson

Less-Advanced Students

Do one of the **Try Your Skill** topics with students and then have them do one with a partner. Go over their pre-writing notes in class to make sure that all steps and materials are included.

Advanced Students

Have students choose two topics for **Try Your Skill.**

Talent Show

Pre-Writing: Planning an Explanation

Here's the Idea   What is your special talent? Do you make the best chocolate-chip cookies in town? Do your friends ask you to show them the latest dance step? Do people seek your help in repairing their stereos or ten-speed bikes?

One way to share your talent or to show your knowledge is by writing an explanatory *how* composition. In this kind of composition, the writer tells the reader how to do something or how something happens or works. In other words, an explanatory *how* composition explains a process.

To write an explanatory *how* composition, you must first select a topic. The process you explain should be one that interests you. Is your hobby computers? You might explain how to design a simple computer game. Do you play baseball? You might write about how to steal second base.

Make sure that your topic can be explained well in the assigned length of your composition. For instance, the subject "how to play football" is too broad. However, a topic limited to a single football skill, such as "the way to make a tackle" is specific. It could be explained well in several paragraphs.

The pre-writing notes you develop for your topic should list all the steps in the process. The list should also include any materials, tools, or ingredients required. Take the time to think carefully about the process you are going to explain. Don't overlook any steps. Write each step simply and clearly.

Check It Out   Read these pre-writing notes.

How To Make a Mobile

1. Collect materials.
   wire, cardboard, tape, paper clips, string, pliers, scissors, wire clippers

2. Prepare mobile.
    cut wire, form loops, and bend wire
    cut cardboard, attach to wire
    find point of balance, bend with pliers
    repeat the process
3. Hang mobile.
    put two sections together—hang mobile from ceiling

· · Do these notes list all the necessary steps in the process? Do the notes include materials needed?

Try Your Skill   Choose one of the following topics for an explanatory *how* composition. Decide how you would develop an explanation. Make a set of pre-writing notes. List the steps in the process. Be sure to include any necessary materials.

how to make brownies	how to wrap a present
how hail is formed	how a jet engine works
how to take good notes	how to make new friends

> ### Keep This in Mind
>
> · An explanatory *how* composition explains a process. It may explain how to do something or how something happens or works.
> · To develop the details for your pre-writing notes, list the steps in the process. Also list any materials, tools, or ingredients required.
> · State each step clearly and simply.

Now Write   Think about some processes that you know well and that you would like to explain. Then, choose a topic for your explanatory *how* composition. Narrow your topic so that it can be explained well in the assigned length of your composition. Make a list of pre-writing details. These will include all the important steps in the process and all the necessary materials. Save your pre-writing notes in your folder.

205

Optional Practice

Have students follow the instructions for **Try Your Skill** for one of the following topics.

   how to make a map
   how to do aerobic dancing
   how to take a photograph
   how to make bread

Extending the Lesson

Find several *how to* articles in magazines or newspapers. Duplicate and distribute copies of the articles to the students. Discuss each example. Ask students to find the topic sentence. Have them list the steps in each process.

Objective

To organize an explanation in a step-by-step order

Presenting the Lesson

1. Read aloud and discuss **Here's the Idea.** Point out that clarity is one of the most important qualities of a composition telling *how* and that it is achieved by organizing the steps telling *how* in the order they are to be done (step-by-step order).

2. Read and discuss **Check It Out.** List the steps on the board as the students answer the questions.

3. Assign **Try Your Skill.** Remind students that not all details are included in this list.

4. Read **Keep This in Mind** and assign **Now Write.** Tell students to read their notes aloud to help find steps that might have been left out.

Individualizing the Lesson

Less-Advanced Students

1. Do **Try Your Skill** as a class exercise. Write the steps on the board as the students correct them. Point out where steps might be confused in order, or where steps might be left out.

2. Go over the students' pre-writing notes for **Now Write** to make sure they are organized correctly and that all the steps are included.

Advanced Students

Have students make pre-writing notes for a composition on how something happens if their **Now**

Follow Me

Pre-Writing: Using Step-by-Step Order

Here's the Idea   Do you know how many steps it takes to program a robot to make toast with jelly? About forty steps are required to direct the robot just to find the jelly and the bread! If a step is missing or in the wrong order, the robot will just stop, and you'll never get your toast.

People, of course, are smarter than robots. However, people still get confused by explanations that are incomplete or jumbled. That is why it is important for you to organize the details in your explanatory *how* composition. You must arrange the steps of the process you are explaining in the order they happen or should be performed. This is called **step-by-step order.**

The first step in organizing your pre-writing notes is to find the two or three most important steps in the process you are explaining. Then group the rest of your pre-writing notes around the major step they help to explain. Each of these idea groups will become a paragraph in your composition. When you have grouped all of your pre-writing notes, arrange the group and the details within them into step-by-step order.

Check It Out   Read the body of the explanatory *how* composition about making a mobile.

> To make a mobile you need wire, cardboard, Scotch tape, paper clips, string, pliers, scissors, and wire clippers. For the wire, you can straighten two coat hangers and cut them with clippers. The cardboard from a plain box will do. If you can find a brightly colored cardboard box, all the better.
>
> To begin, cut an eighteen-inch length of wire. Then form little loops at each end of the wire. Use the pliers to do this. Next,

bend the wire into a graceful arc. Now cut out two shapes about the same size from the cardboard. Firmly tape a paper clip to the center of each shape. Then place the loops of wire through these clips. To find the place on the wire at which the cardboard shapes will balance, tie a string around the wire and move it until the point of balance is found. Form a third loop in the wire at this point, using the pliers. Repeat the entire process with another eighteen-inch wire and two cardboard shapes.

When you have made a loop at the point of balance in the second wire, tie a string to this loop and attach the string to the third loop in the first wire. Then hang the completed mobile from the ceiling. If your mobile doesn't swing in the air currents of your room, you must have missed the point of balance of one of the wires. Try again.

- What steps are explained in the body of this composition?
- Are the steps presented in the right order?

Try Your Skill Here are some jumbled notes for the body of a composition about making lemonade. List the steps below in the correct step-by-step order. Add any other details that seem necessary to you. Keep your work in your folder.

Add sugar. Pour lemon juice into pitcher.
Squeeze three lemons. Fill pitcher two-thirds full with water.
Stir vigorously. Add ice and allow to chill.

> **Keep This in Mind**
> - Use step-by-step order to organize the details of an explanatory *how* composition.

Now Write Look at the pre-writing notes you made in the last section, **Talent Show.** Use step-by-step order to organize your notes. Check them carefully. Add any steps that you may have left out. Save your organized notes in your folder.

Optional Practice

Have students write pre-writing notes for one of the following topics. Then have them mix up the order of the steps and exchange papers with a partner. Have them follow the directions for **Try Your Skill,** making sure they also add any other details that seem to be missing.

how to make a bed
how a tadpole becomes a frog
how to plant a garden
how to study for a test

Extending the Lesson

Instruct students to select one of the following topics and list the steps in the process in step-by-step order.

how to make a pizza	how to trim a Christmas tree
how to wash a car	how to plan a party
how to set a table	how to change a tire

Part 3

Objective

To use transitions that show time order within and between paragraphs in an explanation

Presenting the Lesson

1. Read and discuss **Here's the Idea.** Refer to page 134 to review transitions frequently used in paragraphs and compositions telling *how*.

2. Discuss **Check It Out.** Ask students what other transitions they would have used in these paragraphs.

3. Assign **Try Your Skill.** It is suggested that this exercise be done orally with the class.

4. Read **Keep This in Mind** and then assign **Now Write.**

Individualizng the Lesson

Less-Advanced Students

Guide students through the steps of writing the first draft in **Now Write.** Point out to them that the instructions in **Now Write** are in a step-by-step order.

Advanced Students

Have students write a first draft based on their pre-writing notes from the **Advanced Students** exercise in Part 2. Discuss these drafts in class.

Optional Practice

Duplicate copies of a well-written composition telling *how*. Ask students to underline the transitions

Marking Time

Writing the First Draft

Here's the Idea   Early American explorers marked their trails in a forest by making notches on tree trunks with a hatchet. The notches were a guide for those who followed so they would not get lost. As you write your first draft, remember that you are leading your reader from the beginning to the end of a process. To insure that the reader does not get lost, you have to provide clear transitions. These transitions are like the explorers' notches on the trees. They help to guide your reader through the steps of the process you are explaining.

Transitions can help make clear the order of details within a paragraph. Transitions can also help to link the ideas in one paragraph with those in another.

The transitions used in an explanatory *how* composition should show the natural time order of the process. They should tell the reader *when* to do something or *when* something happens. Transitions words like *first, then, next,* and *finally* are helpful. Transitional phrases such as *to begin, after that, at the same time,* and *the last step* are also useful.

Check It Out   Here are the introduction and conclusion of the composition on making a mobile.

Introduction

A mobile is a special kind of room decoration with a spirit all its own. When properly balanced and hung from the ceiling, it will swing gently with the air currents of any room. A simple mobile is not hard to make, and you might like to try making one yourself.

Conclusion

As soon as your mobile is working properly, you may want to experiment with more complicated models. Instead of using cardboard, you might use Christmas tree ornaments. You might also make your own special figures. You could add a third or fourth section to your mobile. Once you have mastered the art of balancing, your mobile can become as exciting as your imagination.

- What transitions are used within the introduction? within the conclusion?

Try Your Skill   List the transitions used in the body of the composition on mobiles, pages 206–207. Which are used to link ideas within paragraphs? Which are used to link one paragraph to another?

Keep This in Mind

- In an explanatory *how* composition, use transitions to guide your readers through step-by-step order.
- Use transitional words and phrases to link ideas within paragraphs and between paragraphs.

Now Write   Use your organized pre-writing notes to write the first draft of your explanatory *how* composition.

In the introduction, present your topic in a way that will capture your reader's attention.

In the body, give your step-by-step explanation of the process. Don't leave out any steps. Write each step simply and clearly.

In the conclusion, develop the final step of the process.

Use transitions to help your reader move smoothly through the process you are exploring.

Save your first draft in your folder.

used within paragraphs and to circle those used between paragraphs.

Extending the Lesson

Consider having students make up a booklet of explanatory *how* compositions for other classes in the school. First have them choose school-related topics that they think other students would want to know about (how to study for a test, how class scheduling is done, how the school building is heated or cooled, etc.). Assign topics to students, have them make pre-writing notes, organize those notes, write a first draft, and revise it.

209

Part 4

Getting It Right

Revising Your Explanation

Objective

To learn to revise the ideas, organization, and word choice in an explanatory composition telling *how*

Presenting the Lesson

1. Read and discuss **Here's the Idea.** Write each question on the board as you discuss it with the class.

2. Read and discuss **Check It Out.** Carefully go over the changes that were made in the revision of the first draft. Point out that most of the revision had to do with adding transitions and making details more specific.

3. Assign **Try Your Skill.** Have the students write the steps explaining how a pearl is formed to see if anything has been left out or is unnecessary.

4. Read **Keep This in Mind** and then assign **Now Write.**

Individualizing the Lesson

Less-Advanced Students

Have students work in groups to revise the paragraph in **Try Your Skill.**

Advanced Students

Have students revise the composition they have been working on in the **Advanced Students** exercise from Part 3.

Optional Practice

Have students choose an unusual food from another country and write

Here's the Idea Your goal in writing an explanatory *how* composition is to explain a process simply and clearly. You want your reader to be able to successfully follow or understand the process you are explaining. To accomplish your goal, you need to revise your composition so that it is clear, complete, and correct.

Read over your first draft carefully. Ask yourself the following questions.

1. Does the introduction present my topic and capture the reader's interest?

2. Does each paragraph in the body of my composition have an informative topic sentence.

3. Have I included all of the important steps in the process I am explaining?

4. Have I arranged my details in step-by-step order?

5. Have I explained each step simply and clearly?

6. Have I used transitional words and phrases within paragraphs and between paragraphs? Do these transitions lead the reader smoothly from one step to another?

7. Does my conclusion either summarize the process or explain the final step in the process?

When you are sure your explanation is as clear, complete, and correct as it can be, proofread it. Correct any errors in grammar and mechanics.

Check It Out Here is the first draft of the first body paragraph from the composition about mobiles. After reading it, reread the final version of the same paragraph, on page 206.

You need wire, cardboard, scotch tape, paper clips, string, pliers. Straighten two coat hangers. Get cardboard from a plain box. Or a colored box. Cut it into shapes.

- What specific details were added to the final copy?
- What corrections were made during proofreading?

Try Your Skill   Revise this paragraph from an explanatory *how* composition. Refer to the guidelines for revision in this lesson. Remember to proofread the paragraph.

Pearls are formed in oysters. And in other shellfish. A grain of sand gets inside. The grain of sand is covered with nacre. Which is a pearly substance. My sister has a pearl ring. This happens very slowly. A pearl is their in too or three years. Then you can get the pearl out and if its shiny it could be valuable but if its dull its worthless.

Keep This in Mind

- Make sure your explanatory *how* composition is clear, complete, and easy to follow.
- Use step-by-step order to arrange your details.
- Use transitional words and phrases to make the order of your details clear.

Now Write   Use the guidelines in this lesson to revise your explanatory *how* composition. Try to make your explanation as clear as possible. Proofread your composition for errors in grammar and mechanics. When your composition is completely revised, make a final copy. Save your work.

a composition on how to prepare and serve that food.

Extending the Lesson

Working with the science or social studies teacher, decide on a subject that students can write an explanatory *how* composition about. When the papers are finished, grade them for the mechanics of writing and have the other teacher grade them for the accuracy of the information.

Section **18** Objectives

1. To learn to state an opinion clearly and directly

2. To gather reasons, facts, and examples to support an opinion

3. To present supporting reasons and facts in the order of their importance

4. To write an effective introduction, body, and conclusion for an explanatory *why* composition

5. To use transitions to state reasons or facts and to show the order of their importance

6. To revise an explanatory *why* composition

Preparing the Students

Provide these examples to see if students can distinguish facts from opinions.

Susan is a vegetarian.
Everyone should be a vegetarian.

The baseball season ends with the World Series.
The baseball season is too long.

Discuss the difference between facts and opinions. Explain that statements of fact can be proven true or false but that opinions cannot. Point out that an opinion is a belief; to have others accept that belief, the writer must state reasons or facts to support it. Explain that students will be learning how to support opinions effectively in this section.

Additional Resources

Practice Book — pages 87–90
Duplicating Masters — pages 87–90

The Explanatory Composition

Telling *Why*

Teaching Special Populations

LD See **Teaching Special Populations,** page 75.

ESL Those students who still appear hesitant about expressing their own opinions may be helped by class discussion of a topic. As practice, choose a sample topic appropriate to ESL students' background, and write an opinion about that topic on the chalkboard. Then start a class discussion aimed at generating facts in support of the opinion. List the supporting evidence on the chalkboard, and ask students to explain why particular details advance the case being presented.

Review important terms such as *order of importance, body,* and *conclusion,* as well as those transitional words and phrases commonly used in explanatory compositions. Make sure students understand that particular transitions usually occur in the introduction, while others (*as a result, in conclusion, finally,* and so on) tend to be used in the body or conclusion of a composition.

When students revise their final drafts, have them exchange papers with a partner and check each other's work.

NSD See **Teaching Special Populations,** page 75.

Objectives

1. To learn to state an opinion clearly and directly

2. To gather reasons, facts, and examples to support an opinion

Presenting the Lesson

1. Read aloud and discuss **Here's the Idea.** Point out that a *why* composition performs the same function as a *why* paragraph, but that it develops a topic more extensively. Have students discuss the ways to find facts, reasons, and examples.

2. Read and discuss **Check It Out.** Ask students where the author of these notes may have gotten his or her supporting details.

3. Assign **Try Your Skill.** Explain that writing a sentence that clearly and directly states an opinion helps the writer focus his or her ideas.

4. Read **Keep This in Mind.**

5. Assign **Now Write.** If students have trouble finding an opinion, have them do some brainstorming or look in their journals.

Individualizing the Lesson

Less-Advanced Students

Do **Try Your Skill** orally with the students. Help them make the sentences as clear and direct as possible.

Advanced Students

Have students analyze letters-to-the-editor, and editorials from newspapers and news magazines. Ask them to identify the topic of the article and the writer's opinion on the

214

Why, Oh Why?

Pre-Writing: Developing an Opinion

Here's the Idea   One of the most precious freedoms anyone can have is the right to free speech. The United States was founded with the idea that people have different opinions and they have the right to express them. Because you have this right, it is important for you to learn to use it well.

An explanatory *why* composition is one way for you to present an opinion. In this type of composition you explain clearly and directly why you believe something. You also offer reasons to support your belief.

To find a topic for your explanatory *why* composition, think about your own life. What issues do you feel strongly about? How do you feel about your school, your neighborhood, or your town? How do you feel about TV, the space program, industrial pollution, or the draft? Think about the world around you. It is important to choose a topic that has meaning for you.

Once you have selected a topic, write a clear sentence that expresses your opinion. When you write your first draft, this sentence can become the basis for your first paragraph.

Next, gather details to support your opinion. Although everyone has a right to his or her own opinion, opinions should have some evidence to back them up. It is important, therefore, to collect strong, specific facts, reasons, and examples to support your opinion. Make sure that your facts are accurate and your reasons clear and logical.

You may gather your details from direct experience. For instance, if you believe that Lake Crystal is polluted, you could go there and count the number of dead fish on the shore. You may also want to gather details from encyclopedias or other reference books at the library.

Check It Out Read these pre-writing notes for an explanatory *why* composition.

Opinion: The city should install a traffic light at the busy intersection of Third Avenue and Jackson Street.

Support: traffic light would bring order
60% of serious accidents not on highways
improve rush hour flow of traffic
traffic light would protect children
impossible to make left turn
police not always there to direct traffic
traffic light would prevent accidents
children sometimes run into street
accidents include serious injuries, even death
two children hit by cars in last month

- Is the opinion stated clearly and directly?
- Do these notes support the opinion well?

Try Your Skill Write one sentence about each of the following topics. The sentence should clearly and directly state your opinion on the subject.

violence on TV   a woman for President   salaries of doctors

Keep This in Mind

- An explanatory *why* composition presents an opinion.
- State your opinion clearly and directly.
- In your pre-writing notes, gather reasons, facts, and examples to support your opinion.

Now Write List several strong opinions that you have. Choose one that you would like to write about. State your opinion clearly in your pre-writing notes. List the reasons, facts, and examples you will use as support. Save your notes.

Saving the Best

Pre-Writing: Organizing Your Details

Objective

To present supporting reasons and facts in the order of their importance

Presenting the Lesson

1. Read aloud and discuss **Here's the Idea.** Emphasize that *order of importance* means "from the least important idea to most important." Also point out that each supporting idea will become a separate paragraph of the body of the composition.

2. Read and discuss **Check It Out.** Suggest that when it is difficult to decide on the most important idea, it is often helpful to think about which idea would be the most important or convincing to the reader.

3. Assign **Try Your Skill.** Ask volunteers to read their organized reasons or facts to the class.

4. Read **Keep This in Mind** and assign **Now Write.**

Individualizing the Lesson

Less-Advanced Students

Do one of the opinions from **Try Your Skill** with students and then have them do another opinion on their own.

Advanced Students

Explain to students that they must always consider their readers when they are writing an explanatory composition telling *why.* Because they are presenting an opinion, it is important to think about how the

Here's the Idea Have you ever heard someone say, "We're saving the best until last"? The *best* might refer to the best news, the best present, or the best entertainer.

In explaining an opinion, saving the best until last means that you arrange your details so that the most important reason is presented last. When you organize your notes from the least important idea to the most important, you are using **order of importance.**

Order of importance is a powerful way to organize your supporting ideas. It helps you to hold your reader's attention and interest. More important, your reader will be left with your most convincing reason clearly in mind.

Once you have gathered a list of supporting details for your opinion, look them over carefully. Try to identify two or three major ideas. Make these major ideas the main reasons that you use to explain your opinion. Group each of your remaining details around the main reason they help to explain. Each of these idea groups will become a paragraph of support for your opinion.

As a final step, look at your idea groups. Organize them in the order of their importance. Make sure that the best reason is mentioned last.

Check It Out Read these organized pre-writing notes.

1. traffic light would bring order
   –improve rush hour flow of traffic
   –impossible to make left turn
   –police not always there to direct traffic

2. traffic light would prevent accidents
   –60% of serious accidents not on highways
   –accidents include serious injuries, even death
3. traffic light would protect children
   –children sometimes run into street
   –two children hit by cars in last month

- Do you see how these details have been grouped around three main ideas?
- Do you see how each of these idea groups could become a paragraph in an explanatory *why* composition?
- Have these notes been arranged in the order of their importance? Explain your answer.

Try Your Skill   Review the opinions you stated in **Try Your Skill** in the last lesson. Choose one of them. List three specific reasons or facts to support that opinion. Then organize your evidence in order of importance, from the least important idea to the most important.

> **Keep This in Mind**
> - In an explanatory *why* composition, organize your details from the least important idea to the most important.

Now Write   Look at your pre-writing notes from the last lesson, **Why, Oh Why?** What are the main ideas that support your opinion? Write these down. Under them, list the facts and examples that further help to develop each reason. Organize these idea groups in the order of their importance. Save your organized pre-writing notes in your folder.

audience will react. Have students reread the editorials and letters-to-the-editor from the previous **Advanced Students** exercise and determine who the writer thought the audience was for his or her article and why.

Optional Practice

Have students choose one opinion from their journals and make some pre-writing notes about that opinion. Students should then organize their ideas in the order of their importance.

Extending the Lesson

Begin to produce an editorial booklet of student concerns. Discuss various issues in the school and the surrounding community. Ask students to choose an issue that they feel strongly about and to list and organize facts and reasons to support the opinion they want to express.

Part 3

It Stands to Reason

Writing the First Draft

Objectives

1. To write an effective introduction, body and conclusion for an explanatory *why* composition

2. To use transitions to state reasons or facts and to show the order of their importance

Presenting the Lesson

1. Read and discuss **Here's the Idea.** List the parts of the composition on the chalkboard, and then ask students what kind of information belongs in each part. Point out the two different kinds of transitions and their uses.

2. Read **Check It Out.** Ask students to find the transitional words and phrases in the paragraph.

3. Assign **Try Your Skill.** Ask the students how the transitions help to state the reason or show the order of its importance.

4. Read **Keep This in Mind.**

5. Assign **Now Write.**

Individualizing the Lesson

Less-Advanced Students

Go over each step in writing the first draft with students. Do not let them go ahead until they have completed each step successfully.

Advanced Students

Explain that debating is a form of expressing and supporting opinions. Have students browse through newspaper editorial pages and news magazines to find current, controversial topics. Have them discuss or debate these topics in small groups to clarify their opinions.

Here's the Idea   Your first draft gives you a chance to fit your ideas together in the form you will present to your reader. Keep in mind that each part of the explanatory *why* composition has a special role.

It is most important to state your opinion clearly in the **introduction.** Use the sentence from your pre-writing notes or write a slightly different version of that sentence.

In the **body** of your composition, you present the reasons that support your opinion. The idea groups that you organized in your pre-writing notes will become paragraphs in the body.

Make sure that you restate your opinion in the **conclusion.** Sum up your reasons in an effective way.

To link the points of your argument, you will need to use transitions. There are two kinds of transitional words and phrases that are useful in an explanatory *why* composition. One kind helps you to present your reasons in the order of their importance. This kind includes such words and phrases as *the first reason, second, most important,* and *finally.* You may want to use such transitions at the beginning of a new paragraph.

The second kind of transition helps you to state reasons. Some examples are *because, since, if,* and *as a result.*

Check It Out   Read this introduction and conclusion.

Introduction

Traffic is a problem in our neighborhood. It is a source of noise and pollution. Also, the heavy traffic is dangerous. The most serious danger exists at the busy intersection of Third Avenue and Jackson Street. We probably cannot have cars eliminated from this busy intersection. However, we need to make the neighborhood a safer place. Therefore, we should urge the city to install a traffic light at this intersection.

Conclusion

If a traffic light were installed at the intersection of Third Avenue and Jackson Street, drivers would be more cautious. As a result of drivers' caution, there would be fewer traffic jams, fewer accidents, and fewer injuries to children. If these traffic problems are eliminated, we will have a safer neighborhood.

· Does the introduction clearly state an opinion?
· Does the conclusion sum up the argument? How?

Try Your Skill   List the transitions in this paragraph.

The most important reason for putting a traffic light at the intersection is to protect children. The neighborhood around Third Avenue and Jackson Street is heavily populated. Because there is no room anywhere else, children play on the sidewalks. Sometimes they run out into the streets. As a result, two children were hit by cars in the past month.

Keep This in Mind

· In the introduction, state your opinion clearly.
· Use transitions to help state the reasons and to show the order of their importance.
· In the body, give reasons to support your opinion.
· In the conclusion, sum up your opinion.

Now Write   Using your pre-writing notes, write the first draft of your explanatory *why* composition. State your opinion in the introduction. Develop each major reason from your notes into a separate body paragraph. Use transitions to present your reasons and show their order of importance. Sum up your reasons and opinion in the conclusion. Save your first draft.

219

The Final Lap

Revising Your Explanatory *Why* Composition

Objective

To revise an explanatory *why* composition

Presenting the Lesson

1. Read and discuss **Here's the Idea.** Point out that the first two questions deal with the writer's concern for the reader. The other questions listed are concerned more with the ideas and organization of the composition.

2. Read and discuss **Check It Out.** Ask students to point out the reasons for each revision.

3. Assign **Try Your Skill.** If necessary, refer students back to the prewriting notes on pages 216–217, and the introduction and conclusion on pages 218–219.

4. Read **Keep This in Mind** aloud.

5. Assign **Now Write.**

Individualizing the Lesson

Less-Advanced Students

1. Do **Try Your Skill** orally with the students.

2. Have students exchange their **Now Write** compositions with a partner. Have students make suggestions for revision of their partner's paper.

Advanced Students

Have students write a "Letter to the Principal" giving their opinion about something they feel strongly about. They should follow the prewriting, first draft, and revision stages of the process of writing for their letters.

Here's the Idea   All good runners save a little energy for the final stretch of a race. They know they cannot let up until *after* the finish. They know it is important to end well.

The same thing is true in writing. You have put a lot of effort into the first two stages of writing. Do not "let up" during the final stage—revision. With careful revision, you will finish with a composition to be proud of.

As you read your first draft, ask these questions.

Will my reader be convinced that I have good reasons for holding my opinion?

How can I make my opinion even more convincing?

Here are some other questions to ask when revising.

1. Is my opinion stated clearly and directly in the introductory paragraph?

2. Have I given convincing reasons, facts, and examples?

3. Are my reasons clear and logical? Are my facts accurate?

4. Have I organized my reasons from the least important idea to the most important?

5. Have I used transitional words and phrases to show the order of my ideas?

6. Have I used transitions to state my argument clearly?

7. Have I summed up my opinion and reasons in my conclusion?

When you are satisfied that the explanation of your opinion is clearly organized, proofread your composition. Check for errors in grammar, capitalization, punctuation, and spelling.

Check It Out   Notice how this paragraph has been revised.

> *# More important,*
> A traffic light would help to *prevent* ~~stop~~ accidents. According to
> *Safety Commission* *serious traffic*
> ~~statistics~~, over 60% of all accidents ~~did~~ not happen on highways.
> *sixty percent*   *in the last year*
> They happened at intersections like Third and Jackson. These
> *city*   *even*
> accidents caused injuries and deaths. Most of the people injured
> *severe*
> were drivers and passengers. However ‸more than ‸1/4 of those   *one-fourth*
> *pedestrians.*
> hurt were ~~people on the street.~~

- How has this paragraph been improved?

Try Your Skill   Here is another first-draft paragraph. Use the guidelines in this lesson and your other revising skills to help you revise it.

A traffic light would bring order to the corner. The intersection is crowded during rush hour. Traffic gets backed up. Drivers get mad and blow there horns. You cant make a left turn. It gets good when the cops are there. To direct traffic. Lots of times their not there.

Keep This in Mind

- State your opinion clearly in your introduction.
- Present your reasons in order of importance.
- Use transitional words and phrases to highlight the order of your reasons and to present them clearly.
- Sum up your argument in your conclusion.

Now Write   Using the guidelines in this lesson, revise your explanatory *why* composition. When you have done the best job you can do, write your final copy. Proofread this copy one last time. Correct any errors you find. Save your composition.

221

Section 19 Objectives

1. To learn to define a word by giving its general class and specific characteristics

2. To learn how to develop a definition

3. To organize an explanatory *what* composition from the general to the specific

4. To include an introduction, body, and conclusion in the first draft

5. To revise the ideas, organization, and word choice in an explanatory *what* composition

Preparing the Students

Review the definition of the explanatory paragraph telling *what* (Section 13). Explain that the explanatory composition telling *what* gives a fuller definition than a paragraph can. The explanatory *what* composition builds on a general definition by adding supporting ideas. Tell students that this section will teach the skills needed to write an effective explanatory *what* composition.

Additional Resources

Practice Book — pages 91–94
Duplicating Masters — pages 91–94

The Explanatory Composition

Telling *What*

Teaching Special Populations

LD See **Teaching Special Populations,** page 75.

ESL Spend extra time going over the more difficult vocabulary and phrasing in **Check It Out** sections. Make sure students are successful in finding definitions in dictionaries or encyclopedias, and that they are able to incorporate this material into their own writing.

Encourage ESL students to choose topics that relate more directly to their own cultural experience. In the pre-writing stages, you may have to guide students in distinguishing between main ideas and subordinate details. After students have finished their first drafts, have them read their compositions to native English speakers.

NSD See **Teaching Special Populations,** page 75. Pay particular attention to students' revisions, making sure that they are not simply substituting more complicated nonstandard expressions for the original mistakes.

A Chance To Explain

Pre-Writing: Developing a Definition

Part **1**

Objectives

1. To learn to define a word by giving its general class and specific characteristics

2. To learn how to develop a definition

Presenting the Lesson

1. Read and discuss **Here's the Idea.** Point out that the *what* composition begins with a one-sentence definition. Explain that if that definition is complete, the rest of the composition can be easily organized around it. Make sure students understand the term *general class*.

2. Read and discuss **Check It Out.** Ask students whether these notes define a real thing, or an idea.

3. Assign **Try Your Skill.** Encourage students to think of animals other than dogs and cats. You may even want students to do some research on an exotic animal.

4. Read **Keep This in Mind** and then assign **Now Write.** Refer students to their journals for ideas on what to define.

Individualizing the Lesson

Less-Advanced Students

1. Do **Try Your Skill** with students. Encourage them to think of an interesting animal they might know about or want to find out about.

2. For **Now Write,** provide students with several topics that lend themselves to relatively simple definitions. Choose subjects that they would be both familiar and comfortable with.

Here's the Idea Defining things is a part of everyday life. Your teacher may ask you to define a *cloud*, or an *equation*. When you tell your friends about your vacation, they may ask you to define *para-sail, trolley car,* or *silo*. Your brother may ask the mechanic to define *crankshaft* or *idle*.

An explanatory *what* composition is a written definition of something. What is defined may be a real thing, such as a *space station* or a *tropical rain forest*. What is defined may also be an idea, such as *loyalty,* or a term, like *hypnotism*.

When you have decided on a thing, an idea, or a term to define, write a one sentence definition of it. This definition should do three things. First, it should give the name of the thing being defined. Second, it should place the thing being defined into a general class. Third, it should tell how the thing being defined is different from other members of its class. Here is an example of such a definition.

> A space station is a special kind of earth satellite where people live and work on scientific projects.

To gather the details you will use to expand your definition, take some time to think about your topic. If you are defining a real thing, you will want to use facts and figures to develop your definition. A dictionary or an encyclopedia can help you to find accurate information. An idea may be defined in a more personal way. You might use incidents or anecdotes from your own experience to develop this kind of definition. A term is usually defined with specific details. These may come from your own experience or from research.

As you think and read about your topic, write down all of the information you will need to develop your definition.

Check It Out Read these pre-writing notes.

Topic: Grandmother

Notes: "the mother of one's father or mother"
comforts Dad when he worries
tells me stories of when Dad was a boy
knew what to say when I broke my leg
come to all my basketball games
shares her time, gives a calm influence
tells stories of 1930's and 1940's
tells stories of Great-Uncle George
sews on my scout badges
knew what to do when Susan got burned
tells stories of great-grandfather
gives me a sense of history

- What is the writer going to define?
- Do these pre-writing notes come from research or from personal experience?
- Do these notes include information that will give a good definition of the topic? Explain your answer.

Try Your Skill Imagine that you are going to define an animal. Choose an animal you know about. Make pre-writing notes for an explanatory *what* composition.

Keep This in Mind

- An explanatory *what* composition defines a real thing, an idea, or a term.
- Use facts and figures, personal experiences, or specific details to develop your definition.

Now Write Choose a topic for an explanatory *what* composition. You may define a real thing, an idea, or a term. First, write a short definition. Then list pre-writing notes that expand that definition. Save your pre-writing notes.

225

Objective

To organize an explanatory *what* composition from the general to the specific

Presenting the Lesson

1. Read and discuss **Here's the Idea.** Explain that as the definition goes from general to specific, it may use details that further explain why the subject being defined is special, or it may identify the subject's various parts, types, or uses. All of these details make the definition more exact.

2. Read and discuss **Check It Out.** Point out to the students how these notes become more specific through the use of details.

3. Assign **Try Your Skill.** Have students do this exercise in groups in class.

4. Read **Keep This in Mind** and assign **Now Write.**

Individualizing the Lesson

Less-Advanced Students

Do **Try Your Skill** with the students in class. Write the main ideas on the board and then underline the words in the main idea that will be repeated or explained in the details.

Advanced Students

Have students go through their social studies and science texts to find examples of definitions. Discuss how these definitions are organized.

Exactly So

Pre-Writing: Organizing a Definition

Here's the Idea If someone asked you to explain what a space station is, you would probably start out with a very general statement. You might say, "A space station is a place in outer space where astronauts can stay and do scientific experiments." That's actually a pretty good definition. However, if you gave the subject more thought, you could probably say much more about what a space station is. You would add all sorts of specific details that would expand and develop your general statement. In other words, your definition of a space station would go from the **general to the specific.**

Your explanatory *what* composition should be organized in the same way. The introductory paragraph should present a general definition of your topic. The rest of the paragraphs should add specific details to make the definition more exact.

You can start organizing your pre-writing notes by looking them over carefully. Try to find several main ideas that help to define your subject. Then group your remaining details around these main ideas. Each of these idea groups will become a paragraph in your composition.

Check It Out Here are the pre-writing notes for the explanatory composition defining *grandmother.* Notice how they have been organized.

Topic: Grandmother

Gives a Sense of History
   stories of when Dad was a boy
   stories of 1930's and 1940's
   stories of great-grandfather
   stories of Great-Uncle George

Shares Her Time
    comes to all my basketball games
    sews on my scout badges

Provides a Calming Influence
    comforts Dad when he worries about paying the bills
    knows what to do in an emergency (when Susan got burned)
    knew what to say when I was upset about breaking my leg

- What three main ideas have these pre-writing notes been grouped around?
- Do you see how each of these main ideas could become a paragraph in a composition?

Try Your Skill   These pre-writing notes about a space station contain three main ideas. Find them, and group the remaining details around them.

1 space station provides living quarters
   can study the earth, moon, sun, stars 2A
2 space station can be a laboratory
   enough food, oxygen, water for weeks/months 1A
3 space station can be launch base for interplanetary flights
   check laws of nature and test scientific theories 2B
   size of crew limited to size of station 1B
   flights to Venus/Mars might refuel there 3A
   entire families could stay 1C
   send robot probes into deep space 3B

> **Keep This in Mind**
>
> - Organize an explanatory *what* composition from the general to the specific.
> - Group pre-writing notes around two or three main ideas.

Now Write   Look at your pre-writing notes. Find two or three main ideas that define your topic. Group the rest of your details around these main ideas. Save your notes.

Optional Practice

Have students organize the notes they wrote for the **Optional Practice** in Part 1.

Extending the Lesson

Have the class start a list of things or ideas that they would like to know more about; these topics can come from their in-class assignments, from television or radio shows, or from outside reading. At different times during the semester assign these topics to students to report on. The reports should be in the form of an explanatory composition telling *what*.

Which Way Is Best?

Objective

To include an introduction, body, and conclusion in the first draft of a composition that defines

Presenting the Lesson

1. Read and discuss **Here's the Idea.** On the chalkboard write the three parts of the composition and then write what each part should include in an explanatory *what* composition.

2. Read **Check It Out** aloud. Compare the composition with the prewriting notes on pages 226–227. Ask what new details the writer has added.

3. Assign **Try Your Skill.** Write on the board the three things a definition must include.

4. Read **Keep This in Mind.**

5. Assign **Now Write.**

Individualizing the Lesson

Less-Advanced Students

Do one of the definitions for **Try Your Skill** in class with the students. Then have students do a definition on their own.

Advanced Students

Have students write definitions for all the topics in **Try Your Skill.**

Optional Practice

Have students write a one-sentence definition for two of the following topics.

pioneer	circus	weather
planet	camera	freedom

Writing the First Draft

Here's the Idea   When you have organized your notes, begin the first draft of your composition. Remember that your definition should move from the general to the specific.

The **introduction** should include a sentence that gives a clear, general definition of your subject. This definition serves as a starting point for the entire composition.

The **body** should develop the main ideas that define your subject. Each paragraph should explain a different main idea.

The **conclusion** sums up the main ideas. Try to express your ideas in a slightly different way in the conclusion.

Check It Out   Read this explanatory *what* composition.

Have you ever looked up a word in the dictionary and thought, "Technically, that's right, but it doesn't really cover *my* experience"? The dictionary defines *grandmother* as "the mother of one's father or mother." To me a grandmother is this and much more. My grandmother is someone who gives me a sense of history, who shares her time, and who provides calm support.

Talking with my grandmother gives me a personal feeling for history and a sense of my family roots. She tells me what life was like when Dad was young, and what life was like for her during the Great Depression and the second World War. Grandmother is also my link to family history. She remembers her own grandfather, who came from Ireland and worked in the Wisconsin lumber mills. Great-Uncle George becomes more to me than just a photograph in an album.

Not only does Grandmother give me a sense of past times, she also shares her present time. Grandmother is often busy with her computer class and working part-time at the bank. Yet she still finds the time to attend my home basketball games. She also finds the time to sew on the merit badges on my Scout uniform.

Finally, *grandmother* also means a calming influence in troubled times. When Dad wonders how he will pay all of the bills, Grandmother reminds him of how the family managed when Grandpa lost his job. When my cousin Susan was burned, Grandmother gave Susan first aid. When I broke my leg and worried that I would never play ball again, Grandmother knew how to make me feel better.

Grandmother is my father's mother, but that is only the beginning. She is a family historian, a counselor, and a special friend. She is a part of my past, my present, and my future.

- Does the introduction contain a general definition?
- Does the body expand the definition with details?
- Does the conclusion sum up the ideas in the composition? How?

Try Your Skill   Practice writing the kind of one-sentence definition you must include in the first paragraph of your explanatory *what* composition. Write a one-sentence definition for two of the following topics.

dance   diesel   bicycle   winning   credit card

Keep This in Mind

- In an explanatory *what* composition, include a clear, general, one-sentence definition of your subject in the introduction.
- Develop the body with specific details that expand the definition.
- Summarize your definition in the conclusion.

Now Write   Use your pre-writing notes to write a first draft of your explanatory *what* composition. Include a general definition in the introduction. Use the idea groups you organized in your pre-writing notes to develop the body. Sum up your ideas in a slightly different way in the conclusion. Save your work.

Divide the class into groups. Assign each group one of the following categories: *science, space, medicine,* and *computers.* Have each person in the group find a new word in his or her category and write a one-sentence definition for it. Have each group make up a list of its words and definitions to share with the class. If you wish, students may expand their one-sentence definitions into paragraphs. They may also wish to illustrate their definitions.

Objective

To revise the ideas, organization, and word choice in an explanatory *what* composition

Presenting the Lesson

1. Ask students if it is easier to find weaknesses in their writing immediately after they finish writing, or if they go back to it after waiting for a day or two or even a week. Discuss the idea of a "fresh eye." Then read **Here's the Idea** aloud.

2. Read and discuss **Check It Out.** Ask students why these revisions have been made (most are adding more specific details).

3. Assign **Try Your Skill.** Have volunteers read their revisions aloud.

4. Read **Keep This in Mind** and then assign **Now Write.** Remind students to allow some time between writing the first draft and revising it.

Individualizing the Lesson

Less-Advanced Students

Have students do **Try Your Skill** with a partner. Use any mistakes that are not caught as the basis for a review lesson.

Advanced Students

Have students go back to papers they have written and revised earlier in the semester. Ask them to revise and proofread the papers again. When they are finished revising and proofreading the papers, lead a discussion on why they could find errors now that they didn't see the first time they corrected their work.

230

Clean-Up

Revising Your Definition

Here's the Idea When you have completed your first draft, take a break before you begin revising. The break might be as short as half an hour. It might be several days. The length of time is not important. What is important, is that you look over your work with a fresh eye. Then you will be able to check your definition more carefully. To be sure that your subject is clearly defined, ask yourself these questions.

1. Does my introduction contain a general defintion of my subject?

2. Does my general definition have three parts?

3. Have I expanded my general definition with specific details?

4. Does my conclusion sum up the main ideas?

5. Is my composition organized from the general to the specific?

After you are satisfied that you have written a good definition, proofread and correct your composition.

Check It Out Notice how this introduction from an explanatory *what* paragraph has been revised.

It is 1,000 miles above us. It is covered with insulation. It looks like a long pipe. On one end there are antennas. There are also panels for the sunlight to run it. A space shuttle comes to dock with it. It is a space station, a special kind of satellit where people live and work on scientific projects.

230

- In what ways has this paragraph been improved?
- Is this an interesting introduction for an explanatory *what* composition? Explain your answer.

Try Your Skill   Using the guidelines in this lesson and your other revising skills, revise this paragraph from an explanatory *what* composition. Compare your revision with those of your classmates.

> After the cocoa beans are roasted they are ground up. The shells are used as fertilizer. Cocoa beans come from trees. In central and south america. The ground beans are processed. Cocoa powder is one product. Its used for making my favorite drink hot chocolate. Other ground cocoa beans are mixed. With cocoa butter. Also sugar and sometimes milk. This becomes candy. Which is the best use of cocoa in my opinion.

Keep This in Mind

- In an explanatory *what* composition, define your subject clearly and directly in the introduction.
- Expand the definition with specific details in the body.
- Sum up the main ideas in the conclusion.
- Organize your definition from the general to the specific.

Now Write   Use the guidelines in this lesson to revise your explanatory *what* composition. Remember to proofread your definition. When you are satisfied that your definition is as good as it can be, make a final copy. Proofread this copy one last time. Save your completed composition in your folder.

Have students revise the following paragraph from an explanatory *what* composition about an animal called an *okapi*.

> It's body looks like a horse. But it has a long neck and head. Big ears and zebra-stripped legs. I think it looks cute. It lives in tropical forests in Africa and only eats plants. I can't believe it but it's related to a giraffe!

Extending the Lesson

Ask each student to make an illustration to accompany his or her explanatory *what* composition. Explain that it can be a drawing, a collage, a photograph, a cartoon, etc. Then divide the class into groups according to their topics: hobbies, sports, animals, etc. Have each group make a book of their compositions and illustrations. Provide cardboard, contact paper, fabric, hole-punchers, etc., for the binding. Remind the groups to make a table of contents and to make a title for their collection. Display the books in a prominent place in the room. Provide class time to read the books.

Section **20** Objectives

1. To develop techniques for selecting and narrowing a subject for a report

2. To learn where and how to gather information for a report

3. To understand how to write note cards and bibliography cards

4. To learn to organize notes for a report around several main ideas

5. To write the first draft of a report using an introduction, body, and conclusion

6. To improve a report by revising and proofreading it

7. To use a bibliography to name sources at the end of a report

Preparing the Students

Ask students where they could find the details for a composition on space exploration, the history of photography, or how electricity was discovered. Point out that none of these topics can be developed from the students' own experience. Each one requires research from outside sources. Strress that the purpose of a report is always to inform. Explain that in this section, students will learn how to write reports.

Additional Resources

Mastery Test — page 29 in the test booklet

Practice Book — pages 95–100

Duplicating Masters — pages 95–100

Writing a Report

Teaching Special Populations

LD See **Teaching Special Populations,** page 75. Because many LD students are slow readers, you will probably have to provide them with simplified reference materials. Try to make the sheer quantity of reading less intimidating by going over some of it in class. LD students may also benefit from using small spiral notebooks in place of loose note cards that can easily be mislaid.

ESL ESL students might be intimidated by the amount of background reading required for this section. Carefully monitor students' progress during the research stage, and offer them simplified reference materials. Go over summarizing skills with the students and emphasize the necessity of keeping complete notes.

Give ESL students the option of choosing topics that relate to their particular cultural backgrounds. Even those students whose English skills are limited can conduct some form of research on a cultural topic: for example, they can conduct interviews with family members or friends to determine what particular difficulties foreign language speakers have in using facilities such as public transportation or libraries.

Have ESL students with similar linguistic and cultural backgrounds share ideas for topics, and, in the revision stage, pair ESL students with native English speakers.

NSD See **Teaching Special Populations,** page 75.

Objective

To develop techniques for selecting and narrowing a subject for a report

Presenting the Lesson

1. Read and discuss **Here's the Idea.** Once again, stress that reports are based on outside information, not personal experience or opinion. Note that preliminary reading on a general subject is a good way to find a narrowed topic for a report.

2. Read and discuss **Check It Out.** Ask students what the topic of this report is and if it will be narrow enough for a five-paragraph report.

3. Discuss with the students why each topic in **Try Your Skill** would or would not be appropriate for a report.

4. Read **Keep This in Mind** and then assign **Now Write.**

Individualizing the Lesson

Less-Advanced Students

1. Explain that some ways to limit a general topic are to choose a specific example, to pick a particular time period, or to pick a particular place about that topic.

2. Check the topics that students choose for **Now Write.** Help them to determine whether the topics are suitable for a five-paragraph report.

Advanced Students

1. Some students may wish to explore topics that require more than a five-paragraph report. Allow them to

Get the Facts

Learning About Reports

Here's the Idea Now you are going to learn to write a special type of composition called a **report.** In some ways, a report is very much like the compositions you have been writing. A report presents information about a single topic. A report also has an introduction, a body, and a conclusion.

In other ways, a report is very different from a composition. For example, a report is never written from the first-person point of view, as some narratives are. A report also never includes the opinions of the writer.

A report is written entirely from **facts.** A fact is a statement that can be proven true. Facts for a report are gathered from **outside sources.** These sources usually include books, magazines, newspapers, and encyclopedias.

Sometimes a teacher will give you a specific topic for a report. At other times, a teacher will tell you to choose a topic. Then you must first find a subject that interests you. Next you must narrow your subject so that you can cover it properly.

For example, if your teacher has limited you to five paragraphs, you know that you can't handle a subject as general as "Canada," or "Rock Music." One way to narrow a topic is to start reading about it. For instance, suppose you wanted to write about Canada. You could do some reading about Canada in books, magazines, and encyclopedias. As you read, you might discover that you want to write something about the Klondike Gold Rush, or French customs in Quebec.

When you have decided on a topic, you may wish to write a sentence or two that states your topic and your purpose for writing about it. This is called a **thesis statement.**

Check It Out Read this paragraph from a report on the wildlife of Antarctica.

> Antarctica is also home to many species of birds. The best known are the penguins. Penguins cannot fly. They use their wings to help them swim through the water in search of food. Other birds that inhabit Antarctica include cape pigeons, giant fulmars, and skuas. Skuas are hawklike birds. They feed on penguin chicks and eggs. Probably the most amazing birds in Antarctica are the arctic terns. Each year these birds migrate from their breeding grounds in the Arctic to the coast of Antarctica and back again—a journey of 22,000 miles!

- Is this paragraph written from facts?
- Where do you suppose the writer got the facts?

Try Your Skill Here is a list of possible topics for a five-paragraph report. Some of these topics are too general for a report. Some of the topics state personal opinions. Which topics would be just right for a report of this length?

volcanoes	the Tower of London
my personal heroes	music
the destruction of Pompeii	why I don't like science fiction
computers	inventions of Leonardo da Vinci

Keep This in Mind

- A report is written from facts gathered from outside sources.
- A report doesn't include the writer's feelings or opinions.

Now Write Choose a subject that appeals to you and do some reading about it. As you read, try to discover some specific aspect of your subject that would make a good topic for a report. Save your topic.

235

determine their own length for the report, and to choose their topics accordingly.

2. Explain the concept of *thesis statement* more thoroughly to these students. Once they have determined their topic and purpose for writing it, their thesis statement can help them write their introduction and conclusion.

Optional Practice

Have students create two narrowed report topics based on the following general topics. Allow them to use books, magazines, or encyclopedias if necessary.

folk music	weather
mythology	holidays
animals	the ocean
earthquakes	automobiles

Extending the Lesson

Introduce the students to the basics of journalistic news reporting as an adjunct to the report writing skills they learn in this section. Have them analyze several newspaper reports. Through class discussion, bring out the common characteristics of these reports:

objectivity
use of facts that have been researched
organization by order of importance
conciseness of news style

Take Note

Presenting the Lesson

1. Read and discuss **Here's the Idea.** Take the students to the library or bring to class a copy of the *Readers' Guide*. Make sure they understand how to use the card catalog. If necessary, take time to present pages 261–273, **Using the Library.**

When discussing note cards, emphasize that students must use their own wording, and not the exact words of the source. Stress that they are to only put one idea on each note card.

2. Read and discuss **Check It Out.** Point out the difference between a note card and bibliography card. Ask students what a bibliography card for this fact might look like, and what information it should contain.

3. Assign **Try Your Skill.** Ask students why they will be making more than one note card for this paragraph.

4. Write **Keep This in Mind** on the chalkboard for reinforcement.

5. Assign **Now Write.** Have available books and articles that might be helpful for students' topics.

Individualizing the Lesson

Less-Advanced Students

1. Work with these students to help them become familiar with the

Gathering Information

Here's the Idea   Now that you have chosen your topic, you need to find facts to develop it. The library has two general areas where you can start your research. The first area is the reference section. There you will find the encyclopedias and the *Readers' Guide to Periodical Literature*. The *Readers' Guide* will help you to find magazine articles about your topic.

The other area is the card catalog, where you can locate the titles of books on your chosen topic. To find out more about how to use the library, see pages 261–273.

As you read about your topic, write the important facts on note cards. Follow these guidelines.

1. Use a separate 3″ × 5″ note card for each fact or idea.

2. Write down exactly where the fact or idea came from. Include the name of the source, the date if the source is a newspaper or magazine, and the page number where you found the information.

3. Take notes in your own words. It is not acceptable to use another writer's work word for word.

4. Make a bibliography card for each source you use. Write the following information for each type of source. You will need this information when you list your sources.

Book:	author, title, publisher, date published
Magazine:	author of article (if there is one), title of article, name of magazine, date published, page
Encyclopedia:	author of article (if there is one), name of encyclopedia, volume and page, date published
Newspaper:	author of article (if there is one); title of article; name of newspaper; date published; section, page, and column number

Check It Out   Read this note card.

> *There are more than 800 languages spoken in Africa.*
> *World Book*
> *Vol. 1, page 95*

- Does this note card include just one fact?
- Does the card contain the source of the information?

Try Your Skill   A student found this information for a report on stars. Make some note cards using the information.

Stars are glowing balls of gas. They are the basic objects of the universe and exist throughout space. Except for the sun, all stars are too far from the earth for their distance to be conveniently measured in miles or kilometers. For this reason, astronomers measure distances to and between stars in *light-years*.

—*World Book*, Vol. 1, page 802

Keep This in Mind

- As you read about your topic, write the important information, in your own words, on note cards.
- Put one fact on each note card.
- Label each card with the name of the source and the number of the page where the fact is.
- Make a bibliography card for each source you use.

Now Write   Find several outside sources of information for your report. Make note cards as you read about your topic. Make bibliography cards, too. Be sure to follow the guidelines in this lesson. Save your note cards and bibliography cards.

---

library research tools explained in Section 22. Help students to determine appropriate sources, and work with the students in the library as they gather information on their topics.

2. Give students additional practice in paraphrasing material by selecting passages from a textbook and having students rewrite the material in their own words.

Advanced Students

Explain the ideas of skimming and scanning, which are further discussed in Section 23, pages 286–287. Emphasize that students should not try to read every article on their subject word for word.

Optional Practice

Ask students to make note cards and a bibliography card from this information.

The Central African Republic is sparsely populated. In the east an average of only three people live on each square mile. Most of the people live along the Ubangi River, a tributary of the Congo River, and along the northern border. The largest city and capital is Bangui, a port with a population of about 150,000.

Extending the Lesson

Take the class on a tour of the school library or a community library. If possible, have a trained librarian conduct the tour. Be sure the students get an overview of the reference department and the card catalog. Show students how to use the computer catalog, microfilm, and microfiche if available.

Part 3

Sorting It Out

Organizing Your Notes

Objective

To learn to organize notes for a report around several main ideas

Presenting the Lesson

1. Read and discuss **Here's the Idea.** Emphasize that gathering information and organizing a report are two complementary processes: often, as students organize their notes they will find that they need more information or that some of the facts they have gathered are unrelated to their main ideas.

2. Read and discuss **Check It Out.** Discuss the value of outlining as a means of structuring a report. Ask students what else could be added to this "outline" to make it complete (an introduction and conclusion).

3. Assign **Try Your Skill.** Have volunteers share their sentences.

4. Read **Keep This in Mind.**

5. Assign **Now Write.**

Individualizing the Lesson

Less-Advanced Students

For many students, organizing ideas into logically ordered groups is the most difficult part of writing a report. Give students individual attention at this stage of the report and help them to identify the common thread that ties the ideas in each group together. You may want to make up oversized samples of note cards and demonstrate the grouping process.

Here's the Idea   You have finished taking notes on your report topic. Now you must organize your notes. When you arrange your facts in a clear, logical order, you create a plan you can follow as you write your first draft.

The best way to organize your notes is to first spread out your notecards. That way, you have all of your facts in front of you. If you did a good job of gathering information about your topic, you may have twenty or more notecards.

Read your notecards carefully. Try to find two or three main ideas among them. Then arrange your cards into piles. Make a separate pile for each main idea. Each pile of cards will supply the information for one paragraph in your report.

When you have grouped your cards into piles, reread the notes in each pile. Then write a sentence that describes the main idea of each pile. These sentences can become topic sentences when you write your report.

Finally, arrange your notes in the order that you want to present them. First, arrange the piles of cards in the order you will write about them. Then, do the same with facts in each pile.

Take time to arrange your cards in an order that makes sense. You may have to rearrange the cards several times until you are satisfied. Then write an outline from your organized notes. Write down the sentences you wrote to describe each pile of notecards. Then list your facts under each sentence. After you make your outline, you are ready to write your first draft.

Check It Out   Read these organized notes for a report about penguins.

Where Penguins Live

penguins live south of the Equator

they live on the coast of Argentina, New Zealand, Australia, and South America

How Penguins Get Around

on land, they walk awkwardly upright

toboggan down icy hills on their bellies

"fly" through the water with their flippers

Nesting Habits

nests are often piles of pebbles

lay 1 to 3 eggs

both parents incubate eggs

- Do you see how each group of details develops just one main idea?

Try Your Skill Read each group of details in **Check It Out.** Write a sentence that tells about the main idea of each group. Write sentences that could serve as topic sentences in a report.

Keep This in Mind

- Group your notecards in piles. Each pile of cards should develop one main idea.
- Arrange the main ideas and the facts grouped around them in the order you wish to present them.

Now Write Spread your notecards out in front of you. Group the cards into piles. Each pile of cards should develop one main idea. Write a sentence that describes the main idea of each pile. Then arrange your notes in the order that you wish to present them. Use your organized notes to write a simple outline. Save your notes and outline in your folder.

Get It on Paper

Writing the First Draft

Part 4

Objective

To write the first draft of a report using an introduction, body, and conclusion

Presenting the Lesson

1. Read and discuss **Here's the Idea.** Point out that the introduction tells the topic of the report and arouses the reader's interest. The body is developed from the organized note cards (and outline), and the conclusion relates to the body of the report and provides a satisfying ending. Explain that this is no different than any of the other kinds of writing they have already done.

2. Have a volunteer read **Check It Out** aloud. Ask students how the author makes this introduction effective (interesting facts and details).

3. Assign **Try Your Skill.** Explain that the paragraph can be about some of these notes or all of them.

4. Read **Keep This in Mind** and then assign **Now Write.**

Individualizing the Lesson

Less-Advanced Students

Provide individual help guiding students in developing organized ideas into smoothly written paragraphs. Have brief one-on-one conferences with the students as they complete each section of the report: introduction, body, and conclusion.

Here's the Idea Writing the first draft of a report is like writing the first draft of any composition. You follow your organized pre-writing notes as you write the introduction, the body, and the conclusion.

The **introduction** is the first paragraph of your report. This paragraph should tell the reader what your report is about. The introduction should also be interesting enough to capture and hold the reader's attention.

The **body** of your report is made up of several paragraphs. Each paragraph should have a strong topic sentence and should tell about one main idea. Use your grouped notecards to help you to develop these paragraphs.

The **conclusion** is a paragraph that brings your report to a close. The conclusion sums up and ties together everything you have written about your topic.

Check It Out Read this introduction.

> Antarctica is a cold, forbidding land. The entire continent is a mass of ice surrounding the South Pole. Winter temperatures as low as 127 degrees below zero have been recorded. Even in midsummer, inland temperatures remain below zero. Surprisingly, this bleak landscape is home to an astonishing variety of birds, land animals, and marine life.

- Does this introductory paragraph tell the reader what the report is about?
- Is this introduction informative and interesting? Explain your answer.

Try Your Skill Read these pre-writing notes. Then write a paragraph for the body of a report on animal behavior. Include a good topic sentence in your paragraph.

Animal Defenses

Armadillo
  covered with bony armor
  curls up into ball when attached

Porcupine
  quills (sharp, barbed) cause painful wounds
  come off when touched
  can also be shot off

Snakes
  poisonous fangs

Impala
  speed—can outrun attackers

Big Cats
  sharp claws for slashing
  strong, sharp teeth

Keep This in Mind

- In a report, the introduction presents the topic in an informative and interesting way.
- The body develops the topic with facts gathered from outside sources.
- The conclusion sums up and ties together the important information in the report.

Now Write Using your organized pre-writing notes as a guide, write the first draft of your report. Be sure your report has a good introduction, body, and conclusion. Save your first draft in your folder.

Advanced Students

Because a common problem in report writing is the monotonous stringing together of facts, provide instruction in using transitions. Have students list transitional words and phrases, and require them to incorporate some in their first drafts.

Optional Practice

Have students exchange papers and see if they can identify the topic sentences of each other's report. Then have them evaluate whether the details in the paragraphs support the topic sentences.

Extending the Lesson

Have students find and analyze brief encyclopedia articles as examples of reports. Ask students to notice paragraph organization and the development of topic sentences.

Part 5

Objective

To improve a report by revising and proofreading it

Presenting the Lesson

1. Read and discuss **Here's the Idea.** Ask students why checking facts for accuracy is so important in a report. Review the guidelines on pages 174–175 with the class.

2. Read **Check it Out.** Be sure students notice how the paragraph has been improved through the addition of more details and improved word choice.

3. Assign **Try Your Skill.** Have volunteers read their revisions aloud.

4. Read **Keep This in Mind.**

5. Assign **Now Write.**

Individualizing the Lesson

Less-Advanced Students

Use individual conferences to check students' corrections before they make a final copy.

Advanced Students

Encourage students to seek fresh phrases and precise wording. Introduce them to the thesaurus if you have not already done so.

Optional Practice

Have students work with a partner to check corrections and revisions before they make a final copy of their work.

The Last Detail

Revising Your Report

Here's the Idea Throughout this chapter, you have been carefully and thoughtfully developing your report. Now is the time to see how well you've done.

Read your first draft all the way through. What impression does it make on you? You may want to express your ideas more clearly. You may find a paragraph that needs a few more details to develop its main idea. Perhaps you will want to make the language you have used livelier and more interesting. Don't feel discouraged if your report seems to need more work than you thought. Remember, a first draft is just a start.

Use the guidelines on pages 174–175 to help to improve your report. Here are some questions to guide your revision.

1. Is my introduction informative and interesting?
2. Does my report include enough facts to develop my topic?
3. Are my facts accurate? Have I stated them clearly?
4. Does each paragraph in the body tell about one main idea?
5. Do all the facts in each paragraph develop the main idea of that paragraph?
6. Does my conclusion sum up the information in my report?

As you revise your report, make sure that all of your facts are correct. Check the accuracy of dates and figures. Do the same for the spelling of names and special words. Go back to your sources if you are unsure about any of your information.

When you have finished revising the content, language, and organization of your report, proofread it. Correct any errors in grammar, capitalization, punctuation, and spelling.

Check It Out Read this paragraph on a winner of the Nobel Peace Prize. Notice how it has been revised.

In 1960, the commitee gave the prize to Albert John Luthuli. He was an african, He was a zulu chief, He led the African National Congress. He tried to get the South African government to end racial discrimination. Like Dr. King he did peaceful things to meet his goals. He thought everyone sheould be equal.

(handwritten edits: Nobel; peace; a South; who; Luthuli; encouraged; Martin Luther; means; achieve; believed that; in Africa; treated; believed in using)

- How has this paragraph been improved?

Try Your Skill   Here is another paragraph from the report on Nobel Peace Prize winners. Use the guidelines in this lesson as well as your other revising skills to improve this paragraph.

Mother Teresa won the prize in 1979. She was born in Yugoslavia. Mother Teresa is a nun. She works with poor people in India. She is a roman catholic nun. She founded an order of nuns in calcutta. Which is in India. She has won other awards. The Pope John XXIII peace prize and the Jawaharlal Nehru award. The order operates hospitals, schools, orphanages, shelters for lepers. She is known as the *saint of the gutters.*

Keep This in Mind

- When you revise a report, try to improve the ideas, the language, and the organization.
- Proofread the report to correct errors in grammar, capitalization, punctuation, and spelling.

Now Write   Use the guidelines in this lesson as well as the other revising skills you have learned to revise the first draft of your report. After revising and proofreading your report, make a final copy. Proofread this copy once more. Save your work.

Extending the Lesson

1. As an exercise in fact-checking, take students to the library and have them check the accuracy of each other's facts.
2. Have students look through news magazines for articles that present actual reports in an interesting way. Analyze what makes the articles effective.

Part 6

Objective

To use a bibliography to name sources at the end of a report

Presenting the Lesson

1. Read and discuss **Here's the Idea.** Go back over the bibliography cards that the students prepared in Part 2 and have them alphabetize them. Make sure that students understand that a correct bibliography has a proper form that extends even to where periods and commas are to be used.

2. Read and discuss **Check It Out.** Bring to class some books and pamphlets that explain how to write a research paper, and show the various rules that are used to write formal bibliographies.

3. Go over the forms for bibliographies on page 244 again, and then assign **Try Your Skill.**

4. Read **Keep This in Mind.**

5. Assign **Now Write.**

Individualizing the Lesson

Less-Advanced Students

1. Do **Try Your Skill** with the students, using the chalkboard to show the correct form.

2. Have students work on their bibliographies for **Now Write** during classtime. Use examples from their bibliography cards to put the correct bibliography form on the board.

Advanced Students

Point out that bibliographies at the ends of books and articles are often valuable sources for researchers.

Where Credit Is Due

Preparing a Bibliography

Here's the Idea   When you write a descriptive composition, the information in the composition comes directly from you. It comes from your observations or memories. The same is true in most compositions. You, the writer, supply the details that develop the main idea of the composition.

In a report, however, the information that develops the topic comes from outside sources such as books, magazines, and newspapers. When you use information that is not your own, you must tell the reader where the information came from. You must prepare a list of sources. This list is called a **bibliography.**

When you prepare the bibliography for your report, use the bibliography cards that you made as part of your pre-writing notes. First arrange these cards in alphabetical order, according to the author's last name. If no author is mentioned, use the first main word of the title.

When you have arranged your cards in alphabetical order, you are ready to write your bibliography. Each type of source has its own special form. Here are the correct forms. Note the correct punctuation, capitalization, and abbreviations.

Book:	Gilbert, Bil. *Westering Man.* Atheneum Publishers, 1983.
Encyclopedia:	"Cave Life." *Encyclopedia Americana.* Volume 6, p. 105, 1980.
Magazine:	Begley, Sharon. "Jobs." *Newsweek.* 18 October 1982, pp. 87–88.
Newspaper:	Kelly, Nash. "Living with Cancer." *Wanakee Tribune,* 20 May 1984, Sec.1, p. 2, Cols. 1–5.

Check It Out   Look at the bibliography on the next page.

Bibliography

Cunningham, Christy. "The Sun Did It!" *The Altoona Herald Sun*, 12 October 1983, Sec. 2, p. 1, Cols. 1–2.

Marbach, William D. "Steam from the Sunshine." *Newsweek*, 13 December 1982, pp. 92–93.

"Solar Energy." *Colliers Encyclopedia*. Volume 21, p. 167, 1980.

- Are these entries arranged in alphabetical order?
- Does each entry contain the required information?
- Is the information in each entry arranged in order?

Try Your Skill Make a sample bibliography using these sources. Use the correct form for each type of source.

a book titled *Photography in America*, by Robert Doty, published by Random House in 1974.

an article titled "Photography," in *The World Book Encyclopedia*, pages 370–381, Volume 15, 1984.

an article titled "New Photography Draws Critical Fire," in *Photography Review Magazine*, June 6, 1984, pages 45–50.

Keep This in Mind

- If you use outside information in your writing, you must state where it came from.
- The last page of your report should be a bibliography.
- In a bibliography, each type of source has its own special form.

Now Write Use the guidelines in this lesson to prepare a bibliography for your report. Use your bibliography cards to help you. Write your bibliography on a separate sheet of paper and place it at the end of your report. Save your report.

Often one book will not have specific information that someone might need, but the bibliography at the end will tell him or her where to find that information.

Optional Practice

Have students arrange the following items into a formal bibliography:

a magazine article in *Prevention* called "Down-to-Earth Beauty—Clay," September, 1984, pages 33–34

a book by Richard Corson called *Fashions in Makeup: from Ancient to Modern Times*, published by New York Universe Books in 1972

an article by June Weir called "Changing Uses of Makeup during the Centuries," page 75, section VI, column 1 of the September 25, 1983, *New York Times*

an article in *The World Book Encyclopedia*, 1984, on pages 855–856, Volume 4, called "Cosmetics"

Extending the Lesson

Have students find books that contain bibliographies. Discuss the functions of these bibliographies: to document sources of information, to lend credence to the book, and to direct interested readers to further information on the book's topic.

Doty, Robert. *Photography in America*. Random House, 1974.

"Photography." *The World Book Encyclopedia*. Volume 15, pp. 370–381, 1984.

"New Photography Draws Critical Fire." *Photography Review Magazine*. 6 June 1984, pp. 45–50.

Section 21 Objectives

1. To recognize that a fact is a statement that can be proven true

2. To know that facts may be definitions or observations

3. To evaluate statements of fact

4. To differentiate between statements of fact and statements of opinion

5. To recognize judgment and command words

6. To differentiate between sound and unsound opinions

7. To recognize the error of circular reasoning

8. To recognize that unsound opinions can result from loaded language

Preparing the Students

Discuss with students the types of persuasive messages they come in contact with daily: television, magazines, newspapers, radio, and conversations with other people. Ask them how they decide which messages to believe. Explain that this section will help them to judge the accuracy of the information they hear and see, and to use these thinking skills in their writing.

Additional Resources

Mastery Test — page 30 in the test booklet

Practice Book — pages 101–106

Duplicating Masters — pages 101–106

Clear Thinking

Teaching Special Populations

LD LD students may have trouble distinguishing between facts and opinions, and they may struggle to pinpoint the evidence that acts in support of particular propositions. Give these students extra practice in testing statements through personal observation or through the use of reliable sources. Offer LD students a set of statements and guide them as they check the validity of these propositions in an encyclopedia.

ESL Many foreign language speakers find that the difference between facts and opinions in English is an extremely subtle one. Give your students numerous concrete examples. Also try assigning role-playing exercises in which students are required to use words that express judgments, commands, or evaluations. Hand out copies of magazine advertisements and tell students to go through them, picking out facts and opinions. Ask students to underline supporting facts whenever the advertisement relies on them.

NSD Tactfully point out to NSD students that nonstandard dialect can obscure the factual content of a passage or the relationship between opinions and supporting details. Present students with a set of propositions and have them list all the facts and details that might act in support of these statements.

Objectives

1. To recognize that a fact is a statement that can be proven true
2. To know that facts may be definitions or observations

Presenting the Lesson

1. Write the word *fact* and its definition on the chalkboard. Then read and discuss **Here's the Idea.** Discuss the two ways facts may be proven true—by definition or by observation. Make sure students understand what *definition* and *observation* mean.
2. Read **Check It Out.** Ask students what other sources Carlotta could use to find facts about India.
3. Assign **Try Your Skill.** Ask students how each definition can be proven.
4. Read **Keep This in Mind** aloud.
5. Assign **Now Write.** Remind students they are not to use any source more than once.

Individualizing the Lesson

Less-Advanced Students

Do **Try Your Skill** orally with the class and then have them prove each fact. (Supply dictionaries, encyclopedias, etc.)

Advanced Students

Have the students make up six statements of fact, three to be definitions and three to be observations. Make a copy of these facts and have the class identify the definitions and the observations.

248

Nothing but the Facts

Identifying Facts

Here's the Idea   Every day you receive hundreds of pieces of information. Information comes from many sources:

Other people	Movies	Newspapers
Books	Television shows	Signs and posters
Magazines	Advertisements	

You want to be able to use this information well when you write, speak, or make decisions. To do this you have to be able to tell what is fact and what is not.

A **fact** is a statement that can be proven. There are two kinds of facts: definitions and observations. A **definition** simply tells the meaning of a word. An **observation** tells about something that can be seen, tasted, touched, heard, or smelled.

Definition: A *judoka* is an expert in judo.
Observation: Male Siberian tigers average over ten feet in length.

Definitions can be proven by checking a dictionary. Observations can be proven in three different ways:

Proving Observations

1. Make the observation yourself. Use your senses of sight, touch, taste, hearing, and smell.

2. Ask an expert or authority.

3. Check a reliable written source. Such sources include encyclopedias, atlases, almanacs, and dictionaries.

To prove the observation about Siberian tigers, for example, you can visit a zoo. You can ask an expert on big cats. You can also read about these tigers in a book or encyclopedia.

Check It Out   Carlotta was asked to do a report on India for her social studies class. She was having a hard time narrowing her topic, so she spoke with Sashir. Sashir told her that there are many beautiful temples in India.

- What kind of fact is Sashir's comment? Is it a definition or an observation?
- How can Carlotta check this fact? What sources of information can she use?

Try Your Skill   The following statements are facts. Tell whether each is a definition or an observation.

1. A foal is a young horse, mule, or donkey.
2. *Wraith* is a Scottish word for "ghost."
3. Angel Falls, in Venezuela, is over three thousand feet high.
4. Jupiter has rings like those around Saturn.

Keep This in Mind

- A fact is a statement that can be proven true.
- Facts may be definitions or observations.
- Definitions can be checked in a dictionary.
- Observations can be checked personally. They can also be checked by asking an authority or by looking in a written source.

Now Write   Go to the library. Look in encyclopedias, atlases, dictionaries, almanacs, books, and magazines. Make a list of five interesting or unusual facts. On your list, tell the source of each fact. Do not use any source more than once. Label your paper **Nothing but the Facts.** Save it in your folder.

Follow the instructions for **Try Your Skill.**

- 1. Guppies are fish.
- 2. Some dogs are bigger than most people.
- 3. Salt helps melt ice more quickly.
- 4. The White House is in Washington, D.C.
- 5. The moon is a satellite of the earth.

Extending the Lesson

Bring in various books of facts (*The Guiness Book of World Records, The Book of Lists,* etc.). Have students go through them and determine if the facts are definitions or observations. Then have them write a book of facts about their school, using both definition and observation.

Objective

To evaluate statements of fact

Presenting the Lesson

1. Write on the board the two questions students should always have in their minds when reading or writing factual material:

What is the source of this information?

Is the source reliable?

Point out that just because information is in print does not necessarily make it true. Then, read and discuss **Here's the Idea.** Review the definition of *reliable source.*

2. Read **Check It Out.** List on the chalkboard the other sources of information that students suggest. Point out how many ways there are to find good sources.

3. Assign **Try Your Skill.** It is suggested that this be done as an oral exercise.

4. Read **Keep This in Mind** and then assign **Now Write.** Make a list of poor sources for the students to avoid (gossip newspapers, books published before a certain date, books or articles by non-experts).

Individualizing the Lesson

Less-Advanced Students

Provide examples for the guidelines on page 250. Bring to class an old encyclopedia that states that Jupiter has only thirteen moons, an old interview with a TV star ·who claims his or her show is sure to be renewed next season, etc.

Part 2

Says Who?

Using Good Sources

Here's the Idea   Whenever you write, it is important that your facts be accurate. This is especially important when you write a report or an informative talk. To make sure that your facts are correct, check them by using good sources. The following guidelines will help you:

Guidelines for Checking Facts

1. Make sure that your source is reliable. A reliable source is one you can count on to give you the right information. One reliable source is people who have special training, experience, or knowledge. Consider the fact "Jogging on hard surfaces can cause sprains." This fact can be checked by talking to a doctor or to an experienced jogger. Other good sources include the following:

    a. Reference books such as dictionaries, encyclopedias, almanacs, and atlases.

    b. Books, magazines, and newspaper articles written by people with special training, experience, or knowledge.

2. Make sure that your source is up-to-date. A book written in the 1950's will tell you that no one has been to the moon. Of course, this is no longer true. Always use the most recent sources available.

3. Make sure that your source is fair. A fair source is one that doesn't take sides. For example, the son of a political candidate would not be a good source of information on the candidate's abilities. The son couldn't be fair because of the close family connection.

Check It Out   Carlos read an interesting article about building houses. Carlos started thinking about becoming a carpenter someday. He decided to check the facts in the article. He looked under "Carpentry" in an encyclopedia. He talked to the wood-shop teacher at school. He also called the headquarters of the carpenter's union in his town.

- How good are Carlos's sources?
- What other sources of information could Carlos use?

Try Your Skill   Study the following situations. Then explain what is wrong with the sources mentioned.

1. In English class, Phil read a story by Ray Bradbury from *The Martian Chronicles*. He wondered if the story was based on actual facts. He decided to find out everything he could about Mars. At home he found a book called *Our Solar System*. The copyright page had the date 1962.

2. Marsha read an ad for CURES-ALL brand cold remedy. The ad said, "This is the most effective cold remedy on the market today." Therefore, Marsha later bought some CURES-ALL when she became sick.

3. Charmagne did a report on Carrie Fisher. One of her sources was a newspaper that is known for its gossip columns.

Keep This in Mind

- Whenever you write, make sure that your facts are accurate.
- Use sources that are reliable, up-to-date, and fair.

Now Write   Look through some magazines and newspapers. Choose two articles that contain facts. One article should be a good source. The other one should be a poor source. If you have trouble finding a poor source, ask your teacher for suggestions. Write a brief paragraph about each article. Tell why you think it is a good or bad source. Save your paragraphs.

251

Objectives

1. To differentiate between statements of fact and statements of opinion

2. To recognize judgment and command words

Presenting the Lesson

1. Review the definition of *fact*. Then read and discuss **Here's the Idea.** Emphasize that an opinion is a statement about the way someone *feels.* Give the students some additional examples of opinions (summer is a wonderful time; everyone should exercise). Discuss judgement and command words and how they appeal to feelings rather than facts.

2. Discuss **Check It Out.** Point out how opinions cannot be proved through observation.

3. Assign **Try Your Skill.** Have volunteers read their answers to the class. Discuss fully the difference between the facts and opinions.

4. Read **Keep This in Mind.**

5. Assign **Now Write.**

Individualizing the Lesson

Less-Advanced Students

Do **Try Your Skill** as an in-class exercise.

Advanced Students

Have the students change the statements of opinion in **Try Your Skill** to statements of fact by eliminating judgment and command words and rephrasing the sentences.

252

Prove It!

Distinguishing Fact and Opinion

Here's the Idea In Part 1 you learned that a fact is a statement that can be proved. A statement that cannot be proved is an **opinion.** Look at the following examples:

Fact: The guitar was invented in Spain.

Opinion: The guitar is the best of all instruments.

The first statement is a fact because it can be proved. You can check the truth of the statement by looking at an encyclopedia article. The second statement is very different. There is no way to prove it. It just expresses how some people feel. Because there is no way to prove this statement, it is an opinion.

To tell whether a statement is a fact, ask yourself whether it can be proved. If it can be proved, it is a fact. If it can't be proved, it is an opinion.

Opinions often contain **judgment words.** These are words that express personal feelings.

Judgment Words	
good, better, best	excellent, wonderful
bad, worse, worst	terrible, awful
ugly, beautiful	clever, intelligent
valuable, worthless	boring, interesting

Other opinions contain **command words.** These are words that tell what should be done.

Command Words		
should	ought to	must

Check It Out   Study the following dialogue:

Gwen: Michael Jackson is wonderful!

Miguel: You've got to be kidding!

Gwen: I certainly am not! He's got the best voice in popular music, and he does some excellent songs, too.

Miguel: I don't know how you can listen to his terrible music.

Gwen: Terrible? He's fantastic!

- What opinions are given in this dialogue?
- What judgment words can you find?
- Can any of the arguments in the dialogue be proved true? Explain your answer.

Try Your Skill   Tell whether the following statements are facts or opinions. If it is a fact, tell how you could prove it. If it is an opinion, identify any judgment words it contains.

1. Hank Aaron hit more home runs than any professional baseball player in history.
2. Everyone should learn how to swim.
3. Susan Sarandon is a marvelous actress.
4. One painting by Turner was sold for over six million dollars.
5. Barbara Krause won three gold medals in Olympic swimming competition.

Keep This in Mind

- A statement that cannot be proved is an opinion.
- Opinions often contain judgment words or command words.

Now Write   Using the lists of judgment and command words on page 252, write one fact and one opinion about each of these subjects:

arcade games   homework   football   pets

Label your paper **Prove It!** Save it in your folder.

253

Optional Practice

Have the students identify each of the following statements as fact or opinion.

○ 1. All workers should get at least two weeks paid vacation.

○ 2. That salad was the best I've ever eaten.

F 3. More than forty million foreign tourists visited the United States last year.

○ 4. There is life on other planets.

Extending the Lesson

Have the students underline the judgment and command words used in a theater, movie, or restaurant review. Then, have students identify statements of facts and opinion in these reviews.

253

Part 4

The Reasons Why

Ojectives

To differentiate between sound and unsound opinions

Supporting Opinions

Presenting the Lesson

1. Ask students if they believe that "one opinion is as good as another." Then read and discuss **Here's the Idea.** Make sure that they understand that some opinions *are* better than others if they are supported by facts.

2. Read and discuss **Check It Out.** Ask students if they have ever been in a situation where someone tried to influence their ideas with unsupported opinions.

3. Assign **Try Your Skill.** Remind students of the definition of a fact. Refer them to the "Guidelines for Checking Facts" on page 250, if necessary.

4. Read **Keep This in Mind.**

5. Assign **Now Write.**

Individualizing the Lesson

Less-Advanced Students

Do **Try Your Skill** with the students as an in-class exercise. Make sure they use facts to support their opinions, avoiding judgment and command words.

Advanced Students

Have the students bring in editorials and letters-to-the-editor from a local newspaper. Ask them to choose two opinions expressed and to explain whether they are sound or unsound and why.

Here's the Idea All opinions are not created equal. Some opinions are sound. Some are not. A sound opinion is one that can be supported by facts. Such an opinion can be believed. An unsound opinion is one that cannot be supported by facts. Unsound opinions should not be believed. Read these opinions:

Regular exercise is important to a person's health.
Regular exercise is not important to a person's health.

The first opinion is sound. It can be supported by facts such as these:

People who exercise regularly live longer.
Regular exercise strengthens muscles, including the heart.
Regular exercise increases alertness.

The second opinion has no facts to support it.

Whenever you read or hear an opinion, see if it is supported by facts. Whenever you give an opinion of your own, support it with facts that tell why the opinion should be believed.

Check It Out Read about this situation.

The seniors at Morton High wanted to hold a party to welcome the incoming freshmen. Marsha and Alec were chosen to organize the activities. They decided to show a movie. Marsha said, "I know what we ought to show—*Raiders of the Lost Ark.* It's wonderful! It was also a big hit at the box office."

"No," said Alec. "I think we ought to show *A Night at the Opera,* by the Marx brothers."

"But Alec," replied Marsha, "very few students today have even heard of the Marx brothers."

"I don't care," said Alec. "*A Night at the Opera* is great."

- What opinions are expressed by Marsha and Alec?
- Which opinion is supported with facts? Which is not?

Try Your Skill   Write two facts to support each of the following opinions:

1. More people should participate in sports.
2. Many television programs are too violent.
3. Students in shop classes should obey safety rules.
4. Cigarette smoking is harmful.
5. Zoos are fascinating places to visit.

Keep This in Mind

- A sound opinion is one that can be supported by facts.
- An unsound opinion is one that cannot be supported by facts.
- Always support the opinions you give with facts.

Now Write   Write an opinion about one of the following subjects:

automobiles	game shows
club or class	a favorite book
elections	or short story
a career you	a hobby or other
would like	activity that
to have someday	you enjoy

Use this opinion as the topic sentence of a paragraph. In the rest of the paragraph, support your opinion with facts. Label your paper **The Reasons Why.** Save it in your folder.

Objective

To recognize the error of circular reasoning

Presenting the Lesson

1. Read and discuss **Here's the Idea.** Explain to the students that there are many kinds of unsound reasoning, and that this lesson will introduce them to one of the most common kinds: circular reasoning.

2. Read and discuss **Check It Out.** If students are having trouble seeing that an opinion is circular, have them divide the opinion into two parts. Ask them if the second part expresses a different idea than the first part or if it just repeats the first idea in different words.

3. Assign **Try Your Skill.** Have volunteers explain their choices.

4. Read **Keep This in Mind.**

5. Assign **Now Write.**

Individualizing the Lesson

Less-Advanced Students

These students may find it very difficult to understand the concept of circular reasoning. Provide these students with as many examples as they need to understand this concept. Then do **Try Your Skill** with them as a group.

Advanced Students

Introduce students to some other kinds of frequently encountered false reasoning such as cause/effect, either/or, overgeneralization, stereotypes, rationalizing, and bandwagon/snob appeal.

Spinning Wheels

Circular Reasoning

Here's the Idea   Sometimes an unsound opinion comes from an error in reasoning. One common error is circular reasoning. **Circular reasoning** occurs when someone tries to support a statement by repeating it in different words. Read the following example:

> Paul's drum set is better than Lisa's because Paul's is of higher quality.

The opinion given here is that "Paul's drum set is better than Lisa's." Notice that no facts are offered to support this opinion. Instead, the opinion is simply restated in the words "Paul's set is of higher quality." The reasoning is going in circles. It ends up where it began. Therefore, the opinion is unsound.

The error of circular reasoning occurs whenever someone says that something is so simply because it is so. Learn to recognize this error in the speaking and writing of others. Avoid the error yourself by supporting your opinions with facts.

Check It Out   Read the following statements:

1. Juanita is the most valuable player on our team. This is because she is the one who is worth the most to us.

2. Unemployment is a terrible thing because being out of work is awful.

- What is wrong with the reasoning in these statements?
- How could this reasoning be improved?

Try Your Skill   Read the following statements. Tell which ones are examples of circular reasoning. Explain your answers.

1. Literature is an important part of every person's education. This is because everybody needs to be familiar with literature.

2. The United States should develop solar energy resources because there is a limited amount of oil and natural gas.

3. The Cardinals are the most interesting baseball team because they are so fascinating.

4. Martin guitars are the best guitars made because they are constructed better than other guitars.

Keep This in Mind

- Circular reasoning is the error of supporting an opinion by restating it in different words.
- Avoid circular reasoning by supporting your opinions with facts.

Now Write   The following opinions show circular reasoning. Choose one of these opinions. Use the opinion as the topic sentence of a paragraph. In your paragraph, avoid circular reasoning by supporting the opinion with facts. Label your paper **Spinning Wheels.** Save it in your folder.

Students should do their homework regularly because this is what students are supposed to do.

Video games are a lot of fun because they are so enjoyable.

Some television shows are not fit for young children because they are not the sort of programs young children should watch.

Optional Practice

Have the students discuss the reasons they give their parents to explain why they should be allowed to do things such as stay out late or get an increase in their allowance. List the reasons on the board and have students point out any circular reasoning. Explain how much more convincing their opinions would be if supported by facts.

Extending the Lesson

Have the students look through newspapers and magazines for examples of circular reasoning in advertising. Have them make a display of these ads with explanations of why they are faulty.

Snarl and Purr

Recognizing Loaded Language

Objective

To recognize that unsound opinions can result from loaded language

Presenting the Lesson

1. Remind students that different individuals can have opposing but equally valid opinions; that just because one person does not agree with another's opinion does not mean the opinion is wrong or unsound. Then read and discuss **Here's the Idea.** Ask students why they think loaded language is divided into *snarl* words and *purr* words.

2. Read and discuss **Check It Out.** Ask students to give examples from their own experience of the use of snarl words and purr words.

3. Assign **Try Your Skill.**

4. Read **Keep This in Mind** aloud.

5. Assign **Now Write.**

Individualizing the Lesson

Less-Advanced Students

Have students volunteer opinions about various aspects of school, such as gym, the cafeteria, assemblies, etc. Write these opinions on the chalkboard. Then have the students look for snarl words and purr words in the opinions. Have them rewrite the opinions.

Advanced Students

Have students go through the sports pages and movie review pages in their local newspaper. Tell them to find examples of loaded language to share with the class.

Here's the Idea   In Part 5 you learned that unsound opinions can result from circular reasoning. Another common cause of unsound opinions is loaded language.

Loaded language is made up of words and phrases that create strong feelings in the reader or listener. Such words and phrases are sometimes used in place of facts. This is done to sway the opinions of an audience. Read the following selection from a political speech:

> The voters of America are *fed up* with *dishonest* politicians. They are tired of *crooks* like my opponent. Instead, they want *leaders* they can count on, people who will keep their word. They are looking for *honesty* and *integrity*.

In this example the speaker is trying to get the audience to view his or her opponent as someone who can't be trusted. However, notice that the speaker gives no facts to support this opinion. Instead, the speaker uses loaded language to stir up emotion in the listeners. This loaded language is made up of snarl words and purr words.

Snarl words are words that create negative feelings in the audience. Examples from the selection include *fed up, dishonest,* and *crooks.* **Purr words** are words that create positive feelings. Examples from the selection include *leaders, honesty,* and *integrity.*

Whenever a person uses name-calling to make a point, he or she is using loaded language. Such language should be avoided at all times. It is usually used to hide the fact that the speaker or writer has no real facts to support his or her opinions.

Check It Out Read the following selection from an editorial:

> The bleeding-heart liberals in Washington are at it again. This time they want to limit even further the rights of businesses to drill for oil on government land. No decent citizen will allow this. Limiting the activities of business is both un-democratic and un-American. I urge all real patriots to write to Washington. Let's stop this nonsense once and for all.

- What opinions are expressed in this editorial?
- Are any facts offered to support these opinions?
- What loaded words are used to sway emotions? Are these purr words or snarl words?

Try Your Skill Identify the snarl words and purr words in the following sentences:

1. I wouldn't vote for him. He has shifty eyes.
2. Only respectable books should be allowed in libraries.
3. People with real class will not wear such rags.
4. Ms. Jones is fabulously wealthy. Ms. Smith is filthy rich.

Now Write Pick a subject that you feel strongly about. Write an opinion on this subject. Then, support your opinion in a paragraph. Avoid using snarl words and purr words. Instead, support your opinion with facts. Label your paper **Snarl and Purr.** Save it in your folder.

Optional Practice

Have the students rewrite the sentences in **Try Your Skill** to eliminate the loaded language.

Extending the Lesson

1. Have the students go through their social studies or history texts and find at least two statements of opinion. Then have them decide if the opinions are supported by facts.

2. Have the students listen to several commercials on TV or radio. Ask them to find as many examples of poorly supported opinions as they can. Have the students compile a list of these commercials and add to the list during the semester.

Section 22 Objectives

1. To know that fiction is arranged alphabetically by author's last name

2. To know that in most libraries nonfiction is classified and arranged by the Dewey Decimal System

3. To use the card catalog to locate books

4. To know how information is arranged in an encyclopedia

5. To know the major kinds of reference works and how to use them

Preparing the Students

Draw a map of your school library, omitting any labels. Make a copy for each student. Arrange for a class period in the library and ask the librarian to review the facilities available to the students. Then ask the students to label their maps. Ask them to include these basics: the circulation desk, the card catalog, the fiction shelves, the nonfiction shelves, the biography shelves, the encyclopedias, the general reference area, the periodical section, the *Readers' Guide,* and the vertical file. Add any other items that might help the students to know their library better. Tell students to keep their maps for future reference.

Additional Resources

Mastery Test — page 31 in the test booklet

Practice Book — pages 107–110

Duplicating Masters — pages 107–110

Using the Library

Teaching Special Populations

LD Learning to use the library helps reinforce essential skills such as organization and categorization. Carefully work through all the exercises in class with your students. Whenever possible, use actual library materials or take the whole group to the library.

ESL The library can be a formidable place for ESL students, but, once they understand how it functions, their cultural experience will be considerably enriched. Provide as much library practice as possible. Give your students guided tours, and have them make simple plans of the library layout. In fact, you may want to teach this section in the library itself rather than in a classroom.

To help initiate ESL students into research and bibliographic techniques, pair them with native English speakers who are familiar with the card catalog and the overall organization of library materials.

NSD If possible, teach this section in the library itself. Make sure students are coping with the necessary alphabetizing and categorizing skills.

Part 1

Objectives

1. To know that fiction is arranged alphabetically by author's last name
2. To know that in most libraries nonfiction is classified and arranged by the Dewey Decimal System

Presenting the Lesson

1. Read aloud and discuss **Here's the Idea.** Review the definitions of *fiction* and *nonfiction.* Write them on the chalkboard. Next to each, write how it is arranged in the library. Then discuss the elements of a call number.
2. Discuss **Check It Out.**
3. Assign **Try Your Skill.** Ask volunteers to share their answers with the class.
4. Read **Keep This in Mind.**
5. Assign **Now Write.**

Individualizing the Lesson

Less-Advanced Students

1. Make sure students know what the categories in the Dewey Decimal System mean (i.e. *biography, psychology,* etc.).
2. Do the first part of **Try Your Skill** as an in-class exercise. Have students do the second part alone or with a partner.

Advanced Students

Obtain a more detailed breakdown of the Dewey Decimal System from a librarian. Have the students further classify the books in the second part of **Try Your Skill** (810 is American literature, 840 is French literature, etc.).

One for the Books

How To Use the Library

Here's the Idea   When you want something to read, go to the library. There you will find books to read for pleasure or for research. Become familiar with how and where the materials are arranged in the libraries you use.

You will find that library books are classified into two general groups, **fiction** and **nonfiction.** Fiction books have their own section of shelves. The books are arranged alphabetically according to the author's last name. For instance, *No Promises in the Wind,* written by Irene Hunt, would be filed under **H.**

Nonfiction books are arranged on the shelves according to their subjects. Many libraries use a system called the **Dewey Decimal System.** This system groups nonfiction books into ten major, numbered categories. These are the ten categories.

000–099	**General Works**	(encyclopedias, almanacs)
100–199	**Philosophy**	(ethics, psychology, occult)
200–299	**Religion**	(the Bible, mythology)
300–399	**Social Science**	(economics, law, education, government)
400–499	**Language**	(languages, grammars, dictionaries)
500–599	**Science**	(math, biology, astronomy)
600–699	**Useful Arts**	(cooking, farming, carpentry, television, business)
700–799	**Fine Arts**	(music, sports, painting, dance)
800–899	**Literature**	(poetry, plays)
900–999	**History**	(biography, travel, geography)

On the spine of each nonfiction book is its **call number.** This number includes the Dewey Decimal number and other useful information. Some libraries may also add the letter *B* to the spine of a biography or the letter *R* to the spine of a general reference work like an encyclopedia.

Look at this nonfiction book:

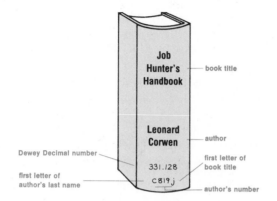

Check It Out Look at the books represented below.

- How can you tell which books are fiction and which are nonfiction?
- How can you tell what the general category of each nonfiction book is?

Have the students assign the correct classification number to each of the following books:

The Good War by Studs Terkel 900
Born Free, A Lioness of Two Worlds by Joy Adamson 500
You and Your Feelings by Eda J. LeShan 100
A Dictionary of Modern English Usage by H. W. Fowler 400

Extending the Lesson

1. Arrange for the students to visit a college or university library. Have them describe the differences they find among the school, community, and university libraries.

2. Make a set of posters for the ten major Dewey Decimal categories. Assign two or three students to each poster. In addition to listing the numbers, general title, and more specific categories, ask students to illustrate the posters with drawings or photographs. To make the posters match, the class as a whole should decide where and how to write the title, etc., on each poster. Display the posters in the library.

Using Books Effectively

Explain to your students that knowing how to use books effectively can help them to get more out of their studying and research. Then introduce them to these important parts of books.

The Table of Contents The table of contents is a list of all of the chapters or sections of a book along with the page numbers on which these chapters or sections can be found. Urge students to consult the table of contents whenever they want a broad overview of the material a book contains.

The Index The index is a detailed, alphabetical list of all of the important subjects a book contains along with appropriate page references. Tell students that the index will help them to discover whether or not a book contains information on a specific topic or person.

The Appendix Some books may contain an appendix. An appendix is a special section of a book, often placed toward the end, that gives important information that supplements or supports the material presented in the book. An appendix may contain graphs, charts, or statistics.

The Bibliography A book may contain a bibliography. A bibliography is a list of books the writer used to prepare his or her book or that the writer feels will be helpful to any one who wants more information about the subject of the book. Tell your students that whenever they want or need more information about the subject of a book, they should check to see if the author has provided a bibliography.

Special Reference Books Many reference books have a special section in the front of the book called "How to Use This Book." This section explains how the book is organized, and the easiest and fastest way to find information in the book. Encourage your students to look for this section whenever they use reference books.

Try Your Skill Write the answers to the following questions.

1. Under what letter on the library shelves would you find the following books of fiction?

Animal Farm by George Orwell O
Leap Before You Look by Mary Stolz S
The Upstairs Room by Johanna Reiss R
Z for Zachariah by Robert C. O'Brien O
A Figure of Speech by Norma Fox Mazer M

2. In which categories of the Dewey Decimal System would you find information on the following subjects?

how to grow vegetables 600
what to see in Washington, D.C. 900
the Greek myths 900
the plays of William Shakespeare 800

Keep This in Mind

· In the library, fiction books are filed alphabetically by the author's last name.
· Nonfiction books may be classified in ten major categories of the Dewey Decimal System. Each nonfiction book has its own call number.

Now Write As your teacher directs, become familiar with your school or public library. Find out where the fiction and nonfiction books are shelved. Find out where reference books and any special collections are kept.

On your visit to the library, find three fiction and three nonfiction books that you might like to read. Write the titles and authors of these books. Copy the call number or special marking that is written on the spine of any of the books. Label your paper **One for the Books,** and put it into your folder.

It's in the Cards

How To Use the Card Catalog

Here's the Idea   To find out if the library has a book you want, use the **card catalog.** This file lists every book in the library at least three times.

Every library book is recorded on an author card, a title card, and at least one subject card. For a nonfiction book, all three kinds of cards include the call number in the upper left corner. The same number appears on the spine of the book and determines where in the library the book is shelved.

All three cards give the author, title, publisher, date of publication, and number of pages in the book. A notation tells whether the book has illustrations or maps. There may also be a description of the book or a list of other related books. Although all three cards contain the same information, the information is arranged differently on each one.

On an **author card,** the author's name is given at the top, last name first. Author cards are filed alphabetically by the author's last name.

Author
Card

650.14 STA	**Stanat, Kirby**
	Job hunting secrets and tactics / by Kirby Stanat, with Patrick Reardon. —Milwaukee: Westwind Press; Chicago: distributed by Follett Pub. Co., c1977.
	iv, 220 p. : ill.; 24 cm.
	O

Part 2

Objective

To use the card catalog to locate books

Presenting the Lesson

1. Read aloud and discuss **Here's the Idea.** Write the three types of cards on the chalkboard. Below each, write how the card is organized. On the title card, point out that if *A, An,* or *The* is the first word of a title, the card is filed under the second word of the title. Review the meanings of *cross reference cards* and *guide cards.*

2. Read and discuss **Check It Out.** Make sure students understand all the abbreviations used on the cards in the catalog (*c1977, ills., iv, 220p.*). Point out that titles are not capitalized.

3. Assign **Try Your Skill.** Give the students index cards to use for their subject, author, and title cards and then display their answers.

4. Read **Keep This in Mind.**

5. Assign **Now Write.** Have volunteers display their cards.

Individualizing the Lesson

Less-Advanced Students

Have students find author or title cards for two of the books listed in the first part of **Try Your Skill** on page 264 and write any other information they can find on the cards.

Advanced Students

Prepare a list of fiction authors whose work has appealed to your students. Have the students find all the fiction books by that author that are in the library. Instruct the students to write down the title and a brief summary of each book.

Optional Practice

Pass out a library book to each student. Ask students to draw three rectangles on their papers and write a title card, a subject card, and an author card for each assigned book.

Extending the Lesson

Ask each student to choose a subject. Take the class to the library and instruct students to make a bibliography of sources on the subject by using the card catalog. (Provide a sample bibliography to illustrate the format for the class.)

On a **title card,** the title appears on the top line. Only the first word of the title is capitalized. Title cards are filed alphabetically by the first word of the title. However, if *A, An,* or *The* appears as the first word in a title, look for the card under the first letter of the second word in the title.

Title Card

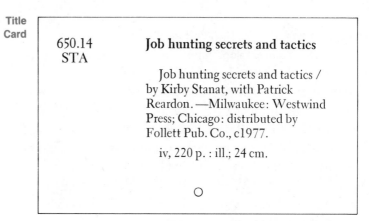

On a **subject card,** the subject appears on the top line. The subject may be written in capital letters or in red. Subject cards are filed alphabetically by the first word of the subject.

Subject Card

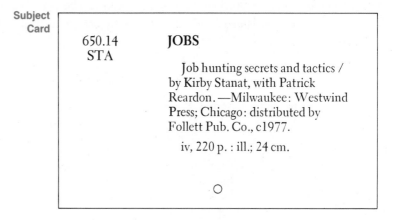

Sometimes you will find a card that states *See* or *See also.* This **cross reference card** refers you to another subject heading closely related to the one you want.

266

Your search for cards in the card catalog will be easier because of **guide cards.** These blank cards have tabs on which are written general subject headings. These headings show you the alphabetical arrangement of the card catalog.

Check It Out   Look at the three sample cards shown, and answer the following questions.

- Under what letter would each card be filed?
- Where would you look for more books by Kirby Stanat?
- Where would you find more books about jobs?

Try Your Skill   Here are the title, author, and call number for a book about astronomy. Draw three rectangles to represent file cards. Use the information below to make an author card, a title card, and a subject card. Make up other details for the cards.

Beyond the Milky Way, by Thornton Page, 523 P145B

Keep This in Mind

- In a library, every book is listed in the card catalog on at least three cards—author, title, and subject.
- Each card gives the author, title, publisher, date of publication, number of pages, and other important information. The card includes the call number of a nonfiction book.

Now Write   Think of a job that interests you. It might be related to music, sports, or medicine. Go to the library. Using the card catalog, find a subject card, title card, and author card related to your possible job. Draw three rectangles to represent the file cards and copy the information from the actual cards. Label your paper **It's in the Cards** and keep it in your folder.

First Stop

Objective

To know how information is arranged in an encyclopedia

Presenting the Lesson

1. Read aloud and discuss **Here's the Idea.** Emphasize that an encyclopedia, like a dictionary, is arranged in alphabetical order. Point out that the letters on the spines of the volumes and the guide words on the pages are aids for using the books. Pay particular attention to the last paragraph, which discusses plagiarism.

2. Read **Check It Out.** Have the students indicate which encyclopedia they have used.

3. Assign **Try Your Skill.** It is suggested you do this as an in-class exercise.

4. Read **Keep This in Mind.**

5. Assign **Now Write.**

Individualizing the Lesson

Less-Advanced Students

Students may have trouble finding the key words in **Try Your Skill.** Discuss each sentence with them, helping them to pick out the main idea to look for. (Would they look up *planet* or *sun* for question 2? Why? Would they look up *coffee* or *Brazil* in question 4? Why?) Give them as many extra examples as they might need until they grasp the concept of *key words.*

Advanced Students

Have the students research the kinds of encyclopedias that their school and public libraries offer.

How To Use an Encyclopedia

Here's the Idea   An encyclopedia is the first source you might want to check for general information. An encyclopedia is a reference work that contains articles on a great many different subjects. The subjects of the articles are arranged in alphabetical order from the first volume through the last. On the spine of each volume is a single letter or guide letters that tell you what subjects are included. Look at the set of encyclopedias arranged below.

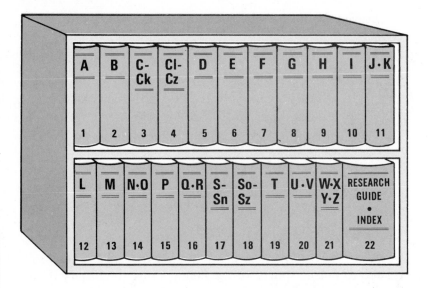

Suppose that you were writing a report on what to see in Washington, D.C. You might use the *World Book Encyclopedia, Collier's Encyclopedia,* or the *Britannica Junior Encyclopaedia.* Find the appropriate volume and look up "Washington,

D.C." Notice that there are guide words at the top of each page, just as there are in a dictionary. These guide words help you to find your subject quickly.

An encyclopedia article on a major subject is usually presented in various parts with subtitles. An article on Washington, D.C. may include such parts as "The City," "People," "History," "Local Government," "Economy," and "A Visitor's Guide." Sometimes you may want to read only the parts related to your specific topic. At other times you may need to read the entire article.

It is always a good idea to check the end of the article for a list of related articles in the encyclopedia or for a list of books for further reading. In addition, some encyclopedias present a guide to help you organize your study of a particular subject.

Many encyclopedias include an index. It may be the first or last volume of the set. You may need the index to find information that is presented under different related subjects in different volumes. Some encyclopedias also publish yearbooks, which contain up-to-date information on certain subjects.

Besides general encyclopedias, there are others that deal with specific subjects. Some of the special encyclopedias may deal with careers, art, sports, or cooking, for example. Others may cover music, animals, or health. These encyclopedias will probably be located in the reference area of the library.

Any large library will have several sets of encyclopedias. Different encyclopedias will have different reading levels. To find the one that will help you, skim through several or ask a librarian for help.

Try to use more than one encyclopedia as a source of information. Check other encyclopedias or kinds of reference books. If different sources give different information, try to use the most recent or most reliable source. Remember that if you use the exact words from any encyclopedia or source, you must use quotation marks. Quotation marks show that you have copied material exactly from an original source.

Make sure they include encyclopedias on specific subjects.

Optional Practice

Have students follow the directions for **Try Your Skill** for the following questions.

1. Which is the oldest college in the United States?
2. Which country first tried to dig the Panama Canal?
3. Who discovered the Hawaiian Islands?
4. Where are the most diamonds mined?
5. Why were the time zones set up in the United States?

Extending the Lesson

Select twenty-six different subjects, each beginning with a different letter of the alphabet. Assign each student a subject and ask him or her to look it up in three different encyclopedias. Then have each student rate the encyclopedias on various dimensions: (1) quality of the information; (2) quantity of information; (3) illustrations; (4) readability (Tell students to consider the use of vocabulary, sentence length, subheadings, and type face.); and (5) listings of additional sources. One way to handle this assignment is to make a rating sheet and distribute three copies to each student. As a follow-up, discuss the strengths and weaknesses of the encyclopedias available to the students.

Check It Out   Look at an encyclopedia in your school or public library. Answer the following questions.

- In what volume will you find information about dancing? spiders? sculpture? the Allegheny Mountains? ancient Egypt? the United Nations?

Try Your Skill   Number your paper from 1 to 8. Write the key word in each question below that tells you what to look up in an encyclopedia.

1. When did the game of <u>basketball</u> begin?
2. What <u>planet</u> is farthest from the sun?
3. Name five animals that are <u>mammals</u>.
4. How many pounds of coffee a year does <u>Brazil</u> export?
5. What common foods are made from <u>flour</u>?
6. What was the total number of home runs that <u>Babe Ruth</u> hit?
7. What is the name of the largest natural <u>lake</u> in the world?
8. What was daily life like in the ancient <u>Roman Empire</u>?

Keep This in Mind

- An encyclopedia is a general reference work that contains information on many different subjects.
- Articles are arranged alphabetically in numbered volumes. Examine a variety of encyclopedias. Choose one that you can read easily.

Now Write   Write the name of the job that you chose in the last lesson. Look up the job or related field in at least two encyclopedias. Jot down a few of the most interesting facts. Compare the information you find in the two encyclopedias. Be sure to list the name of each encyclopedia that you used, the number and guide letters of the volume, the guide words on the page, and the title of any other articles or books on the subject. Label your paper **First Stop** and put it into your folder.

Fact Finding

How To Use Reference Works

Here's the Idea   In addition to encyclopedias, you will find several other kinds of books in the reference section of your library. Each kind of reference work deals with one particular area of information. Most of these specialized books explain the symbols and abbreviations used, how the information is arranged, and show sample entries. When you use any reference work for the first time, examine this introductory explanation so that you can use the book most effectively. There are several major kinds of reference works you will find helpful.

An **atlas** is a book of maps. However, atlases may also contain information about population, weather, and particular places in every part of the world. Some widely used atlases include the *National Geographic Atlas of the World*, *The International Atlas from Rand McNally*, and the *Atlas of World History*.

Almanacs and yearbooks are published each year. They are the most useful source of up-to-date facts and statistics. These reference works contain current information about world events, governments, population, sports, and annual awards. You may want to use the *Guinness Book of World Records*, the *World Almanac and Book of Facts*, the *Information Please Almanac, Atlas, and Yearbook*, or the *Statesman's Yearbook*.

Biographical references are books that contain information about the lives of important people. Usually, these reference works deal with people who are grouped together into one classification, such as presidents or authors. Among the most useful biographical references are *The Book of Presidents*, *Current Biography*, *Who's Who*, *Twentieth Century Authors*, and the *Dictionary of American Biography*.

A **vertical file** is the name of a collection of assorted pamphlets, handbooks, catalogs, and clippings that are kept in a file

271

Part 4

Objective

To know the major kinds of reference works and how to use them

Presenting the Lesson

1. If possible, present this part of the section in the library reference area. If that is not possible, arrange to have as many of the reference works as possible brought to the classroom so that the students can examine the books during the discussion.

2. Read and discuss **Here's the Idea.** Ask students which reference works they may have already used.

3. Read and discuss **Check It Out.** Make sure students know where to find the key to the abbreviations used.

4. Assign **Try Your Skill.** Discuss students' answers in class.

5. Read **Keep This in Mind** and then assign **Now Write.** Have students share the information they find. Emphasize the importance of noting the source of information.

Individualizing the Lesson

Less-Advanced Students

Have the students do **Try Your Skill** with a partner.

Advanced Students

Have the students make an annotated catalog of the most important reference materials in the library. Divide the class into groups, one for each kind of reference work. Have each group list the title of each book or resource, tell how the resource is

271

arranged, and briefly describe the type of information each includes. Compile the information, reproduce it, and give a copy to each student.

Optional Practice

Have the students make up a list of famous people they have studied about or they admire. Have them go to the library and find at least three sources of information on the people on the list. Only one of their sources may be an encyclopedia.

Extending the Lesson

Duplicate the key to abbreviations for the *Readers' Guide* and review it with the class. Then hand out a copy of a page from the *Readers' Guide*. Ask students to write out three entries without using any abbreviations.

cabinet. This collection will vary from library to library. However, it may include special information about careers, travel, and local events, and catalogs of schools and colleges.

Magazines are valuable sources of information about a wide range of subjects. A library may subscribe to any number of the leading magazines published in the U.S. In order to find specific information in magazine articles, you need to become familiar with the *Readers' Guide to Periodical Literature.* The *Readers' Guide* lists the titles of articles, stories, and poems published in more than 100 leading magazines. One hardcover volume of the *Readers' Guide* covers material for an entire year. Several smaller, paperback volumes cover shorter time periods. The *Readers' Guide* is a useful tool to help you research any subject. It is important to learn to use this specially abbreviated source book.

Check It Out   Here is a portion of a page from the *Readers' Guide to Periodical Literature.*

Juniper
Don't overlook the low-growing junipers. N. B. Simpson. il *South Living* 18:114-17 N '83
name of magazine ⎯⎯⎯⎯⎯⎯

Junk
The Age of Junk [symposium] il *Roll Stone* p95+ D 22 '83-Ja 5 '84

Junk food
author ⎯⎯⎯⎯⎯⎯ Life is a hamburger. A. Latham. il *Roll Stone* p103-9 D 22 '83-Ja 5 '84

Junor, Penny
title of article ⎯⎯⎯⎯⎯⎯ Christmas with the royal family. il *McCalls* 111:90-1+ D '83

Jupiter (Planet)
cross reference ⎯⎯⎯⎯⎯⎯ *See also*
Space flight—Voyager flights
Space flight to Jupiter

Atmosphere
volume number ⎯⎯⎯⎯⎯⎯ X-rays from Jupiter. il *Sky Telesc* 66;398-9 N '83

Magnetic properties
Jupiter's tail at Saturn: the clincher [Voyager data] J. Eberhart. *Sci News* 124:215 O 1 '83
page reference ⎯⎯⎯⎯⎯⎯

Ring system
Around and around with planetary rings [Voyager data] J. Eberhart. il *Sci News* 124:295 N 5 '83
date of magazine ⎯⎯⎯⎯⎯⎯

- Read through one listing for an article in this sample and explain completely the information given. Where is the *Readers' Guide* kept in your school or public library? What other kinds of reference works are in the reference section of your library?

Try Your Skill   What reference works would you probably use to answer each of the following questions? Write your answers. Mention a specific reference if possible. If you think magazines might be the best reference, write *Readers' Guide* as the place you would look.

1. How many states in the United States have a city or town named Paris?
2. Who is the current head of state in China?
3. Name two guidelines for jogging safely.
4. What is the area of Texas?
5. Name two books by Pearl S. Buck.
6. Name five current leaders in major United States businesses.
7. What is the most efficient way to insulate a home?
8. What jobs might be listed in a pamphlet called "Careers in the Food Industry"?

Keep This in Mind

- There are several major kinds of specific reference works. Learn to use the ones in your library.

Now Write   Choose a person you admire or a place you'd like to visit. Look up information on your topic in several specific reference works. Jot down at least four interesting facts that you learn. List the references that contain the information. Give their titles, call numbers, and the volumes and page numbers where you find the information. Label your paper **Fact Finding.** Keep your work in your folder.

Section **23** Objectives

1. To understand and record assignments

2. To learn to follow spoken and written directions

3. To choose a study area and a regular study time

4. To understand and use the SQ3R study method

5. To learn how to take notes

6. To learn when and how to adjust reading rates

7. To understand how to use graphic aids

8. To understand how to interpret graphs

9. To understand how to prepare for and take tests

10. To recognize and prepare for objective tests

11. To recognize and prepare for written tests

Preparing the Students

Ask students to discuss the problems they encounter when they complete assignments or take tests. Such problems may include difficulty in following directions, not knowing how to study efficiently, feeling overwhelmed by the assignments, or nervousness. Tell students that this section will help them to learn good study test taking skills.

Additional Resouces

Practice Book — pages 111–121

Duplicating Masters — pages 111–121

Teaching Special Populations

LD This section is crucial for LD students. Because LD students often find it difficult to follow directions, you should pay particular attention to the exercises in Part 2.

274

Study and Research Skills

Make doubly sure that students understand the specific meaning of key words (*analyze, describe, list, compare, organize,* and so on) frequently encountered in written directions. Give students a list of assorted instructions and have them underline the key words in each. Also have them tell specifically what actions should proceed from each set of directions.

Pay particular attention to Parts 9–11. Give students timed practice tests, pointing out that they will be able to answer more questions in a set time if they answer the easy ones first.

ESL Finding time for study and research presents a particular problem for many ESL students. Many of them live in crowded conditions, and may thus have trouble locating a quiet study area. They may also have to work long hours after school or care for younger family members. Try to compensate for this problem by giving students flexible assignment dates. Spend extra time on in-class work and inform students about alternative study areas such as public libraries or reading rooms.

NSD Most of us understand that the language found in instructions or on test questions conforms to a set of commonly accepted academic norms. For NSD students, however, this type of language is particularly intimidating. Give NSD students additional practice in decoding the language of assignments and test questions. Help them familiarize themselves with the highly formal style sometimes encountered in research materials.

Part 1

Note Well

Objective

To understand and record assignments

Presenting the Lesson

1. Ask students what kind of directions, other than schoolwork, that they encounter in the course of a day. Ask them what methods they use to remember those directions. Then read and discuss **Here's the Idea.** Point out that students should not just write down *when* an assignment is due. Explain that it is important to understand *all* the information about the assignment.

2. Read and discuss **Check It Out.** Stress that if students do not understand an assignment, they should ask questions until they do.

3. Assign **Try Your Skill.** Tell students to go over the assignment in their minds, imagining step-by-step what materials they will need.

4. Read **Keep This in Mind.**

5. Assign **Now Write.** Require each student to carry some type of assignment notebook for recording assignments for the rest of the school year.

Individualizing the Lesson

Less-Advanced Students

1. Make sure the students understand the definitions of *resources* and *final product.*

2. Help the students set up their assignment notebooks for **Now Write** by duplicating some pages for a notebook. Check students' assignment notebooks periodically after

Understanding the Assignment

Here's the Idea One of the most important study skills is understanding your assignments. Whenever your teachers give you an assignment, you must listen closely. Then, you must record the assignment carefully in an assignment notebook. Make sure that you record both the subject of the assignment and all specific instructions. You should also record the date the assignment is given and the date it is due. Here is a sample page from an assignment notebook:

Subject	Assignment	Date Given	Date Due
Soc. Studies	Read Chapter 8. Answer questions 1 and 3 on p. 148.	Jan 9	Jan 11
Spanish	Memorize dialogue on p. 218.	Jan. 9	Jan. 12

Before you begin an assignment, ask these questions.

1. Will I have to read, study, or memorize? Will I have to write, answer questions, or make something?

2. Will I hand in a composition, a report, a list of answers, or a written copy of a speech? Will I present a demonstration?

3. Do I need any special supplies? Do I need materials from the library?

4. When is the assignment due? How much time do I have?

Check It Out   Read the following sample science assignment.

Make a chart showing the daily weather forecast and the actual weather for an entire week. Write the forecast in blue ink and the actual weather in red ink. The chart will be due on Friday.

· What does this assignment ask you to do?
· What will the final product be?
· What supplies or resources will you need?
· When is the assignment due?

Try Your Skill   Read the sample English assignment below. What kind of assignment is it? What will your final product be? What materials will you need to complete the assignment? When is it due?

By Wednesday, find two advertisements that use characters or events from ancient myths. The best places to look for these ads are in newspapers, magazines, and the telephone book. Bring the ads to class.

Keep This in Mind

· Write all information about assignments in an assignment notebook.
· Know what to do to complete the assignment.
· Know what your final product will be.
· Know what materials you will need.
· Know the due date of the assignment.

Now Write   Start an assignment notebook. Make four columns on a sheet of paper. Label the columns as shown in **Here's the Idea.** Use these columns to record information about your assignments.

277

you give an assignment to make sure they are recording the information correctly.

Advanced Students

Have the students make up a dictionary of key words often used in assignments: *analyze, evaluate, interpret, review, identify, compare, contrast,* etc. Have the students prepare copies for the entire class.

Optional Practice

Have the students pick out the key words and instructions in each of the following assignments, and answer the questions listed on page 276.

1. Take notes on Chapter Six in your history book and bring them to class tomorrow.
2. Memorize the formula for the perimeter of a rectangle for a test on Thursday.
3. For next Monday, construct a three-dimensional map showing the location of the Rocky Mountains.

Extending the Lesson

Have the students bring textbooks from other classes that list suggested activities and assignments. Ask the students to read sample assignments aloud and ask the class to answer the questions on page 276 about the assignments. Have the students list any questions they would need to ask to clarify the assignments.

Part 2

Part 2

This Way, Please

Objective

To learn to follow spoken and written directions

Presenting the Lesson

1. Read and discuss **Here's the Idea.** Emphasize the importance of listening closely to spoken directions.

2. Read and discuss **Check It Out.** Point out how closely related the "questions for understanding an assignment" on page 276 are to the guidelines on page 278. Explain that understanding an assignment and following directions for an assignment are complementary skills.

3. Have students complete **Try Your Skill.** Point out that not reading all of the directions first often results in more work.

4. Read **Keep This in Mind.**

5. Assign **Now Write.**

Individualizing the Lesson

Less-Advanced Students

1. These students may have trouble dividing an assignment into steps. Give them practice in this and in following directions. Have them bring several textbooks to class or use assignments they have had in other classes. Go over the directions to various activities and exercises. Stress the key word in each step, the materials needed for the assignment, and the final product called for.

2. Do **Now Write** as an in-class assignment. Using students' suggestions, list all the steps in the proper order on the chalkboard.

Here's the Idea   Whenever you play a game, you follow a set of directions. These directions tell you what to do, how to do it, and when it must be done. If you do not follow the directions, the game will not make sense.

The same is true of the directions you are given for completing assignments. You must follow these directions carefully if you want to complete your work correctly. Directions may be either spoken or written.

These guidelines will help you to follow spoken directions:

Following Spoken Directions

1. Listen carefully. Write down the directions as you hear them.
2. Notice what steps are involved in the assignment. Also notice the order of these steps.
3. Listen for the key word in each step. These are words that tell you what to do. Examples are *read, write, organize,* and *memorize.*
4. If you do not understand, ask your teacher to explain the directions.

These guidelines will help you to follow written directions:

Following Written Directions

1. Read all the directions before you begin the assignment.
2. Divide the assignment into steps. Put these steps in a logical order.
3. Ask your teacher to explain any steps that you don't understand.
4. Before you begin work, gather all books and other materials you need to complete the assignment.

Check It Out   Read the following sample assignment.

Make a list of six words that sound like what they describe. Examples include words like *meow* and *buzz*. Make sure that the words you choose can be found in a dictionary. Then, on a separate piece of paper, write three sentences. In each sentence, use at least two words from your list.

- What steps are included in this assignment?
- What materials will you need?
- What questions could you ask to make the assignment clearer?
- Do you know when the assignment is due?

Try Your Skill   Read and follow this set of directions.

1. On a piece of paper, write two last names that are also names of places. (Example: *York*)
2. Write two last names that are also names of colors.
3. If your last name begins with a letter between *A* and *P*, do only number 1, above.
4. If your last name begins with a letter between *Q* and *Z*, do only number 2, above.

Keep This in Mind

- Carefully listen to or read all directions before you begin an assignment.
- Divide your assignments into steps. Place these steps in logical order.
- Ask your teacher to explain if you don't understand.

Now Write   Imagine that you are writing a student handbook to be used by next year's new students. Write directions for checking out a book from your school library. Include all the necessary steps. Place these steps in a logical order. Label your paper **This Way, Please.** Save it in your folder.

279

Have students make up lists of directions on how to move around the classroom (example: go past the first desk on the right, turn around two times, circle the teacher's desk and return to your seat while hopping on one leg). Have one student read his or her directions aloud while the class takes notes. Have one student try to follow the directions from the notes.

Optional Practice

Give students the following oral directions. Give each instruction no more than twice. Discuss with students how well they followed your spoken directions.

1. Take out a sheet of notebook paper and a pencil.
2. On the top line of your paper, on the right hand side, print your name in capital letters..
3. Skip two lines down from your name and list your address, your phone number, and your mother's first name.
4. Skip three lines. Then write down each class you take, skipping two lines between each item.
5. Turn your paper over when you are finished following these directions.

Extending the Lesson

Have four volunteers leave the classroom. Explain a set of directions to one student. Ask him or her to repeat the directions to one of the volunteers who returns to the room. Ask that volunteer to repeat the directions to the next volunteer, and so on. Have the class compare the final set of directions to the original one.

Objective

To choose a study area and a regular study time

Presenting the Lesson

1. Ask students where they usually do their studying. Then read and discuss **Here's the Idea.** Ask students if their study area meets the qualifications on page 280. Make sure they understand the terms *long-* and *short-term goals*.

2. Read and discuss **Check It Out.** Stress that in order to do a good job on long-term projects, students must break the project down into smaller, more manageable tasks. Point out that social events are also included in this study plan.

3. Assign **Try Your Skill.**

4. Read **Keep This in Mind** and then assign **Now Write.**

Individualizing the Lesson

Less-Advanced Students

1. Ask the students to classify these assignments as short-term or long-term: writing a research report, writing an explanatory *how* paragraph, working one page of math problems, memorizing twenty vocabulary words, writing an analysis, and drawing an illustration of a character in a book they are reading. Ask how the larger projects would be broken down into smaller tasks.

2. Help the students set up their study plans for **Now Write.** If students have long-term assignments in any of their classes, help them to break the assignments down into short-term steps.

A Quiet Place

A Time and a Place for Studying

Here's the Idea Studying should be done in a special place. This place may be at home, at school, or in a library. Make sure that your study area meets the following requirements:

The Study Area

1. **A study area should be quiet.** Distractions such as conversation, television, or loud music can hurt your concentration.

2. **A study area should be well lit.** Studying in poorly lighted areas can cause eyestrain and headaches.

3. **A study area should be neat and organized.** Working in a messy study area can cause you to waste time searching for materials.

4. **A study area should be properly equipped.** Keep paper, pens, pencils, a dictionary, and other materials close at hand.

5. **A study area should be available at a regular time.** Set aside a specific time for study each day. Make sure that your study area is available at this time.

In addition to organizing your study area, you must also organize your study time. After school each day, look over your assignments. Think of each assignment as a goal. An assignment that is due the next day is a short-term goal. An assignment that is due after several days or weeks is a long-term goal.

To complete each type of assignment, work out a schedule for yourself. If an assignment is short-term, set a time to complete it before the next day. If an assignment is long-term, divide it into steps. Set a time for completing each step.

To help you to schedule your short- and long-term goals, make a study plan each week. Record the time when you will complete each of your assignments.

Check It Out

Bill was asked to memorize a poem to recite in speech class. He broke this long-term assignment into steps. He included these steps on his study plan, as follows:

Monday	Tuesday	Wednesday	Thursday	Saturday	Sunday
Go to library Get book of poems	Track practice (4:00)	Guitar lesson (5:00)	Finish memoriz- ing poem	Practice poem	Dinner at the Smith's
Study for history test	Study for history test	Study for history test		Danny's birthday party	
	Read poems and choose one				

- How did Bill divide up his long-term assignment?
- Do you see how this study plan made it easier for Bill to complete his assignment?

Try Your Skill

Break up the following sample long-term assignment into several steps. Arrange the steps in order.

Do some research on a famous artist, explorer, or inventor. Write a one-paragraph biography of this person. Tell when and where this person was born. Describe his or her major accomplishments. Today is Monday. The report is due on Friday.

Keep This in Mind

- Choose a study area that is quiet and organized.
- Break all long-term assignments into smaller steps.
- Make a study plan every week.

Now Write

Make a study plan like the one shown in **Check It Out.** Include on this plan all your assignments and major activities for one week. Make a study plan every week.

281

Part 4

Objective

To understand and use the SQ3R study method

Presenting the Lesson

1. Read and discuss **Here's the Idea.** Write the five headings of the method on the board and review what each involves. Emphasize that the SQ3R method helps students get the most from what they read.

2. Read and discuss **Check It Out.** Make sure students see that the more steps of SQ3R that they complete, the more information they will remember.

3. Assign **Try Your Skill.** Use this exercise with an overhead projector, demonstrating the SQ3R procedure.

4. Read **Keep This in Mind.**

5. Assign **Now Write.** After the students have completed this exercise, have them explain how they used SQ3R, and ask them how much it helped them to learn the material.

Individualizing the Lesson

Less-Advanced Students

Discuss how students can identify the main ideas in a section. Help them see that topic sentences, headings, boldface or italic print, and repetition provide clues to an idea's importance.

Advanced Students

Have the students make a bulletin board display illustrating the five steps in the SQ3R method. Use the

Making the Most of It

The SQ3R Study Method

Here's the Idea   Have you ever read an assignment and then forgotten most of what you read? This can be frustrating. It can also lead to poor scores on tests. To avoid this, you should follow a study method. Following a study method can help you to make the most of your reading. One such method is called SQ3R. SQ3R stands for *Survey, Question, Read, Recite,* and *Review.* The following chart describes the SQ3R study method.

Using SQ3R	
Survey.	Look over the material to get a general idea of what you will be reading. Read the introduction and, if there is one, the summary. Check the titles and headings. Look at any illustrations.
Question.	Prepare a set of questions. Decide what questions you should be able to answer at the end of your reading. Use any study questions presented in the book or provided by your teacher. Make up your own study questions by turning each title and heading into a question. Pictures, maps, or charts can also be used to make up questions.
Read.	Look for the answers to your questions as you read. Also identify the main ideas in each section.
Recite.	After you finish your careful reading, recite in your own words the answers to your questions. Make notes on the answers. In addition, make sure you understand any other important points of the selection. Record these too.
Review.	Quickly read over your notes. Look over the main ideas in the book so you will remember them. Look up the answers to any questions you could not answer in the previous step.

Check It Out   Rolanda had to study for a test on Chapter 3 in her biology book. She read the introduction and summary. She glanced at the titles and headings. She made up a list of study questions. Then she read the chapter closely, looking for answers to her questions.

• What else should Rolanda do?

Try Your Skill   Study this passage, using the SQ3R method.

The **alligator** is a large reptile related to the crocodile. It is found in the southeastern United States and in the lower Chang Jiang river valley in China.

Body. Alligators look like enormous lizards. They have short, stocky legs used for walking and long, powerful tails used for swimming. The jaws of an alligator are filled with many sharp teeth. The muscles that close these jaws are very strong. However, once an alligator's jaws are closed, they can easily be held shut by a human being.

Size. Alligators may grow to twelve feet or more in length. An adult male may weigh from 450 to 550 pounds. An adult female usually weighs much less.

Diet. Alligators eat small animals of all kinds. Their diet includes fish, snakes, frogs, turtles, and various small mammals. Large alligators occasionally attack dogs, pigs, or even cattle. However, alligators rarely attack people.

Keep This in Mind

• The SQ3R study method consists of five steps: *Survey, Question, Read, Recite,* and *Review.*
• Use the SQ3R method to study for all your classes.

Now Write   Choose any reading assignment you receive in school today. Using the SQ3R method, study this assignment. First, survey the material. Then, write a list of questions you should be able to answer after you finish reading. Save the list.

display as a reinforcement for the class and to encourage them to use the method.

Optional Practice

Provide the students with duplicates of a brief informative magazine article, and have them practice the SQ3R study method. Help them to formulate questions to answer. When they have completed the assignment, give the students a quiz to see how well they remember the information.

Extending the Lesson

Make sure that students are familiar with the parts of a book that can help them to locate specific material quickly and easily while they study.

1. table of contents–gives summary of book's contents
2. text–contains body of the book
3. appendices–provide additional information, often in the form of graphic aids
4. notes–contains footnotes to works cited in the text
5. bibliography–lists sources used in writing the book
6. glossary–gives definitions of unusual or technical terms
7. index–provides alphabetical list of subjects in the book and their page numbers

Objective

To learn how to take notes

Presenting the Lesson

1. Read and discuss **Here's the Idea.** Go over each paragraph separately, making sure students understand each note-taking technique you are discussing. Point out how important note-taking is for every study and research technique they have learned or will learn.

Emphasize that notes must be legible and abbreviations and symbols understandable, so that students will always be able to read and study their notes effectively.

2. Read and discuss **Check It Out.** Point out how the use of abbreviations saves space and time.

3. Assign **Try Your Skill.** Have volunteers share their notes.

4. Read **Keep This in Mind.**

5. Assign **Now Write.**

Individualizing the Lesson

Less-Advanced Students

Have the students practice taking notes about filmstrips, brief taped lectures, or textbook chapters. Work with them, pointing out important ideas and helping them to decide which are minor details that need not be recorded.

Advanced Students

Have the students consult their notes from other classes and list often-used abbreviations and symbols. Reproduce the lists for the class's use. Point out that special

Remember This

Taking Notes

Here's the Idea Every day in school you read and hear a great deal of information. Remembering all this information can be difficult. If you take good notes, however, you can review the information at a later time. That's why it is important for you to learn how to take good notes.

Always keep your notes in a notebook. Divide your notebook into sections for each class. Write the date and the subject at the top of each page of notes. Take notes on ideas presented in class and in your reading. Include in your notes any questions that arise when you are studying.

In class, listen for clues that tell what information is important. These clues include phrases such as *most importantly, for these reasons, to conclude, for example, the cause was,* and *to review.* Also listen for vocal clues. Your teacher might slow down, repeat a key word or definition, or pause for emphasis.

As you read, take notes on key words, definitions, and main ideas. Also write the answers to any questions that you develop when using the SQ3R study method.

One way to take good notes is to make a rough outline. As you listen or read, jot down main ideas. Under these main ideas, jot down any supporting examples or details.

When taking notes, write neatly. Make sure that you will be able to read your notes later. Do not waste time writing complete sentences. Instead, use phrases, abbreviations, and symbols.

If you wish to do so, make up your own abbreviations. However, make sure that you will be able to understand these abbreviations when you come back to your notes. The following abbreviations and symbols are often used in note-taking.

Abbreviations and Symbols for Note-Taking

w/	with	*info.*	information
w/o	without	*def.*	definition
+	and	*Amer.*	American
bef.	before	*hist.*	history
*	important information	*tho.*	though
		=	is, are, equals

Check It Out   Read these notes in rough outline form.

Science
Nov. 1

Amphibians
– def: animal that lives part of
   life in water, part on land
Types of amphibians
– Frogs and toads (4 legs, w/o tails)
– Salamanders (2 or 4 legs + tails)
– Caecilians (look like earthworms)

- What abbreviations and symbols has this student used?

Try Your Skill   Using the guidelines in this lesson, take notes on the selection on alligators in Part 4.

Keep This in Mind

- Use a rough outline form when taking notes.
- As you take notes, use phrases, abbreviations, and symbols. Do not use complete sentences.

Now Write   Reread Part 2, **This Way, Please.** Take notes on this material, using a rough outline form. Save your notes.

285

abbreviations can be invented for use on specific lectures. For example, if an entire lecture is going to be about electricity, students could use the abbreviation *E* throughout their notes.

Optional Practice

Have students take notes about a magazine article that they find interesting. Then, using their notes, have students give reports to the class on the articles they've read.

Extending the Lesson

Have students take notes on an educational television program, such as *Nova* or a *National Geographic* special. Have them discuss the program the next day, using their notes for reference.

Part 6

Objective

To learn when and how to adjust reading rate

Presenting the Lesson

1. Ask students if they ever read anything very quickly, or very slowly, and when. Tell them that an efficient reader varies his or her reading speed to suit the type of material and the purpose for reading it. Then read and discuss **Here's the Idea.** Write the terms *scanning, skimming,* and *in-depth reading* on the chalkboard. Ask students to define each type of reading and explain when it is used.

2. Discuss **Check It Out.** Point out that this is just one situation where it is not important to read every word.

3. Assign **Try Your Skill.** Make sure students follow the directions for this exercise correctly.

4. Read **Keep This in Mind** aloud.

5. Assign **Now Write.**

Individualizing the Lesson

Less-Advanced Students

1. Point out that the table of contents, index, and heading can help students when skimming.

2. Once students have done the first direction in **Try Your Skill,** give them a time limit of thirty seconds to do the second direction. This will force them to read quickly and not word for word.

Advanced Students

Instruct students to find any book in the library dealing with the Old

286

One Way or Another

Adjusting Your Reading Rate

Here's the Idea   When you are in a hurry, you run or walk quickly. When you are not in a hurry, you walk more slowly. In other words, you change your speed depending on your purpose. Similarly, you can change the way you read depending on what you are reading and why you are reading it.

In-Depth Reading   When you need to learn new or difficult material, read slowly and carefully. Follow the SQ3R method. Read every word. Pay particular attention to definitions, key words, topic sentences, and headings. These will help you to find the main ideas. Once you have identified the main ideas, look for any supporting details.

Fast Reading   Sometimes you may need to use a faster type of reading. Two useful types of fast reading are skimming and scanning.

1. **Skimming** involves moving your eyes quickly over a whole page or selection. When skimming, do not read every word. Instead, note titles, subtitles, headings, pictures, and graphic aids. Use skimming to get a general idea of the content of a selection. You can also use it to survey material as the first step in the SQ3R study method.

2. **Scanning** involves moving your eyes quickly across a line or down a page. It is used to locate specific information. Again, do not read every word. Instead, look for a key word or phrase that shows that you are close to the information you need. When you locate such a clue, read more slowly.

Check It Out   Tim took a test in his science class. One of the questions asked for a definition of the word *Phylum*. Tim

286

couldn't remember the definition. After the test, he checked the definition in his science book. He knew it was in Chapter 2.

- What kind of fast reading should Tim do, skimming or scanning? Explain your answer.

Try Your Skill   Follow these directions one at a time. Do *not* read all of the directions first.

1. Read the passage in depth.
2. Scan to answer the following questions:
   a. How large is the Dismal Swamp?
   b. What plant life grows there?
   c. What animals live there?

One of the most interesting places in America is the Dismal Swamp. This is a wild marshland in northeastern North Carolina and southeastern Virginia. The swamp covers about 750 square miles. It is a tangle of vines and trees. Its trees include pines, junipers, and bald cypresses. Its wildlife includes bears, deer, opossums, raccoons, and snakes.

Keep This in Mind

- Choose a reading speed that suits the material you are reading and your reason for reading it.
- Use in-depth reading when you wish to learn new or difficult material.
- Use skimming to survey material.
- Use scanning to locate specific information.

Now Write   Find a recent copy of a local newspaper. First, scan the front page. Make a list of people whose names are in the news. Second, skim the articles on the front page. Tell what each article is about. Finally, read one article in depth and summarize it. Write your answers on a piece of paper. Label this paper **One Way or Another.** Save it in your folder.

West. Ask them to scan the book and write down whether it contains information on the following:

Mountain Men
Native American Tribes
Early Settlers
Trapping
Legendary Figures

Optional Practice

Ask students to skim reference books to find the following information:

the function of the appendix in the body
the two ways to release atomic energy
the name of the head of the Canadian government

You may want to set a specific, limited time period for this exercise to encourage students to skim rather than read word for word.

Extending the Lesson

Have each student bring a newspaper to class. Ask students to practice different types of reading by:

1. skimming the front page for an understanding of the day's top news
2. skimming the want ads to see what types of ads are there
3. scanning the sports page for the previous day's winning teams
4. finding two articles of special interest to them and reading them in depth

After students complete these activities, discuss how they can use their reading skills to become more efficient newspaper readers.

Part 7

Seeing Is Believing

Using Graphic Aids

Part 7

Objective

To understand how to use graphic aids

Presenting the Lesson

1. Read and discuss **Here's the Idea.** Go over the types of graphic aids and the purposes for which each is used. As you review the four types of graphic aids, direct students' attention to the examples in **Check It Out.**

2. Discuss **Check It Out.** Remind students to look for and read headings, titles, and keys.

3. Assign **Try Your Skill.** Have students explain where and how they found the answers to the questions.

4. Read **Keep This in Mind** and then assign **Now Write.**

Individualizing the Lesson

Less-Advanced Students

1. Project several types of graphic aids using an overhead projector. Lead students through a step-by-step process for reading and interpreting each one. Ask students what the graphics do that written words would not do.

2. Discuss with the students the type of information that needs to be presented in **Now Write.** Help them visualize the graphic aid before they make it.

Advanced Students

Provide the students with an informative magazine or newspaper article and ask them to discuss how graphic aids could be used to visually add information to the article.

Here's the Idea Not all information is presented in words. Some information comes in the form of photographs, illustrations, diagrams, maps, tables, charts, and graphs. Such materials are called **graphic aids.** The following are the most common graphic aids:

Photographs and illustrations are used to show how things look. They are also used to create a mood or a feeling. Always read any captions or labels given with a picture.

Diagrams are drawings that show the parts of a thing. They allow you to identify each part and to see how the parts are related. Always read any captions or labels given with a diagram.

Maps show locations of cities, countries, oceans, mountains, rivers, and other parts of the Earth. They can also show such information as population or climate. Always look for the legend that is found on most maps. The **legend** will help you to figure out distances or directions on the map.

Tables and charts are used to list or compare information. Information is usually presented in labeled columns. Always read any captions or titles given with tables or charts.

Graphs show relationships between facts. Sometimes they show how facts change over time. (See Part 8 for more information on graphs.) Always read any captions, titles, or labels included with graphs.

Check It Out Study the graphic aids on the next page.

- Which graphic aid is a map? an illustration? a diagram? a graph? a table?

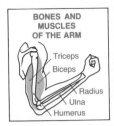

BONES AND
MUSCLES
OF THE ARM

Triceps
Biceps
Radius
Ulna
Humerus

THE HAWAIIAN ISLANDS

KAUAI
OAHU
MOLOKAI
Honolulu
MAUI
Hilo
HAWAII

THE LIBERTY BELL

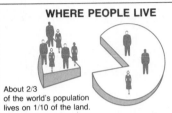

WHERE PEOPLE LIVE

About 2/3
of the world's population
lives on 1/10 of the land.

THE OLDEST U.S. UNIVERSITIES AND COLLEGES	
NAME	CHARTERED
Harvard University	1636
William and Mary College	1693
Yale University	1701
Princeton University	1746
Columbia University	1754

Try Your Skill   Look at the graphic aids in **Check It Out.**
Answer these questions:

   1. On which island is Hilo situated?

   2. What proportion of the world's population lives on 9/10 of the
land?

   3. Name two muscles of the upper arm.

   4. Which is the second oldest university in the United States?

Keep This in Mind

- Graphic aids show information quickly and clearly. Photographs, illustrations, maps, diagrams, tables, charts, and graphs are graphic aids.

Now Write   Make one of the following graphic aids.

   1. **A Map.** Using a ruler, draw a map of the main floor of your
school. Show where important areas, such as the library or gym, are
located. Include a caption and a legend.

   2. **A Diagram.** Trace a picture of a musical instrument or an
automobile. Then, using information from an encyclopedia, label the
parts of your drawing. Write a caption for your diagram.

289

1. Have the students clip examples of the different types of graphic aids used in one day's newspaper.

2. Reproduce an informative article such as one in *National Geographic* that gives a wide range of facts about a subject. Delete all pictures, charts, and graphs. Have the students suggest three graphic aids that would be helpful in presenting the article. You may wish to have students actually create such graphics.

Extending the Lesson

Have the computer teacher or a guest speaker talk to the class about computer graphics. If possible, let the students try a hands-on demonstration.

Part 8

Objective

To understand how to interpret graphs

Presenting the Lesson

1. Read and discuss **Here's the Idea.** Tell the students that although graphs are made so people can draw conclusions from them, they still must be careful that enough information is given in a graph so that the conclusions are valid.

2. Discuss **Check It Out.** Point out captions and labels on the graphs and explain how important it is to read them thoroughly.

3. Assign **Try Your Skill.**

4. Read **Keep This in Mind** and then assign **Now Write.** Explain that there is more than one possible answer for each graph, depending on which factual relationships students want to emphasize.

Individualizing the Lesson

Less-Advanced Students

1. Do **Try Your Skill** as an in-class exercise. Help the students find the answers by pointing out the appropriate labels.

2. Have the students discuss the graphs they find for **Now Write** with the class.

Advanced Students

Have the students find graphs in their textbooks and work together in small groups to draw possible conclusions from the facts presented.

Graphic Descriptions

Reading Graphs

Here's the Idea Graphs are special charts that show relationships between facts.

A **circle graph** uses a circle to show the parts of something. The circle represents all of something. The sections inside the circle represent the parts of the thing.

A **bar graph** shows relationships between two sets of facts. One set of facts is given in numbers. The other is given in words. Bars are used to show how the facts are related.

A **picture graph** is similar to a bar graph. However, it uses pictures instead of bars.

A **line graph** uses a line to show how something has changed over a period of time.

Check It Out Study these graphs.

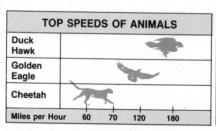

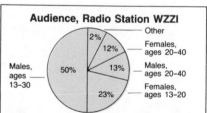

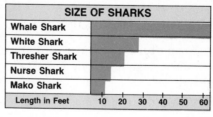

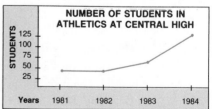

- Which is a circle graph? a bar graph? a picture graph? a line graph?

Try Your Skill   Study the graphs given in **Check It Out.** Then answer these questions:

1. What percentage of the audience of Station WZZT is female?
2. What is the second largest shark?
3. What is the top speed for a land animal?
4. What happened to student athletics at Central High after 1983?

Keep This in Mind

- Graphs show relationships between facts.
- Always read any titles, captions, or labels given with a graph.

Now Write   Find a graph in a newspaper, magazine, or textbook. Copy the graph onto your own paper. Under the graph, describe its purpose. In other words, tell what information it contains. Label your paper **Graphic Descriptions.** Save it in your folder.

Objective

To understand how to prepare for and take tests

Presenting the Lesson

1. First read and discuss the section on "Preparing for Tests" on page 292 in **Here's the Idea.** Help students to see how a good study schedule and the SQ3R method help a student to prepare effectively for tests. Discuss how much time to allow for studying for different kinds of tests in different subject areas.

2. Then read and discuss the section titled "Taking a Test" in **Here's the Idea** on page 293. Compare the process of test-taking to the steps in the SQ3R study method.

3. Read and discuss **Check It Out.** Ask students to discuss how they would have studied for this test.

4. Assign **Try Your Skill.** Ask volunteers to share their guidelines.

5. Read **Keep This in Mind** and then assign **Now Write.**

Individualizing the Lesson

Less-Advanced Students

Ask students to write down the problems they have when taking a test. Discuss each problem and how to avoid it. Be sure to cover these skills:

scheduling time
planning written answers
remembering material
understanding directions

Testing, Testing

Preparing for and Taking Tests

Here's the Idea   Test-taking is a skill, just as playing football or riding a bicycle is. You can improve your performance in any skill by working at it. The way to improve test-taking skills is to learn how to prepare for and complete tests.

Before you take a test, make sure that you are properly prepared. The following guidelines will help you.

Preparing for Tests

1. **Know exactly what you will be tested on.** If you have questions, ask your teacher.

2. **Make a study plan.** Allow yourself plenty of time to review.

3. **When you review, reread your notes.** Skim any reading materials covered by the test. Answer any questions that you wrote while using the SQ3R study method. Also answer any study questions given by your teacher.

4. **Make lists of important names, dates, definitions, or events.** Ask a friend or family member to quiz you on these.

5. **Go over your materials more than once.**

6. **Eat well and get plenty of sleep before the test.**

Knowing what to do before a test is important. So is knowing what to do during a test. The following guidelines will help you to use your test-taking time wisely.

Taking a Test

1. **Survey the test.** Look at the test to see what types of questions are included.

2. **Plan your time.** Decide on the order in which you will answer the questions. Decide how much time you will need for each part of the test. Answer the easiest questions first. Be sure to allow extra time for long or complicated questions.

3. **Read all directions and test questions carefully.** Read all the directions before you answer any of the questions. Make sure that you understand the directions completely.

4. **Save time for review.** Once you have finished, look over the test. Make sure you have not left out any answers. Reread any answers you are unsure of. Try to answer any questions that you skipped.

Check It Out   Larry's history teacher announced a test on Chapter 12, "The Civil War." Larry read the chapter twice.

• What else should Larry have done?

Try Your Skill   Reread the guidelines on these pages. Write a few guidelines that you could add. Compare your list with those of your classmates.

Keep This in Mind

• Prepare carefully before taking tests.
• When taking tests, read all of the directions and plan your time well. Save time for review.

Now Write   Think about a test that you took recently. What could you have done to prepare more fully for this test? Write a paragraph telling what you can do to improve your test-taking skills. Label your paper **Testing, Testing.** Save it in your folder.

293

Objective

To recognize and prepare for objective tests

Presenting the Lesson

1. Write the word *objective* on the board and ask students to define it. Then read and discuss **Here's the Idea.** Tell students to find out before an objective test begins whether there is a penalty for guessing. Ask them why this would be important.

2. Read and discuss **Check It Out.** Ask students what are the key words that tell them how to answer each question (*true or false, not part of, match*).

3. Assign **Try Your Skill.** Ask students *how* they knew what type of test each phrase describes.

4. Read **Keep This in Mind.**

5. Assign **Now Write.**

Individualizing the Lesson

Less-Advanced Students

Divide the students into groups to do **Now Write.**

Advanced Students

Have the students write two or three examples of each type of objective test question. Have them discuss if writing the questions gives them any new insights on how to approach test taking.

Optional Practice

Have students go back over tests they have taken before. Have them apply the guidelines on page 294 to

The Answer Key

Answering Objective Test Questions

Here's the Idea One way to prepare for tests is to learn guidelines for answering the many types of test questions. This chart describes the kinds of questions found on objective tests. **Objective tests** require simple right or wrong answers.

Questions Found on Objective Tests	
Description	**Guidelines**
TRUE/FALSE You are given a statement and asked to tell whether the statement is true or false.	1. Remember that if any part of a statement is false, all of it is false. 2. Words like *all, always, only, never,* and *everyone* often appear in false statements. 3. Words like *some, a few, usually, often,* and *most* often appear in true statements.
MATCHING You are asked to match items in one column with items in another column.	1. Check the directions. See if each item is used only once. Also check to see if some are not used at all. 2. Read all items before starting. 3. Match those you know first. 4. Cross out items as you use them.
MULTIPLE CHOICE You are asked to choose the best answer from a group of answers given on the test.	1. Read *all* choices first. 2. Eliminate incorrect answers. 3. Choose the answer that is most complete or accurate. 4. Pay particular attention to choices such as *none of the above* or *all of the above.*

Check It Out   Read the following test questions.

1. True or False: Norway is located in the northern hemisphere. _T_

2. Which of the following is not part of Scandinavia?
   a. Denmark b. Sweden c. Scotland d. Norway e. Finland

3. Match the country in the first column with its capital in the second column.

Norway   Stockholm
Finland   Oslo
Sweden   Copenhagen
Denmark   Helsinki

- What kind of answer is called for by each of these questions?

Try Your Skill   Tell what type of test each phrase below describes.

1. is often set up in columns
2. can be made false by words such as *all* or *never*
3. may contain answers such as "all of the above"

Keep This in Mind

- There are three types of objective test questions: true/false, multiple choice, and matching.
- Follow specific guidelines for answering different types of test questions.

Now Write   Choose a popular television program or movie. Write an objective test about it. Include three true/false questions and three multiple choice questions. Also include a matching question with a list of five items to match with five other items. Exchange tests with a classmate. Answer the questions on your classmate's test. Return it to be graded.

these tests. Ask them to discuss if and how they would take the test any differently now.

Extending the Lesson

1. Have the students write a script for a "How To Take a Test" filmstrip. Ask them to make drawings or take photographs to illustrate the filmstrip.

2. Have students prepare a humorous skit that shows one group of students that does not prepare for a test correctly, and another that does.

Get It in Writing

Answering Written Test Questions

Objective

To recognize and prepare for written tests

Presenting the Lesson

1. Read and discuss **Here's the Idea.** Point out that for essay tests, students follow pre-writing steps similar to those in the process of writing. Stress the importance of writing in complete sentences for short answer and essay tests.

2. Read and discuss **Check It Out.** Ask students what are the key instructional words in these questions (*explain, define* and *give an example*).

3. Assign **Try Your Skill.** Have students pick out the instructional words before they begin answering the questions.

4. Read **Keep This in Mind** and assign **Now Write.** Remind students to proofread their test essay.

Individualizing the Lesson

Less-Advanced Students

1. Emphasize the importance of identifying key instructional words in essay questions. Have the students pick out these words before they do **Try Your Skill.**

2. Have students pick out the key words in the following sample essay questions.

1. Describe the steps by which a tadpole becomes a frog.
2. Discuss, using at least two examples, why or why not Macbeth is a tragic hero.
3. Compare and contrast tornados and hurricanes.

Here's the Idea Completion, short answer, and essay questions all require written answers. This chart offers guidelines for answering three types of written test questions.

Types of Written Test Questions	
Description	**Strategies**
COMPLETION You are required to add a word or a phrase to an incomplete sentence given on the test.	1. If several words are required, give all of them. 2. Write neatly. Use good spelling, grammar, punctuation, and capitalization.
SHORT ANSWER You are required to write one or two sentences to answer the question.	1. Use complete sentences. 2. Answer the question completely. 3. Use correct spelling, grammar, punctuation, and capitalization.
ESSAY You are required to write one or more paragraphs to answer the question.	1. Follow pre-writing steps before answering the question. 2. Look for action words like *explain* or *compare.* These are words that tell you what to do. 3. Make a rough outline of your essay on a separate sheet of paper. 4. Make sure each paragraph contains a topic sentence. 5. Proofread your completed essay.

Check It Out   Read the following questions.

1. _____ live longer than any other animals.
2. In a paragraph or two, explain what a *barometer* is and how it works.
3. In a couple of sentences, define "myth" and give an example.

- Which of these is an essay question? Which is short answer? Which is completion?

Try Your Skill   Review Part 10, **The Answer Key.** Then, answer the following questions.

1. A question that asks a student to pick the best answer from a list provided on the test is a _____ question.
2. What is a *matching question?* (Answer in a complete sentence.)
3. What strategies can be used to answer a true/false question? (Answer in a complete paragraph.)

Keep This in Mind

- Completion questions are answered with a word or a phrase.
- Short answer questions are answered with complete sentences.
- Essay questions are answered with one or more paragraphs.

Now Write   Choose a reading assignment from one of your classes. Write an essay question that you might be asked on a test covering this material. Then, write an answer to your essay question. Follow the guidelines for answering essay questions given on page 296. Label your completed essay **Get It in Writing.** Save it in your folder.

Section **24** Objectives

1. To use correct form for a friendly letter

2. To address envelopes correctly

3. To know how to write invitations and thank-you notes

4. To know the proper formats, punctuation, and style for business letters

5. To know how to write a letter of request

6. To know how to write a letter of application

7. To know how to complete a job application form

8. To know how to complete work-related forms

Preparing the Students

Select several letters written by famous people and read them to the class. Point out that although their own letters may never be published, they are still important. Explain that this section will review how to write friendly letters, social notes, and business letters. It will also show them how to apply these and other business skills to the practical situation of obtaining a job.

Additional Resources

Mastery Test — pages 32–33 in the test booklet

Practice Book — pages 122–130

Duplicating Masters — pages 122–130

Letters, Forms, and Applications

Teaching Special Populations

LD Combine these lessons with practical demonstrations of how to write and prepare letters for mailing. Also, since many LD students have difficulty filling out forms, it might be wise to amend certain procedures: for instance, in Parts 7 and 8, tell students to first write their answers on a separate piece of paper then copy the information onto the form.

ESL Letter-writing conventions differ from society to society. For instance, many cultures do not use the block and modified block form of American business letters, and most have different conventions for spacing addresses or writing dates, numerals, and salutations. Furthermore, the combination of blunt questioning and comparative informality of address in American business letters would be considered very rude by some cultures. Discuss such differences with your ESL students, and have them read their letters to partners who are native English speakers.

NSD This section will give your NSD students excellent practice in using standard English. Emphasize to them that slang and other forms of nonstandard usage are particularly inappropriate in business letters. Ask your students to write a variety of letters, making sure that they use standard English. Make doubly sure they understand how letter-writing style changes in accordance with the audience to whom one is writing.

299

Mail Call

How To Write a Friendly Letter

Here's the Idea   Writing a letter is one of the best ways of keeping in touch with someone. A letter to someone you know is called a **friendly letter.** A friendly letter should be detailed and lively. It should sound natural and be neat and easy to read.

The form of any friendly letter has five main parts: the *heading*, the *salutation* or greeting, the *body* or main part, the *closing*, and the *signature*.

Presenting the Lesson

1. Read aloud and discuss **Here's the Idea.** Write the five parts of a friendly letter on the chalkboard for emphasis. Refer to the sample letter in **Check It Out** to illustrate each part. When discussing the closing, remind students that only the first word is capitalized.

2. Discuss **Check It Out.**

3. Assign **Try Your Skill.** Ask five volunteers to put the five parts of the letter on the chalkboard in the proper order.

4. Read **Keep This in Mind**.

5. Assign **Now Write.**

The **heading** tells where you are. It consists of three lines: two for your address and one for the date. Do not use any abbreviations. The heading appears at the top right corner.

The **salutation** is your way of saying "hello" on paper. It can be simply "Dear Bob" or "Hi." The salutation is written on the next line below the heading. It starts at the left margin of the page and is followed by a comma.

In the **body,** the main part of the letter, you say what you want to say. Try to be interesting and specific. Imagine that you are in the same room with your friend. What would you talk about? The body begins on the line following the salutation. The first word of the body and of each new paragraph should be indented.

Individualizing the Lesson

Less-Advanced Students

Write the format for a friendly letter on the chalkboard. Then have the students fill in the outline as they do **Now Write.**

Advanced Students

Ask students to locate in their family records, or in a collection of letters from the library, old letters that tell something about the history of our country—even if that history is only a decade or so ago. Discuss the students' findings in class.

The **closing** is your way of saying "goodbye." Common closings are *Sincerely, Yours truly, Love,* or *Your friend.* The closing is written on the line below the last word of the body and is followed by a comma. The first word of the closing should line up with the first words of the heading.

Your **signature** is the last part of your letter. Skip a line after the closing, and sign your name in line with the first word of the closing. If you are writing to someone you know well, use your first name. Otherwise, sign your full name.

Optional Practice

1. Contact a pen-pal service and provide students with an opportunity to correspond with a person

Check It Out   Read this friendly letter.

---

32 Fifth Street
Wheaton, Illinois 60187
February 18, 1985

Dear Dan,

I'm so glad to hear that you will be out of the hospital next week. I imagine you'll be glad to be back at home and school. The whole class has missed your corny jokes.

The school play almost went off smoothly yesterday. Jeff stole the show. He was supposed to fall down and act dead, and he did. Then, about five minutes later, when everyone had assumed he was dead, he gave one enormous shudder and kick. For the rest of the act, everyone kept watching to see if he'd do something else. It was really funny.

Your mom said you would be home on Thursday. See you then!

Your friend,
Jean

- What details make this letter interesting?
- Identify the five parts of the letter.

from another section of the United States, or from another country.

2. Arrange a cooperative exchange with another school and assign pen pals. Ask each of the students to write a friendly letter introducing himself or herself to the pen pal. Have students check their work and make any necessary revisions. When the replies arrive, ask students to check their pen pals' letters for format.

Extending the Lesson

Students may be interested in writing letters to authors of books they have enjoyed, recording artists, or film stars. Offer assistance in obtaining the addr sses. Replies could be used for an interesting display.

Try Your Skill   Put the following information in the correct form.

11 Madison Street, Boston, Massachusetts 02109, July 21, 1985, Dear Greg, I'll be glad to meet your train. Let's plan to meet next to the information booth under the clock. I've had my hair cut, but you'll still recognize me. Your friend, Ben.

> **Keep This in Mind**
>
> · A friendly letter should be lively, natural, and neat.
> · A friendly letter should follow the correct form. The heading, salutation, body, closing, and signature should each be written correctly.

Now Write   Write a letter to a friend or relative. Tell about what you've been doing in school or at home. Use your home address and today's date in the heading. Be sure that the five main parts of your letter follow the correct form. Label your paper **Mail Call** and save it in your folder.

A Proper Send-off

How To Prepare Letters for the Mail

Here's the Idea When you have finished writing a letter, fold it neatly. Choose an envelope that matches the width of the stationery. Insert the folded letter and seal the envelope.

Prepare the envelope carefully. Follow these steps:

1. Address the envelope. Add your return address.
2. Double-check all numbers to make sure they are correct.
3. Include the correct **ZIP** code.
4. Put a stamp on the envelope.

Always check envelopes and packages for accuracy. If you need information about mailing procedures, call your local post office.

Check It Out Look at the envelope below.

Bonnie Calhoun
127 Las Olas Avenue
Orlando, FL 32802

Paul Berman
21 Holden Street
Minneapolis, MN 55401

- Who will receive the letter? Who sent the letter? What state abbreviations are used? How could you check that the ZIP codes are correct?

303

Part 2

Objective

To address envelopes correctly

Presenting the Lesson

1. Read and discuss **Here's the Idea.**

2. Discuss **Check It Out.** Explain that the only abbreviations that may be used are those for states. Point out that the post office will give out zip codes over the phone. Also mention that there are restrictions on envelope size. Ask a volunteer to contact the local post office to find out the restrictions.

3. Assign and review **Try Your Skill.**

4. Read **Keep This in Mind** and then assign **Now Write.** Tell students that they can mail these letters. Ask them to share the replies they get.

Individualizing the Lesson

Less-Advanced Students

Explain that the order of information in an address is from the most specific to the most general. They should begin with the name of the person, go on to where he or she lives, and end with the state and ZIP code (which tells what part of the United States to direct the letter).

Advanced Students

Have students do research to learn what all the numbers in the ZIP code stand for.

Optional Practice

Have each student select five names from the white pages of the

303

local telephone book. Then have them address envelopes to the people they have chosen. Remind the students to include the ZIP code and a return address.

Extending the Lesson

Ask students to bring to class a contest or offer form from a newspaper or magazine. Have each student address an envelope to the proper party. Many offers or contests request a self-addressed stamped envelope (sometimes called a *SASE*). Explain what that is and have each student prepare one.

Try Your Skill   Write each of the jumbled addresses below as it should appear on an envelope. Also write a return address using your own name and address.

    1. Madison, Wisconsin 53705, Chris Dombrowski, 26 Marshall Avenue

    2. Dr. Linda S. Adams, 421 Woodfield Road, Gulfport, Mississippi 39503

    3. 85 East 121st Street, New York, New York 10035, Peter Bucci

    4. Barbara McKenna, Tulsa, Oklahoma 74101, 1728 Columbus Avenue

    5. Mr. and Mrs. Luis Perez, 882 Fairfax Road, San Leandro, California 94577

Keep This in Mind

- Be careful when preparing letters for the mail. Fold your letters neatly. Check addresses for accuracy. Make sure all information is correct and clear.

Now Write   Take out the friendly letter you wrote in the last lesson, **Mail Call.** Address an envelope to your friend or relative. Fold your letter and put it into the envelope.

    Save your letter in your folder.

Thanks So Much

How To Write Social Notes

Here's the Idea A social note is written for a special occasion. Invitations and thank-you notes are social notes. Because they are forms of friendly letters, social notes also have five main parts. The heading, however, may be shortened to the date only.

If you send an **invitation,** you must include specific information about *what, when,* and *where.* When you receive an invitation, you should reply immediately. Tell whether or not you can attend.

You may also send **thank-you** notes. One kind of thank-you note is written after you have received a gift. You do not only thank the sender for the gift. You also thank that person for thinking of you. Maybe the sweater you received is not your favorite color. However, you should say thanks graciously for the time and effort that went into choosing the gift and sending it. If you received a gift that you really do enjoy, tell what makes it so special. Let the sender share your pleasure.

A second kind of thank-you note is a **bread-and-butter** note. It thanks someone for his or her hospitality. If you stayed over-night as a guest in someone's house, you would write this kind of social note.

Whenever you write either of these kinds of thank-you notes, be sure to express your appreciation to the other person. It is also important that you write your thank-you note as soon as possible.

Check It Out Read the social note on page 306.

- What kind of social note is this? How is the form of this letter different from that of the friendly letter shown on page 301?

305

Presenting the Lesson

1. Read aloud and discuss **Here's the Idea.** Point out that the only difference in format between a friendly letter and a social note is that the heading may be shortened to the date only. When discussing invitations, emphasize the importance of including specific information about the time and place of the occasion. Also point out that if students receive an invitation, they may have to write another kind of social note—a letter of regret. Stress that an invitation requires a response as to whether or not the recipient can attend. When discussing thank-you notes, point out that the most important element is to thank the person for his or her thoughtfulness and then for the gift or hospitality itself.

2. Read and discuss **Check It Out.**

3. Assign **Try Your Skill.** Ask volunteers to write their notes on the chalkboard. Discuss the format, punctuation, and content.

4. Read **Keep This in Mind** aloud.

5. Assign **Now Write.**

Individualizing the Lesson

Less-Advanced Students

Discuss which sort of situations require a simple thank-you note, and which require a bread-and-butter note. (Ask students why they think these notes are called *bread-and-butter.*) Be sure that students

305

understand that it is customary and polite to send such notes.

Advanced Students

Have students think of real-life situations in which an informal courtesy note would have been appropriate. Then have students write the note. Point out that these notes are usually very easy and quick to write and are greatly appreciated by the recipients.

Optional Practice

Have the students write a social note for the following situations:

1. A note thanking an aunt for sending a check for their birthday
2. An invitation for a surprise birthday party for their brother
3. A note to a cousin thanking her for letting them visit for the weekend
4. A note thanking the drama teacher for taking them to a popular musical play

Extending the Lesson

Ask students to pretend that they are celebrities. Have each of them write an invitation to themselves from the celebrity, asking them to attend some special occasion. Remind students to include the specific information necessary in an invitation. The second part of the project is to write a thank-you note from a celebrity.

September 5, 1985

Dear Stan,

The box of candy you sent was one of the best birthday presents I've ever received. How did you know how much I like chocolates? What a luxury to have an entire box! I will enjoy every last piece. I only wish you were here to share the candy with me.

Again, thanks for the candy.

Your friend,
Jesse

Try Your Skill You have received a purple sweater as a birthday gift from your best friend. Write a thank-you note.

Keep This in Mind

- Social notes are short forms of friendly letters
- Invitations should include *what, when,* and *where.*
- Thank-you notes should express your appreciation. They should be sent immediately after you receive a gift.

Now Write Label your paper **Thanks So Much.** Write an invitation, a thank-you note, or a bread-and-butter note to someone you know. Use the correct form. Save your work in your folder.

Be Businesslike

How To Write a Business Letter

Here's the Idea Sometimes you may want to order a product by mail, complain about something you ordered, or request certain information. In each of these situations, you would need to write or type a **business letter.**

A business letter has the five parts that a friendly letter has. These parts are the **heading,** the **salutation,** the **body,** the **closing,** and the **signature.** Business letters also have one additional part, the inside address. The **inside address** contains the name and address of the company to which you are writing. Whenever possible, the inside address should also include the name of a particular department or employee within the company. The inside address comes below the heading and above the salutation. It begins at the left margin.

The salutations and closings are more formal in a business letter than in a friendly letter. If you are writing to a specific person, use *Dear Mr., Mrs., Miss,* or *Ms.* before the person's name. Otherwise, use a general greeting like *Dear Sir or Madam.* The salutation appears two lines below the inside address and is followed by a colon (:).

For the closing, use the words *Sincerely, Very truly yours,* or *Yours truly,* followed by a comma. If your letter is typed, leave four lines of space between the closing and your typed signature. Then, write your signature in the space.

A business letter may use one of two forms. The easiest to remember is the *block* form. This should be used only if you type a letter. In a block form, every part begins at the left margin. Two lines of space are left between paragraphs, and the paragraphs are not indented. A *modified block* form may be used either for handwritten or typewritten letters. This form

307

Part 4

Objective

To know the proper formats, punctuation, and style for business letters

Presenting the Lesson

Illustrations of all business letters should be typewritten to show students more realistic examples. Students should know that in the business world letters are almost always typed. However, students should also be told that they are not required—or expected—to type their letters for these lessons.

1. Read aloud and discuss **Here's the Idea.** Write the six parts of a business letter on the chalkboard and explain what is included in each. Pay particular attention to the inside address, the salutation, and the closing because they differ from the friendly letter. When discussing block form and modified block form, pass labeled examples around the room so that the students can see the difference between the two. Point out the last sentence of **Here's the Idea** and stress the importance of keeping copies of all business letters.

2. Discuss **Check It Out.** Ask students how this letter would be arranged if it were written in modified block.

3. Assign **Try Your Skill.** Collect the letters and make duplicates of a sampling of them. Discuss the content, form, and punctuation of the letters.

4. Read **Keep This in Mind.**

5. Assign **Now Write.**

307

Individualizing the Lesson

Less-Advanced Students

Do **Try Your Skill** as an in-class exercise with the students. Make sure they know the difference between block and modified block form. Point out that modified block is the same form that is used in a friendly letter.

Advanced Students

Have the students use the information on the copyright page of this text, their own names and addresses, and today's date, and write a letter to the publisher commenting on this book. Have students use either block or modified block form.

Optional Practice

Display a business letter with obvious mistakes such as colored stationery, uneven margins, cross-outs, red ink, stains, writing on both sides of the paper, etc. Have the students identify the problems and explain how to correct them.

Extending the lesson

Ask students to select a city or state that they would like to visit. Instruct them to write a letter to the Visitors' Bureau or the Chamber of Commerce requesting information about things to do and accommodations in the area. (Bring back issues of the travel section of the newspaper to class to stimulate ideas. Before making the assignment, check with the librarian and/or a travel agent for sources for addresses.) Have students check each other's letters for content, form, and punctuation. Instruct each

puts the heading, closing, and signature at the right side of the page. The paragraphs are indented, and no extra space is left between them.

Whether you write or type a business letter, it is important to make it neat and to use the correct form. Be direct and clear. Always make copies of business letters to keep for your records.

Check It Out   Read this business letter.

1132 Davis Boulevard
Arlington, Virginia 22209
June 3, 1985

Sweetsound Products
43 Chestnut Street
Durham, North Carolina 25710

Dear Sir or Madam:

On March 8, 1985, I sent you an order for the special record album that you advertised in Stereo magazine. The record was called Michael Jackson: The Early Years.

The album has not yet arrived and I have not heard from your company. However, my check for $10 has been cashed. Enclosed is a copy of the canceled check. Please let me know when I may expect to receive the record or a refund.

Sincerely,

Donna Lee

Donna Lee

- What is the purpose of this business letter?
- In what form is this letter typed? Identify the six parts of the letter.

Try Your Skill Write a letter from the sales manager of Sweetsound Products to Donna Lee. Have the company respond to her letter. Make up any necessary details. For this exercise, you may use either the block form or the modified block form.

Keep This in Mind

- A business letter may be written to express a request, to order a product, or to send a complaint. A business letter may be typed or handwritten. Always keep a copy of a business letter.
- *Block* and *modified block* are two forms for writing a business letter. Both forms have six parts, including an inside address.

Now Write Using any newspaper or magazine, find an advertisement for a free booklet or free information. Write a business letter asking for the advertised item. Write the letter in block or modified block form. Make a copy of the letter. Also, address an envelope. Fold your original letter properly and put it in a stamped envelope. Mail the letter. Save the copy of your letter in your folder. When you get the item you ordered, bring it to school to show to your class.

Objective

To know how to write a letter of request

Presenting the Lesson

1. Read aloud and discuss **Here's the Idea.** Point out that the letter assigned in **Now Write** of Part 4 is a letter of request. Emphasize the three important things to remember in writing a letter of request: be specific, be brief, and be polite.

2. Discuss the letter in **Check It Out.**

3. Assign **Try Your Skill.** Make sure students identify themselves, tell why they are contacting the person or company, tell what specific information they need, and explain why they need the information.

4. Read **Keep This in Mind** and then assign **Now Write.**

Individualizing the Lesson

Less-Advanced Students

Go over what should be included in the letter they are writing for **Try Your Skill** before they begin to write. Write their suggestions about the letter on the board, and then have them write the actual letter themselves.

Advanced Students

Have the students brainstorm for a list of hypothetical situations in which they might send a letter of request. Encourage humorous situations. Have the students write the letter, being brief, specific, and polite.

Help!

How To Write a Letter of Request

Here's the Idea   Sometimes you will want to write a letter to request information. You may be planning a trip to another state and want information about its points of interest. Perhaps you would like a company to send you a brochure explaining its products. Maybe you would like a school or camp to send you a catalog describing its program. You can receive this valuable information by writing a **letter of request.**

A letter of request is a type of business letter. It should contain the six main parts of a business letter: *heading, inside address, salutation, body, closing,* and *signature.* You may follow either the *block* or *modified block* form when you write or type a letter of request.

Be specific when you make a request of any kind. Be sure you have included every bit of information necessary to get just what you want. If you are writing to get product information, be specific about the product you are interested in. Include important details about the product such as its size, color, cost, or identification number.

Besides being specific, you should be brief. A letter of request should be direct and to the point. If you want information about motels near Cooperstown, New York, you do not have to explain that you have always wanted to visit the Baseball Hall of Fame. Simply ask the Chamber of Commerce for a list of motels. However, if you want to know what you can see in Cooperstown besides the Baseball Hall of Fame, ask for sightseeing information.

Finally, remember that someone will have to take the time to send you what you have requested. Be sure you have asked for help in a polite way.

Check It Out Read the following letter of request.

11 Lakewood Drive
Lincoln, Nebraska 68501
January 15, 1985

Clowns of America
2715 East Fayette Street
Baltimore, Maryland, 21224

Dear Sir or Madam:

   I am writing a term paper on clowns. I would like to know
what training or schooling is necessary to become a circus
clown. Where can people receive such training? Please
send me whatever information you have available.

Sincerely,

Lee Bowen

Lee Bowen

- Is this letter of request specific, brief, and polite?
- How does the modified block form of this letter differ
from the block form of the letter on page 308?

311

Optional Practice

From the school library borrow a copy of the list of free pamphlets published by the U.S. Information Center. Have the students choose titles of several pamphlets that interest them and write a letter requesting them. (The list is available from the U.S. Consumer Information Center, Pueblo, Colorado 81009.)

Extending the Lesson

Divide the class into four groups, one for friendly letters, one for invitations, one for thank-you notes, and one for business letters. Have each group make a poster outlining the parts of the letter, the kind of information that should be included in that kind of letter, and the proper punctuations, capitalization, and format for the letter. Have them select an example from their **Now Write** folders and copy it on the poster. Display the posters in the class.

Try Your Skill   Write a letter to the Society of American Magicians, 66 Marked Tree Road, Needham, Massachusetts 02192. Ask for information about joining the society. For this exercise you may use either the block form or the modified block form.

Keep This in Mind

- A letter of request should be specific, brief and polite. It may be either handwritten or typewritten.
- The *block* or *modified block* form may be used for this kind of business letter.

Now Write   Write a letter of request to a business or organization in your area. For example, you might want to write to the Chamber of Commerce to ask for a list of local restaurants. Use the phone book to find the address of the business. Address and stamp an envelope. Make a copy of your letter to save in your folder. Mail your letter of request. Bring any reply you receive to class.

312

Letters That Work

How To Write Letters of Application

Here's the Idea   Writing a business letter can be useful when you decide to look for a job. By writing letters of application, you can find out which jobs are available.

When writing to an employer, be neat and careful. This letter will be the first example of your work that the employer sees. The following guidelines will help you.

Guidelines for Letters of Application

1. State the exact title of the job you are seeking. Do you want to be a *bagger?* Do you want to be a *cashier?*

2. Tell the employer whether you want to work part-time or full-time. Also let the employer know if you are seeking a temporary job. A job is **temporary** if it will only last for a short period of time.

3. Give some information about yourself. State your age and grade level in school. Tell the employer why you are qualified for the job. Mention any previous work experience or courses in school that have prepared you for the job. Also mention any special skills or personal qualities that you have. For example, if you are good at math, you could say so.

4. Be specific about when you can work. Let the employer know when you can start and what hours you are available.

5. Request an interview if the job is located near you. If you are writing to a large company, address the letter to the *personnel director.* If you are writing to a small business, address your letter to the *manager* or *owner.* If you are answering a newspaper advertisement, read the ad carefully to find out how you should reply. Send your letter to the address given.

Objective

To know how to write a letter of application

Presenting the Lesson

1. Read and discuss **Here's the Idea.** Explain that a letter of application is a business letter. List the information the letter must contain on the chalkboard. Explain to the students that these guidelines can be modified depending on the type of job they are applying for.

2. Read and discuss **Check It Out.** Have the students point out exactly how the guidelines have been followed in the letter.

3. Assign **Try Your Skill.** Tell students to make up any facts they need to complete this assignment.

4. Read **Keep This in Mind** and assign **Now Write.**

Individualizing the Lesson

Less-Advanced Students

Do one of the letters of application in **Try Your Skill** with the class. Then have students do one on their own.

Advanced Students

Have the students write letters of application for two of the newspaper ads in **Try Your Skill.** Have them share their letters with the class.

Optional Practice

Have students go through the "want ad" section of their local newspaper. Tell them to choose one ad to answer that they think they are qualified for. Have them list all of their qualifications on a separate sheet of paper before they write the first draft of the letter. Then have them follow the process of writing for their letters. Remind them that this is the first impression an employer will have of them. They must be neat, courteous, and honest.

Extending the Lesson

Have the personnel director of a local business give a talk to the students about what a employer looks for when reading letters of application.

Check It Out   Read this letter.

111 Hampton Road
Springfield, IL 62708
April 3, 1985

Ms. Carol Wolf
Sunnyday Camp
29 Capitol Road
Springfield, IL 62708

Dear Ms. Wolf:

I am interested in working as a day camp counselor at your camp this summer. I am 14 years old and a freshman at Liberty High School. I am now taking a course in Child Development. Last summer I worked as a junior counselor for the Park District. I also babysit for several neighbors' children during the school year. You will find that I am reliable and hardworking. I get along well with children and know a great deal about arts, crafts, games, and other camp activities.

I will be available for full-time work on June 12. I can work until the end of the camp session, August 22.

Please contact me for an interview at your convenience. My telephone number is (217) 666-0900.

Thank you,

Sheila Logan

Sheila Logan

- Does this letter follow all of the **Guidelines for Letters of Application?** Explain your answer.

Try Your Skill   Write a letter answering one of the following newspaper ads.

1. Wanted: Groundskeeper for Lakeshore Inn, Seaside Road, Greenlake, Wisconsin 54941. Temporary position: June 5–August 25.

2. Wanted: Dining room help for Redwood Inn. Part-time. Write Mr. Ed Kelly, PO Box 222, Portland, Oregon 97208.

3. Wanted: Cashier. Christmas vacation only. Contact Tiny Tots Toys, 40 Surrey Lane, Augusta, Georgia 30903.

Keep This in Mind

- Letters to employers should be neat, informative, and courteous.
- Include specific information about yourself and about the job you want.

Now Write   Choose a department store or restaurant near or in your town. Write a letter asking for a job. Follow the guidelines given on page 313. Include all the necessary information. Proofread your letter carefully. Title your paper **Letters That Work.** Save it in your folder.

Apply Yourself

How To Complete a Job Application

Objective

To know how to complete a job application form

Presenting the Lesson

1. Read aloud and discuss **Here's the Idea.** Emphasize that advance planning is necessary when applying for a job. Suggest that students make an index card to carry with them on job interviews. The card should contain the information that the student would not have committed to memory: social security number; names, addresses, and phone numbers of former employers; and names, addresses, and phone numbers of references. Explain that one should always ask a person for permission to use his or her name as a reference before listing it on a job application.

2. Discuss the sample application on page 318. Call attention to the use of *Does not apply* and the fact that the writer had to squeeze his printing in order to fit the requested information in the space allowed.

3. Assign **Try Your Skill.**

4. Assign **Now Write.** Real job forms can either be obtained by students or provided by the teacher. Have students check each other's completed application for completeness, accuracy, and neatness.

Individualizing the Lesson

Less-Advanced Students

Sometimes these students have a low level of confidence that might make it difficult for them to present

Here's the Idea   When you write a letter requesting a job, you may get one of several responses. You may be told that there is no job available or that the job is not right for you. You may be asked to come in for an interview. You may receive an application form and be asked to complete and return it. Whatever the response, make sure you follow the employer's instructions exactly.

When it comes time for you to complete a job application form, follow these guidelines.

Completing Job Applications

1. **Read all directions carefully, especially those in fine print.** For example, you may be asked to give your last name first or your first name first. Only by reading the directions can you tell what to do. The ability to follow directions is an important job skill. Show the employer that you can follow directions well.

2. **Be neat.** Print your answers carefully. Use a good pen with blue or black ink. You will find that there is often very little space for the information requested. Therefore, plan your answers before you print them. If you do make an error, erase it. If you cannot erase it, draw a single line through the error and write in the correct information above the line.

3. **Be prepared to answer several basic questions.** Study the sample job application form on page 318. You can expect to have to answer similar questions on most job application forms. Have this information with you when you complete the form. In particular, make sure you have the names and addresses of two or three references. These are people not related to you who have known

you a long time and who would be willing to discuss your abilities. For example, a reference may be a former employer, a teacher, or a clergyman.

4. **Complete every item.** There may be questions that you cannot answer, such as a question about military service. However, you must never leave any space blank on an application. Leaving a blank space is confusing. If an item does not apply to you, write "Does Not Apply" in that space.

5. **Be honest.** You will be asked to sign your name to a statement declaring that all your information is accurate.

Check It Out   Examine the completed job application on the next page.

- Has the application form been filled in neatly and carefully? Have all the instructions been followed?
- Have all items on the application form been answered completely? How might an employer check that the answers are honest and accurate?

Try Your Skill   Suppose you were applying today for a summer job as an assistant at the public library. On a sheet of paper, copy the sample application form as it is shown on page 318. Fill out the application as you would actually complete it.

Keep This in Mind

- Fill in the items on an application by printing as neatly. Read all directions on the form.
- Answer all items honestly and accurately.

Now Write   Obtain a job application form from your teacher or from a local business. Complete the form neatly and honestly. Save it in your folder.

Advanced Students

Have the students research the qualifications for a career in which they are interested. As part of their research, have them list part-time jobs they could apply for now that would enable them to learn more about their chosen career and obtain on-the-job experience.

Optional Practice

Bring to class various job application forms. (Call personnel directors of neighborhood businesses and talk to the job counselor in your school to get these forms.) Use an overhead projector and point out the information requested, as well as specific instructions, such as *print in ink,* or *last name first.*

Extending the Lesson

Invite a qualified person to speak to the class about how to give a good job interview (the work-study program coordinator, the personnel manager of a local business, etc.). After the discussion, hold mock interviews. Use the application filled out in the **Now Write** section to set the scene for the job being applied for. Have the interviewer use the application as a basis for questions.

Application for Employment

Personal Information   Date 9/1/85   Social Security Number 869-28-0827

Name Block   Thomas   Carl
      Last   First   Middle

Present Address 1507 Kennedy Drive, Waltham, Mass. 02154
                 Street   City   State   Zip

Phone Number 555-1742 Date of Birth 3/8/70 U.S. Citizen (Yes) No

Employment Desired

Position part-time kitchen help (after school)   Date You Can Start Monday 9/10/85   Salary Desired open

Are You Employed Now? NO Where? Does not apply Duties Does not apply

Education	Name and Location of School	Years Attended	Date Graduated	Course of Study
Grammar School	Brookside School Merrick, New York	1975-1984	June, 1984	Does not apply
High School	North High School Waltham, Mass.	1984-present	Does not apply	Business Course
College or Trade School	Does not apply			
Military Service	Does not apply			

Former Employers (List your last two employers, starting with the more recent one)

Dates	Name and Address of Employer	Salary	Position	Reason for Leaving
From Christmas To 1984	Simpson's Department Store Arlington, Mass.	$2.90 per hour	Stock boy	Christmas only
From To	Does not apply			

References Name two persons, not related to you, who have known you at least one year.

Name	Address	Business
Ms. Emily Norcott	North High School Waltham, Mass. 02154	math teacher
Dr. John McGrath	173 Wesley Street Waltham Mass. 02154	family doctor

In Case of Emergency Notify Carl and Janet Block 1507 Kennedy Drive Waltham, Mass. 02154 555-1742
                             Name   Address   Phone No.

I authorize investigation of all statements contained in this application. I understand that misrepresentation or omission of facts called for is cause for dismissal.

September 1, 1985   Thomas Carl Block
Date   Signature of Applicant

318

Paperwork

How To Complete Work-Related Forms

Here's the Idea Once you accept a job, you may be asked to complete several other job-related forms. When completing these forms, follow the guidelines for neatness, completeness, and accuracy that you learned in the last lesson.

The following job-related forms are common:

Social Security Card. You need a social security number in order to get paid. To get a number, you must fill out a form. The form asks for information about when you were born. It also asks whether you are a citizen of the United States. You can get this form from your local Social Security office.

Work Permit. In most states, if you are under 16 years old, you'll need a work permit to begin a job. The application for a work permit asks information about your birth date. It also asks about where your job is located, the kind of job you have, and how many hours a week you will work. The application asks about your health and school record. Forms for work permits are available from your school's guidance office.

W-4 Form. Once you are working, you will have to pay taxes. The Federal Government requires every worker to fill out a W-4 form. This form asks you how many people you will support with your salary. There is also a place on the form where you can indicate that you are not self-supporting and earn a minimum amount of money. If your state has a state income tax, you may have to fill out a similar form for your state taxes. Your employer will give these forms to you.

Check It Out Examine the sample W-4 form on the following page.

319

Part 8

Objective

To know how to complete work-related forms

Presenting the Lesson

1. Ask students if they have had any experience filling out forms, possibly for bank accounts, social security cards, etc. Ask if there were any unforeseen difficulties in filling out the forms. Then read and discuss **Here's the Idea.** Ask students if they can think of any other work-related forms they might have to fill out besides those listed (insurance, security clearance, etc.).

2. Read and discuss **Check It Out.** Point out that if students claim an *exempt* status, they will not have income tax deducted from their checks. Also point out that they may have to explain this to their employer.

3. Assign **Try Your Skill.** Make arrangements with the guidance office before assigning this exercise.

4. Read **Keep This in Mind** and then assign **Now Write.**

Individualizing the Lesson

Less-Advanced Students

Tell students that it is often important to make a photo copy of a form when only one copy has been provided. They can use the photocopy as a *working copy* and fill in the blanks for practice before filling in the original form.

Advanced Students

Have students call local businesses and talk to the school's job

319

placement or guidance director to find out what forms are required by various employers. Ask them to bring these forms to class and make a display of their research.

Optional Practice

Tell students to imagine they are starting their own business. Have them design a form for students who want to apply for work at their firm. The form should include such things as the student's year in school, the position the applicant is interested in, previous experience, grade point average, and how the student can be contacted.

Extending the Lesson

Bring to class an income tax refund form and go over it with the students. Explain that they are entitled to a refund if they earn less than a certain amount of money each year. If possible invite an accountant into the class to explain how to fill out the form.

320

6-82
Form **W-4**
(Rev. January 1983)

Department of the Treasury—Internal Revenue Service

Employee's Withholding Allowance Certificate

W-4 1

OMS No. 1545-0010
Expires 8-31-87

1 Type or print your full name
Arletta Vaughn Davis

Home address (number and street or rural route)
800 W. Argyle

City or town, State, and ZIP code
Chicago, IL 60640

2 Your social security number
427-58-9178

3 Marital Status ☒ Single ☐ Married
Note: If married, but legally separated, or spouse is a nonresident alien, check the Single box.

☐ Married, but withhold at higher Single rate

4 Total number of allowances you are claiming (from line F of the worksheet on page 2) ...... │ 0

5 Additional amount, if any, you want deducted from each pay ...... │ $ 0

6 I claim exemption from withholding because (see instructions and check boxes below that apply):

  a ☐ Last year I did not owe any Federal income tax and had a right to a full refund of ALL income tax withheld, AND

  b ☐ This year I do not expect to owe any Federal income tax and expect to have a right to a full refund of ALL income tax withheld. If both a and b apply, enter the year effective and "EXEMPT" here ...... ▲ Year 1985 Exempt

  c If you entered "EXEMPT" on line 6b, are you a full-time student? ...... ☒ Yes ☐ No

Under the penalties of perjury, I certify that I am entitled to the number of withholding allowances claimed on this certificate, or if claiming exemption from withholding, that I am entitled to claim the exempt status.

Employee's signature ▲ Arletta Vaughn Davis Date ▲ December 15 19 85

7 Employer's name and address (Employer: Complete 7, 8, and 9 only if sending to IRS)

8 Office code

9 Employer identification number

- Have all items been answered completely, neatly, and carefully?
- Have all instructions been followed?

Try Your Skill   Ask your school's guidance office for an application for a work permit. Using the guidelines in this lesson, complete the form neatly, completely, and accurately.

Keep This in Mind

- The three most common job-related forms are the social security application, the work permit application, and the W-4 form.
- These forms must be filled out neatly, completely, and accurately.

Now Write   Obtain a social security card form from your local Social Security office. If you don't know where the office is, look up the address in your phone directory. Fill out the form, using the skills you have learned. If you do not already have a card, return the finished form to the Social Security office.

Section **25** Objectives

1. To identify formal and informal talks

2. To prepare for an informal talk

3. To plan a formal talk

4. To gather information for a formal talk and organize it logically

5. To develop the introduction, body, and conclusion of a formal talk

6. To learn to deliver a talk effectively

7. To practice and improve a talk

8. To learn how to listen to and evaluate a talk

Preparing the Students

Ask students how they might feel acting in a commercial or being interviewed for a national news story. Explain that even those who look comfortable in front of a crowd experience some stage fright. These people learn to develop confidence by preparing and practicing their talks. Tell students that this section will help them to become better public speakers.

Additional Resources

Mastery Test — page 34 in the test booklet

Practice Book — pages 131–138

Duplicating Masters — pages 131–138

Teaching Special Populations

LD Those students with emotional problems, speech problems, or behavioral problems, should not

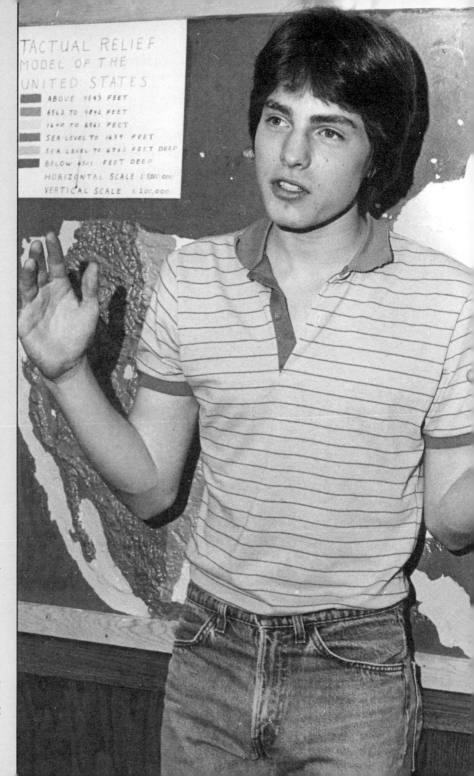

Preparing a Talk

be asked to participate in these exercises. Adjust, shorten, or omit parts of this section in accordance with each student's disability. In some exercises you may want to tape record speeches instead of having students make formal speeches in front of an audience.

ESL Public speaking will help your ESL students gain confidence in their syntax and pronunciation, but at first they will probably be very self-conscious about making mistakes. Begin by having these students address their ESL classmates as a group, then have them graduate to larger audiences. Remember that conventions governing body language (especially eye contact and the use of certain gestures) differ from society to society. Alert all of your students to these differences and make sure they behave in a tolerant, well-mannered fashion when listening to ESL speakers.

As students prepare their speeches, concentrate on helping them with syntax and organization. Encourage students to widen the range of their vocabulary in their speeches. It is also helpful to drill ESL students by having them memorize and deliver a short passage from a work of literature, a magazine article, or some other secondary source.

NSD Nonstandard pronunciation is a troublesome feature of nonstandard dialect. Overuse of elisions and contractions, particularly, also results in students having spelling difficulties. Make it a daily practice to have your NSD students read aloud to their peers. Point out to students (without being too negative) any pronunciation errors.

Part 1

Objective

To identify formal and informal talks

Presenting the Lesson

1. Read aloud and discuss **Here's the Idea.** Ask students which kinds of informal talks they have given recently.

2. Discuss **Check It Out.** Ask students to identify the purpose of the talk.

3. Assign and discuss **Try Your Skill.** Have students identify the types of informal talks described in examples 2 and 3.

4. Read aloud **Keep This in Mind.** Then assign **Now Write.** Ask volunteers to share their paragraphs with the class. Remind students that almost all speakers have experienced stage fright at one time or another.

Individualizing the Lesson

Less-Advanced Students

After reading and discussing **Here's the Idea,** ask the class these questions.

1. What is stage fright?
2. Which is usually longer, a formal talk or an informal talk?
3. Which takes longer to prepare, a formal talk or an informal talk? Why?
4. What are four types of informal talks?

Advanced Students

Ask students how they recognize signs of stage fright in themselves and in other people. Point out that

324

A Manner of Speaking

Formal and Informal Talks

Here's the Idea   Do you know what tops the list of the most commonly reported fears? Fear of the dark? Fear of spiders? Fear of falling? No. The most commonly reported fear is stage fright—fear of speaking in front of people.

There are two ways to overcome stage fright. One way is to give lots of talks. Each talk you give increases your confidence. Another way is to be prepared when you give a talk. You can feel much more at ease if you know exactly what you want to say.

The amount of preparation required for a talk depends on the type of talk you give. **Informal talks** require little preparation. They are short and are used to present information quickly. The following are some types of informal talks:

1. Announcements tell about some past or future event. A talk about an upcoming art fair would be an announcement.

2. Directions tell other people how to do something or how to get somewhere. A talk explaining how to get from your school to a local amusement park would be an example of giving directions.

3. Introductions present people to audiences. A talk presenting a candidate for the student council would be an introduction.

4. Demonstrations show how something is done. A talk showing how to make a videotape would be a demonstration.

Formal talks require more preparation than informal talks. They are also usually longer. They present a specific subject in detail. An in-depth talk on the origins of football would be a formal talk.

324

Check It Out   Read the following selection from a talk.

Ladies and gentlemen of the jury, you have seen much evidence against Mr. Moriarity. This evidence may seem convincing. However, I will now prove that my client is innocent. Let me begin by reminding you that no one saw Mr. Moriarity at the scene of the crime. This is odd, indeed, for the crime took place in broad daylight. (The speaker continues to talk for two hours.)

- Is this an informal talk or a formal talk?

Try Your Skill   Read the following descriptions of talks. Which are informal talks? Which are formal talks?

1. The President of the United States giving the "State of the Union" address formal

2. A play director telling when and where tryouts will be held informal

3. A teacher explaining to a group of new students how to get to the school library informal

4. A student giving a report to her science class on differences between the planets in our solar system formal

---

Keep This in Mind

- Practice and preparation can reduce stage fright.
- Informal talks are short. They require little preparation. They are used to present information quickly.
- Formal talks are longer. They require much more preparation than informal talks. They cover a specific subject in detail.

Now Write   Think of a time when you delivered a talk. What was the subject of your talk? To whom did you give your talk? Was it a formal talk or an informal one? Did you feel stage fright? Why? Answer these questions in a paragraph. Label your paper **Speak Up.** Save it in your folder.

people may have different symptoms of stage fright, but that most people do experience it at some time. Ask the students how they can overcome stage fright.

Optional Practice

Have students identify the following as formal or informal talks. Ask them which types of informal talks are represented.

1. a political candidate presenting his ideas to the public
   formal
2. a salesman showing a customer how to operate a dishwasher
   informal, demonstration
3. a principal closing school for the day because of a storm
   informal, announcement
4. a policeman telling a stranger how to find the museum
   informal, directions

Extending the Lesson

Ask students to think of at least three situations in the future when they will need to give informal talks. Then have them think of at least one time when they might need to give a formal talk. This can be any time in the future, from this month to years from now.

Objective

To prepare for an informal talk

Presenting the Lesson

1. Read aloud and discuss **Here's the Idea.** Point out that for no matter what type of informal talk, preparation helps to make the talk clear and complete.

2. Discuss **Check It Out.** Ask a volunteer to make up clearer directions to the Post Office than those offered by Helene.

3. Assign and discuss **Try Your Skill.** Have volunteers read their questions and their introductions aloud.

4. Read aloud **Keep This in Mind.** Then assign **Now Speak.** Have the students read their announcements and introductions aloud.

Individualizing the Lesson

Less-Advanced Students

Before assigning **Try Your Skill,** have the students interview you. Tell them to ask questions about your interests, activities, and accomplishments. Then have the class, as a group, write a brief introduction using information from the interview. Have a student write the introduction on the board as the class produces it. Encourage revision where necessary.

Advanced Students

Have students choose a fictional or historical figure. Then ask them to write the following informal talks, making up details based on that figure.

326

Look Before You Leap

Preparing an Informal Talk

Here's the Idea   Even informal talks require some preparation. Whenever you are asked to give a talk, first think it through. What do you want to say? What details must you include? The answers to these questions will depend upon the type of talk you are going to give.

1. Announcements should be short and clear. They should answer the questions *who? what? when? where?* and *why?*

> Tomorrow at 2:00 in the gymnasium, the marching band will meet to practice for the Labor Day Parade. Band members, please bring your uniforms and sheet music with you to the gym.

This short announcement answers all five questions.

2. Directions should be exact. They should include all necessary or helpful details. They should not leave out any steps.

> To get to the Lilly Library, walk two blocks north on Dunn Street. At the corner of Dunn and 7th Street, turn right. Walk east on 7th Street, past the Student Union, until you come to a fountain. The Lilly Library will be directly across from the fountain, on the right side.

3. Introductions should be courteous and polite. They should supply information about the person being introduced. Make sure that you have enough information about the person before you begin. If you need more information, interview the person.

> Today's speaker is Mr. Brad Keating. Mr. Keating sings professionally in the Chicago area. Last year he was a finalist in the San Francisco Opera auditions. He is here to speak to you about careers in music. Please welcome Mr. Brad Keating.

326

4. Demonstrations should be well organized. Each step should be performed for the audience and explained as it is performed. Suppose you wanted to demonstrate how to change a bicycle tire. You would actually change a tire, describing each step while performing it. You will find it helpful to practice with such objects before giving the demonstration.

Check It Out   Read this situation.

> Someone stopped Helene on the street and said, "Excuse me. I am from out of town. Will you please direct me to the Post Office?" Helene replied, "Oh, sure, the Post Office is a couple blocks from here. You go that way. It's a big building. You can't miss it."

· What is wrong with the directions given by Helene?

Try Your Skill   Interview one of your classmates. Ask questions about your classmate's interests, activities, and accomplishments. Write a brief introduction using information from the interview. Share your introduction with your classmates.

Keep This in Mind

· Before giving an informal talk, know exactly what you want to say.
· Gather all the information you need. Put this information in logical order.
· Do not leave out any necessary steps or details.

Now Speak   Imagine that one of your favorite entertainers or sports figures is coming to your community. Prepare an announcement telling about this event. Make sure that you include *who, where, what, when,* and *why.* Then, imagine you have been chosen to introduce this person. Write a good introduction. Share your announcement and introduction with your classmates.

1. an announcement stating that the person will speak at the school. (include *who, where, what, when,* and *why*)
2. directions to the auditorium where the speech will be held
3. an introduction about the person

Optional Practice

Ask students to prepare a demonstration. Suggest that they use objects with which they are very familiar and that are relatively simple, such as an egg beater, a needle and thread, a childhood game, a tape recorder, etc. Have the students present their demonstrations in class.

Extending the Lesson

Ask students to find and listen for two of the four types of informal talks on television. Suggest that they pay attention to commercials and to talk shows. Have them prepare summaries of the talks, and discuss them in class.

Objective

To plan a formal talk

Presenting the Lesson

1. Read aloud and discuss **Here's the Idea.** Point out that sometimes the topic of a formal talk is assigned.

2. Discuss **Check It Out.** Point out that a talk about comic book production might be entertaining, but its primary purpose would be to inform (to tell how comic books are made).

3. Assign and discuss **Try Your Skill.** Ask volunteers to read their narrowed topics aloud.

4. Read aloud **Keep This in Mind.** Then assign **Now Write.** Remind students to choose a topic with which they are familiar or for which they can do some research.

Individualizing the Lesson

Less-Advanced Students

1. Have students identify the main purposes of the following topics (to persuade, to entertain, or to inform).
— Let's ban cigarette advertising *persuade*
— How to organize your time *inform*
— I was attacked by a dictionary *entertain*
— Successfully surviving a job interview *inform*
— The school year should be shortened *persuade*

2. Help students choose and narrow their topics for the **Try Your Skill** exercise. Have students brainstorm to create topics from the broad subjects.

A Formal Engagement

Preparing a Formal Talk

Here's the Idea Have you ever been asked to give an oral report? If so, you have already given at least one type of formal talk. In the future you will probably give many such talks. Formal talks are common in classes, at club meetings, and at school assemblies.

When planning a formal talk, follow the pre-writing steps you use when planning a composition.

1. Select an interesting topic. The topic should be of interest to you and to your audience. Try to choose a topic that is fresh and unusual. It should be a subject that you know something about.

2. Narrow your topic. Make sure that your topic fits the time available for your talk. It should not be too broad or too narrow. For example, the topic "Ancient Egypt" would be too broad for a five-minute talk. However, "How Mummies Were Made" would probably be just right.

3. Determine your purpose. The purpose is the reason for your talk. Your purpose may be to inform, to persuade, or to entertain. Your purpose will help you to decide what ideas you will include and what points you will stress in your talk.

4. Identify your audience. Consider the ages, interests, and backgrounds of your audience members. Find out how much they know about your subject. Then, tailor your speech to suit them. Avoid talking about subjects that your audience will not understand or will not be interested in.

Read the following topics.

Why the United States Should Continue Its Space Program
How Comic Books Are Made

- What purpose is indicated by each of these topics?
- Which topic is appropriate to an audience of children?
- Which topic is appropriate to an audience of adults?

Try Your Skill   Read each of the following broad topics for formal talks.

television	hobbies
games	pets
myths	space
school	music

Choose any four topics from this list. Narrow each one for a five-minute talk. Write each narrowed topic. Tell whether the topic is for a talk that informs, persuades, or entertains.

Keep This in Mind

- Choose a topic that interests both you and your audience.
- Choose a topic that you know something about.
- Narrow your topic to fit the available time.
- Decide whether your purpose is to inform, persuade, or entertain.
- Identify your audience before writing your talk.

Now Write   Choose one of your narrowed topics from **Try Your Skill.** Divide a piece of paper into three columns labeled *Topic, Purpose,* and *Audience.* Under *Topic,* write the topic you have chosen. Under *Purpose,* write the purpose of your talk. Under *Audience,* give the average age of people in your class. Then tell why you think your audience will find your talk interesting. Label your paper **A Formal Engagement,** and save it in your folder.

329

Part 4

Objective

To gather information for a formal talk and organize it logically

Presenting the Lesson

1. Read aloud and discuss **Here's the Idea.** Tell students that the same steps they follow to develop compositions and reports can help them to develop formal talks.

2. Discuss **Check It Out.** Bring in a dictionary that tells the meanings of first and/or last names for the students to examine.

3. Assign and discuss **Try Your Skill.** Discuss the results with your students.

4. Read aloud **Keep This in Mind.** Then assign **Now Speak.** Remind the students to use the note-taking skills they have learned.

Individualizing the Lesson

Less-Advanced Students

1. Have the class sort the notes in **Try Your Skill** into the following categories: types of last names, lists of names that fit a particular type, and specific meanings of last names. Then explain that each "types of last names" note will be followed by a "list of names" note which will be followed by "specific meanings" note. Have the students then arrange the notes individually.

2. Help students research their talks by arranging for library time, or by bringing relevant books and magazines to class.

Source Sorcery

Gathering and Organizing Information

Here's the Idea After you have identified your topic, purpose, and audience, you are ready to write a sentence stating the main idea of your talk. This sentence can guide you as you gather the information you need to develop the main idea.

Gathering Information for a Formal Talk

1. Look for information related to your main idea. Information can come from personal experiences, other people, books, magazines, newspapers, encyclopedias, and dictionaries.

2. Take notes on note cards. Write only one piece of information on each card.

3. Organize your notes. Divide the cards into groups of related ideas. If a note is not related to the main idea, leave it out.

4. Organize your groups of note cards. Place them in the order that you want them to appear in the talk. The following orders are common:
   order of importance   spatial order   chronological order

5. Do more research to fill in gaps in your information.

Check It Out Hector was asked to give a formal talk in his English class. He knew that his own last name, *Calderon*, meant "kettle" or "cauldron" in Spanish. He decided to do a talk on the origins and meanings of last names.

- How could Hector state his main idea?
- What sources could he check for information?

Try Your Skill Read the following notes for a talk on the meanings of last names. Copy each note onto a note card. Then, divide these notes into groups of related ideas. Leave out any notes not related to the main idea.

> –A *smith* is someone who works with metals.
> –Some last names are names of places.
> –*Clark* used to mean "priest."
> –A *miller* is a person who grinds grain into flour.
> –Some common English names are *Hill, Brook, Rivers, Lake, Stone,* and *Field*.
> –The name *Taylor* comes from *tailor,* a person who makes clothes.
> –The name *Amy* means "beloved."
> –The name *Deborah* comes from the Hebrew word for "bee."
> –Some names tell about occupations.
> –*Lamb* is a common English name.
> –The following names are common in English—*Carpenter, Cook, Baker*.
> –*Rosenthal* means "red (rosen) valley (thal)."
> –Some names, such as *Swan* or *Wolf,* come from animals.

Keep This in Mind

- The main idea is the subject of your talk. It should be stated in a single sentence.
- The information you gather should be related to your main idea.
- Information may be gathered from personal experience, other people, or written sources.
- Information should be put in a logical order.

Now Write Write a main idea statement for the topic you chose in **A Formal Engagement.** Do research for a talk on this topic. Take notes for your talk. Put these notes in a logical order. Save your notes in your folder.

Part 5

Together at Last

Writing a Formal Talk

Objective

To develop the introduction, body, and conclusion of a formal talk

Presenting the Lesson

1. Read aloud and discuss **Here's the Idea.** Tell the students that the purpose of the talk will have an effect on the way it ends. For example, a persuasive talk will end by asking or reminding the audience to take certain action; a demonstration will sum up the purpose or ease of the process demonstrated.

2. Discuss **Check It Out.** Ask in what other ways a persuasive talk on the space program might be concluded.

3. Assign and discuss **Try Your Skill.** Ask volunteers to read their introductions aloud.

4. Read aloud **Keep This in Mind.** Then assign **Now Write.** Remind students to include the proper types of information in each part of their talks.

Individualizing the Lesson

Less-Advanced Students

As a group, write an introduction for a talk on modern technology, using as a base the notes presented in **Optional Practice** on page 331.

Advanced Students

1. Duplicate a famous talk. Have students analyze the introduction and conclusion.

2. Tell students to assume that they are experts in one of the following subjects: *Martian customs,*

Here's the Idea   After you have organized your notes, you are ready to put together your talk. To do this, you must write an introduction, a body, and a conclusion.

The Parts of a Formal Talk

1. The **introduction** should be short. It should hold the attention of your audience. It should end with a statement of your main idea. There are many ways of introducing a talk:

   a. State an interesting fact.
   b. Ask an interesting question.
   c. Make an interesting comparison.
   d. Tell an interesting story.
   e. Show an interesting object.

2. The **body** should support your main idea. It should present the bulk of your information from your note cards. This information should be organized logically.

3. The **conclusion** can restate your main idea in different words. It can also summarize major points made to support the main idea. If you are speaking to entertain, the conclusion may be a high point of entertainment. It could also be a lesson drawn from the experiences described in the body.

Check It Out   Read the following conclusion to a talk.

I hope that Congress and the President will continue our exploration of space. Then we can continue to enjoy the many new inventions the space program has given us. People will continue to find jobs in space-related fields. Most importantly, our knowledge of the universe will continue to grow. Eventually, we shall make new worlds available for mining and colonization.

- Which sentence restates the main idea?
- What major points are summarized in this conclusion?

Try Your Skill   The following sentences could be the final sentences for the introductions of two talks. Each states the main idea of a talk. Write introductions for each of these main ideas. Use the techniques discussed in **Here's the Idea.**

    1. This is a typical example of the slanted view of teenagers presented by television.

    2. Similarly, you can't become an Olympic athlete without lots of dedication and practice.

Keep This in Mind

- The introduction should state the main idea of your talk. It should also capture the attention of your audience.
- The body should develop your main idea with details.
- The conclusion should restate your main idea. It may also summarize the important points in your talk.

Now Write   Using the notes gathered in Part 4, **Source Sorcery,** write a formal talk. Include an introduction, a body, and a conclusion. Then, revise your first draft. Make sure that each part of your talk contains the information described in **Here's the Idea.** Label your first and final drafts **Together at Last.** Save them in your folder.

333

Objective

To learn to deliver a talk effectively

Presenting the Lesson

1. Read aloud and discuss **Here's the Idea.** Stress the performance aspect of giving a talk. Remind students that they can control many facets of a presentation: how they look, sound, etc.

2. Discuss **Check It Out.** Have volunteers demonstrate the flaws in Pennie's and Ron's presentations.

3. Assign and discuss **Try Your Skill.** Ask volunteers to read the statements clearly. Tell the students that sometimes sentences or phrases that are difficult to pronounce can be conquered by slowing down and practicing before an actual talk.

4. Read aloud **Keep This in Mind.** Then assign **Now Write.** Remind students that gestures and facial expressions should not be so extreme or constant that they detract from the talk itself.

Individualizing the Lesson

Less-Advanced Students

Read the following description to the class.

During a school assembly, Betsy presented a talk on her uncle Alvin, who is a professional clown. She was wearing black, dirty pants and an old black tee shirt. She stared at her notes the whole time, except when she looked at the clock in back of her. She looked grim and unhappy. Her only visual aid was a baby picture of her

334

Special Delivery

Presenting Yourself to an Audience

Here's the Idea　Before a movie director shoots a scene, he or she must plan it carefully. Many questions must be answered. How should the actors act and speak? What clothes should they wear? What gestures should they make? What expressions should they have on their faces? Before you give a talk, you must ask yourself the same questions. You must plan how to present yourself to your audience. The following guidelines will help you:

1. Appearance. Wear clothes that are right for the occasion. Stand up straight, but not rigidly. Try to appear relaxed and confident.

2. Eye Contact. Look directly at audience members or slightly above their heads. This will help keep the attention of your audience. Do not stare at your notes or props.

3. Voice. Speak clearly. Make sure that you can be heard. Pronounce each word precisely. Do not rush. Do not speak in a monotone. Instead, vary your volume, pitch, and rate of speech. Make sure that your tone fits the content of the speech. Pause for emphasis before important points.

4. Gestures and Facial Expressions. Use appropriate gestures and facial expressions. They will relax you and increase your confidence. They will also help you express your feelings. Smile when you talk about something wonderful. Look concerned when you talk about something upsetting. Use your hands to stress important points. Make sure that your gestures and facial expressions are natural.

334

Check It Out   Study the following situations.

1. Pennie gave a speech about safety rules for swimmers. Her written speech was three pages long. However, she gave the entire speech in about one minute.

2. Ron gave a speech on how to do clown makeup. He felt embarrassed as he spoke. He mumbled and kept his head down. His audience had to lean forward to hear him.

- What problems did each speaker have?
- How could these problems be corrected?

Try Your Skill   Practice speaking clearly. Read the following statements aloud. Pronounce all of the words clearly.

1. The six guests sang show tunes.
2. Thelma's father and brothers seem particularly healthy.
3. Bill broke the blue glass fruit bowl.
4. The jeweler filled the kettle with golden, molten metal.

Keep This in Mind

- Whenever you speak, try to look and sound your best.
- Stand up straight. Look at your audience. Speak loudly enough to be heard.
- Use natural gestures and facial expressions to communicate feelings.

Now Write   Study the talk you wrote for **Together at Last.** Make two columns on a piece of paper. Label one column *Gestures.* Label the other *Facial Expressions.* Make a list of facial expressions and gestures that you could use in your talk. Label your list **Special Delivery.** Save it in your folder.

uncle, which she showed briefly at the beginning of her talk.

Ask students to identify at least four flaws in Betsy's performance. Solicit suggestions for improvement.

Advanced Students

Have students choose a short poem to present to the class. Tell them to practice the poem so that they can recite it clearly, without stumbling, and with the appropriate gestures and facial expressions.

Optional Practice

Ask students to practice the following tongue twisters, until they can say them quickly but clearly.

1. Charles shaved sleekly and slowly shortly before Cheryl sadly showed six sick sheep.
2. These sea shells will sit so prettily on the sill, Sally.

Extending the Lesson

If you have access to a videotape camera, tape students as they present talks. You might ask volunteers to deliberately mumble or otherwise deliver poorly. Then have the students, in groups, critique their classmates' performances.

Part 7

Objective

To practice and improve a talk

Presenting the Lesson

1. Read aloud and discuss **Here's the Idea.** Tell students that using a clock or stopwatch might help them to learn to pace themselves as they speak.

2. Discuss **Check It Out.** Point out that practicing in front of friends and relatives might also help to relieve stage fright.

3. Assign and discuss **Try Your Skill.** Have volunteers deliver the introduction in front of the class.

4. Read aloud **Keep This in Mind.** Then assign **Now Speak.** Tell students that they may memorize the body of the talk as well, if they prefer to do so, but caution them that their talk should sound relaxed and natural, not stiff and memorized.

Individualizing the Lesson

Less-Advanced Students

Assign students to teams. Have them help each other memorize and practice their talks. Give individual help to those students who need additional attention.

Advanced Students

Assign brief passages from a Shakespearean play to students (a play the students have studied, if possible). Have them memorize the passages, or practice reading them with the text in front of them. Remind the students to use appropriate facial expressions and gestures.

Mirror, Mirror

Practicing a Talk

Here's the Idea   There's more than a bit of truth in the expression "Practice makes perfect." Sports figures, actors, dancers, musicians, and artists all depend upon regular practice to perfect their skills. Practice is also important to giving a successful talk. The more you practice a talk, the better it will be.

Before you can begin to practice, you must decide how you are going to present your talk. There are two possibilities:

1. Memorize the entire talk. Use the following method.
   a. Read one sentence.
   b. Recite the sentence several times without looking at it.
   c. Read the next sentence.
   d. Recite both sentences without looking at them.
   e. Go through the entire talk in this manner. When you miss a sentence, start all over again.
2. Memorize the introduction and conclusion. Then, make an outline or notes for the body. When you give the talk, refer to your outline or notes as necessary. If you use an outline or note cards, practice with these. Avoid looking at them too often.

To practice your talk, say it aloud several times. If possible, use a tape recorder to check your voice and a mirror to check your posture, facial expressions, and gestures. Make sure you follow the guidelines for giving a talk explained in **Special Delivery.** Ask friends or relatives to listen to your talk. Ask for suggestions for improvement.

Check It Out Kim Li wanted to run for class president. She wrote a campaign speech. She memorized the introduction and conclusion of her talk. Then, she made an outline of the body. She practiced her talk many times in front of a mirror.

- What did Kim Li do to make her talk a success?
- What else could she have done?

Try Your Skill Practice giving the sample introduction from Part 2, **Look Before You Leap.** Write the answers to the following questions.

1. What tone of voice is appropriate for this talk?
2. What facial expressions and gestures could a speaker use when giving this talk?

Keep This in Mind

- You should practice your talk several times before giving it.
- You may memorize the entire talk. You may also memorize just the introduction and conclusion and use notes or an outline for the body.
- Consider your voice, gestures, and facial expressions when practicing a talk.
- Ask your friends or relatives to listen to your talk. Ask them to make suggestions for improvement.

Now Speak Practice the talk you wrote in Part 5, **Together at Last.** Memorize the introduction and conclusion. Use note cards or an outline for the body. Practice your talk alone and then for a relative or friend. List any improvements that you can make on a piece of paper. Label the paper **Mirror, Mirror.** Place it in your folder. If your teacher wishes you to do so, give your talk to your class.

Optional Practice

Duplicate the following sample introduction from a talk about dreams. Have students practice giving this introduction.

After a hard day at school or at work, you enter a world of food—hamburgers, pizza, soda pop, chocolate, your favorites at two or three times their normal size everywhere you look. Or, in spite of an easy, seemingly happy day, you encounter once again giant spiders and slimy monsters. Where are you? You are, of course, in dreamland—and there is a purpose to these dreams.

Extending the Lesson

1. Require students to use at least one audio-visual aid in their speech, and to practice incorporating that item smoothly into their presentation.

2. Tape a portion of a newscast from radio or television. Transcribe and duplicate it. Have students practice giving the talk.

Part 8

Objective

To learn how to listen to and evaluate a talk

Presenting the Lesson

1. Read aloud and discuss **Here's the Idea.** Point out that both the listener and the speaker can benefit from good listening habits.

Stress that an evaluator judges both the talk and its presentation. Remind students that these guidelines apply outside the classroom too.

2. Discuss **Check It Out.** Ask students what they might like to know about their own talks from listeners.

3. Assign and discuss **Try Your Skill.** Point out that the guidelines for evaluating a talk are also useful for practicing a talk.

4. Read aloud **Keep This in Mind.** Then assign **Now Listen.** Collate student responses to the speech. Discuss the difference in responses with the students

Individualizing the Lesson

Less-Advanced Students

Have a student from another class or another teacher present a talk (with or without deliberate flaws). A videotaped presentation would be best. Ask students to evaluate the talk, using the guidelines presented in **Here's the Idea.** Then, go over their evaluations point by point. If the presentation was videotaped, you can go back over the delivery to compare it with the students' evaluations.

338

Have You Heard?

Listening to and Judging Talks

Here's the Idea   An audience should listen closely to a speaker. These guidelines will help you to become a good listener:

Guidelines for Good Listening

1. Sit where you can see and hear. Pay attention.

2. Avoid distracting the speaker. Don't make unnecessary noises or movements.

3. Show the speaker your interest. Look at the speaker as he or she talks. Keep an interested expression on your face.

4. Think about what the speaker is saying. Listen for main ideas and supporting details. You may want to take notes.

5. Be open-minded. Don't judge the speaker's ideas before you hear how they are supported.

If you are asked to judge a talk, use these guidelines:

Evaluating a Talk

CONTENT

Topic:	Was the main point of the talk clear?
Purpose:	Was the purpose of the talk clear? Did the speaker accomplish this purpose?
Audience:	Did the talk suit its audience?
Development:	Did the speaker present enough information? Was any of this information unnecessary?
Organization:	Were the speaker's ideas presented logically?
Introduction:	Did the introduction capture your interest? Did it state the main idea?

338

Body: Did the body offer details to support the main idea? Were the important points clear?

Conclusion: Was the conclusion of the talk satisfactory?

PRESENTATION

Eye Contact: Did the speaker look at the audience? Did the speaker look at his or her notes too often?

Posture: Did the speaker appear confident and relaxed?

Voice: Was the speaker easy to hear and understand? Did the speaker vary his or her voice?

Gestures: Were the speaker's gestures natural?

Facial Expressions: Were the speaker's facial expressions natural? Did they fit the content of the talk?

Preparation: Had the speaker practiced the talk?

Check It Out   Di gave a talk on women in the space program. Later, she asked Joe about her talk. Joe said he liked the talk because it seemed that Di was interested in her subject.

- Why should speakers seem interested in their subjects?
- How could Joe's comments have been more specific?

Try Your Skill   Copy the main headings of the checklist for evaluating talks. Practice the talk that you wrote for Part 7, **Mirror, Mirror.** How can you improve it? Write your ideas next to the correct headings.

> ### Keep This in Mind
> - Good listeners show their interest. They don't distract the speaker.
> - Good evaluators are polite and specific.

Now Listen   Evaluate a talk in class. Use the checklist for evaluating talks. Compare your ratings with those of your classmates. Label your evaluation **Have You Heard?**

339

Advanced Students

Ask students to evaluate each other's listening skills. Have one listen to another tell a story. Ask a third student to keep track of the listener's behavior, and its effect on the speaker.

Optional Practice

Find or write a talk. Present it to the class. Tell them that you are going to deliver the speech in a deliberately flawed manner. Ask them to evaluate your performance. At the same time, have a responsible student evaluate the entire class's listening behavior. Discuss the listening and speaking evaluations in depth.

Extending the Lesson

Tell students to respond inappropriately in a conversation. If the conversation is light, they can look sad; if the topic is interesting, they might look bored and distracted. Have them notice the effect on the speaker. (Tell them also to apologize to the speaker, and to explain their experiment.)

Handbook

A detailed Table of Contents for the Handbook appears in the front of this book.

Section Objectives

1. To identify the subject and predicate of a sentence

2. To know the four kinds of sentences (declarative, interrogative, imperative, and exclamatory) and to use proper end punctuation

3. To identify the simple subject, subject of the verb, and the verb

4. To identify main verbs, helping verbs, and separated parts of a verb

5. To identify compound subjects and compound verbs

6. To identify the subject in unusual positions

7. To identify the subjects and verbs in questions and exclamations

8. To identify the subjects and verbs in sentences beginning with *there*

9. To identify the subjects and verbs in commands

Preparing the Students

Discuss the importance of communication in everyday life, and the various methods of communicating. Ask students for examples of situations where clear communication is necessary, and the method used to accomplish this. List them on the board.

The Sentence and Its Parts

Examples

Situation	Method
Police officer directing traffic	whistle, waving hands
Ambulance on the way to the hospital	flashing lights, siren
Asking someone a question	speaking in a certain tone
Directions on a bottle of medicine	writing

Explain to the students that it is extremely important for written communication to be clear. It must also follow the rules for standard English so that it can be easily understood by the reader.

This section will focus on the sentence. Explain that this section will help students become aware of the parts of the sentence and how they are used. Read and discuss the introduction on pages 343–344.

Additional Resources

Diagnostic Tests — page 1 in the test booklet

Mastery Test — pages 35–38 in the test booklet

Additional Exercises — pages 364–371 in the student text

Practice Book — pages 141–147

Duplicating Masters — pages 141–147

Special Populations — See special section at the back of this Teacher's Edition.

When you speak to someone, you don't always use complete sentences. For example, you can answer a question with a word or two:

    Yes.   No.   Tomorrow.

You can even ask a question without using what are usually considered complete sentences:

    Whose car?   Which girl?   What record?

However, when you write, you must use complete sentences to make your meaning clear. Your reader is not able to ask you to explain what you mean.

Sentences are clear when all the parts are correctly put together. In this section you will study the parts of sentences.

Part 1   The Parts of a Sentence

A sentence is a group of words that expresses a complete thought.

A sentence makes a statement, asks a question, tells someone to do something, or expresses strong feeling. A sentence has two parts. One part names someone or something that the sentence is about. This is the **subject.** The second part tells *what is* or *what happens.* This is the **predicate.**

Subject (*Who* or *what*)	Predicate (*What is* or *what happens*)
Jeff	smiled.
The girl	is captain of the team.
The two cars	nearly collided.
Students in math class	write programs for the computer.

The subject of a sentence tells who or what the sentence is about.

The predicate of a sentence tells what *is* or what happens.

Every sentence must have a subject and a predicate. If one of these parts is missing from a group of words, it is not a complete sentence. It is a **fragment.**

Read these sentence fragments. Notice why each is not a sentence.

Dashed across the finish line. (Who dashed?)
Two girls with a huge banner. (What happened?)

Exercises Find the subjects and predicates.

A. Write each of the following sentences. Draw a vertical line between each subject and predicate.

Example: A flock of geese | flew overhead.

1. Nancy |collects foreign postage stamps.
2. Joe's Labrador retriever |jumped the fence.
3. Thunder |rumbled in the distance.
4. The boy across the street |raises rabbits.
5. Terry |saw the musical on Channel 4.
6. A large crowd |watched the faculty-varsity basketball game.
7. Janet |designed the costumes for the play.
8. Karen |wrote the weekly sports news.
9. One swimmer |broke the school record.
10. The yardstick |snapped in two.

B. Copy these sentences. Draw a vertical line between the subject and the predicate.

Example: The architect | checked her blueprints.

1. Greg's brother |builds historical model boats.
2. The girl in the yellow slicker |missed the bus.
3. Condors |are large vultures.
4. My sister |graduated from high school this year.
5. Several students at Central School |drew the posters for the blood drive.
6. A monkey |chattered in the treetops.
7. An alligator |slid into the water.
8. Elaine |threw the ball to home plate.
9. The roses in our garden |bloom all summer.
10. Two boys from our neighborhood |went on a canoe trip.

Advanced Students

Have each student compose two good sentences. Compile the sentences into one list. Reproduce this list and distribute it to the students. Have them follow the directions for Exercise A.

Optional Practice

Have each student write five sentences about the same subject. Possible subjects could include *the school cafeteria, my best friend, science class,* and so on. Encourage students to write lively sentences with specific verbs. Have students divide each sentence into its subject and predicate.

Extending the Lesson

Write the following groups of words on the board. Ask students to tell whether each group of words is a subject or predicate. Then ask students to complete each group.

S the newspaper photographer
P worked overtime all week
S the inventor of the camera
P makes the hottest chili in town
P landed in the middle of the airfield
S the bookcase in the corner
S the checker in the grocery store

Objective

To know the four kinds of sentences (declarative, interrogative, imperative, and exclamatory) and to use proper end punctuation

Presenting the Lesson

1. Read and discuss page 346. Ask students to supply additional examples for each kind of sentence and explain when they would be used.

2. Assign and discuss Exercises A, B, and C on page 347.

Individualizing the Lesson

Less-Advanced Students

Do Exercise A orally. Have students explain how each sentence matches the definition for its type. Have students complete Exercise B working independently or in pairs. Discuss the exercise in class.

Advanced Students

Have the student compose "Four-Sentence Stories." These stories should be made up of one declarative sentence, one interrogative sentence, one imperative sentence, and one exclamatory sentence. Sentences may be arranged in any order.

Part 2 Kinds of Sentences

You use language for several purposes. Sometimes you want to tell something. Sometimes you want to ask something. Sometimes you want to tell someone to do something. Sometimes you want to show how strongly you feel about something. There is a different kind of sentence for each of these purposes.

1. A sentence that makes a statement is a **declarative sentence.**

   Her story was short.   Tom called the store at noon.

2. A sentence that asks a question is an **interrogative sentence.**

   Was the play a success?   Are you going to camp?

3. A sentence that tells someone to do something is an **imperative sentence.** The subject is not usually stated but is understood to be *you. You* is the person or group spoken to.

   (you) Be here at nine o'clock.   (you) Please open the window.

4. A sentence that is used to express strong feeling is an **exclamatory sentence.**

   How Sherry yawned!   What fun we had!

Punctuating Sentences

Every sentence begins with a capital letter. Every sentence ends with a punctuation mark. Notice the marks at the ends of the sentences above. Remember these rules:

1. Use a period after a declarative sentence.
2. Use a question mark after an interrogative sentence.
3. Use a period after an imperative sentence.
4. Use an exclamation mark after an exclamatory sentence.

Exercises   Learn the kinds of sentences.

A.   Number your paper from 1 to 10. For each of the following sentences, write *Declarative, Interrogative, Imperative,* or *Exclamatory* to show what kind it is. Add the punctuation mark that should be used at the end of each sentence.

Imp. 1. Hold my books for a minute, please.

D. 2. Yes, we took first place in the debate.

Imp. 3. Pour the water into the test tube.

Int. 4. Have you been here before, Sara?

D. 5. We found kindling for our fire in the woods near the lake.

Int. 6. What is the address of that company?

Int. 7. Is your watch running?

Ex. 8. How frightened I was!

Ex. 9. Kate, look out!

Imp.10. Move to the rear of the bus, please.

B.   Follow the directions for Exercise A.

Int. 1. Please don't erase this message.

Imp. 2. Have you heard the new song by Kansas?

D 3. Dad always trims the lilac bush in the fall and in the spring.

Imp. 4. Tell the joke about the elephant again.

Int. 5. Where did you put the Christmas tree lights?

Ex. 6. What big eyes you have!

Imp. 7. Keep your elbow stiff and watch the ball.

Int. 8. When do the miners' shifts change?

Ex. 9. Willie, watch out!

Imp. 10. Have a good day.

C.   Writing   Write three declarative, three interrogative, three exclamatory, and three imperative sentences.

Sentences will vary.

347

Part 3

Objective

To identify the simple subject, the subject of the verb, and the verb

Presenting the Lesson

1. Read and discuss page 348. Be sure students clearly understand the difference between *subject* and *simple subject* and *predicate* and *simple predicate* (verb). Have students divide all sentences into subjects and predicates before attempting to locate the simple subjects and verbs.

2. Assign and discuss Exercises A and B on page 349. During your discussion, ask students to divide each sentence into subject and predicate. Then ask for the verb and its subject.

3. "Diagraming Verbs and Their Subjects." Sentence diagraming is intended as a teaching tool and should be used with students to make the structure of sentences clearer. A minimal amount of diagraming instruction is provided in the text. If students are to diagram, you will need to instruct them in the construction and use of the diagram. It is not advisable for less-advanced students to tackle diagraming at this time.

4. Assign Exercises A and B on page 350 for additional practice.

Individualizing the Lesson

Less-Advanced Students

Have students write out each sentence in Exercise A on page 350 in

In every sentence a few words are more important than the rest. These are the key words that make the group of words a sentence. Study these examples:

A cold, steady **rain**	**fell** throughout the night.
Rain	**fell.**

The subject of the first sentence is *A cold, steady rain.* The key word in this subject is *rain.* You could simply say *Rain fell throughout the night. Rain* is the **simple subject** of the sentence.

The predicate in the first sentence is *fell throughout the night.* The key word is *fell.* You could simply say *A cold, steady rain fell. Fell* is the **simple predicate.**

The key word in the subject of a sentence is called the simple subject. It is also called the subject of the verb.

The key word in the predicate is called the simple predicate. The simple predicate is the **verb.**

To find the simple subject in a sentence, first find the verb. Some verbs tell about action.

Tom *paddled* the canoe.   Ann *caught* the ball.

Sometimes the action shown is an action you cannot see.

Miki *had* a good idea.   Jim *remembered* the story.

Some verbs tell that something *is* or *exists.* Such verbs are **state-of-being verbs.**

The doctor *is* here.   The test *seemed* easy.

To find the verb in a sentence, look for the word that shows action or state of being.

Exercises **Find the verbs and their simple subjects.**

A. For each sentence, write the <u>verb</u> and its <u>subject</u>.

Example: The bus arrived early today.
Verb: arrived   Subject: bus

1. Julie caught the baseball easily.
2. The co-pilot radioed the information to the tower.
3. Nancy plays the flute in the school band.
4. Careful beekeepers wear protective masks.
5. Jack worked at the ice rink after school.
6. The two boys built a chicken coop.
7. A robin built a nest in our cherry tree.
8. The swimmers waited for the starter's signal.
9. Tall elms lined the avenue.
10. The three girls walked home together.

B. For each sentence write the <u>verb</u> and its <u>subject</u>.

1. Martha balanced on the high diving board.
2. The fans in the bleachers roared.
3. The compass pointed north.
4. The coach asked for a timeout.
5. A high fence enclosed the yard.
6. The pilot adjusted his headphones.
7. The helicopter landed on the hospital roof.
8. A heavy rain flattened our tomato plants.
9. Our group gave a report on solar energy.
10. A new member of the club made several suggestions.

Diagraming Verbs and Their Subjects

A diagram helps you see how the parts of a sentence work together. A sentence diagram always begins on a horizontal line. A vertical line cuts the horizontal line in two. It separates

Have students decide which of the words in the following groups can be simple subjects and which can be verbs. Next, they should write a sentence for each group, trying to include the other words given in that group. Remind them that they will have to insert articles and use proper punctuation. Have them underline the subject once and the verb twice.

Example:

is	important
book	dictionary
students	for

The <u>dictionary</u> <u><u>is</u></u> an important book for students.

1. announced	2. winding
principal	curved
assembly	mountains
news	road
good	around
during	
3. old	4. roamed
repaired	in
broken	dinosaurs
car	earth
friend	prehistoric
	times

1. The <u>principal</u> <u><u>announced</u></u> the good news during the assembly.
2. The winding <u>road</u> <u><u>curved</u></u> around the mountain.
3. An old <u>friend</u> <u><u>repaired</u></u> the broken car.
4. <u>Dinosaurs</u> <u><u>roamed</u></u> the earth in prehistoric times.

the subject from the verb. The subject is placed to the left of the vertical line. The verb is placed to the right.

Example: Gerry laughed with his friends.

Gerry	laughed

Exercises   Find the verbs and their subjects.

A. Show the verb and its simple subject in each of the following sentences. Use diagrams or any other method your teacher may suggest. subject | verb

1. Watermelon tastes good in hot weather. Watermelon | tastes
2. Dr. Harvey's cat wore a tin bell. cat | wore
3. A squirrel in the attic started a nest. squirrel | started
4. The clock in the hallway needs a new spring. clock | needs
5. The blower on the furnace stopped. blower | stopped
6. The photographs fell out of the album. photographs | fell
7. Barbara's dresser fit next to the window. dresser | fit
8. The top drawer of the cabinet stuck. drawer | stuck
9. A large, colorful umbrella shaded the chairs. umbrella | shaded
10. Curt wore his favorite sweatshirt. Curt | wore

B. Write the verb and its simple subject in each sentence.

1. A judge read all the contest rules. judge | read
2. The students in our class made a model spaceship. students | made
3. Her pocket bulged with pennies. pocket | bulged
4. Fireworks exploded in the sky. Fireworks | exploded
5. Unexpectedly, the engine stalled. engine | stalled
6. John visited the planetarium in Chicago last summer. John | visited
7. The Moores go to the photography show every year. Moores | go
8. Maria's mother raises vegetables. mother | raises
9. The end of vacation came too quickly. end | came
10. We met Judy at the movie. We | met

Part 4 Main Verbs and Helping Verbs

In some sentences, the verb is one word.

> Meg *visited* Boston.

In other sentences, the verb is two or more words.

> Meg *will visit* Boston.

In this sentence, *visit* is the **main verb.** *Will* is a **helping verb.**

A verb may consist of a main verb and one or more helping verbs.

Certain words are often used as helping verbs.

am	was	has	do	will	could	may	being
is	were	have	does	shall	should	must	been
are	be	had	did	can	would	might	

Some of these verbs can be used alone. Sometimes they are used as **helping verbs** with other verbs:

> The neighbors *have* a new car.   Bill *is* a painter.
> The girls *have finished* their work.   Sue *is going* home.
> We *have been looking* for Tom.

Exercises   Find helping verbs and main verbs.

A. Write the verb for each sentence. Make one column for helping verbs (HV) and one column for main verbs (MV).

Example: Phil is keeping a journal.

HV	MV
is	keeping

1. The weather is becoming cooler.
2. The next players are waiting for the badminton court.

Part 4

Objective

To identify main verbs, helping verbs, and separated parts of a verb

Presenting the Lesson

1. Read and discuss page 351. Ask students if they understand why the words in the list on this page are always verbs. Stress that when these verbs are used alone, they are *main verbs*. It would be helpful for the students to memorize the list.

2. Assign and discuss Exercises A, B and C on pages 351–352.

3. Read and discuss pages 352–353. Emphasize that words that separate parts of the verb are never part of the verb themselves.

4. Assign and discuss Exercises A and B on pages 353–354.

Individualizing the Lesson

Less-Advanced Students

1. For most of the exercises in this part, students should continue to divide sentences into subjects and predicates. They can then go back and underline the simple subjects once and verbs twice.

2. Remind the students to use the list of helping verbs while they do the exercises on pages 351–352.

3. Do Exercise A on page 353 orally. You might have volunteers write the sentences on the chalkboard. For Exercise B on page 353, remind students to check the list of helping verbs on page 351.

Advanced Students

1. Ask students to decide whether each verb in the exercises on pages 353–354 is a main verb or a helping verb. They can do this orally for Exercise A and in writing for Exercise B.

2. Have students write original sentences using the helping verbs *can, could, shall, will, would, may,* and *might.* Discuss their sentences in class.

3. Have students write original sentences with separated verb parts. Use the student sentences for additional practice.

Optional Practice

1. As a class exercise, have students take the basic sentences in Exercises A and B on pages 353–354 and see how many changes they can make by altering the helping verb. First, list some examples of how helping verbs are combined.

have + be + verb

has   been   called
had   been   running

2. Write the following pairs of sentences on the board or on a worksheet. Have students underline the verb in each sentence twice. If the verb consists of only a main verb, students should write **MV** above the verb. If it consists of both a helping verb and a main verb, they should write **HV** over the helping verb and **MV** over the main verb.

             HV   **MV**
Example: The students had often visited
        the zoo.

               HV **MV**
1. a. My uncle has often sung in musical productions.
                MV
   b. My uncle has a beautiful voice.

                   HV   **MV**
3. Four students were serving refreshments.
          HV   **MV**
4. Lou has returned your tape recorder.
                HV
5. My brother did arrive after the thunderstorm.
6. Ted is writing the script for the skit.
                    HV   **MV**
7. The President has visited several countries this year.
         HV   **MV**
8. I have gone to the dentist's office twice this week.
              HV   **MV**
9. Patrick has eaten spaghetti for lunch.
                   HV **MV**
10. The key for the garage is hanging by the back door of the kitchen.

B. Follow the directions for Exercise A.

1. Two ducks were huddling near the pond.
2. The Mulligans have had a good time at Six Flags.
3. The price will include the cost of lunch.
4. The director will select the cast this afternoon.
5. The sky has looked stormy all afternoon.
6. Twice recently the car has needed a new front tire.
7. Really, I do try.
8. At four o'clock the plumber was working on the bathtub drain.
9. Kathy had been ready for over an hour.
10. The outcome had seemed uncertain.

C. Writing Write five sentences. Each sentence should have a main verb and a helping verb. Underline each main verb once. Underline each helping verb twice. Sentences will vary.

Separated Parts of a Verb

Sometimes the parts of a verb are separated from each other by words that are not part of the verb. These words usually tell **when** (*often, always, never*) or **how** (*slowly, scarcely, hardly*). *Not* and the *n't* in contractions are never part of the verb, although they do change the meaning of the verb.

Notice how the parts of verbs can be separated.

That bus **has** *often* **been** late.
During the night, the temperature **had** *suddenly* **dropped.**
We **had** *not* **seen** the accident.

Exercises   Find the verbs.

A. Write the verbs and their simple subjects in these sentences. Underline the subject once and the verb twice. Your teacher may ask you to use diagrams instead.

Example: My cousin had never seen snow before.
cousin   had seen

1. Sara has probably finished the poster by now.
2. Her friend had already opened the window.
3. That class is always going on field trips.
4. Several customers had angrily asked for the manager.
5. Ron was patiently sewing a patch on his jeans.
6. My family has never been to Los Angeles.
7. The dog was carefully burying its bone.
8. The painter had carelessly tossed the brushes away.
9. With little effort, the salmon were leaping the rapids.
10. Under the circumstances, we will certainly help you.

B. Follow the directions for Exercise A.

1. We have never gone to the Milwaukee Zoo.
2. Jane's spirits were obviously rising.
3. The deer have often grazed in that field.
4. I do believe in life on other planets.
5. She had recently photographed the Florida Everglades.
6. Larry will not tell anyone his plans.
7. Trade between the two countries had not begun.

2. a. The rock concert was spectacular.
   b. The band was traveling by train to Seattle.
3. a. The machinist did a good job.
   b. The airline pilot did not fly jumbo jets.
4. a. The capacity crowd had loudly cheered the home team.
   b. The quarterback had a chance for a long pass.
5. a. That color television is the best brand.
   b. The receptionist is leaving on a trip next week.

Extending the Lesson

Many of the sentences in Exercises A and B on pages 353–354 are written with the parts of the verb separated. Have students rewrite those sentences putting the helping verb and the main verb together as a unit. Discuss how this shift changes the meaning or emphasis of a sentence.

8. The waves were constantly pounding the deck.
9. The school is probably closed because of the snow.
10. We have often taken the train to the city.

Presenting the Lesson

1. Read and discuss pages 354–355. The three coordinating conjunctions *and, but,* and *or* should be learned immediately. You may find it valuable to discuss the word *compound* as it is used with other topics (a chemical compound, a building compound, a compound fracture) and relate the meaning to compound subjects and verbs. Also point out that compound subjects share the same verb and compound verbs share the same subject.

2. Read and discuss "Diagraming Compound Subjects and Verbs" on page 355.

3. Assign and discuss Exercises A and B on pages 355–356.

Individualizing the Lesson

Less-Advanced Students

1. Have students work in pairs to complete the exercises on pages 355–356. Have them divide each sentence into subject and predicate before they look for compound parts.

2. If your students have difficulty identifying compound subjects and

Part 5   Compound Subjects and Compound Verbs

Look at these two sentences. How do they differ?

> Two girls tied for first place.
> Kara and Liz tied for first place.

In the first sentence, the subject is *girls.* What is the subject of the second sentence? Both *Kara* and *Liz* are subjects. When a subject has two or more parts, it is called a **compound subject.** The word *compound* means "having more than one part."

Verbs can be compound, too. How do these two sentences differ?

> He directed the movie.
> He directed and produced the movie.

In the first sentence the verb is *directed.* In the second, the verbs are *directed* and *produced.* The words *directed* and *produced* are called a **compound verb.**

Predicates may also be compound. Notice the parts in the following **compound predicate.**

> Dad *assembled the bookcase* and *painted it.*

In the compound subject above, the word *and* joins *Kara* and *Liz.* In the compound verb, *and* joins *directed* and *produced.* In the compound predicate, *and* joins *assembled the bookcase* and *painted it.* Words that join words and groups of words in this way are called **conjunctions.** The word *and* is a conjunction.

When any compound construction has more than two parts, separate the parts with commas.

Carol, Ted, and *Becky* entered the race.
Vince *washed, peeled,* and *chopped* the fruit.
Jan *went home, did her homework,* and *played tennis.*

Diagraming Compound Subjects and Verbs

To diagram the parts of a compound subject, split the subject line. Put the conjunction on a connecting dotted line.

Example: Dean and Mr. York have arrived.

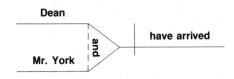

Compound verbs are similarly diagramed.

Example: Cheryl ran, swam, and rested.

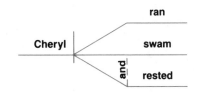

Exercises Find the compound subjects and compound verbs.

A. Write these sentences. Underline the subjects once and the verbs twice.

1. Thunder and lightning preceded the rain. *2, 1*
2. The width and depth of the stage were unusual. *2, 1*
3. The clerk totaled the sale, collected the money, and bagged the groceries. *1, 3*

355

1, 3 4. Everyone swam, played ball, and then ate lunch.

2, 1 5. The speaker's character and energy impressed the students.

2, 1 6. Phil and Jerry carried water for the garden.

2, 2 7. Marie and her father skate and ski together.

2, 2 8. Ruth and Phil stood on the corner and waited fifteen minutes for the bus.

2, 1 9. The wind and the tide were perfect for the race.

1, 2 10. Jack's boat rounded the buoy and finished first.

B. Follow the directions for Exercise A.

1, 2 1. Ann took some grapes and passed the bowl.

2, 1 2. The lamp and the candles threw shadows on the wall.

2, 1 3. Wonderful aromas and happy voices drifted from the kitchen.

2, 1 4. His knees and ankles were weak from the long climb.

1, 2 5. The football players pushed and shoved with their shoulders.

2, 1 6. Trumpets and trombones accompanied the woodwinds.

2, 1 7. By that time Tracy and Luanne were home.

1, 3 8. Jeff walked to the front, looked briefly at his notes, and began his speech.

1, 2 9. The ice-cream vendor rang the bell and pedaled slowly.

1, 2 10. The contestants roped and tied the calves.

Part 6

Objective

To identify the subject in unusual positions

Part 6 Subjects in Unusual Order

In most of the sentences that you have looked at in this book, the subject has come before the verb. All sentences, however, do not follow this same order. Sometimes the subject comes after the verb.

Giving Variety to Sentences

Sometimes, you may want to emphasize certain words in a sentence. Then you may write sentences with the subject after the verb.

	Subject	Verb

Usual Order: A strange *sound came* from the attic.

	Verb		Subject

Unusual Order: From the attic *came* a strange *sound*.

Unusual order does not change the positions of subjects and verbs in diagrams.

Example: Out of the hat popped a rabbit.

rabbit	popped

Exercises   **Find the subjects and verbs.**

A.   Show, as your teacher directs, the subjects and verbs in the following sentences.

1. On the other side of the tracks stood the church.
2. High above our heads stretched the Bay Bridge.
3. At the meeting were boys and girls from every class.
4. Behind his sleepy face was a quick, intelligent mind.
5. From one end of the pipe scampered a frightened squirrel.
6. Close behind the horse trotted a pony.
7. Into Mr. Bevan's office strolled my playful dog.
8. From the sand along the shore came a curious glow.
9. In the corridor were models of boats and a special nautical exhibit.
10. Across the valley stretched fields of beautiful flowers.

357

Presenting the Lesson

1. Read and discuss pages 356–357. Stress that even if the subject is not in its usual position of subject followed by the verb, it still acts as the subject and answers the question *who* or *what*. That is why unusual order of the subject in sentences does not change the positions of subject and verbs on diagrams.

2. Assign and discuss Exercises A, B and C on pages 357–358.

Individualizing the Lesson

Less-Advanced Students

As an in class assignment, rewrite the sentences in Exercise A in usual order. Assign Exercise B to be done independently or in pairs. Discuss the exercise in class.

Advanced Students

Have students rewrite each of the sentences in Exercises A and B on pages 357–358, putting the subject first and then the verb.

1. Ms. Riemer stood behind her desk. Behind her desk stood Ms. Riemer.
2. The runners raced around the track. Around the track raced the runners.
3. The dark clouds road across the sky. Across the sky road the dark clouds.
4. The cuckoo popped out of the clock. Out of the clock popped the cuckoo.

Optional Practice

Have students rewrite each of the sentences in Exercises A and B on pages 357–358 putting the subject first and then the verb.

Extending the Lesson

Have students make sentences out of each of the following groups of phrases. They should place the subject in three different positions.

357

1. burned, in the forest, the brush fire
2. at her desk, the judge, sat
3. the sensational campaign, in the spring, began
4. in the pool, the swimmers, practiced
5. the coconuts, from the trees, dropped
6. roared, the lion, at the trainer

B. Follow the directions for Exercise A.

1. Beyond the spaceship streamed the stars.
2. From the river rose three flamingoes.
3. Beyond the line of hills stood the crimson forest.
4. Suddenly out of the shrubs zoomed our cat.
5. Over the car lot flapped colorful banners.
6. Under the table lurked the gerbil.
7. Far below our campsite lay the rapids.
8. Into the light of the campfire fluttered a moth.
9. Near the barge bobbed a tugboat.
10. Behind the kitchen was the entrance to the cellar.

C. Writing Write five sentences in which the subject comes after the verb. Sentences will vary.

Part 7 Subjects and Verbs in Questions and Exclamations

Some interrogative sentences (questions) are written in normal order: the subject comes first, and the verb second.

Which team won the World Series?

(*Team* is the subject; *won* is the verb.)

Who bought the hamburgers?

(*Who* is the subject; *bought* is the verb.)

Not all questions follow this order. Read the following:

Do you know Mike?

(*You* is the subject; *do know* is the verb.)

Here the subject comes between the parts of the verb.

Part 7

Objective

To identify the subjects and verbs in questions and exclamations

Presenting the Lesson

1. Read and discuss pages 358–359.

2. Assign and discuss Exercises A and B on pages 359–360. In Exercise A, each sentence begins with a helping verb rather than a pronoun. It will be easier for students to find the subject if they find the verb first.

Individualizing the Lesson

Less-Advanced Students

Have students work in pairs first to rearrange the questions and exclamations in the Exercises into

Some exclamatory sentences also have the subject after the verb.

> Was that movie beautiful!   Are you late!

To find the subject and verb in a question or exclamation, try putting the sentence in normal order.

> Has Julie repaired the TV?   Was I upset!
> Julie has repaired the TV.   I was upset.

Diagraming Questions and Exclamations

To diagram a question or exclamation, put the subject and verb in normal order.

> Example: Will you please answer the telephone?

you	Will answer

Exercises   **Find subjects and verbs in questions and exclamations.**

A. Make two columns on your paper labeled *Subject* and *Verb*. Write the subject and verb for each sentence.

1. Does Marilyn study in the library?
2. Have you heard the news?
3. Were we thrilled by the news!
4. Did you watch the television special last night?
5. Does Andrea help in the print shop?
6. Do Mike and Pam work at the pharmacy?
7. Is Jim moving to Arizona?
8. Do the members of the committee know the date?
9. Do we need practice!
10. Do raspberries grow wild in the Midwest?

359

statements and then to find the subjects and verbs. Post a list of helping verbs for students to refer to.

Advanced Students

Diagram several items from one of the exercises for the class. Have them diagram part of one of the exercises independently.

Optional Practice

Have students apply the directions from Exercise A on page 359 to all of the interrogative and exclamatory sentences from Exercises A and B of Part 2 on page 347. (Exercise A: 4, 6, 7, 9; Exercise B: 2, 5, 6, 9)

Extending the Lesson

Have students use each of the following sets of subjects and verbs to write first a statement (declarative sentence) and then a question and an exclamation. Encourage more-advanced students to add adjectives and adverbs to their sentences.   Sentences will vary.

1. author, is writing
2. plane, has arrived
3. medical technician, is bandaging
4. bulls, have trampled
5. governor, was elected
6. conductor, does explain
7. grocer, has displayed
8. leaves, had fallen
9. hurricane, did damage
10. elephants, were following

B. Follow the directions for Exercise A.

1. <u>Has</u> <u>Pedro</u> <u>given</u> his speech?
2. Which <u>movie</u> <u>played</u> first?
3. <u>Do</u> <u>I</u> <u>have</u> a surprise for you!
4. <u>Are</u> <u>winters</u> warmer in Tallahassee than in Corpus Christi?
5. <u>Did</u> the <u>officer</u> <u>question</u> the suspects?
6. <u>Have</u> <u>you</u> <u>had</u> dinner yet?
7. <u>Have</u> <u>you</u> <u>gone</u> to the dentist yet?
8. <u>Are</u> your <u>parents</u> <u>going</u> to the meeting?
9. Which <u>magazine</u> <u>came</u> in today's mail?
10. <u>Who</u> <u>gave</u> the message to Nancy?

Part 8 Sentences That Begin with *There*

Study this sentence. What is the simple subject?

> There are some pencils in my locker.

The subject is *pencils*. The word *there* is not the subject. When the word *there* comes at or near the beginning of a sentence, it often serves just to get the sentence started.

> **Verb**   **Subject**
>
> There *are* some *pencils* in my locker.

Study the following sentences. Notice that the subject is not first when *there* comes near the beginning of the sentence. Point out the subjects.

1. **Are** there any **grapes**?
2. There **are** some **apples** in the bag.
3. There **are** two **birds** at the feeding station.
4. **Were** there many **families** at the picnic?
5. There **were** two **people** in the car.

Part **8**

Objective

To identify the subjects and verbs in sentences beginning with *there*

Presenting the Lesson

1. Read and discuss pages 360–361. Ask students what the verbs are in sentences that begin with *there* (some form of the verb *to be:* usually *is, are, was,* or *were).* Stress that *there* is never a subject. Students who are having difficulty with subjects and verbs may need more review before attempting Part 9. You may want to have them do Exercise A, page 364, first.

2. Assign and discuss Exercises A and B on pages 361–362. Remind students to change questions into statements to make it easier to find the subjects and verbs. Assign and discuss Exercise C on page 362.

Diagraming Sentences with *There*

There is usually just an "extra" word. It is placed on a separate line above the subject in a sentence diagram.

Example: There were many students at the track meet.

Exercises   **Find the subjects and verbs in sentences with *there*.**

A.   Write the subjects and verbs in these sentences.

1. There was a line at the theater.
2. Are there any blossoms on the apple tree?
3. There were several questions after Helen's report.
4. There were two skunks near our cabin.
5. Are there any newspapers in the cellar, Mother?
6. There are some new notices on the bulletin board near the library.
7. Are there any Canadian dimes here?
8. There were two gulls on the pier.
9. Was there any more salad?
10. There are new chairs in the science room.

B.   Write the subjects and verbs in these sentences.

1. There are a few rust spots on our car.
2. There is a charge for children over five.
3. There were several eggs in the basket.
4. Is there anyone home?
5. There have been hornets on the porch again.
6. There is really no reason for concern.

in an article or story. (Descriptive passages are the most likely sources.) If none are available, students may write examples of their own and share them with the class at the board.

7. Were there any <u>problems</u> at the meeting?
8. There was an old <u>bicycle</u> in our garage.
9. Are there <u>pickles</u> in the sandwich?
10. Were there <u>telescopes</u> in the tower?

C. Writing Write lively sentences using the following beginnings. Add the correct punctuation. <small>Answers will vary.</small>

1. There is
2. There would often be
3. There has never been
4. Has there ever been
5. Will there be
6. Were there
7. There has been
8. There will be
9. Have there been
10. Would there ever be

Part 9

Objective

To identify the subjects and verbs in commands

Presenting the Lesson

1. Read and discuss pages 362–363. Stress that imperative sentences (commands) all have the same subject (you). Ask students for an explanation of why this is so. Discuss the purpose of imperative sentences: to command or direct someone to do something. Remind students that the first word of an imperative sentence usually is a verb or the word *please* followed by a verb.

Part 9   Subjects and Verbs in Imperative Sentences

Imperative sentences (commands) usually begin with the verb. For example, in the command *Pay the cashier,* the verb is the first word, *Pay.* What is the subject? There doesn't seem to be any, does there? The subject in the sentence is *you,* even though it is not stated. *You* is the person or group spoken to. The subject *you* is understood.

One-Word Commands

Some imperative sentences consist of only one word—a verb. *Think. Go. Stop.* These are single-word sentences. The subject is the same: *(you) Think. (you) Go. (you) Stop.*

Diagraming Imperative Sentences

When the subject of an imperative sentence is understood, show it in a diagram by writing *(you)*.

Example: Hurry.

Exercises **Find the subjects and verbs in imperative sentences.**

A. Write the <u>subjects</u> and <u>verbs</u> in the following sentences. Use whatever method your teacher suggests.

(You) 1. <u>Tear</u> along the dotted line.
(You) 2. <u>Hold</u> this for a moment.
(You) 3. <u>Put</u> some spruce branches under your sleeping bag.
(You) 4. <u>Stack</u> the dishes in the sink.
(You) 5. <u>Try</u> a bottle opener.

B. Follow the directions for Exercise A.

(You) 1. <u>Have</u> the rest of the casserole for supper.
(You) 2. <u>Ask</u> Nicole her opinion.
(You) 3. <u>Dismount</u> from the parallel bars to your right.
(You) 4. <u>Look</u> this over before the meeting.
(You) 5. <u>Take</u> another apple.

C. **Writing** Write a paragraph on how to get to your house from school. Use only imperative sentences. Underline the verb in each sentence. Sentences will vary.

2. Assign and discuss Exercises A, B, and C on page 363, or discuss the sentences orally, paying particular attention to the understood subject.

Individualizing the Lesson

Less-Advanced Students

These students should do Exercise A orally. If they have trouble with the understood subject, try having them point at someone as they read aloud each command.

Advanced Students

Have the students write five imperative sentences telling someone either how to behave during a fire drill, how to fry an egg, or how to do some other simple task.

Optional Practice

Ask students to list four situations in which an imperative sentence would be used. They should then write an imperative sentence that might be used in each situation. This exercise can be assigned as a written exercise, or you may prefer to do it orally with the class.

Extending the Lesson

Have the students copy five examples of imperative sentences from recipes or instruction manuals. Have them follow the directions for Exercise A on page 363 for these sentences.

Additional Exercises

These Additional Exercises may be used for additional practice of the concepts presented in this Section. Each exercise focuses on a single concept, and should be used after the page number indicated in parentheses.

Review

If you have not assigned these Additional Exercises before this time, you can also use them as an excellent Section Review.

ADDITIONAL EXERCISES

The Sentence and Its Parts

A. Subjects and Predicates Number your paper from 1 to 10. Copy these sentences. Draw a vertical line between the subject and the predicate.

1. Tom | found some wood for the fire.
2. Acorns from red oaks | have dark shells.
3. The girl in the red jersey | won the race.
4. Students | crowded around the bulletin board.
5. Vinegar | softened the eggshell.
6. The gray fish | eats algae.
7. Two of the players | left the game with injuries.
8. Jerome's aunt | writes books for children.
9. Shadows from the clouds | moved across the football field.
10. Maria | kept score for us.

B. Kinds of Sentences Number your paper from 1 to 10. For each of the following sentences, write *Declarative*, *Interrogative*, *Imperative*, or *Exclamatory* to show what kind it is. Add the correct end mark for each sentence.

Int. 1. How did the game end?
Ex. 2. How the movie scared him!
Imp. 3. Set the popcorn on the table.
D. 4. Cork comes from the bark of the cork tree.
Int. 5. Why was the practice session cancelled?
Int. 6. Ramon, may I ask you something?
Imp. 7. Sandy, ask that woman for directions.
Int. 8. What is this knob for?
Ex. 9. What a close call we had!
D. 10. I asked Mr. Loy for help with my history project.

C. Verbs and Simple Subjects Number your paper from 1 to 10. For each sentence write the <u>verb</u> and its <u>subject</u>.

1. Angela draws cartoons for the school paper.
2. A thick fog rolled into the harbor.
3. The sparrows chirped furiously at the dog.
4. The pitcher hurled a no-hitter.
5. Our goalie saved the game.
6. Most students bring their lunches.
7. Our basketball team beat the Dolphins.
8. Some Siamese cats sound like babies.
9. Snowflakes clung to Rosie's hair.
10. A koala bear eats two pounds of leaves each day.

D. Verbs Number your paper from 1 to 10. Write the <u>verb</u> in each of the following sentences.

1. The barber <u>cut</u> Jacob's hair last week.
2. Holly <u>wore</u> a turquoise shirt.
3. This clay <u>hardens</u> quickly.
4. Carolyn <u>removed</u> the film from the camera.
5. Winter <u>came</u> early this year.
6. Tracy's hands <u>were</u> cold.
7. I <u>wonder</u>.
8. You <u>sit</u> at the head of the table.
9. Nick <u>daydreamed</u> all morning.
10. Those slides of onion cells <u>are</u> for my science project.

E. Main Verbs and Helping Verbs Make one column for helping verbs (HV) and one column for main verbs (MV). Find the helping verbs and main verbs in the following sentences. Write them in the proper columns. Some sentences have more than one helping verb.

1. Ryan is joining an archery club.
2. The test papers will be collected in five minutes.

3. I am saying money for a pair of skates.
HV *MV*

4. Jessie did understand you.
HV *MV*

5. The fish should be fed once a day.
HV *HV* *MV*

6. I do surprise myself sometimes.
HV *MV*

7. Somebody is listening at the door.
HV *MV*

8. Our gym class has been practicing backflips.
HV *HV* *MV*

9. Brenda will be told about the new schedule.
HV *HV* *MV*

10. Jake had been thinking about the problem.
HV *HV* *MV*

F. Separated Parts of a Verb Write the verb and its simple subject for each of the following sentences. Underline the subject once and the verb twice.

1. Soccer has recently become a popular game in the United States.
2. Natalie has again won the trophy.
3. Many children have never been to a dentist.
4. Jim was carefully wrapping the glasses.
5. Amy has not missed one rehearsal.
6. Red blood cells will usually live for four months.
7. Bob is probably babysitting tonight.
8. Ms. Koperski does not often speak sharply.
9. Sharon could not remember the lock's combination.
10. The bus had just left.

G. Compound Subjects and Compound Verbs Underline the subjects once and the verbs twice in the following sentences.

1. Records and cassettes were scattered around the room.
2. The mascot and the band marched onto the field.
3. Marty's boots and socks were soaked.
4. The nurse weighed and measured the patients.
5. The ball bounced and rolled into the street.
6. Seedless tangerines and grapes are in the next aisle.

7. The pilot sighted the runway and landed the plane.
8. Both Garfield and Snoopy are popular cartoon animals.
9. The girls waded and splashed across the stream.
10. Detectives and spies think and act fast.

H. Subjects in Unusual Order Underline the subjects once and the verbs twice in the following sentences.

1. Into the alley dashed the child.
2. In the center of the ring stood Chuck.
3. From the ceiling hung colorful banners.
4. In my locker was the library book.
5. On the rose perched a butterfly with yellow wings.
6. Up the ladder went Kay with a bucket in her hand.
7. Almost beyond belief were Houdini's stunts.
8. Far out past the breakers swam the lifeguard.
9. Onto the trampoline leaped Ann.
10. All through the night whined the lonely puppy.

I. Subjects and Verbs in Questions and Exclamations Make two columns on your paper. Write *Subject* at the top of one column and *Verb* at the top of the other. Write the subject and verb for each of the following sentences.

1. Do the Carsons live in the basement apartment?
2. Did we have fun!
3. Are the handlebars too high?
4. Do you smell smoke?
5. Was Amelia Earhart ever found?
6. Which teacher sponsors the club?
7. Does that fish have teeth?
8. How happy we were!
9. Did those runners go fast!
10. Did Barb and Thaddeus choose the props?

367

J. Subjects and Verbs in *There* Sentences Write the subjects and verbs in the following sentences.

1. There was a rainbow over the mountain.
2. Are there rough spots on the ice?
3. There is a penalty for lateness.
4. Is there another exit?
5. There was only one act in the play.
6. Are there cranberries in these muffins?
7. Were there any calls for me?
8. There is really no excuse.
9. There will certainly be fireworks at the picnic.
10. There were several volunteers for the job.

K. Subjects and Verbs in Commands Write the subjects and verbs in the following imperative sentences. Underline the subject once and the verb twice.

(You) 1. Use a red pencil.
(You) 2. Change the station.
(You) 3. Forget it.
(You) 4. Wear boots on the hike.
(You) 5. Help yourself to some lemonade.
(You) 6. Keep your arm perfectly straight.
(You) 7. Please pass the salad.
(You) 8. Never put the sun behind the subject in a photograph.
(You) 9. Keep your eyes on the magician's hands.
(You) 10. Always obey traffic laws on a bike.

MIXED REVIEW

The Sentence and Its Parts

A. Identifying subjects, predicates, simple subjects, and verbs Copy the following sentences. Draw a line between each subject and predicate. Underline each simple subject once and each verb twice. Remember that a verb can be more than one word.

1. Greg|has missed the first inning.
2. Cindy|caught a small brown toad.
3. Many athletes|study ballet.
4. The man in the white car|obviously caused the accident.
5. The grocery store|closes at six o'clock.
6. A family of cats|is living in that old barn.
7. Most of my friends|live nearby.
8. The flowers near the garage|need water.
9. The members of our club|toured the Smithsonian Institute.
10. The bright moon|lit the lake.

B. Finding subjects and verbs Copy the following sentences. Underline each simple subject once and each verb twice. Some subjects and verbs may be compound. Some subjects may be in unusual order. Verbs may include helping verbs.

(You) 1. Print your name in the space below.
2. Is this event sponsored by the PTA?
3. An exhibit of Mexican art will be displayed in the library.
4. Before today, Ben didn't know anyone in our class.
5. This machine chops and grates vegetables.

369

Mixed Review

These exercises provide review of the concepts presented in this Section. Each exercise challenges the students to apply several of the skills they have acquired during previous study. Because the "mixed" feature of these activities makes them more difficult, the teacher may wish to have less-advanced students do them orally or in small groups.

369

6. Who designed the magazine cover?
7. Trish sold twenty magazine subscriptions.
8. Are there any apples in the refrigerator?
9. The members of the team washed and waxed the gym floor.
10. Jim and Sal have started their science projects.

C. Identifying fragments and kinds of sentences Read the following groups of words. If a group of words is a fragment, write *Fragment*. Copy any sentences and punctuate them correctly. Then write *Declarative*, *Interrogative*, *Imperative*, or *Exclamatory* to show what kind of sentence it is.

F. 1. A long, brisk walk in the woods
Int. 2. Where is my apartment key?
F. 3. Rodney, Kay, and all of their friends
D. 4. This brand of paint costs less.
D. 5. We videotaped the program.
F. 6. The shiny, new van in the driveway
Imp. 7. Don't forget your wallet.
F. 8. Waited impatiently for the bus
D. 9. Gretchen collects dolls from foreign countries.
Int 10. Where is the Lincoln Memorial?
E 11. Stop that noise!
D 12. Your camera might need a new battery.

USING GRAMMAR IN WRITING
The Sentence and Its Parts

A. You are a biologist studying life in the Antarctic. One day you are out collecting samples. A sudden blizzard blows up. When you finally get back to your tent, you find that there is a radio message for you. It has been recorded directly onto a cassette. When you play the tape, you find that the message was interrupted by static. Below are the fragments that you hear. Try to make sense out of the message. Supply the missing sentence parts.

_____ when you get back to the tent. We suggest _____. When the storm clears, _____ to get your samples. _____ emergency supplies. Do not, repeat, do not _____.

B. An android is a robot that looks like a human being. Pretend you are a reporter who is doing a story on an android. Complete the following interview. For each question, write the android's answer. For each statement by the android, write the question you might have asked. At the end, write a command you would like to give the android. Give the android a name and use it in the interview.

Q: What kind of music do you enjoy?
A: _____
Q: _____
A: I consume three deep-dish pizzas a day.
Q: What are your plans for the future?
A: _____
Q: _____
A: Most androids get plenty of exercise.
Q: Is it difficult to make friends with human beings?
A: _____
Command: _____

371

Section Objectives

1. To distinguish between fragments and complete sentences

2. To correct run-on sentences

Preparing the Students

Remind the students that in Section 1 they learned what makes a complete sentence. Review the definition of the sentence and its two major parts. Explain that this section will contain more about how to write correct sentences and how to avoid some common mistakes.

Additional Resources

Diagnostic Test — page 1 in the test booklet

Mastery Test — pages 39–40 in the test booklet

Additional Exercises — pages 376–379 in the student text

Practice Book — pages 148–150

Duplicating Masters — pages 148–150

Special Populations — See special section at the back of this Teacher's Edition.

Avoiding Fragments and Run-on Sentences

Sentences tell about facts, ideas, and feelings. When you write sentences, you have the chance to tell about whatever is important to you. You want to make your sentences as clear as you can.

Some sentences are not clear. Confusion may be caused when part of a sentence is left out. Such a group of words is called a **sentence fragment.** Confusion may also be caused when two or more sentences are written as one. Such a group of words is called a **run-on sentence.** In this section you will learn how to avoid these two errors.

Part 1 Avoiding Sentence Fragments

A group of words that is not a complete sentence is called a **sentence fragment.** A fragment is only a part of something. Avoid sentence fragments in your writing.

In a sentence fragment, something important has been left out. Sometimes the subject is missing. Sometimes the verb is left out. As you read a fragment, you may wonder either *What is this about?* or *What happened?*

Fragment: The can of paint (*What happened?*)
Sentence: The can of paint *spilled.*

Fragment: Left the house early (*Who or what?*)
Sentence: *I* left the house early.

Exercises   Recognize sentences.

A. Number your paper from 1 to 10. Write *Sentence* or *Fragment* for each of the following groups of words.

S 1. The parrot is asleep on its perch
F 2. Arrived before the end of the game
F 3. Grandfather in our backyard
F 4. At the pharmacy in the middle of the block
F 5. In the yard the leaves
S 6. We can rent a canoe
F 7. Came up and spoke to us
S 8. Suddenly a fire siren screamed
F 9. Rain, wind, and hailstones
S 10. The branch landed on the garage roof

B. Writing Correct each of the following fragments by adding the words needed to make a sentence. Answers will vary.

1. practiced for two hours

373

Part 1

Objective

To distinguish between fragments and complete sentences

Presenting the Lesson

1. Read and discuss page 373. Ask students for some examples of fragments (part of a letter, part of a conversation, part of a book). Have students explain why these fragments could cause difficulty to a reader. Perhaps introduce the word *fragmented,* and see whether any students recognize it. Discuss its meaning and why the phrase "to piece it together" is frequently heard in reference to something fragmented.

2. Assign and discuss Exercises A and B on pages 373–374. You may wish to have students read these sentences aloud because this usually makes it easier to identify fragments.

Individualizing the Lesson

Less-Advanced Students

Do Exercise A orally with students. Then allow them to work in pairs to complete Exercise B.

Advanced Students

Have students complete each fragment in the exercises in two different ways.

Optional Practice

Have students turn these fragments into sentences.
Sentences will vary.
1. showed the touchdown pass
2. twirled and snapped their fingers

373

3. the winning model plane

4. needs a major overhaul

5. a twenty-one gun salute

6. was signing autographs

Extending the Lesson

Have students look through their composition folders to see if they have written any sentence fragments. Have them write complete sentences to correct any fragments.

Part 2

Objective

To correct run-on sentences

Presenting the Lesson

1. Read and discuss page 374. Remind students to avoid run-on sentences by writing each idea separately and using end marks to show the separations.

2. Review end punctuation if necessary.

3. You may wish to do Exercise A on pages 374–375 with the class. Assign and discuss Exercise B on page 375.

Individualizing the Lesson

Less-Advanced Students

Have the students read the run-on sentences in the exercises aloud to show how difficult it is to follow the thought of the writer without proper punctuation.

Advanced Students

Discuss ways to correct run-on sentences: making two separate

2. earned ten dollars

3. walked cautiously through the dark corridors

4. really likes to sing

5. the mailbox next to the street light

6. designed the yearbook cover

7. near the football field

8. Eliot and his father

9. across the hall from the cafeteria

10. hiked through the hills and valleys

Part 2 Avoiding Run-on Sentences

A **run-on sentence** is two or more sentences written incorrectly as one. Here are some examples:

Incorrect: (*run-on*): Pam arrived, we went cycling.
Correct: Pam arrived. We went cycling.

Incorrect: (*run-on*): Aren't you through let me help.
Correct: Aren't you through? Let me help.

Run-on sentences confuse your readers. Without a period and a capital letter to guide them, they believe they are reading just one thought. Then the words stop making sense.

You can correct run-on sentences by using the proper capitalization and punctuation. Do not use a comma where one is not needed.

Exercises Correct the run-on sentences.

A. Correct the following run-on sentences.

1. We stayed at Elinor Village. we were only two blocks from the ocean.

2. The noise stopped they finished the rest of the work.

3. The refrigerator was broken water was dripping from the freezer.

4. Kay is the sports editor, she is my sister.
5. Everyone was busy. we all had assignments to complete.
6. It rained for days, the soccer field was soaked.
7. There were many balloons strung from the ceiling, they were torn down afterwards.
8. We skated for one hour, we came in to get warm.
9. I have read several biographies, I find them very interesting.
10. Monica and I aren't going skiing. the snow is too slushy.

B. Follow the directions for Exercise A.

1. It snowed throughout the night, most schools were closed the next day.
2. The skyline of Chicago is beautiful. the city has many unusual buildings.
3. Rachel and I ate dinner. then we rushed to the movies.
4. We had basketball practice until noon. we have a game tomorrow.
5. Our class had a bake sale. it was very successful.
6. Ken and Lynn are co-editors, they manage our school newspaper.
7. The doctor X-rayed my arm. she then put a cast on it.
8. Our plane arrived early, we took a bus into the city.
9. Anne is on the volleyball team. she is the captain.
10. The plumber fixed the sink, then he checked the main water pipe.

sentences, making a compound sentence using a comma and a conjunction, or making a compound sentence using a semi-colon. Have the students correct each run-on sentence in the exercises two different ways.

Optional Practice

Tell the students to correctly re-write these run-on sentences.
Answers will vary.
1. The Navy's Blue Angels flew in close formation the stunt pilot flew upside down.
2. Robin Hood won the archery contest he was the most accurate.
3. There are many blind musicians Ray Charles is one of them.
4. My cousin from New York is visiting he will stay for three days.
5. The cherry tomato plant in our garden grew wildly all summer, we harvested more than five hundred tomatoes from it.

Extending the Lesson

Have students look through the compositions they have written for examples of run-on sentences. Have the class decide how these run-ons can best be corrected.

Additional Exercises

These Additional Exercises may be used for additional practice of the concepts presented in this Section. Each exercise focuses on a single concept, and should be used after the page number indicated in parentheses.

Review

If you have not assigned these Additional Exercises before this time, you can also use them as an excellent Section Review.

ADDITIONAL EXERCISES

Avoiding Fragments and Run-on Sentences

A. Sentences and Fragments Number your paper from 1 to 10. Write *Sentence* or *Fragment* for each of the following groups to show what each group is.

F 1. Carried a radio with a long antenna
S 2. The lights are operated by an electric eye
F 3. Enormous stone statues with seashell eyes on Easter Island
S 4. Look at that motorcycle
S 5. Is there a difference between a diary and a journal
F 6. Is often at the recreation center
S 7. The pastor spoke at the ceremony
F 8. Students with early lunch periods
S 9. Straighten the ruler
F 10. Straightened his tie

B. Sentences and Run-ons Number your paper from 1 to 10. Write *Sentence* or *Run-on* for each of the following groups of words to show what each group is.

R 1. Dig for clams at low tide they are easier to find then
R 2. Football helmets are required, they prevent injuries to the players
S 3. Sue raised the seat, oiled the chain, and got on the bike
S 4. With one quick motion Laura captured the monarch butterfly
S 5. The man felt for the curb with his white cane
R 6. Sara has cousins in New York she will stay with them during her visit

R 7. Lou used watercolors, oil paints would have been better

S 8. James walks to school and takes the bus home

S 9. What are you staring at

R 10. Ted works at the supermarket he bags groceries

C. Sentences, Fragments, and Run-ons

Number your paper from 1 to 10. Write *Sentence*, *Fragment*, or *Run-on* for each of the following groups of words to show what each group is.

F 1. People with a lot of free time and nothing to do

S 2. The waters around Antarctica contain many strange life forms

S 3. Sally left, however

R 4. The movie was about Australia, it showed the Great Barrier Reef

F 5. Lacrosse, the national sport of Canada

S 6. Luke added mushrooms to the spaghetti sauce

R 7. A dumbwaiter is a tiny elevator it carries food

F 8. Called just before the game

R 9. The stage crew built the scenery, they painted it, too

S 10. Music blared from a radio outside

Mixed Review

These exercises provide review of the concepts presented in this Section. Each exercise challenges the students to apply several of the skills they have acquired during previous study. Because the "mixed" feature of these activities makes them more difficult, the teacher may wish to have less-advanced students do them orally or in small groups.

MIXED REVIEW

Avoiding Fragments and Run-on Sentences

A. Identifying sentences, fragments, and run-on sentences Write _Sentence_, _Fragment_, or _Run-on_ for each of the following groups of words. Then correct any fragments by adding words to make complete sentences. Correct any run-ons by adding capitalization and punctuation to show where each complete thought begins and ends. Corrected fragments will vary.

R 1. Andy ruined the cake. He used salt instead of sugar

R 2. Carol can't play tennis. She twisted her ankle

F 3. Geese and ducks overhead

S 4. That phone number has been disconnected.

S 5. Is this Room 208 ?

R 6. That's my older brother. He's a sophomore in college.

S 7. The runner tried to steal second but was called out.

R 8. Darci missed the bus. She didn't hear the alarm.

S 9. Chris picked a bushel of apples.

F 10. Pesty flies, curious ants, and busy bees

B. Correcting fragments and run-on sentences Copy the following paragraph. Correct any fragments or run-ons.

My brother and I had one purpose in mind. When we visited Everglades National Park in Florida. We wanted to see an alligator with our own eyes. On our second day there we spotted a seventeen-foot long creature floating lazily along the channel. We knew by the short, blunt snout that this was it. We kept our distance. This large animal looks slow and sluggish but can move very quickly. The park ranger reminded us. That it's against the law to tease alligators. I found that law easy to obey. An alligator will eagerly eat anything it can swallow!

USING GRAMMAR IN WRITING
Avoiding Fragments and Run-on Sentences

A. After winning the Olympic gold medal for the downhill ski race, you breathlessly make this statement to the reporter.

> I can't believe I did it this is a dream come true. All that practice. Really did pay off. I'd like to thank my parents and my coach for their support and help, my friends were behind me too. The most exciting moment of my entire life. I'll never forget it. As long as I live see you all again. In four years.

The reporter who interviewed you rewrote your statement. She corrected all fragments and run-on sentences. Write the statement as it appeared in the newspaper.

B. You are reviewing a new local restaurant, The Round Table, for your school paper. These are the notes you secretly jotted down on a paper napkin. Use them to construct complete sentences. Avoid all fragments and run-ons. Write the review.

> had a twenty minute wait
> a noisy, bustling room
> waiters friendly and attentive
> interesting decorations, looked like a king's court
> the best char-broiled burgers in town
> rich, gooey desserts
> live music is very loud it makes conversation difficult

Using Grammar in Writing

These challenging and enjoyable activities allow the students to see how the concepts of grammar, usage, and mechanics may be applied in actual writing situations. Each exercise is designed to allow students practice in several of the skills they have acquired in this Section. The activities also provide opportunities for students to write creatively about a wide variety of interesting and unusual subjects.

Section Objectives

1. To understand the function of verbs

2. To identify verbs as either main verbs or helping verbs

3. To understand the function of direct objects and to identify them in sentences

4. To differentiate between transitive and intransitive verbs

5. To understand the concept of linking verbs

6. To recognize and use verbs in the present, past, and future tenses

7. To identify the principal parts of verbs and to use a dictionary to find them correctly

Preparing the Students

Display and discuss a picture showing action. List on the board any verbs the students use to describe the picture. Point out that without these words it would be impossible to describe what happens. Read and discuss the introduction on page 380.

Additional Resources

Diagnostic Test — page 2 in the test booklet

Mastery Test — pages 41–42 in the test booklet

Additional Exercises — pages 397–402 in the student text

Practice Book — pages 151–158

Duplicating Masters — pages 151–158

Special Populations — See special section at the back of this Teacher's Edition

Using Verbs

If you do not have a verb, you cannot have a sentence. Even the shortest sentences contain verbs:

Go.   Look.   Try.

You know that the verb is a key word in a sentence. A verb tells of an action or a state of being. Since verbs are so important, you should use them correctly.

In this section you will review what a verb is. You will also learn more about what verbs do. You will learn how verbs work with other words to express your ideas.

Part 1 The Work of Verbs

The verb is one of the main parts of every sentence.
Compare these groups of words. Look at the difference a verb makes.

Without Verbs	With Verbs
The school band well	The school band played well.
Lee over the hoe	Lee tripped over the hoe.
Dan angry	Dan seems angry.

The verb may tell what the subject of the sentence does or what happens. This kind of verb is an **action verb**. The action of the verb may be seen or unseen. Read the following examples:

She *danced*.	Donna *wanted* a job.	I *have* a cold.
Ramon *laughed*.	We *enjoyed* the show.	We *ate*.

A verb may tell that something exists. This kind of verb is a **state-of-being verb**.

Cheryl *is* here.	Jack *seems* happy.
The star *grew* brighter.	The music *sounded* lively.

State of being verbs include *am, is, are, was, were, seem, look, feel, grow, taste, sound, become,* and *appear*.

A verb shows action or state of being.

Use these clues when you look for the verb in a sentence:

- Look for a word that shows action (*ran, walked*).
- Look for a word that shows action you cannot see (*want, have*).
- Look for a word that shows a state of being (*am, is, are, was, were, seem, look, feel, grow, taste, sound, become, appear*).

Examples: Judy *walked* to my house.   We *are* good friends.

Rob *wants* a chance.   You *seem* nervous.

381

Objective

To understand the function of verbs

Presenting the Lesson

1. Read and discuss pages 381–382.

2. Assign and discuss Exercises A and B on page 382. Have students tell you whether the verbs in the sentences are action verbs or state-of-being verbs, and why.

Individualizing the Lesson

Less-Advanced Students

1. For Exercise A, remind students to ask *who* or *what* to find the subject and *is* or *happens* to find the verb. If students are still having trouble, review the explanation of subjects and predicates in Section 1. Then have students write each sentence, drawing a line between the subject and predicate. Then they should underline the verb in each.

2. Allow students to work in pairs for Exercise B. Before having students work independently, discuss where the verb belongs in each sentence. Provide a list of possible verbs to add: *acted, are, played, flew, closed, fell, go, sings, waited, painted, hung.*

Advanced Students

1. Have students write alternative verbs for those used in Exercise A.

2. For Exercise B, have students write these sentences: five declarative, three interrogative, one exclamatory, and one imperative.

Optional Practice

Have students find pictures from newspapers or magazines. Have them list all the verbs they see in the pictures under the headings *Action Verbs* and *State-of-Being Verbs*.

Extending the Lesson

Have students find a paragraph from a newspaper, book, or magazine. Have them number each verb consecutively in the paragraph. Then tell them to list the verbs and write whether each one is an action verb or a state-of-being verb.

When you are looking for verbs, remember that the parts of a verb may be separated. Remember also that the sentence may be in unusual order.

Will he *cook?*   Down the aisle *came* the bride.

Exercises   Find the verbs.

A.   Find the <u>verb</u> in each sentence.

1. The orchestra <u>played</u> country music.
2. Emily <u>is</u> a very good artist.
3. The fire nearly <u>destroyed</u> the fieldhouse.
4. Our class <u>decorated</u> the hall for the bazaar.
5. Marcy <u>hit</u> the ball over the fence.
6. Keith <u>was</u> very quiet.
7. Here <u>is</u> a dozen eggs.
8. Mark's cat <u>climbed</u> the maple tree.
9. Last Sunday we <u>hiked</u> in the woods.
10. During intermission, Erin <u>told</u> us about her canoe trip.

B.   Writing   The following groups of words have subjects but no verbs. Make each group a sentence by adding a verb. Write your sentences and underline the verbs. Add the correct punctuation at the end of each sentence. Answers will vary.

1. The library at noon today
2. A car radio in the background
3. We all Saturday afternoon
4. Dave a letter to his cousin in Texas
5. The boys the back steps
6. Randy very well
7. The bumper sticker off
8. Miriam in a play at school
9. Several of my friends to the rink every Saturday
10. The jet into the air

Part 2 Parts of the Verb

A verb often consists of more than one word. A two-word verb consists of one helping verb and the main verb. Helping verbs include *is*, *do*, and *has*. Some other helping verbs are shown below.

will go	**may** go	**could** go	**must** go
should go	**would** go	**might** go	**can** go

Three-word verbs consist of a main verb and two helping verbs. *Have* is often the middle verb.

will *have* gone	would *have* played	must *have* taken
could *have* gone	can *have* heard	should *have* gone

Do not use *of* for *have*. *Of* is not a helping verb.

Wrong: I could *of* gone   Right: I could *have* gone

Separated Parts of the Verb

The words that make up a verb are not always right next to each other, like *could have done* and *might have seen*. Sometimes the helping verbs and the main verbs are separated by words that are not verbs. *Not* and the ending *n't* are not verbs.

can hardly **wait**	**could** not **have come**
didn't **understand**	**may have** already **arrived**

Exercises Find helping verbs and the main verb.

A. Label two columns *Helping Verbs* and *Main Verb*. Find all the parts of the verb in each of the following sentences. Write them in the proper columns.

Example: We must have waited for an hour.

Helping Verbs	Main Verb
must have	waited

383

Objective

To identify verbs as either main verbs or helping verbs

Presenting the Lesson

1. Read and discuss page 383. Although verb tenses are discussed in Part 6 of this section, you may find it valuable to introduce the idea of tense (time) now. Write the following sentences on the board. Ask students to tell the meaning of each sentence and how the difference in meaning is made.

Jim will repair the gate.
Jim has repaired the gate.
Jim should repair the gate.
Jim can repair the gate.
Jim might repair the gate.

Ask students for other examples of helping verbs used with the verb *repair*. Have them explain the meaning of the complete verb and how the helping verb affects the time of the action.

2. Discuss separated parts of the verb. Stress that *not*, *n't*, and other adverbs are never part of the verb. Use these sentences for examples.

Jim will *not* repair the gate.
Jim has *already* repaired the gate.
Jim ca*n't* repair the gate.

3. Assign and discuss Exercises A and B on pages 383–384.

Individualizing the Lesson

Less-Advanced Students

Do Exercise A orally. Write the columns on the board. Allow students to complete Exercise B independently.

383

Advanced Students

Have students suggest alternative helping verbs for the sentences in Exercises A and B. Discuss how the changes affect the sentence meanings.

Optional Practice

For the following exercise, use the directions for the exercises on pages 383–384. When discussing this exercise, see if students realize that some helping verbs are used as main verbs in other sentences. Ask students to point out those verbs.

1. Did the baby crawl up the stairs? (HV, MV)
2. The racer has run many times before. (HV, MV)
3. The carpenter did a good job on the repairs. (MV)
4. We are members of the school baseball team. (MV)
5. My friend has a unicycle. (MV)
6. The dogs are swimming in the water. (HV, MV)
7. The lions have locks on their cages. (MV)
8. We have planted a small vegetable garden. (HV, MV)

Extending the Lesson

Have students study the following verbs and state which can be used as main verbs, which as helping verbs, and which as both. Then have them write sentences showing how the verbs can be used. If a verb can be used as both, have the students write two sentences for that verb.

wait (MV)	counted (MV)	might (HV)	go (MV)
will (HV)	signed (MV)	has (B)	
had (B)	should (HV)	did (B)	

---

1. I should (HV) be (MV) ready by then.
2. Henry would (HV) not have (HV) forgotten (MV) my birthday.
3. Jeff could (HV) have (HV) told (MV) you that.
4. The driver may (HV) have (HV) put (MV) the package there.
5. Vicki would (HV) like (MV) more blankets.
6. You could (HV) have (HV) fooled (MV) me.
7. Who would (HV) have (HV) told (MV) him?
8. Shall (HV) I bring (MV) my art supplies?
9. The team could (HV) never have (HV) played (MV) in all that mud.
10. We will (HV) never forget (MV) his kindness.

B. Follow the directions for Exercise A.

1. We must (HV) not delay (MV) any longer.
2. We cannot (HV) go (MV) without him.
3. Do (HV) you have (MV) the letter with you?
4. Our neighbors are (HV) always helping (MV) us.
5. The secretary would (HV) have (HV) taken (MV) the message.
6. Didn't (HV) you hear (MV) the explosion?
7. I could (HV) not possibly have (HV) thrown (MV) out my Disneyland T-shirt.
8. The coin may (HV) have (HV) fallen (MV) through the crack.
9. We have (HV) been (HV) planning (MV) the party for weeks.
10. The parade must (HV) be (MV) on Central Street.

Part 3   Verbs and Direct Objects

In many sentences, a verb and its subject are enough to state a complete thought.

Subject	Verb
Snow	fell.
Everyone	laughed.

In other sentences the thought is not complete unless more words are added.

> Roger cut _____.   Linda met _____.

You wonder *what* Roger cut and *whom* Linda met. You could complete the sentences as follows:

> Roger cut the *rope*.   Linda met *Alice*.

In the first sentence, the word *rope* receives the action of the verb *cut*. *Rope* is the **direct object** of the verb.

In the second sentence, *Alice* receives the action of *met*. *Alice* is the **direct object** of the verb.

The direct object tells who or what receives the action of the verb.

Recognizing Direct Objects

To find the direct object in a sentence, first find the verb. Then ask *what* or *whom* after the verb.

Read these examples.

> The engineers studied the plans.
>
> Verb: studied
>   studied *what*? plans
> Direct object: plans

> A reporter interviewed Donna.
>
> Verb: interviewed
>   interviewed *whom*? Donna
> Direct object: Donna

Direct objects only answer *what* or *whom* after the verb. They do not tell *when* or *where* or *how*. You will see that there are no direct objects in the following sentences.

Objective

To understand the function of direct objects and to identify them in sentences

Presenting the Lesson

1. Read and discuss pages 384–386. The concept of the direct object as the receiver of the action in a sentence is sometimes confusing. It may be helpful to ask students for analogies. Have them tell you who or what is doing something, what it is doing, and what completes the action. In the example *The quarterback threw the ball*, *quarterback* is the *who*, *threw* is what he is *doing*, *the ball* is *what* he is throwing or what completes the action.

2. Do Exercise A on page 386 with the class. Discuss the different possibilities for direct objects for each sentence. Assign Exercise B. Assign and discuss Exercise A on page 387 before doing Exercise B on page 387. If finding the direct object in a question is difficult for some students, have them first change the question to a statement.

Individualizing the Lesson

Less-Advanced Students

1. After completing Exercise A as a class, write a chart on the board: *Doer, Action, Receiver of the Action*. Ask for volunteers to fill in the appropriate words for each sentence in Exercise A. Then do Exercise B with the class.

2. Do Exercise A on page 387 orally. For Exercise B, provide the stu-

386

dents with lists of possible subjects (Mr. Schmidt, Anne, Thomas Edison, team, carpenter, Ms. Murphy) and possible direct objects (light bulb, package, flowers, deck, egg rolls, bagels).

Advanced Students

1. In the second set of exercises, have students write an alternative direct object for each sentence.

2. Ask students to write sentences using each of the following verbs with a direct object. Sentences will vary.

bought	prepared
has found	speaks
sees	ate
is washing	played
threw	was cooking

Optional Practice

Put the following pairs of sentences on a worksheet. Tell students to read the sentences carefully. One of the two sentences in each pair contains a direct object, the other does not. Have students underline the direct objects. Sentences will vary.

1. The driver drove the <u>race car</u>.
   The driver drove down the street.
2. The cattle ate the <u>grain</u>.
   The cattle ate outside the barn.
3. The author wrote in her diary.
   The author wrote a terrific <u>story</u>.
4. The actors spoke on stage.
   The actors spoke their <u>lines</u> clearly.
5. The pilot called the control <u>tower</u>.
   The pilot called on her radio.
6. The flagman signaled the <u>engineer</u>.
   The flagman signaled frantically.
7. The professor returned the <u>book</u>.
   The professor returned from the laboratory.
8. The class ended its <u>discussion</u>.
   The class ended last week.

Kelly studies in the afternoon.
They drove around the block.
Andrew whistled sharply.

Exercises Find the direct objects.

A. Copy the following sentences. Underline the verb twice and circle the direct object.

Example: Rita <u>explained</u> her (plan.)

1. A huge puddle <u>hid</u> the (path.)
2. The players <u>rushed</u> the (goalie.)
3. Suddenly a breeze <u>puffed</u> the (sail.)
4. Mud <u>splattered</u> the (windshield.)
5. Dandelions <u>covered</u> the (lawn.)
6. He always <u>starches</u> his (collars.)
7. Allison <u>designed</u> the (covers.)
8. Pete <u>mopped</u> the (floor.)
9. Ms. Marshall <u>lost</u> her (watch.)
10. Judge Harvey <u>takes</u> the (bus) to the courthouse.

B. Number your paper from 1 to 10. Find and write the (direct objects) in these sentences.

1. The dam produces (electricity.)
2. The eagle guarded her (nest.)
3. Why did Tina crumple all that (newspaper?)
4. The store pipes (music) into every department.
5. Don't forget your (appointment.)
6. Did you call (Tony) about track practice?
7. Give an (example.)
8. Have you finished your (project) yet?
9. Mr. White was constantly wiping his (brow.)
10. Bob raised his (eyebrows.)

Exercises

A. Number your paper from 1 to 5. Write direct objects to complete each of the following sentences. Answers will vary.

1. The girls ordered the _____ .
2. The farmer drove his _____ into the field.
3. The police car carried a _____ .
4. Helicopters make short _____ .
5. Do you watch many television _____ ?

B. Writing On a sheet of paper, write sentences using the following verbs. Put a direct object in each sentence. Circle each direct object. Answers will vary.

1. will build
2. photographed
3. is sending
4. invented
5. has made
6. buys

Part 4 Transitive and Intransitive Verbs

A verb that has a direct object is called a **transitive verb.** A verb that does not have a direct object is called an **intransitive verb.** The following pairs of sentences show you the difference between transitive and intransitive verbs.

Some birds sing beautiful songs. (*Sing* is transitive; the direct object is *songs.*)

Some birds sing beautifully. (*Sing* is intransitive; it is used without an object.)

Matt paints houses. (*Paints* is transitive; the direct object is *houses.*)

Matt paints with watercolors. (*Paints* is intransitive; it is used without an object.)

387

intransitive verbs. Have them change the sentences with transitive verbs to sentences with intransitive verbs and vice versa. This may be done orally. This is a helpful preparation for Exercise C which can be difficult for some students.

3. Assign and discuss Exercise C on page 389.

Individualizing the Lesson

Less-Advanced Students

1. Do Exercise A orally. Have students identify the subjects and the verbs. Point out which verbs are transitive and intransitive. Have students ask *whom* or *what* to find the direct objects.

2. Allow students to work in pairs to complete Exercise B.

3. Do Exercise C orally. Write the sentences on the chalkboard as they are developed. Underline the direct object in each sentence that has a transitive verb.

Advanced Students

1. Have the students write ten sentences, five using transitive verbs and five using intransitive verbs. Ask them to underline the verbs and to circle the direct objects of the transitive verbs.

2. Have the students think of three more verbs different from those in Exercise C that can be used as either transitive or intransitive verbs. Ask them to follow the directions for Exercise C with their verbs.

If there is a word in the sentence that answers the question *whom?* or *what?* after a verb that shows action, that word is a direct object, and the verb is transitive.

Notice that *sing* and *paints* in the sentences above are used both as transitive and as intransitive verbs, depending on whether there is a direct object or not.

Some verbs are always used as transitive verbs. They must always have a direct object to complete the thought. An example is *bring*.

Other verbs are always used as intransitive verbs. They can never have a direct object. An example is *arrive*.

Most verbs can be used with or without direct objects. They can be transitive in one sentence and intransitive in another. Here are more examples.

Transitive	Intransitive
Maurita practices her dives.	Maurita practices daily.
Larry ate lunch.	Larry ate already.
Kim reached first base.	Kim reached for the ball.

A transitive verb is an action verb that has a direct object.

An intransitive verb is an action verb that does not have a direct object.

Exercises   **Find transitive and intransitive verbs.**

A.   Make two columns marked *Transitive* and *Intransitive*. Find the <u>verb</u> that shows action in each of the following sentences. If the verb has an object, write the verb under *Transitive* and put its object in parentheses after it. If the verb has no object, write it under *Intransitive*.

Example: John read the map.

Transitive	Intransitive
read (map)	

Trans. **1.** Al <u>built</u> a (bookcase.)

388

388

Trans. 2. The zookeeper <u>fed</u> the(seals.)

Trans. 3. Mark <u>collects</u>(coins.)

In. 4. Bonnie <u>has</u> just <u>moved</u> to Richmond, Virginia, from Tallahassee, Florida.

In. 5. The stamps <u>are lying</u> on the table.

Trans. 6. Craig <u>admired</u> his(grandmother.)

Trans. 7. Jennifer and I <u>ordered</u> a(pizza.)

In. 8. His brow <u>wrinkled</u>.

Trans. 9. Melanie <u>wrinkled</u> her(nose.)

Trans. 10. A good architect <u>designed</u> this(house.)

B. Follow the directions for Exercise A.

Trans. 1. Ned <u>returned</u> the(books)this morning.

In. 2. Kay <u>took</u> the(newspaper.)

Trans. 3. Mr. Thomas <u>laid</u> the(keys) on the TV.

Trans. 4. <u>Rake</u> the front(lawn.)

Trans. 5. We <u>are eating</u>(pancakes) with fresh blueberries for breakfast.

In. 6. Darcy <u>swam</u> across the pool.

Trans. 7. I was <u>unpacking</u> my(suitcase.)

Trans. 8. Do you <u>like</u>(cheesecake?)

In. 9. Barbara <u>stayed</u> at home.

Trans. 10. Wind <u>rippled</u> the(water.)

C. Writing Each of the following verbs can be used either as a transitive verb or as an intransitive verb. For each verb write two sentences. Label the first of the two sentences (*a*) and the second (*b*). Make the verb transitive in the first of the two sentences and intransitive in the second. Write *Transitive* after the first sentence and *Intransitive* after the second.

Answers will vary.

Example: 1. (a) Jack dried his hands. Transitive.
(b) The paint dried. Intransitive.

1. study   2. turn   3. write   4. fly   5. crumble

389

To understand the concept of linking verbs and differentiate them from transitive verbs

Presenting the Lesson

1. Read and discuss page 390. Ask students for examples of sentences using the verbs *seem, appear, taste,* and *sound* as action verbs and then using them as state-of-being verbs. Discuss the meaning of *link* and how it applies to linking verbs. Point out that linking verbs are like equal signs. They show that the subject and the predicate word are alike or similar.

2. Assign and discuss Exercise A and B on page 391.

3. Assign and discuss Exercise C on pages 391–392. Before assigning this exercise, you may find it helpful to review briefly transitive verbs.

Individualizing the Lesson

Less-Advanced Students

1. Do Exercise A as a class. Write the three columns on the board or use an overhead projector. Remind students to think of linking verbs as equal signs in order to find the predicate word, or the word linked to the subject.

2. Allow students to work in pairs to complete Exercise B. Tell them to refer to the list of linking verbs on page 390.

3. For Exercise C, have the students find the verbs independently. Then as a class discuss which

Part 5   Linking Verbs

Verbs that show a state of being are often called **linking verbs.**

Cindy *is* a member.   The soup *tastes* good.

Linking verbs connect the subject with a word in the predicate. The word in the predicate tells something about the subject. In the examples given, *member* tells about *Cindy* and *good* tells about *soup*. *Is* and *tastes* are linking verbs.

The words *is, am, are, was, were, be,* and *become* are often used as linking verbs. The words *seem, look, appear, feel, grow, smell, taste,* and *sound* are sometimes used as linking verbs.

The same verb may be used to show action in one sentence and state of being in another. Notice the following examples:

We *smelled* smoke.   The children *looked* in the box.
The soap *smelled* sweet.   Jean *looked* happy.

Predicate Words

The words that follow linking verbs and tell something about the subject are called **predicate words.** Nouns that follow linking verbs are **predicate nouns.**

Anne *is* a good swimmer.   Larry *was* my classmate.

Adjectives that follow linking verbs are **predicate adjectives.**

The plant *seems* healthy.   David *is* very successful.

Do not confuse linking verbs and predicate words with transitive verbs and direct objects. Remember: A **direct object** answers the question *whom* or *what* after a **transitive verb.**

Connie painted the picture.   Ron won the prize.

A **predicate word** tells something about the subject of a **linking verb.**

Connie is a painter.   Ron was lucky.

Exercises   Find the linking verbs.

A.   At the top of three columns write: Subject, (Linking Verb,) and *Predicate Word*. Find the three parts in each sentence. Write them in the proper columns.

Example: The chili tasted spicy.

Subject	Linking Verb	Predicate Word
chili	tasted	spicy

1. The new store (was) open for business.
2. Margo (is) a volunteer.
3. Thursday (was) Diane's birthday.
4. The temperature (is) unbearable!
5. (Do) you ever (feel) lonesome?
6. Carlos (is) an ambitious worker.
7. Tracy (feels) fine today.
8. Soon Bill (became) sleepy.
9. The air (feels) warmer.
10. Sam (was) by far our best pitcher.

B.   Follow the directions for Exercise A.

1. The cost of the space station (seemed) tremendous.
2. Mrs. Meredith (became) the new principal.
3. Sue and Linda (seemed) anxious at first.
4. The orchids (were) beautiful.
5. (Were) you late for the races?
6. Before the game the team (was) restless.
7. Tony (looks) a little pale this morning.
8. Kristen (is) the manager of the tennis team.
(You) 9. (Do be) careful!
10. Water (is) essential to life on earth.

C.   Copy each of the following sentences. Circle the linking verbs. Underline the transitive verbs.

1. Robin packed the picnic.

verbs are linking verbs and which are transitive verbs.

Advanced Students

1. Have the students copy a favorite poem or song that contains linking verbs. Then underline or list all the linking verbs.

2. Have the students choose three sentences from each exercise to rewrite, using alternative verbs.

Optional Practice

Have students write whether the words linked to the subjects in the sentences in Exercises A and B on page 391 are nouns or adjectives.

Extending the Lesson

Tell students to use their favorite sport or hobby as a subject. Have them write a paragraph of about ten sentences, five of which use linking verbs and five of which use action verbs.

391

Objective

To recognize and use verbs in the present, past, and future tenses

Presenting the Lesson

1. Read and discuss pages 392–393. The perfect tenses are troublesome for some students so it may be helpful to spend some time discussing the time each tense shows and the purpose for the perfect tenses. *Has* and *have* form the present perfect, and *had* forms the past perfect. You may want to teach principal parts first by reversing the order of Parts 6 and 7.

2. You may want to assign Exercises A and B on page 393 now or as a review after studying Part 7.

Individualizing the Lesson

Less-Advanced Students

1. Help students learn the time that each verb tense refers to by adding time references to the examples on page 392.

Present: She sketches every day.
Future: She will sketch tomorrow.
Past: She sketched yesterday.
Present Perfect: She has sketched every day this week.
Past Perfect: She had sketched every day last month.

2. Find the verbs in Exercise A as a class. Have students identify the tense of each verb independently. Do Exercise B orally.

Advanced Students

Have students rewrite each sen-

2. (Am) I late?
3. Pete has the measles.
4. The new puppies (seem) content.
5. The sky (became) dark during the last inning.
6. Dale arranged the meeting.
7. The crowd (seemed) upset.
8. These walnuts (taste) good.
9. Jan tasted the pecans.
10. The lake (appeared) calm.

Part 6   Tenses of Verbs

Verbs change their forms to show the time when an action or state of being occurs. These changes are called **tenses.**

The **present tense** shows present time: *I am. I see.*
The **past tense** shows past time: *I was. I saw.*
The **future tense** shows future time: *I shall be. You will see.*

Tense changes are made in three ways:

1. By changes in spelling: *sing, sang, sung*
2. By changes in ending: *walk, walked*
3. By adding helping verbs: *has walked, will walk*

Here are five important tenses:

Present Tense:	She talks.	We know.
Past Tense:	She talked.	We knew.
Future Tense:	She will talk.	We shall know.
Present Perfect Tense:	She has talked.	We have known.
Past Perfect Tense:	She had talked.	We had known.

You can see that three tenses are used to show different kinds of past time: *past, present perfect,* and *past perfect.* You will learn two things about them:

1. The past tense forms of a verb are used alone. They are never used with helping verbs.

we cleaned   you ran   they brought   she slid

2. The present perfect tense uses the helping verbs *has* and *have*. The past perfect tense uses the helping verb *had*.

Present Perfect	Past Perfect
he has cleaned	you had run
they have brought	she had slid

Exercises Learn to recognize and use tenses.

A. Name the tense of the verb in each sentence.

1. The pitcher caught the ball. past
2. Terry has seen the Painted Desert. present perfect
3. Seth has taken his bicycle. present perfect
4. Toss the ring. present
5. Gayle is happy. present
6. Mr. Gray has an antique car. present
7. Has Rick already gone? present perfect
8. Shall we go too? future
9. You will find it on the table. future
10. We have eaten lunch already. present perfect
11. We almost froze yesterday. past
12. My father had spoken to the club. past perfect

B. Number your paper from 1 to 10. Write the verb tense asked for. Check by reading the sentence to yourself.

1. The hamster (past of *eat*) the food. ate
2. My mother (present of *work*) for that company. works
3. The ship (past of *touch*) the iceberg. touched
4. The plants (past perfect of *grow*) much taller. had grown
5. The PTA (future of *buy*) three new typewriters. will buy
6. I (past of *win*) the prize. won
7. Sue (future of *pick*) up the package tomorrow. will pick
8. The bird (past of *fly*) away. flew
9. We (present perfect of *choose*) new band uniforms. have chosen
10. Tim (past perfect of *do*) twenty pushups. had done

393

tence in Exercise A, changing the tense of the verb.

Optional Practice

Have students underline the verb in each of the following sentences. Then have them write the present, past, future, and perfect tenses of that verb. Answers below.

Example: The judge *rated* all the contestants.
  rate, rated, will rate, has rated, had rated

1. Carol's cat sleeps in a basket.
2. Barbara ran the programs through the computer.
3. The host introduced his guests.
4. Steve ate lunch on the job.
5. We watched the tennis tournaments on television.
6. The flight attendant served our meals.
7. A commercial jetliner lands every minute.
8. The weather forecasters predicted a mild winter.

Extending the Lesson

Give each student a brief newspaper or magazine article. Have the students list all of the verbs used and identify the tense of each one.

1. sleep, slept, will sleep, has/had slept
2. run, ran, will run, has/had run
3. introduce, introduced, will introduce
4. eat, ate, will eat, has/had eaten
5. watch, watched, will watched, has/had watched
6. serve, served, will serve, has/had served
7. land, landed, will land, has/had landed
8. predict, predicted, will predict, has/had predicted

Objective

To identify the principle parts of verbs and to use a dictionary to find them correctly

Presenting the Lesson

1. Read and discuss pages 394–396. Stress that knowing the principal parts of a verb will help students use the verb correctly. Also emphasize that past participles are used only with helping verbs.

2. Review the definition of a *regular verb*. Ask the students to give additional examples of principal parts of regular verbs.

3. Discuss the definition of an *irregular verb*. Study the list of irregular verbs on page 396. Note that *have* is included with each past participle to remind the students that past participles are used only with helping verbs. Explain to students that the principal parts of verbs can be found in a dictionary. Assign each student a verb and have him or her find the principal parts in the dictionary.

4. Have students memorize the list of irregular verbs.

Individualizing the Lesson

Less-Advanced Students

1. Have students practice looking in the dictionary for some of the irregular verbs on page 396. Help them locate the principal parts of the verbs.

Part 7 The Principal Parts of Verbs

Verb tenses are formed from three basic parts of the verb. These parts are called the **principal parts** of the verb. The principal parts are the **present**, the **past**, and the **past participle**.

Present	Past	Past Participle
paint	painted	painted
ring	rang	rung
throw	threw	thrown

By using the principal parts of a verb and different helping verbs, you can make any of the five important tenses.

The principal parts of a verb are the present, the past, and the past participle.

One other part of the verb that is helpful for making verb tenses is the **present participle.** The present participle is the **-ing** form of the verb as in *painting, ringing,* or *throwing.* You use the present participle with helping verbs (*am painting, is ringing, are throwing*).

Learning Principal Parts

There are several thousand verbs in the English language. You won't have any problems using most of them in any tense. They are **regular verbs.** This means that the past is formed by adding *-ed* or *-d* to the present. The past participle is the same as the past form and is always used with a helping verb.

Present	Past	Past Participle
march	march**ed**	(have) march**ed**
plant	plant**ed**	(have) plant**ed**
arrive	arriv**ed**	(have) arriv**ed**

There are a few commonly used verbs, however, whose past forms do not follow this pattern. They are **irregular verbs.**

The list on page 396 gives the principal parts of many irregular verbs. The past participle is always used with a helping verb.

When you use irregular verbs, remember these two important things:

1. The past form is always used by itself, *without* a helping verb.

> Jon *took* our picture.

2. The past participle is always used *with* a helping verb.

> Jon *has taken* our picture.

As you study the list on page 396, you may want to say *have* or *has* in front of each past participle. Then you will not confuse tenses and say, "he seen it," "he done it," "she had stole it," or "she had broke it."

The helping verbs that you will use most often include *has, have, had, is, are, was,* and *were.*

Using a Dictionary To Find Principal Parts

If you are not sure about a verb form, look it up in a dictionary. If the verb is regular, usually only one form will be listed.

If the verb is irregular, the dictionary will give the irregular forms. It will give two forms if the past and past participle are the same: *say, said.* It will give all three principal parts if they are all different: *sing, sang, sung.*

Dictionary Entry for *begin*

present
|
be·gin (bi gin′), **v.** to start being, doing, acting, etc.; get under way [Work *begins* at 8:00 A.M. His cold *began* with a sore throat.]
—**be·gan′**, *p.*; **be·gun′**, *p.p.*
|_____ past participle
|
past

---

2. *Irregular Verb Flash Game.* Make a set of flash cards. On each card, using the list of verbs on page 396, print one principal part of a verb on a side. Print the two other parts on the reverse side. Students can use the cards in small groups as a means of familiarizing themselves with these verbs.

Advanced Students

Have students write original sentences using the present tense, past tense, and past perfect tense of each of the irregular verbs.

Optional Practice

1. Have the students look up the principal parts of these verbs in a dictionary: *make, sell, pull, save, tell, move.* Then have them catagorize the verbs as regular or irregular.

2. Have students make three columns on a sheet of paper. Label them *Present Tense, Past Tense,* and *Past Participle.* Give students the following verbs and ask them to list the other two forms. They may use the dictionary for help.

bite	buy
draw	catch
drive	think
fly	lose

bit, bitten	bought, bought
drew, drawn	caught, caught
drove, driver	thought, thought
flew, flown	lost, lost

Tell students to unscramble each of the following groups of words to make each group into a sentence. Have them use the correct tense of the verb in parentheses.

1. (bloom)
spring
flowers
next
different

2. (collapse)
runners
the race
two
after

3. (have)
strong
acrobats
all
muscles

4. (eat)
cereal
Jason
breakfast
for
always

5. (put)
together
words
correctly
these

6. (make)
cakes
baker
marvelous
that

7. (hit)
a hurricane
yesterday
Florida
early

8. (arrive)
never
this train
time
on

1. Next spring different flowers will bloom.
2. Two runners collapsed after the race.
3. All acrobats have strong muscles.
4. Jason always eats cereal for breakfast.
5. Put these words together correctly.
6. That baker makes marvelous cakes.
7. A hurricane hit Florida early yesterday.
8. This train never arrives on time.

Irregular Verbs

Present	Past	Past Participle
begin	began	(have) begun
break	broke	(have) broken
bring	brought	(have) brought
choose	chose	(have) chosen
come	came	(have) come
do	did	(have) done
drink	drank	(have) drunk
eat	ate	(have) eaten
fall	fell	(have) fallen
freeze	froze	(have) frozen
give	gave	(have) given
go	went	(have) gone
grow	grew	(have) grown
know	knew	(have) known
ride	rode	(have) ridden
ring	rang	(have) rung
rise	rose	(have) risen
run	ran	(have) run
say	said	(have) said
see	saw	(have) seen
sing	sang	(have) sung
sit	sat	(have) sat
speak	spoke	(have) spoken
steal	stole	(have) stolen
swim	swam	(have) swum
take	took	(have) taken
teach	taught	(have) taught
throw	threw	(have) thrown
wear	wore	(have) worn
write	wrote	(have) written

In **Section 4, Using Irregular Verbs,** you will practice using these verbs correctly.

ADDITIONAL EXERCISES

Using Verbs

A. Finding Verbs Number your paper from 1 to 10. Write the <u>verb</u> in each sentence.

1. Johnny <u>tells</u> that story very well.
2. The usher <u>tore</u> the tickets in half.
3. Janet <u>clamped</u> the new pencil sharpener onto the library desk.
4. Dead leaves <u>whirled</u> past.
5. There <u>was</u> a police officer by the meter.
6. She <u>ticketed</u> Mr. Crawford's car.
7. The ball <u>crashed</u> into the pins.
8. For a few minutes Carla <u>seemed</u> uneasy.
9. Good memories <u>are</u> valuable possessions.
10. In the last quarter of the game, Pam <u>had</u> better luck.

B. Main Verbs and Helping Verbs Label two columns *Helping Verbs* and *Main Verbs*. Find all the parts of the verb in each of the following sentences. Write them in the proper columns.

1. Nobody h^{HV}as us^{MV}ed your camera.
2. Tony w^{HV}as b^{MV}oiling some eggs.
3. We h^{HV}ad spr^{MV}ead our beach towels too close to the water's edge.
4. Megan w^{HV}ill probably rem^{MV}ember the address.
5. D^{HV}id you w^{MV}atch the eclipse?
6. The car w^{HV}as just ent^{MV}ering the tunnel.
7. A^{HV}re your parents really s^{MV}elling their van?
8. Carl w^{HV}ould certainly not q^{MV}uit the team.
9. Should^{HV}n't I m^{MV}elt the butter first?
10. I h^{HV}ave often b^{HV}een t^{MV}old that.

Additional Exercises

These Additional Exercises may be used for additional practice of the concepts presented in this Section. Each exercise focuses on a single concept, and should be used after the page number indicated in parentheses.

Review

If you have not assigned these Additional Exercises before this time, you can also use them as an excellent Section Review.

C. Verbs and Direct Objects Write the verb and the direct object for each sentence. Underline the verb and circle the direct object.

1. A lightning bolt <u>hit</u> the (tree.)
2. Nelson <u>collected</u> the (papers.)
3. The judge <u>thanked</u> the (jury) for their hard work.
4. Nobody ever <u>guessed</u> the (truth.)
5. Did the puppy <u>chew</u> its (leash?)
6. Dan <u>called</u> (Ruth) to the phone.
7. Mr. Barnes finally <u>signed</u> the (petition.)
8. I sometimes <u>enjoy</u> the (commercials.)
9. The computer probably <u>made</u> a (mistake.)
10. <u>Measure</u> the (shelves) carefully.

D. Adding Direct Objects Number your paper from 1 to 5. Write direct objects that will complete each of the following.

Answers will vary.

1. Tricia opened the mysterious _____ .
2. Snow covered the _____ .
3. Arthur donated a _____ to the rummage sale.
4. Diane plays the _____ in the band.
5. Joey made a _____ for his mom.

E. Transitive and Intransitive Verbs Label two columns *Transitive* and *Intransitive*. Find the verb in each of the following sentences. If the verb has an object, write it under *Transitive* and put its object in parentheses after it. If the verb has no object, write it under *Intransitive*.

T. 1. A guard <u>stopped</u> the (children.)
In. 2. A taxi <u>stopped</u> in front of our apartment building.
In. 3. The ice cubes <u>melted</u> in a few minutes.
T. 4. The sun <u>melted</u> the (tar) on the roof.
T. 5. The alligator <u>covered</u> its (nest) with leaves.
T. 6. The firefighter <u>swung</u> an (ax.)
In. 7. The street fair <u>ended</u> with a barbeque.

T. 8. Lisa's words <u>ended</u> the (discussion)

T. 9. The mayor <u>presented</u> (medals) to the rescuers.

T. 10. <u>Write</u> your (name) on the list.

F. Linking Verbs and Predicate Words At the top of three columns write: <u>Subject</u>, (<u>Linking Verb,</u>) and <u>Predicate Word</u>. Find the three parts in each sentence. Write them in the proper columns.

1. The full <u>moon</u> (was) <u>bright</u>.
2. Caged <u>animals</u> (are) often <u>nervous</u>.
3. Green <u>vegetables</u> (are) one <u>source</u> of iron.
4. <u>Joyce</u> (seems) <u>happy</u> about something.
5. Last <u>Friday</u> (was) the <u>deadline</u> for the contest.
6. The old <u>school</u> (became) a community <u>center</u>.
7. The <u>cheerleaders</u> (sounded) <u>hoarse</u> by the end of the game.
8. Sometimes the <u>weather</u> (turns) <u>chilly</u> overnight.
9. Those <u>berries</u> don't (taste) <u>ripe</u> to me.
10. The <u>cornbread</u> (smells) <u>wonderful</u>.

G. Verb Tenses Write the <u>verb</u> in each sentence. Then write the tense of the verb.

1. Our school <u>has</u> new computers. present
2. Jeff <u>bought</u> a bag of sunflower seeds. past
3. The parakeet <u>flew</u> out the window. past
4. I <u>had</u> a bad cold last week. past
5. Lauren <u>will be</u> home soon. future
6. Janie <u>has fished</u> for trout before. present perfect
7. <u>Will</u> you <u>sit</u> at our table? future
8. The driver <u>had started</u> the bus. past perfect
9. <u>Is</u> Teresa a baseball fan? present
10. Bill <u>has had</u> a wonderful summer. present perfect

Mixed Review

These exercises provide review of the concepts presented in this Section. Each exercise challenges the students to apply several of the skills they have acquired during previous study. Because the "mixed" feature of these activities makes them more difficult, the teacher may wish to have less-advanced students do them orally or in small groups.

MIXED REVIEW

Using Verbs

A. Identifying verbs Number your paper from 1 to 10. Write the <u>verb</u> from each sentence. Then write whether it is an _Action_ or _State-of-Being_ verb. If it is an action verb, write whether it is _Transitive_ or _Intransitive_.

A., T. 1. Harvey <u>cut</u> the paper into long strips.

A., T. 2. Jan <u>found</u> the key in the bottom of her purse.

A., I. 3. Mr. Thomas <u>works</u> on weekends.

A., I. 4. The film <u>has</u> not <u>been developed</u> yet.

A., I. 5. Rain <u>fell</u> steadily throughout the night.

S.B. 6. <u>Has</u> the TV <u>been</u> on channel 2 or channel 5?

A., T. 7. Donna <u>filled</u> the vase with zinnias and asters.

A., I. 8. John's brother <u>ran</u> in the marathon.

S.B. 9. This camera <u>seems</u> broken.

S.B. 10. The apple pie <u>tastes</u> delicious with cheddar cheese.

B. Recognizing verbs, direct objects, and predicate words Copy the following sentences. Underline the verbs. If a verb is a linking verb, draw an arrow from the verb to the predicate word. If the verb is an action verb, circle the direct object, if there is one.

1. Scott <u>was</u> the best pitcher in the league.
2. Your forehead <u>feels</u> hot.
3. Laura <u>did</u> not <u>hear</u> the (question.)
4. These plums <u>are</u> very ripe.
5. I <u>have written</u> to the editor of the magazine.
6. Mrs. O'Malley <u>is</u> our algebra teacher.
7. <u>Have</u> you ever <u>seen</u> a (bullfight?)
8. The rocket <u>soared</u> into outer space.
9. That man <u>looks</u> familiar.
10. Gwendolyn Brooks <u>is</u> a famous poet.

C. Using verb tenses correctly   Copy the following sentences, using the verb and tense given in parentheses.

1. Dad (present perfect of *miss*) his train. has missed
2. The spout on the teapot (past perfect of *break*). had broken
3. The committee (future of *listen*) to each request. will listen
4. Laura (past of *forget*) the important dates. forgot
5. Dan (present perfect of *fill*) the basket with strawberries. has filled
6. Floyd (present of *listen*) to classical music. listens
7. During the night the pond (past perfect of *freeze*). had frozen
8. Mike (present perfect of *write*) a one-act play. has written
9. The mayor (past of *throw*) out the first ball of the season. threw
10. The players on our team (present of *wear*) blue and white jerseys. wear

These challenging and enjoyable activities allow the students to see how the concepts of grammar, usage, and mechanics may be applied in actual writing situations. Each exercise is designed to allow students practice in several of the skills they have acquired in this Section. The activities also provide opportunities for students to write creatively about a wide variety of interesting and unusual subjects.

USING GRAMMAR IN WRITING
Using Verbs

A. Congratulations! You answered ten trivia questions correctly on the radio. Your prize is a ninety-second free shopping spree in any section of your favorite discount department store. Describe your frantic race to fill the shopping cart. Circle each verb. Label each verb *T* or *I* for transitive or intransitive. Underline each direct object once and each indirect object twice.

B. You are at a carnival. Walking along, you see a mysterious booth draped in black. A sign says "Have Your Future Read by Madame Nozall and Her Crystal Ball." You decide to use your last ticket to have your fortune told. Write a paragraph about some of the things that Madame Nozall tells you about your future. Use verbs in the future tense. Next imagine it is ten years in the future. Write a second paragraph about whether or not the predictions were right. Use the past tense for the verbs in this paragraph.

C. You are applying for a job selling the latest miracle gadget, the Kitchen Shark. To get the job, you have to memorize a list of the things it can do, and the features that it has. Use at least five action words that describe what the gadget can do to different vegetables and fruits. Perhaps it can also open cans and boil eggs. Be as inventive as you want to be. Then use three state-of-being verbs to describe how the object looks or feels.

Using Irregular Verbs

In Section 3, you learned about verbs, especially regular verbs. In this section you will practice using irregular verbs.

When you use irregular verbs, remember these two things:

1. The past tense is always used by itself, *without* a helping verb.

> I *rode* the subway.   Jean *wrote* a poem.

2. The past participle is always used *with* a helping verb.

> I *have ridden* the subway.   Jean *has written* a poem.

Practice Pages on Irregular Verbs

Irregular verbs can cause problems in writing as well as in speaking. Use the exercise on the next page as a test to show how well you can handle these irregular verbs.

403

Section Objective

To become familiar with the principal parts of common irregular verbs

Preparing the Students

You may wish to use this section only with students who need practice in using irregular verbs, or you may wish to use the exercises periodically during the year.

Discuss the meanings of the words *regular* (following a certain order, similar) and *irregular* (out of order, different from the normal). Stress the idea that when the terms *regular* and *irregular* are applied to verbs, they refer only to the form of the verbs, not to their meaning, purpose, or use.

Additional Resources

Mastery Test — pages 43–44 in the test booklet

Additional Exercises — pages 416–418 in the student text

Practice Book — pages 159–164

Duplicating Masters — pages 159–164

Special Populations — See special section at the back of this Teacher's Edition.

Presenting the Lesson

Read and discuss pages 403–404. Nonstandard language habits, including slang and dialect, make the practice pages on pages 405–415 especially useful. The exercise on page 404 can be used as a pretest to determine individual areas of weakness.

Have students work in pairs on

the **Use the Right Word** exercises. One student should read aloud the sample sentences for the other, and then they should switch roles. Emphasize the idea of *say* and *hear.* Then assign each "Write It Right" exercise.

Individualizing the Lesson

Less-Advanced Students

Before discussing the "Say It Right" and "Hear It Right" exercises in this section, you may want to display the three parts of each verb presented on the chalkboard.

Example:

Break	Bring
Broke	Brought
Broken	Brought

Have students do Exercises A and B orally before assigning "Write It Right."

Advanced Students

You may want to assign the exercise on page 404 as a diagnostic test. After correcting the students' papers, you may wish to assign only the exercises on irregular verbs with which the students are having difficulty.

Optional Practice

Have students write sentences of their own using five of the verbs listed in this section. Tell them to write three sentences for each verb: one using the verb in the present tense, one in the past, and one with a helping verb.

If the exercise shows that you do know these verbs, you may refer to this section simply for review. If the exercise shows that you need practice with certain verbs, your teacher may ask you to practice those verbs. For each verb there are sentences that will help you to "say it right," "hear it right," and "write it right." Oral practice is an important way to learn these verbs. Review the oral sections before you do the written work.

Exercise Number your paper from 1 to 22. For each sentence, write the correct word from the two given in parentheses.

1. Dennis (bring, brought) cider for the party.
2. Joe has (broke, broken) the school track record.
3. Ruth had (came, come) to the meeting with us.
4. Rosita has (chose, chosen) a biography for her report.
5. After we had (did, done) the work, we went home.
6. Have you (drank, drunk) all the lemonade?
7. When I came home, everyone had (ate, eaten) dinner.
8. The shallow lake had already (froze, frozen).
9. Mrs. Lorenzo has (gave, given) us our assignment.
10. All of us have (went, gone) to the science fair.
11. Have you (grew, grown) strawberries or raspberries?
12. How long have you (knew, known) the MacArthurs?
13. Sara and Rick have (ran, run) in the relay race.
14. At camp, the dinner bell (rang, rung) every night.
15. I have never (rode, ridden) in a helicopter.
16. Robert had (sang, sung) at the Summer Festival.
17. I have (saw, seen) *E. T.* three times.
18. Ms. Bell has (spoke, spoken) to me about a job.
19. Ginny has (swam, swum) in the Pacific.
20. The umpire (thrown, threw) him out.
21. Have you ever (wore, worn) hiking boots?
22. Mark has finally (wrote, written) his report.

Break
Broke
Broken

Bring
Brought
Brought

Say It Right   Hear It Right

A. Say these sentences over until the correct use of *broke* and *broken* sounds natural to you.

1. Maria broke the glass.
2. The dish is broken.
3. The window had been broken.
4. Break the seal first.
5. The clock was broken.
6. They broke the news.
7. Did Jason break his arm?
8. Christie broke the lamp.

B. Say these sentences over until the correct use of *bring* and *brought* sounds natural to you.

1. Jeff has brought the album.
2. Bring an umbrella.
3. I brought mine.
4. Keith brought his lunch.
5. Laura will bring a camera.
6. Did you bring the tickets?
7. I wish I'd brought my jacket.
8. We brought you a gift.

Write It Right

Write the correct word from the two words given.

1. Did you (bring, brought) the salad?
2. Steve (bring, brought) the badminton set.
3. Have you (bring, brought) the reports to class?
4. I have (bring, brought) a friend along.
5. I have (bring, brought) you a surprise.
6. Haven't you (bring, brought) anything?
7. Peg (bring, brought) her new racket to class.
8. The paramedics had (bring, brought) him to the hospital.
9. Julie has (broke, broken) her wrist.
10. Allen may have (broke, broken) the typewriter.
11. We have (broke, broken) five dishes.
12. Our car had (broke, broken) down on the expressway.
13. That clock has been (broke, broken) for over a year.
14. Ted's fishing pole was (broke, broken) in half.
15. The runner has (broke, broken) the previous record.

Choose
Chose
Chosen

Come
Came
Come

Use the Right Word

Say It Right   Hear It Right

A. Say these sentences over until the correct use of *chose* and *chosen* sounds natural to you.

1. The team was chosen.
2. Fred chose a poem.
3. The class chose these books.
4. Ann has been chosen.

5. Choose a record.
6. Dick chose a yellow shirt.
7. Have you been chosen?
8. Was Liz chosen?

B. Say these sentences over until the correct use of *came* and *come* sounds natural to you.

1. Sue came to the meeting.
2. Will he come with us?
3. He should have come home.
4. Amy and Tad came with me.

5. Has the mail come yet?
6. They came yesterday.
7. Eric has come for his book.
8. Did you come to dinner?

Write It Right

Write the correct word from the two words given.

1. Loud cheers (<u>came</u>, come) from the fans.
2. The exhibit will (came, <u>come</u>) to the museum in July.
3. I wondered why the mail carrier (<u>came</u>, come) so early.
4. They had arrived long before we (<u>came</u>, come).
5. I saw the accident just as I (<u>came</u>, come) along.
6. My sister has (came, <u>come</u>) home from college this week.
7. She (<u>came</u>, come) last weekend, too.
8. We (<u>chose</u>, chosen) to go camping this summer.
9. I (<u>chose</u>, chosen) watermelon instead of pie for dessert.
10. Have you (chose, <u>chosen</u>) the color you want on your walls?
11. The team has (chose, <u>chosen</u>) Chris as captain.
12. We have (chose, <u>chosen</u>) new books for our library.
13. At camp we (<u>chose</u>, chosen) Pablo as our group leader.
14. Ruth has been (chose, <u>chosen</u>) class president.
15. I (<u>chose</u>, chosen) to work on the posters.

Do
Did
Done

Drink
Drank
Drunk

Say It Right   Hear It Right

A. Say these sentences over until the correct use of *did* and *done* sounds natural to you.

1. Sam did his chores.
2. Ellen has done hers.
3. I did the dishes.
4. Lee has done ten problems.
5. Kim did only three.
6. Mark has done only one.
7. Tim did his work quickly.
8. Jim has done the laundry.

B. Say these sentences over until the correct use of *drank* and *drunk* sounds natural to you.

1. I have drunk the juice.
2. Ann has drunk three glasses.
3. Lynn had drunk only one.
4. Carol drank iced tea.
5. Chris drank root beer.
6. Kim and Lisa drank milk.
7. Tim had drunk water.
8. Carla drank ginger ale.

Write It Right

Write the correct word from the two words given.

1. Have you (did, <u>done</u>) the math exercises yet?
2. Juan (<u>did</u>, done) a good job on the model airplane.
3. Have you (did, <u>done</u>) your homework?
4. The team (<u>did</u>, done) the best it could.
5. The school band has never (did, <u>done</u>) so well before.
6. No one could have (did, <u>done</u>) those problems.
7. Jane (<u>did</u>, done) that scale model of a pyramid.
8. The performers (<u>did</u>, done) an excellent job.
9. I have (drank, <u>drunk</u>) eight glasses of water today.
10. Jamie and Steve (<u>drank</u>, drunk) the last soda.
11. Have you ever (drank, <u>drunk</u>) coconut milk?
12. The baby has (drank, <u>drunk</u>) all the juice in the bottle.
13. We (<u>drank</u>, drunk) ginger ale at the picnic.
14. Josh has never (drank, <u>drunk</u>) iced tea.
15. The hikers (<u>drank</u>, drunk) water from the well on the farm.

407

Eat
Ate
Eaten

Freeze
Froze
Frozen

Use the Right Word

Say It Right   Hear It Right

A. Say these sentences over until the correct use of *ate* and *eaten* sounds natural to you.

1. Ted ate the salad.
2. Dana has eaten breakfast.
3. Jim ate later.
4. Beth ate slowly.

5. Shelly had eaten a lot.
6. We had eaten dinner.
7. I eat at noon.
8. We ate hot dogs.

B. Say these sentences over until the correct use of *froze* and *frozen* sounds natural to you.

1. Bus windows were frozen.
2. The fish was frozen.
3. The milk had frozen.
4. Rain froze into hail.

5. It may freeze tonight.
6. Mother froze the meat.
7. The fruit was frozen.
8. The pond froze.

Write It Right

Write the correct word from the two words given.

1. Todd had (ate, <u>eaten</u>) before the game.
2. Stephanie (<u>ate</u>, eaten) the yogurt.
3. I (<u>eat</u>, eaten) too fast sometimes.
4. Scott has (ate, <u>eaten</u>) all the peanut butter.
5. Lucy had (ate, <u>eaten</u>) lunch at a friend's house.
6. She has (ate, <u>eaten</u>) there lots of times.
7. Dave had (ate, <u>eaten</u>) slowly.
8. We (<u>ate</u>, eaten) at my cousin's last night.
9. The lake was (froze, <u>frozen</u>) halfway out from shore.
10. Jan's tears were almost (froze, <u>frozen</u>) on her cheeks.
11. We have (froze, <u>frozen</u>) the leftovers.
12. Waiting for the school bus, we nearly (<u>froze</u>, frozen).
13. Linda's toes were almost (froze, <u>frozen</u>).
14. This is the first winter the river has (froze, <u>frozen</u>).
15. The water pipe has (froze, <u>frozen</u>).

Give
Gave
Given

Go
Went
Gone

Say It Right   Hear It Right

A. Say these sentences over until the correct use of *gave* and *given* sounds natural to you.

1. Liz has given me a gift.
2. Jo gave her speech today.
3. Will you give me a hand?
4. My aunt gave me a watch.
5. I was given the day off.
6. I gave the baby a toy.
7. She has given a party.
8. Sue gave Bob a rare stamp.

B. Say these sentences over until the correct use of *went* and *gone* sounds natural to you.

1. Lisa went home.
2. John had gone last winter.
3. I went to the museum.
4. We went swimming.
5. Did Dee go, too?
6. Mom went to play golf.
7. Have you gone to the zoo?
8. I went there last summer.

Write It Right

Write the correct word from the two words given.

1. We (give, gave) our teacher a present.
2. You should have (gave, given) better directions.
3. Sally (gave, given) me a jigsaw puzzle.
4. Their team seemed to have (gave, given) up.
5. Our coach has always (gave, given) us praise when we win.
6. Sometimes he has (gave, given) us a lecture.
7. Mrs. Hanke (gave, given) us a spelling test.
8. Ann has (went, gone) away for the summer.
9. Jonathan and Liz have (went, gone) fishing.
10. I have (went, gone) fishing only once.
11. Rob has (went, gone) fishing every day this summer.
12. Mary has always (went, gone) to the show on Saturday.
13. The children (went, gone) down the street to get ice cream.
14. My sister has always (went, gone) to summer camp.
15. Jeremy and Beth (went, gone) to the meeting.

409

Know
Knew
Known

Say It Right   Hear It Right

A. Say these sentences over until the correct use of *grew* and *grown* sounds natural to you.

1. The sunflower grew tall.
2. We grew our own lettuce.
3. Did you grow beets?
4. The tree has grown tall.
5. The night grew cold.
6. I had grown tired of weeding.
7. The grass grew quickly.
8. We have all grown a lot.

B. Say these sentences over until the correct use of *knew* and *known* sounds natural to you.

1. Have you known Kim long?
2. I have known her for years.
3. Do you know the results?
4. I had known Jim at camp.
5. Jeff knew Sue from school.
6. I knew the owner.
7. Kay knew her well.
8. They knew it would rain.

Write It Right

Write the correct word from the two words given.

1. Our class (grew, grown) flowers for the army hospital.
2. We have (grew, grown) radishes every summer.
3. Anna (grew, grown) ten kinds of plants for her experiment.
4. George has (grew, grown) two inches since last fall.
5. The Jeffersons (grew, grown) their own vegetables.
6. Mother (grew, grown) catnip for our cat.
7. The corn has (grew, grown) six feet tall.
8. They have (knew, known) each other since fifth grade.
9. I have never (knew, known) a busier person.
10. The hikers (knew, known) they were lost.
11. Kathy (knew, known) how to read at four years old.
12. We (knew, known) the Jacksons.
13. Clara has (knew, known) how to swim since the age of three.
14. We hadn't (knew, known) the game was postponed.
15. Mike had never (knew, known) anyone from Japan before.

Use the Right Word

Run
Ran
Run

See
Saw
Seen

Say It Right   Hear It Right

A.   Say these sentences over until the correct use of *ran* and *run* sounds natural to you.

1. The dog ran outside.
2. Has our time run out?
3. They ran out of ice cream.
4. Al had run very fast.
5. Steve has run three miles.
6. The joggers ran for miles.
7. Barb ran the school store.
8. Has the relay been run yet?

B.   Say these sentences over until the correct use of *saw* and *seen* sounds natural to you.

1. Michelle has seen the play.
2. Have you seen my new puppy?
3. Jay saw the All-Star game.
4. Chris saw it, too.
5. Can you see the screen?
6. Eve saw us at the pool.
7. I saw you yesterday.
8. We haven't seen him.

Write It Right

Write the correct word from the two words given.

1. Ruth had (ran, <u>run</u>) until she was exhausted.
2. When my brother saw Dad, he (<u>ran</u>, run) to meet him.
3. The race was (ran, <u>run</u>) at the high school.
4. Who (<u>ran</u>, run) in the relays?
5. The car has (ran, <u>run</u>) out of gas.
6. Katie and Jeff (<u>ran</u>, run) four miles today.
7. Have you ever (ran, <u>run</u>) in a three-legged race?
8. We (<u>saw</u>, seen) the World Series on television.
9. I (<u>saw</u>, seen) Mr. and Mrs. Barton at the Auto Show.
10. My family (<u>saw</u>, seen) the Olympic Games.
11. Darcy has (saw, <u>seen</u>) the film before.
12. We (<u>saw</u>, seen) an exhibit of American Indian art.
13. I have never (saw, <u>seen</u>) a big league baseball game.
14. Have you (saw, <u>seen</u>) the movie *The Right Stuff?*
15. Ian (<u>saw</u>, seen) the President last week.

Use the Right Word

Say It Right   Hear It Right

A. Say these sentences over until the correct use of *sang* and *sung* sounds natural to you.

1. They sang with the band.
2. Who sang at the concert?
3. We sang in chorus yesterday.
4. She had sung that before.
5. The choir had sung.
6. Can you sing that song?
7. George had sung one song.
8. Have you ever sung here?

B. Say these sentences over until the correct use of *spoke* and *spoken* sounds natural to you.

1. Has Don spoken to you?
2. He spoke to Julie.
3. The principal spoke to us.
4. We had spoken to her.
5. Mother spoke to my teacher.
6. The baby spoke one word.
7. Lou has not spoken to me.
8. Who spoke at the meeting?

Write It Right

Write the correct word from the two words given.

1. The quartet (<u>sang</u>, sung) in the mall last weekend.
2. Have you ever (sang, <u>sung</u>) in a chorus?
3. Her cousin had (sang, <u>sung</u>) just before she did.
4. We (<u>sang</u>, sung) around the campfire.
5. Sara, Lois, Sam, and Chuck (<u>sang</u>, sung) a medley.
6. Ginny (<u>sang</u>, sung) beautifully in her recital.
7. Paul (<u>sang</u>, sung) a solo.
8. Roger and Donna had (sang, <u>sung</u>) a duet.
9. I have (spoke, <u>spoken</u>) to three movie stars.
10. The first speaker (<u>spoke</u>, spoken) on solar energy.
11. The second speaker (<u>spoke</u>, spoken) on nuclear energy.
12. They had both (spoke, <u>spoken</u>) to us before.
13. Tim (<u>spoke</u>, spoken) to the new students.
14. The coach (<u>spoke</u>, spoken) to us enthusiastically.
15. He has often (spoke, <u>spoken</u>) to us that way.

Ride
Rode
Ridden

Ring
Rang
Rung

Say It Right   Hear It Right

A. Say these sentences over until the correct use of *rode*
and *ridden* sounds natural to you.

1. Josh rode the ferris wheel.
2. I have ridden it often.
3. We rode our minibikes.
4. We have ridden them before.
5. Did you ride the train?
6. Have you ridden a mule?
7. Pat has ridden a horse.
8. I rode one last summer.

B. Say these sentences over until the correct use of *rang*
and *rung* sounds natural to you.

1. Who rang the doorbell?
2. The mail carrier rang it.
3. Has the bell rung yet?
4. I thought it rang.
5. The church bells rang.
6. Ring the bell for class.
7. The victory bell rang.
8. It had rung earlier.

Write It Right

Write the correct word from the two words given.

1. That jockey has (rode, ridden) in many races.
2. Have you ever (rode, ridden) in a rodeo?
3. Our club (rode, ridden) in the bike-a-thon.
4. My uncle (rode, ridden) his bicycle to work.
5. Gary has (rode, ridden) in many horse shows.
6. Have you ever (rode, ridden) a horse?
7. My brother (rode, ridden) in a dirt bike race Saturday.
8. The telephone (rang, rung) at midnight.
9. The student (rang, rung) the fire alarm.
10. When the ceremony ended, all the bells (rang, rung).
11. The doorbell (rang, rung) three times.
12. All the church bells had (rang, rung).
13. The fire alarm (rang, rung), but it was a false alarm.
14. The cathedral bells (rang, rung) at Christmas.
15. The camp dinner bell had (rang, rung) twice.

413

Swim
Swam
Swum

Throw
Threw
Thrown

Use the Right Word

Say It Right   Hear It Right

A. Say these sentences over until the correct use of *swam* and *swum* sounds natural to you.

1. Roy swam in the river.
2. Dozens of fish had swum by.
3. We swam after school.
4. Mandy swam for an hour.
5. I can swim three laps.
6. The salmon swam fast.
7. Wayne swam in the pool.
8. Sherry has swum there.

B. Say these sentences over until the correct use of *threw* and *thrown* sounds natural to you.

1. The mayor threw the ball.
2. He threw his cap in the air.
3. Luzinski was thrown out.
4. Bench threw him out.
5. Who threw that pass?
6. Have you thrown it away?
7. I can't throw that far.
8. The pitcher threw a curve.

Write It Right

Write the correct word from the two words given.

1. Curt has (swam, <u>swum</u>) in races for years.
2. The trout (<u>swam</u>, swum) toward the bait.
3. We have (swam, <u>swum</u>) in that race every year.
4. Sally (<u>swam</u>, swum) faster than I did.
5. Only one goldfish (<u>swam</u>, swum) in the bowl.
6. Sharks (<u>swam</u>, swum) in those waters.
7. Our team (<u>swam</u>, swum) laps for an hour.
8. Dolphins (<u>swam</u>, swum) around our boat.
9. Our newspaper had been (threw, <u>thrown</u>) into the bushes.
10. The cargo was (threw, <u>thrown</u>) out of the train by the blast.
11. We (<u>threw</u>, thrown) rice at the bride and groom.
12. Lynn (<u>threw</u>, thrown) the ball to Tanya.
13. The wrestler has (threw, <u>thrown</u>) his opponent.
14. Kent (<u>threw</u>, thrown) the winning pass.
15. They had (threw, <u>thrown</u>) out bread for the birds.

Wear
Wore
Worn

Write
Wrote
Written

Say It Right   Hear It Right

A. Say these sentences over until the correct use of *wore* and *worn* sounds natural to you.

1. They had worn T-shirts.
2. I have worn out my pen.
3. José wore glasses.
4. Gail wore out the battery.
5. May I wear your hat?
6. We all wore sandals.
7. I wore out my shoes.
8. Ryan had worn his jacket.

B. Say these sentences over until the correct use of *wrote* and *written* sounds natural to you.

1. Amy has written a letter.
2. Who wrote this song?
3. Who wrote that play?
4. Shakespeare wrote it.
5. Sue has written a song.
6. We wrote the assignment.
7. I had written two letters.
8. Did you write this poem?

Write It Right

Write the correct word from the two words given.

1. My sister (<u>wore</u>, worn) her new blazer.
2. We had (wore, <u>worn</u>) our heavy gloves to shovel snow.
3. Holly and Juanita were (wore, <u>worn</u>) out from the hike.
4. My sandals (<u>wore</u>, worn) out.
5. I have already (wore, <u>worn</u>) out my jeans.
6. We all (<u>wore</u>, worn) costumes to the party.
7. I have never (wore, <u>worn</u>) roller skates before.
8. To whom have you (wrote, <u>written</u>)?
9. How many letters have you (wrote, <u>written</u>) now?
10. Adam (<u>wrote</u>, written) a science fiction story.
11. We had (wrote, <u>written</u>) to our friends in Indiana.
12. Emily Dickinson (<u>wrote</u>, written) many poems.
13. Have you ever (wrote, <u>written</u>) to the President?
14. Who (<u>wrote</u>, written) "The Raven"?
15. Edgar Allan Poe (<u>wrote</u>, written) it.

415

416

These Additional Exercises may be used for additional practice of the concepts presented in this Section. Each exercise focuses on a single concept, and should be used after the page number indicated in parentheses.

Review

If you have not assigned these Additional Exercises before this time, you can also use them as an excellent Section Review.

ADDITIONAL EXERCISES

Using Irregular Verbs

Irregular Verbs   Write the correct verb from the two forms given.

1. The guests had (bring, brought) food to the party.
2. The doorbell has been (broke, broken) for weeks.
3. Our dog has (come, came) back home.
4. Mike had (chose, chosen) a window seat.
5. The wreckers had (did, done) their job.
6. I (did, done) most of the planning.
7. The robin (drank, drunk) from the puddle.
8. Chip has (ate, eaten) all of the apples.
9. The lock had (froze, frozen).
10. The mayor should have (gave, given) you a medal.
11. Most of the summer workers have (went, gone).
12. Tasha (went, gone) to a gymnastics camp.
13. Mr. Novy has (grew, grown) a beard.
14. Lee (knew, known) the words to every song.
15. Althea has just (ran, run) out of patience.
16. The telephone (rang, rung) only once.
17. Jake had never (rode, ridden) the subway alone.
18. Our choir has often (sang, sung) in other cities.
19. Have you ever (saw, seen) a salt marsh?
20. Many people (saw, seen) strange lights in the sky.
21. The witness had (spoke, spoken) the truth.
22. Nina (swam, swum) from the raft to the pier.
23. I've (threw, thrown) the letter away.
24. I wish I'd (wore, worn) a sun visor.
25. Someone had (wrote, written) to the manager.

MIXED REVIEW

Using Irregular Verbs

A. Using irregular verbs correctly Number your paper from 1 to 12. Write the correct verb from those in parentheses.

1. Brett (<u>chose</u>, chosen) the striped wallpaper.
2. Who (<u>ate</u>, eaten) the last piece of pizza?
3. Jan (<u>broke</u>, broken) her new camera.
4. The runners have (drank, <u>drunk</u>) all the lemonade.
5. Chuck has (went, <u>gone</u>) to the art exhibit.
6. I have (bring, <u>brought</u>) my basketball.
7. Houston has (grew, <u>grown</u>) rapidly.
8. Lynn has (<u>come</u>, came) for her violin lesson.
9. Has Chris ever (ran, <u>run</u>) for president?
10. Walt (<u>did</u>, done) the most work for the homecoming dance.
11. Miss Temple has (rode, <u>ridden</u>) the Orient Express.
12. I (<u>saw</u>, seen) the Big Dipper.

B. Identifying principal parts Number your paper from 1 to 10. Label three columns *Present, Past,* and *Past Participle.* List the three principal parts of the following irregular verbs.

1. speak speak, spoke, spoken
2. wear wear, wore, worn
3. know know, knew, known
4. throw throw, threw, thrown
5. give give, gave, given
6. go go, went, gone
7. swim swim, swam, swum
8. freeze freeze, froze, frozen
9. sing sing, sang, sung
10. write write, wrote, written

Mixed Review

These exercises provide review of the concepts presented in this Section. Each exercise challenges the students to apply several of the skills they have acquired during previous study. Because the "mixed" feature of these activities makes them more difficult, the teacher may wish to have less-advanced students do them orally or in small groups.

Using Grammar in Writing

These challenging and enjoyable activities allow the students to see how the concepts of grammar, usage, and mechanics may be applied in actual writing situations. Each exercise is designed to allow students practice in several of the skills they have acquired in this Section. The activities also provide opportunities for students to write creatively about a wide variety of interesting and unusual subjects.

USING GRAMMAR IN WRITING
Using Irregular Verbs

Two astronauts have been to your school to talk about their trip into space. When you leave school that day, your best friend is waiting to hear all about the talk. Retell some of the things you heard, using at least five of the following irregular verbs. Some of the verbs should be in the past participle form.

choose	have	see
do	go	sing
eat	ride	run
give	say	take
begin	wear	write

Many young people dream of becoming great athletes. Imagine that you have just completed your first big competition. You may pick any sport you like. Write about your experience. How had you felt before the competition began? How did you feel during your performance? Use several of the following verbs in your paragraph. Some should be in the past tense. Some should use the past participle form.

teach	grow	run	throw
break	know	see	wear
bring	ring	steal	take
fall	rise	swim	drink

Using Troublesome Pairs of Verbs

Section Objective

To choose the correct verb from verb pairs that are often confused

Preparing the Students

Point out that this is the third section of the handbook that deals with verbs. This indicates how important they are. It also indicates how many problems verbs can cause. Ask students for specific examples of problems resulting from using the wrong verb at the wrong time.

The title of this section uses the word *troublesome* to describe the verbs because they can be confused or misused in conversation and writing. Read and discuss the introduction on page 419.

Additional Resources

Mastery Test — pages 45–46 in the test booklet

Additional Exercises — pages 426–428 in the student text

Practice Book — pages 165–168

Duplicating Masters — pages 165–168

Special Populations — See special section at the back of this Teacher's Edition.

Presenting the Lessons

1. Read page 420. Ask students to explain the difference in meaning and use between *learn* and *teach*.

2. Assign and discuss the exercise on page 420.

3. Read page 421. Discuss the same questions as for page 420. You may want to take more time with *let* and *leave* since they are sometimes more difficult to differentiate.

Sometimes people confuse certain verbs. For example, they don't know whether to say, "Let me help" or "Leave me help." They aren't sure whether "She lay her books on the table" or "She laid her books on the table" is correct.

In this section you will study six pairs of verbs that are often confused. Learn to use these verbs correctly.

4. If the distinctions appear to be understood, assign and discuss the exercise on page 421. Otherwise, it is suggested that you do part of the exercise with the class first. You may want to ask students to act out the action of some of the sentences.

5. Repeat this procedure for the remaining four verb pairs.

Individualizing the Lessons

Less-Advanced Students

Be sure to discuss the difference between each pair of verbs.

You may want students to work on the exercises in this section in pairs and then share their answers with the class.

Advanced Students

After students have completed the exercises, ask them to prepare cartoon posters illustrating the confusing verb pairs.

Optional Practice

1. Have students write sentences using each of the six troublesome verb pairs correctly. You may want to ask volunteers to write their examples on the chalkboard.

2. Direct students to fill in the blanks with one of the verbs written above each group of sentences.

sit — set

1. _Sit_ on the porch.
2. _Set_ the plate down.
3. _Sit_ in the balcony.
4. _Sit_ on the bench.
5. _Set_ the glass on the table.

may — can

1. _May_ I borrow your radio?
2. Many men _can_ cook well.

Part 1 Using *Learn* and *Teach*

1. *Learn* means "to gain knowledge or skill." Example: I will *learn* French.

2. *Teach* means "to instruct or educate." Example: Kelly *teaches* her friends sign language.

The principal parts of these verbs are:

learn, learned, learned   teach, taught, taught

You use these verbs like this:

Learn

Present: Runners learn to breathe properly.
Past: Britt learned her sister's secret.
Past participle: Lee has learned some words in Spanish.

Teach

Present: That guard teaches the lifesaving course.
Past: Julia Child taught us French cooking.
Past participle: Mr. Mill has taught hundreds of music classes.

Exercise   Use *learn* and *teach* correctly.

Write the correct word from the two words given.

1. Will you (learn, <u>teach</u>) me the new plays before Saturday?
2. We (<u>learned</u>, taught) about dinosaurs at the museum.
3. We (<u>learned</u>, taught) of Ms. Moore's illness.
4. I (learned, <u>taught</u>) myself to play a banjo.
5. Mr. Good has (learned, <u>taught</u>) math for thirty years.
6. The actress had not (<u>learned</u>, taught) her lines.
7. My sister (learns, <u>teaches</u>) people to make clay pots.
8. My camp counselor (learned, <u>taught</u>) us water safety.
9. This course (learns, <u>teaches</u>) woodworking skills.
10. A flight student (<u>learns</u>, teaches) from a trained pilot.

Part 2 Using *Let* and *Leave*

1. *Let* means "to allow or permit." Example: *Let* me go.
2. *Leave* means "to go away (from)." Example: They will *leave* the party early. Leave also means "cause to remain." Example: Leave the books on the table.

The principal parts of these verbs are:

let, let, let   leave, left, left

You use these verbs like this:

Let

Present: This window lets in plenty of air.
Past: Sue's parents let her go on the trip.
Past participle: We have let you win.

Leave

Present: Don always leaves early.
Past: Nora left the breakfast dishes in the sink.
Past participle: Have they left us any chocolate cake?

Exercise   **Use *let* and *leave* correctly.**

Write the correct word from the two words given.

1. Please (<u>let</u>, leave) me help you with that.
2. (<u>Let</u>, Leave) me hold one of the new puppies.
3. Please (let, <u>leave</u>) these paintings dry.
4. We will (let, <u>leave</u>) a note for him.
5. Will you (<u>let</u>, leave) Ralph and Trisha go with you to the movies?
6. (<u>Let</u>, Leave) me take those packages.
7. Shouldn't we (<u>let</u>, leave) the others come?
8. Randy will (let, <u>leave</u>) the package in the hallway.
9. Did you (let, <u>leave</u>) your jacket in your locker?
10. The Jansens will (<u>let</u>, leave) us stay at their house.

---

3. Everyone __may__ have more ice cream.
4. __Can__ you run a mile?
5. __May__ I use your bike?

let — leave

1. __Let__ me know when you are ready to leave.
2. __Leave__ the package next door.
3. __Leave__ your camping gear in the boat.
4. __Let__ me walk to town with you.
5. __Leave__ enough apple juice for the others.

teach — taught — learn

1. __Teach__ us how to play the banjo.
2. The instructor will __teach__ the class traffic safety.
3. The tailor __taught__ her assistant to mend clothes.
4. The nursing student had to __learn__ to give shots.
5. The sculptor __taught__ a new technique.

lie — lay — laid

1. The workers came to __lay__ our new tile.
2. The trainer ordered the dog to __lay__ still.
3. The construction workers __laid__ the foundation for the house.
4. My brother likes to __lie__ in bed and read.
5. The colonel advised the soldiers to __lay__ down their arms.

rise — raise

1. The governor wants to __raise__ the gasoline tax.
2. My cousins wanted to __raise__ the five puppies.
3. Bread dough needs to __rise__.

4. We watched the kite ___rise___ above the trees.
5. The water level in the tank must ___rise___ to the top.

Extending the Lessons

You may want to review briefly transitive and intransitive verbs before doing this lesson. Then have students write sentences of their own using the verbs from this lesson. After each sentence, they should write *T* or *I* (for *Transitive* and *Intransitive*) depending on how the verb is used.

Part 3 Using *Lie* and *Lay*

1. *Lie* means "to recline or rest." It never has a direct object. Its principal parts are *lie, lay, lain.* Example: I *will lie* down for a while.

2. *Lay* means "to put or place." It takes a direct object. Its principal parts are *lay, laid, laid.* Example: *Lay* down your pencils.

Look again at the principal parts of these verbs:

lie, lay, lain   **lay, laid, laid**

You use these verbs like this:

Lie

Present:	My dog rarely lies on the porch.
Past:	The cyclist lay under the tree for a rest.
Past participle:	How long has that shovel lain there?

Lay

Present:	Jan always lays her coat on this chair.
Past:	He laid his books on the table.
Past participle:	She has laid aside her work.

Exercise   Use *lie* and *lay* correctly.

Write the correct word from the two words given.

1. The nurse advised me to (lie, lay) down for a while.
2. Jill's skateboard is (lying, laying) in the driveway.
3. I'm going to (lie, lay) on the beach for an hour or so.
4. Where did you (lie, lay) the scissors?
5. The kittens like to (lie, lay) under the rocking chair.
6. We found a wallet (lying, laying) on the front walk.
7. Please (lie, lay) those photographs on the table.
8. Litter was (lying, laying) all over the picnic area.

9. Several runners (lie, lay) down after the strenuous race.

10. (Lie, Lay) all of the drawings on this counter.

Part 4 Using *May* and *Can*

1. *May* is a helping verb. It is used to show permission. Example: The guard said that we *may* enter. It also shows possibility. Example: According to the forecast, it *may* rain tomorrow. Another form of the verb *may* is *might*. Example: Debbie *might* join the swim team.

2. *Can* is also used as a helping verb. It shows ability to do something. Example: Jim *can* repair bicycles. *Could* is another form of the verb. Example: We *could* hear a strange noise.

The verbs *may* and *can* have no principal parts.

Exercise Use *may* and *can* correctly.

Write the correct form from the two words given.

1. The owner said we (may, can) use his rowboat.
2. Glass and metal (may, can) conduct electricity.
3. I (may, can) see that Anna is angry.
4. Ms. Tower, (may, can) I turn in the paper tomorrow?
5. Ted's parents said that he (may, can) go to the carnival.
6. Now that I've taken swimming classes, I (may, can) do the backstroke.
7. (May, Can) we please stay out late tonight?
8. If you (may, can) jump higher, you will win.
9. If you make noise, the baby (may, can) wake up.
10. Ed is so strong that he (may, can) lift two hundred pounds.

Part 5 Using *Rise* and *Raise*

1. *Rise* means "to get up or to move upward." It has no direct object. Example: The player *rose* from the bench.

2. *Raise* means "to lift." It also means "to grow something." It always takes a direct object. Example: Pam *raised* her arms and cheered.

Look at the principal parts of these verbs:

rise, rose, risen   raise, raised, raised

These verbs are used like this:

Rise

Present: Bread rises because of yeast.
Past: One boy rose from his seat and walked out.
Past participle: After the sun had risen, we began our work.

Raise

Present: Sam raises the curtain at every show.
Past: The rancher raised cattle.
Past participle: The cadets have raised the flag.

Exercise   Use *rise* and *raise* correctly.

Write the correct form from the two words given.

1. Smoke (<u>rose</u>, raised) from the burning building.
2. Ms. Scott (rises, <u>raises</u>) Venus' flytraps in her garden.
3. My parents (rose, <u>raised</u>) my allowance.
4. When Jackson hit a home run, a cheer (<u>rose</u>, raised).
5. The curtain (<u>rose</u>, raised), but the stage was empty.
6. The waves (<u>rose</u>, raised) to a height of five feet.
7. Linda (rises, <u>raises</u>) her voice when she gets angry.
8. Please (rise, <u>raise</u>) the picture higher on the left.
9. A young player (<u>rose</u>, raised) to the major leagues.
10. The thief (rose, <u>raised</u>) the window and looked in.

Part 6 Using *Sit* and *Set*

1. *Sit* means "to be seated." It has no direct object. *Sat* is the past tense of *sit*. Example: We *sat* on the stage.

2. *Set* is a different word entirely. It means "to put or place." *Set* has a direct object. Example: *Set* the package on the counter.

The principal parts of these verbs are:

sit, sat, sat   set, set, set

You use these verbs like this:

Sit

Present:	Our cat always sits in the window.
Past:	Jay sat in the first row.
Past participle:	I have sat there many times.

Set

Present:	Ned usually sets the table.
Past:	I set the packages there last night.
Past participle:	Carol has set the plants on the back porch.

Exercise   **Use *sit* and *set* correctly.**

Write the correct word from the two words given.

1. Tim and Michelle will (<u>sit</u>, set) near the fifty-yard line.
2. Will you (sit, <u>set</u>) the luggage on the curb, please?
3. Please (sit, <u>set</u>) the groceries on the table.
4. We (<u>sat</u>, set) in the front row for the outdoor concert.
5. Do you want to (<u>sit</u>, set) on the front porch?
6. I would prefer to (<u>sit</u>, set) on the main floor.
7. I thought I had (sit, <u>set</u>) my lunch on this table.
8. The drivers (<u>sat</u>, set) waiting for the race to begin.
9. Won't you (<u>sit</u>, set) down and join us for dinner?
10. Sandy (sit, <u>set</u>) the mail on the buffet.

Additional Exercises

These Additional Exercises may be used for additional practice of the concepts presented in this Section. Each exercise focuses on a single concept, and should be used after the page number indicated in parentheses.

Review

If you have not assigned these Additional Exercises before this time, you can also use them as an excellent Section Review.

ADDITIONAL EXERCISES

Using Troublesome Pairs of Verbs

Troublesome Verbs Write the correct verb from the two forms given.

1. Ms. Sims (learned, taught) us how to use a table saw.
2. The lab mice (learned, taught) to run the maze.
3. The mice (learned, taught) themselves to run the maze.
4. Bob (learns, teaches) dances from his sister.
5. That will (learn, teach) him a lesson.
6. Curt (let, left) me play his xylophone.
7. (Let, Leave) Jan stay home if she wants to.
8. Don't (let, leave) your little sister at home.
9. I (let, left) Craig have first choice.
10. The turtle (lay, laid) on its back.
11. Sheila (lay, laid) the turtle right side up.
12. The cat was (lying, laying) in a pile of sweaters.
13. Sue had (lain, laid) her purse on the counter.
14. (May, Can) I please use your pocketknife?
15. JoAnn (may, can) write with either hand.
16. The snake (might, could) be a copperhead.
17. Nobody (might, could) understand why.
18. Steam (rose, raised) from the radiator.
19. The dentist (rose, raised) the chair.
20. Let the pizza dough (rise, raise) for thirty minutes.
21. (Rise, Raise) your left leg.
22. I will (sit, set) in the back seat.
23. Ben had (sat, set) his stopwatch.
24. Jackie (sat, set) down on the diving board.
25. Let's (sit, set) in the shade.

MIXED REVIEW

Using Troublesome Pairs of Verbs

A. Using the correct verb Number your paper from 1 to 12. Write the correct verb from those given in parentheses.

1. (May, <u>Can</u>) you ski down the highest slope?
2. Mrs. Green (<u>teaches</u>, learns) English to adults.
3. (<u>Let</u>, Leave) the child dress herself.
4. (<u>May</u>, Can) we please borrow that tape?
5. I (<u>learned</u>, taught) needlepoint from my sister.
6. The sun is (<u>rising</u>, raising) over the lake.
7. (Lie, <u>Lay</u>) your packages on the table.
8. Paul (<u>let</u>, leave) me use his golf clubs.
9. Gina (<u>raised</u>, rose) guppies last year.
10. The mechanic is (<u>lying</u>, laying) under the car.
11. Ken (<u>sat</u>, set) on the balcony.
12. Gary has (sat, <u>set</u>) the sprinkler in the yard.

B. Using troublesome verbs correctly Five of the following sentences contain errors in their use of verbs. Rewrite correctly any sentences that contain errors. If a sentence is already correct, write *Correct*.

c 1. Dad said that I may wear his parka.
2. Mr. Meyer is leaving us use his typewriter. *(letting)*
3. Ken set in the rocking chair. *(sat)*
c 4. Tina can do many kinds of magic tricks.
5. Ms. Kelly learned us the Morse Code. *(taught)*
c 6. Jerry let us use his stopwatch.
c 7. The dog has lain on the patio all day.
8. The audience raised up and cheered. *(rose)*
9. Sharon lay her bike on the grass. *(laid)*
c10. The builders have raised the roof of the house.

427

Mixed Review

These exercises provide review of the concepts presented in this Section. Each exercise challenges the students to apply several of the skills they have acquired during previous study. Because the "mixed" feature of these activities makes them more difficult, the teacher may wish to have less-advanced students do them orally or in small groups.

USING GRAMMAR IN WRITING
Using Troublesome Pairs of Verbs

A.   Do you remember your first week of school this year? Did you feel unsure of yourself in some ways? Did you have to ask an older student or a teacher for directions or advice? What have you learned about the school that you think a younger student should know? Write a paragraph of good, sound advice for the incoming students. The advice may be funny or serious. In your paragraph, use the following sets of verbs correctly.

learn—teach   let—leave   may—can

B.   You have been changed into a sales item in a large department store. Are you an appliance, a piece of sporting equipment, a toy, or a computer? You may choose to be anything that would be sold in a department store. As soon as someone buys you, the spell is broken. You become yourself again. Write about your experiences on the shelf. Write about the customers who look at you and perhaps try you out. In your paragraph, use the following sets of verbs correctly.

rise—raise   lie—lay   sit—set

Using Nouns

Section Objectives

1. To understand the concept of a noun and to identify nouns in sentences

2. To differentiate between common and proper nouns

3. To identify nouns used as subjects of sentences

4. To identify nouns used as direct objects

5. To identify nouns used as indirect objects

6. To identify predicate nouns

7. To differentiate between singular and plural nouns, and to form plurals correctly

8. To form and use possessive nouns correctly

Preparing the Students

Most students have little difficulty recognizing nouns in sentences at this point. Once the definition of a noun has been established, it is suggested that a class session be spent reinforcing what the students already know about nouns. The **Optional Practice** exercise for Part 1 may be used for this purpose.

Additional Resources

Diagnostic Test — page 3 in the test booklet

Mastery Test — pages 47–48 in the test booklet

Additional Exercises — pages 446–452 in the student text

Practice Book — pages 169–176

Duplicating Masters — pages 169–176

Special Populations — See special section at the back of this Teacher's Edition.

Part 1 What Are Nouns?

Nouns are used to name persons, places, and things.

Persons: friend, pilot, driver, Chris Evert Lloyd
Places: Charleston, beach, field, Disney World
Things: shoe, football, cloud, bread, Oldsmobile

Things named by nouns may be things you can see:

bike belt guitar spoon

429

429

Part 1

Objective

To understand the concept of a noun and to identify nouns in sentences

Presenting the Lesson

1. Read and discuss pages 429–430. Stress that many things that can't be seen, as well as things that can be seen, have names. Those names are nouns. Ask students for additional examples of all three types of nouns: persons, places, and things.

2. Assign and discuss Exercises A and B on pages 430–431.

Individualizing the Lesson

Less-Advanced Students

Have students make collages from old magazines showing as many nouns as possible. Display the collages around the room. Have other students try to list the nouns from these collages.

Advanced Students

Explain the difference between abstract nouns and concrete nouns. As a class, make a list of abstract nouns (examples: *life, reason, love, spirit*). Ask students to define them.

Optional Practice

Within a certain time limit, have individuals or teams gather lists of nouns. Categories for the lists may be assigned, such as nouns that begin with *w*, or nouns that have wheels, or an open category of nouns found in the room. Another variation is to ask students to name

430

Other things named by nouns may be things you cannot see:

pain   science   language   law

Still other things named by nouns are ideas:

friendship   courage   honesty   sadness
freedom   poverty   religion   Christianity

A noun is a word used to name a person, place, or thing.

Exercises   Find the nouns.

A.   Number your paper from 1 to 10. List the nouns in each of the following sentences.

1. Two waiters shoved the chairs and tables against the wall.
2. The wind blew the snow into enormous drifts.
3. The rains made a pond by the side of the road.
4. An hour and ten minutes had passed.
5. The words were on the tip of his tongue.
6. Put your foot on the ladder.
7. A fuzzy orange caterpillar crept up the tree.
8. The meadow behind the barn was covered with flowers.
9. There is a wide porch along the back of the house.
10. The company pumps 80,000 barrels of oil a day.

B.   Follow the directions for Exercise A.

1. Add up the last column again.
2. That news calls for a celebration.
3. The crowd had already left the auditorium.
4. On a clear day you can see the islands.
5. Temperatures in the Antarctic are rarely above zero.
6. The bread was made with bananas.
7. Matthew asked the clerk for change.

430

8. Tina waited for the bus for fifteen minutes in the rain.
9. The truth of the matter is another story.
10. Two sparrows took baths in the puddle.

Part 2 Common Nouns and Proper Nouns

What do you notice about the italicized words in the following sentence?

> One *boy*, *José Rodriguez*, and one *girl*, *Jenny Collins*, come from a nearby *city*, *Lansing*.

The italicized words are nouns. The words *boy*, *girl*, and *city* are called **common nouns.** A common noun is a general name. It does not name a particular boy, girl, or city.

The words *José Rodriguez*, *Jenny Collins*, and *Lansing*, on the other hand, name specific people and a specific city. They are called **proper nouns.** A proper noun always begins with a capital letter.

A common noun is a general name for a person, place, or thing.

A proper noun is the name of a particular person, place, or thing.

Common Nouns	Proper Nouns
team	Georgia Bulldogs
bridge	Golden Gate Bridge
encyclopedia	World Book
company	Jordan Marsh Company
nation	Finland

As the above list shows, a noun may consist of more than one word.

431

Part 2

Objective

To differentiate between common and proper nouns

Presenting the Lesson

1. Read and discuss page 431. Ask students for further examples of common and proper nouns, including some that are more than one word.

2. You may wish to do Exercise A on page 432 with the class. Assign and discuss Exercise B on page 432. Perhaps discuss why proper nouns need to be capitalized and common nouns do not. Exercise C is a good one to do orally and expands well into a class word game which you may wish to use as described below in **Optional Practice.**

Individualizing the Lesson

Less-Advanced Students

Have students make two columns on their papers labeled *Common Nouns* and *Proper Nouns*. They may then list the nouns in the exercises under their appropriate headings. Do Exercise A together. Assign Exercise B for individual work.

Advanced Students

For Exercise C have students write sentences containing both the common and proper nouns.

431

Have them list five more common nouns and ask classmates to give two proper nouns for each category.

Optional Practice

An exercise that is both fun and beneficial to students is to have them see how many different nouns they can use to name themselves. They may need help getting started on the idea. Demonstrate it by doing a sample on the board.

Janis Andersen

student	jogger
sister	gymnast
granddaughter	friend
player	mechanic
singer	neighbor

Extending the Lesson

Give each student a newspaper article. Ask the students to underline all of the common nouns in the article. Have them circle all of the proper nouns.

Exercises   **Find the proper nouns.**

A.   Number your paper from 1 to 10. Write the proper nouns in each sentence. Capitalize them correctly.

1. We saw governor garfield in town.
2. I have never been to the everglades in florida.
3. My family visited toronto, montreal, and niagara falls during our vacation.
4. It was john glenn who became the first american sent into orbit.
5. She was an employee of atlanta national bank.
6. My aunt, vivian taylor, arrived yesterday on the train.
7. The clerk was talking to dan and sheila.
8. The schubert theater has closed.
9. Last night georgetown beat newport in basketball.
10. My parents took a cruise to puerto rico.

B.   Follow the directions for Exercise A.

1. The jefferson public library was open yesterday.
2. We used to go to a library on michigan avenue in chicago.
3. The village called blue hills is near three small lakes.
4. Last summer we went camping near bear lake in rocky mountain national park.
5. We visited sequoia national park in california.
6. I live near the choctawatchee river in florida.
7. We stayed at the holiday inn on market street in san francisco.
8. Our school is on the corner of north street and hickory avenue.
9. We saw the san diego chargers play the green bay packers.
10. That's ellis island and the statue of liberty over there.

C. Writing On a sheet of paper, write each of the following common nouns. Next to each common noun, write the proper noun it suggests to you. Then write a sentence using the proper noun. Answers will vary.

Example: street   Market Street
              We went to the new theater on Market Street.

1. school   3. building   5. book   7. ocean
2. car   4. country   6. magazine 8. company

Part 3 Nouns Used as Subjects

The subject of a sentence tells who or what is being talked about. Nouns are often used as subjects.

The goalie stopped the ball.
(The noun *goalie* is the subject of the verb *stopped*.)

Into the room came Ken and Martha.
(The nouns *Ken* and *Martha* are subjects of the verb *came*.)

In some sentences, the subject may not be right next to the verb. Other words may separate them.

The edge of the rink melted.

What melted? Not the whole rink, just the edge.
Edge is the subject of *melted*.

Exercises **Find the nouns as subjects.**

A. Number your paper from 1 to 10. Write the nouns used as subjects in each of the following sentences.

1. My mother drove slowly around the detour.
2. The kittens were playing with the yarn.
3. The heavy rains forced many cars off the road.

433

Part 3

Objective

To identify nouns used as subjects of sentences

Presenting the Lesson

1. Read and discuss page 433. This lesson should be easy after the extensive work with subjects and simple subjects in Section 1 of the text. Tell students that this section is a review of what they have already studied about subjects. You may want to review briefly the definitions of the terms *subject*, *predicate*, *noun*, and *verb*. Remind students to ask themselves the question *who* or *what is doing something?* in the sentence to find the subject.

2. You may want to do Exercise A on pages 433–434 with the class. Assign and discuss Exercise B on page 434. After picking out the noun that is the subject of the sentence, have students identify all the other nouns in the sentence.

Individualizing the Lesson

Less-Advanced Students

Work orally with students for Exercise A. Have them divide the sentences in Exercise B into subjects and predicates.

Advanced Students

Remind students that the subject does not always precede the verb. (Review pages 356–358.) Have students find the subjects in these sentences.

1. Into the drain swirled the water.
2. There sat Mr. Maloney.

433

3. From the basement came a musty <u>odor.</u>
4. Below the city streets roared the <u>subway.</u>
5. Here is the <u>unicycle.</u>

Optional Practice

Put the following sentences on a worksheet. Have students fill in a subject noun in each sentence. Answers will vary.

1. The huge, furry _____ crashed through the wooden gate.
2. The tall, green _____ stretched to the sky.
3. The bright, twinkling _____ lit up the sky.
4. The small, round _____ growled noisily in its cage.
5. The cool, flashy _____ ambled through the door.
6. The small, speedy _____ raced through the yard.

Extending the Lesson

Ask students to find an article in a newspaper or magazine that is of interest to them. Have them circle all the subject nouns.

Part 4

Objective

To identify nouns used as direct objects

Presenting the Lesson

1. Read and discuss pages 434–436. Since students have already worked with transitive verbs in Section 3, this lesson should not be difficult for them. It is important to re-emphasize, however, the difference

434

4. Our <u>troop</u> is sponsoring a party for the children in the <u>hospital.</u>
5. His <u>pocket</u> was full of nails and washers.
6. The <u>handle</u> of the screwdriver was yellow.
7. The <u>jets</u> thundered off the deck of the carrier.
8. The <u>steps</u> could have been slippery.
9. The <u>bottom</u> of the bag was wet.
10. <u>John Steinbeck</u> wrote the novel *Of Mice and Men.*

B. Follow the directions for Exercise A.

1. The <u>Incas</u> built a great walled city in Peru.
2. The <u>voices</u> of the speakers did not carry to the rear of the <u>gym.</u>
3. At the concert Ms. <u>Maney</u> sat near us on the main floor of the <u>auditorium.</u>
4. In the morning his <u>headlights</u> were still on.
5. The <u>game</u> was delayed because of rain.
6. In England many <u>people</u> like marmalade.
7. Our <u>cafeteria</u> serves the best lasagna.
8. <u>Mercury</u> is the planet nearest to the sun.
9. Which <u>singer</u> is your favorite?
10. The <u>canary</u> in the cage sang continuously.

Part 4 Nouns Used as Direct Objects

A noun used as a direct object receives the action of a transitive verb. A direct object answers the question *whom?* or *what?* after the verb.

> The arrow hit the *target*.   Peggy threw the *basketball*.

The nouns *target* and *basketball* are direct objects. They answer the questions: *Hit what?* and *Threw what?*

434

Now study these examples.

You can buy magazines at the corner store.

Verb: *can buy*
Buy *what:* *magazines*
Direct object: *magazines*

Ramona directed Tom to the turnpike.

Verb: *directed*
Directed *whom:* *Tom*
Direct object: *Tom*

You have learned that subjects and verbs may be **compound,** which means "having more than one part." Direct objects may also be compound. Look at this example.

We saw *Donna, Linda,* and *Pat.*

Verb: *saw*
Saw *whom:* *Donna, Linda, Pat*
Direct objects: *Donna, Linda, Pat*

Diagraming Sentences Containing Direct Objects

When you diagram a sentence, place a direct object on the horizontal line following the verb. Separate it from the verb by a vertical line that does not cut through the subject-verb line.

Example: Shari enjoys music.

Shari	enjoys	music

For compound direct objects, split the horizontal line after the verb. Make as many parallel direct object lines as you need. Put the vertical line before the split, to show that all the words that follow are direct objects.

between subject nouns and object nouns. (Subjects perform the action; objects receive it.) Also review the terms *transitive* and *intransitive*.

2. "Diagraming Sentences Containing Direct Objects," pages 435–436. Diagram form is always helpful in demonstrating the relationships of words in a sentence. Again, however, individual students should not be assigned diagraming exercises unless they demonstrate a thorough understanding of diagraming and find it comfortable to do.

3. Assign and discuss Exercises A and B on page 436.

Individualizing the Lesson

Less-Advanced Students

Have students first find the verbs in the sentences. Then have them read each verb followed by the question *what?* The answer should give them the noun that is the direct object.

Have them list in two columns on their papers the verbs and the direct objects for each sentence in the exercises.

Advanced Students

Write the following verbs on the chalkboard: *kicked, passed, sailed, lifted, drove, scooped.* Have the students write one sentence for each verb. Each verb should have a direct object.

Optional Practice

Follow the directions for Exercise A on page 436.

1. Claudia tried windsurfing.
2. Marcus bought two concert tickets.
3. Pass the carrots, please.
4. Kay plays soccer and volleyball.

5. Mr. Minsky organized the <u>meeting</u>.
6. The elevator operator pushed the emergency <u>button</u>.
7. Some cats sharpen their <u>claws</u> on furniture.
8. Jan stripped the <u>paint</u> off the antique chest.
9. We drove a <u>jeep</u> on the beach.
10. Justin called the <u>play</u>.

Extending the Lesson

Ask students to find an article in a newspaper or magazine that is of interest to them. Have them circle all the direct objects.

Example: We saw Ralph, Sam, and Ed.

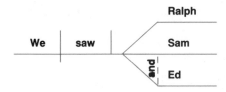

Exercises   Find the nouns used as direct objects.

A. Find the <u>direct objects</u> in the following sentences. Use diagrams or whatever method your teacher suggests.

1. Judy prepared the <u>spaghetti</u>.
2. Our coach clocked the <u>race</u>.
3. The vaporizer cleared my stuffed <u>nose</u>.
4. Adam took a big <u>piece</u> of pizza.
5. Barb suggested a possible <u>solution</u>.
6. The mechanic installed a new <u>muffler</u>.
7. Did you wash the <u>car</u>?
8. I've heard that <u>song</u> before.
9. Bob dropped the <u>book</u> into the return slot.
10. Brenda took a <u>swing</u> at the ball.

B. Follow the directions for Exercise A.

1. You should always use <u>caution</u> in shop class.
2. We climbed the <u>stairs</u> of the lighthouse.
3. Release the <u>clutch</u> slowly.
4. Mozart composed <u>music</u> when just five years old.
5. David could have found the <u>way</u> blindfolded.
6. Polish the <u>candlesticks</u> carefully.
7. Doris bought a <u>coat</u> and a <u>dress</u>.
8. The worker removed the <u>lid</u> from the manhole.
9. Erica and her two cousins solved the <u>puzzle</u>.
10. During the storm, three tugboats entered the <u>harbor</u>.

Part 5 Nouns Used as Indirect Objects

So far you have learned three basic parts of the sentence: *subject-verb-object*. Now you will learn several other parts of the sentence. You will see that nouns can be used in all of these other sentence parts. The part you will learn about first is the **indirect object** of the verb.

The indirect object tells to whom (or to what) or for whom (or for what) about the verb.

Subject	Verb	Indirect Object	Direct Object
Paula	told	her parents	the news.
Linda	showed	Sam	the pamphlet.
Carl	gave	his jade plant	some water.
I	brought	my sister	the tape.

A sentence contains an indirect object only if there is also a direct object. The indirect object comes between the verb and the direct object. The words *to* or *for* never appear before the indirect object.

Nouns used as indirect objects may also be **compound.**

The coach gave *Andy* and *Tim* new equipment.

Diagraming Sentences Containing Indirect Objects

An indirect object is shown on a line below the main line of the sentence.

Alice showed Pat her camera.

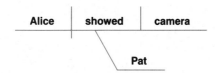

437

Part 5

Objective

To identify nouns used as indirect objects

Presenting the Lesson

1. Read and discuss page 437. Emphasize the difference between indirect objects and objects of prepositions. This is sometimes difficult for students to see. Point out that although an indirect object tells *to whom* (or *to what*) or *for whom* (or *for what*), the indirect object never follows the words *to* or *for*. It should follow the verb, and, in most cases, be followed by a direct object. (All of the exercise sentences have both indirect and direct objects.) Have students locate the direct object first. For example:

Sarah gave Ron a kite.
  Gave what? *kite* (direct object)
  To whom? *Ron* (indirect object)

After the direct object has been identified, the student can determine if there is an indirect object. Present several examples of this kind to the class. Be sure the students recognize that in a sentence, the indirect object comes first and is followed by the direct object.

2. "Diagraming Sentences Containing Indirect Objects," pages 437–438. Use this part of the chapter only with advanced students.

Individualizing the Lesson

Less-Advanced Students

1. For the exercises, ask students to divide their papers into four columns. Label them *Subject, Verb, In-*

437

Notice that the indirect object is connected to the verb by a slanted line.

For compound indirect objects, continue the slanted line a little farther down. Then make as many parallel indirect object lines as you need.

Bob wrote Chris and Jean a letter.

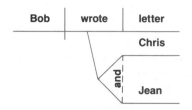

Exercises   **Find the nouns used as indirect objects.**

A. Find the indirect objects in the following sentences. Use diagrams or whatever method your teacher suggests.

1. Tracy threw Mike a curve.
2. My grandmother taught her parakeet two new words.
3. Bill gave Eileen the directions.
4. Carl took the guests their coffee.
5. Ms. Meyers gave the boys a few tennis pointers.
6. Vicki sent Joe and Jim an invitation to the party.
7. We should have offered Sam a ride.
8. The class gave Mr. Collins a gift.
9. Have you given the chair a second coat of paint?
10. Alice sent Ginny several postcards from Texas.

Find any indirect and direct objects in these sentences.

1. Last week Rhoda showed her dog at the dog show.
2. Give Linda a hint.
3. Beth showed signs of progress.
4. Ms. Jamison showed the class some beautiful slides.
5. They sent Mr. McCall flowers.

438

6. Mr. Hoffman sent (Pete) and (Phil) to the store.
7. Cindy gave the <u>subject</u> some (thought.)
8. Have you showed <u>Jack</u> your new (watch?)
9. My little brother pestered (Jim.)
10. Terry baked <u>Nancy</u> some (brownies) for her birthday.

Part 6   Predicate Nouns

You remember that a linking verb links the subject to some word in the predicate. If that word is a noun, it is called a **predicate noun.** It usually means the same thing as the subject. It may explain the subject.

> This machine is a *drill*.
> Jade is a very hard *stone*.
> Sally became *president* of the class today.
> Sylvia has been my best *friend*.

The nouns *drill*, *stone*, *president*, and *friend* are predicate nouns. In many sentences, the predicate nouns and the subject can be reversed without changing the meaning. The two parts are roughly equal.

> The boy is *Jack*.   Jack is the *boy*.

Predicate nouns may also be compound, as in this example:

> Rick is a good *singer* and *musician*.

Diagraming Sentences Containing Predicate Nouns

The diagram for a sentence containing a predicate noun is different from that for a sentence containing a direct object.

> Janet was the leader.

| Janet | was \ leader |

439

Extending the Lesson

Have students write five sentences following this pattern: Subject-Verb-Indirect Object-Direct Object.

Part 6

Objective

To identify predicate nouns

Presenting the Lesson

1. Introduce predicate nouns by providing several examples of sentences containing predicate nouns.

> The leader is Juan.
> Juan is the leader.

Point out that there are three important rules to remember: (1) Predicate nouns follow linking verbs (*be* verbs and similar words); (2) predicate nouns refer to the same person, place, or thing as the subject; and (3) predicate nouns can usually trade positions with the subject. Read and discuss pages 439–440.

2. "Diagraming Sentences Containing Predicate Nouns" (pages 439–440). Carefully point out to the students the difference between a diagram with a predicate noun and one with a direct object.

3. Remind students that linking verbs act as a kind of equal sign. Do Exercise A on page 440 with the students before assigning Exercise B.

Individualizing the Lesson

Less-Advanced Students

1. Skip the section on diagraming with this group.

439

Notice that the predicate noun is on the horizontal line in the same position as the direct object. But the line that separates the predicate noun from the verb slants back toward the subject. This is to show the close relationship between the predicate noun and the subject.

For sentences containing compound predicate nouns, use parallel lines. Place the slanted line before the split in the main line.

Amy is a fine athlete and a loyal friend.

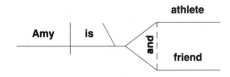

Exercises Find the predicate nouns.

A. Find the predicate nouns in these sentences. Your teacher may ask you to diagram the sentences.

1. The course was a challenge for everyone.
2. Cory McCowan was one tough customer.
3. *Nova* is my favorite television program.
4. The library is the old building on the corner of Orrington Avenue and Church Street.
5. The piano was a Steinway.
6. Muncie is not the capital of Indiana.
7. Rhode Island is the smallest state in the Union.
8. Dr. Patterson is a veterinarian.
9. My sister is a teller at this bank.
10. Dr. Rebecca Barth is our dentist and our neighbor.

B. Some sentences below contain linking verbs, which are completed by predicate nouns. Some sentences contain action verbs, which are completed by direct objects. Find the predicate nouns and (direct objects) in these sentences.

Examples: Julie *ate* a big *lunch.*
    Ate is an action verb.
    Lunch is the direct object.

    Julie *is* a dancer.
    Is is a linking verb.
    Dancer is a predicate noun.

1. Willie became my best friend.
2. Marlene seems an excellent organizer.
3. A job at the pool might be Brad's chance.
4. The council proposed two new laws.
5. Polo is a game for horseback riders.
6. Darren closed the shutters and waited.
7. My father watched the basketball game on TV this afternoon.
8. The Lions Club donated the money for the new children's park.
9. She is the manager at the Holiday Inn.
10. The mayor's action caused an uproar among the city councilmen at the meeting.

Part 7 The Plurals of Nouns

When a word stands for one thing, it is **singular.** These are singular forms: *girl, city, classroom,* and *child.* When a word stands for more than one thing, it is **plural.** These are plural forms: *girls, cities, classrooms,* and *children.*

Here are seven rules for forming the plurals of nouns:

1. To form the plural of most nouns, just add -s:

pencils	cows	buildings	friends
trees	games	roads	logs

441

will confuse students no matter how it is stated because of the large number of exceptions. Point out that musical words, such as *alto, soprano, solo*, always add only an *s*. Use a dictionary exercise to show students how to find noun plurals of which they are not sure. Sometimes dictionaries will give more than one acceptable plural form (*mosquitoes, mosquitos*). Usually the first form is preferred. Stress the importance of using one form consistently in any written piece.

Rule 5 also has many exceptions (*hoofs, hooves*), as does Rule 6 (*fish, fishes*). As before, one form should be used consistently in a single piece of writing. Most noun plurals mentioned in Rule 7 will already be familiar to most students.

2. Assign and discuss Exercises A and B on page 443. Have students check their answers in the dictionary.

Individualizing the Lesson

Less-Advanced Students

Have students refer to the rules as they do the exercises and tell which rule applies to each noun.

Advanced Students

Have students list at least one additional example for each of the seven rules. Have them check each other's examples in a dictionary.

Optional Practice

After students have studied all the rules on pages 441–442, have a spelling bee using only plural nouns. Divide the class into teams. Dictate words from the following word list, from the text, or from the

2. When the singular ends in *s*, *sh*, *ch*, *x*, or *z*, add *-es*:

gases	losses	brushes	churches	boxes
buses	waltzes	rashes	porches	foxes

3. When the singular ends in *o*, add *-s*:

studios	sopranos	Eskimos	solos
radios	altos	egos	silos

Exceptions: For a few nouns ending in *o* with a consonant before it, add *-es:*

potatoes   tomatoes   heroes   echoes

4. When a singular noun ends in *y* with a consonant before it, change the *y* to *i* and add *-es*:

baby—babies	country—countries	hobby—hobbies
army—armies	cry—cries	courtesy—courtesies

When a vowel comes before the *y*, do not change the *y* to *i*. Just add *-s* to the singular.

boy—boys	play—plays	day—days
valley—valleys	monkey—monkeys	tray—trays

5. For most nouns ending in *f*, add *-s*. For some nouns ending in *f* or *fe*, however, change the *f* to *v* and add *-es* or *-s*:

roof—roofs	leaf—leaves	half—halves	self—selves
belief—beliefs	elf—elves	calf—calves	shelf—shelves

6. Some nouns are the same for both singular and plural:

deer	sheep	trout	salmon	moose
tuna	bass	pike	grouse	elk

7. Some nouns form their plurals in special ways:

child—children	foot—feet	woman—women
mouse—mice	tooth—teeth	man—men

Using a Dictionary To Find Plurals

Here is a dictionary entry for the word *knife*. Notice that the entry shows the plural, *knives*. Most dictionaries show the plural of a noun if the plural is formed in an irregular way. When you are in doubt about plurals, check a dictionary.

---

plural

knife (nīf) **n.,** *pl.* **knives** [OE. *cnif*: for IE. base see KNEAD] **1.** a cutting or stabbing instrument with a sharp blade, single-edged or double-edged, set in a handle **2.** a cutting blade, as in a machine —**vt. knifed, knif'ing 1.** to cut or stab with a knife ☆**2.** [Colloq.] to use underhanded methods in order to hurt, defeat, or betray —☆**vi.** to pass into or through something quickly, like a sharp knife —☆**under the knife** [Colloq.] undergoing surgery —**knife' like' adj.**

Exercises   Form the plurals of nouns.

A.   Write the plural of each of these nouns.

1. tomato — tomatoes	5. echo — echoes	9. table — tables	13. company — companies
2. thief — thieves	6. loaf — loaves	10. dress — dresses	14. stay — stays
3. key — keys	7. lady — ladies	11. deer — deer	15. dormouse — dormice
4. daisy — daisies	8. coach — coaches	12. woman — women	16. way — ways

B.   Read the following plural nouns. If the plural has been formed incorrectly, write the correct form. If the plural is correct, write *Correct*.

1. tattoos C	6. selfs — selves	11. churches C	16. skies C
2. joys C	7. boxes C	12. parties C	17. donkies — donkeys
3. buses C	8. patchs — patches	13. crashs — crashes	18. citys — cities
4. babys — babies	9. potatos — potatoes	14. firemans — firemen	19. knifes — knives
5. twos C	10. wolves C	15. moose C	20. flies C

443

---

students' other work. Alternate teams. The winning team will be the one with the most students.

Rule 2:   crosses, boxes, churches, catches, benches, crashes, wishes, dishes, splashes, dresses, touches, flashes, patches, glasses, guesses, mixes, passes, pushes, mashes, circuses, bunches

Rule 3:   zoos, altos, sopranos, solos

Rule 4:   armies, countries, cries, families, histories, parties, stories, tries, worries, babies, industries, puppies, cookies, bakeries, enemies, replies

Extending the Lesson

Put the following words on a worksheet. Have students write *P* after each plural noun and write its singular form, and *S* after each singular noun and write its plural form. If the word is the same form for both singular and plural, students should write *S* and *P*.

S 1. a man — men	P 16. her shoes — shoe
P 2. two churches — church	S 17. your suitcase — suitcases
S 3. our desk — desks	S 18. company — companies
S 4. verb — verbs	S 19. the puzzle — puzzles
S 5. the old goose — geese	S 20. the watch — watches
P 6. several pints — pint	S 21. the circus — circuses
S 7. the red fox — foxes	P 22. pillows — pillow
S 8. his shirt — shirts	S 23. new blanket — blankets
S 9. the bus — busses	S 24. a funny play — plays
SP 10. fish	S 25. new business — businesses
P 11. some pictures — picture	SP 26. deer
S 12. their house — houses	P 27. her children — child
S 13. the young boy — boys	P 28. old buffaloes — buffalo
S 14. airplane — airplanes	P 29. the valleys — valley
SP 15. huge moose	P 30. apostrophes — apostrophe

Part 8

Objective

To form and use possessive nouns correctly

Presenting the Lesson

1. Discuss the meaning of the word *possession*. Show that besides indicating ownership (*the car of my brother*), it can also refer to a relationship (*the sister of Bob*) or other connection (*the friend of my uncle*). *Possess* can also mean "to use" (*the crib of the baby*), or simply "to have" (*the collar of the dog*). Ask students for the shorter way of saying each of these phrases and discuss the idea of possession in each: *the saw of the lumberjack, the ox of Paul Bunyan, the bridle of the horse, the business partner of my aunt.*

Possessive nouns are easy to identify because they always have an apostrophe. They are not, however, as easy to form. Be sure students understand the difference between these different terms: *proper noun, plural noun,* and *possessive noun.*

2. Read and discuss pages 444–445. Be sure students understand the proper formation of possessive nouns: adding only *'s* to the singular noun, adding only an apostrophe to the plural noun ending in *s,* or adding *'s* if it ends in any other letter. Students often become confused if they are asked to change a singular noun to plural possessive. Since this is really two processes, instruct them to perform each step separately. Form the plural first; then, make it possessive. If students

444

Part 8 Possessive Nouns

Nouns can show ownership or possession.

Laura's house   *Bill's* lunch   *Jill's* car

Nouns can also show that something is a part of a person.

Jane's sincerity   *Barbara's* ability   *Tom's* face

The *italicized* words above are called **possessive nouns** because they show possession of the noun that follows.

Forming Possessives of Singular Nouns

Do you see what it is about *Jane's* and *Barbara's* that is a sign of possession? It is the ending—the apostrophe and the -*s.*

To form the possessive of a singular noun, add an apostrophe and -*s.*

Singular Noun	Possessive Form
Sharon	Sharon's
Ms. Hernandez	Ms. Hernandez's
waitress	waitress's
Charles	Charles's

Forming Possessives of Plural Nouns

There are two things to remember in writing the possessive of a plural noun:

If the plural noun ends in s, simply add an apostrophe.

Plural Noun	Possessive Form
teams	teams'
drivers	drivers'
runners	runners'
waitresses	waitresses'

444

If the plural noun does not end in s, add an apostrophe and s.

Plural Noun	Possessive Form
children	children's
men	men's
women	women's

Diagraming Sentences Containing Possessive Nouns

In a diagram, possessive nouns are written on lines slanting down from the nouns with which they are used.

Larry is Jeff's teammate.

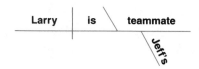

Exercises   Show the possessive forms of nouns.

A.   Write the possessive forms of these nouns.

1. secretaries'
2. banker's
3. James's
4. Peggy's
5. artist's
6. photographer's
7. Mr. Briggs's
8. Ms. Holmes's
9. Charles Smith's
10. customers'
11. day's
12. hours'
13. Lee's
14. Ms. Voss's
15. designers'

B.   Write the possessives of the following nouns.

1. journalist's
2. driver's
3. women's
4. ruler's
5. group's
6. ministers'
7. girl's
8. principal's
9. father's
10. Indians'
11. mothers'
12. teacher's
13. Smith's
14. leaders'
15. Choctaw's

try to perform both processes simultaneously, they are likely to err.

3. "Diagraming Sentences Containing Possessive Nouns" (page 445). Like other modifiers, possessive nouns appear on a slanted line under the words they modify.

4. Assign and discuss Exercises A and B on page 445. Suggest that students examine each word in the exercises to decide whether it is singular or plural before writing its possessive form.

Individualizing the Lesson

Less-Advanced Students

Do Exercise A orally. Then, before assigning Exercise B as independent work, determine as a class which nouns are singular and which are plural.

Advanced Students

Have students complete the singular and plural possessive forms of the following nouns.

child
group
princess
plumber
lawyer
woman
deer

Optional Practice

Have students write sentences to illustrate the various forms of a noun: singular, possessive, plural, and plural possessive. Either have students choose their own nouns or give them a list of ten to choose from.

ADDITIONAL EXERCISES

Using Nouns

A. Identify Nouns   Number your paper from 1 to 10. Write the <u>nouns</u> in each of the following sentences.

1. The mushrooms grew under a log.
2. Dead leaves clogged the sewers on our street.
3. Turn up the radio, Bridget.
4. Jason played his guitar at the assembly.
5. Last year our class took a tour of Gettysburg.
6. Leah saw a game in the new stadium recently.
7. Some students disagreed about the moral of the story.
8. My grandmother has an excellent memory.
9. The mayor asked her aides for an explanation.
10. Floods caused damage throughout the state.

B. Proper Nouns   Number your paper from 1 to 10. Write the proper nouns in each sentence. Capitalize them.

1. Is egypt part of africa?
2. In july we visited storm lake in iowa.
3. On monday the public pools will open.
4. The eagle scouts camped in shawnee national forest.
5. Does chicago have two baseball teams?
6. The city is the home of the cubs and the white sox.
7. Only one yellow chevy was parked on the street.
8. On the front page of the *herald* was a photo of ann.
9. Isn't twelfth street now rosa parks boulevard?
10. The potomac river winds through virginia.

C. Nouns as Subjects   Number your paper from 1 to 10. Write the <u>nouns used as subjects</u> in each of the following sentences. Some subjects may be compound.

1. Sticky liquid oozed from the battery.

2. A long, red <u>car</u> rounded the curve.

3. Beside the basket was a <u>note</u>.

4. Piled on the shelf were <u>hats</u> of all kinds.

5. <u>Liz</u> tied a string to the light switch.

6. The dusty <u>floor</u> showed footprints.

7. There is a <u>picture</u> of Ed in the yearbook.

8. During the movie <u>Bobby</u> and <u>Ray</u> dozed.

9. On the table was a small <u>bell</u>.

10. Does the <u>referee</u> need glasses?

D. Nouns as Direct Objects   Number your paper from 1 to 10. Write the <u>nouns used as direct objects</u> in each of the following sentences. Some direct objects may be compound.

1. Caroline bought a <u>folder</u>.

2. He put the <u>report</u> on her desk.

3. Use exact <u>change</u>.

4. The smoke detector alerted the <u>family</u>.

5. Some reptiles lay <u>eggs</u>.

6. Cass wears bright <u>colors</u> and big <u>hats</u>.

7. Some people really prefer <u>leftovers</u>.

8. She cracked the <u>shell</u> with her teeth.

9. Have you heard the <u>score</u>?

10. Winter turned the <u>rocks</u> into ice castles.

E. Nouns as Indirect Objects   Number your paper from 1 to 10. Write the <u>indirect objects</u> in the following sentences. Some indirect objects may be compound.

1. Chris got <u>Ben</u> a chair.

2. The clerk gave <u>Cheryl</u> and <u>me</u> a funny look.

3. The Red Cross found the <u>family</u> another home.

4. Offer <u>Judy</u> some lemonade.

5. Did Rick lend <u>Jean</u> his umbrella?

6. The class wrote the <u>President</u> a letter.

7. Ms. Carver bought the <u>school</u> a new projector.

447

8. Tell <u>Vince</u> the rest of the story about the haunted house across the road.

9. Rita tossed <u>Alice</u> a pillow.

10. A nurse taught <u>Ms. Pardo</u> and the <u>troop</u> first aid.

F. Predicate Nouns Number your paper from 1 to 10. List the <u>predicate nouns</u> in these sentences. Some predicate nouns may be compound.

1. The truck's cargo was <u>gasoline</u>.
2. That tiny dog is a <u>chihuahua</u>.
3. *Barney Miller* was a popular television <u>show</u>.
4. The math teacher is also the track <u>coach</u> at the community center.
5. Her sister is her best <u>friend</u>.
6. Leslie is an <u>expert</u> in <u>judo</u>.
7. This beach is not private <u>property</u>.
8. Saturday is always a very short <u>day</u>.
9. Are the Riordans your <u>neighbors</u>?
10. Hank's first customers at his lemonade stand were his <u>aunt</u> and <u>uncle</u>.

G. Plurals of Nouns Number your paper from 1 to 30. Write the correct plural form of each word.

1. scratch *(scratches)*	11. fox *(foxes)*	21. tooth *(teeth)*
2. radio *(radios)*	12. potato *(potatoes)*	22. branch *(branches)*
3. child *(children)*	13. moss *(mosses)*	23. foot *(feet)*
4. deer *(deer)*	14. stereo *(stereos)*	24. inch *(inches)*
5. sky *(skies)*	15. county *(counties)*	25. self *(selves)*
6. wrench *(wrenches)*	16. elf *(elves)*	26. lobby *(lobbies)*
7. alley *(alleys)*	17. reef *(reefs)*	27. cross *(crosses)*
8. spy *(spies)*	18. bay *(bays)*	28. butterfly *(butterflies)*
9. hero *(heroes)*	19. dish *(dishes)*	29. maze *(mazes)*
10. mirror *(mirrors)*	20. player *(players)*	30. gentleman *(gentlemen)*

H. Possessives of Nouns Write the following phrases, adding the possessive forms asked for in parentheses.

> Example: the (plural possessive of *team*) schedules
> the teams' schedules

1. the (singular possessive of *city*) budget _{city's}
2. (singular possessive of *Amy*) loafers _{Amy's}
3. the (plural possessive of *class*) field trips _{classes'}
4. the (singular possessive of *glass*) rim _{glass's}
5. (singular possessive of *Jess*) plans _{Jess's}
6. (plural possessive of *deer*) habits _{deer's}
7. (plural possessive of *man*) shirts _{men's}
8. the (singular possessive of *show*) theme song _{show's}
9. the (plural possessive of *country*) leaders _{countries'}
10. Mr. (singular possessive of *Ross*) car _{Ross's}
11. the (plural possessive of *sandwich*) crusts _{sandwiches'}
12. the (singular possessive of *woman*) hands _{woman's}

Mixed Review

These exercises provide review of the concepts presented in this Section. Each exercise challenges the students to apply several of the skills they have acquired during previous study. Because the "mixed" feature of these activities makes them more difficult, the teacher may wish to have less-advanced students do them orally or in small groups.

MIXED REVIEW

Using Nouns

A. Identifying common and proper nouns Label two columns on your paper *Proper Nouns* and *Common Nouns.* Find the nouns in the following paragraph. List them in the correct columns.

In 1983, workers began a big project in New York City. They cleaned and repaired the Statue of Liberty. The statue, designed by Frederic Bartholdi, was a gift from France to the United States in 1884. After nearly a hundred years of service as a symbol of freedom, the statue, made of copper, showed serious signs of age. The Statue of Liberty was closed to visitors during this work. When the job was completed the famous monument once again lit the way into New York Harbor for people seeking freedom.

B. Identifying nouns and their uses Write the nouns from the following sentences. After each, write *Subject, Direct Object, Indirect Object,* or *Predicate Noun* to show how each is used.

1. Your photograph won first prize.
2. Barbara sent her aunt a get-well card.
3. Does Ms. Alvarez teach history?
4. Mrs. Barclay is a detective.
5. Trini served the guests sandwiches and cake.
6. Captain Simon is the pilot.
7. Len and his brother paid the vendor five dollars.
8. Give the baby her bottle.
9. Your jeans need a patch.
10. Eric has two brothers and one sister.

450

C. Using plural and possessive nouns correctly The following sentences contain ten errors in the use of plural and possessive nouns. Copy the sentences, correcting any errors in the use of plurals and possessives. If a sentence is already correct, write *Correct*.

comedies 1. Ellen likes ~~comedys~~ better than dramas.

trains 2. The ~~traines~~ will be late today.

c 3. Jan's arm was fractured in two places.

child's 4. The ~~childs'~~ shoes are too tight.

trout 5. Martha caught two bass and three ~~trouts~~.

editors, 6. The magazine's ~~editor's~~ read the contest ~~entrys~~.
entries
loaves 7. Michael bought four ~~loafs~~ of French bread.

c 8. The school's library is being remodeled.

c 9. Amy and Susan peeled the potatoes and sliced the tomatoes.

woman's 10. The ~~womans'~~ garden contains many varieties of flowers.

USING GRAMMAR IN WRITING
Using Nouns

A. Your class is turning an unused locker into a time capsule. The locker will be filled with carefully selected items that reflect the students' lives today. It will remain locked until your class's twenty-year reunion. Each class member must submit a paragraph that tells what items he or she thinks should be placed in the time capsule. Write your own paragraph. Include some specific names of records, tapes, books, magazines, and clothing brands. Circle each common noun. Underline each proper noun.

B. Imagine that you are a scientist who lives one hundred years in the future. You are visiting the site of an excavation. A house from the 1980's has been discovered there. The excavation team has asked you to analyze some of the odd items that have been found within the house. What do you think each item is? How was it used? Who might have used it?

Write down your comments for four of the items. For each object, first describe what the item looks like. Then answer each of the questions above. Remember that your guesses may be entirely wrong. You may, for example, decide that an egg beater was some sort of noisemaker. When you are finished with your comments, underline the nouns. Label each one S (subject), D.O. (direct object), or I.O. (indirect object).

Using Pronouns

Part 1 What Are Pronouns?

Study these sentences:

> When Roger saw Wendy, Roger spoke to Wendy.
> When Roger saw Wendy, he spoke to her.

The words *he* and *her* are pronouns. They stand for the nouns *Roger* and *Wendy*.

A pronoun is a word used in place of a noun.

A pronoun is a very useful word. It helps you write and talk smoothly and easily without losing track of your ideas and without repeating the same words too often.

Objective

To understand the function of the pronoun and to be able to use pronouns correctly in sentences

Presenting the Lesson

1. Read and discuss pages 453–455. Talk about the definition of the word *personal* and why the pronouns listed on page 454 are called *personal pronouns*. Stress the need to know the noun referred to in order to understand the meaning of the pronoun. If students are not familiar with pronouns, have them memorize the chart.

2. Read the exercise on page 455 aloud with the students and discuss the uses of the pronouns. This will be a good introduction to the rest of this section.

Individualizing the Lesson

Less-Advanced Students

1. You may want to display a chart of the pronouns in the box on page 454 for your students to refer to.

2. Have students complete the exercise on page 455. Afterwards, read a short story to them. Have them pay special attention to pronouns as they listen, and list each pronoun they hear on a sheet of paper. Then go through the story again, reading each pronoun. See which students have the complete list.

Advanced Students

Discuss the personal pronouns in the chart according to *person (first person,* person speaking; *second,*

How Pronouns Differ from Nouns

Nouns change only to show possession and number.

Pronouns differ from nouns. They change form according to their use in a sentence. Study these pairs of sentences to see how pronouns change form and how they differ from nouns.

Nouns	Pronouns
1. *Jerry* pruned the tree.	1. *He* pruned the tree.
2. Mr. Barnes helped *Jerry.*	2. Mr. Barnes helped *him.*
3. Mr. Barnes is *Jerry's* father.	3. Mr. Barnes is *his* father.
4. The *books* came yesterday.	4. *They* came yesterday.
5. Mr. Frank brought the *books*.	5. Mr. Frank brought *them.*

The Forms of Pronouns

Pronouns have three forms: *subject, object,* and *possessive.* Notice how the pronoun *she* changes as its use changes:

She left. (*She* is the subject.)
I saw *her.* (*Her* is the direct object.)
It is *hers.* (*Hers* is the possessive.)

The pronouns listed below are all called **personal pronouns**. Here are the forms you should know.

	Subject	Object	Possessive
Singular:	I	me	my, mine
	you	you	your, yours
	she, he, it	her, him, it	her, hers, his, its
Plural:	we	us	our, ours
	you	you	your, yours
	they	them	their, theirs

Notice the pronoun chosen for each of the following sentences. See how the form of each pronoun depends upon the use of the pronoun in the sentence.

1. The girls are here. *They* arrived early. (subject)
2. The workers left later. Ann saw *them*. (direct object)
3. Sean was early. Terry showed *him* the new aquarium. (indirect object)
4. The Boyles have moved. Caryl has *their* address. (possessive)
5. Karen is my sister. *She* is older than I am. (subject)

Exercise   Use pronouns correctly.

You will study many pronoun forms in the remaining parts of this section. The following sentences use pronouns correctly. Read each sentence aloud.

1. *We* tried the mushroom pizza.
2. The girl on the left is *she*.
3. Sam's friends congratulated *him* for winning the speech contest.
4. John sent *her* a valentine.
5. *We* girls are the winners.
6. *Our* friends are coming today.
7. Tom keeps *his* room clean.
8. The candidates made *their* speeches on cable television last night.
9. *Everybody* liked the movie.
10. *Everybody* has *her* own book.
11. *He* and *I* auditioned for the spring play.
12. The only volunteers were *she* and *I*.
13. Kim saw Todd and *her* together at the movies last Saturday afternoon.
14. Ms. Finch gave *him* and *me* extra help.
15. The yearbook editor gave *us* reporters a new deadline to meet.

person spoken to; *third*, person spoken about) and *number (singular and plural)*. This is a good bridge from grammar to reading and writing. Introduce examples of first-, second-, and third-person writing. Have students rewrite a paragraph, changing it from first to third person or vice versa. Good examples of second-person writing will be found in directions for assembly or recipes. These usually use imperative sentences with the implied *you*.

Optional Practice

Choose the correct pronoun in these sentences.

1. (We, Us) enjoyed the concert.
2. The winner of the contest is (he, him).
3. (She, Her) and (I, me) rode the tandem bicycle.
4. Claire gave (he, him) and (I, me) a ride home.
5. Everyone brought (his or her, their) poncho to the football game.
6. Mr. Marks gave (we, us) boys a job painting his garage.

Extending the Lesson

Have students list five people they know, five things in their homes, and five animals. Next to each noun, have them write every pronoun listed on page 454 that could refer to it. Then have them choose two of their subjects and write one paragraph (4–5 sentences) about each, using as many of the personal pronouns as they can.

Example:

My aunt—she, her, hers, you, your, yours

Objective

To use the subject form of pronouns correctly for subjects and predicate pronouns

Presenting the Lesson

1. Read and discuss page 456. Quickly review the term *linking verb* and the most common linking verbs, the forms of *be*.

2. Assign and discuss Exercises A and B on page 457. Remind students to try the pronoun alone if they are not sure of the correct choice.

Travis and (he, him) went to the store. *He* went to the store. Travis and *he* went to the store.

Individualizing the Lesson

Less-Advanced Students

1. Complete Exercise A orally. Make sure you discuss the three points given on page 456 again. Students should refer to the list of pronouns on page 454. You may want to display the list of subject pronouns for easy referral.

2. Let the students work in pairs to complete Exercise B.

Advanced Students

Have the students rewrite this paragraph substituting subject pronouns for the underlined words.

Karen is a well-rounded person. Karen is an excellent student; Karen is on
the honor roll every grading period.
Karen is also a good athlete. Her
brother Mike agrees. Mike said that
Karen plays basketball better than
most of his friends. Karen also enjoys
music, and Karen is a good musician.

Part 2 Subject Forms of Pronouns

The subject forms of pronouns are used as **subjects** of the verb. Most of the time you use these pronoun forms correctly without difficulty.

The subject forms of pronouns are also used as **predicate pronouns**. A predicate pronoun is a pronoun that follows a linking verb and is linked by the verb to the subject. You may be confused by predicate pronouns because you may often hear the wrong forms used.

The correct use of predicate pronouns is not difficult. But you must be sure that you understand what these pronouns are and how they are used.

Study these examples. Read the sentences aloud.

Subject		Predicate Pronoun	
She and *I*	went	The students were	*she* and *I*
You and *he*	came.	The visitors were	*you* and *he.*

If you have trouble recognizing predicate pronouns, remember these points:

1. Predicate pronouns follow linking verbs, such as *is, was, were,* and *will be.*
2. The predicate pronoun usually means the same thing as the subject.
3. A sentence with a predicate pronoun will usually make sense if the subject and the predicate pronoun are reversed. Study the following example.

Subject	Verb	
He	was	the visitor.
The visitor	was	he.

Always use the subject form of a pronoun for subjects and predicate pronouns.

Exercises Choose the correct pronoun.

A. Number your paper from 1 to 10. Choose the <u>correct</u> <u>pronoun</u> in each of the following sentences. Check your work by reading the sentences aloud.

1. (<u>We</u>, Us) and the Bradleys play touch football every Saturday.
2. It was Todd and (me, <u>I</u>) to the rescue.
3. The base runners were Mark and (<u>I</u>, me).
4. The boys are Al's brothers. Al and (<u>they</u>, them) live next door.
5. Kathy and (<u>I</u>, me) work together.
6. Chris and (her, <u>she</u>) are coming.
7. It is (her, <u>she</u>).
8. There are Ginny and (<u>I</u>, me) on TV!
9. (Him, <u>He</u>) is the boy at the door.
10. The baseball experts are (<u>they</u>, them) and their brothers.

B. Follow the directions for Exercise A.

1. Michael and (<u>he</u>, him) are always together.
2. (Her, <u>She</u>) and (<u>I</u>, me) will see you tonight at the movies.
3. The winners are Trudy and (me, <u>I</u>).
4. Scott and (her, <u>she</u>) are cousins.
5. Robin and (<u>she</u>, her) both roasted marshmallows over the campfire.
6. (Us, <u>We</u>) and about half the class were tennis players.
7. The Big Hawk Pack and (us, <u>we</u>) became friends at camp.
8. The boy on the right is (<u>he</u>, him).
9. Michele and (<u>they</u>, them) kept movie scrapbooks about their favorite actors.
10. Peter and (us, <u>we</u>) were almost late to homeroom because we missed our bus.

too. The winner of the band award was Karen. *(She)* Also, her classmates all like her. Her classmates *(They)* say that Karen is *(She)* the friendliest person in the school.

Optional Practice

Write the following sentences on the chalkboard:

I was the first person in line.
She was the best player.
He was the winner.
We were the youngest ones.
They are the tallest boys.

Have the students reverse these sentences, making the subjects into predicate pronouns. Read aloud the correct answers. Answers below.

Extending the Lesson

Have the students bring a human interest story from a newspaper to class. Ask the students to circle all of the subject pronouns in the article. Point out that a newspaper may repeat a last name instead of using a pronoun in order to avoid confusion.

The first person in line was I.
The best player was she.
The winner was he.
The youngest ones were we.
The tallest boys are they.

Objective

To use the object form of pronouns correctly for direct and indirect objects

Presenting the Lesson

1. Read and discuss page 458. Introduce this lesson with examples of sentences with nouns used as objects. Ask students to substitute pronouns in the sentences. Pronouns may be used as both direct and indirect objects. For example:

Ted saw Jose and Sarah.
Ted saw *him* and *her*.
Lynn asked the teacher a question.
Lynn asked *him* a question.

Review the object pronouns:

Singular: me, you, her, him, it.

Plural: us, you, them

When pronouns are included in a compound object, students should test the pronoun choice by itself. For example: *They saw me* is correct, so it is correct to say, *They saw Terry and me*.

2. Assign and discuss Exercises A and B on pages 458–459.

Individualizing the Lesson

Less-Advanced Students

Do Exercise A orally. Show the students how to break the compound objects into simple objects to determine which pronouns to use. Assign Exercise B.

Advanced Students

Have the students rewrite this paragraph replacing the underlined words with object pronouns.

Part 3   Object Forms of Pronouns

Always use the object form of a pronoun for direct objects and indirect objects.

Direct object: Ted saw *him* and *her*.

Indirect object: Lynn asked *me* a question.

Pronouns in Compound Objects

A compound object may consist of two pronouns joined by *and, or,* or *nor.* A compound object may also consist of a noun and a pronoun. The object form of pronouns is used in all compound objects.

Direct object: They saw *Terry* and *me*.
Virgil questioned *him* and *her*.

Indirect object: Please give *Alice* and *me* your address.
She gave *us* and *them* the records.

Exercises   Use the correct pronoun as object.

A.   Choose the correct pronoun from the two given in parentheses in each of the following sentences. Remember to use the object form of a pronoun for direct and indirect objects.

1. Have you seen John and (he, <u>him</u>) this morning?
2. My uncle sent (he, <u>him</u>) and (I, <u>me</u>) a frisbee.
3. June saw Rosa and (she, <u>her</u>) at the county fairgrounds yesterday.
4. Tim bought (<u>them</u>, they) and their friends ice cream and lemonade.
5. Juan was teaching (he, <u>him</u>) and his sister Spanish.
6. The snow slowed (they, <u>them</u>) and the other hikers down.
7. Tell Linda and (she, <u>her</u>) to wait.

8. Mother gave (they, <u>them</u>) and (<u>us</u>, we) a ride to school.

9. The old man told Jack and (<u>me</u>, I) about the Louistown flood.

10. Give (he, <u>him</u>) and his friend tickets for the tournament.

B. Choose the correct pronoun from the two given in parentheses in each of the following sentences.

1. Kirk helped (he, <u>him</u>) and (she, <u>her</u>) with the dishes.
2. Curtis gave Barry and (I, <u>me</u>) his promise.
3. The architect drew (they, <u>them</u>) and the onlookers a brief sketch.
4. Will you give (she, <u>her</u>) and (I, <u>me</u>) some help with this ladder?
5. The lawyer brought the jury and (<u>her</u>, she) positive proof.
6. Will you give Mary and (<u>me</u>, I) some apples?
7. Mrs. Folette asked (they, <u>them</u>) and Kent to dinner.
8. The parade delayed my grandmother and (we, <u>us</u>).
9. You should have seen (he, <u>him</u>) and (<u>me</u>, I) in our costumes.
10. My mother will call Jim and (they, <u>them</u>) tomorrow.

Part 4 *We Girls or Us Girls; We Boys or Us Boys*

When do you say *we boys* and *we girls*? When do you say *us boys* and *us girls*? You will make the correct choice if you try the pronoun alone in the sentence.

(We, Us) boys walked ten miles.

(*We* walked. Therefore, *We boys walked ten miles* is correct.)

459

Mr. Rosenfield gave Jill and Carol a ride to the park. Travis was waiting for Jill and Carol. They had given Travis a boomerang for his birthday. He wanted Jill and Carol to see how it worked. "Catch the boomerang!" said Travis, as he tossed the boomerang towards Carol. It circled Carol and then flew back to Travis. "Give Travis that thing!" exclaimed Jill. "After I try the boomerang, I'll let Carol try the boomerang. By the end of the afternoon, we'll all be experts!"

Optional Practice

Ask students to substitute an object pronoun for the words in italics in the following sentences.

1. The pilot showed *Manuel* and *Christa* the controls.
2. Attending the concert was a pleasant experience for *Julia* and *Joel*.
3. Sadie gave *Clara* a birthday gift.
4. The employers gave *their employees* a good raise.
5. Jean put *the books* back on the shelf.
6. The teacher gave *the students* the quiz last Friday.
7. The secretary gave *the principal* a message.
8. Sarah baked *the bread*.

Part 4

Objective

To use *we* and *us* correctly

Presenting the Lesson

1. Read and discuss page 459 and the top of 460.
2. Do Exercise A on page 460.

459

with the class. Have students read each sentence once again, leaving out the noun used in combination with the pronoun. Students will see how easy it is to use the correct pronoun by relying on what sounds right.

3. Assign and discuss Exercise B on page 460.

Individualizing the Lesson

Less-Advanced Students

Allow the students to work in pairs to complete Exercise B.

Advanced Students

Have each student write ten sentences using *we (noun)* and *us (noun)* correctly.

Optional Practice

Put the following sentences on a worksheet. Tell students that the sentences use the incorrect pronoun form. Above each incorrect form they should write the correct form.

1. Our pet boa constrictor is fond of Frank and we. [us]
2. Us baseball pitchers warmed up before the game. [We]
3. Only three other students and us scored so high on the test. [we]
4. The task was given to we girls. [us]
5. Us friends would rather stick together. [We]

Extending the Lesson

Have students write a brief speech (possible topics: accepting an award, giving a pep-talk). Explain that they are to use the *we (noun)* and *us (noun)* construction several times.

The music director chose (we, us) sopranos.

(The music director chose *us*. Therefore, *The music director chose us sopranos* is correct.)

Exercises   Use the correct pronoun.

A. Choose the correct pronouns in the following sentences.

1. (We, Us) boys were selected as the finalists.
2. Ms. Gianetti picked (we, us) two for the parts.
3. Take (we, us) boys with you.
4. The winners were (we, us) girls.
5. At first (we, us) receivers were dropping the passes.
6. Give (we, us) members a break!
7. Do (we, us) students have a spelling test today or tomorrow?
8. (We, Us) girls were chosen as representatives.
9. (We, Us) girls are all on the team.
10. Did you see (we, us) boys in the pool?

B. Choose the correct pronouns in the following sentences.

1. (We, Us) girls have all seen the movie.
2. Please take (we, us) boys on the boat, too.
3. (We, Us) two are in the play-offs Saturday.
4. (We, Us) three did all the cleaning up.
5. Give (we, us) boys some help with wrapping these presents.
6. You never told (we, us) class representatives.
7. (We, Us) girls are from Lincolnwood.
8. He is watching (we, us) boys on the bridge.
9. (We, Us) girls have waited half an hour for the school bus.
10. (We, Us) girls are the best.

Part 5 Possessive Forms of Pronouns

The possessive forms of pronouns are these:

my, mine	our, ours
your, yours	
his, her, hers, its	their, theirs

Notice that possessive pronouns have no apostrophes.

Its and It's. Many people confuse the contraction *it's* (meaning *it is* or *it has*) with the possessive *its*. *It's* with an apostrophe always means *it is* or *it has*.

The dog lost *its* collar. (*its* = the collar belongs to the dog)
It's been raining. (*it's* = it has)
The horse turned *its* head. (*its* = the head is part of the horse)
Now *it's* clear again. (*it's* = it is)

Exercises Use *its* and *it's* correctly.

A. Copy the following sentences and insert apostrophes where they are needed.

1. Its about time for the news.
2. The bear could not find its cubs.
3. Its a little too hot for practice today.
4. The long run by the quarterback brought the crowd to its feet.
5. Its either yours or hers.
6. See if its melted yet.
7. The airline will page us when its cargo plane arrives at the loading dock.
8. Its raining again.
9. Give the dog its bath.
10. Its an old story.

461

Part 5

Objective

To use the possessive forms of pronouns correctly, and to differentiate between *its* and *it's*

Presenting the Lesson

1. Read and discuss page 461. You may want to review the concept of *possession* and go over the purpose of contractions. Stress that there are no apostrophes in possessive pronouns.

2. Assign and discuss Exercises A and B on pages 461–462.

Individualizing the Lesson

Less-Advanced Students

Do Exercises A and B with these students.

Advanced Students

Point out that there may also be confusion between *your,* a possessive pronoun, and *you're,* a contraction of *you are.* Remind students that possessive pronouns have no apostrophes. Have the students choose the correct word in these sentences.

1. (Your, You're) coat is in the closet.
2. If (your, you're) leaving now, may I have a ride?
3. What is in (your, you're) bag?
4. (Your, You're) in big trouble now!
5. Can you touch (your, you're) toes?

Optional Practice

Have the students substitute possessive pronouns for the underlined words in this paragraph.

461

Joanne was looking for Joanne's her backpack. "Have you seen Joanne's my backpack?" she asked Joanne's sister her Meg.

"No," Meg replied, "that one is mine Meg's. Did you leave Joanne's yours at camp?"

"I don't know," Joanne said, "but I'll ask Ted if I can borrow Ted's his for the camping trip."

Extending the Lesson

Have students write a sentence for each of the possessive pronouns listed on page 461. Point out that some are used in front of nouns and some are used alone.

Part 6

Objective

To understand the function of the antecedent of a pronoun, and to identify antecedents in sentences

Presenting the Lesson

1. Write a sentence on the board containing a pronoun and its antecedent. For example: *Mike found his boots.* Ask students to identify the pronoun *(his).* Then ask them who or what *his* refers to—whose boots? *(Mike's).* Explain that every pronoun used must clearly refer to some noun in the same sentence or in the preceding one. Tell them that the noun referred to is called an *antecedent.* Discuss other examples with the class.

2. It might be helpful to do Exercise A on page 463 with the class,

462

B. Follow the directions for Exercise A.

1. It's good to know a foreign language.
2. Bill thinks it's his football, but it's mine.
3. That bat is theirs. It's much newer than ours.
4. The robin left its nest too soon.
5. According to the weather report, it's supposed to rain all weekend.
6. It's not an impossible dream.
7. The marathon is Sunday; its distance is 26 miles and 385 yards.
8. The new record shop opens Saturday, and all of its albums will be on sale.
9. It's usually warm in San Diego.
10. The kitten was lying on its back.

Part 6 Pronouns and Antecedents

The **antecedent** of a pronoun is the noun or pronoun that it replaces or to which it refers.

1. *Larry* came today and brought *his* tools.
   (*Larry* is the antecedent of *his.*)
2. *Debbie* and *Tom* came in. *They* were laughing.
   (*Debbie* and *Tom* are the antecedents of *they.*)

The antecedent usually appears before the pronoun. Sometimes, as in the second example, the antecedent is in the sentence before it.

Singular and Plural Pronouns

Use a singular pronoun for a singular antecedent. Use a plural pronoun for a plural antecedent.

462

The *runner* talked about *his* Olympic medals.
(*Runner* is singular; *his* is singular.)

The *actors* learned *their* lines.
(*Actors* is plural; *their* is plural.)

Exercises Find the antecedents.

A. Number your paper from 1 to 10. Make two columns, and label one *Pronouns* and the other *Antecedents*. Place the pronouns in one column and their antecedents in the other.

Example: Aunt Carol and Uncle Jim like Susan. They told her many stories about the old mining town.

Pronouns	Antecedents
they	Aunt Carol
	Uncle Jim
her	Susan

1. Mr. Mulligan planted more soybeans last year. They brought him a good price. They / soybeans / him / Mr. Mulligan
2. That tree lost all its berries overnight. its / tree
3. Tim and Rick didn't bring their raincoats. their / Tim and Rick
4. Here is the tent Bill's grandparents lent him. He brought it with his sleeping bag. him / Bill / He / Bill / it / tent / his / Bill
5. Steel mills can create a serious problem. They pollute the air. They / Steel mills
6. The thief erased his fingerprints from the windowsill and the door handle. his / thief
7. Owen had the injured sparrow with him. He carried it carefully. He / Owen / It / Sparrow
8. Joan has had her bike repaired. her / Joan
9. Rex showed Al his hockey trophy. They talked about the championship game. They / Rex and Al
10. Ann won the citizenship award. It was given to her at the city council meeting. It / award / her / Ann

463

2. You should ask *them* for replacement batteries.

3. Try to understand what *they* have written.

4. The newsboy delivered newspapers to *them* for five years.

5. *They* have raised the price of gas again this week.

6. Be sure to write to *them* before next week.

7. My family had *them* over for lunch yesterday.

8. The sports store had *them* on sale just last week.

9. *They* crocheted one hundred hats for the church bazaar.

10. The fisherman tried to catch the fish with *it*.

Extending the Lesson

Duplicate a passage from a short story or from a newspaper or magazine article. Have the students underline each pronoun and draw an arrow from the pronoun to its antecedent.

Part 7

Objective

To understand the function of compound personal pronouns, and to identify them in sentences

Presenting the Lesson

1. Read and discuss page 464. Stress that compound personal pronouns are not used as substitutes for other personal pronouns but for emphasis. For example, *I bought myself a pair of gloves*, not *I bought me a pair of gloves*, and *Joshua and*

B. Follow the directions for Exercise A.

1. Jim and Liz brought their dog. They kept it on a leash.
   <small>their   Jim and Liz
They   Jim and Liz
it   dog</small>

2. Wayne sanded and painted the birdhouse. He had made it in shop class. <small>He Wayne
it birdhouse</small>

3. My father held the needle at arm's length. Then he poked the thread at it. <small>He Father
it needle</small>

4. Marsha and Jack are here now. She is washing the apples, and he is peeling them. <small>She Marsha
he Jack</small>

5. Even before Mary got there, Jay and Frank had started their breakfast. <small>their   Jay and Frank</small>

6. Carla grabbed her end of the rope. <small>her   Carla</small>

7. The boys saw Nancy. They asked her how she liked the movie. <small>They boys
her Nancy
she Nancy</small>

8. Peter left his camera on Sheila's desk. When she came in, she found it. <small>his Peter   she Sheila
she Sheila it camera</small>

9. Mrs. Foster bought all those bananas for a dollar. They were certainly worth it. <small>They bananas
it dollar</small>

10. Ann let Ned try her skateboard. He couldn't keep his balance on it. <small>her Ann
He Ned
it skateboard</small>

Part 7 Compound Personal Pronouns

A **compound personal pronoun** is formed by adding *-self* or *-selves* to certain personal pronouns.

myself	ourselves
yourself	yourselves
himself, herself, itself	themselves

Here are some examples.

We always do the repairs *ourselves*.
(You) Read the story *yourself*.
She weighs *herself* every day.

Exercise   **Use compound personal pronouns.**

Number your paper from 1 to 10. Beside each number write the correct compound personal pronoun for each of the following sentences. After it, write the noun or pronoun to which it refers.

Example: She made (pronoun) a big breakfast. (herself, She)

1. Nancy thought of (pronoun) as everyone's friend. herself—Nancy
2. She bandaged the cut (pronoun). herself—She
3. The wolves threw (pronoun) against the cage in an attempt to escape. themselves—wolves
4. A motor-driven robot can walk by (pronoun). itself—robot
5. Cut (pronoun) another piece of cake. yourself—(You)
6. We made (pronoun) at home. ourselves—We
7. Jim looked at (pronoun) in the mirror while putting on a tie. himself—Jim
8. You made this sled (pronoun), didn't you? yourself—You
9. Kevin pushed (pronoun) to run farther and faster around the track. himself—Kevin
10. The campers arranged (pronoun) in a circle around the fire. themselves—campers

Part 8   Demonstrative Pronouns

The pronouns *this*, *that*, *these*, and *those* are used to point out which persons or things are referred to. They are called **demonstrative pronouns**.

This and *these* point to persons or things that are near. *That* and *those* point to persons or things farther away.

This is our campsite.   **These** should be packed.
That was a rattlesnake.   **Those** are pine trees.

465

I like science fiction, not *Joshua and myself like science fiction*. Discuss why these pronouns are called compound personal pronouns.

2. Read and discuss the exercise on page 465.

Individualizing the Lesson

Less-Advanced Students

Do the exercise orally.

Advanced Students

Add these items to the exercise on page 465.

11. I (pronoun) inspected the machinery. myself, I
12. Len poured (pronoun) a glass of juice. himself, Len
13. We pride (pronoun) on our workmanship. ourselves, we
14. The computer (pronoun) can plot a graph. itself, computer
15. Can you tear (pronoun) away from that book? yourself, you

Optional Practice

Have students write a sentence of their own for each of the compound personal pronouns in the list on page 464.

Extending the Lesson

Have the students look through their literature books to find sentences that use compound personal pronouns. Discuss them in class.

Part 8

Objective

To understand the function of the demonstrative pronouns *this, that,*

465

these, and those, and to use them correctly in sentences

Presenting the Lesson

1. Read and discuss page 465.
2. Assign and discuss the exercise on page 466.

Individualizing the Lesson

Less-Advanced Students

Do the exercise on page 466 orally with the class.

Advanced Students

Have students write two sentences for each demonstrative pronoun.

Optional Practice

Follow the instructions for the exercise on page 466.

1. _____ are my new barbells.
2. _____ is the freight elevator.
3. _____ over there are hippos.
4. _____ is the casserole dish.
5. Would _____ be better than _____ for a costume?

Extending the Lesson

Have the students find examples of demonstrative pronouns in a newspaper or magazine.

Part 9

Objective

To use interrogative pronouns correctly in sentences, particularly *who* and *whom*

Exercise **Use demonstrative pronouns.**

Number your paper from 1 to 10. Write the correct demonstrative pronoun for the blank space in each sentence.

1. ___These___ on my feet are wooden shoes from Holland.
2. ___Those___ were the days when cowboys roamed the West.
3. Now ___this___ is the moment I have been waiting for.
4. ___These___ in my hand are rare coins.
5. ___Those___ that we saw yesterday were counterfeit bills.
6. Look over there. ___That___ must be a gold nugget.
7. ___That___ is his picture, right there.
8. Right here, ___this___ is the spot where they landed.
9. ___Those___ over there are Jonathan's boots.
10. Is ___that___ Mt. Rainier in the distance?

Part 9 Interrogative Pronouns

The pronouns *who, whose, whom, which,* and *what* are **interrogative pronouns**. Interrogative pronouns are used to ask questions.

Who plays tennis?   *Which* came first?
Whose is this bike?   *What* is the answer?
Whom did you call?

Exercise **Find the interrogative pronouns.**

Find the interrogative pronoun in each sentence.

1. Who made these delicious tacos?
2. Of the two sweaters, which do you prefer?
3. What is the best way to learn to ski?
4. Who planned the picnic?

5. If that bike is Jack's, whose is this?
6. Whom did you invite to the party?
7. Which of the players scored the goal?
8. Whose are these?
9. What caused the explosion?
10. Who invented the parachute?

Using *Who* and *Whom*

The interrogative pronouns *who* and *whom* are often confused. Study these examples. They will help you to use *who* and *whom* correctly.

Use *who* as the subject of the verb.

> *Who* is coming today?   *Who* gave you that sweater?

Use *whom* as the direct object of the verb and as the object of the preposition.

> *Whom* were you describing?   With *whom* did you dance?
> *Whom* did Jim call?   To *whom* was she talking?

Exercise   Use *who* and *whom*.

Choose the correct interrogative pronoun from the two given in parentheses.

1. (Who, Whom) recorded that album?
2. At (who, whom) did the bus driver yell?
3. (Who, Whom) ate all the bananas?
4. (Who, Whom) did Emily invite to the dance?
5. To (who, whom) did Eva pass the ball?
6. (Who, Whom) plays first base?
7. (Who, Whom) did Ramon ask?
8. (Who, Whom) was Butch Cassidy's sidekick?
9. For (who, whom) are you babysitting?
10. (Who, Whom) did the Emmy winner thank?

467

Presenting the Lesson

1. Read page 466. Discuss the use of the interrogative pronouns in the examples: *who, which,* and *what* as subject pronouns; *whose* as a possessive pronoun; and *whom* as an object pronoun.

2. Assign and discuss the exercise on pages 466–467. Have students point out the grammatical uses of the interrogative pronouns.

3. Read and discuss page 467.

4. Assign and discuss the exercise on page 467. Again have students point out the grammatical uses of the interrogative pronouns.

Individualizing the Lesson

Less-Advanced Students

Complete the exercises orally. Stress the use of *who* as the subject and *whom* as the direct object.

Advanced Students

Add this instruction to both exercises: "State whether the pronoun is used as a subject, a direct object, or the object of a preposition."

Optional Practice

Have students choose the correct interrogative pronoun.

1. From (who, <u>whom</u>) did you hear the news?
2. (<u>Who</u>, Whom) answered it?
3. (Who, <u>Whom</u>) did Myra choose?
4. (<u>Who</u>, Whom) was that masked man?

Extending the Lesson

Ask students to write two sentences for each of the interrogative pronouns listed on page 466.

Part 10

Objective

To identify indefinite pronouns and to use the correct possessive pronouns with them

Presenting the Lesson

1. Read and discuss page 468. Stress that many of these indefinite pronouns are only referred to with singular pronouns. Widespread nonstandard use of plural pronouns may increase the students' resistance to the correct form.

2. Assign and discuss Exercises A and B on page 469.

Individualizing the Lesson

Less-Advanced Students

Do Exercise A orally. Allow the students to work in pairs to complete Exercise B.

Advanced Students

Point out that *each, both, many, few, several, all, any,* and *some* function as adjectives when they modify a noun, but they are always indefinite pronouns when they stand alone. Put the following sentences on the board and ask students whether *some* is being used as an indefinite pronoun or an adjective.

Some of the guests arrived late. (pronoun)

I would like *some* lunch now. (adjective)

Put the following exercise on a worksheet. Next to each sentence have students write whether the italicized word in each sentence is being used as an *adjective* or a *pronoun.*

Some pronouns do not refer to a particular person. They are called **indefinite pronouns**. The following indefinite pronouns are singular:

anybody	each	everything	no one
anyone	everybody	neither	somebody
anything	everyone	nobody	someone

Because they are singular, use the singular possessive pronouns *his, her,* or *its* to refer to them. Perhaps these sentences will help you to remember. Read each of them aloud.

Everybody took *his* turn.   Something had *its* burrow here.

Someone left *her* raincoat.   No one had *his* or *her* ticket.

Notice that the phrase *his or her* may be used when the person referred to could be either male or female.

A few indefinite pronouns are plural. They refer to more than one person or thing:

both	many	few	several

Both raised *their* hands.   Few stopped *their* cars.

Many of the fans left *their* seats.   Several offered *their* help.

Four indefinite pronouns may be either singular or plural, depending on their meaning in the sentence:

all	any	some	none

All of the salad *was* eaten. (singular)

All of the seats *were* empty. (plural)

Does any of this newspaper need to be saved? (singular)

Do any of these songs sound familiar? (plural)

Some of the jewelry *is* missing. (singular)

Some of the plants *need* direct sunlight. (plural)

None of the food *was* left. (singular)

None of the planes *were* taking off. (plural)

Exercises

Use the correct possessive pronouns with indefinite pronouns.

A. Choose the correct possessive pronoun for each sentence from those in parentheses. Write the pronoun. Then read each sentence aloud, using the correct form.

1. Somebody lost (his or her, their) hockey stick.
2. Both of the referees blew (his or her, their) whistles.
3. Many of the runners clocked (his or her, their) best times.
4. All of the snakes shed (its, their) skins.
5. Did everyone bring (his or her, their) permission slip?
6. Each of the boys displayed (his, their) drawing.
7. Some of the plants dropped (its, their) leaves.
8. No one raised (his or her, their) hand.
9. Can anyone touch (his or her, their) toes?
10. Neither of the twins remembered (her, their) locker number.

B. Follow the directions for Exercise A.

1. Each of the panthers must stay in (its, their) cage.
2. Did any of the truck drivers stop (his or her, their) rigs?
3. All of the photographers snapped (her, their) shutters.
4. Will somebody lend me (his or her, their) compass?
5. Both of the police officers jumped in (his, their) cars.
6. Somebody broke (his or her, their) leg on the ski slope.
7. All of the campers cooked (his or her, their) own food.
8. Several of my teammates offered (his, their) help.
9. Everyone brought (her, their) favorite record to the party.
10. Some of the punch has lost (its, their) flavor.

469

ADDITIONAL EXERCISES

Using Pronouns

A. Pronouns Rewrite the following sentences, changing all the words in italics to pronouns.

1. *Susan* looked up *Greg's* address.
2. *Matthew* enjoyed reading *the book*.
3. *Janet* and Mary waded across Blue Creek.
4. *Mr. and Mrs. Bailey* sent *Dan* a telegram.
5. The award was given to *Ellen* by Mr. *Scott*.

B. Subject Pronouns Number your paper from 1 to 10. Choose the correct pronoun in each of the following sentences.

1. Carmen and (she, her) crossed the swinging bridge.
2. Ellis and (me, I) are in the same history class.
3. Marsha and (he, him) set up the badminton net.
4. Jenny and (them, they) are the backup singers.
5. (I, Me) was the only survivor.
6. The Browns and (us, we) share the garage behind the apartment building.
7. Connie and (her, she) are at the counter.
8. (Them, They) were the winners of the relay race.
9. Shawn and (she, her) were on the bus.
10. Bill and (he, him) went ice skating this afternoon.

C. Predicate Pronouns Choose the correct pronoun from the two given in parentheses.

1. The team captains were Lonny and (he, him).
2. Our choice for class president is (she, her).
3. The starting forwards in Friday night's game will be (we, us).

470

4. Tubman High's newest National Honor Society members are (they, them).
5. The auto shop teachers are Ms. Rodriquez and (he, him).
6. The ushers for the school musical will be the Key Club and (we, us).
7. Our best wide receiver is (he, him).
8. The winner of this year's perfect attendance award was (she, her).
9. The homecoming dance committee includes Mr. and Mrs. Nelson and (they, them).
10. Ms. Jacob's secretary is (he, him).

D. Object Pronouns Choose the correct pronoun from the two given in parentheses.

1. The director gave Tony and (me, I) our cues.
2. The principal congratulated Vicky and (he, him).
3. The dog was chasing Bonnie and (them, they).
4. Ms. Tesser knitted Ron and (she, her) sweaters for Christmas.
5. We soon spotted Carol and (they, them).
6. Show Gwen and (I, me) the photograph from the party.
7. Are you following Mike and (me, I)?
8. Ask Charles and (he, him) for the information.
9. The manager gave Nina and (we, us) refunds.
10. An usher seated Jackie and (she, her).

E. We and Us Choose the correct pronoun from the two given in parentheses.

1. (We, Us) girls are in the same homeroom.
2. The waiter gave (we, us) girls another table.
3. (We, Us) people in the back can't hear you.

471

4. Mr. Nakai chose (we, <u>us</u>) three for the judo demonstration.
5. Are (<u>we</u>, us) boys still on the team?
6. (<u>We</u>, Us) swimmers must wear lifejackets, too.
7. Watch (we, <u>us</u>) boys at the track meet.
8. Don't forget (we, <u>us</u>) girls.
9. (<u>We</u>, Us) patients can get very lonely.
10. The teacher saved (we, <u>us</u>) latecomers some seats.

F. *Its* and *It's* Copy these sentences. Insert apostrophes where needed. If the sentence is correct, write *correct*.

C 1. The spider spun its delicate web.
2. It's a soccer ball.
C 3. Jody caught the duck and banded its leg.
C 4. Its mane was braided.
5. It's a grand old flag.
C 6. The pine was shedding its needles.
C 7. I can't find its leash.
C 8. Riley put the album back in its cover.
9. We know it's snowing.
10. Surely it's a joke of some kind.

G. Pronouns and Antecedents Number your paper from 1 to 10. Make two columns. Label one column *Pronouns* and the other *Antecedents*. Place the pronouns in one column and their antecedents in the other.

1. Darlene displayed her collection of arrowheads. _{her} _{Darlene}
2. Several animals escaped from their cages. _{their} _{animals}
3. A hurricane destroyed the shed, but Grandpa rebuilt it. _{it} _{shed}
4. Karen watched the robin gather twigs for its nest. _{its} _{robin}
5. Clark never looks at his opponent during a match. _{his} _{Clark}
6. Lucy and her sister share a room. They divide the space. _{her} _{Lucy and sister} _{They}

7. Marvin pushed his sunglasses up. his   Marvin

8. Where have you been, Rachel? you   Rachel

9. Stephen lost his gloves. He can't remember where he
   left them. his   Stephen   he   Stephen
   He   Stephen   them   gloves

10. Paul asked Angie if she remembered their zip code.
    she   Angie
    their   Paul and Angie

H. Compound Personal Pronouns Number your paper
from 1 to 10. Beside each number write the correct compound
personal pronoun for each of the following sentences. After it,
write the noun or pronoun to which it refers.

1. Ken forced (pronoun) to dive. himself—Ken

2. The squirrels found (pronoun) a new tree. themselves—squirrels

3. The referee (pronoun) will keep score during the
   basketball game. himself or herself—referee

4. Ms. Sedik drove (pronoun) to the emergency room
   after the accident. herself—Ms. Sedik

5. Don't cut your hair (pronoun), Molly. yourself—Molly

6. We appointed (pronoun) leaders. ourselves—We

7. I (pronoun) called the station. myself—I

8. The store calls (pronoun) a junior department store. itself—store

9. Runners time (pronoun), don't they? themselves—Runners

10. Andrew weighed (pronoun). himself—Andrew

I. Demonstrative Pronouns Number your paper from 1 to
10. Add the correct demonstrative to the blank in each sentence.

1. ___That___ is the bus stop across the street.

2. Isn't ___that___ Sal way over there?

3. Are ___those___ the Blue Ridge Mountains ahead?

4. ___This___ is the best place right here.

5. ___Those___ were harder times back then.

6. ___These___ over here are for pierced ears.

7. Wasn't ___that___ your cousin that I met last week?

8. ___This___ is a shortcut that I'm showing you.

9. ___That___ is what you said last month.
10. ___This___ is a garter snake I am holding.

J. Interrogative Pronouns Choose the correct interrogative pronoun from the two given in parentheses.

1. (Who, Whom) scored the last touchdown?
2. For (who, whom) is the flag at half-mast?
3. You asked (who, whom) to the dance?
4. With (who, whom) was Ralph walking?
5. To (who, whom) should I give the note?
6. (Who, Whom) did you meet?
7. (Who, Whom) solved the Rubik's cube?
8. (Who, Whom) talked with Milo last?
9. With (who, whom) were you talking?
10. At (who, whom) is Gayle smiling?

K. Possessive Pronouns with Indefinite Pronouns
Number your paper from 1 to 10. Choose the correct possessive pronouns from those given in parentheses.

1. Nobody knows (his or her, their) topic yet.
2. Somebody was muttering (his, their) locker combination.
3. Both of the men overcame (his, their) handicaps.
4. Neither of the teams regained (its, their) standing.
5. Some of the cake had mysteriously lost (its, their) icing.
6. Anyone can lose (his or her, their) job.
7. All the girls carried (her, their) own luggage from the airport to the car.
8. Everybody made a tape of (his or her, their) speech.
9. Some of the swimmers broke (her, their) own records.
10. Several of the musicians rent (his or her, their) instruments.

MIXED REVIEW

Using Pronouns

A. Using personal pronouns For each of the following sentences, write the correct pronoun from the two given in parentheses. Then, write the antecedent if one is given.

1. Emma and (I, me) couldn't stay for lunch.
2. (We, Us) disagree with your position on this issue.
3. After lunch, Mr. Regis gave (I, me) a tour of the stables.
4. Kara read her lines. The director asked (she, her^{Kara}) to repeat them.
5. Kelly took the keys from Vera and (her, she).
6. Jamie met (we, us) at the bus station.
7. Give the final copy of the report to (he, him) before you leave.
8. (We, Us) and they worked extra hard.
9. The most reliable babysitters are Liz and (her, she).
10. Chris and Tom read the telegram. (They, ^{Chris and Tom} Them) were shocked.

B. Using the correct pronoun Write the correct pronoun from those given in parentheses.

1. (My, Mine) idea was not very practical.
2. Kelly's dog has chewed (its, it's) leash.
3. (We, Us) girls helped decorate the cafeteria.
4. Mr. Jeffers chose (we, us) debaters to represent our school.
5. (It's, Its) not your turn to bat.
6. The blue woolen mittens are (her, hers).
7. (We, Us) runners never break training.
8. Jill told us her story, and (it's, its) unbelievable.

These exercises provide review of the concepts presented in this Section. Each exercise challenges the students to apply several of the skills they have acquired during previous study. Because the "mixed" feature of these activities makes them more difficult, the teacher may wish to have less-advanced students do them orally or in small groups.

9. The fields beyond this fence are (<u>theirs</u>, their's).
10. Give the job to one of (<u>us</u>, we) boys.

C. Using pronouns For each sentence, write the <u>correct pronoun</u> from those given in parentheses.

1. (<u>Who</u>, Whom) locked the cabin door?
2. To (who, <u>whom</u>) do you wish to speak?
3. They built the campfire (<u>themselves</u>, theirselves).
4. (<u>Those</u>, These) planes over there are flying awfully low.
5. Many of my friends earn (his, <u>their</u>) own spending money.
6. He helped (hisself, <u>himself</u>) to another burrito.
7. (<u>Who</u>, Whom) brought these ice skates?
8. (This, <u>That</u>) player at third base is my cousin.
9. These ovens can turn (<u>themselves</u>, theirselves) off.
10. Everybody in the class cast (<u>his or her</u>, their) ballot.

D. Choosing pronouns correctly Number your paper from 1 to 11. Read the following paragraph. Write the correct pronouns from those given in parentheses.

(<u>Who</u>, Whom) said that bees are busy? (<u>We</u>, Us) know that a queen bee has a lazy existence. (<u>She</u>, Her) only lays eggs and lets the worker bees feed and care for (<u>her</u>, she). The workers are females, too, but (<u>they</u>, them) are smaller. (<u>Their</u>, They're) chores are many: caring for the nest, gathering nectar, and waiting on the queen. But (who, <u>whose</u>) fate can be worse than that of the drone? (<u>He</u>, Him) is the male honeybee. In autumn, the workers let (he, <u>him</u>) starve. (<u>They</u>, Them) are afraid (<u>he</u>, him) will eat too much of the stored honey.

USING GRAMMAR IN WRITING
Using Pronouns

A. Write six questions for use on a game show. In each question, use one of these subject form pronouns: *I, he, she, we, it,* and *they.* Then use other pronouns as necessary. Exchange papers with a partner. See if you can answer each other's questions.

> Examples: *I* am a famous baseball player. *My* home run record is better than Babe Ruth's. Who am *I?* (Answer: Hank Aaron)
>
> *It* is the largest mammal in the world today. *Its* home is the ocean. What is *it?* (Answer: a whale)

B. Pronouns make our language flow more naturally and easily. This is especially true in poetry. The following poems have been rewritten incorrectly without pronouns. Correct them by replacing the italicized words with pronouns.

The Moon (use feminine pronouns)

The moon was but a chin of gold
   A night or two ago,
And now *the moon* turns *the moon's* perfect face   she, her
   Upon the world below.

EMILY DICKINSON

Paper Dragons

In March, kites bite the wind
and shake *kites'* paper scales.   their
Kites strain against *kites'* fiber chains they, their
to free *kites'* dragon tails.   their

SUSAN ALTON SCHMELTZ

477

Using Grammar in Writing

These challenging and enjoyable activities allow the students to see how the concepts of grammar, usage, and mechanics may be applied in actual writing situations. Each exercise is designed to allow students practice in several of the skills they have acquired in this Section. The activities also provide opportunities for students to write creatively about a wide variety of interesting and unusual subjects.

Section Objectives

1. To understand the function of adjectives and to identify them in sentences

2. To understand the function of predicate adjectives and to identify them in sentences

3. To identify possessive pronouns used as adjectives and to use them correctly

4. To differentiate between demonstrative pronouns and demonstrative adjectives and to use them correctly

5. To form the comparative and superlative forms of adjectives, particularly irregular comparisons, and to use them correctly

6. To use *them* and *those,* and *here* and *there* correctly, and to use the correct demonstratives with *kind* and *sort*

Preparing the Students

Explain that modifiers make the meaning of a word definite and specific. A word that is modified becomes a clearer, better defined word. An adjective is a word that is used to modify a noun or pronoun.

Additional Resources

Diagnostic Test — page 4 in the test booklet

Mastery Test — pages 51–52 in the test booklet

Additional Exercises — pages 491–495 in the student text

Practice Book — pages 185–190

Duplicating Masters — pages 185–190

Special Populations — See special section at the back of this Teacher's Edition.

478

Using Adjectives

Part 1 What Are Adjectives?

Nouns and pronouns name and identify people and things. Verbs tell what the people and things are or what they do.

Adjectives describe people and things.

When you write the noun *hills,* you probably have a picture of certain kinds of hills in your mind. Will your reader have the same picture? He or she may not. Do you mean *rolling* hills, *distant* hills, or *steep* hills? Do you mean *purple* hills, *bare* hills, or *rocky* hills? Each one of the words in italics describes the word after it. Each word in italics is an adjective.

478

Adjectives help to give your readers a clear picture of what you are writing about. They add to the meaning of another word. They make the meaning more exact. When one word adds to the meaning of another word, it *modifies* that word. It is called a **modifier**.

An adjective is a word that modifies a noun or a pronoun.

Adjectives can tell three things about the words they modify.

> **Which one or ones?**
> *this* book, *that* jet, *these* shoes, *those* passengers
>
> **What kind?**
> *blue* sky, *hot* oven, *small* jar, *old* house, *beautiful* sunrise
>
> **How many?**
> *four* bicycles, *several* cars, *many* people, *few* children

Look at the adjectives in italics in these sentences:

> This street is the *dividing* line.
> One lucky day they found *buried* treasure.

You can see that some adjectives come from verbs and have verb endings. *Dividing* and *buried* are two examples. Here are three more:

> *running* water   *toasted* muffin   *broken* glass

Most adjectives from verbs have *-ing* and *-ed* endings. Some have irregular forms, as *broken* does.

Proper Adjectives

Proper adjectives are adjectives formed from proper nouns.

Proper adjectives are always capitalized. Here are some examples:

a Chinese puzzle	the Atlantic coast	a Swedish ship
a Mideast peace	the French language	a Roman coin

479

To understand the function of adjectives and to identify them in sentences

Presenting the Lesson

1. Read and discuss pages 478–480.

2. "Diagraming Sentences Containing Adjectives," page 480. It is suggested that this instructional tool be employed cautiously. Only students with previous diagraming experience should be asked to do individual diagrams. You may wish to put the diagram form on the board, however, to illustrate the relationship between modifiers and the words they modify.

3. Assign and discuss Exercises A and B on pages 480–481. Point out that most adjectives fall into the *what kind* category.

Individualizing the Lesson

Less-Advanced Students

1. Instruct students in the correct use of *a* and *an*.

2. Have students first identify nouns and pronouns in the exercises and then look for words that tell *what kind*, *how many*, or *which one*.

Advanced Students

1. Point out that suffixes they previously learned can form adjectives. They are *-less*, *-able*, *-ful*, and *-ous*. Have students form adjectives using these suffixes and use each in a sentence.

480

2. Have students write a short descriptive paragraph. Ask them to use as many adjectives as possible.

Optional Practice

Have students write five sentences using at least five different adjectives to describe themselves.

Extending the Lesson

Adjective Riddles. Each student must choose five objects that can be found in the classroom and think of three adjectives that describe each object. For example, adjectives for a window might be *square, glass,* and *clear.* Each student in turn tries to stump the class on the identity of one of the objects by asking What is _____, _____, and _____ ? (filling the blanks with the list of adjectives). Whoever names the object gets the next turn. If the class cannot discover the object from five adjective clues, the first student tells the answer and chooses the student who gets the next turn.

Articles

The adjectives *a, an,* and *the* are called **articles.** *The* is the **definite article.**

> This is *the* shirt that I want. (one specific shirt)

A and *an* are **indefinite articles.**

> I would like to ride *a* horse. (any horse)
> Please bring me *an* orange. (any orange)

Use *a* before a consonant sound (*a* horse, *a* jar, *a* leg). Use *an* before a vowel sound (*an* orange, *an* ounce, *an* umbrella).

The sound, not the spelling, makes the difference. Do you say *a* honorable man or *an* honorable man? *a* hour or *an* hour?

Diagraming Sentences Containing Adjectives

In a diagram, write an adjective on a line that slants down from the noun it modifies.

> An elm tree shades the front porch.

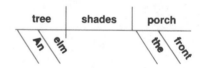

Exercises   Find the adjectives.

A.   Find the <u>adjectives</u> in the following sentences. Show in writing, as your teacher directs you, how they modify nouns.

1. The red car had a flat tire.
2. Sherry is an early bird.
3. The sheep and their lambs went in the empty shed.
4. Our old car needs new brakes.
5. Rob whipped up a hot, peppery sauce.
6. The fat, laughing clown led the parade.

7. Black soot coated the old fireplace.
8. The ancient Dutch windmill made a screechy sound.
9. A young otter splashed in the small pond.
10. A playful young husky pranced ahead of the sled.

B. Writing Copy the following sentences. Write a clear, exact adjective in place of each blank. Answers will vary.

1. A _____ statue stood at the _____ intersection.
2. The sky was filled with _____ stars.
3. The _____ clock has a _____ dial.
4. Have you ever seen such a _____ collection of bottles?
5. The _____ town had _____ buildings.
6. A _____ string dangled from the light fixture.
7. The _____ basket was full of _____ clothes.
8. The _____ ship sailed rapidly through the _____ sea.
9. _____ gophers sat upright in the _____ pasture.
10. A _____ car was parked near the _____ house.

Part 2   Predicate Adjectives

When a noun follows a linking verb and refers to the subject of the sentence, that noun is called a predicate noun.

> Mark is our *treasurer*. (The noun *treasurer* follows the linking verb *is* and modifies the subject *Mark. Treasurer* is a predicate noun.)

When an adjective follows a linking verb and modifies the subject of the sentence, that adjective is called a **predicate adjective.**

> Nancy is *funny*. (The adjective *funny* follows the linking verb *is* and modifies the subject *Nancy. Funny* is a predicate adjective.)

481

Part 2

Objective

To understand the function of predicate adjectives and to identify them in sentences

Presenting the Lesson

1. Read and discuss pages 481–482. Discuss the similarity in structure between predicate nouns and predicate adjectives. This is a good time to review linking verbs and predicate nouns.

2. Do Exercise A on page 482 with the students. Assign and discuss Exercise B on pages 482–483.

481

3. "Diagraming Sentences Containing Predicate Adjectives," page 483. Point out to students the slanted line that points back to the subject being modified. Compare diagraming predicate adjectives with diagraming adjectives (page 480).

4. Assign and discuss the exercise on pages 483–484. It provides additional practice in seeing the relationship between predicate adjectives and the subjects of sentences. Have students point out the linking verb in each sentence.

Individualizing the Lesson

Less-Advanced Students

1. Review the fact that linking verbs can be followed by predicate nouns. They can also be followed by adjectives.

2. Guide the students through Exercise A, putting the three columns on the board. If necessary, review the list of linking verbs on page 390.

3. Assign Exercise B for independent practice, then have students share their answers with the class. It may help students to first divide the sentence between the subject and the predicate.

Advanced Students

Have students suggest synonyms for the predicate adjectives in the exercises as a way of developing their vocabulary. They may find the thesaurus helpful.

Optional Practice

Refer the students to Exercises A and B on page 391. Instruct them to find which sentences contain predicate adjectives.

Here are some more sentences that contain predicate adjectives. What is the predicate adjective in each sentence? What word does it modify?

The windows were dirty.
This room smells musty.
Rich looks sick.
Sean appears calm.

A predicate adjective is an adjective that follows a linking verb and that modifies the subject.

Exercises **Find the linking verbs and predicate adjectives.**

A. On your paper, label three columns *Subject, Linking Verb,* and *Predicate Adjective.* Find these words in each sentence below. Write them in the column where they belong.

Example: This water is salty.

Subject	Linking Verb	Predicate Adjective
water	is	salty

1. My shoes felt tight.
2. The possibilities are endless.
3. After the rain, the basement smelled damp.
4. The plant looked dry.
5. The spinach tastes gritty.
6. His story sounds fishy to me.
7. This cocoa tastes bitter.
8. Does the old rug look clean?
9. Emily seemed happy tonight.
10. That mosquito is pesky.

B. Follow the directions for Exercise A.

1. This board still feels rough.
2. The rice looks sticky.

3. That siren (sounds) close.
4. On Thursday my mother (is) busy with her patients.
5. Your topic (sounds) good to me.
6. (Is) the knife sharp?
7. The applause (seemed) endless after her performance.
8. On stage Sharon (felt) confident.
9. That canoe (appears) unsafe.
10. These flowers (smell) good in the spring.

Diagraming Sentences Containing Predicate Adjectives

Show predicate adjectives in diagrams just as you show predicate nouns. Place them on the horizontal line following the verb. Separate them from the verb with a slanted line that points back toward the subject.

The slanting line shows the relationship between the predicate adjective and the subject.

The morning was cool.

Exercise   Find the predicate adjectives.

Copy these sentences. Show the relationship of the predicate adjective to the subject as your teacher directs.

Example: John is musical.

1. That room seemed stuffy.
2. Does the raft look safe?
3. That milk is sour.
4. Is your pencil sharp?

483

Have students complete these sentences with predicate adjectives: Sentences will vary.

Sports are _____.
The lake looks _____.
Saturdays are _____.
Winter seems _____.
I feel _____.

The students may work in groups to think of as many vivid predicate adjectives as they can. A thesaurus may be helpful. You can also have them develop one of the sentences into a topic sentence for a short paragraph.

Part 3

Objective

To identify possessive pronouns used as adjectives and to use them correctly

Presenting the Lesson

1. Assign and discuss page 484. Some students will resist the idea that a pronoun can also be considered an adjective. Remind them that the function of a word gives it its identity in a sentence. A pronoun may function as an adjective in some sentences.

2. Assign and discuss the exercise on page 484.

Individualizing the Lesson

Less-Advanced Students

Do the exercise as a class, writing the sentences on the chalkboard.

Advanced Students

After completing the exercise on page 484, turn back to the exercise on pages 483–484. Ask students to find the sentences in that exercise that use pronouns as adjectives.

Optional Practice

Have students write a sentence of their own for each of the possessive pronouns used as adjectives listed on page 484.

Extending the Lesson

Select a newspaper column and display it to the class using an opaque projector. Read it together. Have the students pick out all of the pronouns used as adjectives.

484

5. The teams appeared unequal in strength and speed.
6. In response to my question, Glenda's reply was frank.
7. The lake seems rough today.
8. During the race, his knees felt wobbly.
9. Under the microscope, the ant looked huge.
10. The Johnsons were nervous after the accident.

Part 3 Pronouns Used as Adjectives

Possessive pronouns are used as adjectives. As you can see from the following examples, a possessive pronoun is a modifier because it makes the meaning of a noun more exact.

my book	*our* room
your game	*your* trophies
his house, *her* ruler, *its* foot	*their* school

The words *my, your, his, her, its, our,* and *their* are possessive pronouns used as adjectives.

Exercise   **Find the pronouns used as adjectives.**

Copy the following sentences. Draw arrows from the possessive pronouns to the words they modify.

1. Dick and Elsie brought their stamps.
2. My new book has a red leather cover.
3. The horse has losts its rider.
4. My watch is on the mantel.
5. Did you wash your car?
6. The girls are repairing their bicycles.
7. These pants should have their cuffs fixed.
8. Our bicycles were chained to the parking meter.
9. The computer stored its information.
10. Jane left her bracelet on the chair.

484

Part 4 Demonstrative Adjectives

The words *this*, *that*, *these*, and *those* may be used as modifiers with nouns to point out specific things.

> I liked *this* book, but I really didn't like *that* one.
> *These* peas are fine, but *those* beans are tasteless.

When used as modifiers, these four words are called **demonstrative adjectives.** They tell *which one* or *which ones* about the nouns they modify. (When they are used by themselves, instead of as modifiers, these words are called **demonstrative pronouns:** I like *that.* *This* is better.)

Demonstrative Adjective	Demonstrative Pronoun
I liked *this* book.	I liked *this.*
We saw *that* play.	We saw *that.*

Exercise **Find demonstrative pronouns and demonstrative adjectives.**

On your paper make two columns: *Demonstrative Adjectives* and *Demonstrative Pronouns*. Write the demonstrative words in these sentences in the correct columns.

DP 1. These are my friends Terry and JoAnn.

DP 2. That was my final trip to the orthodontist.

DP 3. This is the field where we play softball.

DA 4. That woman told my fortune.

DA 5. This moped runs well.

DA 6. That motor should be oiled.

DA 7. Don't these pictures remind you of summertime?

DP 8. This is the second time I've lost my bike.

DA 9. Do you see those airplanes flying in formation over the lake?

DA 10. Can you knock over those bowling pins all at once?

485

Part 4

Objective

To differentiate between demonstrative pronouns and demonstrative adjectives and to use them correctly

Presenting the Lesson

1. Read and discuss page 485.
2. Assign and discuss the exercise on page 485.

Individualizing the Lesson

Less-Advanced Students

1. Have students practice using demonstrative adjectives orally. Have them point out objects in the classroom, such as *this* pencil, *that* eraser, *those* kinds of shoes.
2. Do the exercise on page 485 orally placing the two columns on the chalkboard.

Advanced Students

Add these items to the exercise on page 485.
11. These are the best burritos in town. *D.P.*
12. This insect repellent works well. *D.A.*
13. Isn't that car a convertible? *D.A.*
14. What are those? *D.P.*
15. These shoes are comfortable. *D.A.*

Optional Practice

Have students write two sentences using each of the demonstratives *(this, that, these,* and *those),* first as pronouns and then as adjectives.

Extending the Lesson

Have students find the demonstrative pronouns and the demon-

485

strative adjectives in the following sentences.

^{D.A.} This umbrella is mine, and that ^{D.P.} is yours. These boots ^{D.A.} are mine, and those are yours. That ^{D.A.} coat on the hook is mine. That ^{D.A.} one on the chair is yours. Do we have everything? I think we're ready for a walk in the rain now.

Part 5

Objective

To form the comparative and superlative forms of adjectives, particularly irregular comparisons, and to use them correctly

Presenting the Lesson

1. Read and discuss pages 486–488.

2. You may wish to do Exercise A on page 488 with the class. Then assign and discuss Exercise B on pages 488–489.

3. Point out that the word after a comparative adjective is always *than*, not *then*, which means *later*.

Individualizing the Lesson

Less-Advanced Students

1. At this time you may want to review spelling rules for adding endings. If a word ends in *y*, change the *y* to *i* before adding the ending: *happy = happier.*

When a word ends with a short vowel and consonant, double the final consonant: *wet = wetter.*

2. Have students give examples of comparative and superlative

Part 5 Adjectives in Comparisons

Comparing people and things is one way of learning about the world. You often compare new things with things you already know. You might say, for example, "These new stereo speakers are *better* than the old ones. The sound is *clearer,* but they are *more expensive.*" Or you might say, "The new singer is the *best* one in the group."

In comparisons, adjectives have special forms or spellings.

The Comparative

When you compare one person or thing with another, use the **comparative** form of the adjective.

> Rob is *taller* than John.
> My dog is *smarter* than yours.

The comparative form is made in two ways:

1. For short adjectives like *calm* and *slow,* add *-er.*

   calm + er = calmer   slow + er = slower
   happy + er = happier   bright + er = brighter

2. For longer adjectives like *delicious,* use *more.*

   more delicious   more enjoyable

Most adjectives ending in *-ful* and *-ous* form the comparative with *more.*

   more thoughtful   more gracious

The Superlative

When you compare a person or a thing with all others of its kind, use the **superlative** form of the adjective. In fact, whenever you compare a person or thing with more than one other person or thing, use the superlative.

Lynn is the *tallest* person in the class.
The tiger seems to be the *most ferocious* animal in the zoo.

The superlative form of adjectives is made by adding *-est* or by using *most*. For adjectives that take *-er* in the comparative, add *-est* for the superlative. Those that use *more* to form the comparative use *most* for the superlative.

Adjective	Comparative	Superlative
full	fuller	fullest
dim	dimmer	dimmest
pretty	prettier	prettiest
practical	more practical	most practical
courageous	more courageous	most courageous

Remember three things in using adjectives for comparison:

1. Use the comparative to compare two persons or things. Use the superlative to compare more than two.

This year's model is *sleeker* than last year's.
Jenny is the *youngest* member of our family.

2. Do not leave out the word *other* when you are comparing something with everything else of its kind.

Wrong: I like Mark Twain better than any author.
(This sentence says that Mark Twain is not an author.)
Right: I like Mark Twain better than any *other* author.

Wrong: Sequoias grow taller than any tree.
(Are sequoias trees?)
Right: Sequoias grow taller than any *other* tree.

3. Do not use both *-er* and *more* or *-est* and *most* at the same time.

Wrong: Lead is more softer than steel.
Right: Lead is *softer* than steel.

Wrong: Science is the most easiest subject for me.
Right: Science is the *easiest* subject for me.

forms. Stress that the superlative is only used when comparing three or more things.

3. Do Exercise B orally with the class.

Advanced Students

1. Inform students that some words such as *perfect* do not have comparative or superlative forms. One thing cannot be more *perfect* than another. Ask students to think of other adjectives of this type.

2. Have students write five sentences using comparative forms of adjectives and five sentences using superlative forms of adjectives.

Optional Practice

1. Make up a worksheet including three columns labeled *Adjective*, *Comparative Form*, and *Superlative Form*. For each item give one of the forms and have students fill in the other two. This will reinforce the spelling of the adjectives.

2. Have students fill in the comparative form of the adjective in parentheses in sentences 1 to 8 and the superlative form in sentences 9 to 16.

1. The home team was (lucky) luckier. than the visiting team.

2. The ballerina seemed (beautiful) more beautiful than ever.

3. This winter is (cold) colder than last winter.

4. Some guests arrived (early) earlier than others.

5. The meals in this restaurant are much (good) better than in most other places.

6. I like brocolli (little) less than I like spinach.

7. Joy and Amy go roller skating (much) _more_ often than ice skating.

8. The marathon winner ran (fast) _faster_ than anyone else.

9. The giraffe is the (tall) _tallest_ living animal.

10. The (long) _longest_ river in the world is the Nile.

11. The (common) _common_ Chinese name is Chang. ^{most}

12. The (long) _longest_ leap by a frog recorded at the annual Calaveras County Jumping Frog Jubilee was 17 feet, 6¾ inches.

13. Our swimming team was the (successful) _successful_ this year. ^{most}

14. The world's (busy) _busiest_ airport is O'Hare International Airport in Chicago.

15. The (large) _largest_ mammal is the blue whale.

Extending the Lesson

Have students clip pictures from magazines showing the three forms of an adjective. Have them display their findings around the room. Example: *happy, happier, happiest.*

Irregular Comparisons

You form the comparative and superlative of certain adjectives by changing the words:

	Comparative	Superlative
good	better	best
well	better	best
bad	worse	worst
little	less *or* lesser	least
much	more	most
many	more	most
far	farther	farthest

Exercises

A. Write the correct form of the <u>adjective</u>.

1. My suitcase is (heavier, heaviest) than yours.
2. It was (warmest, warmer) in Texas than in Florida.
3. Wilson's store was always the (busiest, busier) in town.
4. Of the two parks, I like this one (best, better).
5. This is the (worse, worst) program I've ever seen.
6. Jill was the (youngest, younger) of the two.
7. These socks are the (softer, softest) of all.
8. This traffic is the (worst, worse) in the area.
9. That was the (shorter, shortest) night of the year.
10. Jan's room is (more cluttered, most cluttered) than mine.

B. Write the correct form of the adjective, following the directions in parentheses.

Example: He runs (comparative of *fast*) than I.
Answer: faster

1. We need a (comparative of *narrow*) board than this. ^{narrower}
2. Lunch was (comparative of *good*) than breakfast. ^{better}

3. The lake was (comparative of *rough*) than usual. rougher
4. It was the (superlative of *funny*) movie I've ever seen. funniest
5. No school in town has (comparative of *beautiful*) grounds than ours. more beautiful
6. Greg politely took the (comparative of *small*) piece. smaller
7. That's the (superlative of *bright*) star in the whole sky. brightest
8. This soda tastes (comparative of *creamy*) than that. creamier
9. He was (comparative of *underweight*) than his brother. more underweight
10. The bus driver was (comparative of *careful*) than most I have seen. more careful

Part 6 Special Problems with Adjectives

Them and *Those*

Them is always a pronoun. It is used as an object.

Those is an adjective if it is followed by a noun. It is a pronoun if it is used alone.

> We asked *them* for a ride. (pronoun)
> *Those* cans fell to the floor. (adjective)
> *Those* are my books. (pronoun)

Never substitute *them* for *those*.

> Wrong: *Them* boys brought the canoe.
> Right: *Those* boys brought the canoe.

The Extra *Here* and *There*

Have you ever heard someone say, "This here pen" or "That there car"? The word *this* includes the meaning of *here*. The word *that* includes the meaning of *there*. Never use *this here* or *that there* before a noun.

Part 6

Objective

To use *them* and *those*, and *here* and *there* correctly, and to use the correct demonstratives with *kind* and *sort*

Presenting the Lesson

1. Read and discuss pages 489–490.
2. Do Exercise A on page 490 with the class. Assign and discuss Exercise B on page 490.

Individualizing the Lesson

Less-Advanced Students

Write the following sentences on the board. See if students can find the error in each. Discuss the problems with each sentence while correcting them.

1. This ~~here~~ wire should be replaced.
2. Mario doesn't like these sorts of games.
3. The committee never purchases those kinds of supplies.
4. Did you read that ~~there~~ poster about the tournament?
5. You should take some photographs of ~~them~~ those puppies.

Advanced Students

Have students rewrite this paragraph, correcting the errors made in the use of adjectives.

Them totem poles are over two hundred years old. This here pole was carved from a solid block of wood. That there pole was painted with vegetable dyes. Those kind of dyes produce beautiful colors.

489

Have students circle any words in the following sentences that are incorrect and rewrite the sentences correctly.

1. These ~~here~~ dinosaur bones are prehistoric.
2. Look at ~~them~~ photos of the moon's surface. *(those)*
3. Sometimes the farm stand sells ~~them~~ kinds of vegetables. *(those)*
4. I like this ~~here~~ kind of bicycle best.
5. We bought ~~them~~ new tennis balls on sale. *(those)*
6. These ~~kind~~ of puzzles confuse me. *(kinds)*
7. Cora enjoys those sort s of Hardy Boys' mystery stories.
8. The young kitten clawed ~~them~~ new drapes into shreds. *(those)*
9. ~~Them~~ apples are only for cooking. *(Those)*
10. The car dealer ordered ~~this~~ special accessories for his own car. *(these)*

Extending the Lesson

Have students write a sentence for each of the following: *this kind, these kinds, this sort, these sorts, those* (adjective), *those* (pronoun) *them* (pronoun).

Kind and Sort

Kind and *sort* are singular. Use *this* or *that* to modify *kind* and *sort*.

Kinds and *sorts* are plural. Use *these* or *those* to modify *kinds* and *sorts*.

I enjoy *this* kind of movie.   *Those* kinds of games tire Spot.

Exercises   Use modifiers correctly.

A.   Choose the right word from the two given in parentheses in each of the following sentences.

1. (<u>This</u>, This here) cake is made from carrots.
2. Did (them, <u>those</u>) raccoons raid the garbage cans?
3. Have you seen (them, <u>those</u>) magazines?
4. (<u>That</u>, That there) biplane crossed the Atlantic.
5. Our gym class does (that, <u>those</u>) kinds of exercises.
6. (Them, <u>Those</u>) plums look fresh and juicy.
7. Actors wear (<u>that</u>, those) kind of makeup.
8. I like (them, <u>those</u>) commercials better than the show.
9. (<u>That</u>, That there) roller coaster goes very fast.
10. (This, <u>These</u>) kinds of tapes don't have good sound.

B.   Choose the right word in these sentences.

1. Lola can do (<u>that</u>, those) kind of back dive.
2. Someone should wash (them, <u>those</u>) windows.
3. Football players wear (<u>this</u>, these) kind of shoe.
4. (Them, <u>Those</u>) sponges grow on the ocean floor.
5. Campers use (this, <u>these</u>) kinds of wood for fires.
6. The forest ranger spotted (them, <u>those</u>) bears.
7. (<u>That</u>, That there) bicycle belongs to Brian.
8. (<u>This</u>, This here) train runs between here and Boston.
9. Terry's stereo has (that, <u>those</u>) kinds of speakers.
10. The Dodgers train at (<u>that</u>, that there) stadium.

ADDITIONAL EXERCISES

Using Adjectives

A. Adjectives Number your paper from 1 to 10. Make two columns. Put the adjectives in one column and the nouns they modify in the other. Ignore any articles.

1. The fence had sharp spikes on top.
2. The two hikers dropped the heavy backpacks.
3. These books have good photographs.
4. The gym echoed with the lively beat of the music.
5. You need a lighter hammer for those tiny nails.
6. The bright sun melted the snow despite the low temperature.
7. A weary young man was picking the ripe berries.
8. I bought Swiss cheese and one loaf of French bread.
9. The moon made a narrow gold path on the water.
10. We packed the fragile glasses in a sturdy crate.

B. Predicate Adjectives Label three columns *Subject,* *Linking Verb,* and *Predicate Adjective.* Find these words in each sentence below, and write them in the appropriate columns.

1. Your map is too old.
2. Lake Huron was once clear.
3. The butter knife is smaller.
4. These drums are African.
5. My closet is full of junk.
6. Maybe that box is empty.
7. Sandy's balance has always been poor.
8. The child star grew too tall for the part.
9. Her remarks sounded rude.
10. The stars were visible last night.

491

Additional Exercises

These Additional Exercises may be used for additional practice of the concepts presented in this Section. Each exercise focuses on a single concept, and should be used after the page number indicated in parentheses.

Review

If you have not assigned these Additional Exercises before this time, you can also use them as an excellent Section Review.

491

C. Pronouns Used as Adjectives Number your paper from 1 to 10. Label two columns *Possessive Pronoun* and *Word Modified.* Put the possessive pronouns and the words that they modify in the correct columns.

1. Our (kite) soared above the trees.
2. The siren screamed its (warning.)
3. Ducklings follow their (mother) almost everywhere.
4. Betsy bought some buttons for her (shirt.)
5. The students cleaned out their (lockers) before vacation.
6. Mr. Cabrera usually enjoys his (job.)
7. The janitor washed our (windows.)
8. The garter snake raised its (head) and looked around.
9. Did you finish your (math) yet?
10. I found my (scarf) at Kitty's house.

D. Demonstrative Adjectives Number your paper from 1 to 10. Label two columns *Demonstrative Adjective* and *Word Modified.* Put the demonstrative adjectives and the words that they modify in the correct columns.

1. This (splinter) will be hard to remove.
2. Did you see that (motorcycle?)
3. Take these (clothes) to the dry cleaner's.
4. Those (holes) in the net won't hurt the game.
5. That (song) gets on my nerves.
6. Our doctor has an office in this (building.)
7. Doesn't that (van) belong to the school?
8. Some of those horror (movies) are funny.
9. Shall I give out these (booklets?)
10. Throw away those (rags) with paint on them.

E. Adjectives in Comparisons Number your paper from 1 to 10. Choose the correct form of the adjective from the two given in parentheses.

1. That was the (hottest, most hottest) day of summer.

2. Tara is the (more athletic, most athletic) of the twins.

3. Does an album or a cassette cost (more, most)?

4. Gold is (heavier, more heavier) than silver.

5. Mr. Ridolfi tells the (worse, worst) jokes.

6. Of the three dogs, Scout is the (shyer, shyest).

7. Of these two books, which is (best, better)?

8. Pete is (courteouser, more courteous) when he's happy.

9. This roller coaster is the (most best, best) I've ridden.

10. That is the (least, leastest) of my worries.

F. Special Problems with Adjectives Number your paper from 1 to 10. If there is a mistake with the way an adjective is used, write the sentence correctly. If the sentence is correct, write *Correct*.

1. I will send them this here card.

2. Them seeds should be planted in the shade.
   Those

c 3. These kinds of moccasins wear out quickly.

4. Some of them electronic eyes can identify colors.
   those

5. This here is your seat.

6. That there door leads to the basement.

7. Not many of them Canadian Mounties still ride horses.
   those

c 8. The dentist recommended this sort of toothbrush.

9. Don't give him those kind of gift.
   that

10. Don't them there peaches look good?
    those

These exercises provide re-view of the concepts pre-sented in this Section. Each exercise challenges the stu-dents to apply several of the skills they have acquired dur-ing previous study. Because the "mixed" feature of these activities makes them more difficult, the teacher may wish to have less-advanced stu-dents do them orally or in small groups.

MIXED REVIEW

Using Adjectives

A. Finding adjectives Write all of the adjectives in the following sentences. Include proper adjectives, articles, pro-nouns used as adjectives, and demonstrative adjectives. After each adjective, write the word it modifies.

1. The tourists ate in a small Chinese restaurant.
2. An entire city was buried by the huge volcano.
3. The students, rested and prepared, took the exam.
4. The mountaintops were snowy.
5. That magazine has a wide circulation.
6. My mother will be running in our local marathon.
7. This sauce tastes delicious.
8. Your music is disturbing my sleep.
9. Are my books in the cafeteria?
10. A colorful quilt covered the old brass bed.

B. Using adjectives correctly The following paragraph contains nine errors in the use of adjectives. Rewrite the paragraph, correcting any errors you find.

The first~~est~~ question people ask me about ^{my} ~~mine~~ dog, Pedi, is always the same: "What breed of dog is that ~~there~~ dog?" I don't enjoy ^{these} ~~this~~ kinds of questions. You see, breeds are a delicate subject for me. Don't misun-derstand. I'm not ashamed of Pedi's poodle, spaniel, and terrier background. He's bright, obedient, and ^{healthy} ~~healthier~~. With his shiny black coat, Pedi is the ^{handsomest} ~~handsomer~~ dog I know. Like most mixed breeds, he's calm~~est~~ and good-natured. To show how much I care for him, I named him Pedigree. It's the only pedigree he'll ever have, but he's the ^{best} ~~bestest~~ dog in this ~~here~~ world.

USING GRAMMAR IN WRITING
Using Adjectives

A. The things we own and the way we dress often tell others a lot about us. For example, a guitar, frayed jeans, and a short-wave radio might be clues to someone's personality and interests. What do you own that tells something about you? What might someone learn about you if he or she peeked into your closet or your school locker? Write a paragraph that tells what this person might see and what conclusions he or she might draw. Use plenty of adjectives to describe your closet or locker and its contents.

B. Imagine that you have been chosen as a set designer for the class play. The setting for this one-act play is the attic of a large, old house. You must create an atmosphere of mystery and suspense. Before visiting the prop room, you make a list of items you might need. Rewrite the list, using adjectives to further describe these key elements of the setting.

trunk	barrel of clothes	doll
mannequin	chair	boxes
newspapers	lamp	painting
phonograph	mirror	rocking horse

These challenging and enjoyable activities allow the students to see how the concepts of grammar, usage, and mechanics may be applied in actual writing situations. Each exercise is designed to allow students practice in several of the skills they have acquired in this Section. The activities also provide opportunities for students to write creatively about a wide variety of interesting and unusual subjects.

Section Objectives

1. To understand the function of adverbs, to identify them in sentences, and to use them correctly

2. To form the comparative and superlative forms of adverbs and to use them correctly

3. To differentiate between adverbs and adjectives and to use them correctly

4. To correctly use *good* and *well*, *bad* and *badly,* and to avoid the double negative

Preparing the Students

Review the function of modifiers: to limit the meaning of a word and make that meaning more definite. Explain that adverbs, like adjectives, are used to modify other words. They enrich the meaning of verbs, adjectives, and other adverbs.

Additional Resources

Diagnostic Test — page 4 in the test booklet

Mastery Test — pages 53–54 in the test booklet

Additional Exercises — pages 510–513 in the student text

Practice Book — pages 191–195

Duplicating Masters — pages 191–195

Special Populations — See special section at the back of this Teacher's Edition.

Using Adverbs

Part 1   What Are Adverbs?

You have already studied adjectives, which modify nouns and pronouns. In this section you will learn about a second kind of modifier: **adverbs.** Adverbs modify verbs, adjectives, and other adverbs.

In order to make your meaning clear, vivid, and complete, you often use words that tell *how, when, where,* or *to what extent*. These words are called adverbs.

Adverbs Modify Verbs.

We *walked.*

How? We walked *slowly.*

When? We walked *yesterday.*

Where? We walked *out.*

Adverbs Modify Adjectives.

It was a *clear* day.

How clear? It was a *fairly* clear day.

The problem was *difficult.*

How difficult? The problem was *too* difficult.

I was *late.*

To what extent? I was *very* late.

Adverbs Modify Other Adverbs.

Joe talked *fast.*

How fast? Joe talked *extremely* fast.

The senators agreed *enthusiastically.*

How enthusiastically? The senators agreed *most* enthusiastically.

The ball rolled *away.*

To what extent? The ball rolled *far* away.

Adverbs are words that modify verbs, adjectives, and other adverbs.

Exercises **Find the adverbs.**

A. Copy each sentence. Draw an arrow from the adverb to the word it modifies.

Example: Ms. James came home early.

1. Our puppy barked eagerly.

497

Objective

To understand the function of adverbs, to identify them in sentences, and to use them correctly

Presenting the Lesson

1. Read and discuss pages 496–497.

2. Assign and discuss Exercises A and B on pages 497–498. Point out that a great many adverbs end in the suffix *-ly.* Often an adjective may be changed into an adverb by adding *-ly (fair* to *fairly, clear* to *clearly).* You may want to do part of each exercise with the class. In Exercise A, every adverb modifies a verb. In Exercise B, adverbs modify verbs, adjectives, and other adverbs. When checking Exercise B, you might find it helpful to have the students identify each word modified by adverbs and identify which of the three types it is.

3. Read and discuss page 498. Positioning of adverbs can be a valuable lesson for increasing sentence variety in student compositions. Adverbs modifying verbs are most commonly located at the beginning or end of a sentence. Go back to the exercises on pages 497–498 and see if the adverbs assume any other positions in the sentences. Tell students that when there are alternatives, personal taste and a writer's style often dictate which of the positions will be appropriate.

4. Read and discuss "Diagraming Sentences Containing Adverbs," page 499. By this time the sentence diagram has become fairly complex. All students will benefit, however, from sample diagrams drawn on the board to illustrate the relationships between the various parts of the sentence. Only the more-advanced students should be assigned diagrams to complete independently.

5. Assign and discuss Exercise A on pages 499–500. Only single-word adverbs should be accepted for this exercise. Avoid confusion by making this clear at the beginning of the exercise. Review student responses orally, gathering as many possible answers for each sentence as you can. Point out how the meaning of a sentence is altered by using different adverbs. Assign and discuss Exercise B on page 500 which asks students to write sentences using the list of adverbs. When discussing what has been written, ask students to explain what question each adverb answers.

6. Read and discuss page 500. Ask students for other examples of adjectives that can be changed to adverbs by adding -ly.

7. Assign and discuss the exercise on page 501. Stress the spelling change necessary when the adjective ends in y.

Individualizing the Lesson

Less-Advanced Students

1. Have students work in pairs to complete Exercises A and B on pages 497–498.

2. Now have students make four columns on their papers labeled *How, When, Where,* and *To What Extent.* Ask them to list the appropriate adverbs from the sentences in their proper columns.

498

2. Sandra and Andy play tennis regularly.
3. Rain fell heavily during the night.
4. They ran swiftly from the car to the house.
5. The Warners had parked nearby.
6. Ben scored easily from mid-court.
7. The water rose steadily.
8. He will leave tomorrow for San Francisco.
9. Have you skied lately?
10. The skiers raced daringly down the slopes.

B. Follow the directions for Exercise A.

1. The movie was terribly funny.
2. Chris and Bruce are definitely running for office.
3. The gymnast gracefully performed her floor exercise.
4. Scott was extremely quiet during the class discussion.
5. A performance by that symphony orchestra is always beautiful.
6. To our surprise, Luanne's speech was quite short and very interesting.
7. The cowboy hat looked simply ridiculous on him.
8. The closet is cleaner now.
9. His report on the battles of the Civil War was very long.
10. The base runner easily stole second.

The Position of Adverbs

When an adverb modifies an adjective or another adverb, it usually comes before the word it modifies:

very hot   *quite* still   *not* often

But when an adverb modifies a verb, its position is not usually fixed:

I see *now.*   *Now* I see.   I *now* see.

Diagraming Sentences Containing Adverbs

Adverbs, like adjectives, are shown in diagrams on lines slanting down from the words they modify. The following diagram shows an adverb modifying a verb.

Finally the shy boy asked a question.

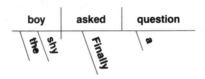

Notice that *Finally*, the first word in the sentence, keeps its capital *F* in the diagram.

That fairly young boy plays the violin quite well.

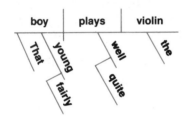

This diagram shows an adverb modifying a verb (*plays*). It shows an adverb (*fairly*) modifying an adjective (*young*). It also shows an adverb (*quite*) modifying another adverb (*well*). Notice how *fairly* is attached to *young*. Notice how *quite* is attached to *well*.

Exercises   Use adverbs.

A.   Rewrite the following sentences, supplying adverbs that answer the questions in parentheses. Answers will vary.

> Example: Wash the dishes. (*When?*)
> Wash the dishes *now*.

1. Bring your books. (*When?*)

3. Help students decide which part of speech the adverb modifies. You may want to add another column for this.

4. Have students select only eight of the adverbs for Exercise B on page 500.

Advanced Students

1. After completing the exercise on page 501, students will have lists of adjectives and adverbs. Have them use each in a sentence.

2. Have students list five more adjectives that can be changed into adverbs. Then have them exchange lists with classmates and write sentences for each adverb.

3. Have each student underline every adverb in a newspaper sports report or a short article in a sports magazine.

Optional Practice

1. Have students clip pictures from magazines or newspapers for which they could write captions containing adverbs. For example: The student is studying *quietly*. Have them write the sentence under the clipping. Display their work.

2. Show students a picture showing action. Ask them to list words that tell about the action (verbs). Then, next to each verb, have them write a single-word adverb that describes that verb.

3. Have students make four columns on their paper labeled *How, When, Where,* and *To What Extent*. Ask students to list each of the following adverbs in the correct columns:

down, strongly, very, inside, there, cleverly, here, badly, then, swiftly, weekly, accurately, quietly, eagerly, around, wide, actively, indoors, perfectly, later, loosely, yesterday, happily, sleepily, forever, immediately, incorrectly, today, softly, too

Extending the Lesson

1. Have students imagine a super-machine they would like to invent, give it a name, and write at least eight sentences, each telling something different that it does. They should use at least one adverb in each sentence to describe the action.

2. Tell students that each of the following sentences contains an incorrectly placed adverb. Have them draw a line through the adverb, then place the adverb in a new location by writing it on the line above the sentence and indicating exactly where it should go with a caret (∧).

1. The disc jockey∧played quickly the newest record.
2. The neighbor∧walked briskly her dog∧
3. We planted early the vegetables∧
4. Bring immediately me some ice∧
5. The chef cooked thoroughly the pork roast∧
6. The skier∧sprained badly her ankle∧
7. Marcia ordered early the tickets∧
8. The entertainer played excellently the piano.∧
9. The carpenter∧built skillfully his own garage∧
10. Dwayne was∧raking happily all the leaves in his yard.

500

2. The monkey climbed. (*How?*)
3. The elevator stopped. (*Where?*)
4. Did your cousin arrive? (*When?*)
5. The bird flew. (*Where?*)
6. The runners rounded the turn. (*How?*)
7. Jack slept soundly. (*How soundly?*)
8. The small deer raised up its head and looked. (*Looked where?*)
9. The sunset was beautiful. (*How beautiful?*)
10. The damaged plane arrived. (*When?*)

B. Writing Write sentences using the following adverbs. You have seen that certain adverbs may appear in three positions: after the verb (I see *now*), at the beginning of a sentence (*Now* I see), and just before the verb (I *now* see). Try to experiment with the position of these adverbs in the sentences you write. Answers will vary.

1. closely	5. finally	9. quietly	13. fairly
2. speedily	6. forcefully	10. often	14. quite
3. now	7. nearly	11. sometimes	15. soon
4. never	8. loudly	12. always	16. lately

Forming Adverbs

Many adverbs are made by adding -*ly* to an adjective:

plain + -ly = plainly
brave + -ly = bravely

Sometimes the addition of -*ly* involves a spelling change in the adjective:

noisy + -ly = noisily (*y* changed to *i*)
terrible + -ly = terribly (final *e* dropped)
dull + -ly = dully (*ll* changed to *l*)

500

Exercise Form adverbs.

Change the following adjectives into adverbs by adding -*ly*. Use a dictionary to check your spelling.

pure — purely
crazy — crazily
full — fully
thoughtful — thoughtfully

nice — nicely
open — openly
shy — shyly
double — doubly

large — largely
merry — merrily
evil — evilly
capable — capably

gloomy — gloomily
speedy — speedily
loose — loosely
playful — playfully

Part 2 Adverbs in Comparisons

Adverbs are used to compare one action with another. You might say, "This engine runs *smoothly,* but that one runs *more smoothly.*"

Or you might say, "Julie planned her exhibit *more carefully* than any other student in the class."

Adverbs have special forms or spellings for use in making comparisons, just as adjectives do.

The Comparative

When you compare one action with another one, use the **comparative** form of the adverb. The comparative form is made in two ways:

1. For short adverbs like *high* and *early,* add -*er.*

The rocket soared *higher* into space.
Betsy left the party *earlier* than Sue.

2. For most adverbs ending in -*ly,* use *more* to make the comparative.

Stores handle eggs *more carefully* than other foods.
The instructor skied *more smoothly* than his pupils.

501

Objective

To form the comparative and superlative forms of adverbs and to use them correctly

Presenting the Lesson

1. Read and discuss pages 501–503. Point out that, as with adjectives, there are comparative and superlative forms for adverbs. The comparative is used to compare two things. The superlative is used to compare three or more things. Point out that the rules for making the comparative and superlative forms of adverbs are the same as for adjectives (add -*er* or -*est*) except when the adverb ends in -*ly* (add *more* or *most* before the adverb). Remind students that it is incorrect to use -*er* and *more* or -*est* and *most* together. Also, the -*ly* ending of an adverb is never removed to form the comparative or superlative form (*happily* becomes *more happily,* not *happier*).

2. You may wish to assign and discuss Exercise A on page 503 first, and then assign Exercise B on pages 503–504.

1. Do Exercise A orally. Have students choose the correct answer and tell if it is in the comparative form or the superlative form.

2. Have students list their answers for the exercises in four columns on their papers. Label them *How*, *When*, *Where*, and *To What Extent*.

3. Ask students to write sentences for each of the irregular adverbs listed on page 503.

Advanced Students

1. After completing Exercise B, have students write the other two forms of each adverb. They should also write each of the other forms in a sentence.

2. Have students make charts of the comparative and superlative forms of various adverbs.

3. Have students form sentences from each adverb below. Write three sentences using each of the forms.

Example: *Sentences will vary.*

John arrived early.
John arrived earlier than Fran.
John arrived earliest of all.

quick	soon
often	swift
late	sweetly

Optional Practice

All of these sentences contain errors in the use of adverbs. Rewrite each sentence correctly.

1. Sally can add ~~more~~ faster on the calculator.
2. Lance types ~~carefuller~~ than Kitty. *(more carefully)*
3. This shirt is the ~~least~~ expensive of the two. *(less)*

The Superlative

When you compare one action with two or more actions of the same kind, use the **superlative** form of the adverb.

Of all the clerks, Debbie works *most efficiently.*
Connie and Dave try hard, but Joe tries *hardest.*

The superlative form of adverbs is formed by adding *-est* or by using *most.* Adverbs that form the comparative with *-er* form the superlative with *-est.* Those that use *more* for the comparative use *most* for the superlative.

Adverb	Comparative	Superlative
late	later	latest
fast	faster	fastest
fiercely	more fiercely	most fiercely
softly	more softly	most softly

In using the comparative and superlative forms of adverbs, keep in mind the following three points.

1. Use the comparative to compare two actions and the superlative to compare more than two.

Jenny runs *faster* than Emmy.
Of all the runners, Jenny moves the *fastest.*

2. Do not leave out the word *other* when you are comparing one action with every other action of the same kind.

Wrong: A cheetah travels faster than any animal.
Right: A cheetah travels faster than any *other* animal.

3. Do not use both *-er* and *more* or *-est* and *most* at the same time.

Wrong: Bill sprints more faster.
Right: Bill sprints *faster.*

Irregular Comparisons

Some adverbs make their comparative and superlative forms by complete word changes. For example:

Adverb	Comparative	Superlative
well	better	best
much	more	most
little	less	least

Exercises **Use the correct forms of adverbs.**

A. For each of the following sentences, write the correct form of the adverb from the two given in parentheses.

1. I walked into the library (<u>more quietly</u>, most quietly) than before.
2. Nobody can count money (best, <u>better</u>) than she.
3. My mother exercises (<u>more regularly</u>, most regularly) than I do.
4. Our relay team could run the (faster, <u>fastest</u>) of all.
5. He wrapped my package the (more carefully, <u>most carefully</u>) of all.
6. Watch this film (<u>more closely</u>, most closely) than that.
7. Mark ran (best, <u>better</u>) than anyone in the group.
8. Ray cleared the jump (most easily, <u>more easily</u>) than I.
9. My dog drinks (<u>less</u>, least) than any other dog I know.
10. Sally tried (hardest, <u>harder</u>) than anyone.

B. For each of these sentences, write the correct form for the adverb, following the directions in parentheses.

1. Ted usually wakes up (superlative of *early*). earliest
2. A snail walks (comparative of *fast*) than Joe. faster
3. Our friends stayed (comparative of *long*) than usual. longer
4. Dr. Parr arrived home from Brazil (comparative of *soon*) than her postcards. sooner

4. The librarian asked us to speak softly.
5. Mark gives directions ~~good~~. well
6. Of the five runners, Danielle ran ~~more~~ quickly. most
7. No copying machine operates more ~~easier~~ than this one. easily
8. The windows shone brightly in the sunlight.

Extending the Lesson

Have students take a newspaper or magazine article of some length and circle all the adverbs. Then they should write each one in a list and write whether it answers the question *how?*, *when?*, *where?*, or *to what extent?*

Objective

To differentiate between adverbs and adjectives and to use them correctly

Presenting the Lesson

1. Read and discuss pages 504–505.

2. Assign and discuss Exercises A and B on pages 505–506. Remind students to find what word is being modified to determine whether the modifier is an adjective or an adverb.

3. Then assign Exercises A and B on pages 506–507. When students have completed them, discuss their answers.

4. Discuss the fact that the correct use of adjectives and adverbs is a problem for many students in their own written work. Conversational English often uses the adjective form when the adverb form is called for *(move quick* is used instead of *move more quickly)*. Impress upon students the importance of using the standard forms in more formal situations, both spoken and written.

Avoid using the words *right* and *wrong* when discussing English usage. Instead the appropriateness for a particular situation must always be considered. Be sure that students consider the degree of formality of a situation when making any decisions concerning the use of language.

5. That package took the (superlative of *long*) time to arrive. longest

6. No one draws (comparative of *well*) than Sue. better

7. I reread the short story (comparative of *carefully*) the second time. more carefully

8. She speaks (comparative of *distinctly*) than he does. more distinctly

9. That driver approached the bridge (comparative of *cautiously*) than anyone. more cautiously

10. This door opened (comparative of *easily*) than the other. more easily

Part 3   Adjective or Adverb?

An adverb tells	An adjective tells
how when where to what extent	what kind how many which one
about a verb, adjective, or adverb.	**about a noun or pronoun.**

Study the following sentences. Which sentence sounds right to you?

> Our team won *easy.*
> Our team won *easily.*

The second sentence is the correct one. An adverb (*easily*) should be used, not an adjective (*easy*).

It is sometimes difficult to decide whether an adjective or an adverb should be used in sentences like the two given above. When you are not sure which modifier to use, ask yourself these questions:

1. Which word does the modifier describe? If it describes a verb (like *won* in the sentences above), it is an adverb. It is also an adverb if it describes an adjective or another adverb. If it describes a noun or a pronoun, it is an adjective.

2. What does the modifier tell about the word it describes? If the modifier tells *how, when, where,* or *to what extent,* it is an adverb. If it tells *what kind, how many,* or *which one,* it is an adjective. In the sentences above, the modifier tells *how* our team won. Therefore, it must be an adverb: *easily.*

Exercises   Find the adjectives and adverbs.

A. Number your paper from 1 to 10. Make two columns. Label one *Adjectives* and one *Adverbs.* List the adjectives and adverbs from each sentence in the proper columns. Do not list articles.

1. The sportscaster talked endlessly about the new season.
2. A single sailboat drifted on the peaceful lake.
3. Suddenly, a heavy rainstorm flooded the streets.
4. The tiny car left a gray cloud of smoke as it quickly pulled away.
5. This salesperson seems too pushy.
6. An extremely deep hit by Garvey scored two runs.
7. Rapidly and skillfully, the farmer steered a huge tractor through the fields.
8. The gray horse responds more gently than the brown one.
9. Jed was pleasantly surprised by very good grades last semester.
10. Kris usually studies in the quietest room in the house.

Follow the directions for Exercise A.

1. Of the fifty jumpers, Molly leaped highest.

Individualizing the Lesson

Less-Advanced Students

For Exercises A and B on pages 505–506, stress that the first step in determining whether a word is an adjective or an adverb is deciding whether the verb is a linking verb or an action verb. Tell students that confusion often arises from verbs that can be either linking or action *(look, appear, smell, taste).* Give examples of these words used both with predicate adjectives and with adverbs. Discuss how the verbs used in the following samples determine which modifier is correct.

1. He writes (good, well). (The word *well* is an adverb modifying the verb *writes.*)
2. Roses smell (sweet, sweetly). (*Sweet* is a predicate adjective.)
3. We were (terrible, terribly) late. (*Terribly,* an adverb, modifies *late,* a predicate adjective.)
4. It tastes (good, well). (*Good* is a predicate adjective.)

Work with students to choose the correct words for each of the sentences in Exercises A and B on pages 506–507. Have them refer to the chart on page 504.

These exercises provide a good review of all the grammar covered thus far in this section.

Advanced Students

Have students divide their papers into three columns while working on the exercises on pages 505–506. Label the columns *Adjective, Adverb, Word It Modifies.* Also, they should tell whether the modified word is a noun, verb, adjective, or other adverb.

Optional Practice

On a sheet of paper write adjectives or adverbs that fit into the spaces in the following sentences.
Sentences will vary.

1. A _____ _____ car came _____ down the road.

2. _____ stapler works _____ _____.

3. _____ chicken looks _____ and _____.

4. _____ people _____ seem _____.

5. Have you _____ ridden a _____ horse?

6. A _____ light shone throughout the _____ room.

Extending the Lesson

1. Have students think of an occupation: firefighter, police officer, football player, musician, etc. Tell them to write eight sentences: four sentences using adjectives to describe different things a person in that occupation needs or uses; and four sentences using adverbs to describe actions a person in that occupation does. Students should identify the adjectives and adverbs they use, and tell what word each modifies.

Examples:

The referee uses a *loud* whistle.
(*loud* modifies *whistle*)
The referee watches the action *carefully*.
(*carefully* modifies *watches*)

2. Put the following sentences on a worksheet. Have students fill in each blank with the correct form of the base word in parentheses.

(quickly)   1. The train traveled
more quickly
_____ than the car.

2. The confused driver (mistakenly) dumped gravel in our front yard.

3. The boys mowed the tall grass (swiftly) but (neatly).

4. It was a cold and rainy day, and we walked (quickly) to the bus stop.

5. Carrie smiled (broadly) as she (happily) held the trophy in her hands.

6. Jeff (finally) bought the dark brown boots.

7. The sunbathers lay on the hot beach and (slowly) sipped lemonade.

8. The teacher (quietly) opened the door, and the class (calmly) filed in.

9. One canteen is (almost) empty, and the other is (nearly) full.

10. The parachute billowed and (then) (slowly) drifted to the ground.

Exercises   Choose the right modifier.

A.   Write the correct word for each of the following sentences. Be ready to tell why it is correct.

Example: White's Pond looks (clean, cleanly) enough for swimming.
Clean is a predicate adjective modifying *White's Pond*.

1. He lined up his airplane collection (neat, <u>neatly</u>).
2. May plays the piano (good, <u>well</u>), doesn't she?
3. This way is (more quickly, <u>quicker</u>).
4. That's a (real, <u>really</u>) tough question.
5. The bread smells (<u>fresh</u>, freshly).
6. Are you (near, <u>nearly</u>) through?
7. The new girl watched the preparations (shy, <u>shyly</u>).
8. The puppy appeared (<u>hungry</u>, hungrily).

9. The graduates walked (proud, <u>proudly</u>) through the corridors to the auditorium.
10. Mr. Murphy argued (<u>more strongly</u>, stronger) than Ms. Kimball about the council's decision.

B. Follow the directions for Exercise A.

1. My dog soon became (<u>smarter</u>, more smarter).
2. John felt (<u>bad</u>, badly) about the accident.
3. This building is (<u>bigger</u>, more bigger) than that one.
4. Your centerpiece looks (<u>beautiful</u>, beautifully).
5. Ms. Becket answered (<u>more gently</u>, more gentle).
6. The squad looked (envious, <u>enviously</u>) at the trophy.
7. The auctioneer gave the (most brief, <u>briefest</u>) nod to the bidder.
8. That pie smells (wonderfully, <u>wonderful</u>)!
9. He didn't do so (good, <u>well</u>) this time.
10. The students moved (quiet, <u>quietly</u>) through the halls.

Part 4   Special Problems with Modifiers

Good and Well

Good is used only as an adjective to modify nouns and pronouns. It is used after linking verbs.

> This book is *good*.   I feel *good*.

Well is an adjective when it means "in good health." *Well* is used as an adverb to modify an action verb when it means that the action was performed properly or expertly.

Adjectives	**Adverbs**
I feel *well*.	The baby walks *well* now.
Karen looks *well*.	The battery works *well*.

507

(loud)   2. The music was <u>louder</u> than usual.

(clearly)   3. Of all the people at the meeting, Reuben spoke the <u>most clearly</u>.

(well)   4. This candidate's campaign was <u>better</u> organized than his opponent's.

(high)   5. The planes flew <u>higher</u> than ever before.

(delicious)   6. This peach tasted <u>more delicious</u> than that one.

Part 4

Objective

To correctly use *good* and *well*, *bad* and *badly,* and to avoid the double negative

Presenting the Lesson

1. Read and discuss page 507. Remind students that the comparative and superlative forms of *good* and *well* are the same. Put the following sentences on the board and have students fill in the blanks. Adjective: This book is *(good)*. That one is *(better)*. This one is the *(best)* of all. Adverb: Janine dances *(well)*. Clem dances *(better)*. John dances *(the best)* of all.

2. Assign and discuss Exercise A on page 509.

3. Read and discuss page 508. Point out how double negatives in a sentence actually contradict the meaning the sentence is trying to communicate.

507

4. Assign and discuss Exercise B on page 509.

Individualizing the Lesson

Less-Advanced Students

Do the first half of each exercise orally. Allow the students to work in pairs to complete the exercise.

Advanced Students

Have the students rewrite this paragraph, correcting the errors.

"I don't want ~~no~~ ^{any} part of flying," said Tim as I walked him onto the plane. He looked ~~badly~~ as he put on his seat belt. "There isn't ~~no~~ ^{any} parachute here!" he exclaimed. "I certainly hope the pilot flies ~~good~~ ^{well}," he remarked. "I wouldn't want ~~no~~ ^{any} trip without ~~no~~ ^a parachute!"

Optional Practice

1. Have students underline the correct adjective or adverb in parentheses. Then use the correct comparative or superlative form of that word in the next sentence.

1. Anna plays soccer (good/<u>well</u>).
   Sarah plays <u>better</u>.
2. The Pittsburgh Pirates played as (good/<u>well</u>) as they could.
   The Baltimore Orioles played <u>better</u>.
3. Those paintings look (<u>good</u>/ well).
   The abstract oil is <u>best</u> of all.
4. Everyone works as (good/<u>well</u>) as he.
   Nobody works <u>better</u>.
5. We were shown some (good/ <u>well</u>) trained horses.
   Your horse is the <u>best</u> trained one we have seen.

Bad and *Badly*

Bad is used only as an adjective to modify nouns and pronouns.

> This tape sounds *bad*.   Karen felt *bad*.

Badly is an adverb. It is used with action verbs.

> The orchestra played *badly*.   The gymnast performed *badly*.

The Double Negative

A **double negative** is the use of two negative words together when only one is needed. Good speakers and writers take care to avoid the double negative.

Wrong: This orange *doesn't* have *no* seeds.
Right: This orange doesn't have any seeds.

Wrong: I *haven't never* missed a football game.
Right: I haven't ever missed a football game.

Wrong: After his dental work, Keith *couldn't* eat *nothing*.
Right: After his dental work, Keith couldn't eat anything.

The most common negative words are *no, none, not, nothing, never,* and contractions with *n't* (for *not*).

After contractions like *hasn't* and *didn't*, use words such as *any, anything,* and *ever*. Do not use *no, nothing, never,* or any other negative words with such contractions.

> The motel *hasn't any* empty rooms.
> The team *didn't* score any hits.
> Laura *hadn't ever* eaten curry.
> The mechanic *didn't* fix *anything*.

Hardly, barely, and *scarcely* are often used as negative words. Do not use them with contractions like *haven't* and *didn't*.

Wrong: Megan *couldn't hardly* wait for her fifteenth birthday.
Right: Megan could hardly wait for her fifteenth birthday.

Wrong: The man *hadn't barely* any friends.
Right: The man had barely any friends.

Wrong: Kevin *couldn't scarcely* remember his first day of school.
Right: Kevin could scarcely remember his first day of school.

Exercises Use modifiers correctly.

A. Choose the correct modifier in these sentences.

1. The teacher knew her subject (good, <u>well</u>).
2. That new paint job looks (<u>bad,</u> badly).
3. Cindy types (good, <u>well</u>).
4. A (<u>good</u>, well) photo tells a story.
5. Oil doesn't mix (good, <u>well</u>) with water.
6. Terry asked a (<u>good</u>, well) question.
7. Danny felt (<u>bad,</u> badly).
8. John pitches as (good, <u>well</u>) as Lee.
9. Kim had a (<u>good</u>, well) chance to win the election.
10. The papers we wrote in class were quite (<u>good</u>, well).

B. Number your paper from 1 to 10. Write the following sentences, correcting the double negatives. If a sentence contains no double negative, write *Correct*.

1. Connie had~~n't~~ never flown in an airplane.
2. The injured horse could~~n't~~ barely walk.
c 3. Some people don't eat any meat.
4. The car didn't stop for ^{any} ~~no~~ stoplights.
5. Bert won't read ^{any} ~~no~~ love stories.
6. We can~~'t~~ barely hear the speaker.
7. Seniors don't have ^{anything} ~~nothing~~ to complain about.
8. We don't have ^{any} ~~no~~ time for lunch.
c 9. The deep-sea divers couldn't find the sunken ship.
10. The band ^{played} ~~didn't play~~ hardly any popular music.

509

509

Additional Exercises

These Additional Exercises may be used for additional practice of the concepts presented in this Section. Each exercise focuses on a single concept, and should be used after the page number indicated in parentheses.

Review

If you have not assigned these Additional Exercises before this time, you can also use them as an excellent Section Review.

ADDITIONAL EXERCISES

Using Adverbs

A. Adverbs Number your paper from 1 to 10. Write the adverbs in the following sentences. After each <u>adverb</u>, write the (word it modifies.) Some sentences have more than one adverb.

1. The referee <u>quickly</u> (blew) her whistle.
2. Denny (could) <u>hardly</u> (open) his eyes.
3. Cynthia (is swimming) <u>too</u> (far) from the boat.
4. The laundry (flapped) <u>gently</u> in the breeze.
5. I (feel) lucky <u>today</u>.
6. The angry customer (walked) <u>away</u>.
7. <u>Fortunately</u>, a taxi <u>finally</u> (appeared)
8. Tim (walked) <u>very</u> (slowly) on his crutches.
9. A hubcap (fell) <u>off</u> the old car.
10. Justine (strolled) <u>lazily</u> down the sunny boardwalk.

B. Adverbs in Comparisons For each sentence, write the correct form of the adverb from the two given in parentheses.

1. Cocoa is (more better, <u>better</u>) than cider on cold days.
2. Can the fullback run (<u>faster</u>, more fast)?
3. Hold the racquet (<u>more firmly</u>, firmlier).
4. Jessica played (least often, <u>less often</u>) than the other drummer.
5. Of the four girls, Sara draws (better, <u>best</u>).
6. Tie the tourniquet (tightlier, <u>more tightly</u>).
7. Hank exercises (<u>less</u>, littler) than Perry.
8. Of the two boys, Vic bowls (<u>better</u>, best).
9. Lynn sang (more beautifully, <u>most beautifully</u>) than any other contestant.
10. Of all the debaters, Ron spoke (less confidently, <u>least confidently</u>).

510

C. Adjective or Adverb?
Choose the correct word from the two given in parentheses in each of the following sentences. Write whether you have chosen an adjective or an adverb.

1. Penny looked (careful, carefully) for her lost contact lens.
2. Skateboarding appears (easier, more easily) than it is.
3. The last problem was (real, really) difficult.
4. Ken speaks (quick, quickly) when he is nervous.
5. Shellfish are becoming (scarce, scarcely) in the bay.
6. Rescuers worked (desperate, desperately) to save the miners.
7. The tunnel had collapsed (sudden, suddenly).
8. Line up the numbers in (even, evenly) columns.
9. Ginger (scarce, scarcely) had time for lunch.
10. Ocean breezes smell (salty, saltily).

D. Special Problems with Modifiers
Number your paper from 1 to 10. If the sentence is correct, write *Correct*. If there is an error, write the sentence correctly.

1. The cottage looks ~~well~~ good with new shutters.
2. Our goalie defends the goal ~~good~~ well.
3. He couldn't ~~hardly~~ squeeze through the trapdoor.
4. Tammy sings ~~good~~ well in the school musical.
c 5. I can't pedal any faster.
6. Mel's idea sounds ~~well~~ good to me.
c 7. Erin saw nothing she liked at the store.
8. I didn't say ~~nothing~~ anything.
9. Don't ~~never~~ ever forget to wear your safety glasses in wood shop.
c 10. You won't find prices as good anywhere else.

Mixed Review

These exercises provide review of the concepts presented in this Section. Each exercise challenges the students to apply several of the skills they have acquired during previous study. Because the "mixed" feature of these activities makes them more difficult, the teacher may wish to have less-advanced students do them orally or in small groups.

MIXED REVIEW

Using Adverbs

A. Finding adverbs Write all of the adverbs in the following sentences. After each adverb, write the word it modifies. Then write *how*, *when*, *where*, or *to what extent* to show what each adverb tells.

1. Kyle read the material slowly and carefully. how, how
2. The paramedics arrived very quickly. to what extent, how
3. I'll frost the cake now. when
4. Dana looked up and smiled warmly. where, how to what extent, how
5. This instrument measures more exactly than that one.
6. The box of cereal was almost empty. to what extent
7. Occasionally we have ice cream for dessert. when
8. These shoes are too tight. to what extent
9. The jazz band practices daily. when
10. George speaks well before a group. how

B. Using adverbs correctly The following paragraph contains errors in the use of adverbs. Rewrite the paragraph, correcting any errors.

The runner training serious^{ly} for the 26-mile marathon must be dedicated and determined. He begins by increasing his daily running distance. This is done gradual^{ly} Then he works on his speed. A potential marathon runner should be able to run ten miles in an hour easy^{ly} He carefully must also pace himself. The first few miles pass quick^{ly} But energy and willpower are needed desperate^{ly} for that twenty-sixth mile.

USING GRAMMAR IN WRITING
Using Adverbs

A. Your friend Tracy has maintained a perfect driving record during her first year behind the wheel. The following paragraph states some of the things Tracy does when she drives. Rewrite the paragraph, adding one of the following adverbs to each sentence. *Note:* The fifth and seventh sentences won't make sense in your story until you add the adverbs:

> Adverbs: often usually slowly rarely
> never always carefully

> Tracy wears her seatbelt. She asks her passengers to buckle up, too. Tracy backs the car up. She watches the road. Tracy exceeds the speed limit. She checks the mirrors. She laughs and jokes while she drives.

B. You just got home from an exciting movie. It was called *Superchase.* Someone asks you what the movie was about. Who was chasing whom? Was the chase on foot? Did it involve bicycles, cars, or motorcycles? Maybe it was an inter-galactic space chase. Write a vivid description of the chase. Include adverbs in your description that answer *when, where, how,* and *to what extent* the action happened. Underline every adverb.

C. You are a junior reporter for a major newspaper. Your boss sends you to do a story on a fire in an old warehouse. Because you are inexperienced, he tells you that the story should be no longer than five lines. When you turn in your story, however, he is so pleased that he asks you to double its length.

Make a copy of both versions of your story. The first should contain only basic information. This information might include the time and place of the fire, who was involved, and when the firefighters arrived. Your second version should include striking and original adjectives that bring the scene to life.

513

Section Objectives

1. To identify prepositions and prepositional phrases and to understand their function

2. To identify nouns and pronouns as objects of prepositions

3. To identify prepositional phrases used as modifiers

4. To correctly place prepositional phrases within sentences

5. To differentiate between the use of a word as a preposition and its use as an adverb

Preparing the Students

Write the following sentences.

The apple fell *under* the tree.
The squirrel *in* the tree chattered noisily.
The top branch *of* the tree is dead.

Ask students to identify the parts of speech used in these sentences: nouns, verbs, adjectives, and adverbs. Ask students what the remaining words, *under, in,* and *of* do. Make sure that they see that they do not function like any of the other four groups, but are new types of words called *prepositions.*

Additional Resources

Diagnostic Test — page 5 in the test booklet

Mastery Test — pages 55–56 in the test booklet

Additional Exercises — pages 527–531 in the student text

Practice Book — pages 196–202

Duplicating Masters — pages 196–202

Special Populations — See special section at the back of this Teacher's Edition.

514

Using Prepositions

Sometimes you are able to communicate an idea clearly by using short sentences.

> David won.   We will go.

Often you have to provide more information.

> David won first prize.   We will go there today.

You can add some information by using adjectives and adverbs (*first, there, today*).

Another way to express more information is to use words that show relationships.

> *At the science fair*, David won first prize.
> We will go there *by train* today.

In this section you will learn about a part of speech that shows relationships: **prepositions.**

514

Part 1 What Are Prepositions?

Prepositions are words that show how one word is related to another word. Read these sentences. Notice how each expresses a different relationship.

The radio is *on the table*.
The radio is *near the table*.
The radio is *beside the table*.

Dorothy pulled a muscle *before the final race*.
Dorothy pulled a muscle *after the final race*.
Dorothy pulled a muscle *during the final race*.

Katy spoke *to him*.
Katy spoke *for him*.
Katy spoke *against him*.

In the first group of sentences, you can see that the words *on*, *near*, and *beside* show the relationship of *table* to *radio*. In the next group, *before*, *after*, and *during* show the relationship of *race* to *pulled a muscle*. In the last group, *to*, *for*, and *against* relate *him* to *spoke*.

You can see that prepositions do not show relationships by themselves. They begin a **phrase,** a group of words that belong together but do not have a subject and verb. *On the table*, *before the final race*, and *to him* are examples of the prepositional phrases in the sentences above.

A preposition is a word used with a noun or pronoun, called its *object*, to *show how* the noun or pronoun *is related to* some other word in the sentence.

A prepositional phrase consists of a preposition, its object, and any modifiers of the object.

Here is a list of words often used as prepositions. Most of these prepositions show relationships of place or time. Some show other relationships among people and things. Study the prepositions and see the relationship that each shows.

515

Part 1

Objective

To identify prepositions and prepositional phrases and to understand their function

Presenting the Lesson

1. Read and discuss pages 514–516. Have students take turns making phrases with the prepositions in the list on page 516. Remind them that an object must follow the preposition.

2. Do Exercise A on page 516 with the students. Encourage the use of the list of prepositions. Ask students to identify the object of each preposition. Assign and discuss Exercise B on pages 516–517.

Individualizing the Lesson

Less-Advanced Students

1. Do Exercise A on page 516 orally. Write the prepositional phrases on the board. Have volunteers underline the object of the preposition. Discuss the relationship of the phrase with another word in the sentence.

2. Assign Exercise B on pages 516–517. Remind students that there may be more than one prepositional phrase in a sentence. Have them refer to the list on page 516.

3. Make flash cards with prepositions on them. Have the students flash the cards to each other. They must then make up sentences using those prepositions.

Advanced Students

Add these sentences to the instructions for Exercises A and B on

515

"Next to each prepositional phrase, write the word to which it relates. Then state whether the preposition shows a relationship of place, time, or some other relationship."

Optional Practice

1. Have students complete the following sentences using as many of the prepositions from page 516 as possible. Answers will vary.

Example:

Put the paper _____ the book. (in, on, under, beside, over, with)

1. Joe read the exercise _____ his sister.

2. The mice played _____ the woodbox.

3. I sat _____ Nancy and Bill.

4. Tony's kite dived _____ the trees.

5. The snow fell _____ the roof.

6. These five boys played _____ us.

7. _____ the field we found a meadowlark's nest.

8. There was one white horse _____ the black ones.

2. Have students identify the prepositional phrase or phrases in each of the following sentences. They should write the phrases and next to them write *time, place,* or *other relationship* to identify the use of each phrase.

Example:

The book is on the table.
on the table—place

P 1. Greg climbed the rugged side of the mountain.

T,P 2. The traffic during rush hour moved slowly down the street.

P,T 3. The movie at that theater lasted for three hours.

Words Often Used as Prepositions

about	before	down	of	throughout
above	behind	during	off	to
across	below	except	on	toward
after	beneath	for	onto	under
against	beside	from	out	until
along	between	in	outside	up
among	beyond	inside	over	upon
around	but (*except*)	into	past	with
at	by	like	since	within
		near	through	without

Exercises

A. Write all the prepositional phrases you find in the following sentences.

> Example: He ran out the door without his shoes.
> out the door, without his shoes

1. Attach the shells to the frame with this glue.
2. Gail was waiting for the special dessert with raspberry sauce.
3. The picture fell off the wall during the night.
4. Behind the garage is a row of sunflowers.
5. The Cullens went from Seattle to San Diego by train.
6. A batting cage is behind home plate.
7. Terry slid into second base.
8. There was dust under the bed.
9. The sailboat was drifting toward the breakwater.
10. Brad is waiting for you in the lobby.

B. Follow the directions for Exercise A.

1. Juanita fed the dollar into the change machine.

2. The program began after a brief announcement by the principal.
3. They built their Fourth of July bonfire by the light of the moon.
4. Go through that door and up the stairs, and leave the package there.
5. The group of skiers was taking the bus to Aspen.
6. The band marched briskly down the street toward the reviewing stand.
7. We visited Lincoln's home in Springfield, Illinois.
8. Under the bridge the river flowed swiftly.
9. My brother was babysitting with Drew.
10. Never look a gift horse in the mouth.

Part 2   Objects of Prepositions

Objects of prepositions are the nouns or pronouns within prepositional phrases. Objects complete the meaning of prepositions. Objects may or may not be modified.

Using Nouns as Objects of Prepositions

You have seen that nouns are used as subjects, direct objects, and indirect objects of the verb. Nouns are also used as objects of prepositions. Look at the nouns used as objects in the following prepositional phrases.

behind *Jenny*   without a *doubt*
in the *World Series*   by *Thanksgiving*

Like nouns used in other ways, objects of prepositions also may be compound. Look at these examples:

to *teachers* and *students*
toward her *house* and the new *library*
like *Paul* and *Danny*

517

and add one or more adjectives to each object of the preposition.

3. Read and discuss pages 518–519. Remind students that pronouns substitute for nouns in sentences. If a noun is an object of a preposition, a pronoun can take its place. The object forms of the pronouns are the only ones used.

4. Assign and discuss Exercises A and B on pages 519–520. Students should be able to choose the correct pronoun if they remember that only the pronouns listed on page 518 can be objects. Choosing pronouns by the way they sound will work for some students, but remind them to test pronouns in compounds separately.

Individualizing the Lesson

Less-Advanced Students

1. For the exercise on page 518, have students refer to the list of prepositions on page 516. You may want to display a chart of these prepositions in the room.

2. You may want to review the list of pronouns in Section 7 on page 454 before beginning Exercises A and B on pages 519–520. Stress that only object forms of pronouns can be used as objects of prepositions in a sentence. List them on the board.

Do Exercise A on page 519 orally. Have students point out the prepositions. Have them test for compound objects by saying the pronoun alone with its preposition. Assign Exercise B for independent work.

Advanced Students

1. Have students rewrite this paragraph correcting the errors made in the use of pronouns.

518

Exercises   **Find the objects of prepositions.**

In these sentences nouns are used as objects of prepositions. Write the prepositional phrases in each sentence. Circle the object of each preposition.

1. Joan climbed up the ladder and onto the roof.
2. After school, we went to the pool.
3. Pat and Leslie walked along the beach with their dog.
4. Kevin looked closely at the big bluefish.
5. The jet landed on the runway and taxied to the terminal.
6. They walked along the edge of the lagoon.
7. Jay rushed into the waiting room with the timetable.
8. Bob sat beside the fire and talked to Christine.
9. A spider crawled across the ceiling and down the basement wall.
10. Ten kinds of tropical fish were swimming in the huge tank.

Using Pronouns as Objects of Prepositions

Pronouns are also used as objects of prepositions.

The object forms of pronouns are the only forms used for objects of prepositions.

Here are the object forms of pronouns:

me	us	whom
you	you	
him, her, it	them	

Pronouns are used as objects in the following prepositional phrases.

to *me*	with *whom*
through *us*	like *her*
from *them*	toward *you*

518

Compound Objects

You seldom make mistakes in using a single pronoun directly after a preposition. But you may be confused when the object of a preposition is compound.

Simple Object	Compound Object
Take it to *her*.	Take it to *Mary* and *her*.
Come with *me*.	Come with *her* and *me*.
We worked for *him*.	We worked for *Homer* and *him*.

Here is a way to know if you are using the correct pronoun in a prepositional phrase with a compound object. First say the pronoun alone after the preposition. If it sounds right, then that is the correct pronoun to use in the compound object.

These tickets are for Pam and (he, him).

These tickets are for *him*.
These tickets are for *Pam* and *him*.

Exercises Use pronouns as objects of prepositions.

A. Choose the correct pronoun from the two given in parentheses. Write the prepositional phrase.

1. The Junior Achievement presentation was given by Sara and (her, she).
2. Nobody was there except Mr. Parks and (I, me).
3. Finally the nurse looked at Bill and (I, me).
4. Beside Karen and (he, him) were their parents.
5. I almost fell over Amy and (she, her).
6. Ms. Sims bought tickets for Judy and (I, me).
7. Hal stood behind Tracy and (we, us).
8. We gave the winners' score sheets to the coach and (he, him).
9. The ball fell between Steve and (he, him).
10. Roger was talking about Robin and (she, her).

519

Mark gave Sue and me a ride home from school today. We had stayed late to make a banner to welcome the band members back. The state music association gave a first place prize to the band leader and them. The lift home was a big favor to her and me because it had started to rain. Thanks to his car and him, we stayed dry and got home on time.

2. After completing Exercise B on page 520 have students write complete sentences using the prepositional phrases given.

Optional Practice

Ask students to complete the following by filling in one blank in each sentence with an object pronoun and the other with an object noun. Point out that there is more than one possible answer. Suggest that students use a variety of pronouns. Answers will vary.

1. The librarian at _____ showed the books to _____.
2. We walked along _____ near the _____.
3. People took pictures of _____ during the _____.
4. The adults played baseball with _____ at the _____.
5. John takes the bus with Dan and _____ to _____.

Extending the Lesson

Explain to students that the use of prepositional phrases can make their writing more descriptive. It is also a way to eliminate short, choppy sentences. Have students combine each of the following pairs of sentences into one sentence by using a prepositional phrase.

1. The frightened girl stood in the corner. She held a battered suitcase. *with a battered suitcase*

2. Mark bought a new car. ~~It has four-wheel drive.~~ *with four-wheel drive.*
3. We read the best novel in English class. ~~It described the old West.~~ *about the old West*
4. I noticed the man standing in the rain. ~~He did not have an umbrella.~~ *without an umbrella*
5. You can't leave for the party yet. ~~You can leave at 5:00.~~ *until 5:00*

Part 3

Objective

To identify prepositional phrases used as modifiers

Presenting the Lesson

1. Read and discuss pages 520–521. Remind students that prepositional phrases always begin with a preposition; the preposition is followed by an object. The object may be a noun or a pronoun, and the nouns may have adjective modifiers. Point out that the prepositional phrase itself always functions as a modifier. If the phrase modifies a noun, the phrase is an adjective phrase. If it modifies a verb, adjective, or adverb, it is an adverb phrase.

2. Students who have successfully diagramed sentences with single-word adjectives and adverbs should be able to do the diagrams in "Diagraming Sentences Containing Prepositional Phrases," pages 521–523. The placement of the words on the diagram is extremely important if the diagram is to serve its purpose of illustrating the rela-

520

B. Choose the correct pronoun from the two given.

1. to him and (I, <u>me</u>)
2. past them and (we, <u>us</u>)
3. for you and (we, <u>us</u>)
4. between Joy and (she, <u>her</u>)
5. beside them and (we, <u>us</u>)
6. toward Sally and (I, <u>me</u>)
7. between Carl and (he, <u>him</u>)
8. near Ellen and (I, <u>me</u>)
9. to Jim and (he, <u>him</u>)
10. at Sam and (I, <u>me</u>)

Part 3 Prepositional Phrases as Modifiers

A modifier may be a group of words as well as a single word. Frequently a prepositional phrase is a modifier. Prepositional phrases do the same work in a sentence as adjectives and adverbs.

A prepositional phrase that modifies a noun or pronoun is called an adjective phrase.

The procession passed the statue *of Lincoln.*

He was washing the window *over the sink.*

A room *on the third floor* is available.

Like adjectives, adjective phrases tell *which one, what kind,* or *how many.*

A prepositional phrase that modifies a verb is called an adverb phrase.

The crowd ate *in shifts.*

The geyser erupted *at noon.*

They swam *under the bridge.*

Like adverbs, adverb phrases tell *how, when, where,* and *to what extent* about verbs.

Often you will find two prepositional phrases in a row. Sometimes the second phrase is an adjective phrase modifying the object of the first phrase.

The grocer put a sign *on the basket of apples.*

(*On the basket* is an adverb phrase telling *where* about the verb *put.*)

(*Of apples* is an adjective phrase modifying *basket.* It tells *which* basket.)

The car streaked away *in a cloud of smoke.*

(*In a cloud* tells *how* the car streaked.)

(*Of smoke* modifies *cloud.* It tells *what kind* of cloud.)

Diagraming Sentences Containing Prepositional Phrases

Since a prepositional phrase does the work of an adjective or an adverb, you diagram it like an adjective or an adverb. Write the preposition on a line slanting down from the word modified. Then, on a horizontal line attached to the preposition line, write the object. Anything modifying the object slants down from it. Notice in the following diagram that the object of a preposition (*rim*) may be modified by another phrase (*of the volcano*).

In the morning we walked to the rim of the volcano.

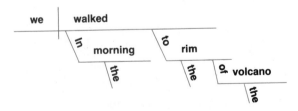

A prepositional phrase containing a compound object is diagramed in a similar way.

tionship between words in a sentence. Remind students that any noun (not only the subject) can have an adjective or adjective phrase modifier. Point out that in the first example on page 521 *of the volcano* modifies the object of the adverb phrase *to the rim.*

3. It may be helpful to do Exercise A on pages 522–523 with the class. Review briefly the functions of adjectives and adverbs. Ask students to tell you the questions that adverbs and adjectives answer in sentences. Assign and discuss Exercise B on page 523.

Individualizing the Lesson

Less-Advanced Students

1. Do Exercise A on pages 522–523 with the group, writing the columns on the board. Have them refer to the list of prepositions on page 516 while they are doing the exercise.

2. Have the students identify the prepositional phrases independently in Exercise B on page 523. Then work with them to distinguish between adjective and adverb phrases.

Advanced Students

Read a short magazine or newspaper article with the class. Have students find all of the prepositional phrases and identify each phrase as an adjective phrase or an adverb phrase. Also, have students state what word each phrase modifies.

Optional Practice

Have students copy the prepositional phrases from the following sentences and write whether they are used as adverbs or adjectives.

1. The meteors <u>from outer space</u> [Adj.]
   bombarded the earth's atmosphere
   <u>with amazing speed</u>. [Adv.]
2. His forehand is his best stroke <u>in</u> [Adj.]
   <u>tennis</u>.
3. We bought some tape <u>in a dis-</u> [Adj.]
   <u>penser</u> <u>at the stationery store</u>. [Adv.]
4. The painting <u>on</u> the wall [Adj.] was
   painted <u>by an old friend</u>. [Adv.]
5. We should return that sweater <u>to</u> [Adv.]
   <u>the store</u>.
6. The guest speaker arrived <u>at six</u> [Adv.]
   <u>o'clock</u> <u>in a limousine</u>. [Adv.]
7. That student <u>in the other class</u> used [Adj.]
   three prepositional phrases <u>in one</u> [Adj.]
   <u>sentence</u>.
8. The telephone repairwoman
   climbed <u>up the pole</u> [Adv.] <u>with her spiked</u> [Adv.]
   <u>boots</u>.
9. It does not usually snow much <u>in</u> [Adv.]
   <u>Washington, D.C.</u>
10. The stripes <u>in the curtains</u> [Adj.] clashed
    <u>with the flowers</u> <u>in the wallpaper</u>. [Adv.] [Adj.]

Extending the Lesson

Have students put a single-word
modifier or a prepositional phrase in
each blank as directed.
Answers will vary.
Example: The *young* girl watched the
game. (adjective)
The girl *on the bench*
watched the game. (adjec-
tive prepositional phrase)

1. The _____ airplane was diverted to
   another airport. (adjective)
   The airplane _____ was diverted to
   another airport. (adjective prepositional phrase)
2. Cora gave the money to the _____
   salesclerk. (adjective)
   Cora gave the money to the salesclerk _____. (adjective prepositional phrase)

Trucks with fruits and vegetables attracted the passers-by.

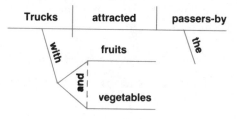

In this sentence, the phrase *with fruits and vegetables* is an adjective phrase modifying the noun *trucks*. The preposition line therefore slants down from the word *trucks*. Because of the compound object, the line for the object of the preposition is split.

Exercises **Find adjective and adverb prepositional phrases.**

A. Make three columns marked *Phrase*, *Word Modified*, and *Kind of Phrase*. For each prepositional phrase in the following sentences, fill in the information under the three columns. (Before you begin the exercise, review what questions adjectives and adverbs answer.)

Example: Under the planks, Gary could always find
         worms for bait.

Phrase	Word Modified	Kind of Phrase
under the planks	could find	adverb
for bait	worms	adjective

1. The (buttons) on his sleeve caught in the door. [Adj.]
2. I (saw) a strange Siamese cat in the alley. [Adv.]
3. At the corner they (built) a new sign. [Adv.]
4. The bacon (sizzled) in the frying pan. [Adv.]
5. Someone (called) about noon. [Adv.]
6. The (hikers) without maps [Adj.] (returned) at sunset. [Adv.]
7. Gulls (flocked) around the fishing boats. [Adv.]

8. The Mannings (went) through the Blue Ridge Mountains on their trip. [Adv / Adv]

Adv 9. Dad (had) already (put) the pizzas in the oven.

10. On his birthday, he (has) (cake) with chocolate icing. [Adv / Adj]

B. Find the prepositional phrases in the following sentences. Tell whether each phrase is used as an adjective or adverb. Write the answers as your teacher indicates.

Adv 1. Put Jack's books behind the big chair.

2. In the afternoon, the class went to a museum. [Adv / Adv]

Adv 3. Sheila waited patiently on the landing.

4. After a while, the cars moved at a snail's pace. [Adv / Adv]

5. Four girls on the team waited in the office. [Adj / Adv]

Adj 6. The Brown County art colony in Indiana is famous.

Adv 7. He didn't look under the couch.

Adj 8. The closet beneath the stairs is full.

9. In the greenhouse, they grew three kinds of violets. [Adv / Adj]

10. In the fifth inning, the first batter for the Tigers hit a home run. [Adv / Adj]

Part 4 Putting Prepositional Phrases in the Right Place

Sometimes, the position of a prepositional phrase makes a great deal of difference in the meaning of the sentence.

The trainer signaled the dolphins on the platform.
The trainer on the platform signaled the dolphins.

The first sentence is unclear because the phrase *on the platform* seems to modify *dolphins*. The second sentence brings the phrase where it should be: closer to *trainer*, the word it modifies. As with other modifiers, a prepositional phrase should be placed as close as possible to the word it modifies.

523

3. The _____ Volkswagen was in the repair shop for two weeks. (adjective)
   The Volkswagen _____ was in the repair shop for two weeks. (adjective prepositional phrase)

4. The _____ circus performed twice yesterday. (adjective)
   The circus _____ performed twice yesterday. (adjective prepositional phrase)

5. The biology class gave a present to the _____ teacher. (adjective)
   The biology class gave a present to the teacher _____. (adjective prepositional phrase)

6. The clown on the stilts walked _____. (adverb)
   The clown on the stilts walked _____. (adverb prepositional phrase)

7. The drummer played the bass drums _____. (adverb)
   The drummer played the bass drums _____. (adverb prepositional phrase)

8. The bell on the alarm clock rang _____. (adverb)
   The bell on the alarm clock rang _____. (adverb prepositional phrase)

Part 4

Objective

To correctly place prepositional phrases within sentences

Presenting the Lesson

1. Read and discuss page 523. Point out that sometimes the incorrect placement of a prepositional phrase will make a sentence awkward or ambiguous. This is most common if an adjective phrase is not placed close enough to the word it modifies. Ask students to explain why. Have them note that in the example on page 523, the adjective phrase functions clearly only when it is directly before or after the noun.

2. It will be helpful to do Exercise A on page 524 with the class and then assign and discuss Exercise B. Reading the sentences aloud will help identify the problems.

Individualizing the Lesson

Less-Advanced Students

Work together on the exercises. Point out the humorous interpretations that are possible for some of the sentences.

Advanced Students

Have these students make up their own sentences containing misplaced modifiers. Have the students exchange papers and rewrite the sentences placing the prepositional phrases correctly.

Optional Practice

Put the following exercise on a worksheet. Have students rewrite the sentences, correctly inserting the prepositional phrases.

1. The rocket was launched from Cape Canaveral. (from Cape Canaveral) (at 6:00 A.M.)
2. The seagulls picked open the oyster shells with their beaks. (on the beach) (with their beaks)
3. The escalator in the store will be repaired. (in the store) (before tomorrow)
4. There were monsters roaming the earth in the science fiction movie. (in the science fiction movie) (with weird shapes)

524

Exercises   Place prepositional phrases correctly.

A. Writing   The following sentences are awkward. Change the position of one phrase in each sentence to make the meaning clear. Rewrite each sentence.

1. The boys hurried after the ice-cream truck (on their bikes.)
2. Jean wrote several long letters to the director (on her typewriter.)
3. John stood on tiptoe and reached for the string beans (with raised arms.)
4. David mailed his request to the senator (at the post office.)
5. (With his big straw stomach) Al laughed at the scarecrow.
6. There is some orange juice for the boys (in the refrigerator.)
7. We saw a big white horse beside a brook (with a long tail.)
8. Alice searched for rare birds (with powerful binoculars.)
9. A rabbit ran across the street (with long ears.)
10. Grandpa picked up the baby (with his pipe in his mouth.)

B.   Follow the directions for Exercise A.

1. The baby wanted its mother (in the highchair.)
2. Kathy has a letter from a friend (in her desk.)
3. That tall girl caught the ball (with the striped T-shirt.)
4. The game was played at the stadium (between Detroit and Cleveland.)
5. The clock stopped (by the water fountain) at 3:30.
6. Was he the only one who could do cartwheels (on the gymnastics team?)
7. Dan told everyone about his high dive (at breakfast.)

524

8. The woman looked at the garden (in the green jacket.)
9. Carol and I startled the mail carrier (in our costumes.)
10. That money is for the tollbooth (on the dashboard.)

Part 5 Preposition or Adverb?

Many words used as prepositions may also be used as adverbs. A preposition never appears alone. It is always followed by its object, a noun or pronoun. If the word is in a phrase, it is a preposition. If it is not in a phrase, it is probably an adverb.

The carpenter climbed *in the window.*
Grandfather walked *in.*

Uncle Frank fell *down the stairs.*
Put your pencils *down,* please.

Outside the stadium the crowd waited.
The puppy followed the children *outside.*

Exercises Find prepositions and adverbs.

A. In each pair of sentences that follows, there is one adverb and one preposition. Number your paper from 1 to 10. After each number, write *a* and *b*. After each letter, write *Preposition* or *Adverb*, depending on which you find.

Example: (a) He heard a noise below.
         (b) He heard a noise below the window.

         (a) adverb
         (b) preposition

1. (a) We climbed óut. (b) We climbed out the window.
2. (a) The ball fell through the net. (b) The ball fell through.
3. (a) Terry walked along. (b) Terry walked along the shore.

Extending the Lesson

Have students check their writing folders for misplaced modifiers in their papers. Have students correctly rewrite those sentences.

Part 5

Objective

To differentiate between the use of a word as a preposition and its use as an adverb

Presenting the Lesson

1. Read aloud and discuss page 525. Remind the students that adverbs tell *how, when, where,* and *to what extent* about verbs.
2. Assign and discuss Exercises A and B on pages 525–526.

Individualizing the Lesson

Less-Advanced Students

Stress that a preposition never stands alone. If it is used alone it is probably an adverb. Review that an adverb is a word that modifies verbs, adjectives and other adverbs. Work together on Exercise A on pages 525–526. Assign Exercise B.

Advanced Students

After completing the exercises, have students make up sentences of their own using words that can be used as both prepositions and adverbs.

Optional Practice

Make a copy of these sentences for the students. Have them decide whether the underlined words in these sentences are adverbs or prepositions.

Adv. 1. Mr. Murphy paced <u>around</u> nervously.

Adv. 2. Eliot walked <u>out</u> without a word.

Prep. 3. The boulder rolled <u>over</u> the cliff.

Prep. 4. Kenny works <u>at</u> the university medical center.

Adv. 5. We heard a creaking noise <u>above</u>.

Prep. 6. A gangway runs <u>between</u> the old brownstone houses.

Adv. 7. The reception will be held <u>outside</u>.

Prep. 8. The electrician switched <u>off</u> the power.

Prep. 9. The temperature has been dropping <u>since</u> sunset.

Prep.10. Refreshments were served <u>during</u> the meeting.

Extending the Lesson

Have students look at the list of prepositions on page 516. Tell them to decide which ones can be used as both adverbs and prepositions. For the words that can be used as both, have the students write sentences showing each usage.

4. (a) ^{Adv.}Behind came Joanne. (b) ^{Prep.}Behind us came Joanne.

5. (a) ^{Prep.}Above our heads shone the sun. (b) ^{Adv.}Above, the sun shone.

6. (a) The bear cub rolled ^{Adv.}over. (b) The cub rolled ^{Prep.}over its brother.

7. (a) We had not met ^{Prep.}before the game. (b) We had not met ^{Adv.}before.

8. (a) The red blanket goes ^{Adv.}beneath. (b) The red blanket goes ^{Prep.}beneath the saddle.

9. (a) Come ^{Prep.}up the stairs. (b) Come ^{Adv.}up.

10. (a) Bob stayed ^{Prep.}in the house all day. (b) Bob stayed ^{Adv.}in.

B. Follow the directions for Exercise A.

1. (a) They went ^{Prep.}inside the house. (b) They went ^{Adv.}inside.

2. (a) The train went ^{Adv.}through. (b) The train went ^{Prep.}through the mountain village.

3. (a) ^{Adv.}Beyond lay the Smoky Mountains. (b) ^{Prep.}Beyond the town lay the Smoky Mountains.

4. (a) The picture fell ^{Adv.}off. (b) The picture fell ^{Prep.}off the wall.

5. (a) The doctor is ^{Adv.}in. (b) Dr. Rayner is ^{Prep.}in her office.

6. (a) The dog ran ^{Prep.}beside the motorcycle. (b) The dog ran ^{Adv.}beside.

7. (a) They drove ^{Adv.}past. (b) They drove ^{Prep.}past the old theater.

8. (a) The boys waited ^{Prep.}outside the gym. (b) The boys waited ^{Adv.}outside.

9. (a) We went ^{Adv.}inside. (b) We went ^{Prep.}inside the gymnasium.

10. (a) I've heard that song ^{Adv.}before. (b) I've heard that song ^{Prep.}before today.

ADDITIONAL EXERCISES

Using Prepositions

A. Prepositional Phrases   Number your paper from 1 to 10. Write the prepositional phrases in the following sentences. Underline the object of each preposition.

1. Simon drew boundary lines in the dust.
2. The empty highway stretched before us.
3. We inched our way to the back.
4. Trisha stepped carefully onto the roof.
5. During a storm, Mother unplugs the television.
6. Hang the blankets in the sun.
7. The rear wheel of the car was on the sidewalk.
8. Wait for me by the fountain.
9. Laura kept the news to herself without difficulty.
10. Monty talks about himself.

B. Pronouns as Objects of Prepositions   Choose the correct pronoun from the two given in parentheses. Write it with the preposition.

1. The block party was planned by the Rays and (they, them).
2. Stacey dribbled past the forward and (I, me).
3. At the assembly we sat behind Jess and (she, her).
4. To (he, him), the news was a shock.
5. To (who, whom) do you wish to speak?
6. It sounds like (he, him).
7. Nobody admitted sending the Valentines to Ed and (I, me).
8. I ordered pizza for you and (her, she).
9. The Bellaks share the cottage with the Haines and (we, us).
10. The sponsor with (who, whom) I spoke liked the plan.

527

Additional Exercises

These Additional Exercises may be used for additional practice of the concepts presented in this Section. Each exercise focuses on a single concept, and should be used after the page number indicated in parentheses.

Review

If you have not assigned these Additional Exercises before this time, you can also use them as an excellent Section Review.

C. Adjective and Adverb Prepositional Phrases Find the underlined prepositional phrases in the following sentences. Write *adjective* or *adverb* to describe each phrase.

Adj. 1. The woman in the trenchcoat is Ms. Lorca.

Adv. 2. Cary put his earnings into the bank.

Adv. 3. Our parrot escaped from its cage.

Adj. 4. Neal boiled five pounds of potatoes.

Adv. 5. The table was near the restaurant's kitchen.

Adj. 6. The constant drone of the mosquitoes woke me up.

Adv. 7. Don't swim past the rope.

Adv., Adv. 8. We huddled under the canoe during the rain.

Adv. 9. Dark clouds were massing in the east.

Adj., Adj. 10. The boy in the blue jacket is a student from Brazil.

D. Correct Use of Prepositional Phrases The following sentences are awkward. By changing the position of one prepositional phrase in each sentence, you can make the meaning clear. Rewrite each sentence in this manner.

1. The spaceship was aimed for the moon with an unusual wing design.

2. Joannie bit into the plum with a wide grin.

3. The headlights shined dimly in the fog on the jeep.

4. There is tuna casserole for your brother Chris in the oven.

5. Donald wore his new parka on the camping trip with the fur hood.

6. We sent the card to Grandma in a perfumed envelope.

7. A wrestling match was held in the gym between Ted and Vic.

8. The acrobat landed on the chair with the sequined tights.

9. The batter hit the ball out of the park in the red uniform.

10. Martha told me about the track meet in art class.

E. Preposition or Adverb? Decide whether the italicized words in these sentences are adverbs or prepositions. Write *Adverb* or *Preposition* for each sentence.

Prep. 1. Derek flashed a light *around* the dark warehouse.

Adv. 2. *In* strolled Marilyn.

Prep. 3. Carrie vaulted *over* the hurdle.

Prep. 4. Ivy grew *up* the brick walls.

Prep. 5. Can we wade *across* the stream?

Adv. 6. The bag of groceries toppled *over*.

Prep. 7. *Down* the alley strolled the tomcat.

Adv. 8. Flies were buzzing *around*.

Prep. 9. Carter put the violets *in* a little pitcher.

Adv. 10. The audience stood *up* and applauded.

Mixed Review

These exercises provide review of the concepts presented in this Section. Each exercise challenges the students to apply several of the skills they have acquired during previous study. Because the "mixed" feature of these activities makes them more difficult, the teacher may wish to have less-advanced students do them orally or in small groups.

MIXED REVIEW

Using Prepositions

A. Finding prepositions and adverbs Copy each sentence. Underline any prepositional phrases. Put an *O* over the objects of the prepositions. Circle any adverbs.

1. The judge walked in.
2. Please leave the air conditioner off.
3. The address book is in the top drawer.
4. Let's go inside.
5. The contest is over.
6. Janet stumbled and fell off the diving board.
7. Our plane flew over the Rocky Mountains.
8. The musicians put their instruments down.
9. We found shelter inside the old cabin.
10. Peter lives in the new building down the street.

B. Using adjective and adverb phrases Rewrite the following sentences, adding the prepositional phrases shown in parentheses. Be sure to place the phrase in the correct place. After each sentence, write *Adverb* or *Adjective* to show what kind of phrase you have added.

Adj. 1. The new girl is in our homeroom. (from Tulsa)
Adj. 2. The dog barked at me. (on the leash)
Adv. 3. Josh captured a yellow and red butterfly. (in his net)
Adj. 4. The new emergency center treats many patients. (on Washington Street)
Adv. 5. My pencil broke. (before the test)
Adj. 6. Susan frightened the children. (in a scary costume)
Adv. 7. Marc told us about the secret. (in a whisper)
Adj. 8. The books are on the second shelf. (about old coins)
Adv. 9. Bill asked his boss during their meeting. (for a raise)
Adv. 10. The crew saved the boat. (during the storm)

USING GRAMMAR IN WRITING
Using Prepositions

A. Imagine that you have just seen the magician David Copperfield. He pulled objects from many different places only to make them disappear again. Write a paragraph describing part of the routine in which the magician used several props. Tell how the props were used and how or where things were concealed from the audience. Underline prepositional phrases. Here are some prepositions you might use.

from	under	off	in
into	over	around	up
of	with	through	during
with	at	to	toward

B. The following story needs descriptive phrases to make it more interesting. Rewrite the paragraph, adding at least eight prepositional phrases. You may use some of the prepositions above. Underline the prepositional phrases. Label them *Adjective* or *Adverb* to tell how the phrases are used.

> It was almost dark. A full yellow moon hung low. Annette was walking. She heard a rustling noise.
> "It's nothing," she told herself.
> She began walking again, more quickly this time. The noise returned. Annette peered. There was something hiding. It was low and dark. It moved. Suddenly it jumped. Annette laughed.
> "OK, Pepper," she said, "you can come. You've scared me so much, I need a watchdog now!"

These challenging and enjoyable activities allow the students to see how the concepts of grammar, usage, and mechanics may be applied in actual writing situations. Each exercise is designed to allow students practice in several of the skills they have acquired in this Section. The activities also provide opportunities for students to write creatively about a wide variety of interesting and unusual subjects.

Section Objective

To understand the function of conjunctions and to identify conjunctions and compound constructions

Preparing the Students

Put the following sentences on the board:

Either Paul or Sara will go to the library.

The picnic was held for both us and the team.

The story was long but fascinating.

Ask students to explain the function of the underlined words in each sentence. Ask them to tell about the relationships among the words in these sentences.

If the students have not yet identified the words as conjunctions, tell them the term. Explain that they will be learning about two kinds of conjunctions in this section, coordinating conjunctions and correlative conjunctions.

Additional Resources

Diagnostic Test — page 5 in the test booklet

Mastery Test — pages 57–58 in the test booklet

Additional Exercises — pages 535–537 in the student text

Practice Book — pages 201–202

Duplicating Masters — pages 201–202

Special Populations — See special section at the back of this Teacher's Edition.

Using Conjunctions

You have learned that prepositions show relationships between words in a sentence. Relationships are also shown by another kind of word: **conjunctions.**

Read these examples:

The students *and* the teacher laughed.
Before the opening, the actors were nervous *but* happy.
Jason *or* Brooke will know the answer.

In the examples, you can see how the conjunctions *and, but,* and *or* are used. *And* connects *students* and *teacher. But* connects *nervous* and *happy. Or* connects *Jason* and *Brooke.*

A conjunction is a word that connects words or groups of words.

Coordinating Conjunctions

Coordinating conjunctions join only words or groups of words that are of equal importance. The coordinating conjunctions are *and, but,* and *or.* The words joined by coordinating conjunctions are called **compound constructions.** These sentences show how coordinating conjunctions connect words of equal importance.

Mark *or* **she** will fix it. (*Or* connects *Mark* and *she,* the compound subject of the verb *will fix.*)

Kent **shot** *and* **scored.** (*And* connects *shot* and *scored,* verbs that form the compound verb.)

We need **string** *and* **tape.** (*And* connects *string* and *tape,* the compound direct object of the verb *need.*)

Give **Susan** *or* **her** the mail. (*Or* connects *Susan* and *her,* the compound indirect object of *give.*)

The suitcase was **light** *but* **awkward.** (*But* connects *light* and *awkward,* compound predicate adjectives.)

He spoke **briefly** *but* **well.** (*But* connects the adverbs *briefly* and *well.*)

Send it to **Andrea** *or* **him.** (*Or* connects *Andrea* and *him,* the compound objects of the preposition *to.*)

Correlative Conjunctions

A few conjunctions are used in pairs:

both . . . and	neither . . . nor	not only . . . but (also)
either . . . or	whether . . . or	

Such conjunctions are called **correlative conjunctions.**

Cal ordered *both* bacon *and* eggs.
Either Debbie *or* Eric will win the election.
Neither the drugstore *nor* the market had any cough drops.
I like *not only* rock music *but also* classical music.
The question is *whether* Karen *or* Beth should receive the award.

Presenting the Lesson

1. Read and discuss pages 532–533.

2. You may want to do Exercise A on page 534 with the class, discussing the kind of compound construction in each sentence to prepare students for doing Exercise B on their own. It may also be helpful to have students label all the words before they decide what kind of compound construction is used.

Individualizing the Lesson

Less-Advanced Students

1. Work with students to complete Exercises A and B. First have them identify the conjunction in each sentence. Then have them tell what words are joined by the conjunction. Finally, have them tell what kind of compound construction each is.

2. Have students write six sentences of their own using conjunctions.

Advanced Students

Have students write ten sentences containing correlative conjunctions.

Optional Practice

Have students write sentences including these elements. Answers will vary.

1. Compound subject/coordinating conjunction
2. Compound subject/correlative conjunction
3. Compound verb/coordinating conjunction
4. Compound verb/correlative conjunction
5. Compound direct object
6. Compound predicate adjective

Extending the Lesson

Have the students page through the short story section of their literature anthology. Ask each student to find a sentence with a compound construction. Discuss each sentence. (Be prepared to discuss compound sentences in case someone uses one as an example of a compound construction.)

Exercises **Recognize conjunctions and compound constructions.**

A. Find the conjunctions in the following sentences. Be prepared to tell what (words) or word groups are connected by each conjunction.

1. In the past, people either (hunted) or (went hungry.)
2. The (President) or (Vice-President) will travel to Russia.
3. Candy has both a (sled) and (ice skates.)
4. Beth put on the horse's (saddle) and (bridle.)
5. Some stars appear both (on television) and (in films.)
6. Neither (jokes) nor (riddles) could make Lynn laugh.
7. The math test was (long) but (easy.)
8. Ernie reads sports (stories) or (biographies.)
9. Whether he is (happy) or (sad,) Tom always smiles.
10. Leslie takes not only (ballet) but also (voice lessons.)

B. Number your paper from 1 to 10. Write the compounds you find in each sentence. Circle the conjunction. Then write *Subject, Verb, Direct Object, Indirect Object, Predicate Adjective, Adverb,* or *Object of a Preposition* to identify each compound.

Example: Wear a dress or jeans.

dress (or) jeans: direct object

1. The lettering on the posters (and) banners is too small.
2. Slowly (and) thoughtfully he repaired the clock.
3. His story was unbelievable (but) true.
4. Lori carefully (but) quickly explained the answer.
5. The travelers waved (and) smiled.
6. Dad (and) Mother bought a rocking chair.
7. Janet found the address (and) telephone number.
8. We waited throughout the afternoon (and) evening.
9. The biggest tractor on the lot was green (and) yellow.
10. She could have given you (or) Pat a chance.

ADDITIONAL EXERCISES

Using Conjunctions

Conjunctions and Compound Constructions   Write the compound construction in each sentence. Underline the conjunction. Underline every word of a correlative conjunction.

1. Yvonne practiced on the parallel bars and the rings.
2. Cold nights and warm days are good for maple sap.
3. The fugitive either swam or rowed across the river.
4. I waited but got no answer.
5. The girls washed and waxed Mom's new car.
6. The hawk swooped toward Adam and me.
7. Red and yellow lights flashed on the control panel.
8. Neither aspirin nor rest helped his headache.
9. This peanut butter contains neither salt nor sugar.
10. Joy worked slowly but steadily on the model ship.
11. The hailstones destroyed not only the soybean crop but also the sweet corn.
12. This switch turns the furnace on and off.
13. I wonder whether the dust or the cat is making me sneeze.
14. We studied not only history but also geography.
15. Kip asked whether milk or juice had more calories.
16. Jerry reads well but writes poorly.
17. The team and the coach huddled during the timeout.
18. Is the snow wet or powdery?
19. Dwight neither knows nor cares.
20. Nicole washed not only the apples but also the grapes.
21. The detective was polite but persistent.
22. First, turn over the soil and then remove the stones.
23. Sacajawea guided Lewis and Clark.
24. The seahorse swims upright and grasps with its tail.
25. Both Brenda and Carol play softball.

535

These Additional Exercises may be used for additional practice of the concepts presented in this Section. Each exercise focuses on a single concept, and should be used after the page number indicated in parentheses.

Review

If you have not assigned these Additional Exercises before this time, you can also use them as an excellent Section Review.

Mixed Review

These exercises provide review of the concepts presented in this Section. Each exercise challenges the students to apply several of the skills they have acquired during previous study. Because the "mixed" feature of these activities makes them more difficult, the teacher may wish to have less-advanced students do them orally or in small groups.

MIXED REVIEW

Using Conjunctions

A. Identifying compound sentence parts Copy the following sentences. Underline the compound sentence parts. Circle the (conjunctions.) After each sentence, write what the compound part is.

> Example: Stephen wrote the letter quickly (but) neatly.
> Compound Adverb

1. Mr. Jacobs researched (and) wrote the article about vampire bats. Verb
2. Marion (or) Colette will represent our neighborhood at the meeting. Subject
3. The opposing team wore blue (and) gold uniforms. Adjective
4. I enjoy reading mysteries now (and) then. Adverb
5. Stu collects matchbooks (and) menus from famous restaurants. Direct Object
6. The service in this store is slow (but) dependable. Predicate Adjectives
7. Katherine said her lines smoothly (and) distinctly. Adverb
8. (Neither) he (nor) I actually saw the accident. Subject
9. Beth designed (and) built an unusual doghouse. Verb
10. Dad gave Sam (and) me haircuts. Direct Object

B. Using conjunctions and compound sentence parts Write sentences using compound sentence parts according to the directions that follow. Answers will vary.

1. Compound indirect object. Use a noun and a pronoun.
2. Compound predicate noun. Use proper nouns.
3. Compound object of a preposition. Use two pronouns.
4. Compound subject. Use *either, or.*
5. Compound verb. Use *but.*

USING GRAMMAR IN WRITING
Using Conjunctions

A. Following are instructions for making fresh applesauce. These instructions were written for a child. Therefore, the sentences are short and simple. Rewrite the instructions for an adult, combining ideas into compound constructions.

> Peel several apples. Core the apples. Slice the apples. Set the slices aside. Pour one-fourth cup of apple juice in a blender. You can use water instead. Add the apples one at a time. Blend the mixture until it is smooth. Pour it into a saucepan. Cook over low heat. Add some cinnamon to taste. Add some honey to taste. Add a dash of lemon juice.

B. The last ten seconds changed the outcome of the basketball game between your team, the Jays, and your arch rivals, the Falcons. Write a paragraph that describes the last ten seconds of the game. Use the following compound constructions in your sentences.

> shot and scored
> both the referee and the coach
> missed the shot and fouled
> tired but happy
> must either pass or shoot
> our forward and their guard

C. You are listening to a speaker who tries to impress listeners by using long, involved sentences. Here is the first sentence of today's speech. Write out what you think the rest of it might be. Use the same style. When you are done, underline the conjunctions you used.

> "My friends and fans, I come before you today not as a celebrity or a star, but as a friend."

537

Using Grammar in Writing

These challenging and enjoyable activities allow the students to see how the concepts of grammar, usage, and mechanics may be applied in actual writing situations. Each exercise is designed to allow students practice in several of the skills they have acquired in this Section. The activities also provide opportunities for students to write creatively about a wide variety of interesting and unusual subjects.

Section Objectives

1. To recognize the eight parts of speech, including interjections
2. To recognize the use of a single word as different parts of speech

Preparing the Students

Discuss how each word in a sentence has a particular job to do. Ask students to tell you what each word in the sentence below is, and what its function is.

John and I raced quickly across the wide field.

List the seven groups of words as the students name them. Explain that almost every word in our language can be placed in one of these groups. This section will give more information about identifying words as one of the parts of speech. Stress the importance of identifying a word according to its function in a sentence. This section will also introduce the eighth part of speech, the interjection.

Additional Resources

Mastery Test — pages 59–60 in the test booklet
Additional Exercises — pages 542–544 in the student text
Practice Book — pages 203–205
Duplicating Masters — pages 203–205
Special Populations — See special section at the back of this Teacher's Edition.

Using the Parts of Speech

Part 1 The Parts of Speech

You have studied verbs, nouns, pronouns, adjectives, adverbs, prepositions, and conjunctions. You have been learning to recognize words in these groups and to use them correctly in sentences.

In this section, you will learn about an eighth group of words called **interjections.**

The name used for all of these groups of words is **parts of speech.** Here are the eight parts of speech:

nouns	**verbs**	**adverbs**	**conjunctions**
pronouns	**adjectives**	**prepositions**	**interjections**

A word fits into one of the groups because of the way it is used in a sentence.

What Are Interjections?

In addition to the seven parts of speech you have studied, there is a group of words called **interjections.**

An interjection is a word or short group of words used to express strong feeling. It may be a real word or merely a sound. It may express surprise, joy, longing, anger, or sorrow. An interjection is usually followed by an **exclamation mark (!).**

Read these examples of interjections:

> *Hooray!* We won the game.
> *No way!* I'm not riding that roller coaster.
> *Congratulations!*
> *Ouch!* That hurts.

Exercises Recognize the parts of speech.

A. Read each sentence. Then write the italicized word. Beside each word, write what part of speech it is.

1. Margaret is locked *in* her room. Preposition
2. The hermit is irritable *and* unfriendly. Conjunction
3. Jody *whistled* for her dog. Verb
4. A *shaggy* dog ran through the yard. Adjective
5. Rain *gently* tapped on the windows. Adverb
6. A performer walked on broken *glass.* Noun
7. *He* was not scratched or cut. Pronoun
8. *Ugh!* This is disgusting! Interjection
9. *Marcus* saw a strange flying object. Noun
10. A *silver* racer streaked around the curve. Adjective

B. Follow the directions for Exercise A.

1. The soccer players *scrambled* down the field. Verb
2. These new rules are *strict.* Adjective
3. The *mayor* appointed a new aide. Noun
4. Opera fans applauded *her* enthusiastically. Pronoun

Part 1

Objective

To recognize the eight parts of speech, including interjections

Presenting the Lesson

1. Read and discuss pages 538–539. Ask students when interjections are most likely to be used. Ask them to give other examples of interjections and to explain why they should be followed by exclamation points. Discuss what it means to *interject* something into a conversation.

2. Assign and discuss Exercise A and B on pages 539–540.

Individualizing the Lesson

Less-Advanced Students

Do Exercise A orally. Allow students to work in pairs to complete Exercise B.

Advanced Students

Review with the students where to find the part of speech in a dictionary entry. This will be a good lead-in to Part 2 of this section.

Optional Practice

Make copies of these sentences. Have students name the part of speech of the underlined word in each sentence.

Adj. 1. The <u>new</u> red Frisbee whizzed by his outstretched hand.

Pro. 2. <u>They</u> practiced diving with the coach and her yesterday.

Conj. 3. The rocket has to be dismantled <u>and</u> moved.

4. Check the condition of your tires <u>regularly</u>. Adv.
5. The <u>mechanic</u> and his helper fix Noun cars, motorcycles, and minibikes.
6. <u>Yes</u>! Hurry! Get here quickly! Excl.
7. The skaters <u>glided</u>, turned, and spun around on the ice. Verb
8. <u>At</u> the lake there were sailboats docked at the marina. Prep.

Extending the Lesson

Select a paragraph or short article that the students would enjoy reading. Underline fifteen to twenty words, several of each part of speech. Reproduce the work or use an overhead projector. Have students identify the parts of speech.

Part 2

Objective

To recognize the use of a single word as different parts of speech

Presenting the Lesson

1. Read and discuss pages 540–541. Ask students for examples of other words that can be used as different parts of speech.

2. Assign and discuss Exercises A and B on page 541. Students should be ready to explain how they know what part of speech the word is.

Individualizing the Lesson

Less-Advanced Students

Work together with students on the exercises. Have them write the sentences on the board. Discuss

5. Vincent painted the sign *neatly.* Adverb
6. Two men escaped *into* the jungle. Preposition
7. Sunglasses *or* a visor shades the sun. Conjunction
8. *Wow!* You dance so well! Interjection
9. The hikers *finally* found the waterfall. Adverb
10. Bonnie lit the charcoal *with* a match. Preposition

Part 2   Words Used as Different Parts of Speech

You cannot tell what part of speech a word is, of course, until you see how the word is used in a sentence. Many words may be used in different ways.

Read these examples:

Dennis took a *break* from his homework.
   (*Break* is used as a noun.)

Don't *break* the cookie jar.
   (*Break* is used as a verb.)

Money is kept in a *safe.*
   (*Safe* is used as a noun.)

Lexington is a *safe* town with little crime.
   (*Safe* is used as an adjective modifying *town.*)

The gymnast soared *high* into the air.
   (*High* is an adverb modifying the verb *soared.*)

Horses jumped the *high* hurdles.
   (*High* is an adjective modifying *hurdles.*)

The ice skater whirled *around.*
   (*Around* is an adverb telling *where* about the verb *whirled.*)

The sentry paced *around* the fort.
   (*Around* is used as a preposition.)

This is our lunch hour.
   (*This* is used as a pronoun, the subject of the sentence.)

We will take a field trip *this* week.

(*This* is used as an adjective modifying *week*.)

The enemy will *free* its prisoners of war.

(*Free* is used as a verb.)

Paula received a *free* T-shirt.

(*Free* is used as an adjective modifying *T-shirt*.)

Exercises   Decide the part of speech.

A.   Write the italicized word in each sentence. After it, write its part of speech.

1. The center took one free *throw*. Noun
2. Children *throw* peanuts to the elephant. Verb
3. Your arrow came *close* to the bull's-eye. Adverb
4. *Close* friends talk honestly. Adjective
5. Monopoly uses *play* money. Adjective
6. We girls often *play* soccer. Verb
7. *Which* is the best restaurant? Pronoun
8. *Which* films are playing downtown? Adjective
9. Seagulls flew *by* the beach. Preposition
10. Suddenly a fire engine sped *by*. Adverb

B.   Follow the directions for Exercise A.

1. A huge jade *plant* grows in the greenhouse. Noun
2. Did the gardener *plant* tulips? Verb
3. The twins strolled *in*. Adverb
4. The freshman class held a party *in* the gym. Preposition
5. Put the *cover* on the jar. Noun
6. *Cover* the flowers before winter. Verb
7. I *long* for some privacy. Verb
8. Beth wore a *long* scarf around her neck. Adjective
9. This wallet is *his*. Pronoun
10. Lou threw *his* cards on the table. Adjective

each word and its part of speech. If the word is a modifier, ask for the word it modifies. You may want to have them first identify the subject and predicate in each sentence.

Advanced Students

Have students use their dictionaries to determine how many different parts of speech these words can be: *wake, check, lean, hurrah, inside, silence.*

Optional Practice

Have students write two sentences for each of the following words, using the word as one of the parts of speech listed at the top of the column. Have them underline the word in each sentence, and write what part of speech the word is used as. Answers will vary.

Noun/Verb	Adjective/Verb
1. paint	1. clean
2. turn	2. dry
3. land	3. clear

Preposition/Adverb
1. outside
2. above
3. down

Extending the Lesson

Have each student choose a word that can be used as at least two parts of speech. Then have him or her write sentences showing each use of the word. Then have the student make an illustration for each sentence (stick-figure cartoon, cutouts, etc.). Display the work in the classroom.

542

ADDITIONAL EXERCISES

Using the Parts of Speech

Parts of Speech Number your paper from 1 to 25. Write the part of speech of the italicized word in each sentence.

Adv. 1. Francine put a jacket *on.*

Prep. 2. Sea holly grows *on* the beach.

Adj. 3. *That* noise was thunder.

Pro. 4. *That* sounded like thunder.

N. 5. Dave's *curls* lay around the barber's chair.

V. 6. Our terrier *curls* her tail when she's happy.

Inter. 7. *Well!* Did you see that?

Adv. 8. Leslie can't see that *well* without her glasses.

Adj. 9. That mousey little animal is a miniature *Siamese* cat.

N. 10. The *Chinese* are more likely to own bikes than cars.

N. 11. Shirley made a good *move* with her pawn.

V. 12. Jeff *moved* closer to the microphone.

V. 13. *Flip* the coin again.

N. 14. Juan did a *flip* from the high diving board.

Adj. 15. Freddie waxed his new *leather* boots.

N. 16. *Leather* has become expensive.

Prep. 17. A satellite revolves *around* the earth.

Adv. 18. The seeing-eye dog led its master *around.*

Pro. 19. *Which* is the starter switch?

Adj. 20. *Which* league is he in?

V. 21. Mark *skated* across the pond.

Adj. 22. Molly borrowed my *skate* key.

N. 23. Lee found only one *skate* in the garage.

N. 24. There was no *screen* on the window.

V. 25. Ms. Washington *screened* all applicants.

Additional Exercises

These Additional Exercises may be used for additional practice of the concepts presented in this Section. Each exercise focuses on a single concept, and should be used after the page number indicated in parentheses.

Review

If you have not assigned these Additional Exercises before this time, you can also use them as an excellent Section Review.

MIXED REVIEW

Using the Parts of Speech

A. Identifying parts of speech   Number your paper from 1 to 15. Copy the words in italics. Decide how each word in italics is used. Then write its part of speech.

Adj.   1. Do you have *enough* warm clothing?

Adv.   2. Carol worked *hard* on her acceptance speech.

N.   3. Mom paid the *bill* promptly.

V.   4. Ben's cat *scratches* the furniture.

Adj.   5. We had a *great* day at the beach.

N.   6. This small *print* is difficult to read.

Adj.   7. *Dry* brown leaves rustled in the wind.

V.   8. We must *clean* the stables before sundown.

N.   9. Scott painted the fence with firm, even *strokes*.

Prep.   10. A light shone *above* the door.

Adj.   11. Your application is *complete*.

Adv.   12. Move *over*, please.

Adj.   13. The judges praised Dad's *giant* marigolds.

Adj.   14. This pillow is stuffed with *goose* feathers.

N.   15. The two sides reached a settlement by *morning*.

B. Using words as different parts of speech   Write two sentences for each of the following words. In each sentence, use the word as a different part of speech. Underline the word, and then write what part of speech it is used as in that sentence.   Answers will vary.

1. thought
2. below
3. brush
4. lost
5. call

These challenging and enjoyable activities allow the students to see how the concepts of grammar, usage, and mechanics may be applied in actual writing situations. Each exercise is designed to allow students practice in several of the skills they have acquired in this Section. The activities also provide opportunities for students to write creatively about a wide variety of interesting and unusual subjects.

USING GRAMMAR IN WRITING
Parts of Speech

A. There are many kinds of codes. This one is based on words that can be used as different parts of speech. For example, you want to relay this message:

My cover is broken. I will fly to a safe area.
<small>N ... V ... V ... Adj.</small>

You could write it in code this way, using the underlined words as different parts of speech:

Cover the broken bed. The fly on the safe can be found.
<small>V ... Adj. ... N ... N</small>

The following are important messages. Write them in the code, using the underlined words as different parts of speech. Label what part of speech each of the code words is now used as.

1. Thieves may break into the safe. Place money in the wall.
2. They demand a raise. Pay by check.
3. Leads are few. Must fly back.
4. Hit the jackpot. Will stop at your place.

B. Each word below can be used as at least two different parts of speech. Some can be used as verbs, nouns, or adjectives. Some can be used as all three. Write two or three sentences for each word, using that word as a different part of speech in each sentence.

Example: Place the money over there.
          I hid in a safe place.
          My mother bought new place mats.

1. plant   4. safe
2. cover   5. sail
3. play   6. meet

Sentence Patterns

Part 1 Word Order and Meaning

Sentences are made up of words that are arranged in order. However, not just any order will do. To make sense, the words must be put together in order according to certain patterns. Read the groups of words below. Which groups make sense?

Rain fell heavily.   Ms. Parker hired Louis.
Fell heavily rain.   Ms. Parker Louis hired.

545

545

Presenting the Lesson

1. Ask the class to listen carefully and follow the instructions below. Read them no more than twice, and wait for students to figure them out.

1. Book your hold up.
2. Hand raise your other.

Discuss why they had difficulty understanding the directions.

2. Read and discuss pages 545–546.

3. Assign and discuss the exercise on page 546.

Individualizing the Lesson

Less-Advanced Students

Do the exercise on page 546 orally with the class.

Advanced Students

Have students make up their own exercise like the one on page 546. Then have them exchange papers and rewrite the sentences.

Optional Practice

Tell students to unscramble the words below, and write them in two different orders for two correct sentences.

1. his customer the waiter the plate took from
   The waiter took the plate from his customer. or The customer took the plate . . .
2. with doctor her the tests discussed patient the
   Her doctor discussed the tests with the patient or The patient discussed . . .
3. that book the author is who of
   Who is the author of that book? or The author of that book is who?
4. patted nose the lion lion's tamer the
   The lion tamer patted the lion's nose or The tamer lion patted the lion's nose.

Extending the Lesson

Explain that every language has a certain word order. Have students who know a foreign language point out how that language differs from English.

The first group in each pair makes sense because the words are in the right order for one of the patterns of an English sentence. The second group in each pair does not make sense because the words are not in the right order. From your experience with English sentences, you know what the right order is. You can see at once when the order is wrong.

Sometimes there is more than one right order for the words in a sentence. Each order makes sense and expresses an idea. However, when the order is changed, the ideas expressed may change, too. Read the following pairs of sentences.

Kathy held the baby.   Benson watched the creature.
The baby held Kathy.   The creature watched Benson.

The words are the same in each sentence, but the word order is not. The difference in word order makes a difference in meaning.

Exercise   Change word order to change meaning.

Read each sentence. Then change the order of the words to change the meaning. Write each new sentence on your paper.

1. Rachel ignored Albert.
   Albert ignored Rachel.
2. The climbers saw Bigfoot.
   Bigfoot saw the climbers.
3. That dog chased the jogger.
   The jogger chased that dog.
4. Mike burned the cookies.
   The cookies burned Mike.
5. Laura petted the cat.
   The cat petted Laura.
6. Diane called the captain.
   The captain called Diane.

Part 2   The N V Pattern

In English sentences, words are arranged in a certain order to make sense. The word order of most sentences follows a pattern. In this section, you will study five **sentence patterns**.

One simple pattern for English sentences is called the **N V pattern.** Every sentence has a subject and a verb. The subject is usually a noun or a pronoun. In this chart, N stands for the noun (or pronoun) in the complete subject. V stands for the verb in the complete predicate.

N	V
The crowd	applauded.
Loretta	left.
She	walked slowly.

The word order above follows the N V pattern.

Exercises Use the N V pattern.

A. Make a chart for the N V pattern. Label one column *N*. Label the other *V*. Write these sentences on the chart.

1. Walter | understands.
2. Spring | arrives tomorrow.
3. Time | flies.
4. New shoes | may hurt.
5. The sink | overflowed.
6. Madeline | ran by.

B. Copy this chart. Complete each N V pattern.

Answers will vary.

N	V
1. _____	flew away.
2. Three runners	_____.
3. _____	listened carefully.
4. Daniel	_____.
5. _____	sneezed.

Part 3 The N V N Pattern

A sentence in the **N V N pattern** has three parts. The first *N* stands for the subject noun or pronoun. The *V* stands for the verb. The second *N* stands for the direct object. The sentences in the following chart are in the N V N pattern.

547

Part 2

Objective

To recognize the NV sentence pattern

Presenting the Lesson

1. Read and discuss pages 546–547. Read the examples on page 547 in reverse order (verb first) and discuss why it is much more difficult to understand them.

2. Assign and discuss Exercises A and B on page 547. Do Exercise B with the class.

Individualizing the Lesson

Less-Advanced Students

Do Exercise A orally. Then have students do Exercise B in groups.

Advanced Students

Ask students to write 5 original NV sentences.

Optional Practice

Ask students to write five original NV sentences.

Extending the Lesson

Have each student find examples of sentences using the NV pattern in a newspaper article.

Part 3

Objective

To recognize the N V N sentence pattern

547

Presenting the Lesson

1. Read and discuss pages 547–548. Make it clear that each of the three parts in the N V N pattern may have one or more words.

2. Assign and discuss Exercises A and B on page 548.

Individualizing the Lesson

Less-Advanced Students

Do Exercise A orally. Have students complete Exercise B in groups.

Advanced Students

Have students follow the directions for Exercise A on page 548 using sentences 5, 6, 8, 9, and 10 of Exercise B on page 349.

Optional Practice

Have students write ten sentences using the N V N pattern.

Extending the Lesson

Have students find examples of sentences using the N V N pattern in their literature anthologies.

Part 4

Objective

To recognize the N V N N sentence pattern

Presenting the Lesson

1. Read and discuss page 548. Remind students that the indirect object comes before the direct object in a sentence.

N	V	N
Elizabeth	heard	a crash.
Many people	will see	that movie.
Everyone	wanted	a rest.

Exercises   Use the N V N pattern.

A. Make a chart for the N|V|N pattern. Label the three columns *N*, *V*, and *N*. Write these sentences on the chart.

1. Terry|has|a cold.
2. My aunt|built|some shelves.
3. He|climbed|the ladder.
4. I|cooked|the hamburgers.
5. Roger|borrowed|my pen.
6. Thelma|can fix|your bike.

B. Copy this chart. Complete each N V N pattern. Answers will vary.

N	V	N
1. _____	dropped	the mirror.
2. Fran	sold	_____.
3. _____	caught	_____.
4. _____	_____	the boat.
5. _____	operated	the machine.

Part 4   The N V N N Pattern

A sentence in the **N V N N pattern** has four parts. The first *N* stands for the subject noun or pronoun. The *V* stands for the verb. The second *N* stands for the indirect object. The third *N* stands for the direct object. Read the sentences in the following chart. They are in the N V N N pattern.

N	V	N	N
Sue	gave	Joan	a scarf.
The waiter	brought	us	the menu.
I	sent	the company	a complaint.

Exercises   Use the N V N N pattern.

A.   Make a chart for the N|V|N|N pattern. Label the four columns *N*, *V*, *N*, and *N*. Write these sentences on the chart.

1. Pollen|gives|me|hay fever.
2. My aunt|brought|me|an album.
3. Someone|sent|Caroline|a note.
4. I|made|myself|a sandwich.
5. Tom|told|Ted|your secret.
6. The judges|gave|the winner|a perfect score.
7. We|sent|Ms. Samuelson|a get-well card.
8. Midnight snacks|give|Hubert|nightmares.
9. The manufacturer|sent|me|a replacement.
10. A victory|will earn|us|the championship.

B.   Copy this chart. Complete each N V N N pattern. Answers will vary.

N	V	N	N
1. _____	gave	Lucille	_____.
2. Rick	told	_____	_____.
3. Someone	_____	_____	a gift.
4. _____	_____	me	two letters.
5. I	taught	_____	_____.

C.   Writing   Make a chart of your own for the N V N N pattern. Write five sentences in the N V N N pattern. Answers will vary.

Part 5   The N LV N Pattern

A sentence in the **N LV N pattern** has three parts. The first *N* stands for the subject noun or pronoun. *LV* stands for a linking verb. The second *N* stands for the noun or pronoun that follows the linking verb. The sentences in this chart are in the N LV N pattern.

549

2. Assign and discuss Exercises A, B and C on page 549.

Individualizing the Lesson

Less-Advanced Students

Work with students to complete the exercises, placing the columns on the board. For Exercise C suggest the following verbs: *give, hand, send, bring, show,* and *offer.*

Advanced Students

Have the students expand the sentences they wrote for Exercise C, adding modifiers.

Optional Practice

Have students rewrite the following sentences in the N V N N pattern.

1. The star forward on the basketball team passed the ball to his teammate.
2. Gino's friends gave a birthday present to him.
3. The guard tossed the keys to his relief man.
4. Julie mailed a letter to her friend.
5. Mike's uncle bought some roller skates for him.

Extending the Lesson

Have students find sentences written in the N V N N pattern in the sports section of a newspaper.

Part 5

Objective

To recognize the N LV N sentence pattern

Presenting the Lesson

1. Read and discuss pages 549–550. Point out that each part of a N LV N sentence may have more than one word.

2. Assign and discuss Exercises A, B, and C on page 550. Stress that the first and second noun should be interchangeable.

Individualizing the Lesson

Less-Advanced Students

Do Exercises A and B orally. Write the charts on the chalkboard.

Advanced Students

Have students follow the directions for Exercise A on page 550 but use items 2, 3, 6, and 10 from Exercise A, and items 2 and 8 from Exercise B on page 391.

Optional Practice

Have students write as many N LV N sentences as possible using these nouns (Ralph, skier, Connie, singer, swimmer, student) and these verbs (is, was).

Extending the Lesson

Have each student find five sentences in print using the N LV N pattern.

Part 6

Objective

To recognize the N LV Adj sentence pattern

N	LV	N
Rita	is	our pitcher.
She and I	are	co-captains.
The cold lemonade	was	a treat.

Exercises   Use the N LV N pattern.

A.   Make a chart for the N|LV|N pattern. Label the three columns *N*, *LV*, and *N*. Write these sentences on the chart.

1. Don|was|the winner.
2. They|are|the only volunteers.
3. This book|is|a thriller.
4. Betsy|is|a good bowler.
5. Soccer|is|my favorite sport.
6. Snakes|are|reptiles.

B.   Copy this chart. Complete each N LV N pattern. Answers will vary.

N	LV	N
1. _____	is	the owner.
2. Babe Ruth	was	_____.
3. _____	are	_____.
4. Claudia and Bill	_____	marathon runners.
5. _____	were	_____.

C.   Writing   Make a chart of your own. Label the columns *N, LV,* and *N.* Write five sentences in the N LV N pattern.

Answers will vary.

Part 6   The N LV Adj Pattern

Sentences in the **N LV Adj pattern** have three parts. The *N* stands for the subject noun or pronoun. *LV* stands for the linking verb. *Adj* stands for the predicate adjective. The sentences in the following chart are in the N LV Adj pattern.

N	LV	Adj
Bald Mountain	is	steep.
Your brother	seems	certain.
Kathleen	sounds	quite worried.
Our pizza	will taste	superb.
You	have been	helpful.

Exercises   Use the N LV Adj pattern.

A. Make a chart for the N|LV|Adj pattern. Label the three columns *N*, *LV*, and *Adj*. Write these sentences on the chart.

1. Marge|looks|curious.
2. These pickles|are|sour.
3. The crisp lettuce | tasted|fresh.
4. Snails|are| slow.
5. Joel|seemed|eager.
6. The movie|was|hilarious.
7. The sunrise|was|brilliant.
8. She|will be|busy.

B. Make a chart like the one below. Complete each sentence in the N LV Adj pattern. Answers will vary.

N	LV	Adj
1. _____	is	quiet.
2. The wind	became	_____.
3. Mustard	tastes	_____.
4. The shelves	_____	sturdy.
5. _____	sounded	_____.

C.   Writing   Make a chart of your own. Label the columns *N*, *LV*, and *Adj*. Write five sentences in the N LV Adj pattern.
Answers will vary.

Presenting the Lesson

1. Read and discuss pages 550–551. Remind students that adjectives following linking verbs describe the subject.

2. Assign and discuss Exercises A, B, and C on page 551.

Individualizing the Lesson

Less-Advanced Students

Allow the students to work in pairs to complete Exercises A and B.

Advanced Students

Add these sentences on page 391 to Exercise A: Exercise A, items 1, 4, 5, 7, 8, and 9; and Exercise B, items 1, 3, 4, 5, 6, 7, 9, and 10.

Optional Practice

Have students write sentences using the N LV Adj pattern. Tell them to use nouns from the following list. They should choose a linking verb and an adjective that goes with each noun. Sentences will vary.

1. the last performance
2. the rescuers
3. the water wheel
4. some ghost stories
5. pizza
6. wallpaper
7. photography
8. Greek mythology
9. colonial times
10. five library books

Extending the Lesson

Have the students find five examples of sentences written in the N LV Adj pattern in the newspaper.

552

Additional Exercises

These Additional Exercises may be used for additional practice of the concepts presented in this Section. Each exercise focuses on a single concept, and should be used after the page number indicated in parentheses.

Review

If you have not assigned these Additional Exercises before this time, you can also use them as an excellent Section Review.

ADDITIONAL EXERCISES

Sentence Patterns

Sentence Patterns Number your paper from 1 to 25. Write the pattern for each sentence. Each sentence fits one of these patterns:

N V   N V N   N V N N   N LV N   N LV Adj

1. Your brother will be furious. N LV Adj
2. The sign collapsed. NV
3. Harper caught the pass. NVN
4. The rebels fought fiercely. NV
5. Randy became weary. N LV Adj
6. I recognized Sherry's voice. NVN
7. The class bought the principal a birthday cake. NVNN
8. Marva Collins is a well-known teacher. N LV N
9. Freckles dotted his nose. NVN
10. The judge gave the lawyer a lecture. NVNN
11. I passed Cara the ball. NVNN
12. Cara passed the ball to Jessica. NVN
13. My aunt is a minister. N LV N
14. Somehow the flowers survived under the snow. NV
15. The hurricane season had begun. NV
16. Ashes from the volcano covered the streets. NVN
17. San Juan is a seaport. N LV N
18. Kate is arguing with Mimi again. NV
19. The sergeant showed us her badge. NVNN
20. The street is noisy in summer. N LV Adj
21. People sat on the front porch. NV
22. Cheryl sounded sincere. N LV Adj
23. Bert sounded the alarm. NVN
24. Donna walked slowly to the board. NV
25. I told you the truth. NVNN

MIXED REVIEW

Sentence Patterns

A. Finding sentence patterns Decide what sentence pattern is used in each of the following sentences. Write *NV*, *NVN*, *NVNN*, *N LV N*, or *N LV Adj*. Then write another sentence with the same pattern. Sentences will vary.

1. Meg knit Clara leg warmers. NVNN
2. The officer gave Dad directions. NVNN
3. The hamburgers burned. NV
4. Gail's sister is a dental hygienist. N LV N
5. The storm raged throughout the night. NV
6. My tennis shoes are clean. N LV Adj
7. I will be ready at ten. N LV Adj
8. Andrew mailed the invitations. NVN
9. Todd showed the class pictures from his vacation. NVNN
10. These children are first graders. N LV N

B. Using sentence patterns Write two sentences using each of the following sentence patterns. Answers will vary.

1. N V
2. N V N
3. N V N N
4. N LV N
5. N LV Adj

Mixed Review

These exercises provide review of the concepts presented in this Section. Each exercise challenges the students to apply several of the skills they have acquired during previous study. Because the "mixed" feature of these activities makes them more difficult, the teacher may wish to have less-advanced students do them orally or in small groups.

USING GRAMMAR IN WRITING
Sentence Patterns

A. You can use the different sentence patterns to write a nature poem. Choose a subject in nature and follow the sentence patterns given in this example.

Rain

NV	Clouds form.
NVN	The sun leaves the sky.
NVNN	The trees give the wind their branches.
N LV Adj	The rains are furious.
N LV N	The storm is a lion.

Your last sentence, the N LV N pattern, should compare your subject with something else. The comparison should not use the words "like" or "as." This kind of comparison, used often in creative writing, is called a *metaphor.*

B. When you apply for a job, you must usually state your qualifications. Think of a job for which you are qualified. Using each of the five basic sentence patterns, state your qualifications for that job. Remember, you may substitute personal pronouns for nouns.

Example: Job—announcer on the school's radio station, WIGH.

Radio interests me. (NVN)
My drama teacher gave me a recommendation. (NVNN)
My voice is clear. (N LV Adj)
I am a hard worker. (NLVN)
I can work after school. (NV)

Using Verbals

Section Objectives

1. To understand the function of gerunds and gerund phrases and to identify them in sentences

2. To understand the function of participles and participial phrases, to identify them in sentences, and to distinguish them from gerunds and gerund phrases

3. To understand the function of infinitives and infinitive phrases and to identify them in sentences

4. To review the functions of gerunds, participles, and infinitives

Preparing the Students

Stress that words may be used as different parts of speech depending on their use in a sentence.

If students understand the concept of parts of speech, ask them what part of speech the word *swimming* looks like; it appears to be a verb. Put *Swimming is my favorite sport* on the board. Have students identify each word except for *swimming*. Then ask them what is missing (the subject). Students will see that *swimming* is being used as a noun.

Read and discuss the introduction on pages 555–556.

Additional Resources

Mastery Test — pages 61–62 in the test booklet

Additional Exercises — pages 567–573 in the student text

Practice Book — pages 206–209

Duplicating Masters — pages 206–209

Special Populations — See special section at the back of this Teacher's Edition.

Many words are used as different parts of speech. You can determine the part of speech of a word only when you see how the word is used in a sentence.

In this section, you will study some special kinds of words that seem to be one part of speech but are used as a different part of speech. These words are called **verbals.**

A verbal is a word that is formed from a verb, but that acts as another part of speech. Verbals may look like the verbs in a sentence, but they are never used as verbs.

There are three kinds of verbals:

gerunds   participles   infinitives

Part 1

Objective

To understand the function of gerunds and gerund phrases and to identify them in sentences

Presenting the Lesson

1. The concept that a word can be used as a noun and at the same time have the properties of a verb is usually confusing to most students. Concentrate on the concept of how words can be used as different parts of speech. Read and discuss pages 556–557.

2. Assign and discuss Exercises A and B on pages 557–558. You may wish to do Exercise A with the class first, and then assign Exercise B. During the discussion, have students identify everything in each sentence except for the gerund phrase. This may make it easier for them to see how the gerund phrase is being used in the sentence.

Individualizing the Lesson

Less-Advanced Students

1. Write these examples on the board. Discuss the use of the gerund in each.

1. Jack enjoys *hunting.* (object)
2. *Studying* will help you pass tests. (subject)
3. She was trying to win the contest with her loud *singing.* (object of the preposition *with*)

Part 1   Gerunds

A gerund is a verb form that is used as a noun. Gerunds end in *-ing.* Gerunds can be used in any way that nouns are used.

Like nouns, gerunds may be used as subjects.

> *Running* is good exercise.
> (*Running* is a gerund, the subject of the verb *is.*)

Like nouns, gerunds may be used as objects.

> Kelly likes *reading.*
> (*Reading* is a gerund, the direct object of the verb *likes.*)

Like nouns, gerunds may be used as objects of prepositions.

> The time for *swimming* is too short.
> (*Swimming* is a gerund, the object of the preposition *for.*)

The Gerund Phrase

Gerunds are not always used alone. Because gerunds are formed from verbs, they can have objects. A gerund with its objects and modifiers is called a **gerund phrase.**

> *Playing the piano* relaxes me.
> (*Playing the piano* is a gerund phrase used as the subject of *relaxes; piano* is the object of *playing.*)

Because gerunds are formed from verbs, they can be modified by adverbs.

> *Parking here* is difficult.
> (*Parking here* is a gerund phrase used as the subject of *is; here* is an adverb modifying *parking.*)

Because gerunds are used as nouns, they can be modified by adjectives.

> *Careful planning* is necessary.
> (*Careful planning* is a gerund phrase used as the subject of *is; careful* is an adjective modifying *planning.*)

Gerunds can be modified by prepositional phrases.

> Mr. Lane allowed *talking after the test.*
> (*Talking after the test* is a gerund phrase used as the direct object of *allowed; after the test* is a prepositional phrase modifying *talking.*)

In all of these examples you can see that gerunds are verb forms, but they are never used as verbs. Because *running, reading, swimming, playing, parking, planning,* and *talking* are used as nouns in the example sentences, they are gerunds.

Exercises   Find the gerunds and gerund phrases.

A.   Write the gerund or gerund phrase in each of the following sentences. Then write whether the gerund or gerund phrase is used as a subject, a direct object, or the object of a preposition.

> Example: Shoveling snow is hard work.
> *Shoveling snow:* subject

S. 1. Chasing rabbits is our dog's favorite pastime.

S. 2. Digging for clams is done at low tide.

O.P. 3. That team won by playing good defense.

S. 4. Wearing contact lenses is convenient.

D.O. 5. The coach recommended running.

S. 6. Rebuilding engines is Janet's hobby.

S. 7. Sewing clothes saves money.

O.P. 8. There are trails for horseback riding.

S. 9. Dancing builds grace and control.

O.P. 10. After washing the walls, Chris painted them.

557

Have students substitute new words in place of the gerunds to create new sentences.

Then discuss these gerund phrases. Write them on the board.

1. *The loud knocking on the door* frightened the babysitter. (subject)
2. I hate *getting up early for school.* (object)
3. He earns money by *delivering the newspaper.* (object of the preposition *by*)

2. Do Exercises A and B with the class.

Advanced Students

Have students write ten original sentences using gerunds and gerund phrases. Encourage them to use the gerunds and gerund phrases as subjects, objects, and objects of prepositions.

Optional Practice

Have students fill in the blanks with a gerund in the first five sentences, and a gerund phrase in the second five sentences.
Answers will vary.

1. _____ is hard work.
2. Neither Joel nor his friends enjoy _____ .
3. The news article was written about _____ .
4. The band practices _____ in the afternoon.
5. _____ is good exercise.
6. _____ is her favorite sport.
7. The class enjoyed _____ last week.
8. _____ is the best way to get there.
9. We like _____ every week.
10. _____ is an interesting hobby.

Extending the Lesson

Have students underline the gerunds and gerund phrases in the following paragraph.

Talking on the phone is one of my favorite pastimes. I enjoy gabbing with a friend any time. They like receiving my calls, too. However, my parents don't allow phoning during the dinner hour. They also feel that late night is not the time for calling friends. Therefore, I do most of my conversing in the early evening.

Part 2

Objective

To understand the function of participles and participial phrases, to identify them in sentences, and to distinguish them from gerunds and gerund phrases

Presenting the Lesson

1. Read and discuss pages 558–559. Stress that a participle is always used as an adjective in a sentence.

2. If students are having difficulty with this part, do Exercise A on page 560 with them before assigning Exercise B. Have students identify the subject and verb in each sentence. This may make it easier for students to see how the participial phrase is being used.

3. Read and discuss pages 560–561. Remind students of the importance of identifying words according to their use in a sentence.

4. Do the exercise on page 561 with the students. Discuss how each word is used in the sentence.

B. Follow the directions for Exercise A.

D.O. 1. Melissa enjoys taking pictures of babies.

O.P. 2. Bob is known for being friendly.

O.P. 3. Craig earns money by moving furniture.

S. 4. Sailing on rough water is dangerous.

D.O. 5. Did you ever try tobogganing?

O.P. 6. Inez stays informed by reading magazines.

O.P. 7. The library is a place for quiet studying.

S. 8. Flying is one method of travel.

O.P. 9. We get to the island by taking a ferry.

S. 10. Seeing a dentist regularly is important.

Part 2 Participles

A participle is a verb form that is used as an adjective.

You remember that one of the principal parts of the verb is the **past participle.** The past participle is formed by adding -d or -ed to the present tense: *walk–walked.* The past participles of irregular verbs do not follow this rule and have to be learned separately: *bring–brought, ring–rung.*

There is another kind of participle, called the **present participle.** All present participles are formed by adding -ing to the present tense of the verb: *bring–bringing, ring–ringing, walk–walking.*

Look at these additional examples.

Verb	Past Participle	Present Participle
talk	talked	talking
go	gone	going
give	given	giving
write	written	writing

(If you need more review, see **Sections 3** and **4** on verbs and irregular verbs.)

Participles are always used as adjectives. They can modify nouns or pronouns:

> *Laughing,* the speaker turned away.
> (*Laughing* is a present participle modifying the noun *speaker.*)

> The truck hit a *parked* car.
> (*Parked* is a past participle modifying the noun *car.*)

> *Waving,* the police officer signaled us to stop.
> (*Waving* is a present participle modifying the noun *officer.*)

The Participial Phrase

Participles are not always used by themselves. They may be part of a phrase. The participle with its objects and modifiers is called a **participial phrase.** Because participles are formed from verbs, they may have objects.

> *Wearing high boots,* the fisherman waded into the stream.
> (*Wearing high boots* is a participial phrase, modifying the noun *fisherman; boots* is the object of the participle *wearing.*)

Because participles are formed from verbs, they may be modified by adverbs.

> A *badly dented* bicycle was left at school.
> (*Badly dented* is a participial phrase modifying the noun *bicycle; badly* is an adverb modifying *dented.*)

Participles may be modifed by prepositional phrases.

> *Listening to the radio,* Tom heard the final score.
> (*Listening to the radio* is a participial phrase, modifying *Tom; to the radio* is a prepositional phrase modifying *Listening.*)

In all of these examples you can see that participles are verb forms, but they are never used as verbs. Because *laughing, parked, waving, wearing, dented,* and *listening* are used as adjectives, they are participles.

559

2. After completing the exercise on page 561, have students write six sentences of their own using the same word, first as a gerund and then as a participle. Have them exchange papers with a classmate to be checked.

Optional Practice

Have students fill in the blanks in the following sentences with participles or participial phrases.

Answers will vary.

1. _____, Joan stumbled on a rock.
2. Did you see the _____ plane?
3. The speaker, _____, looked at the audience.
4. The engineer, _____, climbed down from the train.
5. _____, the roast beef looked like a lump of coal.

Extending the Lesson

Have students skim the short story section of their literature anthologies to find sentences that include participial phrases and/or gerund phrases. Using an overhead projector, write each sentence, and discuss it with the class.

Exercises   **Find the participles and participial phrases.**

A.   Write the participle or participial phrase in each of the following sentences. Write the word modified.

Example: Bowing, the lord greeted the queen.
Bowing: modifies *lord*

1. Hearing the alarm, Toni jumped out of bed.
2. The boy pumping gas is my brother.
3. Bitten by a snake, Cara was rushed to the hospital.
4. Dribbling, the forward stalled for time.
5. The teacher found her class telling jokes.
6. Linda Ronstadt, singing sweetly, opened the show.
7. Kathy listened at the slightly opened door.
8. Salted popcorn is tasty.
9. Hitting a home run, Cruz tied the score.
10. The villain, played by Brian, twirled his moustache.

B.   Follow the directions for Exercise A.

1. No one noticed the shooting star.
2. The expertly coached team won all its games.
3. Hoping for a victory, the team practiced daily.
4. The man riding a motorcycle stopped suddenly.
5. Circling, the plane was running out of fuel.
6. The person wearing the best costume wins a prize.
7. One patient, covered with a blanket, lay on the floor.
8. Sitting on the bench, Ted hoped he would play.
9. The woman campaigning for mayor shook my hand.
10. Cleverly drawn cartoons appear in the newspaper.

Gerund or Participle?

You have studied two of the three kinds of verbals. The gerund, like the present participle, is formed by adding *-ing* to the present tense of the verb. How can you tell whether a word is a gerund or a participle? It depends upon how the word is used. If it is used as a modifer, it is a participle. If it is used as a noun, it is a gerund. Study these examples:

Walking is good exercise.
(*Walking* is a gerund, the subject of *is*.)

Walking, we could take the shortcut.
(*Walking* is a participle modifying *we*.)

Climbing the stairs is slower than taking the elevator.
(*Climbing* is a gerund, the subject of *is*.)

Climbing the stairs, Ellen spotted a dollar bill.
(*Climbing* is a participle modifying *Ellen*.)

Exercise   **Distinguish between gerunds and participles**

For each sentence, write the gerund or participle and tell which it is. Be prepared to explain why it is a gerund or a participle.

G, O.P. 1. After fixing the TV, the repairman left.
P, Adj. 2. Lying on the beach, Willy read a book.
P, Adj. 3. Training for the Olympics, Sarah skates each day.
P, Adj. 4. Stamping her feet, the child would not move.
G, Subj. 5. Exercising in gym class is required.
G, Subj. 6. Taking the school bus saves time.
P, Adj. 7. Walking to the bus stop, Shawn met a friend.
G, Subj. 8. Throwing snowballs is against school rules.
G, Subj. 9. Running daily built Ann's endurance.
P, Adj. 10. Hosting the debate, the senator introduced her guests.

Part 3   Infinitives

The third kind of verbal is the **infinitive**.

An infinitive is a verbal that usually appears with the word *to* before it. *To* is called the **sign of the infinitive**.

Part 3

Objective

To understand the function of infinitives and infinitive phrases and to identify them in sentences

Presenting the Lesson

1. Read and discuss pages 561–564. Infinitives are sometimes easier for students to recognize than other verbals, but they can still be confusing. Ask students to tell you how they can differentiate between a prepositional phrase that begins with *to* and an infinitive phrase.

2. Have students think of examples of infinitives used as nouns, adjectives, and adverbs.

3. Assign and discuss Exercises A and B on pages 564–565.

Individualizing the Lesson

Less-Advanced Students

Do the exercises on pages 564–565 orally with the class. Guide them in finding the subject and verb first. This will make identifying the infinitive easier. Once they have chosen the infinitive, have them explain how it is used in the sentence.

Advanced Students

Remind students that infinitives can be confused with prepositional phrases. Discuss the difference between the two. Work with the students on Exercise A. Have them identify the infinitive and tell whether it is used as a subject, an object, an adjective, or an adverb. If the infinitive is an adjective or adverb, they should indicate the word being modified.

Optional Practice

Have students put an infinitive or infinitive phrase in each blank to complete the following sentences.
Answers will vary.
1. The supervisor expects _____ .

The following are examples of infinitives.

to be	to give	to want	to run
to go	to have	to see	to ask

Note: You already know that the word *to* is often used as a preposition. *To* is a preposition if it is followed by a noun or pronoun that is its object. *To* is the sign of the infinitive if it is followed by a verb. Notice the difference in these examples:

Prepositional Phrases	**Infinitives**
We are going *to the game.*	Dee and Jim want *to go.*
Jim ran *to the door.*	I plan *to study.*

When you see the word *to,* look to see if it is used as a preposition or as a sign of the infinitive.

The Infinitive Phrase

Like the other verbals, the infinitive is not always used alone. The infinitive with its objects and modifiers is an **infinitive phrase.** Because the infinitive is formed from a verb, it is also like a verb in several ways. An infinitive may have an object.

> Kris wanted *to own a dog.*
> (*Dog* is the direct object of the infinitive *to own.*)
> Sue planned *to give her friends gifts.*
> (*Friends* is the indirect object and *gifts* is the direct object of the infinitive *to give.*)

Because the infinitive is formed from a verb, it may be modified by adverbs.

> The batter tried *to swing hard.*
> (*Hard* is an adverb modifying the infinitive *to swing.*)
> Sunshine helps plants *to grow quickly.*
> (*Quickly* is an adverb modifying the infinitive *to grow.*)

Infinitives may also be modified by prepositional phrases.

We'd like *to fly in a helicopter.*

(*In a helicopter* is a prepositional phrase modifying the infinitive *to fly.*)

Ken volunteered *to work in the library.*

(*In the library* is a prepositional phrase modifying the infinitive *to work.*)

Uses of the Infinitive Phrase

Unlike the other verbals, infinitives and infinitive phrases can be used as more than one part of speech. Infinitives can be used (1) as nouns, (2) as adjectives, or (3) as adverbs.

You remember that nouns are used as subjects and direct objects of verbs. Infinitives and infinitive phrases can be used as subjects, as direct objects, and in other ways that nouns are used.

Subject: *To become a mechanic* is Lou's goal.
         (*To become a mechanic* is the subject of *is.*)

Direct Object: The girls wanted *to eat pizza.*
         (*To eat pizza* is the direct object of *wanted.*)

Infinitives and infinitive phrases can also be used as modifiers. If the infinitive or infinitive phrase modifes a noun or pronoun, it is used as an adjective. If it modifies a verb, adjective, or adverb, it is used as an adverb.

Adjective: My friend brought a magazine *to read.*
       (*To read* modifies *magazine.*)

Adverb: Laughter is good *to hear.*
       (*To hear* modifies *good.*)

Adverb: The fans came *to hear a jazz concert.*
       (*To hear a jazz concert* modifies the verb *came.*)

Adverb: A lathe is hard *to use.*
       (*To use* modifies the adjective *hard.*)

563

2. The hockey player pretended
_____ .

3. The owner of the team offered
_____ .

4. The publisher could not afford
_____ .

5. The star player promised _____ .

6. The vacationers hoped _____ .

7. Some people offered _____ .

8. During practice each player tried
_____ .

9. The committee decided _____ .

10. The radio announcer continued
_____ .

11. _____ is my goal.

12. Aunt Martha gave me a book
_____ .

13. Larry arranged _____ .

14. _____ is her favorite pastime.

15. Lemonade is refreshing _____ .

Extending the Lesson

Have students underline the word *to* in the following sentences. If *to* is used as the sign of the infinitive, have them write *I* after the sentence. If *to* is used as a preposition have them write *P.* If the sentence contains an infinitive or an infinitive phrase, have the students state whether it is used as a subject, a direct object, an adjective, or an adverb.

I 1. I want to leave the house early. D.O.

P 2. We went straight to the store.

P 3. The cat climbed to the top of the tree.

I 4. We had to call the fire department. D.O.

I 5. How much will it cost you to fix the television? Adv.

I 6. The customer asked the waiter to bring her soup right away. D.O.

I 7. I need to practice more often. D.O.

P 8. She goes to the community meetings every month.

P 9. Alice walked up to me and asked a question.

I 10. The magician wants to take three rabbits out of that top hat. *D.O.*

P11. We came to the engineering building.

P12. Everyone is going to the game.

P13. A box of grapefruit was sent to our house by mistake.

I 14. Everyone was glad to see the sun. *Adv.*

I 15. The algebra students tried everything to solve that problem. *Adj.*

P16. I read that article to the end.

P17. Most of us went to the free concert.

I 18. There weren't enough books to go around. *Adv.*

I 19. One of my aunts is coming to visit next week. *Adv.*

I 20. Skaters need to have strong legs. *D.O.*

In all of the examples given, you can see that infinitives are verb forms, but they are never used as verbs. Infinitives are used as nouns, as adjectives, or as adverbs.

The Split Infinitive

Sometimes a modifier is placed between the word *to* and the verb. A modifier in this position is said to split the infinitive. A split infinitive sounds awkward and should be avoided.

> Awkward: Sue learned to *rapidly* type.
> Better: Sue learned to type *rapidly.*

Exercises Find the infinitives and infinitive phrases.

A. Write the infinitive or infinitive phrase in each of the following sentences. Tell how it is used.

1. Sandra likes to fish on the lake. N., direct object
2. Tracey learned to paddle a canoe. N., direct object
3. To settle disputes is the referee's job. N., subject
4. Scheduling is the main issue to discuss. Adj., modifies issue
5. The map showed the road to take. Adj., modifies road
6. To tell jokes well requires good timing. N., subject
7. Cary wanted to play darts. N., direct object
8. The air controller watches to prevent accidents. Adv., modifies watches
9. To get good grades takes effort. N., subject
10. Grapes are good to eat. Adv., modifies good

B. Follow the directions for Exercise A.

1. A kiln is used to bake clay. Adv., modifies is used
2. The engineer decided to stop the train. N., direct object
3. Money is easy to spend. Adv., modifies easy
4. The movers used dollies to carry the furniture. Adv., modifies used
5. A guitar is fun to play. Adv., modifies fun
6. I bought pants to match the sweater. Adj., modifies pants

7. Speakers are designed to amplify sound.
   Adv., modifies are designed
8. The lifeguard rushed to save the swimmer.
   Adv., modifies rushed
   Adv., modifies used
9. To level the street, the crew used a steamroller.
10. To see relatives is the purpose of a family reunion.
    N., subject

Part 4   A Review of Verbals

You have learned that verbals are special kinds of words. Verbals are verb forms, but they are never used as verbs in a sentence. Verbals are used as other parts of speech.

There are three kinds of verbals: gerunds, participles, and infinitives. All three verbals may be used by themselves. They may also be used in phrases. These phrases are gerund phrases, participial phrases, and infinitive phrases. Because they are like verbs, all three kinds of verbals may take objects and they may have modifers.

A **gerund** is a verb form used as a noun. (Gerunds end in -*ing*.) A gerund may be used in all the ways a noun used.

> *Reading* is fun.
> I enjoy *reading*.
> I enjoy *reading aloud*.
> I have a question about *your reading*.

A **participle** is a verb form used as an adjective. (Past participles of regular verbs end in -*d* or -*ed*. Past participles of irregular verbs must be learned individually. Present participles end in -*ing*.) Participles, like adjectives, modify nouns or pronouns.

> *Reading his assignment*, Jim fell asleep.
> *Reading too quickly*, Jim made a mistake.
> *Reading by the fire*, Jim fell asleep.
> *Reading by the fire*, he fell asleep.

An **infinitive** is the verbal that usually appears with the word *to* before it. Infinitives may be used as nouns, as adjectives, or as adverbs.

Part 4

Objective

To review the functions of gerunds, participles, and infinitives

Presenting the Lesson

1. Read and discuss pages 565–566. Put the following sentence on the board: *The man crossing the street likes to exercise by jogging.* Ask students to point out the verbals, identify what kind they are, and what their functions are in the sentence. With the class, construct at least two other sentences that contain all three verbals.

2. Assign and discuss Exercises A and B on page 566.

Individualizing the Lesson

Less-Advanced Students

You may want to list on the board or display a chart showing the examples of verbals as given on pages 565–566. The students can refer to this while doing the exercises. Work with them in identifying the verbals. Then they should tell whether the verbal is a gerund, participle, or infinitive.

Advanced Students

1. Once students have identified the verbal in the exercises and told what type of verbal it is, have them be more specific and tell how the gerund, participle, or infinitive is used in the sentence.

2. Have them write sentences of their own containing different types of verbals. They can exchange sentences with classmates for checking.

Optional Practice

Have students complete each of the following sentences with the verbal or verbal phrase indicated in parentheses.   Sentences will vary.

1. My cousins all tried _____ in the race. (gerund)
2. The auto mechanic remembered _____ . (infinitive)
3. Being in such a hurry, I almost forgot _____ . (infinitive)
4. _____ mountains takes skill and endurance. (gerund)
5. I don't like _____ television the night before a big exam. (infinitive)

Extending the Lesson

Have the students write the verbal or verbal phrase in each sentence. Then have them tell whether the verbal is a gerund, participle, or an infinitive.

I 1. It was too soon to know the winner of the contest.
G 2. Running quickly got Elaine to school on time.
P 3. Talking very loudly, no one noticed the teacher enter the room.
P 4. The garbage can was filled with broken glass.
I 5. Her dream was to live in Paris.
P 6. After baking two loaves of bread, we ate them both.
G 7. Swimming is a healthy sport.
I 8. Marc did not want to sing that song.

566

To read is fun.
To read a mystery is enjoyable.
I like *to read*.
The funniest book *to read* is this one.
This novel is hard *to read*.

Exercises   Find the verbals.

A.   Find the verbal in each sentence. Write the verbal or verbal phrase. Tell whether the verbal is a gerund, participle, or infinitive.

i 1. John is likely to succeed.
p 2. Tired of the city, the Browns moved to the country.
i 3. The visitors hated to leave.
p 4. Expecting a call, Don waited by the phone.
g 5. Tanning makes leather flexible.
g 6. These paths are for snowmobiling.
p 7. Gliding gracefully, Wendy skied down the hill.
p 8. People opposing the new law held a rally.
g 9. Hang gliding is a new sport.
i 10. Lee learned to use sign language.

B.   Follow the directions for Exercise A.

g 1. Working hard usually pays off.
i 2. Autumn is the time to harvest pumpkins.
p 3. Turning sideways, the model posed for a picture.
i 4. Casts allow bones to heal.
g 5. Recording an album is done in a studio.
p 6. The people standing in line were waiting for tickets.
i 7. The youth center is a place to meet friends.
p 8. Winning four straight games, the Yankees took the World Series.
g 9. Doing crossword puzzles can build your vocabulary.
p 10. Guided by radar, the shuttle landed on target.

ADDITIONAL EXERCISES

Using Verbals

A. Gerunds and Gerund Phrases   Write the gerunds and gerund phrases in these sentences.

1. Collecting stickers is my little sister's hobby.
2. Teasing the cat is mean.
3. Hal did not enjoy weeding the garden.
4. Gwen was paid five dollars for addressing the envelopes.
5. Running has become a popular sport.
6. Bullfighting involves great risk.
7. Mr. Novo disapproves of bullfighting.
8. A blizzard hit without warning.
9. Before leaving, Cal washed the dishes.
10. Jeanie was saving bus fare by walking to school every day.

B. Participles and Participial Phrases   Write the participles and participial phrases in these sentences. Some sentences have more than one participle or participial phrase.

1. The whining, injured dog was taken to the vet.
2. Have you ever seen a flying saucer?
3. Paul repaired the broken radio.
4. Taking a corner too fast, the cyclist skidded.
5. A driving rain flattened the plants.
6. A guard caught the boys climbing the tower.
7. The arresting officer wrote the report.
8. Does the city or the school pay crossing guards?
9. Blushing, Patrick joined in the laughter.
10. The ingredients include beaten eggs and sifted flour.

567

Additional Exercises

These Additional Exercises may be used for additional practice of the concepts presented in this Section. Each exercise focuses on a single concept, and should be used after the page number indicated in parentheses.

Review

If you have not assigned these Additional Exercises before this time, you can also use them as an excellent Section Review.

C. Gerund or Participle? Write the gerund or participle in each sentence, and write which it is. Tell what part of speech each is used as.

P, Adj. 1. A <u>winding</u> staircase led to the attic.

G, D.O. 2. Digital watches do not need <u>winding</u>.

P, Adj. 3. William swept the <u>dining</u> room.

G, Subj. 4. <u>Dining</u> out was a rare treat.

P, Adj. 5. Blake waited at the <u>starting</u> line.

G, D.O. 6. Try <u>starting the motor</u> again.

G, D.O. 7. I still like <u>wading in the creek</u>.

P, Adj. 8. A limp, plastic <u>wading</u> pool hung over the bench.

P, Adj. 9. <u>Grinding his teeth</u>, Carl said nothing.

G, Subj. 10. <u>Grinding the peanuts</u> takes a long time.

D. Infinitives and Infinitive Phrases Write the <u>infinitives</u> and infinitive phrases in these sentences.

1. These dogs are trained <u>to attack</u>.
2. Use a calculator <u>to do the last problem</u>.
3. Melissa had planned <u>to put her stuffed animals away</u>.
4. The old jeans are too comfortable <u>to throw away</u>.
5. Ms. Kung offered <u>to drive me to the stadium</u>.
6. <u>To get there on time</u>, Martha took a taxi.
7. <u>To smile</u> can take a lot of effort sometimes.
8. Judy likes <u>to go out</u>, but Mae prefers <u>to stay home</u>.
9. Curtis has yet <u>to hit a home run</u>.
10. After a tiring day at work, Mom does yoga <u>to relax</u>.

E. Kinds of Verbals Write the <u>verbal</u> in each sentence. Label the verbal *Gerund, Participle,* or *Infinitive.*

G 1. <u>Cleaning my room</u> will take an hour.

I 2. I didn't mean <u>to forget you</u>.

P 3. <u>Feeling sick</u>, Joe stayed home from work.

P 4. <u>Whistling happily</u>, Cathy started down the path.

P 5. A hiker noticed the rising river.

P 6. Ryan shoved his clenched fists in his pockets.

I 7. You can't use a stick to paddle a raft.

I 8. Rebecca forced herself to pay attention.

G 9. We passed the time by playing cards.

G 10. Learning English was hard for the refugees.

I 11. I want to eat lunch right now.

G 12. Playing tennis is strenuous exercise.

P 13. Looking for firewood, Alan came across a nest of mourning doves.

G 14. Hurrying through a job often causes mistakes.

I 15. Is Amy to meet you before or after school?

P 16. Laughing, Andy grabbed the pillow from his brother.

G 17. Bob got paid for mowing and then raking the yard.

I 18. The principal said that no one is allowed to run through the halls.

G 19. Our dog got out of the yard by pushing at the gate's lock with her paw.

P 20. The papers from Cyna's notebook went flying around the room.

MIXED REVIEW

Using Verbals

A. Identifying verbals Write the verbals and verbal phrases from the following sentences. Then write whether the verbal or verbal phrase is a *gerund, gerund phrase, participle, participial phrase, infinitive,* or *infinitive phrase.*

1. Asking questions is important for students. gerund phrase
2. The freshly painted car looks new. participial phrase
3. Clutching the grocery bag, Martha ran to the car. participial phrase
4. Talking to the counselor helped David. gerund phrase
5. Learning a new language is a challenge. gerund phrase
6. I want to learn that song. infinitive phrase
7. Taking long walks relaxes me. gerund phrase
8. Dee plans to visit us this summer. infinitive phrase
9. Smiling happily, Jenny told us the story. participial phrase
10. I'd like to ask a question. infinitive phrase

B. Using verbals in sentences Complete the following sentences by adding the verbal or verbal phrase asked for.

Answers will vary.

Example: _____ is my favorite sport. (gerund)
Swimming is my favorite sport.

1. Ms. Keene asked me _____. (infinitive phrase)
2. Susan wants _____. (infinitive phrase)
3. _____, Jeff scored a goal. (participial phrase)
4. _____, Denise told the joke. (participle)
5. _____ is a popular hobby. (gerund phrase)
6. _____ is important in any sport. (gerund)
7. _____, the gymnasts impressed the crowd. (participial phrase)
8. My favorite job is _____. (gerund phrase)

USING GRAMMAR IN WRITING
Using Verbals

A. Are you an excellent basketball player or a gymnast? Is a friend of yours a fine musician or artist? If you could pick any one skill to excel in, what would it be? Write a paragraph about it. Give reasons why you wish you had that particular skill. In your paragraph include at least one infinitive, two gerunds, and two participles. Underline the verbal phrases.

B. You are at the homecoming football game. The score of the game is tied. By the third quarter, almost everyone in the stands is hoarse. Describe the behavior of the fans during the last quarter. Use at least five of the following verbals in your paragraph. Use at least two as gerunds. Use at least two as participles. Your paragraph should convey plenty of excitement.

laughing	shouting	cheering	jumping
screaming	yelling	clapping	watching

C. If you could spend a day anywhere you like, doing whatever you want, how would you spend it? Use at least three infinitive phrases in your description. At least one should be the subject of a sentence. At least one should be a direct object.

These challenging and enjoyable activities allow the students to see how the concepts of grammar, usage, and mechanics may be applied in actual writing situations. Each exercise is designed to allow students practice in several of the skills they have acquired in this Section. The activities also provide opportunities for students to write creatively about a wide variety of interesting and unusual subjects.

These exercises are designed to cover broad areas of grammar, usage, and mechanics. They require the application of skills taught thus far in the text. The exercises may be used for testing purposes, or as an excellent resource for review.

CUMULATIVE REVIEW
The Parts of Speech

A. Identifying parts of speech There are twenty underlined words in the following paragraph. Decide what part of speech each word is used as. Number your paper from 1 to 20. Write *Noun, Verb, Pronoun, Adjective, Adverb, Preposition,* or *Conjunction* for each word. Be sure to notice *how* the word is used in the sentence.

Many people do not get enough exercise. It is
    N   Adj   Pro
      1   **2**   **3**

important to get regular exercise in order to look good
Adj
  4

and to feel good. Some people do not know how to
Conj
 5

exercise to get the most benefit. You need at least
                                N   Pro
                                6 Prep **7**

three thirty-minute sessions of exercise a week. A session
                                  8

sion should consist of a five-minute warm-up, twenty
       V
     9   Adj
              10

minutes of vigorous exercise, and a five-minute cool-
           Adj
           11

down. The best type of exercise is an aerobic exercise
     Adj   V   Adj
     12   **13**   **14**

like walking, jogging, swimming, or jumping rope.
                                  Conj
                                  15

These exercises really get your heart and lungs work-
Adj   Adv
16   Adv   **17**

ing efficiently. A sweaty brow and a strongly beating
    Adv   Adv
    18   Adj   **19**

heart are signs of a good workout.
                      20

B. Recognizing how words are used Each of the following sentences contains an underlined word. Number your paper from 1 to 15. Write *Subject, Verb, Direct Object, Indirect Object, Object of the Preposition, Predicate Noun,* or *Predicate Adjective* to show what each word is.

1. Zeke made his brother an egg sandwich.
                    IO

2. Running is not a good sport for people with back trouble.
   [S above Running]

3. That specimen box contains my insect collection.
   [DO above collection]

4. A puffin is a bird with a short neck and a large, grooved bill.
   [PN above bird]

5. The pilot landed the helicopter on the roof of the skyscraper.
   [DO above helicopter]

6. Rob gets around in a motorized wheelchair.
   [OP above wheelchair]

7. Have the pears ripened yet?
   [S above pears]

8. After the storm, the beach looked deserted.
   [PA above deserted]

9. Sam was revising his composition.
   [V above revising]

10. Marla wants to win the speech contest.
    [DO above to win]

11. The marine gave his commanding officer a salute.
    [IO above officer]

12. Virgil I. Grissom was one of the first astronauts.
    [PN above one]

13. The bulldozer leveled the building.
    [V above leveled]

14. The clown's hair was pink.
    [PA above pink]

15. Ross enjoys cross-country skiing.
    [DO above skiing]

1. To understand the use of singular and plural verb forms

2. To understand and apply the rules for making the subject and verb agree

3. To understand and apply the rules for making a verb agree with a compound subject

4. To understand and apply the rules for making the subject and verb agree in inverted sentences

5. To understand and apply the rules for making the subject and verb agree in sentences beginning with *there*

6. To understand and apply the rules for making an indefinite pronoun subject and the verb agree

Preparing the Students

Discuss the fact that the subject and the verb are the most important parts of the sentence. They should agree to avoid confusion. Ask students to tell you what kind of confusion could result from incorrectly matched subjects and verbs.

Additional Resources

Diagnostic Test — page 6 in the test booklet

Mastery Test — pages 63–64 in the test booklet

Additional Exercises — pages 585–591 in the student text

Practice Book — pages 210–214

Duplicating Masters — pages 210–214

Special Populations — See special section at the back of this Teacher's Edition.

Making Subjects and Verbs Agree

You have studied the sentence and its parts. In this section you will look closely at how subjects and verbs work together.

Part 1 Singular and Plural Forms

Here is a brief review for you:

When a noun stands for one thing, it is **singular.**

> dog   student   city   classroom

When a noun stands for more than one thing, it is **plural.**

> dogs   students   cities   classrooms

Verbs, too, have singular and plural forms:

> Singular: The class *votes*.   Plural: The classes *vote*.
> The team *practices*.   The teams *practice*.

The *s* at the end of a verb, such as *votes* or *practices*, shows that it is singular. Unlike nouns, most verbs drop the *s* to form the plural.

Special Forms of Certain Verbs

A few verbs have special forms that you should keep in mind. These verbs are used frequently.

Is, Was, Are, and Were:

The verbs *is* and *was* are singular. The verbs *are* and *were* are plural.

> Singular: Pat *is* here.   Plural: They *are* here.
> Pat *was* here.   They *were* here.

Has and Have:

The verb *has* is singular. The verb *have* is plural.

> Singular: She *has* a bicycle.   Plural: They *have* bicycles.

Does and Do:

The verb *does* is singular. The verb *do* is plural.

> Singular: He *does* the dishes.   Plural: They *do* the dishes.

575

Part 1

Objective

To understand the use of singular and plural verb forms

Presenting the Lesson

Read and discuss page 575.

Individualizing the Lesson

Less-Advanced Students

Make a list of singular nouns and their plurals on the chalkboard. Ask students to suggest a verb for each singular noun. Change the verb to agree with the plural noun.

Advanced Students

Explain that although the collective noun indicates more than one thing, it is considered singular. Have the students make a list of collective nouns.

Optional Practice

Have students use each of the following verbs in two sentences, one with a singular subject and another with a plural subject.
Answers will vary.

build	sound
store	rescue
has	believe
is	compare
dream	perform

Extending the Lesson

Have students write ten sentences with singular subjects and verbs and ten sentences with plural subjects and verbs. Discuss the sentences with the class to reinforce the notion of agreement.

575

Part 2

Objective

To understand and apply the rules for making the subject and verb agree

Presenting the Lesson

1. Read and discuss pages 576–577. Remind students that the verb must agree with its subject in number.

Students who rely exclusively on the sound of a sentence to choose the correct verb forms may have difficulty when the sentence contains an adjective prepositional phrase following the subject. Emphasize that the agreement must be between the verb and the subject, and not with any other noun or pronoun in the sentence. Examine the sample sentences on page 576.

Point out that the pronoun *you* is always used with plural verbs. Ask students to give you examples of sentences with *you* as the subject.

2. Do Exercise A on page 577 with the class, discussing reasons for each answer. Assign and discuss Exercise B on page 578.

Individualizing the Lesson

Less-Advanced Students

Work with students to follow these three steps to complete the exercises:

1. Copy the sentence, eliminating all prepositional phrases.
2. Find the subject.
3. Choose the right verb.

Have students read the sentences aloud.

When you say that a word is singular or plural, you are saying that the word tells about one or more than one thing or action. This is called the **number** of the word. When one word **agrees** with another, it is the same in number.

A verb must agree with its subject in number.

Singular: *She does* an excellent job.
Willy has a new car.
Was Dan at home?

Plural: *Students do* homework.
The *Yankees have* a good pitcher.
Were the *uniforms* clean?

Beware of Phrases

When you are making subjects and verbs agree, beware of phrases. Often a phrase appears between the subject and the verb. The subject is never part of such a phrase. Look for the subject outside the phrase.

The subject of the verb is never found in a prepositional phrase.

One of the glasses *was* broken.

The *pictures* on the desk *were* torn.

Phrases beginning with the words *with, together with, including, as well as,* and *in addition to* are not part of the subject.

The *principal,* in addition to the teacher, *is* here.

Mr. Casey, together with his children, *has* left.

The Pronouns *You* and *I*

Unlike other pronouns, *you* is the same for both singular and plural. But *you* is never used with a singular verb. It is always used with plural verbs.

> You have (*not* has) my best wishes.

> You were (*not* was) next on the list.

The pronoun *I* is also used with plural verbs.

> I *do* lawn work.
> I *have* a collie.

The only singular verb forms used with *I* are *am* and *was*.

> I *am* a member.
> I *was* in the band.

Exercises   Make the subject and verb agree.

A.   Choose the right verb for each sentence. Write the subject and the verb. Beware of phrases that come between the subject and the verb.

> Example: The vase of roses (were, was) lovely.
>   vase, was

1. These sets of books (are, is) to be returned to the library.
2. You (was, were) late today.
3. The chances for a victory (is, are) good.
4. One of the motors (need, needs) oil.
5. The footprints in this cave (seem, seems) very large.
6. Several houses in our block (is, are) for sale.
7. This group of skiers (give, gives) lessons to beginners.
8. The pond by the willow trees (were, was) deep.
9. I (sing, sings) a solo in the second act.
10. The paper on the walls (was, were) silvery.

578

5. (After an early dinner)we went(to the movies.)

6. Baseball games are held(at the park)(by the expressway.)

7. One(of the players)disagreed(with the referee's call.)

8. (In the evenings)she takes courses (at a college)(in the city.)

9. The end (of the book)was exciting.

10. (In the safe)(under the floor)he had hidden the gold.

Part 3

Objective

To understand and apply the rules for making a verb agree with a compound subject

Presenting the Lesson

1. Read and discuss page 578. Go over the two rules carefully.

2. Assign and discuss Exercises A and B on pages 579–580. You may wish to do part of Exercise A with the class. Remind students to change questions into statements before trying to determine the correct form of the verb.

Individualizing the Lesson

Less-Advanced Students

Tell students to find the conjunction in the compound subject first, then to decide which verb form is correct. Help students change the questions in the exercises into statements before they choose the appropriate verb form.

B. Follow the directions for Exercise A.

1. The bag of grapes (is, are) beside the nectarines in the refrigerator.

2. This kind of sundae (is, are) best.

3. I (was, were) the only person home.

4. The rungs in the ladder (was, were) loose.

5. Terri and Kate (works, work) at the dairy.

6. (Were, Was) you at the concert, too?

7. The boys in the park (has, have) a soccer ball.

8. This pair of gloves (look, looks) like yours.

9. The cars in the garage (needs, need) new tires.

10. (Has, Have) you any more paint?

Part 3 Verbs with Compound Subjects

You will remember that a compound subject is two or more subjects used with the same verb.

A compound subject that contains the conjunction *and* is plural. Therefore, a plural verb must be used with it.

Examples: Marie and Lynn *are* here.

He and she *work* at the supermarket.

The tomatoes and peppers *were* ripe.

When the parts of a compound subject are joined by *or* or *nor*, the verb agrees with the subject nearer to the verb.

Examples: Lisa or Ted *is* coming.

Neither Beth nor her sisters *are* here.

Three oranges or one grapefruit *makes* enough juice for the punch.

Exercises   Use the right verb with a compound subject.

A.   Choose the correct form of the verb, from the two given in parentheses.

1. The band and the chorus (is, <u>are</u>) performing tonight.
2. The older men and Jack (<u>walk</u>, walks) home along Plymouth Street.
3. Steve and I (is, <u>are</u>) both busy.
4. My mother or my older brothers always (<u>meet</u>, meets) Dad at the airport.
5. (Have, <u>Has</u>) either Carol or Brenda heard that record?
6. Either the Taylors or my parents (<u>are</u>, is) going with us.
7. Neither the mushrooms nor that chicken (<u>is</u>, are) fresh.
8. The cottonwood trees and the elm (is, <u>are</u>) budding out.
9. Ellen and her mother (was, <u>were</u>) here.
10. The president or the vice-president usually (<u>takes</u>, take) charge.

B.   Follow the directions for Exercise A.

1. Neither Jane nor her sister (<u>is</u>, are) at home.
2. Sarah's cat and puppy (<u>don't</u>, doesn't) like each other.
3. (Do, <u>Does</u>) your mobile and that poster always hang there?
4. Either my cousins or Kathy (phone, <u>phones</u>) every week.
5. (Do, <u>Does</u>) either Bob or Larry play soccer?
6. Neither Alicia nor I (believes, <u>believe</u>) in ghosts.
7. My bedspread and rug (<u>match</u>, matches) the curtains.
8. (<u>Does</u>, Do) either Colleen or her sisters practice on Tuesday?

579

9. Bob and his guitar (is, are) inseparable.
10. The treasurer's figures and the secretary's report (agree, agrees).

Presenting the Lesson

1. Putting the verb in front of the subject may sound unusual to many students, but they should be familiar with the construction and be able to identify it. Read and discuss page 580. Encourage students to go back to the system of locating simple subjects and verbs by using the *who/what* and *is/happens* process.

2. Assign Exercises A and B on pages 580–581. Afterwards, be sure to discuss the reason for each verb choice.

Individualizing the Lesson

Less-Advanced Students

Have students first find the subject of each sentence in the exercises and then choose the verb that agrees with it.

Advanced Students

Have the students write five original sentences in inverted order.

Optional Practice

Have students choose the proper present tense form of the verb in parentheses and then rewrite the sentence in inverted form.

Part 4   Agreement in Inverted Sentences

In most sentences, the subject comes before the verb. A person is likely to say, for example, "The glider soars over the hill." For emphasis, however, a writer or speaker might say, "Over the hill soars the glider." The second sentence is called an **inverted sentence.** In each sentence the subject is *glider* and the verb is *soars*.

In inverted sentences, as in ordinary ones, the subject and verb must agree.

> Examples: Up above *flutter* a thousand *flags*. (flags flutter)
>
> Through the museum *stream tourists* by the thousands. (tourists stream)
>
> In the yard *is* a *pile* of leaves. (pile is)

Exercises   **Use the right verb in inverted sentences.**

A.   Number your paper from 1 to 10. Read each sentence. Find the subject. Write the correct form of the verb for each sentence.

1. To each of you (go, goes) the speaker's thanks.
2. Down the stretch (thunder, thunders) the horses.
3. On and on (go, goes) the story.
4. After all that baking (come, comes) the best part.
5. Out of the birdbath (jump, jumps) one goggle-eyed frog.
6. After the Marshfield band (comes, come) the 4-H float.

7. Round and round (go, <u>goes</u>) the Ferris wheel.
8. Beside the bench (is, <u>are</u>) the toolbox.
9. With each of the games (go, <u>goes</u>) an instruction booklet.
10. Under the street (rumble, <u>rumbles</u>) the subway.

B. Follow the directions for Exercise A.

1. Between the cushions (was, <u>were</u>) some pennies and a key.
2. Around the bend (come, <u>comes</u>) two buses.
3. Over the fire (hang, <u>hangs</u>) an old iron pot.
4. On either side of Trisha (sit, <u>sits</u>) her brothers.
5. At the end of the two-by-fours (flap, <u>flaps</u>) a red flag.
6. After the chapter on oceans (come, <u>comes</u>) one on mountains.
7. Beside their house (flow, <u>flows</u>) the Wabash River.
8. Over the chimney (<u>curls</u>, curl) the smoke.
9. High above the peaks (<u>soar</u>, soars) two eagles.
10. There on the windowsill (lie, <u>lies</u>) the stopwatch.

Part 5   Verbs with *There*

The word *there* often comes where you expect the subject to be. As you will remember, *there* is often used simply to get a sentence started. When *there* begins a sentence, look for the subject farther on in the sentence.

Examples: There is a book on the table.
(*Book* is the subject; *is* is the verb.)

There are no questions.
(*Questions* is the subject; *are* is the verb.)

In the first example, notice that the correct verb is *is*, because the subject, *book*, is singular. In the second example, *are* must be used because the subject, *questions*, is plural.

581

and discuss pages 581–582. Remind students that *there* is never the subject of the sentence.

2. Do Exercise A on page 582 with the students. Discuss the reason for each verb choice by first identifying the subject of the sentence. Assign Exercise B.

Individualizing the Lesson

Less-Advanced Students

Work with students to find the subject in each sentence. Have them then select the correct verb.

Advanced Students

Have students write complete sentences to answer the questions in Exercises A and B.

Optional Practice

1. Have students fill in the proper form of the verb *be* and circle the subject.

1. There ___was___ an interesting program on TV last night.
2. There ___were/are___ many people at the basketball game.
3. There ___was/is___ a good response to the questionnaire.
4. There ___were___ beautiful quilts on display.
5. ___Are___ there many questions?

2. Have students rewrite these sentences, changing singular subjects to plural, and plural to singular.

1. Were there rainbows after that storm? Was there a rainbow . . . .
2. Is there an extension on that phone? Were there extensions . . . .
3. There were boxes next to the refrigerator. There was a box . . .
4. There is a hole in this umbrella. There were holes
5. Will there be a good rock group at the concert? Will there be good rock groups . . . .

582

When *there* is used at the beginning of a sentence, be careful to make the verb of the sentence agree in number with the actual subject of the sentence.

Exercises   Use the correct verb with *there*.

A.   Read each sentence. Choose the correct form of the verb. Write the subject and verb for each sentence.

Example: There (is, are) some new notices on the
bulletin board.

subject: notices

verb: are

1. There (is, are) no reason for that.
2. Often there (is, are) people on the pier.
3. There (is, are) someone looking for you.
4. (Are, Is) there any toothpicks in the box?
5. (Was, Were) there no ushers?
6. There (is, are) a second-hand, three-speed bike for sale.
7. (Were, Was) there two windows in the stage set?
8. There (weren't, wasn't) many fans in the stadium.
9. (Is, Are) there any oranges?
10. Sometimes there (is, are) taxis waiting here.

B.   Follow the directions for Exercise A.

1. There (is, are) just two pages left in my notebook.
2. There (was, were) several witnesses to the accident.
3. (Is, Are) there four rows of seats in the balcony?
4. (Is, Are) there any strawberry jam left?
5. There (were, was) extra hangers in the closet.
6. (Are, Is) there a second for the motion?
7. (Was, Were) there a cap on the oil can?

582

8. (Weren't, Wasn't) there <u>pyramids</u> before the <u>Egyptians</u>?

9. There (wasn't, weren't) another <u>marina</u> on the lake.

10. There (is, are) a <u>chance</u> of rain.

Part 6   Indefinite Pronouns

Making subjects and verbs agree may be more difficult if the subject is an indefinite pronoun. You will remember that some indefinite pronouns are singular, some are plural, and some may be either singular or plural. Study these examples.

The indefinite pronouns in the list below are **singular:**

another	each	everything	one
anybody	either	neither	somebody
anyone	everybody	nobody	someone
anything	everyone	no one	something

Examples: *Each* of the customers *was* given a number.
Everybody has a report to do.
Neither of us *has* a good plan.

The indefinite pronouns below are **plural:**

both   few   many   several

Examples: *Both* of the boys *were* sick.
Several of us *have* vacations soon.

These indefinite pronouns are **singular** if they refer to one thing. They are **plural** if they refer to several things:

all   any   most   none   some

Examples: *All* of the paper *was* yellow.
All of the supplies *were* here.

Most of the work *is* mine.
Most of the books *are* new.

Some of the jewelry *has* diamonds.
Some of the cookies *have* walnuts.

583

the subject in each sentence is singular or plural. Refer the students to page 583 to check the lists of singular and plural indefinite pronouns. Then they can choose the correct verb that agrees with the subject.

Advanced Students

Have students rewrite this paragraph correcting the errors made in the use of indefinite pronouns.

The annual masquerade party at school is a lot of fun. Each of the guests wears a mask until midnight. Everyone keeps his or her identity a secret. Some of the people dresses as historical figures. Usually somebody comes as Napoleon. Many of the guests comes as sports figures or movie stars. All of the guests seems to enjoy themselves immensely.

Optional Practice

Have students choose as many pronouns as they can from the ones listed on page 583 that can be followed by a prepositional phrase beginning with *of.* Have them write sentences of their own using each pronoun with an *of* prepositional phrase.

Extending the Lesson

Have students write two sentences of their own for each of the indefinite pronouns that may be singular or plural: *all, any, most, none, some.* The first sentence should use the pronoun as a singular subject, and the second sentence as a plural subject.

Exercises   Make verbs agree with their subjects.

A.   Choose the verb that agrees with the subject, which is an indefinite pronoun.

1. Somebody (has, have) broken the window on the back porch.
2. Nobody (likes, like) being criticized.
3. All of the prizes (was, were) hidden.
4. Everything (seems, seem) peaceful.
5. Neither of the pictures (is, are) flattering.
6. (Was, Were) any of the food left?
7. One of my favorite programs (begins, begin) at eight o'clock.
8. Both of the boys (has, have) a soccer ball.
9. Most of the sophomores (takes, take) driver's education.
10. Either of the keys (opens, open) the front door.

B.   Follow the directions for Exercise A.

1. Both of her ears (was, were) red.
2. (Does, Do) everyone have a schedule?
3. Some of the clubs (sells, sell) refreshments.
4. Most of the record (sounds, sound) distorted.
5. (Has, Have) any of the exchange students from France or Germany arrived?
6. Many of my friends (wears, wear) braces.
7. Few of the tourists (climbs, climb) to the top of the monument.
8. Each of the club members (was, were) going to bake something for the sale.
9. Everybody (knows, know) the procedure for fire drills.
10. One of their starters (was, were) injured in last night's game.

ADDITIONAL EXERCISES

Making Subjects and Verbs Agree

A. Singular and Plural Forms Number your paper from 1 to 20. Write the <u>subject</u> and <u>verb</u> for each sentence. Tell whether they are <u>singular</u> or <u>plural</u>.

P 1. The steps were high and narrow.
S 2. Linda studies Spanish.
P 3. These vitamins contain no sugar.
S 4. The saber-toothed tiger is extinct.
S 5. Rory does the laundry at the laundromat.
S 6. A boomerang is an Australian weapon.
P 7. They do exercises every morning.
S 8. This horn sounds funny.
S 9. It was my mistake.
S 10. The picture needs a larger frame.
S 11. The telephone is in the kitchen.
S 12. The water is icy.
P 13. The picnic tables are near the shelter.
S 14. Miguel has the tickets.
S 15. Sarah was in a fashion show.
P 16. Ants live in colonies.
P 17. Bees have remarkable abilities.
P 18. Some bakeries sell milk.
S 19. Donna has a typewriter.
P 20. Melinda's toes were cold.

B. Agreement of Subjects and Verbs Number your paper from 1 to 10. Choose the correct form of the verb for each sentence.

1. Carly (<u>does</u>, do) a good routine on the balance beam.
2. The cords on the parachute (was, <u>were</u>) twisted.

585

Additional Exercises

These Additional Exercises may be used for additional practice of the concepts presented in this Section. Each exercise focuses on a single concept, and should be used after the page number indicated in parentheses.

Review

If you have not assigned these Additional Exercises before this time, you can also use them as an excellent Section Review.

3. A wreath of pine cones (hangs, hang) on our door.
4. The bouquet of flowers (was, were) from Darcy.
5. The patch of weeds (was, were) wet and tangled.
6. Two of the drains (is, are) clogged.
7. You still (is, are) missing that high note.
8. The coach, together with the players, (plans, plan) the strategy.
9. You (was, were) reading the wrong chapter.
10. All the students, including Judy, (seems, seem) glad.

C. Verbs with Compound Subjects Number your paper from 1 to 10. Choose the correct form of the verb for each sentence.

1. The leaves and the grass (is, are) turning brown.
2. The stars and moon (was, were) shining.
3. Flags and a banner (was, were) waving in the breeze.
4. The parrot and the parakeet (does, do) not talk to each other.
5. The McBrides and she (has, have) had some problems.
6. My mother or my brothers always (meets, meet) me there.
7. Neither Marge nor Stu (remembers, remember) the phone number.
8. Either sharks or dolphins (follows, follow) boats.
9. Popcorn or peanuts (is, are) for sale.
10. Either goggles or a face mask (is, are) required.

D. Agreement in Inverted Sentences Number your paper from 1 to 10. Use the correct form of the verb for each sentence.

1. Up the mountain (winds, wind) a narrow road.
2. Under the stone bridge (is, are) the rod and reel.
3. Around the corner (is, are) three apartment buildings.
4. In the cave (sleeps, sleep) hibernating skunks.

5. Behind the garage (is, are) the children's playhouse.
6. Behind the house (is, are) a spacious patio.
7. In the doorway (hangs, hang) wind chimes.
8. On the windowsill (is, are) a bowl of flowers.
9. At the top of the steeple (is, are) a big clock.
10. Over the dam (pours, pour) the torrents of water.

E. Verbs with *There* Choose the correct verb from the two in parentheses.

1. There (goes, go) the stock cars.
2. On holidays there (is, are) many relatives to visit.
3. (Is, Are) there a thirteenth floor in this building?
4. There (is, are) extra test booklets.
5. There (is, are) no ice cubes left.
6. (Is, Are) there bobcats in these woods?
7. There (is, are) no snakes in Ireland or New Zealand.
8. There (was, were) chicken and ham in the refrigerator.
9. There (was, were) no return address on the envelope.
10. (Was, Were) there complaints about the noise?

F. Verbs with Indefinite Pronouns Number your paper from 1 to 10. Write the correct form of the verb.

1. Someone in the audience (was, were) coughing.
2. Everyone (meets, meet) at the bus stop after school.
3. (Does, Do) anybody play the banjo?
4. (Has, Have) all of your friends seen the circus?
5. Another of my favorite television shows (has, have) been canceled.
6. Most of the records (is, are) on sale.
7. All of the snow (has, have) melted.
8. Several of the rescue workers (was, were) injured.
9. Either of those times (is, are) convenient.
10. (Do, Does) each of the pockets have a hole in it?

MIXED REVIEW

Making Subjects and Verbs Agree

A. Making subjects and verbs agree For each sentence, write the verb that agrees with the subject.

1. The hamsters in that cage (is, are) hungry.
2. The students at our school (study, studies) French.
3. (Do, Does) Amy live near you?
4. Joan (keep, keeps) her diary in her room.
5. Neither Brendan nor James (want, wants) to play.
6. Elephants (live, lives) longer than many animals.
7. Parts of London (was, were) rebuilt after the war.
8. One of my sisters (attend, attends) Wright College.
9. Only two people (fit, fits) in this canoe.
10. I (wake, wakes) up every morning at 6:30.

B. Using verbs correctly Six of the following sentences contain errors in subject-verb agreement. If a sentence contains an error, rewrite it correctly. If a sentence is already correct, write *Correct*.

c 1. The team members respect Coach Myers.
2. Dozens of apples remains unpicked.
c 3. There is a good reason for his error.
4. Ten rolls of film was needed to photograph the wedding.
c 5. Paperback books are less expensive than hardcover books.
6. Orange, purple, and green is secondary colors.
7. Most of my friends babysit on weekends.
8. With every ten-dollar purchase comes a coupon.
c 9. On the shores of Lake Michigan stands Chicago.
10. There is several good comedians in the show.

USING GRAMMAR IN WRITING
Making Subjects and Verbs Agree

A. Do you have an opinion about how some part of the government should be run? There is probably at least one thing you wish the President or Congress would change. Write a letter to the President or your state representative. Tell him or her what you think needs improvement, and why. Suggest how the situation could be changed for the better. Begin at least one sentence with *There.* Also use at least four of the following indefinite pronouns in your letter. Be sure all verbs agree with their subjects.

anyone	each	everybody	nobody	somebody
few	many	several	all	most	none	some

B. This letter appeared in an Alison's Advice column:

Dear Alison,
    My sister and I share a room. One of our biggest problems is that I am extremely neat and Chris is not. Her clothes cover the floor. Her books and records are thrown all over. Even our dog can't handle the mess. When he sees it, he whimpers and runs away.
    I discuss this problem with Chris daily. She says she can't change. Our parents want us to solve this without their interference. What do you suggest?

Desperately,
Kara

Write a reply from Alison. Use the following as sentence subjects in the reply. Make sure the verbs you use agree with the subjects.

you	Chris	her belongings
you and your sister	your parents	you or Chris
either of you	the dog	every member of the family

Using Grammar in Writing

These challenging and enjoyable activities allow the students to see how the concepts of grammar, usage, and mechanics may be applied in actual writing situations. Each exercise is designed to allow students practice in several of the skills they have acquired in this Section. The activities also provide opportunities for students to write creatively about a wide variety of interesting and unusual subjects.

These exercises are designed to cover broad areas of grammar, usage, and mechanics. They require the application of skills taught thus far in the text. The exercises may be used for testing purposes, or as an excellent resource for review.

CUMULATIVE REVIEW
Usage

A. Choosing the correct word Write the correct word from the two given in parentheses.

1. Surgeons wear (this, these) kinds of gloves.
2. Mrs. Casselli plays chess (good, well).
3. The kitten licked (its, it's) paws.
4. (May, Can) we (sit, set) in the front row?
5. Have you seen (them, those) new video games?
6. (Its, It's) my bicycle (laying, lying) on the front lawn.
7. This bread smells (fresh, freshly).
8. You should (let, leave) Jim (teach, learn) you guitar.
9. Our school colors look (good, well) together.
10. Clare hasn't (never, ever) seen (them, those) snapshots.
11. (Lie, Lay) the packages under the Christmas tree.
12. The dog doesn't have (any, no) water in (its, it's) bowl.
13. Larry feels (bad, badly) about losing (them, those) papers.
14. (Let, Leave) Ida (rise, raise) the issue in Student Council.
15. You look (good, well) in (that, those) kind of sweater.
16. One of the bushes (were, was) in full bloom.
17. There (is, are) some tickets for the operetta for Mother and (I, me).
18. Everybody from the nearby high schools (was, were) there that day.

19. Neither the Halloween witches nor the ghost (look, looks) very realistic.

20. Behind the oak tree (run, runs) two small streams.

B. Using words correctly Twenty words are underlined in the following paragraph. Ten of the underlined words contain errors in the use of verbs, nouns, pronouns, adverbs, and adjectives. Ten of the words are correct. Proofread the paragraph. Rewrite it, correcting the errors.

Zack looked happily at the calendar and realized that it was the day he was going to the circus with his dad. When they arrived, Zack asked ~~quick,~~ quickly "~~Can~~ May I have some of ~~them~~ those peanuts?" The circus parade started the show. Zack thought the chain of elephants wouldn't never end. Finally the show ~~begin.~~ began It ~~were~~ was not possible to watch everything going on in all three ~~ring~~ rings at one time. Zack kept looking from the ~~farther~~ farthest ring to the middle ring to the nearest ring. Zack's favorite act was the tigers. When they performed, each of the tigers had ~~their~~ its own stand to sit on. "The tigers really move ~~graceful,~~ gracefully" said Zack, "but there's no way you'd ever get me in the cage with those cats!"

Section Objectives

1. To review the definition of a simple sentence and its possible compound parts

2. To understand the definition of a compound sentence, to differentiate it from a compound predicate, and to use correct punctuation in a compound sentence

Preparing the Students

Review the meaning of the word *compound* (Section 1). Ask students to tell you what parts of the sentence they already know can be compound, and have them give you examples. In each case, carefully point out how the conjunction joins words or phrases of equal importance. Ask students what they think a compound sentence should be and why. Ask for examples and put them on the board.

Read and discuss the introduction on page 592.

Additional Resources

Diagnostic Test — page 7 in the test booklet

Mastery Test — pages 65–66 in the test booklet

Additional Exercises — pages 604–606 in the student text

Practice Book — pages 215–218

Duplicating Masters — pages 215–218

Special Populations — See special section at the back of this Teacher's Edition.

Using Compound Sentences

You use sentences to communicate information, ideas, and feelings. You know that there are many differences among the sentences you use. In this section, you will learn about two kinds of sentences. The kinds of sentences you will study are called simple sentences and compound sentences.

Part 1 Review of the Sentence

Throughout this book you have been studying sentences. You know that a sentence has two basic parts, the **subject** and the **predicate**.

Subject	Predicate
Nancy	sang.
Kevin	shouted.
Winter	arrived.
Parrots	talk.
Actors	spoke.
The actors	spoke their lines.
The actors on the stage	spoke their lines with emotion.

The subject of a sentence names the person or thing that the sentence talks about. The predicate tells what the subject is, what the subject did, or what happened.

The **simple predicate** is the verb. The **simple subject** is also called the subject of the verb.

In the subject of a sentence, you will find the simple subject and words that modify it. In the predicate of the sentence, you will find verbs, objects, predicate words, and their modifiers.

Compound Parts in a Sentence

You also know that all of the parts of a sentence may be **compound**. That is, they may themselves have more than one part.

Compound Subject:	The *coach* and the *team* discussed strategy.
Compound Verb:	The girls *talked* and *laughed.*
Compound Object:	The store accepts *cash* or *credit.*
Compound Predicate Word:	The tacos were *hot* and *tasty.*

593

Part 1

Objective

To review the definition of a simple sentence and its possible compound parts

Presenting the Lesson

1. Read and discuss pages 593–594. It is important to review the simple sentence because students must understand what a simple sentence is in order to understand what a compound sentence is.

2. Assign and discuss Exercises A and B on page 594. When discussing these exercises, be sure to have students point out the compound parts in some of the sentences and tell you what those parts are.

Individualizing the Lesson

Less-Advanced Students

Work with these students on the exercises. First have them divide the sentences into subject and predicate parts. Then have them identify any compound parts.

Advanced Students

After students have identified subjects and verbs in the sentences from the exercises, tell them to label the other words in the sentences.

Optional Practice

Have students fill in the blanks in the compound parts of the following sentences. Next to each sentence have them write the kind of compound part in that sentence.

Answers may vary.

593

1. Mercury and _____ are two planets in our solar system. subject
2. My favorite sports are _____ and _____. predicate noun
3. Jerry washed and _____ the vegetables. verb
4. We ate too many pears and _____. direct object
5. Carla and _____ had tacos for lunch. subject
6. The spaceship and the _____ were on display at the museum. subject
7. The kites flew _____ and _____ in the wind. adverb
8. That team needs more practice and _____ this season. predicate
9. We painted _____ and _____ for scenery in the play. direct object
10. The lions and _____ roared when it was mealtime. subject

Extending the Lesson

Have students write original sentences with compound parts. Have them write one sentence for each of the following compound parts.

a. compound subject
b. compound verb
c. compound direct object
d. compound indirect object
e. compound predicate noun
f. compound predicate adjective
g. compound object of a preposition
h. compound adverb
i. compound subject and compound verb
j. compound subject and compound direct object

Definition of the Sentence

You can see that each of these sentences expresses one main idea. These sentences, like all of those you have been studying, are called **simple** sentences.

Now you are ready for a definition of the simple sentence:

A simple sentence is a sentence that contains only one subject and one predicate. The subject and the predicate, or any part of the subject or predicate, may be compound.

Exercises   Review simple sentences.

A. Find the subjects and verbs in each of the following simple sentences.

1. Sid brushed and groomed the horse.
2. My favorite place is a riverbank in the woods.
3. In our town, nothing ever happens.
4. Rain battered the windows.
5. Did Evan pass the test?
6. My family enjoys practical jokes.
7. The bullfighter shook the cape and waited for the bull to charge.
8. Katie rode her bike to the store.
9. In 1861 the Civil War began.
10. Several miners were trapped by a fall.

B. Follow the directions for Exercise A.

1. The club outing was a dinner and a hayride.
2. Someday humans will land on Mars.
3. Why do people explore caves?
4. The train of wagons headed west.
5. Ruth painted the walls and ceiling.
6. Each lighthouse flashes a different signal.

7. <u>Geronimo</u> <u>was</u> a leader and warrior.
8. <u>Vegetables</u> <u>fill</u> the basket.
9. <u>Ray Bradbury</u> <u>is</u> a science fiction writer.
10. The American <u>cowboy</u> <u>is</u> a folk hero.

Part 2 What Is a Compound Sentence?

Sometimes two sentences are so closely related in thought that you join them together. Then you have a different kind of sentence. You have a sentence that has more than one subject and more than one predicate. This is called a **compound sentence.**

A compound sentence consists of two or more simple sentences joined together.

The parts of a compound sentence may be joined by a coordinating conjunction or by a semicolon (;). Study the following examples.

My uncle gave me a book, **and** I read it from cover to cover.
We need scientists, **but** we need laboratory workers even more.
You can take the course now, **or** you can wait until next year.
Mother threw the coat away; it was worn out.

All of the main parts of the compound sentences above could be written as separate sentences without conjunctions.

My uncle gave me a book. I read it from cover to cover.
We need scientists. We need laboratory workers even more.
You can take the course now. You can wait until next year.
Mother threw the coat away. It was worn out.

Why not, then, write only simple sentences? Why bother with compound sentences? You will see the answer as soon as you read this passage:

595

Part 2

Objective

To understand the definition of a compound sentence, to differentiate it from a compound predicate, and to use correct punctuation in a compound sentence

Presenting the Lesson

1. Read and discuss pages 595–596. Review the usage of the three main conjunctions: *and, but,* and *or.* Ask students for compound sentences using each of the conjunctions.

2. The diagraming instruction in "Diagraming Compound Sentences," page 596, is intended only for those students who have had previous experience with sentence diagrams. The example on page 596 may be a good visual model for the class.

3. Do Exercise A on page 597 with the class. Emphasize that a complete thought is located on either side of the conjunction. Assign and discuss Exercise B.

4. Read and discuss page 598. Identifying compound constructions is a difficult task for many students. Sentences with compound predicates are easily confused with compound sentences. Caution them not to be misled by the length of a predicate, but to be sure that there is a complete thought—a subject and a predicate—on each side of the conjunction.

Do Exercise A on pages 598–599 with the students. Assign and discuss Exercise B.

595

I earned four dollars last weekend. I decided to buy a Mother's Day present with it. My mother doesn't like candy. She does like flowers. My brother drove me into town. I went to the florist's shop. All the nice flowers cost too much. Finally, I decided to buy a box of candy for the whole family.

A long series of short sentences is monotonous and choppy. Joined into compound sentences, they sound much better.

I earned four dollars last weekend, *and* I decided to buy a Mother's Day present with it. My mother doesn't like candy, *but* she does like flowers. My brother drove me into town. I went to the florist's shop, *but* all the nice flowers cost too much. Finally, I decided to buy a box of candy for the whole family.

Diagraming Compound Sentences

It is not difficult to diagram compound sentences if you can already diagram simple sentences. A compound sentence is two or more simple sentences joined together. Therefore, you draw the diagram for the first half of the sentence, draw a dotted-line "step" for the conjunction, and then draw the diagram for the second half.

Example: Elaine ran swiftly, but she couldn't catch the other girls.

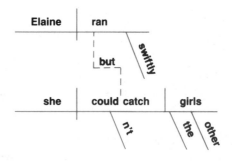

Exercises   Analyze compound sentences.

A. Number your paper from 1 to 10. Label three columns *Subject/Verb,* (*Conjunction,*) and *Subject/Verb*. For each sentence, fill in the columns.

Example: Greg went to the library, but I stayed home.

Subject/Verb	**Conjunction**	**Subject/Verb**
Greg/went	but	I/stayed

1. The clouds are low, (but) it still isn't raining.
2. He's buying radish seeds, (but) I'm getting green beans.
3. Debby shut the curtain, (and) the crew changed the props.
4. Cheryl plays checkers, (but) she prefers chess.
5. The commercial came on, (and) we headed for the kitchen.
6. The bluejay called, (and) three other jays answered.
7. Five cars passed us, (but) we took our time.
8. Either I broke my watch, (or) it needs a new battery.
9. Tracy mowed the front lawn, (and) Jim weeded the garden.
10. Wendy washed the car, (and) Kim cleaned the garage.

B. Follow the directions for Exercise A.

1. The stars were out, (but) the southern sky was cloudy.
2. Scott flew to Miami, (but) we took the train.
3. He painted the wall yellow, (and) his brother liked it.
4. Kate arranged the meeting, (but) Sue organized it.
5. Mom and I played records, (and) Dad read the newspaper.
6. Bill painted the back porch, (and) he sanded the front steps.
7. The dog barked, (but) the cat just arched its back.

597

them point out the conjunction. Help them decide which sentences are compound. Assign Exercise B.

4. Have volunteers write the exercises from pages 602 and 603 on the board. Discuss the uses of *, and, , but,* and *, or,* and the semicolon. Work together on Exercise A helping students choose the best coordinating conjunction.

Advanced Students

1. Have students decide which sentences in the exercises on pages 597–598 would sound acceptable with semicolons. Have them substitute other conjunctions in the sentences and discuss the changes in meaning of the sentences. For example, substitute *but* for *and* in sentences 5, 9 and 10 in Exercise A.

2. Do Exercise A on pages 598–599 orally with the class. Assign Exercise B on page 599. Have students first divide the sentences between the subject and the predicate. Then they can decide whether they are simple or compound sentences. Then have students write five original compound sentences.

3. After completing Exercises A and B on pages 600–601, have each student compose two very brief compound sentences that do not require commas.

Have students write a simple sentence. Then tell them to exchange papers and make the sentences they receive into compound sentences.

4. After completing Exercises A and B on pages 602–603, have students write short paragraphs and

597

exchange them for editing. Have students look for choppiness resulting from too many simple sentences, for overuse of conjunctions, and for joining of unrelated ideas.

1. Have students copy the following sentences. Next to each one, have students write *simple,* if it is a simple sentence, or *compound,* if it is a compound sentence. Then have them underline the subject(s) once and the verb(s) twice. They should also insert any necessary commas.

S 1. *Star Wars* and *E.T.* are my two favorite movies.

C 2. The batter hit a home run and the fans screamed with delight.

S 3. The mountain climbers and the skiers like lots of snow.

C 4. The government task force studied solar energy but their report is not finished yet.

S 5. The firefighter raced up the stairs of the burning building and into the children's room.

S 6. Everyone in our neighborhood saves newspapers and bottles for recycling.

S 7. Strong bridges and good roads are necessary for a good transportation system.

C 8. I liked that movie a lot and I want to see it again soon.

S 9. The airport buses and taxis were filled to capacity.

C10. The critics praised the concert but it didn't seem that special to us.

2. Tell students that the following paragraphs could be improved by the use of some compound constructions. They should rewrite each paragraph, using what they have learned about compound constructions. Remind students that they will

8. The program was on at eight, (but) we weren't home.

9. The paintings were mostly oils, (but) there were several watercolors.

10. The nozzle came off, (and) Terry got all wet.

Compound Predicate or Compound Sentence?

You should know the difference between a compound sentence and a simple sentence with a compound predicate. Read these sentences:

> s.   v.   v.
> The girls *painted the posters* and *tacked them to the bulletin boards.*
> (This is a simple sentence. The conjunction *and* joins two parts of a compound predicate.)

> s.   v.   s.   v.
> The girls *painted the posters,* and *the boys tacked them to the bulletin boards.*
> (Here are two simple sentences, each with a subject and verb. They are joined by the conjunction *and* into a compound sentence.)

Exercises   Compound predicate or compound sentence?

A.   Number your paper from 1 to 10. Decide whether the following sentences are compound sentences or simple sentences with compound predicates. Write *Compound Sentence* or *Compound Predicate.*

CP 1. They sat down and waited for the train.

CS 2. We enjoyed the show, but it was too long.

CP 3. Julia and Jerry cleaned the garage and went home at eight o'clock.

CS 4. It is early, but we'd better leave anyway.

CP 5. I enjoy movies but don't go often.

CP 6. We started early for the game but got there late.

CS 7. Jan likes dramatics, and she enjoys singing, too.

CP 8. The llama looked very proud and kept his long neck stiff.

CS 9. Larry rang the doorbell twice, but no one came to the door.

CP 10. In no time the elephant reached out for the hay and stuffed it into his mouth.

B. Follow the directions for Exercise A.

CS 1. The tank was empty, and we were far from a gas station.

CP 2. Laura closed the window and locked it.

CP 3. We rowed out to the middle of the lake and fished until noon.

CS 4. We called twice, but there was no answer.

CS 5. The whistle blew suddenly, and everyone in the room was quiet.

CS 6. Our dog barks furiously at strangers, but he never bites.

CS 7. Our bus was late, and we missed our flight.

CP 8. Dave opened his wallet and took out his money.

CS 9. Our wrestling team won the district meet, and we were second in the regionals.

CS 10. Kristie and I went to the concert, but we missed the first group's performance.

Punctuating Compound Sentences

Since compound sentences are made up of two or more simple sentences, they may be long. To help the reader keep the thoughts in order, put a **comma** before the coordinating conjunction in a compound sentence.

Patty did a routine on the parallel bars **,and**
Liz and Amy performed on the trampoline.

599

need to consider choice of conjunction, use of comma, and appropriateness of combined sentences. There is more than one way of rewriting the paragraphs.

Paragraphs will vary.

Paragraph #1

The real show was along the lake front. You hardly knew where to look. There were big rockets shimmering like jewels. Some of them flashed green. A fraction of a second later they turned pink. Some were a bright orange. They left long star-shaped clouds. Another kind was very bright. It was a burst of huge, multi-colored sparks. The rockets were mostly red, white, and blue. The very best rockets were brilliant bursts of fiery white stars.

Paragraph #2

Many early attempts were made with a flying machine. The Wright brothers are credited with the invention of the airplane. They were aviation pioneers. They were gifted with unusual mechanical aptitude. Orville and Wilbur Wright worked together to develop a powered aircraft. They built three biplane gliders first. They had to design propellers. They had to build an engine. In 1903 they completed their first powered biplane. It was called the "Kitty Hawk."

Extending the Lesson

1. Have students write compound sentences by combining each of the sentences in Column 1 with a related sentence in Column 2.

Column 1

1. The dinosaur lashed the ground with his gigantic tail. 3
2. We had a great time at Great America amusement park in Illinois. 6
3. Cross-country skiing is becoming a very popular sport. 5
4. The photos of Mars were disappointing. 2

5. An autobiography is the story of someone's life written by that person. 1

6. We donated a dozen sweaters to the clothing drive. 4

Column 2

1. An autograph is a person's signature.

2. The rings of Saturn showed clearly.

3. The brontosaurus shook the forest with his mighty roar.

4. Our neighbors contributed five jackets.

5. Many people like downhill skiing, too.

6. We also had fun at Opryland in Nashville.

2. Review the definitions of *run-on sentences* (two complete thoughts joined without semicolon or conjunction) and *fragments* (incomplete thoughts with only the subject or only the predicate). After each sentence below, have students write whether it is a *run-on* or a *fragment*. Then have them rewrite the sentence correctly. Answers will vary.

R 1. The gymnasts did a superb job on the mats our team won first prize.

R 2. One performer did a triple somersault on the trampoline another did a strenuous exercise on the rings.

F 3. Whirled and jumped and leaped into the air before our eyes.

F 4. The audience, the performers, the coaches, and the judges at the meet.

R 5. The audience was very enthusiastic, they clapped and cheered after each performance.

R 6. Everyone watched the competition on the parallel bars and the uneven bars closely no one could tell who would win.

Sometimes the parts of a compound sentence are joined by a **semicolon (;)** instead of by a conjunction and a comma.

> Patty did a routine on the parallel bars;
> Liz and Amy performed on the trampoline.

The only compound construction you have studied that requires a comma is the compound sentence. You do not need a comma to separate two subjects, two predicates, or two of any of the other compound constructions you have studied. Look at these examples.

> The students from the seventh grade and those from the eighth formed a baseball team.

> We walked into the office and talked with the manager.

Finally, the comma is not necessary in a very short compound sentence, unless it is joined by *but*.

> We skated and we skied.
> You can play or you can watch.
> The movie was short, but it was fascinating.

Exercises   Punctuate compound constructions.

A. In the following sentences, commas have been omitted from all the compound constructions. If a sentence is correct, write *Correct*. If it needs a comma, write the two words between which the comma belongs, and put in the comma.

> Example: The class was preparing a program and the class sponsors were helping with it.
>
> program, and

c 1. They took pictures of the activity groups and put them on display.

2. The Hiking Club has taken several training walks lately, and it is planning a walkathon for next month.

c 3. We could hear the rumbling of thunder and see flashes of lightning across the lake.

c 4. Ms. Hart and the members of the camera club will be putting on an exhibit of indoor photography.

5. The program was interesting, but we couldn't hear some of the speakers.

6. The walls were concrete, and the windows were narrow.

7. The old bathtub had legs on it, and its feet were imitation lion's paws.

8. The old pie safe had tin ends on it, and Carrie was fascinated by the interesting designs cut through the tin.

9. I like all sports, but I really enjoy baseball.

c 10. Dennis wears hip boots and fishes right in the stream.

B. Follow the directions for Exercise A.

1. We went to the drugstore for our photos, but the film hadn't come back yet.

2. Carlos tuned his guitar, but it still sounded flat.

c 3. A chain saw can be dangerous and can cause accidents.

4. A lion is a huge cat, but a bobcat is rather small.

c 5. An electric typewriter is very sensitive and types at the slightest touch.

6. They folded the raft, and Russ stowed it in the trunk.

7. Steve was the villain in the play, and he wore a long brown cape.

c 8. The lawyer approached the bench and spoke with the judge.

c 9. We repaired our bikes and rode to the lake.

10. Our cat poked a hole in the screen door, and mosquitoes flew in.

R 7. The contestants were all in excellent physical condition, they had practiced hard for this meet.

R 8. The three judges gave each gymnast a score for his or her performance the head judge announced the scores from the stand.

R 9. We were excited we congratulated the members of the team.

F 10. Crowded lot next to the gym.

601

Combining Related Thoughts

You have learned that the parts of a compound sentence are related grammatically. That means they are simple sentences, each with a subject and a predicate. The parts of a compound sentence must also be related in thought.

Some pairs of sentences make good compound sentences, and some do not.

> It looked like rain. We went anyhow.
> (Will these two simple sentences make a good compound sentence? Yes, because they are closely related in thought. Use *but* to join them.)

> I like horseback riding. Deep-sea fish are often big.
> (The ideas are not related. These two sentences should not be joined into a compound sentence.)

> Pete flew his kite. The rain got the car wet.
> (The ideas are not related. These two sentences should not be joined into a compound sentence.)

> Give me your boat. I'll give you my ski poles.
> (These two may be joined into a compound sentence because they are related in thought. Use *and* to join them.)

Exercises **Make compound sentences.**

A. Rewrite the following sentences as compound sentences. Pick the best coordinating conjunction for each.

1. Marilyn and Phillip were going to the carnival, but The thunderstorm changed their plans.
2. Charlene was talking to Joey, but Joey wasn't paying any attention.
3. The fan belt on the old Chevy was worn out, but There was nothing wrong with the engine.
4. The car wash is finally open, but Now the line is too long.
5. The wood in that pile is hickory, and This pile is maple.

6. Builders use those concrete blocks for walls$_{,}$ ^{but} My older brother uses them with boards for bookcases.

7. The swimming pool is crowded$_{,}$ ^{and} The water is cold.

8. She put the test booklet on the desk$_{,}$ ^{and} The students picked them up.

9. Ann went horseback riding every weekend$_{,}$ ^{and} She rode in the annual horse show every summer.

10. Dad has gone to PTA$_{,}$ ^{and} Mom is going to the League of Women Voters.

B. Writing Find the six pairs of sentences that are related in thought. Write them as compound sentences. Use a good coordinating conjunction. Remember to use commas correctly.

1. Elizabeth has the mumps$_{,}$ ^{but} She is not very sick.

2. Most trees lose their leaves$_{,}$ ^{but} Evergreens live up to their name.

3. Todd and Doug were the winners. It started to snow after the match.

4. Have a good time in New York$_{,}$ ^{and} See all you can.

5. You can make it this way$_{,}$ ^{or} You can try another way.

6. The potatoes were raw$_{,}$ ^{but} Some of the meat was burned.

7. Arizona is a beautiful state. Rhode Island is on the east coast.

8. Lori and Jovita walked to the basketball game$_{,}$ ^{and} Lori's mother picked them up when it was over.

9. The feature of the game was the raising of the flag. Our cheerleader sprained his ankle.

10. Cross-country skiing is a popular winter sport$_{,}$ ^{and} Many Midwestern states provide excellent skiing trails.

ADDITIONAL EXERCISES

Using Compound Sentences

Compound Sentences Copy each sentence. Decide whether it is a compound sentence or a simple sentence with a compound predicate. Write *Compound Sentence* or *Compound Predicate* after each sentence. Add a comma in the right place for each compound sentence.

CS 1. The telephone rang, and Tara answered it.

CS 2. Diana built a table, but most of the class made lamps.

CS 3. Jason listens to the radio, but he doesn't read a paper.

CP 4. The skater held one arm forward but kept the other back.

CP 5. They live in town during winter but move to the shore during the summertime.

CP 6. Shawn looked around the store but bought nothing.

CS 7. The end reached for the pass, but he missed it.

CS 8. John either types his homework, or he prints it neatly.

CS 9. The school library didn't have the book, but the public library did.

CS 10. The diver saw an eel, but she didn't see the octopus.

CP 11. Everybody was clapping and dancing in the aisles.

CS 12. Mom chose the pattern, but I picked out the material.

CP 13. He went home and sulked for a few hours.

CS 14. I called Kevin, but his phone was busy.

CP 15. The portrait is beautiful but doesn't resemble her.

CP 16. Julie makes up tongue-twisters and tries them on us.

CS 17. Choctaw Indians used two sticks for lacrosse, but some other tribes used one.

CS 18. Food was scarce, and there were long lines at stores.

CP 19. The rabbit plucks her fur and lines the nest with it.

CP 20. We brushed the snow off the car and scraped the ice from the windows.

MIXED REVIEW

Using Compound Sentences

A. Identifying simple and compound sentences Copy the following sentences. If a sentence is simple, write *S*. If a sentence is compound, write *C*. Underline all subjects once and all verbs twice. Add any necessary commas to compound sentences.

S 1. The boys sold hot dogs and hamburgers at the picnic.

S 2. Yvette and Cheryl teach arts and crafts on Saturdays.

C 3. Birds came to the feeder, but none were cardinals.

S 4. Rita washed and dried her hair before the party.

S 5. The students write and edit our school newspaper.

C 6. Mr. Healy invented the device, and he sold it.

S 7. Jorge took the exam and passed it.

C 8. We left the house on time, but the snow delayed us.

S 9. The night air was damp and chilly.

C 10. Dad and I repaired the shutters, and we painted them.

B. Combining sentences Combine the following simple sentences into compound sentences. Punctuate them.

1. We can wait for Bob's call. or We can call him ourselves.

2. Camping is a fun vacation. but It's inexpensive.

3. Ellen wants those boots. but She can't afford them.

4. Jack chopped the wood. and We stacked it on the porch.

5. Harold practiced the concerto. but He made several mistakes.

6. Jodie wants to play by the rules. or She won't play.

7. Dr. Hines examined my throat. and It was not infected.

8. The senator campaigned vigorously. and She won the election.

9. Dan can accept this. or He can wait for a better offer.

10. Rick wound the old watch. and It worked.

605

Mixed Review

These exercises provide review of the concepts presented in this Section. Each exercise challenges the students to apply several of the skills they have acquired during previous study. Because the "mixed" feature of these activities makes them more difficult, the teacher may wish to have less-advanced students do them orally or in small groups.

USING GRAMMAR IN WRITING
Using Compound Sentences

A. Your town officials are discussing the possibility of building an indoor ice rink. You and your friends are stopped by a
reporter and asked for your opinions on this issue. Complete
the five replies by making them compound sentences.

1. (Use *and*) It would encourage more people to skate
2. (Use *or*) We should improve our outdoor rinks
3. (Use *but*) It would increase taxes
4. (Use *and*) An indoor rink would attract skaters from other
towns
5. (Use *but*) Ice skating is really an outdoor sport

B. Your best friend has decided to run for a class office. He
or she has asked you to help write campaign slogans. These
slogans will be put on posters. Write five campaign slogans for
your friend. Your slogans may rhyme, and they may be funny or
serious. Each one should be a compound sentence. Use the
conjunction *or* in at least one slogan. Use *but* in at least one.

C. Old mail order catalogues contained many amusing ads for
strange medicines and gadgets. These ads often made out-
rageous claims about the products. Help make the following
ads more truthful by changing each claim into a compound
sentence. Use the conjunctions *and, but,* and *or.*

> **Example:** Clark's Cleaning Compound removes any stain . . .
> *and* takes the material with it.

1. Dr. Doolittle's Elixer cures any sickness
2. The Kitchen Wizard was designed to do fifty tasks
3. Professor Clef's Band-in-One lets you sound like three
instruments at once
4. Magic Brush will groom and clean your hair each morning
5. The Excel-Exerciser can change the way you look

Using Complex Sentences

Section Objectives

1. To understand the definition of complex sentence and to recognize subordinate clauses

2. To recognize adverb clauses and punctuate them correctly

3. To recognize adjective clauses and to understand the function of relative pronouns

4. To recognize noun clauses and to understand how they are used

5. To be able to identify the three kinds of subordinate clauses: the adverb clause, the adjective clause, and the noun clause

6. To be able to recognize and correct subordinate clause sentence fragments

7. To be able to identify the three kinds of sentences: simple, compound, and complex

Preparing the Students

Write the word *complex* on the board. Ask students what it means. Ask them to explain what might make a writing style complex. Ask students what a complex sentence would be.

Additional Resources

Diagnostic Test — page 7 in the test booklet

Mastery Test — pages 67–68 in the test booklet

Additional Exercises — pages 623–630 in the student text

Practice Book — pages 219–226

Duplicating Masters — pages 219–226

Special Populations — See special section at the back of this Teacher's Edition.

You have studied simple sentences and compound sentences. Another kind of sentence that will help you to express your ideas is the **complex sentence**. In this section, you will learn about complex sentences.

To understand the definition of a complex sentence and to recognize subordinate clauses

Presenting the Lesson

1. Read and discuss pages 608–609. Stress that the term *independent clause* is another name for a sentence.

Read and discuss pages 609–610. Discuss the definition of *subordinate*. Ask students for examples of things that are subordinate to something else (on the job, ideas in an outline). Relate the discussion to subordinate clauses.

2. Do the exercise on page 610 with the class, and have students tell why each subordinate clause they make is incomplete. Discuss the definition of the complex sentence on page 611. Have students make complex sentences orally by completing some of the subordinate clauses they wrote in the exercise on page 610.

3. Do Exercise A on page 611. with the class. Then assign and discuss Exercise B on pages 611–612. If students have problems recognizing the subordinate clauses, have them identify each word in the sentences according to its part of speech. This will help them become aware of the words that begin subordinate clauses in a sentence.

Part 1 What Is a Complex Sentence?

Before you can know what a complex sentence is, you should know what a clause is.

A clause is a group of words that contains a verb and its subject.

From this definition you can see that a simple sentence is a clause. It has both a verb and a subject.

> s.   v.
> We heard a loud explosion.

> s.   v.
> The blacksmith forged a horseshoe.

Your study of sentences will be clearer, however, if you think of a clause as a part of a sentence. A clause is a group of words containing a subject and a verb within a sentence.

Do compound sentences contain clauses? Do they contain groups of words that have a subject and a verb? Look at these examples:

> s.   v.   s.   v.
> Tall tales are not true, but they are amusing.

> s.   v.   s.   v.
> Don walked into the store, and he asked for a job.

The answer is clear. Compound sentences do contain groups of words that have their own subjects and verbs.

See what happens when you divide the compound sentences above into their main parts.

> Tall tales are not true. They are amusing.

> Don walked into the store. He asked for a job.

Each one of the clauses in the compound sentences can become a sentence by itself.

Phrases and Clauses

Can you tell the difference between a *phrase* and a *clause?* Read these examples.

Phrases: in the river
            with friends

                  s.   **v.**
Clauses: when she was busy

              s.   **v.**
              who planned the party

A clause has a subject and a verb. A phrase does not.

Main Clauses

A clause that can stand as a sentence by itself is a **main clause**. All the clauses in compound sentences are main clauses. They can all stand as simple sentences by themselves. For that reason, they are sometimes called **independent clauses**.

Subordinate Clauses

Now look at clauses of a different kind.

       s.   **v.**
as the clock struck twelve

         s.   **v.**
after the movie was over

Neither group of words above is a complete thought. Each leaves you wondering: "Then what?"

Now, with your finger, cover the first word in each group of words. What happens? Each group of words becomes a complete sentence. You can see, then, that words like *as* and *after* are important in a clause.

When a word like *as* or *after* introduces a clause, it *subordinates* the clause. That is, it makes the clause depend on a main

8. _____, working conditions improved in the factory.

9. _____, you should organize your study time.

10. _____, the vegetables did not grow well.

2. *Challenge Game.* Using index cards, make up a set of flash cards containing the list of subordinating conjunctions from page 610. Divide the class into two teams. Flash a card to a team member and, in one minute, he must make up a sentence using that subordinating conjunction and a subordinating clause. Members from the other team may challenge the answer.

Extending the Lesson

Have each student find five examples of complex sentences in print. (Use magazines or textbooks instead of newspapers for this search.) Discuss the sentences in class.

clause to complete its meaning. Words like *as* or *after* are called **subordinating conjunctions**. They introduce **subordinate clauses**.

Subordinate clauses are clauses that cannot stand alone as sentences.

Not every subordinate clause begins with a subordinating conjunction, but many do. The following words are used frequently as subordinating conjunctions.

Words Often Used as Subordinating Conjunctions			
after	because	so that	whatever
although	before	than	when
as	if	though	whenever
as if	in order that	till	where
as long as	provided	unless	wherever
as though	since	until	while

Caution: These words are subordinating words only when they introduce a clause. Some can be used in other ways.

Not all subordinate clauses begin with subordinating conjunctions. The following words can also introduce subordinate clauses:

that	who, whom, whose	which
what	whoever, whomever	how

Exercise Make subordinate clauses.

Writing Use a variety of subordinating words to make subordinate clauses out of these sentences. Answers will vary.

1. My shoes are tight.
2. The bus pulled away.
3. The Ferris wheel stopped.
4. The cookies are done.
5. There is no answer.
6. The battery works.
7. Some insects bite.
8. We ate the cake.
9. The buzzer sounded.
10. It snowed last night.

Definition of the Complex Sentence

Now that you know about main clauses and subordinate clauses, you are ready to learn what a complex sentence is.

A complex sentence is a sentence that contains one main clause and one or more subordinate clauses.

Main Clause	Subordinate Clause
We left	before you came.
We'll go to the carnival	unless it rains tonight.
We were on the lake	when the storm began.

Exercises   Recognize subordinate clauses.

A.   Find the (subordinate clause) in each sentence. Copy it. Underline the <u>subject</u> once and the <u>verb</u> twice.

1. The crowd cheered (after the game ended.)
2. Carlos wears a strange hat (when he fishes.)
3. People dream (while they sleep.)
4. (Although she was tired,) the mountaineer continued.
5. I have days (when nothing goes right.)
6. The diver (who came ashore) had seen a shark.
7. The trout is a fish (that lives in fresh water.)
8. The balloon rose (when we filled it with helium.)
9. David was scared, (although he pretended not to be.)
10. Jane pulled the parachute cord (as she jumped.)

B.   Follow the directions for Exercise A.

1. The water is shallow here (because the tide is out.)
2. Call a plumber (if the pipes leak.)
3. Planes will land (if the fog clears.)
4. The audience hissed (when the villain appeared.)
5. Carolyn waved (as the ship pulled out.)

Objective

To recognize adverb clauses and punctuate them correctly

Presenting the Lesson

1. Read and discuss page 612.
2. It may be helpful to do Exercise A on page 613 with the class and have students identify each word in the adverb clause. Stress that there must be both a subject and a verb in the adverb clause as well as in the main clause. Also, point out the use of commas after introductory adverb clauses (items 3, 8, and 9). Assign and discuss Exercise B on page 613.

Individualizing the Lesson

Less-Advanced Students

Have students refer to the list of subordinating conjunctions on page 610 while working on the exercises. Work with students to identify the adverb clauses. It may help them to first pick out the verbs and subjects in the sentences before trying to identify the adverb clauses.

Advanced Students

Have students add a main clause to each of the following adverb clauses. Tell them to vary the position of the adverb clause in the sentence.

1. if you say so
2. because Marci was a nurse
3. since the boys arrived
4. while he answered the phone
5. unless you prefer hot cocoa

612

6. Aretha Franklin brings music to life (when she sings.)
7. We grilled the red snapper (that Dave caught early this morning.)
8. Bob left for basketball practice (when it was four o'clock.)
9. Mimes do not talk (while they act.)
10. Morse code, (which was developed in 1840) was once used for sending telegrams.

Part 2 Adverb Clauses

You know that every complex sentence contains a subordinate clause. There are three kinds of subordinate clauses. The first kind you will study is the adverb clause.

An **adverb** is a word that modifies a verb, an adjective, or another adverb.

Adverb: A fire started *suddenly*.

An **adverb phrase** is a prepositional phrase used as an adverb. Adverb phrases usually modify verbs.

Adverb phrase: A fire started *in the forest*.

An adverb clause is a subordinate clause used as an adverb.

When an adverb clause begins a sentence, use a comma to separate the clause from the rest of the sentence.

Adverb clause: A fire started *when lightning struck*.

When lightning struck, a fire started.

Adverbs and adverb phrases or clauses tell *when, where, how,* or *to what extent* about the word they modify.

Remember that a *clause* contains a subject and a verb. A *phrase* has neither a subject nor a verb.

612

Exercises Recognize adverb clauses.

A. Copy the (adverb clause) from each sentence. Underline its <u>subject</u> once and its <u>verb</u> twice. Circle the subordinating conjunction.

Example: Although the lights were on, no one was home.
(Although) the lights were on

1. His nickname is Rocket (because) he <u>moves</u> fast.
2. Our dog barks (if) it <u>sees</u> strangers.
3. (If) <u>I</u> could <u>move</u>, I'd live in Australia.
4. Water looks blue (since) it <u>reflects</u> the sky.
5. I follow rules (if) <u>they</u> <u>are</u> necessary.
6. We awoke (when) the <u>tent</u> <u>collapsed</u>.
7. Dana shopped (while) <u>Cathy</u> <u>waited</u>.
8. (When) <u>Liz</u> <u>can't sleep</u>, she reads.
9. (While) <u>everyone</u> <u>slept</u>, snowplows cleared the main streets.
10. Ships send signals (when) <u>they</u> <u>need</u> help.

B. Follow the directions for Exercise A.

1. Travelers were trapped (when) the <u>blizzard</u> <u>hit</u> without warning.
2. (Although) <u>Tim</u> <u>hits</u> well, his fielding is weak.
3. The door swung open (when) <u>we</u> <u>knocked</u>.
4. A siren screamed (as) the <u>ambulance</u> <u>raced</u> down the street.
5. Use candles (if) the <u>electricity</u> <u>goes</u> off.
6. We stopped (where) the <u>road</u> <u>forked</u>.
7. (After) the <u>battle</u> <u>was lost</u>, the army retreated through the forest.
8. Maureen tripped (as) <u>she</u> <u>reached</u> for the ball.
9. We sang carols (while) <u>we</u> <u>decorated</u> the tree.
10. The rookies were learning (while) <u>they</u> <u>worked</u>.

613

613

Part 3

Objective

To recognize adjective clauses and to understand the function of relative pronouns

Presenting the Lesson

1. Read and discuss pages 614–615.

2. It may be helpful to do Exercise A on pages 615–616 with the class and have students identify each word in the adjective clause. Stress that there must be both a subject and a verb in the adjective clause as well as in the main clause. Assign and discuss Exercise B.

Individualizing the Lesson

Less-Advanced Students

1. Help students find the adjective clauses in Exercise A on pages 615–616. On the board list the words that introduce most adjective clauses: *where, when, who, whom, whose, that,* and *which.* Once they've identified the adjective clause, help them find the noun or pronoun that it modifies.

2. Work together on Exercise B. Have students write the adjective clause for each sentence. Then they should underline the subject and verb of each clause. Help them find the word each adjective clause modifies.

Advanced Students

Have students write five original complex sentences using adjective clauses.

The second kind of subordinate clause is the adjective clause. An **adjective** is a word that modifies a noun or pronoun.

a *delicious* lunch   the *exciting* book

An **adjective phrase** is a prepositional phrase that modifies a noun or pronoun.

the message *in the mailbox*   the load *of gravel*

An adjective clause is a subordinate clause used as an adjective to modify a noun or pronoun.

Usually, an adjective clause comes immediately after the word it modifies. Study the examples.

This drive-in has a computer *that takes food orders.*

We learned the metric system, *which is used worldwide.*

Anyone *who is late* will miss the field trip.

Some adjective clauses start with *where* and *when.*

The cafeteria is the place *where friends meet.*

September is the month *when school begins.*

Who and Whom in Clauses

The words *who, whose,* and *whom* are often used to begin adjective clauses. They tie the clause to the word it modifies in the main clause. When used in this way, *who, whom,* and *whose* are called **relative pronouns**. They relate the clause (called a **relative clause**) to the word it modifies. *That* and *which* may also be relative pronouns.

Relative Pronouns

who   whom   whose   that   which

Relative pronouns have three jobs:

1. They begin an adjective clause.
2. They relate the adjective clause to a word in the main clause.
3. They act as subject, object, predicate pronoun, or the object of a preposition in the adjective clause.

> Curtis is the player *who won the match.*
> (*Who* is the subject of *won.*)

> Is Gayle the girl *whom you met?*
> (*Whom* is the direct object of *met.*)

> That is the senator *to whom I wrote.*
> (*Whom* is the object of the preposition *to.*)

The subject form is *who.* The object form is *whom.* Which form you use depends upon how the word is used in the clause.

> Eric Heiden is an athlete (who, whom) I admire.
> (An object of the verb *admire* is needed. *Whom* is the object form.)

> Eric Heiden is an athlete *whom* I admire.

Exercises   Recognize adjective clauses.

A.   Copy the (adjective clause) from each sentence. Underline the subject once and the verb twice. Before the clause, write the (word it modifies.)

> Example: She is the guitarist who will perform with the Atlanta Symphony.
> (guitarist—who will perform with the Atlanta Symphony.)

1. Melissa wears (clothes) (that are very stylish.)
2. (Someone) (who draws well) will design the stage sets.
3. Nurses are (people) (whom I admire.)
4. Jenny is the only (one) (who found a job.)
5. The (apples) (that we picked are crisp and juicy.)

615

Have students complete the following sentences by writing an adjective clause in each blank. Tell them to write a clause that modifies the noun that precedes it.
Answers will vary.

1. The engineer blew the train whistle _____.
2. The referee called a foul _____.
3. The pianist played the concerto _____.
4. The announcer introduced the speaker _____.
5. The bus waited for passengers _____.
6. The class interested the students _____.
7. The plane took off from the airport _____.
8. The teller counted the money ____.
9. The movie astounded people ____.
10. The batter hit a high fly ball ____.

Extending the Lesson

1. Have students rewrite each pair of sentences as a complex sentence, using the italicized sentence as the subordinate clause.

Example:

John scored the winning touchdown. *He is the captain of the football team.* (who)
John, who is the captain of the football team, scored the winning touchdown.

1. The biology teacher‸carefully explained the muscle system of the frog. *She is an interesting lecturer.* (who)
   who is an interesting . . . .
2. My little brother screamed in fright at the big dog. *The dog was running towards him.* (that)
   that ‸ who was
3. The young mountain climber‸ showed us how to scale a peak. *He was an expert. (who)*
   who was an expert.

615

4. The plants ^that had not been .... were turning brown. ~~They had not been watered enough.~~ (that)

5. The city had to cut down hundreds of trees. ^that ~~They~~ had Dutch elm disease. (that)

2. On index cards, write several pairs of sentences. Hand a card to the first person in every row of students. They must combine the sentences on a piece of paper to make a complex sentence. Then tell them to pass the card on to the person behind them until the entire row is finished. The first row to correctly complete the sentences wins.

Part 4

Objective

To recognize noun clauses and to understand how they are used

Presenting the Lesson

1. Be sure students have a firm grasp of adverb and adjective clauses before beginning this lesson. The concept of a noun clause is usually much more difficult for students to understand.

Discuss the function of a noun in a sentence. Point out that a noun clause does the same thing, only it contains a subject and a verb that together act as a noun. Read and discuss pages 616–617. Ask students for examples of sentences with noun clauses that begin with the introductory words listed on page 617. Make sure they understand that some of the same introductory words can also be used to

6. Zappo is a (magician)(who does many amazing tricks.)

7. The robber stole (everything)(that was valuable.)

8. (Skateboarding,)(which was a fad years ago,)is popular again.

9. Here is the (newspaper)(that you wanted.)

10. (Jimmy Carter,)(who was the thirty-ninth President of the United States,)wrote that book.

B. Follow the directions for Exercise A.

1. The (fish)(that we catch)with nets are smelts.

2. The class (notes)(that I took are messy.)

3. Mom brought (plates)(that don't break easily.)

4. Meryl Streep is an (actress)(who has appeared on the stage, on television, and in movies.)

5. One (tribe)(that lives mainly in Oklahoma)is the Cherokee.

6. The (astronaut)(who returned from the moon)gave a speech.

7. We rode the toboggan (slide,)(which is very steep.)

8. Mary Shelley is the (author)(who wrote *Frankenstein*.)

9. The (doctor)(whom we consulted)made a diagnosis.

10. The Milky Way is a group of (stars)(that includes our sun.)

Part 4   Noun Clauses

The third kind of subordinate clause is the noun clause.

You will remember that nouns can be used as subjects, as objects of verbs, as predicate words after linking verbs, and as objects of prepositions.

A noun clause is a clause used as a noun in a sentence. The noun clause can be used in any way that a noun is used. Noun clauses do not modify anything because nouns are not modifiers.

Uses of Noun Clauses

Subject: *What the club needed* was a new president.
Whoever guesses the correct number wins a prize.

Direct Object: The teacher asked *who had read the story.*
A beekeeper explained *how honey is made.*

Object of Preposition: Tammy waved at *whomever she knew.*
(The clause is the object of the preposition *at.*)
A guide pointed to *where the exhibit was.*
(The clause is the object of the preposition *to.*)

Predicate Noun: His message was *that he would not be home for dinner.*
The outcome is *what matters.*

You can see that a great many noun clauses are introduced by *that* and *what*. Some are introduced by *whatever*, *whoever*, and *whomever*. Other noun clauses are introduced by *who*, *whose*, and *whom*. Some are introduced by *where*, *when*, and *how*.

Exercises Recognize noun clauses.

A. Copy the (noun clauses) in these sentences. Underline the subject once and the verb twice. Tell how the clause is used.

Example: What I want is a warm hat.
What I want (used as subject)

D.O. 1. No one knows (how we won.)

D.O. 2. Merle never discovered (who sent the Valentine.)

D.O. 3. Mike claims (that horses have feelings.)

O.P. 4. Gene brought cupcakes for (whoever wants one.)

S. 5. (What Judy did) was a surprise to everyone.

S. 6. (Where we sat) was just fine.

D.O. 7. Do you know (where she works?)

introduce adjective clauses and adverb clauses.

2. Do Exercise A on pages 617–618 with the class. Assign and discuss Exercise B.

Individualizing the Lesson

Less-Advanced Students

List the words that introduce noun clauses on the board for the students to refer to: *that, what, whatever, whoever, whomever, who, whose, whom, where, when* and *how*. Work with students in identifying the noun clauses in the exercises. Discuss how each clause is used in the sentences.

Advanced Students

1. Work orally in completing Exercise A. Have the students identify each noun clause and tell how it is used in the sentence. Assign Exercise B.

2. Have students search newspaper or magazine articles for sentences containing noun clauses.

Optional Practice

Have students underline the noun clauses in the following paragraph. You might also wish to have them identify the kind of noun clause.

D.O. Whoever said that circuses are just for little kids? I had a great time last week at the Ringling Brothers-Barnum and Bailey Circus. When we arrived, Subj. we saw the animals. What excited me most was the trained tiger act. I asked D.O. who the trainer was. I discovered that D.O. it was the famous Gunther Gebel- Subj. Williams. Whoever designed the beautiful costumes should have been honored. They were extraordinary, just like the different acts. I still don't under- D.O. stand how the man survived his blast

out of the cannon. I thought that he
D.O.
would never get up from the net
across the ring. My family and I hope
that the circus will return next year.
One can never see everything in just
one visit. D.O.

Extending the Lesson

Have students write eleven complex sentences with noun clauses. Have them write the sentences using each of these words that introduces a noun clause: *that*, *what*, *whatever*, *whoever*, *whomever*, *who*, *whose*, *whom*, *where*, *when*, and *how*. Encourage students to try using the noun clauses in various places in the sentences.

Part 5

Objective

To be able to identify the three kinds of subordinate clauses: the adverb clause, the adjective clause, and the noun clause

Presenting the Lesson

1. Read and discuss page 618.
2. Assign and discuss Exercise A on pages 618–619. Have students circle the word that introduces the subordinate clause in each sentence. During your discussion have them also tell what the main clause of each sentence is. Assign and discuss Exercise B on page 619.

618

O.P. 8. Connie laughs at (whatever her baby brother does)
D.O. 9. The lumberjack showed (how he cuts down a tree)
D.O. 10. I couldn't read (what the billboard said)

B. Follow the directions for Exercise A.

S. 1. (Whoever wins the race) will get a gold medal.
D.O. 2. We didn't know (who was in charge of the ballot box)
S. 3. (Whatever you decide) is all right with me.
O.P. 4. Save these coupons for (whoever wants them)
S. 5. (Whoever finds Kathy's watch) will receive a reward.
S. 6. (Why they chose me) is hard to understand.
D.O. 7. I was wondering (how you did that)
D.O. 8. Sally doesn't know (where the supplies are)
O.P. 9. Sign the papers for (whoever needs them)
S. 10. (How you finished so quickly) is beyond me.

Part 5 A Review of Subordinate Clauses

There are three kinds of subordinate clauses. They are the adverb clause, the adjective clause, and the noun clause.

You cannot tell the kind of clause from the word that introduces it. You can tell the kind of clause only from the way it is used in the sentence. If the clause is used as a noun, it is a noun clause. If the clause is a modifier, it is either an adverb or an adjective clause.

Exercises   Identify subordinate clauses.

A. Write each subordinate clause from the following sentences. If a clause is used as a noun clause, tell how it is used in the sentence. If a clause is used as an adjective or adverb clause, tell what it modifies.

1. The test, which was about the Civil War, was easy. adj., test

2. We went to the circus <u>when it came to town</u>. adv., went
3. The bait <u>that worked best</u> was shrimp. adj., bait
4. Everyone <u>who travels</u> needs a map. adj., everyone
5. No one saw Diane <u>after she left practice</u>. adv., saw
6. The wolf attacked <u>because it was trapped</u>. adv., attacked
7. The robot will do <u>whatever you ask</u>. noun, direct object
8. Len claims <u>that he knows judo</u>. noun, direct object
9. Amy blushed <u>when she was announced as the winner</u>. adv., blushed
10. <u>What I like best</u> is talking on the phone with friends. noun, subject

B. Follow the directions for Exercise A.

1. Jeff's sister is the one <u>who plays the guitar</u>. adj., one
2. A person <u>who designs buildings</u> is an architect. adj., person
3. The champ beat <u>whomever he fought</u>. noun, direct object
4. <u>Whoever returns the stolen jewels</u> will get a reward. noun, subject
5. The mutt followed Jeff <u>wherever he went</u>. adv., followed
6. <u>Although she prefers hockey</u>, Grace plays baseball. adv., plays
7. Many people watch television <u>because they are bored</u>. adv., watch
8. We could see the lake from <u>where we stood</u>. noun, object of preposition
9. I don't know <u>what you mean</u>. noun, direct object
10. Radar, <u>which locates distant objects</u>, is used to track spacecraft. adj., Radar

Part 6 More About Sentence Fragments

The sentence fragments that you studied in Section 1 were easy to spot. They were fragments because they lacked a verb or the subject of a verb.

Another kind of sentence fragment is the subordinate clause. A subordinate clause has both a verb and a subject. By itself, however, it is still a fragment because its meaning is not complete. Look at the groups of words below. Which is a

619

Individualizing the Lesson

Less-Advanced Students

Do Exercise A orally. Allow the students to work in pairs to complete Exercise B.

Advanced Students

Have each student write three original sentences, one with a noun clause, one with an adjective clause, and one with an adverb clause. Compile the sentences and have the students follow the instructions for Exercise A using the student-written sentences.

Optional Practice

Have students make posters defining the three kinds of subordinate clauses and their uses. Have them write sample sentences illustrating each type of clause and each use. Display the posters in the classroom.

Part 6

Objective

To be able to recognize and correct subordinate clause sentence fragments

Presenting the Lesson

1. Read pages 619-620 with the class.

2. Assign and discuss Exercise A on page 620. Have students point out subjects and verbs. Remind them to place a comma at the end of the subordinate clause if it is used before the main clause. Assign and discuss Exercise B.

619

Individualizing the Lesson

Less-Advanced Students

Help students decide whether the word groups in the exercises are sentences or fragments. Have them write the fragments on the chalkboard adding words to make complete sentences.

Advanced Students

After having completed the exercises, have students write sentence fragments of their own. Have them exchange papers and make the fragments they received into complete sentences.

Optional Practice

Have students write *S* next to sentences, and *F* next to fragments.

F 1. After traveling through the dangerous snowstorm for miles.

S 2. It began to make strange noises.

S 3. She is the professor.

F 4. How to turn on the tape recorder.

S 5. The explorers managed to reach safety.

Extending the Lesson

Have students rewrite this paragraph eliminating the sentence fragments.

When we went to the amusement park/ It was a rainy day. My brother Pete/ Who is a pessimist/ Thought we should go home. I wouldn't hear of it. Although it was raining/ We could still enjoy the many indoor attractions. Also, there were no crowds or lines/ Which is the usual state of affairs on a nice day. That he enjoyed himself/ Was obvious by the smile on Pete's face. He even remarked/ That we should always go to the amusement park on a rainy day.

complete sentence? Which is a subordinate clause?

> The bell rang
> When the bell rang

A subordinate clause must not be written as a complete sentence. It must always be joined to a main clause.

Fragment: When the bell rang
Sentence: When the bell rang, the school emptied.

Fragment: Although candy tastes good
Sentence: Although candy tastes good, it causes tooth decay.

You can see that it is important to be able to recognize subordinating conjunctions.

Exercises   Recognize sentence fragments.

A. Write each of the following groups of words. If the group of words is a sentence, write *S* and add the correct punctuation. If the group of words is a fragment, write *F*. Then add words to make each fragment a complete sentence. Punctuate and capitalize where necessary. Sentences will vary.

F 1. How the drill on the wall works

S 2. Smile for your picture

S 3. The attic holds many treasures

S 4. Have you seen this movie?

F 5. Because the ending is a surprise

F 6. That manufactures fireworks

F 7. Where the trunk was hidden

F 8. That the doctor prescribed

S 9. The photos were blurry

F 10. When the waves hit the rocks

B. Follow the directions for Exercise A.

S 1. Today machines make most goods

F 2. Until the judge rules

F 3. Because the pitcher balked
F 4. Where the icicles hung
S 5. Will the prisoner be released ?
S 6. Have a good day !
S 7. In the United States bullfights are banned .
F 8. Although they are popular events in Spain and Mexico
F 9. As everyone expected
S 10. The jury made its decision .

Part 7 A Review of Sentences

In this section you have learned about three kinds of sentences that you use.

You know that a **simple sentence** contains one subject and one predicate. A simple sentence expresses one main idea. You will remember, however, that parts of the simple sentence may be compound.

s.   s.   v.
The basketball team and the hockey team won yesterday.

s.   s.   v.   v.
Mark and Donna read and discussed the history assignment.

You have learned that a **compound sentence** consists of two simple sentences. These simple sentences are joined by a coordinating conjunction or by a semicolon. A compound sentence expresses two main ideas that are related in thought.

s.   v.   s.   v.
The basketball team won yesterday; the hockey team lost.

s.   v.   s.   v.
Mark studied history, **but** Donna studied math.

You have also learned that a **complex sentence** contains one main clause and one or more subordinate clauses. (The subordinate clauses may be used as nouns, as adjectives, or as adverbs.) A complex sentence expresses one main idea and one or more ideas that depend on the main idea.

Part 7

Objective

To be able to identify the three kinds of sentences: simple, compound, and complex

Presenting the Lesson

1. Read and discuss pages 621–622.

2. Assign and discuss Exercises A and B on page 622. If a sentence is compound, have students point out the coordinating conjunction. If complex, have students point out the subordinate clause.

Individualizing the Lesson

Less-Advanced Students

Work orally with students in completing the exercises. Help them look for clues that may aid in their decisions. Discuss each answer.

Advanced Students

1. Provide students with an article or paragraph that contains examples of each kind of sentence. Have them identify those sentences.

621

2. Have students write sentences of their own showing examples of each type of sentence. When writing complex sentences, they must tell how the clauses are used.

Optional Practice

Put the following sentences on a worksheet. Have students write *Simple*, *Compound*, or *Complex* next to each sentence. Then have them underline each subordinate clause, and identify what kind it is (adjective, adverb, or noun).

Example:
adverb
Bob locks his bicycle <u>whenever he parks it outside</u>. —Complex

Cx 1. The glasses <u>that are in the dish drainer</u> were just washed.
     ^{Adj}

Cx 2. <u>As the ambulance came racing down the street</u>, it sounded its siren.
     ^{Adv}

S 3. The desert air became cold after the sun set.

S 4. The steak knives were all in a box in the drawer.

Cp 5. Sometimes we take the bus, but we usually take the train.

Extending the Lesson

Play a challenge game. Make up a set of cards each containing one kind of sentence. Divide the class into teams. Show a card to a member of one team who scores a point if he or she correctly identifies the kind of sentence on the card. Each team member may score a bonus point for identifying the subordinating clause and a bonus point for telling what kind it is (adjective, adverb, or noun).

S. V. S.
Although the basketball team won yesterday, the hockey team

V.
lost.

S. V. S. V.
Tom made a salad *while Donna grilled the hamburgers.*

Exercises   Recognize the kinds of sentences.

A. Number your paper from 1 to 10. For each sentence, write <u>Simple</u>, <u>Compound</u>, or <u>Complex</u> to show what kind it is.

Cx. 1. If I close my eyes, a roller coaster doesn't scare me.

Cx. 2. Do you know when vacation starts?

S. 3. Have you ever seen a sunrise from a lighthouse?

Cx. 4. Everyone who campaigns makes promises.

S. 5. This area is perfect for cross-country skiing.

Cp. 6. Kelly enjoys Monopoly, but she dislikes Scrabble.

S. 7. Julie rode a unicycle in the parade.

Cp. 8. The wind grew fierce, and several trees fell.

Cp. 9. Mary washed the car, and Todd repaired his bike.

S. 10. The cast and crew worked hard in rehearsal.

B. Follow the directions for Exercise A.

S. 1. Molly owns and operates a ham radio.

Cx. 2. Australia has summer when we have winter.

Cp. 3. The tightrope walker fell, but she landed in a net.

Cx. 4. We had fun when we were at camp.

Cp. 5. Will you walk home, or do you have a ride?

S. 6. The hermit loved animals but disliked people.

S. 7. The talent show was scheduled for Friday and Saturday.

S. 8. Our school newspaper has articles about student opinions.

Cp. 9. A hurricane struck Florida, and then it moved south.

Cx. 10. Migrant workers move to wherever there is work.

ADDITIONAL EXERCISES

Using Complex Sentences

A. Subordinate Clauses Copy the (subordinate clause) in each sentence. Underline the subject of the subordinate clause once and the verb twice.

1. Kelly hummed (as she raked the leaves.)
2. I will get a job (when I am sixteen.)
3. (Whatever the problems are,) Rob will do his best.
4. Lena is the one (who is eating an apple.)
5. (When the alarm rings,) the firefighters move fast.
6. People (who believe in magic) are superstitious.
7. (That he won) is exciting.
8. (Since the buzzer had sounded,) Chip's shot didn't count.
9. The dog (that ran away) is mine.
10. I looked more carefully for my contact lens (than I had before.)

B. Adverb Clauses Copy each (adverb clause) in the following sentences. Underline the subject of the clause once and the verb twice. Then write the word or (words the clause modifies.)

1. (Because Rhonda was late,) she (missed) lunch.
2. (When autumn came,) the birds (flew) south.
3. (Since we had time,) we (saw) the movie twice.
4. We (could) barely (keep) our balance (when we walked on the ice.)
5. (Wherever Mary went,) her dog and cat (would follow) her.)
6. Everyone (stood) (when the judge entered the court-room.
7. Some people (worry) (when they must give a speech.)

623

Additional Exercises

These Additional Exercises may be used for additional practice of the concepts presented in this Section. Each exercise focuses on a single concept, and should be used after the page number indicated in parentheses.

Review

If you have not assigned these Additional Exercises before this time, you can also use them as an excellent Section Review.

8. Laura (cried) (as she peeled the onions.)
9. (Until everyone is home,) Dad (cannot) (sleep.)
10. Jack (painted) the house (after we bought a new ladder.)

C. **Adjective Clauses**   Copy the (adjective clauses) in the following sentences. Underline the subject of the clause once and the verb twice. Write the (word) each clause modifies.

1. This is the (school) (that won the championship.)
2. The (bicycle) (that you wanted) has been sold.
3. (Aaron,) (who is only five years old,) found a dollar bill.
4. Do you know the name of the (person) (who invented the television?)
5. The (bus) (that is parked at the corner) only goes down State Street.
6. Do you remember the (day) (that you met Emily?)
7. Washington was a (man) (who was known for his honesty.)
8. Meet me at the (shop) (that has a blue awning.)
9. The (plane,) (which was running short of fuel,) landed.
10. This is my friend (Davis,) (whom I told you about.)

D. **Noun Clauses**   Copy the noun clause in each sentence. Underline the subject of the clause once and the verb twice. Tell whether the clause is used as a subject, direct object, object of a preposition, or predicate noun.

S. 1. (How viruses make us sick) is a mystery.
D.O. 2. Vin asked (if he could replace the broken window.)
D.O. 3. I wonder (where fireflies go during the day.)
O.P. 4. Ms. Nolan does not agree (with what you said.)
S. 5. (Whoever comes in the room) next wins the door prize.
P.N. 6. That is (what I would like.)
D.O. 7. Maria said (that she had run four miles.)
D.O. 8. Marshall shouted (that there was danger ahead.)
D.O. 9. Mom asked (where we had been.)
S. 10. (Whoever washed those windows) did a good job.

MIXED REVIEW

Using Complex Sentences

A. Finding subordinate clauses Copy the (subordinate clause) from each of the following sentences. Underline the subject once and the verb twice.

1. (After she practiced,) Alice recited her lines smoothly.
2. Karl is the player (who scored the winning touchdown.)
3. (Since we all agreed,) we decided to work together.
4. Call me (if you need advice.)
5. Adam made the error (because he didn't follow directions.)
6. Aunt Susan will meet us in St. Paul (if she can.)
7. (When we reached the top of the hill,) we rested in the shade.
8. Students (who lose their ID cards) must pay for new ones.
9. (If those gloves are too big,) try this pair.
10. The hat (that she wore) attracted attention.

B. Identifying subordinate clauses Copy the (subordinate clauses) from the following sentences. Label each *Adverb*, *Adjective*, or *Noun* to show what kind of clause it is.

Adv. 1. Pam took notes (while she listened to the lecture.)
N. 2. (That he won) surprised us all.
Adv. 3. I brought my boots (because it might snow.)
Adj. 4. People (who are busy) must be well organized.
Adv. 5. James cheered (when he heard the news.)
N. 6. My little sister does (whatever I do.)
Adj. 7. The fabric that I used) is very inexpensive.
Adv. 8. (When Wendy (studies,) she needs complete quiet.
N. 9. No one knew (how the fire started.)
Adj. 10. Is she the woman (who interviewed you?)

625

C. Identifying fragments and kinds of sentences
Decide whether the following groups of words are sentences or fragments. Copy any sentences and punctuate them correctly. Then write *Simple*, *Compound*, or *Complex* to show what kind of sentence each is. If a group is not a sentence, write *Fragment*.

F. 1. Whenever I hear a siren

Cp. 2. We tried to make applesauce, but it didn't taste right.

Cx. 3. No one who saw the movie liked it.

S. 4. This suitcase has not been claimed.

Cx. 5. I'd like to see how Brenda cuts hair.

F. 6. That we wanted for the display

S. 7. London, Bristol, and Manchester were the main stops on their tour of Great Britain.

Cx. 8. The umpire who made the call admitted his mistake.

Cp. 9. Sandra started the job, and Megan finished it.

S. 10. I called the doctor and made an appointment.

D. Using subordinate clauses Write a complex sentence for each of the following subordinate clauses. Sentences will vary.

1. while the snow fell
2. where this highway ends
3. what the symbols represent
4. that the storm is moving closer
5. which I applied for
6. when the band played
7. until the road is repaved
8. before the movie begins
9. whoever finds my ring
10. although the news was good

USING GRAMMAR IN WRITING
Using Complex Sentences

A. In China, the most respected people are the oldest people. Grandparents have the most honored place in each family. Think of someone you know who is at least sixty years old. Write a paragraph that tells why you respect him or her. You might write about his or her accomplishments. You might mention some good advice this person gave you. Maybe you admire the way this older person treats other people. Include at least three complex sentences. Listed below are some subordinating conjunctions that you can use in those sentences.

although	if	whatever	while
as long as	so that	when	that
because	until	whenever	who, whom, whose
before	unless	wherever	which

B. You are a famous mystery story writer. Your editor gives you the beginning of a mystery story. Complete the sentence as you wish. Then continue the story. Include at least four complex sentences in the story. Some of the subordinate clauses should be adjective and adverb clauses.

Although the windows of the old house were boarded up, —————————.

C. One of the differences between stories written for children and stories written for adults is word choice. Another is sentence length. Think of a famous fable, such as "The Tortoise and the Hare." First write it for children. Then write it for older readers. In your second version, use a more advanced vocabulary. Also use several complex sentences.

Using Grammar in Writing

These challenging and enjoyable activities allow the students to see how the concepts of grammar, usage, and mechanics may be applied in actual writing situations. Each exercise is designed to allow students practice in several of the skills they have acquired in this Section. The activities also provide opportunities for students to write creatively about a wide variety of interesting and unusual subjects.

627

CUMULATIVE REVIEW
The Sentence

A. Identifying kinds of sentences Copy the following sentences. Insert the correct punctuation. After each sentence, write *D* for declarative, *INT* for interrogative, *IMP* for imperative, or *E* for exclamatory. Underline each subject once and each verb twice.

IMP 1. Plan your route carefully. (You)

D 2. Dr. Watanabe is a dentist.

INT 3. Where is the suntan oil?

E 4. What a remarkable athlete he is!

D 5. Brenda planted an herb garden.

IMP 6. Prepare the outline for your speech tonight. (You)

INT 7. Is that stone an emerald?

E 8. Look out for those wasps! (You)

D 9. Waterfowl decoys are used by hunters.

IMP 10. Turn on the projector, please. (You)

B. Understanding agreement in sentences Number your paper from 1 to 15. Write the correct word from the two given in parentheses.

1. There (was, were) forty members in Pep Club last year.
2. He and she (does, do) a skit about news anchor people.
3. The short stories in this book (is, are) all science fiction.
4. Here (is, are) the markers and the name tags.
5. Each of the men carried (his, their) own canoe.
6. You (was, were) the first runner to cross the finish line.
7. Either Bess or her brothers (walk, walks) the dog.
8. He (don't, doesn't) appreciate modern art.

628

9. Few of the movies (seem, <u>seems</u>) recent.

10. The pasta in those packages (<u>is</u>, are) homemade.

11. One of my friends (play, <u>plays</u>) the oboe in the community orchestra.

12. The grown chimpanzees shared (its, <u>their</u>) bananas with the baby chimps.

13. Where (was, <u>were</u>) the tickets to the play?

14. The piano and your desk (<u>need</u>, needs) polishing.

15. Have the ushers taken (<u>their</u>, its) places yet?

C. Correcting fragments and run-on sentences The following paragraph contains fragments and run-on sentences. Rewrite the paragraph. Use capitalization and punctuation to correct the fragments and run-ons. Do not add or change any words.

The potato, a vegetable familiar to everybody, originally grew wild in South America. When the Spanish conquered the Incas in Peru in the 16th century, They introduced the potato to Europe. It is an amazing vegetable; it is quite nutritious. An average-sized potato, without rich toppings, contains only about 100 calories. And is 99.9 percent fat-free. One potato provides 50% of the daily adult vitamin C requirement, a potato also provides many of the B vitamins and iron. In addition, potatoes will grow almost anywhere. Except in a jungle. A potato crop, Matures faster than corn, wheat, or rice; the potato is a great bargain!

D. Writing good sentences Rewrite each of the following sentences. Follow the directions in the parentheses.

1. Belinda ordered two posters from the catalog. for her bedroom. (Add the prepositional phrase *for her bedroom*.)

2. Mrs. Hopper peeled the apples. and She made apple crisp. (Combine these two simple sentences into one with a compound predicate.)

629

3. Mr. Schwartz raced through the airport. *[, but]* His plane had already left. (Combine these two simple sentences into a compound sentence using **,but**.)

4. Debby *[∧ and Fred]* raked the leaves. ~~Fred did, too.~~ (Combine these two simple sentences into one with a compound subject.)

5. The taxes must be raised. *[, or]* The educational programs will be cut back. (Combine these two simple sentences into one compound sentence using **,or**.)

6. The Washington Monument *[∧ which has 898 steps,]* is 555 feet, 5⅛ inches tall. ~~It has 898 steps.~~ (Combine these two simple sentences into one complex sentence using *which*.)

7. Sally has found a summer job already. *[∧ although]* Kevin and Naomi have not. (Combine these two simple sentences into one complex sentence using *although*.)

8. Johnny Morris *[∧ , who once played professional football,]* reports on sports for a Chicago television station. ~~He once played professional football.~~ (Combine these two simple sentences into one complex sentence using *who*.)

9. Peter studied last night. (Change this NV sentence to one with a NVN pattern.) Sentences will vary.

10. Coach Jaworski is a patient man. (Change this N LV N sentence into one with a N LV ADJ pattern.) Sentences will vary.

Capitalization

Section Objectives

1. To understand and apply the general rules for capitalizing proper nouns and adjectives, the pronoun *I*, and abbreviations

2. To understand and apply the rules for capitalization of first words and for capitalization in letters, outlines, and titles

Preparing the Students

Students have been dealing with capitalization since they first began to read and write, so they should already have some appreciation for the aid it provides in communicating ideas clearly. Ask them to list as many situations as they can think of that require the capitalization of words. Have students give specific examples for each situation. Read the introduction on page 631.

In student writing, many of the errors of capitalization are due to carelessness. Once the basic rules have been reviewed in this section, encourage students to proofread and edit all written work. Students should also be on the lookout for unnecessary capitalization.

Additional Resources

Diagnostic Test — page 8 in the test booklet

Mastery Test — pages 69–70 in the test booklet

Additional Exercises — pages 646–650 in the student text

Practice Book — pages 226–232

Duplicating Masters — pages 226–232

Special Populations — See special section at the back of this Teacher's Edition.

The use of capital letters is called **capitalization**. When you use a capital letter at the beginning of a word, you *capitalize* the word.

Capital letters are used to make reading easier. They call attention to the beginnings of sentences and to certain special words.

Objective

To understand and apply the general rules for capitalizing proper nouns and adjectives, the pronoun *I*, and abbreviations

Presenting the Lesson

1. Read and discuss pages 632–633. The correct capitalization of titles and of names that indicate family relationships may need some extra discussion.

2. Assign and discuss Exercises A and B on page 634. They provide good proofreading practice. Allow students to complete them independently before discussing them with the group. Be sure students are able to support their corrections with rules.

3. Read and discuss the capitalization rules on pages 635–636. Ask students to give you other examples of words following each rule.

4. Assign and discuss Exercises A and B on pages 636–637. Again be sure students are able to support their corrections with rules.

5. Read and discuss page 637. Ask students for other examples.

6. Assign and discuss Exercises A and B on page 638.

7. Read and discuss pages 638–639. Have students explain why some names of school subjects are capitalized and others are not.

8. Assign and discuss Exercises A and B on page 640. Be sure students are able to support their corrections with rules.

632

Proper Nouns and Adjectives

Capitalize proper nouns and proper adjectives.

A **proper noun** is the name of a particular person, place or thing.

> Victoria   **S**weden   **C**ongress

A **common noun** is the general name of a person, place, or thing. It is not capitalized.

> woman   nation   government

A **proper adjective** is an adjective formed from a proper noun.

> **V**ictorian   **S**wedish   **C**ongressional

Names of Persons

Capitalize the names of persons and also the initials or abbreviations that stand for those names.

> Linda **S. A**dams   **W**illiam **J. F**ranklin, **J**r.
> Linda **S**usan **A**dams   **W**illiam **J**ames **F**ranklin, **J**unior

Capitalize titles used with names of persons and abbreviations standing for those titles.

> **D**octor Maria A. Sandquist   **R**ev. M. R. Eaton
> **D**r. John J. DeBender   **P**resident Lincoln

The titles **M**r., **M**rs., **M**s., and **M**iss are always capitalized.

> **M**r. Kotter   **M**iss Brooks   **M**s. Gloria Thomas

Do not capitalize a title that is not followed by the name of a person.

> One of our police **c**aptains is Daniel Jeffries.
> The **p**resident was Mary Gomez.
> My mother is a **d**octor.

632

Capitalize titles of people and groups whose rank is very important.

Titles of important people, such as those of the President and Vice-President of the United States, are capitalized even though these titles are used without proper names.

> The **V**ice-**P**resident presides over the sessions of the Senate. The **Q**ueen attended the opening of Parliament.

Family Relationships

Capitalize such words as *mother, father, aunt,* and *uncle* when these words are used as names.

> Hello, **M**other. Is **D**ad home yet?

These words are not used as names when they are preceded by a possessive or by such words as *a* or *the*.

> I talked with my **m**other about it.

The Pronoun I

Capitalize the pronoun I.

> Did you get the postcard that **I** sent?

The Supreme Being and Sacred Writings

Capitalize all words referring to God, to the Holy Family, and to religious scriptures.

God	the **B**ible	the **T**orah
the **F**ather	the **G**ospel	the **T**almud
the **L**ord	**A**llah	the **K**oran
Jesus **C**hrist	the **H**oly **S**pirit	the **B**lessed **V**irgin

633

Individualizing the Lesson

Less-Advanced Students

1. Work with students in completing the exercises. Have them tell which rule applies whenever they capitalize a word.

2. Have students search newspapers and magazines for examples of the different types of capitalized words. Discuss the rules that apply to each.

Advanced Students

1. Have students make maps of your community, labeling points of interest with properly capitalized names. Display the maps in the classroom.

2. Have students write reports on geographical or historical topics. Ask them to exchange reports to check for proper capitalization.

3. Have students make up sets of flashcards with sentences that contain words which need capitalizing. Also, have them include words that are capitalized and shouldn't be. These cards can then be used with your less-advanced students.

Optional Practice

Have students copy the following list, changing small letters to capital letters where necessary.

1. margaret thatcher, the prime minister of england
2. king khalid of saudi arabia
3. dwight d. eisenhower, a general who became president
4. senator gary hart, a senator from colorado
5. thomas bradley, the mayor of los angeles
6. professor william lapinski, a math instructor at washington university

633

7. mother teresa, winner of the nobel peace prize

8. george orwell, a well known english writer

2. Have students list names and titles to identify themselves, such as *Sue, Mrs. Stover's daughter, a student.* Have them review their lists, making sure they have capitalized each proper noun.

3. Divide the class into four teams. On the chalkboard list four categories such as *cars, movies, countries, singers.* The teams must write as many proper nouns as they can think of that fit into the categories in a given time. The team that comes up with the most correct answers wins. Have the winning team list their answers on the board.

4. Conduct a capitalization bee, following the procedures for a spelling bee. Provide names and titles to each team alternatively, drawing from the examples given in this section. Ask whether the word should be capitalized. Students who give incorrect answers are eliminated from the game.

Extending the Lesson

1. Distribute copies of the following paragraph. Have students find the errors in capitalization and write the words correctly.

Our class took a great trip to washington, d.c. last spring. We stayed at the mayflower hotel, which was close to everything. During our tour of the white house, we were surprised when the first lady made an unexpected appearance. We visited the national zoological park and were amazed at how large the chinese pandas were. Two students got lost that afternoon at rock creek park, but we soon found them at

Exercises   Use capital letters correctly.

A.   Number your paper from 1 to 10. Write the following sentences, changing small letters to capital letters wherever necessary. One sentence is correct.

1. The president of the united states was there.

2. My mother said, "Ask dad if he brought the camera."

3. Four players in the baseball hall of fame are ernie banks, jackie robinson, sandy koufax, and mickey mantle.

4. Do you know the prince of monaco's last name?

5. We made french onion soup last night.

6. My sister linda is personnel director.

7. My favorite aunt is aunt ginny.

C 8. She is my father's sister.

9. Moslems study the koran; jews study the torah.

10. Two well-known women in the game of golf are babe didrikson zaharias and patty berg.

B.   Write the following sentences, changing small letters to capital letters wherever necessary. One sentence is correct.

1. Prince charles and queen elizabeth attended the reception.

2. On monday i had an appointment with the dentist.

3. The names on the door were dr. natalie j. sanders and martin able, jr.

4. Christopher columbus sailed under the spanish flag.

5. The coast was explored by portuguese sailors.

6. Edmund p. hillary climbed mt. everest.

7. The queen of england made him a knight.

8. Once he was a british spy.

C 9. Cheryl was elected president of our club.

10. Last spring, we saw hana mandlikova and chris evert lloyd play in several tennis tournaments.

Geographical Names

In a geographical name, capitalize the first letter of each word except articles and prepositions.

The article *the* appearing before a geographical name is not part of the geographical name. Therefore, it is not capitalized.

Continents:	North America, South America, Asia, Europe
Bodies of water:	the Indian Ocean, Lake Superior, the Jordan River, Cape Cod Bay, the Caspian Sea
Land forms:	the Rockies, the Sinai Peninsula, the Grand Canyon, the Syrian Desert
Political units:	Delaware, the District of Columbia, the British Isles, the Commonwealth of Massachusetts, the West Indies, San Francisco
Public areas:	Gettysburg National Park, Fort Niagara, Mount Rushmore, Statue of Liberty
Roads and highways:	Central Avenue, Route 66, Garden State Parkway, Van Buren Avenue, the Ohio Turnpike, State Street

Directions and Sections

Capitalize names of sections of the country.

Cotton was king in the South.
Cities in the Southwest are flourishing.
The legends of the West are fascinating.

Capitalize proper adjectives derived from names of sections of the country.

an Eastern school   a Western concept   Southern hospitality

635

the spot where the creek flows into the potomac river. Several students were able to climb to the top of the washington monument. The rest of us, who took the elevators, laughed when we saw how out of breath the climbers were.

When we went on a walking tour of embassy row, we saw sheik yamahmi entering the saudi arabian embassy. At our farewell dinner that evening, we all sampled maryland crabcakes for the first time at phil's restaurant. There was still so much to see. As we rode home on the amtrak train the next day, many of us dreamed of a return visit.

2. You may want to have your more-advanced students work on this exercise or divide the class into small groups. Give students copies of the following list of countries. Instruct the students to write the proper adjective that describes people and things of each country. Make sure they know where they can look to find the information (dictionary, encyclopedia, social studies text). Remind them to capitalize when necessary. After everyone is finished, discuss the answers.

china, mexico, austria, norway, japan, sweden, italy, france, spain, ireland, britain, australia, brazil, africa, poland, canada, india, egypt, russia

Chinese, Mexican, Austrian, Norwegian, Japanese, Swedish, Italian, French, Spanish, Irish, British, Australian, Brazilian, African, Polish, Canadian, Indian, Egyptian, Russian

Do not capitalize directions of the compass.

They flew **e**ast through the storm.
Sue lives on the **n**orth side of the street.
The hurricane moved **n**orthward.

Do not capitalize adjectives derived from words indicating direction.

a **s**outherly course   an **e**astern route

Exercises   Use capital letters correctly.

A.   Number your paper from 1 to 10. Find the words in the following phrases that should be capitalized. Write the words after the proper number, using the necessary capital letters.

1. near the gulf of mexico
2. represents the seventh congressional district
3. pike's peak near colorado springs
4. the pacific coast beaches
5. one block north of first avenue
6. in the catskill mountains
7. a street in paris, france
8. donner pass over the rockies
9. the transamerica pyramid in san francisco
10. across the great plains of the west

B.   Follow the directions for Exercise A.

1. Colonel Powell explored the grand canyon in arizona.
2. The gateway arch in st. louis, missouri, is 630 feet high.
3. In the carolinas we found out about southern hospitality.
4. The southernmost continent is antarctica.
5. We drove from toronto to detroit on the macdonald-cartier highway.

636

6. We saw buffalo at ^{C}custer ^{N}national ^{M}monument.

7. A toll bridge extends over the ^{S}straits of ^{M}mackinac.

8. The ^{A}arlington ^{M}memorial ^{B}bridge extends across the ^{P}po-
    tomac ^{R}river to the ^{L}lincoln ^{M}memorial.

9. Our new neighbors come from ^{S}southeast ^{A}asia.

10. Is the ^{U}united ^{N}nations ^{B}building on ^{F}fifth ^{A}avenue in ^{N}new
    ^{Y}york ^{C}city?

Names of Organizations and Institutions

Capitalize the names of organizations and institutions, including political parties, governmental bodies or agencies, schools, colleges, churches, hospitals, clubs, businesses, and abbreviations of these names.

General Motors Corporation   Stacy Memorial Hospital
Nichols Junior High School   Burns and White, Inc.

Do not capitalize words such as *school, college, church,* and *hospital* when they are not used as names.

the emergency entrance at the hospital
the basketball team at our school

Names of Events, Documents, and Periods of Time

Capitalize the names of historical events, documents, and periods of time.

Industrial Revolution   Bill of Rights
World War II   Middle Ages

Months, Days, and Holidays

Capitalize the names of months, days, and holidays.

February   Wednesday   Labor Day
April   Sunday   New Year's Day

637

Exercises   **Use capital letters correctly.**

A.   Copy the following, changing small letters to capitals or capitals to small letters where necessary.

1. the house of represen-
   tatives
2. a Weekend in june
3. Eisenhower high school
4. the Battle of bunker
   hill
5. fire prevention Week

6. Industries and Colleges
7. Louisiana state university
8. the month of march
9. veterans' day, novem-
   ber 11
10. the civil war

B.   Write each sentence, using the necessary capital letters.

1. We saw the chicago bears play the new york jets.
2. One of the largest companies is xerox corporation.
3. The emancipation proclamation was written during
   the civil war.
4. The middletown team will play washington high.
5. In new orleans, mardi gras is celebrated with parades.
6. The first ten amendments to the constitution of the
   united states are called the bill of rights.
7. The first monday in september is labor day.
8. In our anthology, *Black Roots*, we read selections by
   maya angelou and anne moody.
9. Our class will visit the museum in april.
10. The period of the 1930's in the united states was
    known as the great depression.

Languages, Races, Nationalities, Religions

Capitalize the names of languages, races, nationalities, and religions, and also adjectives derived from them.

Irish linen	German band	French language
Italian heritage	Lutheranism	African art

School Subjects

Do not capitalize the names of school subjects, except course names followed by a number.

Algebra I   History of Civilization II   social studies

Remember that the names of languages are always capitalized.

English   Spanish   Hebrew   German

Ships, Trains, Airplanes, Automobiles

Capitalize the names of ships, trains, airplanes, and automobiles.

U.S.S. Constitution   *City of New Orleans*   *Concorde*
Firebird

Abbreviations

You know that an **abbreviation** is a shortened form of a word. You also know that abbreviations of proper nouns and proper adjectives are capitalized.

Capitalize the abbreviations *B.C.* and *A.D.*

Julius Caesar was born in the year 100 **B.C.**
Christopher Columbus landed on San Salvador in **A.D.** 1492.

You know that *B.C.* and *A.D.* are used to refer to time. *B.C.* is the abbreviation for *before Christ*. *A.D.* stands for Latin words meaning "in the year of the Lord."

Capitalize the abbreviations *A.M.* and *P.M.*

The bus leaves at 8:05 **A.M.** and returns at 5:30 **P.M.**

Exercises   Use capital letters correctly.

A.   Number your paper from 1 to 15. Copy each of the following groups of words. Wherever necessary, change small letters to capitals.

1. ^Rroman ^Ccatholic
2. ^Iitalian food
3. studying ^Hhistory I
4. bought a new ^Fford
5. the ^Sspanish language
6. 2:30 p.m. ^{P.M.}
7. 10:00 a.m. ^{A.M.}
8. the year 40 b.c. ^{B.C.}
9. a.d. 300 ^{A.D.}
10. the s.s. *france* ^{S.S. F}
11. math problems
12. ^Ffrench bread
13. printed in ^Eenglish
14. a ^Sscottish writer
15. ^Aamerican citizen

B.   Number your paper from 1 to 10. Copy each of the following sentences. Wherever necessary, change small letters to capitals.

1. Although ^Iillinois is called the ^Lland of ^Llincoln, ^Aabraham ^Llincoln was born in ^Kkentucky.
2. A ^Rroman emperor gave his name to the month of ^Aaugust.
3. This year I am taking ^Wworld ^Hhistory II, ^Eenglish, math, and art.
4. The sign said that banking hours are from 8:30 a.m. ^{A.M.} to 5:00 p.m. ^{P.M.}
5. We rode the ^Ssan ^Ffrancisco ^Zzephyr to ^Ddenver.
6. Every ^Ttuesday and ^Tthursday the ^Ggerman band plays polkas.
7. My sister can speak ^Sspanish, but she cannot write it.
8. We will see the ^Qqueen ^Eelizabeth II the first weekend in ^Mmay.
9. Mother will complete her master's degree at ^Ppurdue ^Uuniversity next ^Aaugust.
10. The ^Ddatsun is a ^Jjapanese automobile.

First Words

Sentences

Capitalize the first word of every sentence.

My sister plays basketball. **S**he is the captain of the team.

Poetry

Capitalize the first word in most lines of poetry.

A word is dead
When it is said,
　Some say.
I say it just
Begins to live
　That day.
　　　　　　—EMILY DICKINSON

Sometimes, especially in modern poetry, the lines of a poem do not begin with capital letters.

Quotations

Capitalize the first word of a direct quotation.

When you use a **quotation,** you use the words of a speaker or writer. If you give the *exact* words of the speaker or writer, you are giving a **direct quotation**. If you change the words of the speaker or writer to your own words, you are giving an **indirect quotation**. Be sure that you can tell the difference between the two kinds.

Here are two examples of direct quotations:

"**C**lose the window, please," Ms. Smith said to Jerry.
Sarah said, "**M**y parents bought a new car."

Objective

To understand and apply the rules for capitalization of first words and for capitalization in letters, outlines, and titles

Presenting the Lesson

1. Read and discuss pages 641–642. Discuss with the students that capitalization in poetry is a matter of a poet's style. Many contemporary poets have abandoned traditional forms for the sake of originality. Explain to students that breaking these rules is done purposely and that for a poet to make the creative choice, he or she must first be aware of the standard rule.

2. It might be helpful to do Exercise A on pages 642–643 with the class and then assign and discuss Exercise B.

3. Read and discuss pages 643–645.

4. Assign and discuss Exercises A and B on page 645.

Individualizing the Lesson

Less-Advanced Students

1. Work with students in completing the exercises. Have them identify which rule is applied each time they capitalize a word.

2. Provide students with examples of poems and outlines with all capital letters missing. Have students rewrite the examples putting in the correct capital letters.

Advanced Students

Here are two examples of an indirect quotation:

> Ms. Smith asked Jerry to close the window.
> Sarah said that her parents had bought a new car.

Notice that the first word of an indirect quotation is not capitalized.

Sometimes a direct quotation is interrupted by explanatory words like *she said*. Here is an example

> "Well," she said, "you may be right."

Notice that the first word of the second part of this direct quotation is not capitalized since it is not the first word of a sentence. When a direct quotation is interrupted in this way, it is called a **divided quotation**.

If the second part of a divided quotation begins a new sentence, capitalize the first word as you would in any sentence.

> "I don't know," he said. "You may be right."
> "We met Ellen," said Jane. "She was with her father."

Exercises   Use capital letters correctly.

A.   Using correct capitalization, write the words that need capital letters.

1. sailing is a favorite sport for visitors to cape cod.
2. uganda, kenya, and chad are nations in africa.
3. thanksgiving is always the fourth thursday in november.
4. a harvest mouse goes scampering by
   with silver claws and a silver eye.
5. the doors open early. no one can enter after 2 p.m.
6. "hi," said bill. "we won. are mom and dad home?"
7. hope is the thing with feathers
   that perches in the soul,
   and sings the tune without the words,
   and never stops at all.

8. ^Y"you are late," said ^Bb. ^Jj. ^Ppate.
9. ^T"there's no school tomorrow," said ^Hheather. ^I"it's ^Vvet-
erans' ^Dday."
10. ^Wwhat's that old saying about "a month of ^Ssundays"?

B. Follow the directions for Exercise A.

1. ^Wwhat do the shoppers want? ^Tthey want more parking.
2. ^Bbarton ^Iindustries, ^Iinc., is constructing a new plant
near ^Cchicago.
3. ^Tthe ^Ggrand ^Ccanyon is a national park. It is in north-
western ^Aarizona.
4. ^Yyou can see the ^Ccolorado ^Rriver from ^Ttoroweap ^Ppoint.
5. ^Ssome ^Hhavasupai ^Iindians live at the foot of the gorge.
6. ^Mmany years ago, ^Mmother ^Sshipton made rhymes about
the future.
7. ^Ffor every parcel ^Ii stoop down to seize,
^Ii lose some other off my arms and knees.
8. ^Ccall ^Ddisc ^Jj. ^Ddan. ^Aask him to play your favorite song.
9. "^Nnurse," said ^Ddr. ^Ddee, "hold this while ^Ii get some alco-
hol."
10. ^Iit was many and many a year ago,
^Iin a kingdom by the sea,
^Tthat a maiden there lived whom you may know
^Bby the name of ^Aannabel ^Llee;

Letters

Capitalize the first word, words like *Sir* and *Madam,* and the name of the person addressed in the greeting of a letter.

Dear **S**ir or **M**adam: **D**ear **M**rs. **C**ooper: **D**ear **R**ick and **J**ohn,
Dear **M**r. **H**errara: **D**ear **M**s. **A**shley: **D**ear **A**unt **M**arge,

In the closing, capitalize the first word only.

Sincerely yours,   **Y**ours very truly,

Outlines

Capitalize the first word of each line of an outline.

    II. Things to be considered
       A. Breed

          1. Kinds of dogs
          2. Uses of dogs
       B. Training

Titles

Capitalize the first word and all important words in chapter titles, titles of magazine articles, titles of short stories, essays, or single poems, and titles of songs or short pieces of music.

Chapter:	Chapter 2, "The First Settlers"
Magazine article:	"Taking Color Pictures"
Short story:	"To Build a Fire"
Essay:	"On the Importance of Friendship"
Poem:	"Richard Cory"
Song:	"The Star-Spangled Banner"

Capitalize the first word and all important words in titles of books, newspapers, magazines, plays, movies, titles of television and radio programs, works of art, and long musical compositions.

When you write titles like these, underline them. (When these titles are printed, they are *italicized*.)

Book:	*I Am the Cheese*
Newspaper:	*Boston Globe*
Magazine:	*Reader's Digest*
Play:	*The Miracle Worker*
Movie:	*Raiders of the Lost Ark*
Televison program:	*Today*
Work of art:	Rodin's *The Thinker*
Long Musical Composition:	*Amahl and the Night Visitors* [opera]

The words *a, an,* and *the* (called **articles**) are not capitalized unless they come at the beginning of a title. Conjunctions and prepositions (such as *and* and *of*) are not capitalized either, except at the beginning of a title.

Exercises Use capital letters correctly.

A. Copy the following, using the correct capital letters.

1. sincerely yours,
2. the poem, "my last duchess"
3. a *reader's digest* article
4. the painting, *blue boy*
5. *rocky*, the award-winning film
6. a *daily news* subscription
7. the magazine article "sailing the skies of summer"
8. the cast of *our town*
9. an early novel, *the deerslayer*
10. dear ms. martin

B. Follow the directions for Exercise A.

1. mother and dad went to see *the wiz* in chicago.
2. they sang "the sounds of silence" for an encore.
3. *the girl at the open half door* is in the Art Institute.
4. our copy of *the detroit free press* ended up on the roof.
5. during christmas vacation, we saw *the nutcracker suite.*
6. read "builders for a golden age" in *american heritage.*
7. dear mrs. gomez:
   your subscription to *national geographic* ends today.
8. "the outcasts of poker flat"
9. mother reads *the wall street journal.*
10. dear sir:
    have you read *the daily times* lately?

Additional Exercises

These Additional Exercises may be used for additional practice of the concepts presented in this Section. Each exercise focuses on a single concept, and should be used after the page number indicated in parentheses.

Review

If you have not assigned these Additional Exercises before this time, you can also use them as an excellent Section Review.

ADDITIONAL EXERCISES

Capitalization

A. Capital Letters Copy the following sentences. Change small letters to capital letters wherever necessary.

1. Some of harriet s. adam's pen names were laura lee hope, franklin dixon, and carolyn keene.
2. The atlanta falcons will play the new orleans saints on sunday, december 10.
3. They asked for god's blessing on their work.
4. Should i use an irish accent to read my lines?
5. Did you videotape the wedding of prince charles and princess diana?
6. Our family doctor is dr. lopez.
7. Maybe mr. and mrs. moss have no telephone.
8. On her patrols, sergeant pahls uses a two-way radio.
9. Did father sweeney read from the bible in latin?
10. My father got a letter from the president of the united states.

B. Capital Letters Copy the following sentences, changing small letters to capital letters wherever necessary.

1. The first nation in which women got the right to vote was new zealand.
2. Are the west indies in the caribbean sea?
3. The train crossed the rio grande into mexico.
4. Mr. davis now has an office on wall street.
5. Do people from florida have southern accents?
6. My cousin owns a farm in the midwest.
7. Villagers in uganda built a runway so that a doctor could visit by plane.
8. One seaport city in poland is named gdansk.

9. We drove south through the great smoky mountains.
10. Lake mead is near grand canyon national park.

C. Capital Letters Copy the following sentences, changing small letters to capital letters wherever necessary.

1. Jim is an orderly at community general hospital.
2. The fourth of july is a holiday celebrating the signing of the declaration of independence.
3. On the first monday in september, labor day is observed.
4. Sandra Day O'Connor was appointed to the supreme court on september 25, 1981.
5. When was the period of history known as the dark ages?
6. My mother is a student at savannah state college.
7. At sundown, passover will begin.
8. My uncle is a member of the urban league, a national organization.
9. When did that war become known as world war I?
10. April fool's day began as a celebration of spring.

D. Capital Letters Copy the following sentences, changing small letters to capital letters wherever necessary.

1. Next year I will take woodworking 200 and art 201.
2. Ty's favorite subjects are history and english.
3. The *invincible* is a british battleship.
4. The *cardinal* pulled out of the station at 6:00 p.m.
5. The Wailing Wall is part of a temple built in 515 b.c.
6. Is your jazz dance class at 8:00 a.m. or 8:00 p.m.?
7. A german ship sank the *lusitania*, a british ship, in 1915.
8. By a.d. 500, Ireland had become a christian country.
9. Mecca and Medina are holy places to moslems.
10. An early compact car was the volkswagen.

647

E. Capital Letters
Copy the following sentences. Change small letters to capital letters wherever necessary.

1. a late blizzard struck. the first game was cancelled.
2. "we're lost," lee said. "who has a compass?"
3. "that," said betsy, "is none of your business."
4. dr. sanders said he would be happy to meet with us.
5. who said, "lafayette, we are here"? what did it mean?
6. "watch willy," said the coach. "he dribbles perfectly."
7. Cora asked if she could borrow my mexican necklace.
8. "nobody," said sonya, "is angry with you."
9. pandora promised that she would not open the box.
10. will there really be a morning?
    is there such a thing as day?
    could I see it from the mountains
    if I were as tall as they?

                             —EMILY DICKINSON

F. Capital Letters
Follow the directions for Exercise E.

1. the chapter in the manual is "know your computer."
2. dear ms. taylor:
    it's time to renew your subscription to *ebony*.
3. dear madam or sir:
    you can have *the herald* delivered to your doorstep.
4. the novel *the hobbit* is by j. r. r. tolkien.
5. there are many choruses to "yankee doodle."
6. the class discussed "the black madonna," a short story.
7. carl's essay was titled, "the end of summer."
8. here are your tickets to *a raisin in the sun*.

                                 sincerely yours,
                                 robert c. stone

9. "point of no return" is a short poem by mari evans.
10. III. kinds of religious art
    A. statues
    B. frescoes

MIXED REVIEW

Capitalization

A. Using capitalization correctly Copy the following sentences, changing small letters to capitals where necessary.

1. The ᴰdallas ᶜcowboys play at the ˢsilverdome.
2. The 1984 ˢsummer ᴼolympics were held in ᴸlos ᴬangeles.
3. My ᵁuncle ᴶjosh toured ᶜcanada in a ᶜchevy van.
4. Turn south on ᶠfreeport ᴰdrive.
5. Marge wrote to ᴴhoward ᴸl. ᴮbyrne, ᴶjr., of ᴳgreenleaf ᴮbooks.
6. We listened as ᴿreverend ᴮbrooks read the gospel.
7. Diana, the ᴾprincess of ᵂwales, is married to ᴾprince ᶜcharles.
8. Sam and ᴵi met last summer at ᶜcamp ᴸlincoln.
9. Can ᴰdad drive me to the dentist's office on ˢsaturday morning?
10. I haven't eaten at ᴮburger ᴷking since ᴶjune.

B. Using capitalization correctly in proofreading Proofread the following paragraph. Copy it, using correct capitalization.

My favorite ᴮBaseball team resides in a city ᴵi've never visited. This may seem strange unless you know that the ᴸlos ᴬangeles ᴰdodgers were once a ᴮbrooklyn team. That's right, the ᴮbrooklyn ᴰdodgers were our family team for generations. ᴬa simple move to the ᵂwest ᶜcoast couldn't change that tradition. Another ᶜcalifornia team, the ᴼoakland ᴬathletics, once hailed from ᴷkansas ᶜcity, ᴹmissouri. Professional ᵀTeams are bought and sold often. New owners can take the ᵀTeam to another ᶜCity in the ᵁunited ˢstates. You never know when your loyalty as a ᶠFan will be put to this test.

649

Mixed Review

These exercises provide review of the concepts presented in this Section. Each exercise challenges the students to apply several of the skills they have acquired during previous study. Because the "mixed" feature of these activities makes them more difficult, the teacher may wish to have less-advanced students do them orally or in small groups.

These challenging and enjoyable activities allow the students to see how the concepts of grammar, usage, and mechanics may be applied in actual writing situations. Each exercise is designed to allow students practice in several of the skills they have acquired in this Section. The activities also provide opportunities for students to write creatively about a wide variety of interesting and unusual subjects.

USING MECHANICS IN WRITING
Capitalization

A. The opening sentences of a news story contain the important facts of the story. The sentences often tell *who, what, where, when, why,* and *how.* Write the opening sentences for a story in each of the following sections of a newspaper. Follow the rules for capitalization.

> front page (include the names of a famous person and a country)
> sports section (include the names of a city and a team)
> food section (include a nationality, such as French)
> business section (include the name of a company and a quote by its president)
> entertainment section (include the name of a movie or play, the names of its stars, and a comment by a critic)

Example: **front page**
           In India this morning,
           Mother Teresa of Calcutta
           learned that she had won
           the Nobel Peace Price.

B. What is your favorite magazine? How would you convince others to buy and read it? Using a copy of the magazine, write a short paragraph that will "sell" your magazine. Tell what types of stories are included. Use titles of articles and authors' names in your paragraph. Quote satisfied readers. Remember to follow the rules for capitalization.

Punctuation

Section Objectives

1. To use end marks correctly

2. To use the comma correctly

3. To use the semicolon and the colon correctly

4. To use the hyphen correctly in word division at the end of a line and in compound numbers and other words

5. To use the apostrophe correctly to form possessives, contractions, and plurals

6. To use quotation marks correctly in direct quotations, and to use quotation marks and underlining correctly in titles

Preparing the Students

Present the material in this section periodically rather than as a single unit. If you overview this section at the beginning of the year, you can have students use it as a reference independently.

When introducing the section, discuss the importance of using correct punctuation so that what is written will be clear to anyone who reads it. Read the introduction on page 651.

Additional Resources

Mastery Test — page 9 in the test booklet

Mastery Test — pages 71–72 in the test booklet

Additional Exercises — pages 683–691 in the student text

Practice Book — pages 233–243

Duplicating Masters — pages 233–243

Special Populations — See special section at the back of this Teacher's Edition.

Punctuation is the use of commas, periods, semicolons, and other marks in writing. The marks used are called **punctuation marks.**

Good punctuation will help your readers understand what they read. It will show them where to pause or stop. It will tell them whether they are reading a statement, an exclamation, or a question.

To use end marks correctly

Presenting the Lesson

1. The four kinds of sentences were discussed in Section 1, Part 2. Periods, question marks, and exclamation points were introduced at that time. You may wish to review page 346 while covering the material on pages 652–655.

2. Have students complete Exercises A and B on pages 655–656 themselves. Discuss the exercises. Students should be able to explain the reasons for each punctuation mark used.

Individualizing the Lesson

Less-Advanced Students

1. Write the three end marks on the chalkboard. Review the four types of sentences and their end marks on page 346. Provide several examples of each.

2. Work with students to read the sentences in the exercises aloud and decide what type of sentence each is. Then have the students complete the exercises independently.

Advanced Students

After completing the exercises, have students write two examples of their own for each rule presented in this part. Then they should write the reason for using each end mark.

652

End Marks

The punctuation marks that show where a sentence ends are called **end marks.**

There are three very important end marks: (1) the **period,** (2) the **question mark,** and (3) the **exclamation point.**

The Period

Use a period at the end of a declarative sentence.

A **declarative sentence** is a sentence that makes a statement. It is the kind of sentence you use when you want to tell something.

My sister plays the piano.

A declarative sentence is often shortened to one or two words, for example, in answering a question.

Where are you going to put the ladder?

Over there. (*I am going to put it over there.*)

Use a period at the end of an imperative sentence.

An **imperative sentence** is a sentence that requires or tells someone to do something.

Please open the window.

If the imperative sentence also expresses excitement or emotion, an exclamation point is used after it.

Look out!

Use a period at the end of an indirect question.

An **indirect question** is the part of a statement that tells what someone asked, but that does not give the exact words of the person who asked the question.

652

Judy asked *whether the movie was worth seeing.*

Now compare the indirect question with a **direct question:**

Judy asked, "Is the movie worth seeing?"

A direct question gives the exact words of the person who asked the question. It is always followed by a question mark, as in the above example.

Use a period after an abbreviation or after an initial.

An **abbreviation** is a shortened form of a word. You should know the correct abbreviations for many words.

<blockquote>
in. (*inch or inches*)   Dr. (*Doctor*)

Sept. (*September*)   Tues. (*Tuesday*)
</blockquote>

A name is often shortened to its first letter, or **initial.**

<blockquote>
O. J. Simpson (*Orenthal James Simpson*)

Susan B. Anthony (*Susan Brownell Anthony*)
</blockquote>

Sometimes an abbreviation is made up of two or more parts, each part standing for one or more words. A period is then used after each part.

<blockquote>
B.C. (*Before Christ*)   S. Dak. (*South Dakota*)
</blockquote>

Periods are omitted in some abbreviations. If you are not sure whether an abbreviation should be written with or without periods, look up the abbreviation in your dictionary.

<blockquote>
FM (*frequency modulation*)   UN (*United Nations*)
</blockquote>

Use a period after each number or letter that shows a division of an outline or that precedes an item in a list.

(Outline)	(List)
I. Trees	1. meat
A. Shade trees	2. potatoes
1. Elms	3. ice cream

The Question Mark

Use a question mark at the end of an interrogative sentence.

An **interrogative sentence** is a sentence that asks a question.

> Has anyone seen my dog?

The above sentence gives the exact words of the person who asked the question. It is called a *direct question*. A question mark is used only with a direct question.

Do not use a question mark with an indirect question. Instead, use a period.

An *indirect question* is the part of a statement that tells what someone asked, without giving the exact words.

> Kelly asked *whether anyone had seen her dog.*

The Exclamation Point

Use an exclamation point at the end of an exclamatory sentence.

An **exclamatory sentence** expresses strong feeling, such as excitement or fear.

> What a terrific game that was!

An exclamation point is also used at the end of an imperative sentence that expresses excitement or emotion.

> Hurry up!

Most imperative sentences, however, should be followed by a period.

> Please shut the door.

Use an exclamation point after an interjection or after any other exclamatory expression.

An **interjection** is a word or group of words used to express strong feeling. It is one of the eight parts of speech. Words often used as other parts of speech may become interjections when they express strong feeling.

Oh! How beautiful!   Wow! What an exciting movie!

Avoid using the exclamation point too frequently. Use it only when you are sure it is needed.

Exercises   Use periods, question marks, and exclamation points correctly.

A. Copy these sentences. Supply the missing punctuation.

1. Help! This carton is too heavy for me.
2. On the card was printed "Dr. Stephanie James, D.D.S."
3. Mr. and Mrs. T. A. Stock, Miss Sarah Temple, and Dr. G. B. Torker spoke at the board meeting.
4. How did the cat get into the birdcage?
5. Write to J. B. Lippincott Co., publishers of the book.
6. We listened to the news broadcast at 7:30 A.M.
7. Ms. Sue M. Horton teaches swimming at the Y.M.C.A.
8. Was Mr. J. E. Edwards in Buffalo on June 19, 1985?
9. Look out! That shelf is falling!
10. How peaceful it is here! Is it always this way?

B. Follow the directions for Exercise A.

1. Please let me see that book. Is it yours?
2. Pete asked me whether I had seen Dr. M. J. Thomas.
3. Wow! That was an exciting race!
4. Did Ms. Bryant call Dr. Loras about the appointment?
5. How dare you say that!
6. She lives at 1720 Pennsylvania Avenue, Washington D.C.

Objective

To use the comma correctly

Presenting the Lesson

1. Point out how confusing our written language would be without commas (July 41826 as compared to July 4, 1826; 1000000000 as compared to 1,000,000,000). Read and discuss page 656. Stress the purpose of a comma in clarifying a writer's thoughts.

2. Assign and discuss the exercise on page 657.

3. Read and discuss pages 657–658. Explain that commas used to separate adjectives before a noun give the reader time to see each word separately. If two words belong together to create a single image, the comma is not needed.

4. Assign and discuss Exercises A and B on pages 658–660. You may wish to use the sentences in these exercises for a *Comma Bee* (see **Optional Practice** 1).

5. Read and discuss page 660. Point out how commas are used to set off words in a sentence to insure clarity of thought. Stress the pause and voice-level drop that occurs with interrupters.

6. Assign Exercises A and B on pages 660–661.

7. Read and discuss page 662. Have students think of original sentences using nouns of direct address and appositives.

8. Assign Exercises A and B on pages 663–664.

9. It is suggested that this part of the section, "Commas with Quota-

---

7. My plane left Boston at 11:45 A.M. and arrived in St. Louis at 2:15 P.M.
8. Do Mr. and Mrs. F.L. Schaefer live here?
9. This map of Fresno, California, is drawn on a scale of 1 in. to ¼ mi., isn't it?
10. Sue asked Mr. Cassini if he knew Ms. Williamson or Mrs. Marshall.

The Comma

When you speak, you do not say everything at the same speed. You pause to show that there is a break in your thought. You put words into groups, pausing at the end of the group. You use the pause to help your listeners understand which words go together.

In writing, the comma is used to show which words go together. Commas also show your readers where to pause. If they read right on without pausing, they will be confused.

The Comma To Avoid Confusion

Some sentences can be very confusing if commas are not used in them. Read these two examples of such sentences:

In the morning mail is delivered.

After eating my dad takes a nap.

Now notice how much clearer a sentence is when a comma is used. Read the sentences again.

In the morning, mail is delivered.

After eating, my dad takes a nap.

Use a comma whenever the reader might otherwise be confused.

Exercise   Use a comma to avoid confusion.

Read each of the following sentences. Then write each sentence, using commas to make the meaning clear.

1. When we approached,the house was dark.
2. Before coloring,her little sister put away all her toys.
3. After they had finished,the table was cleared.
4. Sue ordered hot chocolate,and Jo ordered ice cream.
5. By the time she woke up,the neighborhood was very quiet.
6. Circling,the airplane approached the field.
7. When we entered,the room was empty.
8. When the climbers reached the top,coats were necessary.
9. No matter what,I do not want another milkshake.
10. While painting,my sister accidentally broke a window.

Commas in a Series

Use a comma after every item in a series except the last.

In writing, a series consists of three or more items of the same kind. These items may be nouns, verbs, modifiers, phrases, or other parts of the sentence.

A comma is placed after every item in a series except the last. Read these examples:

> We packed, ate, and left for home.
> (The three items in this series are verbs.)

> Tom, Mary, Eve, and Ray won prizes.
> (The four items in this series are nouns.)

> The arms of the machine moved up and down, in and out, and back and forth.
> (The items in this series are the groups of adverbs *up and down, in and out,* and *back and forth.*)

657

tions," be used with the lesson on quotation marks on pages 676–677. You may wish to present it briefly now, and then refer to it later, or save it all for one joint lesson. Read and discuss pages 664–665. Have students look at a section of dialogue in their literature textbooks and examine the punctuation.

10. Assign and discuss the exercise on page 665. Alternate directions for this exercise are to have the students write out the entire sentence each time. This provides practice in placing quotation marks correctly.

11. Read and discuss pages 665–666. Commas in compound sentences were discussed in Section 16. Review the difference between a compound sentence and all other types of compound constructions.

12. Assign and discuss Exercises A and B on pages 666–667.

13. Read and discuss the other uses of commas on pages 667–668. Stress that no comma is needed between the house number and the street name or between state and zip code.

14. Assign and discuss Exercises A and B on pages 668–669.

1. Work with students, having them read each sentence aloud before deciding where the commas should be placed.

2. When discussing the exercises, have the students tell why each comma is placed where it is and which rule applies.

3. Before students begin work on Exercise B on pages 663–664, have them determine which nouns are the appositives.

4. For Exercises A and B on pages 666–667, have the students first identify the conjunction in each sentence and determine whether the conjunction joins two sentences.

Advanced Students

1. For Exercises A and B on pages 658–660, have students tell whether the items in the series are used as nouns, verbs, modifiers, phrases, or other parts of a sentence (omit numbers A1, 4, 6, 8 and B1).

2. After completing the exercise on page 665, have students rewrite three of the direct quotations as indirect quotations.

3. Have students skim through almanacs and other references to find interesting places and dates. Have them copy these, placing the commas in the correct places.

Optional Practice

1. *Comma Bee.* Use sentences from the various exercises from pages 656–669. Divide the class into two teams. The first student on one team is assigned one of the sentences to punctuate. If he or she

We could not decide whether to ride to the old mill, to the beach, or to Sunset Park.

(The items in this series are the phrases *to the old mill, to the beach,* and *to Sunset Park.*)

It was getting dark, a wind blew down from the mountain, and Henry began to wonder where he was.

(The items in this series are sentences.)

Use commas after the adverbs *first, second, third,* and so on.

We had three reasons: first, we weren't interested in fishing; second, we had no transportation; third, we had other things to do.

When two or more adjectives precede a noun, use a comma after each adjective except the last one.

It was a bright, brisk, beautiful day.

Sometimes two adjectives are used together to express a single idea made up of two closely related thoughts. Adjectives used in this way are not usually separated by a comma.

A *little old* man knocked at the door.
A *big red* truck pulled into the driveway.

When you say the two sentences above, notice that you do not pause between the adjectives.

Exercises   Use commas correctly to separate items.

A. Read the following sentences. Write each of the sentences, adding commas where they are needed.

1. These three girls were with us: Michelle Richards, Martha Rose, and Joanne Cary.
2. In his pockets Terry had a bent penny, a pencil stub, about a yard of string, a comb, and two rubber bands.

3. Mrs. Harrison ordered the ginger ale and cola, checked on the supply of paper plates and cups, and called the farmer to get permission for us to picnic.

4. Here are the kinds of sandwiches we had: peanut butter and jelly, tomato and bacon, ham and cheese, and egg salad.

5. Last summer Ted helped with the haying, fed the chickens, went after the cows, and hoed the garden.

6. Do three things: first, get the book from the library; second, make an outline; third, write the report.

7. The three pairs were Bill and José, Jim and Tony, and Bob and Carl.

8. Please check the addresses of these persons: Ms. Sondra Jackson, Dr. Joyce L. Rainer, and Mr. and Mrs. George Abel.

9. That was a long, hard train ride.

10. I saw them slide, scramble, and tumble down the slope.

B. Follow the directions for Exercise A.

1. About midnight I woke up. First, there was a loud crash outside; second, the dog barked; third, things rustled on the table.

2. In the morning the sun rose over the hills, the birds were singing in the trees, and fish jumped in the lake.

3. You may go to the pool, to the park, or into town.

4. Karen, Jack, and Juanita went swimming; my mother, my father, and I went to the store.

5. For supper we had hot dogs, pickles, and baked beans.

6. That evening we unloaded the car, set up the tent, climbed into our sleeping bags, and went to sleep.

7. When I looked out, the garbage can was overturned, and two curious, black-masked raccoons were on the picnic table.

does so correctly, a point is scored and a second sentence is assigned to the first person on the other team. If the sentence is incorrectly punctuated, the other team gets to try. This procedure continues until the sentence is punctuated correctly.

2. Have students use the following sentence pattern, and fill in the blanks with appropriate items from each number using commas correctly. On *(date)* we celebrated *(name of celebration)* in *(place)* and saw *(items in a series)*.

1. July 14 1971
   Bastille Day
   Paris France
   parades air shows other patriotic events

2. March 17 1953
   St. Patrick's Day
   Dublin Ireland
   green hats shamrocks green decorations

3. January 14 1985
   the Winter Carnival
   Minneapolis Minnesota
   sleigh rides skating contests ice sculptures

4. August 5 1967
   the Calgary Stampede
   Calgary Alberta
   rodeos square dancing cowboys in western gear

5. November 12 1979
   my birthday
   Disney World Florida
   Adventureland Tomorrowland
   many Walt Disney characters

3. Test the mastery of direct and indirect quotations by asking students to identify sample sentences. Have students change direct to indirect and vice versa. You may wish to have them simply rewrite the sentences in the exercise on page 665 as indirect quotations.

8. Slowly, quietly, and thoroughly they investigated the house.
9. They nibbled the cookie, argued over an apple, and turned up their noses at a piece of pickle someone had dropped.
10. Dad said, "At least it wasn't a bobcat, a skunk, or a big bear."

The Comma After Introductory Words, Phrases, or Clauses

Use a comma to separate an introductory word, phrase, or clause from the rest of the sentence.

Yes, Paula is my sister.

Climbing down the tree, I ripped my jacket.

Because I studied hard, I passed the test.

The comma may be omitted if there would be little pause in speaking.

At first Nancy was frightened.

Commas with Interrupters

Use commas to set off words or groups of words that interrupt the flow of thought in a sentence.

This bike, however, is in better condition than that one.

The answer, I suppose, will never be known.

Exercises   Use commas to set off words correctly.

A. Write the following, adding commas where necessary.

1. However, Jan prefers to work on her own.

2. The library, Bill had said, was closed for the last two weeks.
3. Janet's absence is excusable, I am certain.
4. The Safety Committee, of course, needs good equipment.
5. The test results, I suppose, will be posted tomorrow afternoon.
6. The Assembly Committee, as I said earlier, will meet on Thursday.
7. No, I haven't seen that movie.
8. Several of the hikers, nevertheless, made the trip in an hour.
9. This paper, for example, has no watermark.
10. After all, Maria is a college senior.

B. Write the following sentences, adding commas where necessary. (One sentence does not need any commas.)

1. Running to third base, I tripped and sprained my ankle.
2. Maybe Sue will join us.
3. In slalom skiing, on the other hand, you use only one ski.
4. Mary has a Siamese cat, I think.
5. Did you hear, by the way, that there was a sellout crowd at the game last night?
6. Pat, I hope, will make a better shortstop than Chris.
7. No, you may not stay at Ellen's for dinner this evening.
8. Finally, the last marathon runner entered the Olympic Stadium.
9. Yes, the game has been postponed until we can find a referee.
10. While vacationing in Montreal Allison and I met many French-speaking people.

Commas with Nouns of Direct Address

Use commas to set off nouns of direct address.

When you are speaking to someone, you use that person's name. When you do, you use a **noun of direct address.**

Call me tonight, Jane, if you can.

In the above sentence, *Jane* is the noun of direct address. It names the person the speaker is addressing (speaking to).

If commas are omitted with nouns of direct address, the sentence may confuse the reader. Read this example of such a confusing sentence:

Help me bake Jon and you may have some cookies.

Now read the sentence with commas correctly placed:

Help me bake, Jon, and you may have some cookies.

Commas with Appositives

Use commas to set off most appositives.

Appositives are words placed immediately after other words to make those other words clearer or more definite. Most appositives are nouns. Nouns used as appositives are called **nouns in apposition.**

Our science teacher, Miss Bell, will not be back next year.

Karen and Maria, our co-captains, accepted the trophy.

When an appositive is used with modifiers, the whole group of words is set off with commas.

Joe, the boy in the blue shirt, is Dave's cousin.

When the noun in apposition is a first name, it is not usually set off by commas.

This is my friend Tony.

Exercises **Use commas with nouns of direct address and with appositives.**

A. Copy the following sentences. Add commas wherever necessary. After each sentence, give your reason for using commas in it. direct address = D.A. appositive = App.

1. Mrs. Harmon,^{D.A.} I'd like you to meet my sister Robin.
2. Mary,^{D.A.} this is my classmate,^{App.} Tanya Jefferson.
3. Mr. Ingram,^{App.} our English teacher,^{App.} is here now,^{D.A.} Dad.
4. Dad,^{D.A.} this is Mr. Ingram,^{App.} our English teacher.
5. Don Jenkins,^{D.A.} this is Cynthia,^{App.} my sister.
6. Mother,^{D.A.} have you met Mr. Gillespie,^{App.} our music teacher?
7. Carla Mantoya,^{D.A.} this is my father,^{App.} Ken Brown.
8. Mrs. Doyle,^{App.} our math teacher,^{App.} is from Alaska.
9. Beth,^{D.A.} dinner will be ready any minute now.
10. José,^{D.A.} this is my brother Larry.

B. Rewrite the following pairs of sentences. Combine each pair into a single sentence by using an appositive.

There may be more than one way to combine sentences.

Example: Jill Douglas is the mayor of our town. She will speak next.

Jill Douglas, the mayor of our town, will speak next.

There was only one hit, a single, against Wills.
1. There was only one hit against Wills. It was a single.
Karen, my classmate, is on the swimming team.
2. Karen is on the swimming team. She is my classmate.
The author, Mark Twain, knew a lot about people.
3. The author is Mark Twain. He knew a lot about people.
The girl in the third row, Paula, likes to go camping.
4. The girl in the third row is Paula. She likes to go camping.
The fastest runner, Penny Tate, is on the track team.
5. The fastest runner is on the track team. She is Penny Tate.
We have a favorite horse, Daisy Belle.
6. We have a favorite horse. Her name is Daisy Belle.

663

The second largest city in the United States, Chicago, was founded in 1803.

7. The second largest city in the United States is Chicago. It was founded in 1803.
   Our pitcher, Bill Phillips, injured his arm.
8. Our pitcher is Bill Phillips. He injured his arm.
   Ms. Parsons, our music teacher, plays the piano.
9. Ms. Parsons is our music teacher. She plays the piano.
   One of my favorite plays, The Miracle Worker, is about Helen Keller and Annie Sullivan.
10. One of my favorite plays is *The Miracle Worker*. It's about Helen Keller and Annie Sullivan.

Commas with Quotations

Use commas to set off the explanatory words of a direct quotation.

Remember that when you use a quotation you are giving the words of a speaker or writer. You are *quoting* the words of the speaker or writer. If you give the *exact* words, you are giving a **direct quotation.** Usually you include explanatory words, like *Joyce said, Peggy answered,* or *Bill asked.*

Jeff said, "Mother and I are going to the store."

In the above sentence, the explanatory words come *before* the quotation. A comma is then placed after the last explanatory word.

Now look at this quotation:

"Let's visit the zoo," suggested Joe.

In the above sentence, the explanatory words come *after* the quotation. A comma is then placed after the last word of the quotation, as you can see.

Sometimes the quotation is separated into two parts.

"If it rains," he said, "it'll probably be just a shower."

The above sentence is an example of what is called a *divided quotation*. It is called "divided" because it is made up of two parts that are separated by the explanatory words. A comma is used after the last word of the first part. Another comma is used after the last explanatory word.

The quotations you have just looked at are all direct quotations. A quotation can be either *direct* or *indirect*. In an **indirect quotation** you change the words of a speaker or writer to your own words. No commas are used.

Ms. Mooney said *that she enjoyed visiting our class.*

Exercise   **Use commas with direct quotations.**

Write each of the following sentences, adding commas where they are needed. If a sentence needs no commas, write the word *Correct* after it.

1. Jim said, "Everyone has gone to the beach today."
c 2. Dr. Gonzales said that Sandy had broken her arm.
3. Liz asked, "Won't your mother let you have a dog?"
4. "But London Bridge is no longer in London," Art said.
5. "Did you know," asked Angie, "that Alpha Centauri is the nearest star?"
6. "I like the climate of Seattle best of all," answered Tom.
7. Denise asked, "Have you ever flown in a helicopter?"
8. "I can fix that faucet in ten minutes," Mary boasted.
c 9. Ken asked if we could drop him off first.
10. "I believe," shouted the announcer, "that we have a winner!"

The Comma in a Compound Sentence

You will remember that a **compound sentence** consists of two simple sentences joined together.

Use a comma before the conjunction that joins the two simple sentences in a compound sentence.

Chris got back from his trip, and now he's sleeping.

665

The comma is not necessary in very short compound sentences when the parts are joined by *and*.

> We were thirsty and we were hungry.

However, always use a comma before *but* or *or*.

> We were thirsty, but we weren't hungry.

Do not confuse a compound sentence with a sentence that has only a compound predicate. The two parts of a compound predicate are *not* joined by commas.

> We can stop here or go on to Toronto.

If a compound predicate has more than two parts, the parts are joined by commas.

> We came early, worked hard, and left late.

Exercises   **Use commas correctly.**

A.   Write each of the following sentences, adding commas where they are needed. Two sentences have compound predicates and need no commas. Write the word *Correct* after those sentences.

1. Can you stay for dinner, or are you leaving early?
2. The coach drew a diagram, and the players studied it.
3. We stopped on the side of the road and ate our lunch.
4. On the moon the temperature rises to over 200° in the daytime, but it drops far below zero at night.
5. There was an annoying noise in the car, but we could not locate the cause.
6. You can have two large containers or use three small ones.
7. I'd like to go to the show, but I have too much work to do.
8. The movie was excellent, but I didn't enjoy waiting in line.

9. We raked the leaves into neat piles, but the wind blew them away.
10. Ellen played the piano, and Laura performed a Mexican folk dance.

B. Follow the directions for Exercise A. (Here, also, are two sentences that have compound predicates and need no commas.)

1. The book wasn't very long, but she couldn't finish it.
2. The mail carrier delivered two small packages, and he asked me to sign for them.
3. I don't really want to go, but I will if you come with me.
c 4. We went to the state fair yesterday and spent the day.
5. Is a meter shorter than a yard, or is it longer?
6. Are you in a hurry, or can you stop for some ice cream?
7. At first she couldn't dance at all, but now she's pretty good.
c 8. He flew to San Francisco and took a bus from there.
9. Nancy brought lemonade, but she forgot the glasses.
10. These jeans are too long, and they don't fit at the waist.

Commas in Dates

Use commas to set off the parts of dates from each other.

Tuesday, November 9, 1978

If a date is used in a sentence, place a comma after the last part of the date.

February 20, 1962, was the day on which the first American orbited the earth.

667

Commas in Locations and Addresses

Use commas between the name of a city or town and the name of its state or country.

> Des Moines, Iowa
>
> London, England

Use commas to separate the parts of an address.

> 1943 Meech Road, Williamston, Michigan 48895

If an address is used in a sentence, also place a comma after the last part of the address.

> From Omaha, Nebraska, we drove to Wichita, Kansas.
>
> Please send the order to 125 West Lincoln Highway, DeKalb, Illinois 60115, as requested.

Commas in Letter Parts

Use a comma after the greeting of a friendly letter and after the closing of any letter.

> Dear Dana,   Sincerely yours,

Exercises   Use commas correctly.

A. Write the following sentences, adding commas where they are needed.

1. Does this address say Gary, Indiana, or Cary, Illinois?
2. My older brother was born on February 29, 1968.
3. Sherlock Holmes lived at 221B Baker Street, London.
4. Dear Diana,
   Let me know if you can babysit on Friday.
                              Yours truly,
                              Margaret Findley

5. He was born on April 3,1967,so he's an Aries.
6. Ed lives at 4652 Orchard Street,Oakland,California.
7. We're going to the museum on Thursday,May 5.
8. The first Boston Marathon was held on April 19,1897.
9. Are you talking about Kansas City,Missouri,or Kansas City,Kansas?
10. Someday my address will be 1600 Pennsylvania Avenue,Washington,D. C.

B. Follow the directions for Exercise A.

1. Where were you on Friday,June 24,1979?
2. Reno,Nevada,is farther west than Los Angeles,California.
3. Eleanor Roosevelt was born on October 11,1884,and died on November 7,1962.
4. My cousins were both born on September 4,1964.
5. Why is 10 Downing Street,London,famous?
6. Saturday,July 26,is Kathryn's birthday party.
7. The best hot dogs are at Petey's,110 Washington Street,Elm Forest.
8. Dear Helen,
   Thank you for the sweater. It fits perfectly.

   Love,
   Marsha
9. We lived at 130 Rand Road,Austin,Texas,from May 1, 1973,to April 30,1977.
10. July 4,1776,is the only historical date I can remember.

The Semicolon

Use a semicolon to join the parts of a compound sentence when no coordinating conjunction is used.

Mother threw the coat away; it was worn out.

669

They may experience trouble with its use for introducing a list of items. Explain that the statement before a list must clearly indicate that a list will follow.

It is suggested that you discuss the exercise on page 670 aloud as part of the class lesson.

Individualizing the Lesson

Less-Advanced Students

As a class, compose sentences that call for the use of the semicolon and the colon.

Advanced Students

Have students write original sentences using the semicolon to punctuate compound sentences and using the colon to introduce lists of items.

Optional Practice

Put the following exercise on a worksheet. Have students put either a colon or a semicolon in each of the sentences.

1. For our hiking trip we took the following essentials : good shoes, some light clothing, dried food, and a well-stocked backpack.
2. I have to go to the store ;I need some eggs and milk right away.
3. Your car must have a major overhaul ;the transmission is all worn out.
4. At the athletic equipment sale I bought the following items :a volleyball, a soccer ball, a football and a hockey stick.
5. The Chicago Bears quarterback threw the ball to Walter Payton ;he made the winning touchdown in the last minute and a half.

The Colon

Use a colon after the greeting of a business letter.

Dear Sir or Madam: Gentlemen:

Use a colon between numerals indicating hours and minutes.

9:30 A.M.

Use a colon to introduce a list of items.

We need the following items: paintbrushes, tubes of paint, a palette, and canvas.

Exercises   **Use semicolons and colons correctly.**

Copy the word before and after the missing punctuation mark and add the correct punctuation mark.

1. Mary Ann is my sister; Dan is my twin brother.
2. The last vote was counted; Jane was elected by a large majority.
3. Class will be held at 2:15 P.M. in the music room.
4. The pupils with the highest marks are these: Michael Karantz, Susan O'Brien, and Janet Newcombe.
5. Here is what Jack wants: a compass, a pencil, and ink.
6. The game will begin at 1:00 P.M.
7. Sally decided against the 3-speed bike; she's going to get a 10-speed instead.
8. My grandfather grows a lot of vegetables in his garden: peas, lettuce, beets, carrots, and sweet corn.
9. Gentlemen:
   The payment for your bill is enclosed.

   Sincerely,
   Jack Parsons
10. Which of the following flavors is your favorite: boysenberry, chocolate, vanilla, or strawberry?

The Hyphen

Use a hyphen to divide a word at the end of a line.

> My father gets extra pay when he has to work over-
> time at the office.

Only words of two or more syllables can be divided at the
end of a line. Never divide words of one syllable, such as *school*
or *worse*. A single letter must not be left at the end of a line.
For example, this division would be wrong: *a-waken*. A single
letter must not appear at the beginning of a line, either. It
would be wrong to divide *slippery* like this: *slipper-y*.

**Use a hyphen in compound numbers from twenty-one
through ninety-nine.**

> thirty-two seconds   forty-three pencils

Use a hyphen in fractions.

> We have a three-fourths majority.

Use a hyphen or hyphens in certain compound nouns.

> sister-in-law   commander-in-chief   great-aunt

**Use a hyphen or hyphens between words that make up a
compound adjective used before a noun.**

> I rode my ten-speed bike to school.
>
> It was a well-written letter.

When a compound adjective comes after a noun, it is usually
not hyphenated.

> The phone call was long distance.
> My sister is ten years old.

The Hyphen

Objective

To use the hyphen correctly

Presenting the Lesson

1. Explain that the hyphen has
several specific and well-defined
functions. Read and discuss each
of the rules on page 671. Encourage
use of the dictionary when students
are unsure of where to divide words.

2. Assign and discuss the exercise on page 672. Have students
identify reasons for each hyphen
used.

Individualizing the Lesson

Less-Advanced Students

Use the following list of words to
have students practice finding correct syllabification in the dictionary.
Then have them write the one word
which cannot be divided at the end
of a line (a-loud).

weather	bedlam
blanket	demon
preseason	family
fishing	aloud

Advanced Students

Have students look through the
newspaper and find examples of
each of the five uses of the hyphen.
In addition, have them look for errors in the division of words at the
end of a line. This type of error is
occasionally found in newspapers
that are set by computers.

Optional Practice

For each of the following numbers, have students decide if the
word is hyphenated correctly at the

end of a line. If it is, they should write C before the number. If it is not, they should write out the word with a hyphen where it would be broken correctly.

1. unint-eresting   unin-teresting
2. com-mitted   C
3. swi-ng   swing
4. co-mb   comb
5. col-lapse   C
6. t-rial   tri-al
7. se-arches   search-es
8. cap-tain   C
9. ni-nety   nine-ty
10. miss-pelling   mis-spelling

Extending the Lesson

Have students make compound words by combining words from Column A with words from Column B. They should write the word using a hyphen if necessary. Remind them to check the dictionary.

Column A	Column B
1. heavy-duty	a. wave
2. monkey wrench	b. out
3. newsman self-	c. self
4. confidence	d. duty
5. grand piano	e. piano
6. follow-through	f. man
7. heat wave	g. through
8. through out	h. wrench

The Apostrophe

Objective

To use the apostrophe correctly to form possessives, contractions, and plurals

672

Exercise   Use hyphens correctly.

Copy the words in each sentence that need hyphens and add them.

1. A two-thirds majority vote by Congress is needed to override the President's veto.
2. Nora's great-grandparents came here from Norway in 1892.
3. Today only, felt-tip pens are reduced from eighty-nine cents to fifty-nine cents.
4. Marilyn's sister-in-law worked as a police officer before she became a lawyer.
5. The trip back to Bob's took forty-five minutes by express bus.
6. I hope those money-hungry, cattle-rustling outlaws meet up with The Kid.
7. Eileen's mother bought her a peach-colored blouse and a lime-green jumper.
8. An eight-cylinder engine has more power, but a six-cylinder engine will burn less gas.
9. The Mason-Dixon line, which divides the North and South, was surveyed by Charles Mason and Jeremiah Dixon.
10. The President is also commander-in-chief of the armed forces.

The Apostrophe

To form the possessive of a singular noun, add an apostrophe and an s.

girl + **'s** = girl's   man + **'s** = man's

boy + **'s** = boy's   Charles + **'s** = Charles's

To form the possessive of a plural noun that ends in s, add only an apostrophe.

$$\text{friends} + \text{'} = \text{friends'} \qquad \text{countries} + \text{'} = \text{countries'}$$

To form the possessive of a plural noun that does not end in s, add an apostrophe and an s.

$$\text{women} + \text{'s} = \text{women's} \qquad \text{mice} + \text{'s} = \text{mice's}$$

Exercises   Form the possessives of nouns correctly.

A. On a piece of paper, write the possessive form of the following nouns.

1. editor's
2. counselor's
3. producer's
4. elephant's
5. Dana's
6. electrician's
7. Ms. Prentiss's
8. Randy's
9. employee's
10. architect's
11. manager's
12. conductor's
13. artist's
14. librarian's
15. reporter's
16. horse's
17. doctor's
18. writer's
19. Mrs. Thomas's
20. principal's

B. On a piece of paper, write the plural form of each of the following nouns. After the plural form, write the plural possessive for each noun.

1. dentist — dentists, dentists'
2. man — men, men's
3. county — counties, counties'
4. nurse — nurses, nurses'
5. woman — women, women's
6. optometrist — optometrists, optometrists'
7. astronaut — astronauts, astronauts'
8. teacher — teachers, teachers'
9. bookkeeper — bookkeepers, bookkeepers'
10. salesperson — salespeople, salespeople's
11. company — companies, companies'
12. family — families, families'
13. student — students, students'
14. accountant — accountants, accountants'

cactuses	cactuses'	(same)	deer's
cactus	deer		
(same)	salmon's		brothers-in-law
salmon	brother-in-law		
indexes	indexes'		brothers-in-law's
index	layman		
(same)	moose's	laymen	laymen's
moose	mouse		
		mice	mice's

Optional Practice

Ask students to identify all the phrases in the following list that indicate possession, and write them in a column, using apostrophes where necessary. In a second column, have them list all the phrases that contain contractions, adding the necessary apostrophes. You may have students change each phrase into a complete sentence.

C 1. shouldn't have run so fast
P 2. the comedians old jokes *, or comedians'*
C 3. after we've seen the movie again
P 4. the baseball players mitt
P 5. an astronauts space vehicle *, or astronauts'*
C 6. hadn't ever seen skydivers before
P 7. his sisters guitar *, or sisters'*
P 8. the lead singers recent hit song
C 9. couldn't have done it better
C 10. didn't have the correct address

Extending the Lesson

Have students add apostrophes to the following paragraph.

Its a rare day when my brother offers to help me with my chores. Last Saturday I couldnt meet my friends until Id finished raking the leaves. Thats when Jeremy volunteered to help me. Im always suspicious of Jeremys motives. "Hes up to something, no ifs, ands, or buts about it," I thought. "Hes being so nice." Well, I didnt have to wait long to find out. He wanted a ride in my friends new sports car. I guess the old saying is true— you dont get something for nothing.

674

	cities, cities'		journalists, journalists'
15.	city	18.	journalist
	lawyers, lawyers'		orthodontists, orthodontists'
16.	lawyer	19.	orthodontist
	paramedics, paramedics'		carpenters, carpenters'
17.	paramedic	20.	carpenter

The Apostrophe in Contractions

Writing contractions is not at all difficult if you understand that the apostrophe simply replaces one or more omitted letters.

we're = we are	where's = where is
she's = she is	they're = they are
here's = here is	can't = cannot
there's = there is	couldn't = could not
I'd = I would	won't = will not
we'll = we will	wasn't = was not
they'll = they will	wouldn't = would not

Look out, too, for *it's* and *its*. Remember:

It's (with an apostrophe) always means *it is* or *it has*.
Its (without the apostrophe) is the possessive of *it*.

It's time for the dog to have *its* bath.

Remember, too, that no apostrophe is used with the possessive pronouns *ours, yours, hers, theirs*.

These magazines are *ours*.
Those on the table are *theirs*.

Look out for *who's* and *whose*. Remember:

Who's (with an apostrophe) means *who is* or *who has*.
Whose (without the apostrophe) is the possessive of *who*.

Who's going with you to the movie?
Whose house is that?

Two other contractions that you should watch are *you're* and *they're*. *You're* means *you are*. Do not confuse it with the possessive pronoun *your*. *They're* means *they are*. Do not

674

confuse it with the possessive pronoun *their*.

> *You're* now in *your* own classroom.
> *They're* visiting *their* aunt.

Use an apostrophe to form the plurals of letters, figures, and words used as words.

> Children used to be told to mind their *p*'s and *q*'s.
> Carol should form her *3*'s and *8*'s more carefully.
> Pam's story was full of *but*'s.

Exercises **Use apostrophes correctly.**

A. Copy these sentences, inserting apostrophes where they are needed.

1. Wheres the paint for the puppets faces?
2. Its on the garage shelf. Its Ms. Steins paint. Dont waste it.
3. Were going to keep working until weve finished.
4. Ill turn on Carls desk lamp. Wont that help?
5. Thats fine. Well work much faster now.
6. Jim cant go because hes helping his parents.
7. Its late. Havent you finished yet?
8. My puppet wont sit up. Its back isnt stiff enough.
9. Heres the book you wanted. Its been checked out in your name.
10. Wheres the paste? Im ready. Lets go.

B. Write each of the following sentences. Choose the correct word from the two given in parentheses.

1. (You're, Your) the one (who's, whose) going to Mexico, aren't you?
2. Kathy and Peg are going to the play, but they (don't, dont) have (they're, their) tickets yet.
3. Which poster is (her's, hers)?

675

4. (It's, Its) hard to believe that the car has lost (it's, <u>its</u>) muffler already.
5. (<u>Here's</u>, Heres) the pump for (you're, <u>your</u>) tire.
6. (<u>We'll</u>, Well) all be happy if it (<u>doesn't</u>, doesnt) rain.
7. (<u>Wasn't</u>, Wasnt) Mr. Lopez (they're, <u>their</u>) teacher?
8. (<u>Who's</u>, Whose) going with you to the concert? I hope (<u>you're</u>, your) able to find someone.
9. Mrs. Larette (<u>doesn't</u>, doesnt) know (who's, <u>whose</u>) bike is in the driveway.
10. (They're, <u>Their</u>) team has had much more practice than (our's, <u>ours</u>).

Quotation Marks

Use quotation marks at the beginning and at the end of a direct quotation.

Quotation marks [" "] consist of two pairs of small marks that resemble apostrophes. They tell a reader that the exact words of another speaker or writer are being given.

> Matt said, "I'm going to wash the family car."

Quotation marks are not used with indirect quotations:

> Matt said *that he was going to wash the family car.*

Explanatory words before a direct quotation are followed by a comma. The period at the end of the sentence is placed *inside* the quotation marks.

> My uncle answered, "I'll send you a postcard."

Explanatory words after a direct quotation are followed by a period. The words of a direct quotation are followed by a comma *inside* the quotation marks.

> "I'll send you a postcard," my uncle answered.

Quotation Marks

Objective

To use quotation marks correctly in direct quotations, and to use quotation marks and underlining correctly in titles

Presenting the Lesson

1. Two previous lessons in the text have dealt with the writing of direct quotations. Capitalization was discussed on pages 641–642, and commas on pages 664–665. You may want to refer to this material as needed to complete this lesson. Stress that quotation marks enclose only what is actually spoken. Make it clear that if the actual quotation is one sentence, it should be treated as one sentence even if it is interrupted by explanatory words such as *he answers, she said,* or *he replied.* If there are two sentences, they should be treated as two sentences, each beginning with capital letters and ending with proper

Divided Quotations

Sometimes a direct quotation is divided into two or more parts by explanatory words. In such cases use quotation marks before and after each part of the quotation.

"If that team wins," Patty whispered, "I'll be surprised."

The second part of a divided quotation is not capitalized unless it is a proper noun or unless it starts a new sentence.

"If you're ready," said Paul, "we can leave now."

"I saw Mr. Prichard," said Amy. "He was in the supermarket."

After the first part of a divided quotation, place a comma *inside* the quotation marks.

"When you wash the car," Jan said, "use a soft cloth."

In a divided quotation use either a comma or a period after the explanatory words. Use a comma after the explanatory words if the second part of the quotation does not begin a new sentence. Use a period after the explanatory words if the second part of the quotation is a new sentence.

"Help me set the table," said Peter, "and then call the others."

"I've finished my homework," Dan said. "It was easy."

Exercise   Use quotation marks correctly.

Writing   Write each sentence three ways as a direct quotation. Answers will vary.

Example: Of course you can go.
　　　a. "Of course you can go," he said.
　　　b. He said, "Of course you can go."
　　　c. "Of course," he said, "you can go."

1. If you like, we will stay.
2. At least you like potatoes.

punctuation. Write some direct quotations with explanatory words on the board. Leave out the needed punctuation and capitalization. Discuss what is needed for each item and why it is important.

2. Before students do the exercise on pages 677–678, discuss the three placements of explanatory words. Then assign and discuss the exercise.

3. Assign and discuss Exercises A and B on pages 678–679.

4. Read and discuss pages 679–680. Ask students to explain why the quotation marks are used as they are, and why in writing conversation it is necessary to begin a new paragraph every time the speaker changes.

5. Assign and discuss the exercise on page 680.

6. Read and discuss pages 680–681. Some discussion of titles has already taken place in Section 18 on capitalization. Ask students for other examples of each category.

7. Assign and discuss Exercises A and B on pages 681–682.

Individualizing the Lesson

Less-Advanced Students

1. Work with students on Exercises A and B on pages 678–679. Have them read each sentence aloud before deciding where to put the quotation marks. Be sure they place the punctuation marks in the correct places.

2. Use the overhead projector to show the paragraph on page 680. Work with students in selecting the right punctuation.

3. While working on Exercises A

and B on pages 681–682, have students identify each kind of title.

1. Have students use alternatives for *said* in the explanatory words they add to the sentences in the exercise on page 677.

2. Have them change all direct quotations in the exercises on pages 678 and 679 to indirect quotations and indirect quotations to direct quotations.

3. Have students write two new examples of each title listed on page 681.

Optional Practice

1. Explain that one of the two sentences in each of the following pairs is correct, but that the other needs quotation marks and may need capitalization. Students should write *C* after the correct sentence in each pair. In the space below each pair, students should rewrite correctly the sentence that contains errors.

Example:
a. Earl wanted to know what movie was at the theater.
b. What movie is at the theater? Earl asked.
   "What movie is at the theater?" Earl asked.

1. a. The robber told them to put up their hands.C
   b. The robber said, stick 'em up. "
2. a. He asked if we wanted to go to the airport.C
   b. He asked, do you want to go to the airport? "
3. a. The sportscaster announced that there were five minutes left in the game. C
   b. The sportscaster announced, there are five minutes left in the game."

3. Well, there's another way to do it.
4. At noon the pool will open.
5. Aunt Mary is going to visit us.

Punctuating Direct Quotations

Place question marks and exclamation points inside quotation marks if they belong to the quotation itself.

> Mother said to Tim, "Have you finished the dishes?"
>
> "Look out!" Dad shouted.

Place question marks and exclamation points outside quotation marks if they do not belong to the quotation.

> Did Rachel say, "Meet me in the library"?
> The teacher said, "There is no homework tonight"!

Exercises   Punctuate correctly.

A. Punctuate these quotations correctly. (There are three indirect quotations that only need periods.)

1. "Did you notice," Inspector Blaine asked, "anything peculiar about the suspect?"
2. "Just that he wore a raincoat and a hat that hid his face," I replied.
3. "Are you certain that he was tall and that he limped as he ran?" Blaine asked.
4. "Correct," I answered. "I also believe he favored his left side."
5. I reminded the Inspector that I had caught only a glimpse of the mysterious person.
6. "Oh, by the way," I added, "he was carrying a small suitcase, too."
7. "Would you mind coming down to the station and making a statement?" Blaine asked.

8. I told him that I wouldn't mind, but that I preferred to keep my name out of the newspapers .

9. "No need to worry,"he remarked as he opened the squad car door for me .

10. I thanked him for his courtesy and got in .

B. Writing Write each of the following sentences as a direct quotation. In some examples, put the quotation first. In others, put the quotation last. Also, for variety, divide some quotations. Answers will vary.

Example: Next week I start my new job.

Possible Answers:
"Next week I start my new job," Sally said.
Sally said, "Next week I start my new job."
"Next week," Sally said, "I start my new job."

1. The shirts are dirty, but the slacks are clean.
2. By the way, that clock is ten minutes fast.
3. After lunch should we go to the movies?
4. Thank goodness my glasses didn't break!
5. Last night I had a terrible dream.
6. Walk three blocks and turn right.
7. Next summer my whole family is driving to California.
8. Perhaps poodles are smarter, but I still prefer collies.
9. Do green apples give you a stomachache?
10. All it takes to open that paint can is a screwdriver.

Punctuating Dialogue

Notice how the following quotation, which contains more that two sentences by one speaker, is punctuated.

"Can the repairman come tomorrow?" asked Jean over the telephone. "Mother needs to use the washing machine. She can't use it at all now."

Only one set of quotation marks would be needed if the example read as follows:

> Over the telephone Jean said, "Can the repairman come tomorrow? Mother needs to use the washing machine. She can't use it at all now."

In writing *dialogue* (conversation), begin a new paragraph every time the speaker changes:

> "Lynn invited us to the lake for the afternoon," said Jean.
> "How was it?" asked Barbara.
> "Well, the car broke down on the way. We had to walk three miles to the lake," replied Jean.

Exercise   **Punctuate dialogue correctly.**

Writing   Rewrite the following conversation. Make correct paragraph divisions and use the right punctuation.

> Home Run Reilly stepped up to the plate. He was facing Lightning Louie, the fastest pitcher in baseball. The first pitch was a blur. Strike one! the umpire called. Reilly gripped the bat, and the second pitch streaked by. Strike two! the umpire said. Reilly frowned as he heard the third pitch thunk into the catcher's mitt. Strike three! the umpire shouted. You're out! Reilly turned to the umpire and asked, Could you see those pitches? No, the umpire confessed. I couldn't either, said Reilly, but the last one sounded a little high to me.

Using Quotation Marks for Titles

Use quotation marks to enclose chapter titles, titles of magazine articles, titles of short stories, essays, or single poems, and titles of songs or short pieces of music.

Chapter:	Chapter 8, "The Revolution Begins"
Magazine article:	"Space Age Tour"
Short Story:	"The Lady or the Tiger?"
Essay:	"The English Language Today"
Poem:	"The Raven"
Song:	"America"

Underline the titles of books, newspapers, magazines, plays, movies, titles of television and radio programs, works of art, and long musical compositions.

When you are writing or when you are typing, underline these titles, like this: <u>Light in the Forest</u>.

When these titles are printed, they are printed in *italics*, rather than underlined.

Book:	*The Pearl*
Newspaper:	*Los Angeles Times*
Magazine:	*Newsweek*
Play:	*Julius Caesar*
Movie:	*Butch Cassidy and the Sundance Kid*
Television program:	*Great Performances*
Work of art:	Grant Wood's *American Gothic*
Long Musical Composition:	*William Tell*

Exercises Use quotation marks and underlining correctly.

A. Copy the following sentences, adding quotation marks around titles or underlining titles where necessary.

1. The chorus sang "My Old Kentucky Home."
2. "The Catbird Seat" is a funny story by James Thurber.
3. Karen's picture was in the local paper, the <u>Leesburg Advance</u>.
4. Did you read <u>My Darling, My Hamburger</u> for your book report?

5. The drama department is presenting <u>The Miracle Worker</u> as the spring play.
6. Our teacher assigned the second chapter, "Families of Man", in our social studies book.
7. Robert Redford won the Academy Award as best director for <u>Ordinary People</u>.
8. Estelle used <u>Time</u> and <u>Newsweek</u> to write her report.
9. No one can even estimate the value of the <u>Mona Lisa</u>, which is in the Louvre museum.
10. The play <u>Romeo and Juliet</u> was the basis for the movie <u>West Side Story</u>.

B. Follow the directions for Exercise A.

1. One article in this month's <u>Seventeen</u> is "Are You a Good Friend?"
2. We are reading a science fiction novel, <u>The Time Machine</u>, in English class.
3. Shirley Jackson's story "The Lottery" has a shocking ending.
4. Before the game began, everyone sang "The Star-Spangled Banner."
5. One <u>Nova</u> program explained sunspots.
6. My favorite poems are "Dreams" by Langston Hughes and "Space Man" by Babette Deutsch.
7. The longest running play is <u>The Mousetrap</u> by Agatha Christie.
8. We listened to the orchestra play Schubert's <u>Unfinished Symphony</u>.
9. Dan has seen <u>Star Wars</u>, <u>The Empire Strikes Back</u>, and <u>The Return of the Jedi</u> three times each.
10. My father reads the <u>Chicago Tribune</u> and the <u>New York Times</u> every Sunday.

ADDITIONAL EXERCISES

Punctuation

A. Periods, Question Marks, and Exclamation Points
Copy the following sentences. Supply the missing punctuation.

1. Donna explained why she was late.
2. Please pull up a chair.
3. What a hot day it is!
4. What is the forecast for tomorrow?
5. Wow! Is it really 2:00 A.M.?
6. The speaker is Bonita Pamatz, M.D.
7. Did you learn to swim at the Y.W.C.A.?
8. Dr. Hill and Ms. Wirtz are the chaperones for the freshman dance.
9. Chuck Berry recorded "Johnny B. Goode" long ago.
10. The Great Wall of China, built before 200 B.C., is the only human structure visible from outer space.

B. Commas Copy each of the following sentences. Use a comma to make the meaning clear.

1. Since Irv left, Spot has been lonesome.
2. While juggling, Mark talks to the audience.
3. Sandra can't stand cheese, and Mimi dislikes milk.
4. Outside, the lawn was being mowed.
5. While the turkey was roasting, Kay opened a window.
6. Instead of moping around, Kelly went biking.
7. Almost falling down, Len regained his balance on his skateboard.
8. Running behind, Nicole got her second wind.
9. When you finish, the tests will be collected.
10. Tripping, Lori stumbled into the Christmas tree.

683

These Additional Exercises may be used for additional practice of the concepts presented in this Section. Each exercise focuses on a single concept, and should be used after the page number indicated in parentheses.

Review

If you have not assigned these Additional Exercises before this time, you can also use them as an excellent Section Review.

C. Commas Copy the following sentences. Add commas where they are necessary.

1. We caught a bass, a trout, and a catfish.
2. Megan found a carton, cleaned it out, and packed the books.
3. The Barbary States were Algiers, Tunis, and Tripoli.
4. First, slice the eggplant; second, drain it; third, brush it with oil.
5. I looked under the cushion, beneath the rug, and in the wastebasket.
6. The farm offers rides on a hay wagon, a tractor, or a horse.
7. Why did George sit through that long, boring, pointless movie?
8. Leon brought a red rubber ball, Kristy brought a striped beach ball, and Sabrina brought a Frisbee.
9. His plump, freckled, solemn face was on the front page.
10. Arlene and Vivian made up funny, catchy, campaign slogans.

D. Commas Copy these sentences. Add commas where necessary.

1. You are, I'm sure, telling the truth.
2. No, the snow has not stopped.
3. The Packers, however, have an excellent chance of winning the championship.
4. For example, Dracula movies are still being made.
5. Part of the mistletoe, as you may know, is poisonous.
6. Because Gerri is an usher, she sees many plays.
7. Stuck under the viaduct, the truck blocked traffic.
8. Helping himself to my popcorn Kent, told me the ending of the movie.
9. Consequently, the jury found her innocent.
10. Miriam, yawning loudly, looked at the clock.

E. Commas Copy these sentences. Add commas where necessary.

1. Danny, where are you going?
2. Have you had lunch, Maria?
3. Remember, Charley, to use hand signals.
4. Richard Pryor, the comedian, was the star.
5. Mrs. Owens, this is my friend, Nina.
6. Carol, meet Olga Herrera, my new neighbor.
7. I quickly spotted Al, the only boy wearing a tie.
8. The award was presented by Gwendolyn Brooks, the poet from Illinois.
9 Alice fed the garter snake a goldfish, its favorite food.
10. Japanese children learn *origami*, the art of folding paper.

F. Commas Copy these sentences. Add commas where necessary. If a sentence needs no comma, write *Correct*.

1. "Actually", said Jo, "the sun is nearer the earth in winter."
c2. Marla said that dinner would be late.
3. "I iron my own shirts", Art said.
c4. Wendy asked if she was in the way.
5. Mr. Tijani asked, "Do all of you see this line?"
6. "When I sing", said Laura, "I forget myself."
7. "The coast is clear", Adrienne told us.
c8. Walt told us that he was allergic to bee stings.
c9. Michelle promised that she would shovel the walk.
10. Olsen promised us, "I will not let you down."

G. Commas Copy these sentences. Add commas where necessary. If a sentence needs no comma, write *Correct*.

1. We practiced hard all week, and our coach was pleased.

2. O. J. Simpson used to play football, but now he's a sports commentator.

c 3. A rock hit the windshield and shattered it.

4. Carly and Lisa accepted, but Nell declined the party invitation.

5. You'd better explain to Sid, or he will be hurt.

6. Harry was talking fast, and we were listening hard.

c 7. Jody and Fred were talking and laughing at the same time.

8. The ramps are meant to help people in wheelchairs, but cyclists also like the smooth slopes.

c 9. Ian will wait in the car or walk around the block.

10. Did you mean that, or were you joking?

H. Commas Copy the following sentences. Add commas where necessary.

1. There is a game preserve near Nairobi, Kenya.

2. Hitler invaded Poland on September 1, 1939.

3. On January 3, 1959, Alaska joined the Union.

4. Contributions can be sent to UNICEF, 331 East 38th Street, New York, New York 10016.

5. Wednesday, April 8, was the night of the full moon.

6. Beverly Hills, California, is on the outskirts of Hollywood.

7. Our address will be 10 Sugar Pine Road, Medford, Oregon 97501, as of June 25.

8. Dear Sally,

   I hope that I will be able to attend a performance of your play on Saturday, January 20.

   Sincerely,
   Linda

9. Ginger moved to Vose Farm Road, Peterborough, New Hampshire, on May 1, 1985.

10. Cairo, Illinois, is very different from Cairo, Egypt.

I. Semicolons and Colons Copy these sentences, adding the missing punctuation mark.

1. The race was over; the jockey jumped from her horse to accept the medal.
2. Bring the following supplies: wood, nails, a hammer, and glue.
3. The plane didn't leave the runway until 5:30 P.M.
4. Dear Mrs. Kohl:
   Your appointment is on March 12 at 9:00 A.M.
5. These students should report to the gym before the assembly: Ben Evans, Josh Shapiro, and Lois Sims.
6. Stay on the right side of the road; ride in a single file.
7. This is all you need: salt, flour, and vinegar.
8. The hay got wet; it might rot.
9. The clock struck 12:00; it was Christmas.
10. The camp will provide sheets and pillows; you must bring your own towels, however.

J. Hyphens Copy the words that need hyphens and add the hyphens.

1. My great-aunt is celebrating her ninety-fifth birthday on January 23.
2. It was an attention-catching sign.
3. The gravity of the moon is one-sixth that of the earth's gravity.
4. My great-grandmother rides a ten-speed bike.
5. The living room has built-in bookcases.
6. Reporters began predicting the winner when only one-fourth of the votes were in.
7. The Vice-President now has an official residence.
8. Gray-brown dust was blowing everywhere.
9. Two-thirds of the books are out-of-date reference works.
10. The co-captains are half-sisters.

K. Plurals and Possessives Write the plural form of each of the following nouns. After the plural form, write the plural possessive for each noun.

1. doctor — doctors, doctors'
2. puppy — puppies, puppies'
3. heroine — heroines, heroines'
4. seamstress — seamstresses, seamstresses'
5. man — men, men's
6. child — children, children's
7. painter — painters, painters'
8. contestant — contestants, contestants'
9. panther — panthers, panthers'
10. member — members, members'
11. eagle — eagles, eagles'
12. mouse — mice, mice's
13. lady — ladies, ladies'
14. writer — writers, writers'
15. electrician — electricians, electricians'

L. Apostrophes Copy the following sentences, inserting apostrophes where they are needed.

1. Can't you see that I'm busy?
2. I'll keep your secret.
3. You're sure it's a diamond, aren't you?
4. The two girls' mittens are missing.
5. Michael's dog isn't welcome here.
6. Europeans make their 7's differently.
7. Whose ice cream hasn't melted yet?
8. Who's playing those steel drums? They're Liz's.
9. Its feathers feel oily, don't they?
10. Ours has lost its cover. Yours hasn't.

M. Quotation Marks Copy and punctuate the following sentences.

1. "I have homework to do," Mother said.
2. Charlene said that she was trying out for the cheerleading squad.
3. Hal said, "That Harley-Davidson is a classic."
4. "Watch out for shaving cream!" Toby yelled. "It's Halloween!"
5. Chief Joseph told his warriors, "From where the sun now stands, I will fight no more forever."
6. Mr. Rizal asked if we had any questions.

7. Hattie asked,"Is the dolphin a mammal?"

8. "When the snow thaws," said Leah,"our street floods."

9. "Renault said that he would be here," said Emma.

10. "I measured the doorway," said Ann."It's too narrow."

N. Dialogue Rewrite the following conversation. Make correct paragraph divisions and use the right punctuation.

"Did you hear that storm last night?" asked Janet at breakfast.
Pam answered, "I certainly did not."
"Well," said Janet, "the thunder almost shook the house, and lightning streaked right into our room. I was afraid the hailstones would break the windows."
"Why didn't you wake me up?" asked Pam indignantly. "You know I can't sleep during a storm."

Did you hear that storm last night asked Janet at breakfast Pam answered I certainly did not Well said Janet the thunder almost shook the house and lightning streaked right into our room I was afraid the hailstones would break the windows Why didn't you wake me up asked Pam indignantly You know I can't sleep during a storm

O. Titles Copy the following and fill in the blanks. Punctuate the titles correctly.

1. My least favorite televison program is _____ . Use quotation marks.

2. Joan has a subscription to _____ magazine. Underline.

3. The best movie that I ever saw was _____ . Underline.

4. The title of Monty's essay was _____ . Use quotation marks.

5. One book that held my attention was _____ . Underline.

MIXED REVIEW

Punctuation

A. Using punctuation correctly Copy the following sentences, adding end marks, commas, apostrophes, and quotation marks, and underlining where necessary.

1. Pete, Diane, and Evan all have the flu.
2. Have you read any poems by T. S. Eliot?
3. Oh, no! I forgot the tickets.
4. Laura has just finished the novel <u>Little Women</u>.
5. Keep your eyes on the ball, not on the pitcher.
6. "Before you leave," said Dad, "clean your room."
7. Yes, I can go camping on Wednesday, September 22.
8. His argument, I believe, is logical.
9. Sandra is a dancer, a singer, and an actress.
10. "There's a squirrel in the fireplace!" shouted Kevin.

B. Using punctuation correctly in proofreading Proofread the following letter. Copy it, using correct punctuation.

Camp Willowbrook
P. O. Box 2112
Whitewater, Wisconsin 51620

Dear Ellen,

You were so right! Being a camp counselor is better than babysitting. Where else could I teach swimming, diving, and gymnastics every day? The campers are bright, active kids. Sometimes, however, their creativity leads to some unusual pranks. I did have a reward last weekend when a camper said to her parents, "I'll come back next year if Beverly does."

Please write soon, Ellen. I miss our phone calls.

Sincerely,
Bev

USING MECHANICS IN WRITING
Punctuation

A.   Marty was nervous but confident before the typing test. He knew he was faster and more accurate than anyone else in class. Fingers flying, he completed the test with a full minute to spare. But his heart sank as he reviewed his paper. He had forgotten to capitalize and punctuate. Rewrite Marty's test, making all necessary corrections.

what do michelangelo ringo starr gerald ford and harpo marx have in common they all have one simple trait shared by millions of others theyre left-handed no one is sure why some of us prefer our left sides to our right sides many stories and superstitions have arisen because of the mystery the bible tells of sharp shooting left-handed warriors in the middle ages some people even believed that left-handed warriors had magic powers on the contrary lefties have problems with simple things such as cutting with scissors knitting and dining next to right-handed people benjamin franklin an early champion of left-handed people encouraged tolerance most lefties today are proud of their distinction for them its the right way.

B.   A reporter has stumbled on an exciting story. She has discovered a scientist who has invented a machine that can control weather. The scientist is pleading with the reporter not to reveal the secret. He is afraid of what others might do with the knowledge. Write their conversation. Have each character speak at least four times. Include at least four divided quotations. Invent details to make the conversation interesting and realistic.

Using Mechanics in Writing

These challenging and enjoyable activities allow the students to see how the concepts of grammar, usage, and mechanics may be applied in actual writing situations. Each exercise is designed to allow students practice in several of the skills they have acquired in this Section. The activities also provide opportunities for students to write creatively about a wide variety of interesting and unusual subjects.

Section Objectives

1. To develop good spelling habits

2. To learn to spell particularly difficult words

3. To understand and apply common spelling rules

4. To distinguish between words often confused

Preparing the Students

Read and discuss the introduction on page 692. Point out that the rules to be discussed in this section will not tell how to spell every word, but will make the spelling of most words easier to figure out.

It is not necessary to teach this chapter in its entirety to classes that regularly use a structured, sequential spelling program. It may serve as a good year-end review for this kind of program or as a handy reference section for students who have specific spelling problems.

Additional Resources

Diagnostic Test — page 10 in the test booklet

Mastery Test — pages 73–74 in the test booklet

Additional Exercises — pages 706–710 in the student text

Practice Book — pages 244–250

Duplicating Masters — pages 244–250

Special Populations — See special section at the back of this Teacher's Edition.

Spelling

It is important to have good spelling skills. You will use these skills when you write reports for school. You will use them when you write friendly letters and business letters, and you will use them when you fill out job applications. If you care what others think of you, you will want to be able to spell words correctly.

Being a good speller doesn't just happen. It takes practice, and you have to remember a few simple rules. If you do have trouble spelling, you may be relieved to know that generations of students have shared the same problem. Many of those students have learned to be good spellers. You can, too.

There is no simple way to teach you how to spell. However, there are several methods you can use to attack your spelling problems. These methods of attack are discussed in this chapter.

A General Method of Attack on Spelling

To improve your spelling, follow these helpful guidelines:

1. Find out what your personal spelling demons are and conquer them. Go over your old composition papers and make a list of the words you misspelled on them. Keep this list and master the words on it.

2. Pronounce words carefully. It may be that you misspell words because you don't pronounce them carefully. For example, if you write *probly* for *probably*, you are no doubt mispronouncing the word.

3. Get into the habit of seeing the letters in a word. Many people have never really looked at the word *similar*. Otherwise, why do they write it *similiar?*

Take a good look at new words, or difficult words. You'll remember them better. Copy the correct spelling several times.

4. Think up a memory device for difficult words. Here are some devices that have worked for other people. They may help you, either to spell these words or to make up your own memory devices.

princi**pal** (*pal*)	The princi**pal** is my *pal*.
fri**end** (*end*)	I will be your fri**end** to the *end*.
bus**i**ness (*i*)	*I* was involved in big bus**i**ness.
bel**ie**ve (*lie*)	There is a *lie* in bel**ie**ve.

5. Proofread everything you write. In order to learn how to spell, you must learn to examine critically everything you write.

To proofread a piece of writing, you must read it slowly, word for word. Otherwise, your eyes may play tricks on you and let you skip over misspelled words.

693

A General Method of Attack on Spelling

Objective

To develop good spelling habits

Presenting the Lesson

1. Read and discuss the suggestions on pages 693–694. Point out that everyone has some personal spelling demons to conquer. Ask students for some of the words they have difficulty spelling.

2. This is a good time to discuss use of the dictionary as an aid to better spelling. If dictionaries are available for class use, you may wish to prepare some practice drills on locating words by sounding out approximate spellings.

Individualizing the Lesson

Less-Advanced Students

Work with students to compile a class list of words that are frequently misspelled in the students' writing. Practice each step on this page to begin work on conquering these problems.

Advanced Students

Have students proofread each others' compositions for spelling. Then have them review their own papers and make lists of words they often misspell.

Optional Practice

Have a spelling bee using the list of spelling problems made up by the class.

693

A Method of Attack on Specific Words

Objective

To learn to spell particularly difficult words

Presenting the Lesson

Read through the steps on page 694 with the class. Discuss why each step should be helpful. Emphasize how important it is to be able to *say* the word correctly, to *hear* the word correctly, as well as to *write* the word correctly.

Individualizing the Lesson

Less-Advanced Students

Choose several new spelling words and have students try this method for learning them.

Advanced Students

Have students choose difficult words from their science texts and then try this method to learn how to spell the words.

Optional Practice

Divide the class into small groups. Have each student list five words he or she finds difficult to spell. The groups should discuss ways that might be helpful to remember the correct spellings. Compile a list of words noting the learning suggestions next to them. Make copies for the entire class.

Extending the Lesson

Conduct a spelling bee, using the lists compiled by students in **Optional Practice.**

6. Use a dictionary. You don't have to know how to spell every word; no one spells everything correctly all the time. A good dictionary can help you to be a better speller. Use a dictionary whenever you need help with your spelling.

7. Learn the few important spelling rules given in this chapter. Refer to these guidelines until you begin to follow them naturally on your own. You'll see that you will become a good speller.

A Method of Attack on Specific Words

To spell a specific word that is difficult for you, follow these steps:

1. Look at the word and say it to yourself. Be sure you pronounce it correctly. If it has more than one syllable, say it again, one syllable at a time. Look at each syllable as you say it.

2. Look at the letters and say each one. If the word has more than one syllable, separate the word into syllables when you say the letters.

3. Write the word without looking at your book or list.

4. Now look at your book or list and see whether you spelled the word correctly. If you did, write it again and compare it with the correct form again. Do this once more.

5. If you made a mistake, note exactly what it was. Then repeat steps 3 and 4 above until you have written the word correctly three times.

By following these steps, you will have mastered the difficult word. You will be able to spell it correctly whenever you use it.

Rules for Spelling

The Final Silent e

When a suffix beginning with a vowel is added to a word ending in a silent e, the e is usually dropped.

relate + -ion = relation   believe + -ing = believing
amaze + -ing = amazing   create + -ive = creative
fame + -ous = famous   continue + -ing = continuing

When a suffix beginning with a consonant is added to a word ending in a silent e, the e is usually retained.

hope + -ful = hopeful   waste + -ful = wasteful
state + -ment = statement   move + -ment = movement
noise + -less = noiseless   wide + -ly = widely

The following words are exceptions:

truly   argument   ninth   wholly

Words Ending in *y*

When a suffix is added to a word ending in *y* preceded by a consonant, the *y* is usually changed to *i*.

easy + -ly = easily   happy + -ness = happiness
sixty + -eth = sixtieth   clumsy + -ly = clumsily
city + -es = cities   marry + -age = marriage

Note the following exception: When -*ing* is added, the *y* does not change.

hurry + -ing = hurrying   worry + -ing = worrying
study + -ing = studying   copy + -ing = copying

When a suffix is added to a word ending in *y* preceded by a vowel, the *y* usually does not change.

enjoy + -ed = enjoyed   play + -ing = playing
employ + -er = employer   destroy + -er = destroyer

695

Optional Practice

Copy this list of words. Have students write *C* after each word that is spelled correctly. If the word is not spelled correctly, they should put a line through it and rewrite it correctly.

1. brief c
2. cheif *chief*
3. decieve *deceive*
4. handkercheif *handkerchief*
5. reciept *receipt*
6. sieze *seize*
7. grieve c
8. wieght *weight*
9. mischief c
10. seive *sieve*
11. yield c
12. neice *niece*
13. conciet *conceit*
14. thier *their*
15. frieght *freight*
16. retrieve c
17. shield c
18. theif *thief*
19. vien *vein*
20. believe c
21. cieling *ceiling*
22. iether *either*
23. weird c
24. eight c
25. field c
26. recieve *receive*
27. achieve c
28. neither c
29. siege c
30. sleigh c

Extending the Lesson

1. Have students list examples of verbs ending in *-ing* and *-ed* in a newspaper or magazine or one of their textbooks. Next to each word they should write the base word.

2. Discuss how the various suffixes change words from one part of speech to another. For example, the *-ly* ending may change an adjective to an adverb. Ask for examples.

Exercises   Spell words and their suffixes.

A.   Find the misspelled words in these sentences. Spell them correctly.

1. Our class is competeing in the state science fair. *competing*
2. The magician's performance was truely amazeing. *truly, amazing*
3. My brother and I had an argument about rakeing the leaves. *raking*
4. The nurse placed the baby carfully against her shoulder. *carefully*
5. By the seventh inning, the game was hopless for our team. *hopeless*
6. The troop leaders are arrangeing chairs for tonight's scout meeting. *arranging*
7. The dareing circus performers walked easyly across the tightrope. *daring, easily*
8. My grandparents were gratful for the pictures we sent them. *grateful*
9. The chef's createion looked terrific but tasted awful. *creation*
10. It was truly exciteing to meet the actors and actresses backstage. *exciting*

B.   Add the suffixes as shown, and write the new word. Remember to change *y* to *i* wherever it is necessary.

1. silly + -ness *silliness*
2. messy + -est *messiest*
3. twenty + -eth *twentieth*
4. marry + -ing *marrying*
5. crazy + -ly *crazily*
6. relay + -ed *relayed*
7. spray + -ing *spraying*
8. beauty + -ful *beautiful*
9. glory + -ous *glorious*
10. hasty + -ly *hastily*
11. play + -ful *playful*
12. supply + -ing *supplying*
13. employ + -ment *employment*
14. fly + -er *flier*
15. lazy + -er *lazier*
16. dirty + -est *dirtiest*
17. fancy + -ful *fanciful*
18. study + -ous *studious*
19. enjoy + -able *enjoyable*
20. pretty + -er *prettier*

696

The Suffixes -*ness* and -*ly*

When the suffix -*ly* is added to a word ending in *l*, both *l*'s are kept. When -*ness* is added to a word ending in *n*, both *n*'s are kept.

actual + -ly = actually   thin + -ness = thinness
real + -ly = really   even + -ness = evenness

The Addition of Prefixes

When a prefix is added to a word, the spelling of the word remains the same.

mis- + spell = misspell   mis- + place = misplace
il- + legal = illegal   im- + perfect = imperfect
im- + mobile = immobile   dis- + approve = disapprove
pre- + record = prerecord   ir- + regular = irregular

Exercise   **Spell words with prefixes and suffixes.**

Find the misspelled words in these sentences and write them correctly.

1. Our car is parked legally, but yours is in an ilegal [illegal] space.
2. The blue vase is slightly mishapen. [misshapen]
3. In English class we are learning about iregular [irregular] verbs.
4. The uneveness [unevenness] of our sidewalk makes skateboarding dangerous.
5. We were practicaly [practically] finished eating when it began to rain.
6. The owner is disatisfied [dissatisfied] with the people who live upstairs.
7. We received a thoughtfuly [thoughtfully] written thank-you note.
8. Scrooge's meaness [meanness] was replaced by kindness and charity.

9. Dr. Martin's handwriting is almost ilegible. _illegible_

10. I mispelled two words in my essay because I misspro- _misspelled_ _mispronounced_
    nounced them.

Words with the "Seed" Sound

Only one English word ends in *sede: supersede.*
Three words end in *ceed: exceed, proceed, succeed.*
All other words ending in the sound of *seed* are spelled *cede*:

concede   precede   recede   secede

Words with *ie* and *ei*

When the sound is long *e* (*ē*), the word is spelled *ie* except after *c*.

I Before E

believe   shield   yield   fierce
niece   brief   field   pier

Except After C

receive   ceiling   perceive   deceit
conceive   conceit   receipt

The following words are exceptions:

either   weird   species
neither   seize   leisure

Exercise   Spell words with the "seed" sound and words with *ie* and *ei*.

Find the misspelled words in these sentences and write them correctly.

1. My mother's salary excedes that of many people. _exceeds_
2. There are leaks on the cieling of the locker room. _ceiling_

698

3. I lost the ^receipt reciept for the hockey equipment I rented.
4. Bikers should yeild ^yield the right of way to pedestrians.
5. The Student Council will ^proceed procede with its plans.
6. The doctor gave me a prescription to ^relieve releive my pain.
7. ^Neither Niether Missouri nor Kentucky seceded from the Union during the Civil War.
8. My aunt bakes special cookies for all her ^nieces neices.
9. The playing feild ^field was too wet for the game to proceed.
10. The candidate did ^concede conceed the victory.

Doubling the Final Consonant

In words of one syllable that end with one consonant preceded by one vowel, double the final consonant before adding -ing, -ed, or -er.

bat + -ed = batted   bed + -ing = bedding
get + -ing = getting   grab + -ed = grabbed
big + -er = bigger   slim + -er = slimmer
put + -ing = putting   run + -er = runner

The following words do not double the final consonant because *two* vowels precede the final consonant:

treat + -ing = treating   loot + -ed = looted
feel + -ing = feeling   near + -er = nearer

Exercise Doubling the Final Consonant

Add the suffixes as shown and write the new word. Remember to double the final consonant wherever it is necessary.

1. dig + -ing ^digging
2. fear + -ing ^fearing
3. fat + -er ^fatter
4. slap + -ed ^slapped
5. pair + -ed ^paired
6. hop + -ing ^hopping
7. bat + -er ^batter
8. creep + -ing ^creeping
9. wrap + -ed ^wrapped
10. dim + -er ^dimmer

Objective

To distinguish between words often confused

Presenting the Lesson

1. Even good spellers have trouble with some of the words on pages 700–703. Have students note those words in the list with which they have little difficulty. Have them try to find reasons for the difficulties they may have with other words.

After going through the list with the class, have students close their books. Read the definition and sentence for each word. Have students spell the word orally and then write it correctly.

2. Assign and discuss Exercises A and B on pages 704–705. Be sure that students can give reasons for all answers.

Individualizing the Lesson

Less-Advanced Students

Have students use flashcards to help them quiz each other on the spellings and definitions of these words. Also have them write each word in a sentence.

Advanced Students

Have students brainstorm for ideas to help them remember the definitions and spellings of these words.

Words Often Confused

Study each group of words and meanings. Learn to spell these words that are often confused.

accept means "to agree to something" or "to receive something willingly."

except means "to exclude" or "omit." (As a preposition, *except* means "but" or "excluding.")

> Kay did *accept* the Hansens' invitation to go camping with them.
> The ninth grade will be *excepted* from locker inspection.
> Everyone *except* the team will sit in the bleachers.

all ready expresses a complete readiness or preparedness.

already means "previously" or "before."

> The pilots and their crew were *all ready* for the landing.
> We had *already* made arrangements to take the early train.

capital means "most important" or "most serious." It also refers to the city or town that is the official seat of government of a state or nation.

capitol is a building in which a state legislature meets.

the Capitol is the building in Washington, D. C., in which the United States Congress meets.

> Montpelier is the *capital* of Vermont.
> Use a *capital* letter to begin every line of poetry.
> The thief had previously been arrested for a *capital* offense.
> The committee held a special meeting at the *capitol* building.
> We visited the *Capitol* in Washington, D. C., last summer.

des′ert means "a wilderness or dry, sandy region with sparse, scrubby vegetation."

des·ert′ means "to abandon."

dessert (note the change in spelling) is a sweet, such as cake or pie, served at the end of a meal.

The Mojave *Desert* is part of the Great American *Desert* in southern California.

When we ran out of fuel, we *deserted* our car to find gas.

Jon and Sue baked a strawberry pie for *dessert*.

hear means "to listen to" or "take notice of."

here means "in this place."

Because of a poor sound system, we couldn't *hear* the band.

We finally arrived *here* in Seattle after a flight delay in Denver.

its is a word that indicates ownership.

it's is a contraction for *it is* or *it has*.

The city lost *its* power during the thunderstorm.

It's almost noon, and I haven't finished my work.

lead (lēd) means "to go first."

led (lĕd) is the past tense of *lead*.

lead (lĕd) is a heavy, silvery-blue metal.

A circus wagon pulled by horses will *lead* the parade.

This wagon had *led* the parade for many years.

Lead is one of the heaviest metals, yet it melts at a very low temperature.

lose means "to misplay" or "suffer the loss of something."

loose means "free" or "not fastened."

Our car began to *lose* some of its power as we reached the top of Pike's Peak.

The hinges on the back gate are quite *loose*.

past refers to that which has ended or gone by.

passed is the past tense of *pass* and means went by.

Our *past* experience with that team has taught us to use a different defense.

We *passed* through the Grand Tetons on our vacation last summer.

Optional Practice

1. Have students choose groups of these words and illustrate the meanings with pictures clipped from magazines. Post these to help students associate a visual image with each spelling.

2. Write each of the words on a slip of paper. Place the slips of paper in a grab bag. Have each student draw a word and write a sentence that clearly applies the definition of that word. Have each student read his sentence and have another student spell the word.

3. Repetition is important for learning the words. Have students design their own personal set of flash cards with the word on the front and its correct use on the back. They can then be used for individual practice drill.

4. Ask students to write one sentence for each of the following groups of words.

Example:

Everyone *except* John will *accept* your apology.

lose	its	plane
loose	it's	plain
past	hear	your
passed	here	you're
to	their	who's
too	there	whose
two	they're	
		all ready
		already

Extending the Lesson

1. Encourage students to look through newspapers and magazines and bring in examples of misspellings they find. Have them make a display using both the misspelled words and their corrections.

2. Ask students to be on the look-out for misspelled words in signs and advertising. Billboards and local businesses may be the targets for student scrutiny. Ask them to bring examples to class.

piece refers to a section or part of something.

peace means "calm" or "quiet" or "freedom from disagreements or quarrels."

> We cut each *piece* of lumber into several smaller *pieces*.
> I felt a certain *peace* as I sat and watched the sunrise.

plane is a flat, level surface or a carpenter's tool.

plain means "clearly understood," or "simple," or "ordinary." It can also refer to an expanse of land.

> In geometry, we learned how to measure a *plane*.
> In shop, we used a *plane* to smooth and trim boards.
> Milton likes *plain* foods; he won't try anything unusual.
> The farms were scattered across the *plain*.

principal describes something of chief or central importance. It also refers to the head of an elementary or high school.

principle refers to a basic truth, standard, or rule of behavior.

> The *principal* cities of France include Paris, Marseilles, Lyons, and Nice.
> The *principal* of our school presented the awards.
> We will study the *principles* of democracy in our American government class.

quiet refers to no noise or to something rather peaceful or motionless.

quite means "really" or "truly," and it can also refer to a considerable degree or extent.

> Everyone was *quiet* during the graduation ceremony.
> We were *quite* sure that the school bus would be late.

stationary means "fixed" or "unmoving."

stationery refers to paper and envelopes used for writing letters.

> The new digital scoreboard will be *stationary* in the large gym.
> Two students in my art class designed the school *stationery*.

there means "in that place."

their means "belonging to them."

they're is a contraction for *they are*.

> Please put the groceries over *there* on the counter.
>
> In 1803, the explorers Lewis and Clark led *their* expedition to the western United States.
>
> Sue and Pam are skiing, and *they're* going snowmobiling on Saturday.

to means "toward," or "in the direction of."

too means "also" or "very."

two is the number 2.

> We all went *to* the zoo last weekend.
>
> It was much *too* cold to go cross-country skiing.
>
> *Two* television stations carried the President's last press conference.

weather refers to atmospheric conditions such as temperature or cloudiness.

whether helps to express choice.

> Daily *weather* reports are studied by meteorologists all over the world.
>
> *Whether* we call or write for our vacation reservations, we must do it soon.

whose is the possessive form of *who*.

who's is a contraction for *who is* or *who has*.

> Do you know *whose* bicycle is chained to the parking meter?
>
> *Who's* going to volunteer to help at the children's Christmas party?

your is the possessive form of *you*.

you're is a contraction of *you are*.

> Please take *your* books back to the library today.
>
> *You're* going there right after school, aren't you?

Exercises   Spell words often confused.

A. Choose the correct word from the words in parentheses.

1. This (past, passed) year I had a special tutor to help me in math.
2. Three summers have (past, passed) since I went away to camp.
3. Be sure to check your paper for the correct use of (capital, capitol) letters.
4. This is no time to (desert, dessert) our baseball team!
5. We ran out of gas while crossing the (desert, dessert).
6. The weather (hear, here) has been extremely cold.
7. (It's, Its) hard to remember certain dates in American history.
8. Our puppy wags (it's, its) tail as soon as I enter the room.
9. Theodore Roosevelt (lead, led) the charge up San Juan Hill.
10. A drum majorette will (lead, led) the marching band.
11. The latch on the door is (lose, loose) and needs to be fixed.
12. Every winter I (lose, loose) at least two pairs of gloves.
13. All of the players (accept, except) the goalie were involved in the argument.
14. The refreshments are (all ready, already) for the parent-teacher meeting.
15. Loretta has (already, all ready) decided that she wants to be a veterinarian.

B. Choose the correct word from the words in parentheses.

1. The carpenter used a (plane, plain) to trim the top of the door.
2. Would you like to try a (piece, peace) of pecan pie?

3. The two leaders signed a (piece, peace) treaty.
4. We studied the (principles, principals) of government in social studies.
5. The (principle, principal) actors took their bows.
6. Call us when (your, you're) ready.
7. The coach says (your, you're) the best hitter on the team.
8. Our neighbors never let (their, there) cat out at night.
9. (They're, There) widening Main Street to provide more parking places.
10. That movie was (to, too) funny for words.
11. If the (weather, whether) permits, we will have a picnic.
12. The police officer wondered (whose, who's) fingerprints were on the door.
13. (Whose, Who's) making all that noise?
14. I am (quiet, quite) nervous about going to high school.
15. I received a letter from the mayor on her official (stationery, stationary).

Additional Exercises

These Additional Exercises may be used for additional practice of the concepts presented in this Section. Each exercise focuses on a single concept, and should be used after the page number indicated in parentheses.

Review

If you have not assigned these Additional Exercises before this time, you can also use them as an excellent Section Review.

ADDITIONAL EXERCISES

Spelling

A. Spelling   Find the <u>misspelled words</u>. Spell them correctly.

1. You surely don't <u>beleive</u> those stories! believe
2. The garden apartment is <u>actualy</u> the basement. actually
3. A <u>rageing</u> fire destroyed the department store. raging
4. Expressways are used <u>heavyly</u> at rush hour. heavily
5. A referee shouted "<u>ilegal</u> motion." Illegal
6. Am I really <u>mispronounceing</u> that word? mispronouncing
7. As the tide <u>receeds</u>, we go digging for clams. recedes
8. The <u>arguement</u> was completely silly. argument
9. <u>Finaly</u> my niece stopped crying. Finally
10. Rose <u>succedes</u> when she tries. succeeds
11. Someone who <u>recieves</u> stolen goods is also a thief. receives
12. I could <u>easyly</u> give you a receipt. easily
13. The bus had <u>stoped</u> for the twentieth time. stopped
14. I mistakenly thought I would become <u>fameous</u> overnight. famous
15. He <u>beleives</u> some truly amazing things. believes

B. Words Often Confused   Choose the correct word from the two given in parentheses.

1. Everyone could attend (accept, <u>except</u>) Cal.
2. The concert is (all ready, <u>already</u>) sold out.
3. Rich didn't want to (loose, <u>lose</u>) your friendship.
4. We (past, <u>passed</u>) many vacant lots.
5. The empty gym was still and (<u>quiet</u>, quite).
6. My new (stationary, <u>stationery</u>) is gray with a black border.
7. I asked (<u>whether</u>, weather) the gerbils would bite.

MIXED REVIEW

Spelling

A. Spelling words correctly Pick out any <u>misspelled words</u> from the following sentences. Write them correctly. If there are no misspelled words in a sentence, write <u>Correct</u>.

1. ^{Their} <u>There</u> phone is out of order.
2. Our dog chewed ^{its} <u>it's</u> leash.
3. Children ^{accept} <u>except</u> only sealed candy on Halloween.
4. Taylor had a piece of cake for ^{dessert} <u>desert</u>.
5. ^{Whose} <u>Who's</u> report was the most ^{carefully} <u>carefuly</u> prepared?
6. Cheating on a test is against my <u>principals</u>.^{principles}
7. Stan ^{passed} <u>past</u> his ^{driving} <u>driveing</u> test easily.
8. Our team suffered ^{quite} <u>quiet</u> a loss on Saturday.
c 9. Blair doesn't know whether she'll enter the contest.
10. Wayne ^{led} <u>lead</u> the discussion.

B. Using spelling in proofreading Proofread the following paragraph. Copy it, spelling all words correctly.

Every ^{amusement} amusment park from Six Flags ^{to} too Great America boasts a thrilling roller coaster. Although simple gravity was and is the force that propels the ride, the first roller coasters would not seem ^{exciting} exciteing today. An ^{inclined} inclineed railway in Pennsylvania, once used ^{to} too transport coal, became the first roller coaster in the United States. Called the Switchback, this ride ^{chugged} chuged along at five miles per hour. In 1884, the Gravity Pleasure Railway at Coney Island, New York, had ten-passenger cars. The speed of this roller coaster did not ^{exceed} excede six miles per hour. At midpoint, the cars had ^{to} too be pushed up a hill until gravity could take over again. The only ^{enviable} envyable thing about that old roller coaster was the price. Can you ^{believe} beleive it only cost five cents a ride?

Mixed Review

These exercises provide review of the concepts presented in this Section. Each exercise challenges the students to apply several of the skills they have acquired during previous study. Because the "mixed" feature of these activities makes them more difficult, the teacher may wish to have less-advanced students do them orally or in small groups.

These challenging and en-
joyable activities allow the students to see how the con-
cepts of grammar, usage, and
mechanics may be applied in
actual writing situations. Each
exercise is designed to allow
students practice in several of
the skills they have acquired
in this Section. The activities
also provide opportunities for
students to write creatively
about a wide variety of interesting and unusual subjects.

USING MECHANICS IN WRITING
Spelling

A. Write a thank-you note to someone who has taken you on a wonderful weekend trip. Make up the details yourself, but use one of the following pairs of words in each sentence. One or both of the words in each pair is misspelled. Correct the misspelled words. Use all five pairs.

truely enjoied   createive planing   actualy studying
amazing citys   realy believe

(corrections shown above the words: truly enjoyed, creative planning, actually, cities, really)

B. The following paragraph contains some words that are often confused. Those words are underlined. Some are spelled correctly, but others are not. Find the mistakes in this paragraph. Rewrite those sentences correctly.

I enjoy seeing disaster movies. The <u>reel</u> world seems so full of <u>peace</u> when compared to the events in these action-<u>packed</u> movies. Somehow the movie always ends with a happy <u>seen</u>, too. This happens <u>whether</u> heroes or heroines are trapped in a skyscraper, threatened by a fire, or surprised by an iceberg <u>braking</u> up a ship.

In one typical film, a <u>hole</u> is blown out of the rear of a <u>plain</u> by a passenger who hates airplane food. Of course, that causes the jet engines to become <u>lose</u>, too. And <u>whose</u> <u>their</u> to save everyone? That job falls to the quiet, misunderstood pilot who had been <u>passed</u> by for promotion. He <u>excepts</u> his assignment to <u>save</u> the passengers; he <u>waists</u> no time. The plane is already diving toward the <u>dessert</u> below. <u>Its</u> hard to believe, but the pilot saves everyone but the angry passenger <u>who's</u> plans are all <u>waisted</u>. If <u>your</u> depressed, go <u>sea</u> a disaster movie. It will cheer you up.

(corrections shown: real, scene, breaking, plane, loose, who's, there, accepts, wastes, desert, It's, whose, wasted, you're, see)

CUMULATIVE REVIEW
Capitalization, Punctuation, and Spelling

A. Using capitalization, punctuation, and spelling correctly Copy the following sentences, correcting the errors in capitalization, punctuation and spelling.

1. Étienne and ~~j~~(J)oseph ~~m~~(M)ontgolfier launched the first hot-air balloon in ~~f~~(F)rance, 200 years ago.

2. Cary ~~g~~(G)rant, whose real name is ~~a~~(A)lexander ~~a~~(A)rchibald ~~l~~(L)each is an ~~a~~(A)merican movie actor.

3. Is ~~you're~~(your) ~~reciept~~(receipt) stapled to the bag?

4. "~~j~~(J)ane ~~f~~(F)onda ~~excepted~~(accepted) the ~~o~~(O)scar for her father, ~~h~~(H)enry ~~f~~(F)onda," said Mavis.

5. "I ~~beleive~~(believe)," remarked ~~l~~(L)arry, "that camels are called ships of the dessert."

6. Mike ~~tryed~~(tried) a triple somersault, but he ~~didnt~~(didn't) succeed.

7. Jane bought ~~copys~~(copies) of ~~t~~(T)ime, ~~n~~(N)ewsweek, and ~~u s~~(U. S.) news and ~~w~~(W)orld ~~r~~(R)eport from the newsstand.

8. "I've typed ~~you're~~(your) business address on the office ~~stationary~~(stationery)," said the secretary.

9. The tourists visited ~~c~~(C)oit ~~t~~(T)ower and the ~~t~~(T)ransamerica ~~b~~(B)uilding in ~~s~~(S)an ~~f~~(F)rancisco, ~~c~~(C)alifornia.

10. What ~~amazeing~~(amazing) facts about ~~t~~(T)okyo, ~~j~~(J)apan, are in this book?

11. I drew a map showing how the strait of ~~g~~(G)ibraltar connects the ~~m~~(M)editerranean ~~s~~(S)ea and the ~~a~~(A)tlantic ~~o~~(O)cean.

12. ~~Accept~~(Except) for Stephen, everyone had ~~all ready~~(already) eaten ~~desert~~(dessert).

13. Our ~~principle~~(principal), ~~m~~(M)s. Kahn, gave me a copy of ~~p~~(P)resident Lincoln's ~~g~~(G)ettysburg ~~Adress~~(Address).

14. Many of the world's largest and most ~~fameous~~(famous) diamonds come from the ~~k~~(K)imberly mine in ~~c~~(C)ape province, South Africa.

709
Cumulative Review

These exercises are designed to cover broad areas of grammar, usage, and mechanics. They require the application of skills taught thus far in the text. The exercises may be used for testing purposes, or as an excellent resource for review.

709

15. "that is correct," said Mrs Dawes, "computors are not difficult to use if you follow there instructions carefully."
16. The Five Nations was a confederation of iroquoian Indians including the mohawks, Oneidas, Cayugas, and senecas.
17. "When we were in new mexico I saw an amazeing indian mound," said Marsi.
18. They're is no place to put the radio that their fixing," said mother.
19. The president takes his oath of office on inauguration Day, January 20.
20. Michael jackson sang the song "Thriller."

B. Using proofreading skills Proofread the following paragraph. Copy it, correcting the errors in capitalization, punctuation, and spelling.

Have you ever been in a hot-air balloon? Well it is quiet an experience. my first flight was out in the colorado rocky mountains. The balloon that carryed me into the air was ninty feet tall. i had to stand in an open wicker gondola, or basket. "Your not getting me in their, I cryed when i first saw it. When i finaly got in the pilot turned on the propane burner to warm the air in the balloon. We floated high above the ground, and then we descended and skimed the treetops. What an exhilarating experience it was. the landing was the scaryest part. When we finaly bumped to a stop, I shouted, "lets do it again. that was realy great."

in possessives, 672–673
Articles, 266, 480
Assignments, understanding, 276–277
Atlas, 271
Audience
of a composition, 166–167
of a paragraph, 82–83
of a speaker, 328
Author card in card catalog, 265
Auxiliaries. See Helping verbs.

B

bad/badly, 508
Base words, 16–17
be, forms of, 381, 390
See also Irregular verbs.
Bibliography cards, 236–237
Bibliographies, 244–245
Biographical references, 271
Body
of a business letter, 307–308
of a composition, 160–161, 166–167, 184–185, 196–197, 218–219, 228–229
of a friendly letter, 300–302
of a report, 240–241
of a speech, 332
Books, finding and using in the library. *See* Library, using the.
Borrowed words, 2
Brainstorming, 78–79
Bread-and-butter notes, 305–306
Business letters, 307–308

C

Call numbers, 262
can/may, 423
capital/capitol, 700

Capitalization, 631–650
days, 637–638
directions, 635–636
direct quotations, 641–642
events, 637
family relationships, 633
first words
of outlines, 644
of poetry lines, 641
of quotations, 641
of sentences, 641
geographical names, 635
holidays, 637–638
I, 633
initials, 632
languages, 638
in letters, 643
months, 637–638
names, 632–633
nationalities, 638
organizations and institutions, 637
periods (of time), 637
proper adjectives, 632
proper nouns, 632
races, 638
religions, 638
school subjects, 639
and sections of the country, 635–636
Supreme Being and sacred writings, 633
titles of persons, 632–633
titles of written works, 644
Card catalog, 265–266
Characters, 178–179
Charts, *See* Graphic aids.
Chronological order
in narrative compositions, 180–181
in paragraphs, 88–89, 108–109, 112–113, 198

Circular reasoning, 256–257
Clauses
adjective, 614–616
adverb, 612–613
independent, 609–610
main, 609–610
noun clauses, 616–618
relative, 614–615
subordinate, 609–610, 618–619
Closing of letters, 300–302,
307–308
colons with, 307–308
commas with, 300
Colon, 307, 670
Combining sentence parts, 56–57
Combining sentences, 54–55
Commas, 656–669
with adjectives, 658–659
with adverbs, 658–659
with appositives, 662–663
to avoid confusion, 656–657
with city, state, and country,
668
in compound constructions, 354
in compound predicates, 600
in compound sentences,
599–601, 665–666
with dates, 667
with direct address, 662–663
with direct quotations, 664, 676
with indirect quotations, 665
with interrupters, 660–661
with introductory words, 660
in letters, 669
in a series, 657–660
to set off *names*, 662–663
after *yes, no*, 660
Common nouns, 431–433
Comparisons
using adjectives, 486–488
using adverbs, 501–502
as context clue, 10–11

Complete predicate of a sentence,
348
Complete sentence, 344–345
Complete subject of a sentence,
344
Completing applications and work-
related forms, 316–320
Completion, or fill-in-the-blank
tests, 296–297
Complex sentences, 607–627, 621
and clauses, 609–610
definition of, 608, 611
and sentence fragments,
619–620
Compositions, 159–231
body of, 160, 166–167, 184–185,
196–197, 218–219, 228–229
chronological order in, 180–181
characters in, 178–179
choosing point of view for,
182–183
choosing subjects for, 162–163,
194–195, 214
conclusion of, 160–161,
166–167, 184–185, 196–197,
218–219, 228–229
conflict in, 178–179
definition of, 160–161
descriptive, 193–201. *See also*
Descriptive compositions.
details in, 180–181, 194–195
development of, 162–163
dialogue in, 186–187
explanatory
how, 203–211
what, 223–232, 231
why, 213–221
final copy of, 172–173, 175
first drafts of, 166–167, 174–175
descriptive, 196–199
explanatory, 134–135, 144–145,
154–155

narrative, 184–189

first-person point of view in,
182–183

flashback, use of, 180–181,
188–189

general-to-specific organization,
226–227

guidelines for writing, 162–163,
174–175

introduction in, 160–161,
166–167, 184–185, 196–197,
218–219, 228–229

main ideas in, 160–161,
164–165

narrative, 177–191. *See also*
Narrative compositions.

narrowing topic for, 194–195

omniscient point of view in,
182–183

opinion in, 213–221

order of importance as method
of organization in, 216–217

organizing ideas, 164–165

parts of, 160–161

planning, 178–179, 204–205

plot in, 178–179, 180–181

point of view in, 182–183

pre-writing, 160–165, 174

revision of, 168–169, 175,
190–191, 200–201, 210–221,
230–231

sensory details in, 194–195

setting in, 178–179

spatial order in, 194–195

step-by-step order in,
206–207

third-person point of view in,
182–183

time sequence in. *See* Chronological order.

title for, 170–172

topic sentence in, 160, 214

transitions in, 188–189,
208–209, 218–219
See also Writing, Pre-writing, *and* Transitions.

Compound direct object, 533

Compound object of prepositions,
519, 533

Compound object of verb, 533

Compound predicate, 533, 593,
598

Compound predicate adjective,
533, 534

Compound predicate noun, 536

Compound sentences, 592–606,
621

combining related thoughts,
602–603

commas in, 665–667

or compound predicate,
598–599

definition of, 595–596

diagraming of, 596

punctuation of, 599–601

Compound subjects, 354–356, 533,
578–580

diagraming, 355–356

Compound verbs, 354–356, 533

diagraming, 355–356

Conclusions

in compositions, 160–161,
166–167, 184–185, 196–197,
218–219, 228–229

in paragraphs, 92–93

in reports, 240–241

in speeches, 332, 333

Conflict, in stories, 178–179

Conjunctions, 532–537

in compound constructions, 533

in compound sentence parts,
532–535, 594

in compound sentences,
595–596

coordinating, 533
correlative, 533
definition of, 532–533
subordinating, 610
Context
clues, 6–13
definition of, 6
learning word meanings from
comparison, 10–11
contrast, 10–11
definition, 6–7
examples, 8–9
inference, 12–13
restatement, 6–7
Contractions
apostrophe in, 674–675
list of, 674
negatives, 508–509
n't not included in verb, 383,
508–509
Cross-reference card, 266
Cumulative review
capitalization, punctuation,
spelling, 709–710
parts of speech, 572–573
sentence, 628–630
usage, 590–591

D

Dates
capitalization of, 637–638
commas in, 667
Declarative sentences, 346–347
definition of, 346
periods in, 346
Definition
as context clue, 6–7
in dictionary, 29
in explanatory *what* paragraph,
150–153

Demonstrations, 324, 327
Demonstrative adjectives, 485
Demonstrative pronouns, 465–466,
485–486
Descriptions, 117–127
Descriptive compositions
ending a description in, 198–199
first draft of, 196–197
revising, 200–201
using sensory details, 194–195
Descriptive paragraphs, 72–73,
117–127
first draft of, 124–125
gathering sensory details,
118–119
mood in, 122–123
revising, 126–127
using spatial order, 120–121
using transitional words,
124–125
Details
descriptive, in paragraphs,
86–87, 106–107
organizing, 88–89
sensory, 70, 86, 118–119,
194–195
in speeches, 330–331
Dewey Decimal System, 262–264
Diagraming, 349–350
adjectives, 480
adverbs, 499
compound sentences, 596
compound subjects and verbs,
355
direct objects, 435
imperative sentences, 363
indirect objects, 437–438
interrogative sentences, 359
possessive nouns, 445
predicate adjectives, 483
predicate nouns, 483
prepositional phrases, 521–522

questions. *See* Interrogative
sentences.
subjects in unusual word order,
356–357
verbs and their subjects,
349–350
Diagrams. *See* Graphic aids.
Dialogue, 186–187
Dialogue tags, 186–187
Dictionary, 23–33
abridged, 24
accent marks in, 28
alphabetical order in, 24
abbreviations and symbols in, 24
antonyms in, 29
definition of, 24
definitions in, 29
entries, information in, 28–33
entry word, 28
guide words, 26–27
irregular verbs in, 395
meaning, choosing right one,
31–33. *See also* Context clues.
origin of word in, 28
part of speech listed in, 28
plurals in, 443
principle parts in, 395
pronunciation in, 28
special forms or endings in, 28
syllables in entries, 28
synonyms in, 29
types of, 24
unabridged, 24
See also Words *and* Vocabulary.
Directions
following, 278–279
giving (in a speech), 324, 326
for reading forms, 316–320
Direct objects, 384–387, 434–436
compound, 458–459
definition of, 385
diagraming, 435

nouns as, 434–436
predicate words or, distinguishing, 390
pronouns as, 454–455, 458–459
recognizing, 385–388
Direct quotations,
capitalization of, 641–642
commas in, 676
punctuation of, 676–678
Discovery draft. *See* First draft.
does/do, 575
Double negatives, 508

E

Empty sentences, 46–47
Encyclopedia, 268–269
Ending compositions. *See* Conclusions in compositions; *see also*
Compositions, conclusions.
Ending sentences in paragraphs,
92–93
English language
as a living language, 2–3
jargon, 40–41
nonstandard, 36–37
slang, 38–39
standard, 36–37
English language words. *See*
Words.
Entry words in a dictionary, 28
Envelope, addressing, 303–304
Essay tests, 296–297
Examples
as context clue to meaning of
word, 8–9
used to develop a paragraph,
70–71, 86–87
except/accept, 700
Exclamation mark, or point,
with exclamatory sentences, 346
with interjections, 538–540

sensory details in, 70, 118–119
spatial order in, 88–89, 120–121
step-by-step order in, 132–133
third-person point of view in, 110–111
time sequence in, 88–89
topic for, narrowing, 80–81
topic sentence in, 68–69, 84–85
transitions in, 112–113, 124–125, 132–133, 144–145
unity in, 66–67
Participle, 555, 558–561, 565
Participial phrase, 559–560
Parts of speech, 28–29, 538–544
definition of, 538
as shown in dictionary entries, 28
using words as different, 540–541
See also the particular parts of speech.
Past participle of verbs, 394–395
Past tense of verbs, 392–393
peace/piece, 702
Period, 652–653
with quotation marks, 676
Personal observation to attain information, 86
Personal point of view. *See* First-person point of view.
Phrases and clauses, 609
Phrases, transitional
in compositions, 188–189
in paragraphs, 112–113, 124–125, 132–133, 144–145
piece/peace, 702
Plot in stories, 178–179
Plural forms
of nouns, 441–443
of pronouns, 462–463, 583–584
of verbs, 575

Poetry lines, capitalization of, 641
Point of view
first-person, 110–111, 182–183
omniscient, 182–183
third-person limited, 182–183
third-person, 110–111, 182–183
Possessive nouns, 444–445
Possessive pronouns, 454–455, 461–462
Predicate
complete, 348
compound, 354–355, 533, 593
definition of, 344
simple, 348–350, 593
Predicate adjectives, 390, 481–484
compound, 533
definition of, 390, 481–482
diagraming, 483
Predicate nouns, 390, 439–441
compound, 533
definition of, 390
diagraming, 483
Predicate pronouns, 456–457
Predicate words, 390
Prefixes, 18–19
and spelling, 697
Prepositional phrases, 515, 520–525
Prepositions, 514–531
adverbs or, distinguishing, 525–526
compound objects of, 519
definition of, 514–515
list of, 517
objects of, 517–520
nouns as, 517–518
pronouns as, 518
Present tense of verbs, 392–393
Pre-writing
as part of a process, 76–77, 98–99

choosing a point of view,
110–111, 182–183
choosing a subject, 78–79,
140–141, 162–163
for compositions, 162–165
creating mood, 122–123
definition of, 76, 98
for descriptive writing, 118–121,
194–197
developing a definition, 152–153
developing an opinion, 140–141,
214–215
developing a paragraph, 86–87
for explanatory writing,
130–133, 140–143, 150–153,
204–207, 214–217, 224–227
gathering ideas, 86–87,
162–163
gathering sensory details,
118–119
guidelines, 162–163
for narrative writing, 106–107,
178–183
narrowing a topic, 80–81,
106–107
notes, 106–107, 164–165
organizing paragraphs
chronological order, 88–89,
108–109
general-to-specific order,
88–89
order of importance, 88–89,
142–143
spatial order, 88–89, 120–121
step-by-step order, 130–133
stating definitions, 150–151
using sensory details, 194–195
writing a topic sentence,
84–85
Principal parts of verbs, 394–396
principal/principle, 702
Process of writing

pre-writing, 76–77, 98–99. *See
also* Pre-writing.
proofreading, 101
revising, 76–77, 100–101. *See
also* Revising.
steps in, 76–77
writing the first draft, 76–77,
99–100. *See also* First draft.
See also Writing.
Pronouns, 453–477
as adjectives, 484
and antecedents, 462–464
as compound objects of preposition, 519
compound personal, 464–465
definition of, 453
demonstrative, 465–466, 485
indefinite, 468–469, 583–584
interrogative, 466–467
after linking verbs, 456–457
as objects, 454–455, 458–459
of prepositions, 519
of verbs, 458–459
plural, 462–463, 583–584
possessive, 454–455, 461–462
predicate, 456–457
relative, 614–615
singular forms of, 462–463,
583–584
as subjects, 454–457
agreement with verbs,
583–584
with point of view, 110–111,
182–183
substituting nouns, 453
we/us, 459–460
Pronunciation of words, as shown
in dictionary entries, 28
Proofreading, 101
Proper adjectives, 479–481
capitalization of, 479
definition of, 479

Proper nouns, 431–433
  capitalization of, 431
  definition of, 431
Punctuation, 651–691
  accent mark, 28
  apostrophe, 672–676
  to avoid confusion, 656
  colon, 307, 670
  comma, 656–669. *See also*
    Comma.
  in compound sentences, 53–55,
    599–601
  at end of a sentence, 346,
    652–656
  exclamation mark, or point,
    654–655
  hyphen, 671–672
  in letters, 299–315
  period, 652–653
  question mark, 654–655
  quotation marks, 676–681
  semicolon, 600, 669
  and underlining, 681
Purr words, 258–259

Q

Question mark, 346
Questions. *See* Interrogative
  sentences.
quiet/quite, 702
Quotations
  capitalization in, 641–642
  commas with, 676, 644–645
  definition of, 676–677
  direct, 676, 678–680
  divided, 677
  punctuation with, 644–645
Quotation marks, 676–681
  commas with, 676
  in dialogue, 679–680

with divided quotations, 677
exclamation marks with, 678
question marks with, 678
for titles, 680–681

R

raise/rise, 424
*Readers Guide to Periodical Liter-
  ature*, 272
Reading, 286–287
Real life narrative compositions,
  178–179
Real life subjects for paragraphs,
  106–107
Reference works, 271–272
Regular verbs, 394–395. *See also*
  Verbs.
Relative clauses, 614–615
Religions, capitalization of,
  638
Reports, 233–245
Research, 86, 236–237. *See also*
  Study and research skills.
Restatement, as context clue to
  word meaning, 6–7
Return address on envelope,
  303–304
Revision
  definition of, 76–77
  of compositions, 168–169, 175,
    190–191, 200–201, 210–211,
    220–221
  of descriptive writing, 126–127,
    200–201
  of explanatory writing, 136–137,
    146–147, 156–157, 210–211,
    220–221
  of first drafts, 94–95, 126–127,
    200–201, 220–221
  of narrative writing, 114–115

of paragraphs, 94–95, 100–101,
114–115, 126–127, 136–137,
146–147, 156–157
as part of a process, 76–77,
100–101
of a report, 242–243
rise/raise, 424
Run-on sentences, 374–375

S

s'/s, 444–445
Salutation in letters, 300, 307
Scanning, 286–287
Schedules for study, 280–281
Semicolon, 600, 669
Senses, as basis for gathering detail, 118–119
Sensory details, 70, 118–119,
194–195
Sentence fragments, 344, 372–374,
619–621
Sentence patterns, 545–554
N LV Adj., 550–551
N LV N, 549–550
N V, 546–547
N V N, 547–548
N V N N, 548–549
Sentences, 43–61, 343–379
by adding single words, 58–59
beginning with *there,* 360–361
capitalization of, 641
combining, 54–55
by adding single words, 58–59
sentence parts, 56–57
complete, 344–345
complete predicate in, 344
complete subject in, 344
complex, 607–627
compound, 53–55, 60–61,
592–606, 621

compound predicate in,
354–355, 533
compound subject in, 354–355
correct use of, 42–51, 344–349
declative, 346
definition of, 44, 344, 594
diagraming, 349–350. *See also*
specific sentence parts.
empty, 46–47
ending, in paragraphs, 92–93
end punctuation in, 346
exclamatory, 346, 358–361
fragments, 344, 372–374,
619–621
imperative, 346, 362–363
interrogative, 346, 358–361
overloaded, 50–51
padded, 48–49
in paragraphs, 64–67
parts of, 344–345
patterns of, 345–354
predicate in, 344–345
punctuation in, 346. *See also*
specific punctuation.
run-on, 374–375
simple, 621
simple predicate (verb) in,
348–349, 593–594
simple subject in, 344–345,
348–349, 593–594
topic, 68–69, 84–85
writing, 43–61
set/sit, 425
Setting in stories, 178
Short-answer tests, 296–297
Signature in letters, 300, 307
Simple predicate (the verb),
348–349
Simple sentences, 354–355, 621
Simple subject, 344–345, 348–349
Singular forms of nouns, 441–443
sit/set, 425

simple, 348–349, 593
understood (you), 346, 362–363
in unusual positions, 356–358
of the verb, 348
Subordinate clause, 609–612,
618–619
Suffixes, 20–21, 479, 697
Superlatives
adjectives as, 486–487
adverbs as, 502–503
Syllables
in dictionary entries, 28
dividing words into, 671–672
Synonyms, 14–15, 29

T

Tables. *See* Graphic aids.
Talks. *See* Speech.
teach/learn, 420
Test taking, 292–297
Thank-you notes. *See* Letters.
their/they're 674–675
them/those, 489
there, here, where introducing
sentences, 581–582
Thesis statement, 234
Third-person point of view
in compositions, 182–183
in paragraphs, 110–111
those/them, 489
Time Sequence. *See* Chronological
order.
Title card, 266
Titles
capitalization of, 632–633
of compositions, 170–171
of persons, 632–633
of written works, 680–681
to/too/two, 703
Topic, choosing, 78–79

Topic, narrowing the
for compositions, 162–163
for paragraphs, 78–79
Topic sentences
in compositions, 160–214
in paragraphs, 68–69, 84–85
Transitions
showing chronological order,
112–113, 188–189
in compositions, 188–189,
208–209, 218–219
showing order of importance of
reasons, 218–219
in paragraphs, 112–113,
124–125, 132–133
showing spatial order, 124–125,
193–194
showing step-by-step order,
132–133, 208–209
True-false tests, 294–295
two/to/too, 703

U

Underlining titles for italics, 681
Understood subject (you), 346,
362–363
Unity in paragraphs, 66–67
Using grammar in writing. *See* end
of each lesson.
Using mechanics in writing
capitalization, 650
punctuation, 691
spelling, 708

V

Verb (simple predicate), 348–349
Verbals, 555–574
Verbs, 380–428
action, 381–382

727

after *there*, 581–582
agreement with subject,
   574–577
be, 381, 390
   See also State-of-being verbs,
      Linking verbs *and* Irregular
      verbs.
in a clause, 608–611
compound, 354–355
with compound subjects,
   578–580
contractions, 383
definition of, 380–382
diagraming, 349–350
using dictionary to find principal
   parts, 395
direct objects of, 384–387
helping, 351–354, 383–384, 394,
   403
in imperative sentences,
   362–363
intransitive, 387–389
irregular, 403–418, 383,
   394–395, 396
linking, 381, 390–392
main, 351–354, 383–384
in negative contractions, 383,
   508–509
number, definition of, 576
object of, 384–387
past paticiple of, 394–395
plural forms of, 575
present part, 394–395
principal parts of, 394–396
regular, 394–395
in sentence patterns, 345–354
separated parts of, 352–353, 383
singular forms of, 575
state-of-being, 348, 381–382,
   390–392
subjects of, 348
tenses, 392–393

transitive, 387–389
troublesome, 419–427
using negatives, 508
   See also Irregular verbs.
Vertical file, 271–272
Vocabulary, 1–21
   See also Words *and* Dictionary.

W

we/us, 459–460
weather/whether, 703
well/good, 507
whether/weather, 703
who/whom, 467, 614–615
who's/whose, 674, 703
what compositions, 223–231
what paragraphs, 149–159
why compositions, 213–221
why paragraphs, 139–147
Word endings as shown in dictionary entries, 28
Word order and sentence meaning, 545–546
Word parts, 16–21
Words, English language
   antonyms, 14–15, 29
   base, 16–17
   borrowed, 2–3
   clipped, 2
   context clues to meaning of,
      6–13
   entry words in dictionary, 28
   as different parts of speech,
      540–541
   guide words, 26–27
   homographs, 31–32
   jargon, 40–41
   origin of, 2,
   from people's names, 2
   purr words, 258–259
      snarl words, 258–259

for special fields, 4–5
synonyms, 14–15, 29
slang, 38–39
transitions
 in compositions, 188–189,
  208–209, 218–219
 in paragraphs, 112–113,
  124–125, 132–133
Work-related forms, 319–320
Writing
 choosing a point of view,
  110–111, 182–183
 choosing a subject, 162–163,
  194–195, 214
 compositions. *See* Compositions.
 final copy, 103, 172–173, 175
 first drafts
  of compositions, 166–167,
   174–175, 184–189,
    196–199, 208–209,
     218–219, 228–229
  of paragraphs, 90–93,
   144–145, 154–155
 narrowing a topic, 78–79, 80–81,
  162–163
 paragraphs, 63–159. *See also*
  Paragraphs.

pre-writing, 76–77, 78–89,
 98–99, 162–165, 194–197,
 214–215. See also Pre-writing.
as a process, 76–77, 98–103
proofreading, 101
revision
 of compositions, 168–169,
  175, 190–191, 200–201,
  220–221, 230–231
 of paragraphs, 76–77,
  100–101, 114–115,
  126–127, 136–137,
  146–147, 156–157
sentences, 43–61
using combining skills in, 60–61
Written tests, 296–297

Y

you
 as understood subject, 346,
  362–363
 and agreement with verb, 577
your/you're, 674

Z

ZIP code, 303–304

Acknowledgments

Open Court Publishing Company: for "Paper Dragons" by Susan M. Schmeltz, from *Cricket* Magazine, vol. 6, no. 7, March 1979; copyright © 1979 by Susan M. Schmeltz.

Photographs

Tom McCarthy/Hillstrom Stock, ii; Alex Webb/Magnum, xviii; Jim Whitmer, 22, 34, 96, 212, 232; James L. Ballard, 42, 176; Norma Morrison/Hillstrom Stock, 52, 298; Jacqueline Durand, 62, 260, 274, 322; Brent Jones, 74, 116, 202, 222; Paul Damen/Click Chicago, 104; Don & Pat Volenti/Hillstrom Stock, 128, 148; Don Smetzer/Click Chicago, 138, 340; Frank Siteman/Marilyn Gartman Agency, 158; Ray F. Hillstrom, Jr., 192; David Borth/Hillstrom Stock, 246.

Cover

Sinjerli Variation IIA, 1977. Frank Stella. Petersburg Press, London and New York, © Vert Foncé, 1977.

Editorial Credits

Editor-in-Chief: Joseph F. Littell
Editorial Director: Joy Littell
Administrative Editor: Kathleen Laya
Managing Editor: Geraldine Macsai

Director of Secondary English: Bonnie Dobkin
Editors: James M. LiSacchi, Mary Schafer
Associate Editor: Robert D. Shepherd
Associate Designer: Mary E. MacDonald
Assistant Designer: Debbie Costello
Cover Design: Joy Littell, Mary E. MacDonald

Teaching Special Populations: Specific Suggestions

Section 1: The Sentence and Its Parts

LD   LD students will find it easier to distinguish between a sentence and a fragment if you stress that a fragment contains only part of an idea. Demonstrate this by giving them an incomplete and a complete request.

> EXAMPLE: Don't do. (incomplete)
> Don't do the first assignment. (complete)

Discuss what information these two groups of words present.

You may want to limit your LD students to the simple subject-verb diagrams. Introduce other elements when and if your students are ready for them.

ESL   ESL students will have trouble distinguishing sentence fragments from sentences, since their command of syntax is likely to be poor. Provide extra practice using the diagram on page 344 and the questions *who?* and *what?* until the difference is clear. Use a scrambled sentence exercise; give sentences with scrambled word order (*bike a tire flat has the*) and have students unscramble them (*the bike has a flat tire*).

Stress word order in each of the four types of sentences. Demonstrate differences in intonation. Practice with scrambled sentences and substitution drills. In the latter, the teacher provides a model sentence; students substitute cue words (from the teacher) to make new sentences.

> MODEL: Elaine won an award yesterday.
> CUES: drove car I
> STUDENT RESPONSE: I drove a car yesterday.

Stress the logic of punctuation, which is common to all languages that use punctuation.

ESL students may find the English verb system confusing. Demonstrate usage and correct form, and provide practice as needed. Give additional practice placing *who?* or *what?* before the verb in order to identify the subject. Stress the exercises in which the students must find the subject in unusual positions, and add to them if possible.

ESL students will find diagraming especially helpful because it provides visual representations of difficult syntactical patterns.

NSD   NSD students frequently have difficulty with the use of helping verbs. The lesson on *Main Verbs and Helping Verbs* can be used as a diagnostic exercise, to determine where students' difficulties lie.

Section 2: Avoiding Fragments and Run-on Sentences

LD and ESL   Because LD and ESL students will do a number of the exercises in this text orally, it will be helpful to spend some time on the lesson *Avoiding Run-on Sentences*. Run-on errors, which are readily apparent in written work, are not easy to detect in oral work.

When teaching ESL students, see comments in preceding section. Identifying fragments and run-ons requires comprehension of examples. Check for understanding of vocabulary. Do many exercises orally, encouraging the use of logic. ESL students may not be able to generate their own sentences. Provide them with native English-speaking partners, or help them yourself.

Section 3: Using Verbs

LD   LD students may require additional explanation and drill in order to master state-of-being verbs. Instructions for exercises may have to be more explicit. These students will need more explanation and examples of separated parts of verbs and predicate words in order to complete the exercises.

ESL   ESL students frequently omit forms of *be*, drop *s* from third-person singular present tense, or drop *ed* from regular past tense. Go over rules very carefully and provide extra practice: scrambled sentences, fill-in sentences, substitution drills.

In some languages the pronoun is indicated in the verb ending, so these students may omit the pronoun in English. As far as possible, compare English forms with forms in other languages.

ESL students will have many difficulties with helping verbs. Only extensive practice will solve them. You might analyze questions in several word orders.

Can he run?
Does he run?
Did he run?

In some languages gender and number determine the form of the predicate word. Explain that English relies on the meanings of the subject and the predicate word to establish their relationship. Give oral practice before requiring written responses. Extensive use of the sentence pattern chart will benefit ESL students immensely; be sure, however, that they first recognize parts of speech.

NSD NSD students, as already noted, have many difficulties with main verbs and helping verbs. If you have already used Section 1 as a diagnostic test, use Part 2 of this section to concentrate on specific problems. Be especially aware of the faulty use of *be*.

Section 4: Using Irregular Verbs

LD LD students will require extensive practice. Additional exercises can be found in this book and in the Practice Book.

ESL ESL students may have trouble distinguishing between past and past participle forms. Provide extensive oral drills and substitution drills. These students will not be good judges of what "sounds right." Give supplementary oral practice before assigning written exercises, or do some written exercises together as a class.

NSD Many NSD students will be more familiar with deviant rather than with standard usage of irregular verbs. They may not be able to distinguish aurally between standard and nonstandard usage. Emphasis must be placed on both the written and the oral exercises. Repetition and patience will be essential when attempting to modify linguistic habits.

Section 5: Using Troublesome Pairs of Verbs

ESL Allow ESL students ample time for practice with confusing pairs of verbs. Review and practice with extra exercises.

NSD This lesson is of particular importance to NSD students. Many nonstandard dialects regularly substitute one verb for another similar verb. (Example: *lay* for *lie*). Remember that these are not eccentric habits in the student; rather, the student is obeying semantic rules acquired over many years. If necessary, spend extra time on this lesson.

Section 6: Using Nouns

LD LD students may have difficulty using dictionaries. Thus, frequent repetition and reinforcement will be necessary when teaching singular and plural nouns, particularly for irregular examples.

Use diagrams only when and if your students are ready for them.

ESL ESL students will understand proper and common nouns and possessives more readily through comparisons and contrasts with their own languages. They will need extra practice with forming plurals, the irregular ones in particular. Using a dictionary may be beyond their skills; a partner could help.

Word order will continue to be a problem. Be alert for negative transfer from the student's native language: for example, word placement according to a different system.

NSD NSD students will need to spend some additional time working on *The Plurals of Nouns*. Encourage these students to use a dictionary. You may wish to work through or review the lesson **Using a Dictionary** (Writing Section 2) before attempting this section.

Section 7: Using Pronouns

LD LD students should be allowed to do several exercises orally, to make sure that they understand the directions.

ESL ESL students will find this section difficult because pronouns are much more complicated in English than in many other languages. These students are likely to mistake case and gender and to omit pronouns. Review the rules, stressing that pronouns are not dropped in English. Provide extensive practice: scrambled sentences, cloze exercises, substitution drills.

ESL students cannot usually judge what "sounds natural." Encourage them to refer to the chart on page 454. Practice possessive pronouns, especially *its*, extensively.

Some ESL students will substitute a pronoun for the verb *be* forming a double subject. (*Mary, she nice.*) Be aware of this problem, too, when teaching linking verbs.

NSD NSD students will have difficulty determining when to use the object form and when to use the subject form of pronouns. Pay particular attention to Parts 2 and 3 of this lesson.

Section 8: Using Adjectives

LD LD students will have trouble generating and writing sentences as instructed in Exercise B on page 481. Either omit it or do it as a group exercise.

ESL ESL students will have trouble using articles and placing adjectives in the sentences correctly. Practice with scrambled sentences and expansion drills. In an expansion drill, the teacher gives a base sentence (*I see him*), the student repeats it, the teacher gives a new word (*always*), and the student inserts it in the correct place in the sentence (*I always see him*).

ESL students may be slow to master English conventions governing proper adjectives, but experience will eventually teach them. Unlearning the rules from their native language may be harder than learning new ones.

Make sure that these students know the vocabulary in this section, and also concepts such as *what kind, how many,* and *which ones*.

Agreement in gender and number between an adjective and the noun it modifies is much simpler in English than in many other languages. Point out that English does not require distinct forms for gender and number (except for demonstratives *this, these, that,* and *those*).

Give many examples of predicate adjectives, and use arrows, as in the exercise on page 483, to indicate the word modified.

Part 5 will be more accessible to these students if taught with ample supplementary illustration (That student over there is *taller* than this one over here).

Section 9: Using Adverbs

ESL ESL students may confuse adverbs and predicate adjectives, especially when they are used with linking verbs. Focus on the words modified. As you present the examples and the exercises, ask the questions *how, when, where,* or *to what extent,* and encourage the students to do so. Give these students ample practice (scrambled sentences, fill-in sentences) using adjectives and adverbs before moving on to comparative forms.

Section 10: Using Prepositions

ESL For ESL students the functions of prepositions in English may be very confusing because their native languages use them quite differently. Contrast the usages whenever possible, and emphasize memorizing the list on page 516. Pace this material very cautiously, since the concepts presented are numerous and difficult to see in relation to one another. Correct placement of prepositional phrases may require more sensitivity to English word order than these students have developed. Do many of the sentences orally, discussing the relationships among sentence parts and, when possible, the contrasts with the native language. You may need to review terminology and give additional examples.

Section 11: Using Conjunctions

LD   Students may have trouble understanding relationships between sentence parts. Use extra examples to help recognition of correlative conjunctions.

ESL   Use of conjunctions in English may be very different for ESL students than in their native languages. See comments in preceding section. You may also have to review *and, but,* and *or.*

Section 12: Using Parts of Speech

LD   LD students will require some review of parts of speech before they can do the first exercise. Perhaps you can use the exercise as the basis for an oral review.

ESL   ESL students will find this review very helpful. Stress the material on multiple functions of words, which is very important for non-native speakers.

Section 13: Sentence Patterns

LD   LD students may have trouble completing pattern charts in exercises. Do them orally as class exercises.

ESL   This section will be helpful but difficult for ESL students. They will not know what word order makes sense, or how a word's position in a sentence changes the meaning of the sentence. Use word pictures to explain how ideas change with word order. Switch pictures to show who does action and who receives action (example: *Kathy held the baby* and *The baby held Kathy*).

Pair ESL students with native English-speaking partners, or help them yourself.

NSD   Review verb forms with NSD students, specifically the use of *be,* before you begin *LV* patterns.

Section 14: Using Verbals

LD   You may wish to limit your LD students to just finding verbals in a sentence rather than identifying the kind of verbal and its uses. You will have to modify exercises to your students' abilities, and do most of the exercises orally.

ESL   Review the concept of words used in more than one way before starting (Handbook Section 12).

Call attention to spelling changes in verbs that are made into gerunds and participles. Give extra exercises and practice.

Give extra exercises and practice.

NSD   NSD students frequently drop the *-ing* ending of verbals to an *in'* sound (*runnin', singin'*). These students will need reinforcement in the spelling and pronunciation of participles and gerunds in order to recognize them aurally.

Section 15: Making Subjects and Verbs Agree

LD   For LD students, emphasize the rules. Use examples to illustrate conditional statements such as "When a subject noun or pronoun is singular, the verb must also be singular."

ESL   ESL students may need some review. The concepts *singular* and *plural* will be familiar, but the students may need to be reminded of their application to English words. Third person singular present tense verbs end in *s*, as do plural nouns, a fact that may cause confusion. Practice with substitution drills and fill-in sentences.

Special verb forms and compound subjects may require practice; encourage use in classroom conversation.

The plurality and singularity of certain indefinite pronouns may be confusing to ESL students. Provide extra practice with these words, and encourage students to refer to the lists on page 583.

NSD Stress the necessity of agreement between subject and verb, especially the state-of-being verbs.

Section 16: Using Compound Sentences

ESL ESL students may need careful explanation of the nuances in the uncombined sentences before they can combine them with the correct conjunction. Review uses of *and, but*, and *or*.

If students find combining sentences difficult, present an add-on sentence exercise: start with a noun or verb and have students place additional words where they belong in a sentence. After building two related sentences, have students add a conjunction to join them.

Section 17: Using Complex Sentences

LD Work slowly through this section with LD students. Do all exercises orally with the class. You may want to review the definition of a sentence before teaching main and subordinate clauses. Present two simple sentences and show different ways they can be put together.

ESL Encourage ESL students to practice writing complex sentences. Additional exercises will be found at the end of this Section and in the Practice Book.

Make sure students understand that a subordinate clause does not have only one position in a sentence, that it can appear first, last, or in the middle of a sentence.

It is important to make ESL students aware of which subordinating words are to be used when referring to people (*who, whom*, etc.).

Section 18: Capitalization

LD LD students will have trouble copying all the sentences. Assign fewer sentences, or allow these students to complete them orally.

ESL ESL students will find some personal titles, proper nouns, outline/letter forms, and literary titles unfamiliar. Have these students work with native speaking partners who can explain this material. The rules must be practiced to be learned.

Section 19: Punctuation

LD Again, LD students will have trouble copying all the sentences. Assign fewer sentences, or allow these students to complete them orally.

ESL ESL students will benefit from emphasis on the logic that governs punctuation in all languages. Point out any marks whose use may be unfamiliar, such as the hyphen or the apostrophe in possessives, and give extra practice in using them. Again, a native English speaking partner may be helpful, especially in using the dictionary.

Section 20: Spelling

ESL ESL students must learn English spelling through written use and practice. Discuss the rules at a leisurely pace, using a multi-sensory approach: see, hear, say, write.

NSD Most likely NSD students will need additional work in spelling. Encourage the use of the dictionary through dictionary drills. Spelling Bees are also helpful. (Be sure students have a list of words to study before each Bee.)

Guidelines for Evaluating Composition

Adapted from Teaching and Evaluating Student Writing,
copyright © 1985 by McDougal, Littell & Company

Types of Evaluation

In order to give student writers the constant practice and feedback they need, teachers must have a practical method of evaluation. Obviously, if the student will be writing constantly, a teacher cannot be expected to evaluate each piece in a line-by-line, word-by-word manner. Nor would such an evaluation necessarily be useful to the developing writer. It is therefore suggested that a teacher learn to use two different evaluation methods—the holistic method and the more detailed analytic method.

Holistic evaluation of writing is a quick, guided method of rating pieces of writing. It can best be used to evaluate daily writing samples or first drafts of more complex pieces. With holistic evaluation, an evaluator reads the written piece as a whole, considers certain features, and immediately assigns a grade. The grade may be a single rating for the entire piece of writing or a set of ratings for the different features being considered.

Analytic evaluation should occur only when the student has turned in the clean, final copy of a piece of writing. In this detailed type of evaluation, the teacher analyzes each aspect of a piece of writing, including both content and mechanics.

Evaluators

The evaluation process can be utilized by three types of evaluators: the writer of the piece, other students, and the teacher. Each type of evaluation offers unique benefits to the developing writer.

1. Self-Evaluation. In this type of evaluation, a writer comments on his or her own work, noting which parts were successful and which unsuccessful.

2. Peer Evaluation. Evaluating the writing of others is often a strong learning experience. In peer evaluation, students work together in small groups to improve a piece of writing. Student evaluators should always be given a list of specific criteria that the writing is expected to meet, and should then comment on how well each paper succeeds.

3. Teacher Evaluation. The teacher's comments and suggestions may be incorporated at any point in the writing process. Studies indicate that evaluation by the teacher is most successful when it is done in combination with self- and peer evaluation. The evaluation that follows provides for such a combination of evaluation procedures.

Teacher evaluation should also involve direct communication with every student. Such help can be provided in student-teacher conferences.

Keeping a Record of Improvement

Both the teacher and students benefit when writing folders are maintained throughout the school year. A piece of writing from early in the year, along with its evaluations, can be compared with later pieces. Progress from one piece to the next will be erratic, as the writer takes risks using new techniques and appears to move backwards until gaining mastery of each new technique. However, over the course of the year, progress should be evident.

BIBLIOGRAPHY

Cooper, Charles R. and Lee Odell, eds. *Evaluating Writing: Describing, Measuring, Judging.* Urbana, Illinois: National Council of Teachers of English, 1977.

Graves, Donald H. *Balance the Basics: Let Them Write.* New York: The Ford Foundation, 1978.

Murray, Donald M. *A Writer Teaches Writing: A Practical Method of Teaching Composition.* Boston: Houghton Mifflin, 1968.

Payne, Lucile Vaughn, *The Lively Art of Writing.* Chicago: Follett, 1965.

Using the Evaluation Form

The following form for composition evaluation may be used at any stage of the writing process, and may be re-used after each revision.

The form should be filled out by the student and turned in with the writing. There is also space on the form for peer evaluation, if desired. The teacher may ask students to turn in only final copies, or may ask to see work in progress. The student states whether the submitted writing is the final copy.

On the evaluation form, content may be rated at any point; mechanics should be graded only on a final copy.

Self-Evaluation: Besides the questions on the form, the student can ask himself or herself the questions concerning revising listed in the relevant composition chapter. The student may use 1, 3, and 5 subjectively.

Peer Evaluation: Members of the peer group should rate each feature as objectively as possible. In order to focus on ideas and organization, the group should evaluate content only.

Teacher Evaluation: The following standards for evaluating composition are provided to assist the teacher in rating papers with objectivity and consistency. In a conference, the teacher might discuss one or two of these areas in detail.

Standards for Evaluation

Content

	1—Low	3—Average	5—High
1	Unclear, unimaginative writing.	Understandable but unimaginative writing.	Imaginative, interesting writing.
2	Boring or poorly defined topic.	Topic adequately limited and defined.	Well-chosen, precisely developed topic.
3	Purpose unclear, or not achieved in the writing.	Purpose defined adequately. Not completely achieved.	Clear, well-defined purpose. Writing achieves purpose successfully.
4	Writing so lacking in detail that topic remains undeveloped.	Incomplete development. More information needed.	Topic thoroughly covered. Writing is rich in detail and supporting information.
5	Many irrelevant sentences or details.	Few irrelevant sentences or details.	Well-chosen, relevant sentences and details.
6	Disjointed ideas. No transitional words, phrases, or ideas.	Inconsistent flow. Some transitional devices.	Ideas flow well. Good use of transitional devices.
7	Lack of any logical organization of ideas.	Some organization of ideas evident.	Well-organized ideas. Type of organization suited to topic and purpose.
8	Dull, general words, poorly chosen. Inappropriate to audience.	Suitable but unimaginative language. Generally appropriate to audience.	Specific, vivid language. Appropriate to audience.

Mechanics

1	Many fragments and run-on sentences. Frequent mistakes in the use of nouns, verbs, pronouns, and subject-verb agreement.	Few fragments and run-ons. Some mistakes in the use of nouns, verbs, pronouns, and subject-verb agreement.	No fragments or run-ons. Few mistakes in the use of nouns, verbs, pronouns, and subject-verb agreement.
2	Frequent mistakes in capitalization.	Occasional mistakes in capitalization.	Infrequent mistakes in capitalization.
3	Punctuation marks frequently misused or missing.	Punctuation marks usually used correctly.	Infrequent mistakes in punctuation.
4	Frequent mistakes in spelling, without any indication of awareness of spelling patterns.	Occasional misspellings, usually indicating an approximation of the correct spelling and an awareness of spelling patterns.	Infrequent spelling mistakes.
5	Paragraphs not indented. Writing illegible. Incorrect headings or margins.	Some carelessness or inconsistency in form. Occasionally hard to read.	Correct form. Neat, legible handwriting.

Composition Evaluation Form

Writer _____

Date _____

Title _____

Circle one: Unfinished   Final Copy

Evaluation Symbols
1 Needs a great deal of work
3 Acceptable—could be improved
5 Very good. Needs no further revision.

Content

	Writer's Opinion	Peer Group Opinion	Teacher's Evaluation	Teacher's Comments
1. **Interest.** Is the writing interesting and understandable? Does it hold the reader's attention?				
2. **Topic.** Is the topic a good one? Has it been narrowed sufficiently?				
3. **Purpose.** Is the purpose of the writing clear? Has the writer accomplished this purpose?				
4. **Development.** Has the topic been developed well? Is there sufficient information?				
5. **Unity.** Are all ideas and details related to the topic? Do they all help to develop or strengthen the main idea?				
6. **Continuity.** Do ideas flow smoothly? Has the writer avoided any breaks in thought?				
7. **Organization.** Were ideas arranged in a logical order? Does this order suit the purpose of the writing?				
8. **Language.** Is the language appropriate to the writing? Does it suit the audience? Are the words vivid?				
Additional Guidelines				

Mechanics (to be graded by teacher on final copy only)

	Writer's Opinion	Peer Group Opinion	Teacher's Evaluation	
1. **Grammar and Usage.** Are there any fragments or run-ons? Is the correct form of every pronoun or verb used? Are adjectives and adverbs used correctly?				
2. **Capitalization.** Are all first words, initials, proper nouns, proper adjectives, and titles capitalized?				
3. **Punctuation.** Does each sentence have the proper end mark? Are all punctuation marks used correctly?				
4. **Spelling.** Are all words spelled correctly? Are plurals and possessive forms spelled correctly?				
5. **Form.** Is the writing legible? Is the heading correct? Are there sufficient margins?				